The United States, 1763–2001

The United States, 1763–2001 is a new approach to teaching and learning US history from 1763 to 2001 at A-level. It meets the needs of teachers and students studying for today's revised AS and A2 exams.

In a unique style, *The United States, 1763–2001* focuses on the key topics within the period. Each topic is then comprehensively explored to provide background, essay writing advice and examples, source work and historical skills exercises.

From 1763 to 2001, the key topics featured include:

- The struggle for the Constitution, 1763–1877
- The American Civil War, its causes and aftermath
- The 'Roaring Twenties'
- Franklin D. Roosevelt and the New Deal
- Foreign policy, 1890–2001
- Civil rights, 1863–2001
- Domestic policy, 1960–2001

Using essay styles and source exercises from each of the exam boards, AQA, Edexcel and OCR, this book is an essential text and revision guide for students and teachers.

John Spiller is Course Leader in History and Politics at Ashton-under-Lyne Sixth Form College. He has written articles for A-level magazines, including *History Review* and is an A-level examiner.

Tim Clancey teaches History at Edinburgh Academy and has been an A-level examiner.

Stephen Young teaches History and Politics at Ashton-under-Lyne Sixth Form College.

Simon Mosley teaches History at Babington Community Technology School, Leicester.

Spotlight History

John Spiller, Tim Clancey, Stephen Young
and Simon Mosley

The United States,
1763–2001

Routledge
Taylor & Francis Group

LONDON AND NEW YORK

First published 2005
by Routledge
2 Park Square, Milton Park, Abingdon, Oxon OX14 4RN

Simultaneously published in the USA and Canada
by Routledge
270 Madison Ave, New York, NY 10016

Routledge is an imprint of the Taylor & Francis Group

© 2005 John Spiller, Tim Clancey, Stephen Young and Simon Mosley

Typeset in Minion and Helvetica Neue by
Florence Production Ltd, Stoodleigh, Devon

Printed and bound in Great Britain by
St Edmundsbury Press, Bury St Edmunds, Suffolk

British Library Cataloguing in Publication Data
A catalogue record for this book is available from the British Library

Library of Congress Cataloging in Publication Data
The United States, 1763–2001/John Spiller . . . [*et al.*].
        p. cm. – (Spotlight history)
    Includes bibliographical references and index.
    1. United States – History – Textbooks.   2. United States – History – Study
and teaching (Secondary).   I. Spiller, John.   II. Series.
    E178.1.U544 2004
    973 – dc22   2004004552

ISBN 0–415–29028–7 (hbk)
ISBN 0–415–29029–5 (pbk)

Contents

List of Illustrations

Acknowledgements

The author and publishers would like to thank the following for permission to reproduce material:

Bettmann/CORBIS (Figures 2.2, 3.1, 4.2, 4.3, 6.1, 6.2, 8.1, 10.2); CORBIS (Figure 9.2); The Library of Congress (Figures 3.4, 4.1, 7.1); Monticello/Thomas Jefferson Foundation, Inc. (Figure 2.3); Denver Public Library (Figure 5.3); Brown Brothers Stock Photos (Figures 5.2, 10.1); popperfoto.com (Figure 10.3); Rex Features Limited (Figures 11.1, 11.2); AP Photo/Bud Krogh/White House (Figure 11.3).

While every effort has been made to trace and acknowledge ownership of copyright material used in this volume, the publishers will be glad to make suitable arrangements with any copyright holders whom it has not been possible to contact.

General Introduction

The aim of this book is to help prepare you for exam board modules in AS and A-level History. Each chapter is divided into standard parts, the purpose of which is to combine essential knowledge and the various skills necessary to achieve the highest grade in line with the AS and A-level specifications. This General Introduction concentrates on AS format but most chapters in the book also contain A2 content as well as A2 question formats, and A2 techniques will be dealt with in the General Conclusion.

The first page of each chapter takes the form of a 'map' or outline of the chapter. The purpose is to enable the reader to 'navigate' through each topic, and to see which aspects of the subject form the focus of each part.

The structure of the chapters

Part of the chapter	Purpose	Method
Part 1: Historical background	To provide the basic, factual backgrounds and issues related to each topic. This may also be relevant to some questions of the simpler format.	The factual narrative is structured to include all the key themes. A chronological summary is also provided to give perspective at a glance.
Part 2: Essays	To provide worked answers to the major aspects of each topic. These provide examples of interpretation and factual support.	The wording of the question varies to allow for different types of examination response. Further questions are provided for term-work and examination practice; these can be prepared through the further reading recommended.
Part 3: Source analysis	To provide a selection of some of the key sources for each topic and to examine the different types of questions which can be asked about these.	Each set of sources has two sets of questions: one with worked examples and one without. The questions without worked examples allow for class discussion or for individual practice.
Part 4: Historical skills	To provide some suggestions about how the topic can be used as a focus for selected skills not already covered in Parts 2 and 3.	The types of skills covered vary from chapter to chapter: they include discussion and presentation.

Part 1: Historical background

A good understanding of the topic in each chapter is essential before any meaningful analysis can be done. This involves three main approaches.

The approach of the historical background

Type of approach:	Reason for this:	How it is accomplished:
1 Outline perspective	An ability to visualise the structure of the topic covered in the chapter and the way in which components of the topic fit together.	Through the chronological summary, the headings and sub-headings, and the introductory paragraphs of each section.
2 Knowledge in depth	An ability to focus on parts of the topic in depth.	Through careful and systematic development of details. These are grouped within an overall structure.
3 Integrating perspective and depth	An ability to combine the overall perspective with a focus on specific selected details.	By relating the details to the interpretations in the essays.

Understanding of the historical background is also assisted by two sections at the end of the book. First, significant individuals are discussed in brief Biographies, beginning on p. 308. Second, there is a Glossary of Key terms, which begins on p. 319. Words and phrases which are explained in the glossary are printed in bold on the first occasion that they appear in the text. The glossary is in alphabetical order, for ease of reference.

 ## Part 2: Essays

What is an essay?

An essay is a formal attempt to answer a question or to provide a solution to a problem; the term derives from the French '*essayer*' and the Latin '*exigere*', the latter meaning 'to weigh'. The better the attempt, the higher the mark will be. There is usually no right or wrong solution. But there can be a solution which is presented well or badly, or which makes good or poor use of supporting material.

An essay should always be written in full sentences and paragraphs and should not normally include notes or bullet points. Appropriate lengths vary considerably, but some idea can be gained by the worked answers in Part 2 of each chapter. Relevance is vital throughout. This means keeping exactly to the confines of the question asked. The answer should be direct and should start within the first sentence or two. You should also keep the question in mind throughout the essay, answer all parts of it and include nothing which is not relevant to it. Think in terms of '*The question, the whole question and nothing but the question*'.

Instructions in essay questions and what they mean

Instruction	Meaning of instruction	Examples
Outline . . . Describe . . . What . . .?	Provide a coherent summary of the topic or issue in the question. It is important to include at least some specific factual references. ('Outline', does not mean 'be vague about'.) This type of instruction is less common than the others and, if it does appear, is more likely as a short question.	Ch. 2: 1b; Ch. 3: 2; Ch. 4: 1a, 2a; Ch. 5: 4, 9a; Ch. 6: 1; Ch. 9: 1b, 2a, 2b, 4a, 5a, 10b; Ch. 10: 1, 5a; Ch. 11: 1

Examine . . . Why. . .? Explain why . . .	The emphasis switches from 'describing' to 'providing reasons for'. This means looking at the question as a problem to be solved by a direct answer based on an argument which selects relevant factual information to support it.	Ch. 3: 9, 11; Ch. 4: 7a; Ch. 5: 1; Ch. 7: 2b, 7a, 9a; Ch. 8: 4b, 5; Ch. 9: 6, 8b, 9b; Ch. 11: 6; Ch. 2: 1a, 2a; Ch. 3: 1; Ch. 4: 2b; Ch. 5: 10a; Ch. 6: 6; Ch. 7: 2a, 7b; Ch. 8: 1a, 1b, 1c, 2a, 2b, 2c, 4a; Ch. 9: 1a, 10a; Ch. 11: 12
Account for . . .		Ch. 5: 3a, 9b; Ch. 6: 2, 4, 5; Ch. 11: 2
Identify . . . and 　 explain TWO . . .	In addition to the previous instruction, this involves choosing two areas to 'explain'. Make sure that they are relevant to the question and that they can both act as a base for argument. This is common as a second question in a two-part structure.	
Assess To what extent . . .? How far . . .? How far do you 　 agree . . .? How valid is the view 　 that . . .? Discuss . . . How successful/effective 　 was . . .? How serious were . . .? How important was . . . ? With what justification 　 . . . ? Comment on . . .	This group of instructions involves more directly the notion of 'weighing'. It is therefore essential to have a clear idea of the 'extent' to which you 'agree' with the proposition put in the rest of the question. The extremes are 'entirely' or 'not at all'. If you adopt one of these, you need to explain why the alternative is not acceptable. More likely are 'to a very limited extent' or 'to a large extent, but not entirely.' In 'weighing' two arguments you need to explain: why one is 'heavier' or 'lighter' than the other. In terms of style, it is better to avoid using 'I' in the answer even if there is a 'you' in the question.	Ch. 4: 1b, 4a, 9a; Ch. 5: 2, 5a; Ch. 7: 6b; Ch. 9: 4b, 7a, 8a; Ch. 10: 6a; Ch. 11: 4, 10 Ch. 2: 1c, 2c, 3b, 4, 5, 7; Ch. 3: 4; Ch. 4: 6a, 6b, 7b, 8a; Ch. 5: 5b, 10b; Ch. 6: 3; Ch. 7: 3, 4a, 5, 10, 11, 12; Ch. 9: 1c, 7b; Ch. 10: 3; Ch. 11: 5, 9, 11 Ch. 2: 2b; Ch. 3: 3, 5, 6, 8, 10; Ch. 4: 3a, 3b, 5a, 9a; Ch. 5: 3b, 7; Ch. 6: 7, 8; Ch. 7: 8; Ch. 9: 3; Ch. 10: 2, 5b Ch. 2: 8, 10; Ch. 4: 5a Ch. 4: 5b; Ch. 11: 7 Ch. 2: 6, 9; Ch. 3: 7; Ch. 4: 8b; Ch. 5: 8; Ch. 6: 8; Ch. 11: 8 Ch. 5: 6; Ch. 7: 1, 4b, 6a; Ch. 9: 5b Ch. 4: 4b; Ch. 9: 9a; Ch. 10: 5b, 6b
Compare . . . Compare and contrast . . . Compare the importance 　 of three reasons . . . Assess the relative 　 importance of . . . How similar were . . .? How different were . . .?	The approach will involve the process of 'weighing', as with the previous set of questions. There are, however, two or more specific items to 'weigh'. These may be policies, or they may be arguments about policies. They may be named in the question, or you may be asked to select your own. Whatever the case, you need to consider the two against each other;	

at all costs avoid a description of the two separately. 'Compare and contrast' (or 'compare' by itself) involves finding similarities and differences between items, as do 'how similar were' and 'how different were'.

Argument and support

Since most essays involve an attempt to solve a problem, the solution should be clearly presented and well supported. The structure should be argument backed up by factual examples. This is much more effective than factual narrative followed by deduction. For most types of question you should argue then support; do not *narrate then deduce*.

Appropriate and inappropriate essay technique

Appropriate essay technique	Inappropriate essay technique
Argument	Narrative
Factual detail supporting the argument	Argument deduced from the narrative
Argument	Narrative
Factual detail supporting the argument	Argument deduced from the narrative

To become accustomed to writing in this way it can be helpful to outline or highlight *argument* in red and *factual detail supporting the argument* in blue; there will, of course, be some overlapping between the two. For each issue covered in the essay the red should come *before* the blue.

Stages in the essay

Stages	Appropriate development
Introduction	Mostly argument: considering the meaning of the question and offering an outline answer without detail.
Each subsequent paragraph	A part of or stage in the argument. The first sentence of each paragraph is based on argument. The rest consists of argument supported by factual detail. It should not normally be factual detail followed by deduction.
Conclusion	Need not repeat the arguments already provided, but may pull together any threads. The final sentence should be a generalisation. Never write 'unfinished'.

The introductory paragraph is vital since it will usually provide the direction for the rest of the essay; it will also provide the initial impression for the person reading or marking it. It should be a single paragraph and of immediate relevance to the question rather than leading gradually to the point. It should be largely argument, attempting to consider *all* the key words and concepts in the question and to provide a brief outline answer to it. This can then be developed in the rest of the essay. All this means that the introductory paragraph can and should be quite short.

The main section of the essay (about 90 per cent) will consist of several paragraphs that will develop the issues raised in the introduction. Ideally, each paragraph should start with a stage in the argument, with the rest of the paragraph comprising a combination of the argument in more detail and relevant factual support. Paragraphs therefore need to be seen as units within the answer. The reason for starting another paragraph is usually to move on to another unit. A sequence of very short paragraphs usually shows a disjointed argument, and a complete absence of paragraphs makes it difficult to follow the stages in the argument at all.

It is important to have some sort of conclusion and not to stop suddenly. This should round the essay off by pulling threads together and giving a final assessment in any 'to what extent?' essays. It might also be a fitting place for a quotation, especially one which complements or contradicts any quotation included in the question. Never write 'unfinished'; in the event of mistiming, use a rounding off sentence rather than a full conclusion.

Part 3: Source analysis

Questions are set on primary sources, secondary sources or both. There are different styles of source-based questions. Despite contrasts in wording, however, they do have certain common features.

Types of source-based questions

Type of question	Examples of question structure	General advice on the answer
The Source used for information and inference.	• What can you learn from this Source about . . . ? • What evidence is there in Source 1 to suggest that . . . ?	Identify implications as well as information. This means inferring, not describing.
The Source used as a stimulus for further knowledge. Usually this means explaining a particular sentence or phrase in the Source: this will involve further material outside the Source.	• Using Source A and your own knowledge, explain the meaning of '. . .' [a phrase in quotation marks]. • Using your own knowledge, explain briefly, why '. . .' [an event or development in quotation marks].	Identify precisely what is required and confine the use of 'your own knowledge' to explain the words in the quotation marks. This will, however, need accurate detail rather explain than vague generalisation.
Questions on a Source's 'usefulness' and 'reliability'.	• How useful is Source A about . . . ? • How reliable is Source A about . . . ? • How useful are these Sources to the historian studying . . . ?	For usefulness distinguish between internal criteria (i.e. content) and external criteria (i.e. the type of Source). Reliability can also be assessed by referring to whether the content is accurate and the circumstances in which the source was produced. A source may be unreliable but still useful.
Questions asking for comparisons between Sources. These may concern similarities, or differences, or both. They may involve an explanation of the reasons for similarities or differences.	• Compare . . . according to Sources A and B. • How would you explain the differences? • What evidence in Source 1 supports the view in Source 5 that . . . ? • Explain how the judgement in Source A challenges the judgement in Source C that . . .	'Compare' or 'compare and contrast' mean finding similarities and differences. These may involve details or general arguments. In either case precise references are needed, using brief quotations from the sources. Reasons for differences in the content of sources usually involve a comment on the differences in the type of source.

Questions which provide a viewpoint that needs to be tested against the Sources and against additional knowledge beyond the Sources.

- Use Sources A to D, and your own knowledge, to explain whether the view that '. . .' is accurate.
- Study Sources A, B and C and use your own knowledge. How important . . .
- Refer to Sources A, B and C and use your own knowledge. Explain . . .
- Do you agree that '. . .' Explain your answer, using the sources and your own knowledge.

The answer needs two dimensions.
- The content and your own knowledge of the sources should be 'used' to test the viewpoint in the question. At the same time, the reliability of this content should be briefly assessed: does the source apparently support . . . and does it really support . . .?
- 'Own knowledge' should have the same amount of time and space as the 'use of sources' and should include material beyond the sources.

How does this book combine the different approaches of the boards to essays and source questions?

The use by the boards of different styles is an opportunity to see common objectives from slightly different angles. It is very likely that an approach used by a board you are not following will clarify at least one approach used by the board that you are. At the very least, you will learn a great deal about what essay and source skills mean by comparing the ways in which they are approached. This is because you will be doing the most important thing you can do: you will be thinking about what the skills actually *mean*.

This book attempts to use all the approaches of the boards in a way in which they relate to each other and reinforce each other. At the same time, it intends to give precise examples of how the questions of specific boards can best be approached. A subject area which is not represented in a board's specifications may not contain essays or Source questions in that board's question style.

AS question styles of the boards and where they are located in this book

Board	Styles of answers	Where located in chapters
OCR	Essays (one-part)	Chs 2, 6, 8
	(two-part) 30/60 minutes	Chs 4, 5, 7, 8, 9, 10
	Sources (3 questions)	Chs 4, 5, 7
AQA	Essays (one-part) AS (20)	Chs 3, 5, 6, 7, 10, 11
	Essays (three-part)	Chs 8, 9
	Sources (3 questions)	Chs 2, 8, 9, 10
Edexcel	Essays (two-part)	Chs 7, 9, 10
	Essay/source combination (3 questions)	Ch. 9

Part 4: Historical Skills

History is a diverse subject with wide-ranging skills. There is also much more emphasis on academic skills within the context of the sixth form. The two can be closely connected and the purpose of Part 4 of each chapter is to suggest how specific skills can be developed both within the History course and with a close connection to more general sixth-form courses. The intention is to enhance techniques already developed in essay-writing and source-analysis – but also to go beyond them in anticipating the needs of students of higher education. The focus of Part 4 of the various chapters is summarised below. These overlap – but are not intended to duplicate – the various patterns of key skills.

Each chapter considers the development of a different skill. The historical context may not be directly relevant to what you are studying, but the skill will be transferable to the area that is. This has the added benefit of making you think about the process of transferring ideas from one context to another and, in the process, changing and refining them. This, as much as anything else, is what History is about.

Skills covered in this book

Type of skill	What it is that is covered	Where it is covered
1 Essay-writing	• Purpose of essays. • Preparation and structure; analysis and factual support. • Precise coverage of the requirements of different styles of question. • Thematic approach to answer.	Introduction: Part 2; and Chs 2–11: Part 2. Ch. 5: Part 4.
2 Source-analysis	• Types of sources and techniques of analysis. • Different types of question. • Contextual knowledge. • Comparison between sources. • Usefulness and reliability of sources. • Use of sources and own knowledge in an overall assessment.	Introduction: Part 3; and Chs 2–11: Part 3. Chs 4, 6, 7 and 11: Part 4.
3 Writing different types of document	• Producing a report.	Ch. 6: Part 4.
4 Oral contributions	• Contributing to a discussion or debate.	Chs 2 and 8: Part 4.
5 Numerical skills	• Use of bar charts. • Use of tables. • Use of graphs.	Chs 4 and 6: Part 4. Ch. 6: Part 3. Ch. 11: Part 4.
6 Weighting the importance of different factors or individuals	• Assessing the roles or significance of individuals. • Weighing up the relative importance of factors as causes.	Chs 3, 8 and 11: Part 4.
7 Working with others towards an agreed objective	• Group work involving decision-making.	Ch. 2: Part 4.
8 Research skills	• Use of websites. • Synthesis of information. • Textbook reading.	Chs 3, 5, 6, 9, 10 and 11: Part 4.

| 9 | Empathy | • To understand differing perspectives on issues. | Chs 3, 9 and 10, Part 4. |
| 10 | Anticipating the skills required for A2 | • Historiography and the study of different interpretations.
• Synoptic approaches to a period of about 100 years.
• How the study of AS History leads conceptually to A2 History. | Conclusion: Part 2. |

Chapter 1

An Introduction to the Period

Independence

In the mid-eighteenth century the inhabitants of the thirteen colonies along the Atlantic seaboard of America still regarded themselves as British, but the society in which they lived was far from similar to that in Britain, and in fact major differences had emerged between northern and southern colonies, with such issues as slavery having a profound effect upon the diversity of life in the Americas. The end, in 1763, of the French and Indian War (or Seven Years War, depending on one's perspective), changed the relationship between the colonies and the mother country, but rather than putting relations on a firmer footing it hastened the process by which the colonies became independent.

The British had no plans to destroy liberty in North America and until the winter of 1775/6 very few colonists favoured independence; yet between 1775 and 1781 the Americans, with the help of the French, defeated the greatest military power in the world at that time and achieved their independence. In the years that followed independence there was initially little support for the expansion of central power and the writing of a new **constitution**. The 'Founding Fathers' however, who met in Philadelphia in the summer of 1787, changed all of that and by the end of 1789 the Constitution had been ratified, and George Washington had been elected the first **President** of the US. The new Constitution and accompanying Bill of Rights ensured that the American Revolution would be a strictly political event, with the social order remaining firmly intact. It contained compromises on major issues such as slavery, the representation of the large and small states, the extent of federal power, and trade; but they were not all compromises which could be laid to rest, and in the years to come the struggle for the Constitution would almost destroy the Union it had created.

Expansion, war and Reconstruction

The first half of the nineteenth century was dominated by westwards expansion, with two large tracts of land accruing to the US as a result of the Louisiana Purchase of 1803 and the buying of land from Mexico following the peace treaty of 1848. As territories further west applied to join the Union as states, the question of whether they would be 'slave' or 'free' states became a thorny issue, particularly as abolitionists, who opposed slavery on moral grounds, grew more vocal. Until the 1850s, when the Whig Party collapsed and the Republican Party came into existence, the party system that had evolved from the end of the eighteenth century managed to prevent slavery from becoming the sectional issue it had always threatened to become. Anti-Catholicism moved from centre stage and gave way to the issue of slavery, which became linked to that of states' rights versus federal rights, and also to wider questions on the nature of individual freedom, culminating in eleven Southern slave states leaving the Union in the months following Abraham Lincoln's election in 1860.

In the decades before the American Civil War (1861–5) the beginnings of industrial development had been more noticeable in the North and it was this greater capacity for production of the materials of war that allowed the North to make more guns and boats than the South. The larger population of the North also allowed it to recruit more soldiers, and these advantages ultimately proved to be crucial to the outcome of the war.

The war was to prove a watershed in terms of resolving some of the issues over which the Constitution had attempted compromise. Slavery was abolished, and the supremacy of federal rights over states' rights was secured, along with the future dominance of the North and the Republican Party. Not all Americans however would be reconciled to the verdict the war had brought, and the period of Reconstruction following war witnessed prolonged bitterness on the part of Southern whites, as well as the first impeachment of a President, and culminated in a 'corrupt bargain' in 1877 between Democrats and Republicans, largely at the expense of **African Americans**.

The rise to power – 'boom and bust'

In the years between 1865 and the close of the century the US became the most powerful industrial nation in the world. The closing of the frontier in 1890 seemed to reinforce the dominance of industrialisation and urbanisation. The pejoratively termed 'Gilded Age' had been largely powered by massive immigration, and had brought with it great wealth for the few, social problems on a scale never seen before, and political corruption at the highest level. A kind of backlash came with the Progressives, who prompted greater state intervention to curb the worst excesses of the capitalist system and championed social and political reform.

The 1890s also saw early attempts at empire-building, with intervention in the Civil War in Spanish Cuba by which the US gained certain Caribbean colonies and power in the Pacific. The reluctance of the government to become involved in the First World War was finally overcome and the US emerged from isolation to play a crucial part in the outcome. America reaped the rewards of victory and was also soon to experience the industrial boom of the 1920s – a decade which also brought with it intolerance, repression, Prohibition and female suffrage. The prosperity of the 1920s however was not widely enough dispersed and this was partly what led to the Great Depression that haunted 1930s America. Franklin Roosevelt's 'New Deal' was only partially successful, but demonstrated the extent to which federal government could intervene to improve quality of life and set a precedent for the post-war era. The prosperity of the country was ironically restored by a war that it had, once again, hoped to avoid, with the US eventually being shaken out of its isolationist complacency by the Japanese attack on Pearl Harbor.

The Cold War and beyond

With the advent of the **Cold War**, foreign policy took an anti-communist direction, against the backdrop of **McCarthyism** during the 1950s. The decade also brought major **civil rights** agitation particularly on the part of African Americans. In the 1960s, Kennedy and Johnson expanded government intervention but their domestic legislation was overshadowed by involvement in Vietnam. Watergate in turn overshadowed the cessation of hostilities with Vietnam, as well as the Nixon Presidency, and seriously undermined the faith of the American people in the way the country was governed. The years of Ford and Carter were followed by the emergence of the 'New Right', personified by Ronald Reagan. In 1992, in the aftermath of the LA riots that left 55 dead, Bill Clinton was elected President. He was a 'New Democrat' who claimed the era of 'big government had ended', but will be best remembered for being only the second President in US history to be impeached. Like Andrew Johnson before him, he may have survived the trial but the whole affair left a sour taste in the mouths of voters.

At the beginning of the twenty-first century the US could still be described as an 'unfinished nation', to borrow the title of Alan Brinkley's excellent book. The US had emerged from the Cold War as the world's only superpower but the richest 1 per cent of its population held 38 per cent of its wealth, and there were also signs that some of the lessons of the past had not been learned: a movement seeking **reparations** for the families of former black slaves strove to make its case; the number of black males in prison exceeded the number in higher education; and tens of thousands of neo-confederates continued to call for independence from the control of a federal government which had apparently ceased to represent Southern values; while the election of George W. Bush in 2000 and the repercussions of '9/11' appear to have ushered in a new era for the United States and the wider world.

The fundamental aims of this textbook are to deal with the issues covered by the examination boards in a concise but interesting way. In many ways the Presidency, the wider federal government and the Constitution is all that Americans have in common, which is why history has often been written from the top down. We hope that in the following pages we have managed to do more than this, and have succeeded in raising issues that may provide students with the impetus to find out more about the fascinating history of the United States of America.

Chapter 2

The Struggle for the Constitution, 1763–1877

This chapter will cover the build-up to the War of Independence and the subsequent writing of the US Constitution. The problems that the Constitution failed to resolve will be examined, along with the changing nature of American society and politics. An assessment of the impact of the Constitution and its amendments on the political development of the US, the significance of the Civil War for the country, and the changing role of the Presidency will also be undertaken.

 Historical background

 Sources

 Historical skills

 Essays

Chronology

1754	French and Indian War began
1756	Seven Years War began
1763	Peace of Paris ended 'Seven Years War' between Britain and France
1764	Sugar Act
1765	Stamp Tax levied on colonists by British government
	Stamp Act Congress met at New York with nine colonies represented
1766	Stamp Act repealed by British but Declaratory Act confirmed subordinate status of colonies
1770	Boston Massacre – five colonists killed
1773	Boston Tea Party
1774	First Continental Congress met at Philadelphia with 12 colonies represented
1775	First shots fired at Lexington in War of Independence
	Second Continental Congress met at Philadelphia
1776	Declaration of Independence
1777	Articles of Confederation agreed by most states
1783	Treaty of Paris – Britain formally recognised US independence
1786	Shays' Rebellion against taxes in Massachusetts
1787	Philadelphia Convention met and wrote the new Constitution
1789	George Washington chosen to be first President and First Congress elected
1798	Alien and Sedition Acts passed (impinged on free speech)
1798–9	Kentucky and Virginia Resolutions advocated nullification of federal laws by states
1800	Thomas Jefferson elected President
1802	Louisiana Purchase doubled size of US territory
1803	Supreme Court established right of judicial review to overturn an Act of Congress
1812	War of 1812 started against the British
1819	Florida acquired from Spain
1828	Andrew Jackson elected President
1845	Texas admitted to Union
1846	Oregon territory acquired
1846–7	War with Mexico
1848	Mexican land purchased
1860	Abraham Lincoln, first Republican to be elected President
1861	American Civil War began
1862	Homestead Act passed by Congress
1863	Emancipation Proclamation
1865	End of Civil War
	Lincoln assassinated
	13th Amendment (abolished slavery)
1867	Andrew Johnson impeached but not found guilty
1868	Ulysses S. Grant elected President
1870	15th Amendment stated that right to vote could not be denied on grounds of race
1877	Compromise between supporters of Presidential candidates Hayes and Tilden

Part 1: Historical background

 Introduction

By the middle of the eighteenth century there existed 13 colonies on the Atlantic seaboard of the North American continent all nominally under British rule. They had been established for a range of reasons in the seventeenth century, except for Georgia which was created in 1733 as a colony for deported debtors. Trade and profit had been the motivation for the setting up of New York, New Jersey and South Carolina, for example, while many of those who set up home in Massachusetts, Connecticut and Pennsylvania did so in order to practise their religious beliefs freely. The colonies each had different customs, currencies and laws, as well as varying climates, which all contributed to economic differences – including the use of African slaves in the southern colonies – and the possibility that one day they might unite to break the shackles of their mother country seemed highly unlikely.

The Treaty of Paris in 1763 has been a convenient event for historians who wish to study the birth of an independent United States of America, given that it formalised the end of the Seven Years War, but there were signs before 1763 that relations between the British and their American cousins were not exactly cordial. In the summer of 1754 a force of the Virginia militia was despatched under the command of a young colonel called George Washington to limit French expansion into the Ohio Valley. Washington's surrender of Fort Necessity marked the beginning of what colonists called the French and Indian War though it was not until 1756 that the British became formally involved in military action against the French and their Indian allies. Many Americans had hoped the British might get involved sooner, but when they did finally appear, great offence was caused to the very colonists they were supposed to be protecting. The requisition of supplies, impressment of troops and reimposition of Crown authority caused a great deal of friction, and Prime Minister Pitt acted swiftly: reimbursing colonists for supplies; allowing the colonial assemblies to take control of recruitment; and sending greater numbers of soldiers from Britain. There is no doubt that the cessation of the struggle between France and Great Britain for global dominance marked a turning point, and in the aftermath of the war, relations between the 13 colonies and their mother country began to decline markedly. For the British, the defeat of the French was expected to give the Crown greater power in America; whereas for the American colonists, the French defeat seemed to reduce their dependence on Britain for protection.

 The road to independence

By the terms of the Treaty of Paris, the French ceded all of Canada and the land east of the Mississippi to the British, who established the Proclamation Line near the crest of the Allegheny Mountains and declared all land to the west to be Indian territory. This was partly in response to the uprising led by Pontiac, chief of the Ottawa, against frontiersmen who had crossed into tribal lands, but served merely to annoy the independent-minded colonists who sought to move west. In addition the exertions of war had more than doubled the national debt of Britain and it was felt that the American colonists should contribute more towards paying off the debt for a war from which they had clearly benefited, as well as to the upkeep of a standing army to guard the frontier. Increasing tax demands, trade controls to reduce manufactures that competed with British goods, clamping down on smuggling, and maintaining a standing army that might even be used against them, all served to further aggravate anti-British feeling among the colonists.

The most notorious of the measures designed to increase revenue from the under-taxed Americans was the Stamp Act of 1765, which levied a tax on all printed documents and thereby offended a range of influential colonials. It led to the calling of the Stamp Act Congress in New York to which nine colonies sent representatives who agreed that they should only be taxed if their own assemblies approved. This was

Figure 2.1 **Map illustrating how the United States was formed**

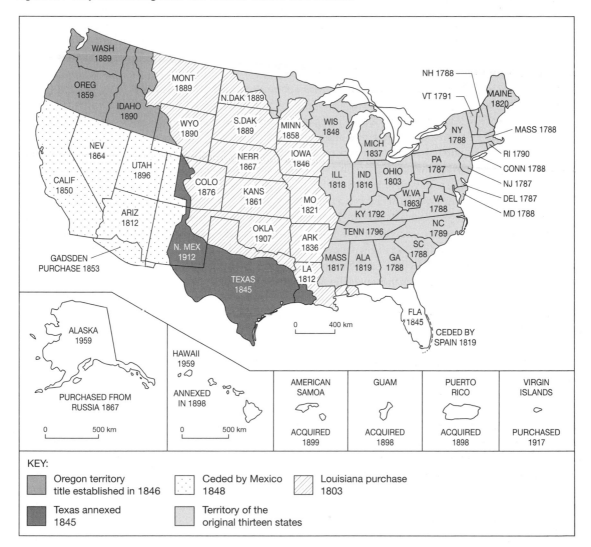

significant in that it was the first formal attempt the colonists had made to organise themselves. The Stamp Act was repealed by the British, but soon the colonists were paying perhaps ten times as much as they had done before 1763. Despite the revision of the Proclamation Line in 1768 to open areas for colonisation, Americans were not satisfied. Even worse, the 1774 Quebec Act seemed designed to cause offence, for as well as recognising Roman Catholics, leaving French civil law in force, giving authority to a governor of Quebec without an elected assembly, and limiting trial by jury, it re-expanded the boundaries of the Canadian province as far south as the Ohio and Mississippi rivers, which was regarded as damaging to the western ambitions of Virginia and Pennsylvania.

The colonies had faced their fair share of internal unrest in the past. In 1763 the Paxton Boys had marched on Philadelphia to demand tax relief and financial support, while in 1771 a small-scale civil war had erupted in North Carolina, but the actions of the mother country gradually brought the squabbling colonists together. The British refused to give way, and relations gradually deteriorated with such events as the Boston Massacre and the Boston Tea Party, followed by the Intolerable Acts which further increased tensions. Americans called the First Continental **Congress** at Philadelphia in September 1774, petitioned King George III for a return to their 1763 status, demanded no taxation without representation and boycotted British goods. In April 1775 the first military skirmishes of the War of Independence took place at Lexington and Concord, persuading undecided colonists to join the radicals. Englishman Thomas Paine's pamphlet 'Common Sense' – considered widely to have been a great inspiration to revolutionaries – went through an astonishing 25 editions in 1776, selling hundreds of thousands of copies. Although it actually worried revolutionaries such as John Adams of Massachusetts in case it encouraged too much democratic thought.

On 2 July 1776 Congress approved Virginian Richard Henry Lee's resolution that 'these United Colonies are, and of right ought to be free and independent states'. This vote formally marked the birth of the United States, but it is 4 July that is remembered for the Declaration of Independence (only a full declaration of independence would have won over French support), which was mainly the work of another Virginian, Thomas Jefferson. It proclaimed the existence of 13 free and independent states and drew on English philosopher John Locke's belief that a government could be overthrown when it ceased to preserve the lives, liberty and happiness of its people. However, of those who signed the document, 69 per cent had held colonial office under the Crown. And in Boston, within a week of the Declaration, it was decided that the rich could avoid the military draft by paying for substitutes, whereas the poor had no choice (a similar system would operate years later during the Civil War). It was therefore clear from an early stage that there would be no great social changes to match the political ones.

Some historians see the origins of the War of Independence in political, intellectual and constitutional terms, while others tend to emphasise social and economic causes, arguing that the colonists had more material interests at heart, but it is possible to see a combination of both interacting.

 ## The winning of independence and subsequent problems

It is argued that between one-fifth and one-third of white colonists remained loyal to Britain during the Revolution and up to 100,000 colonists left the country in its aftermath. Indians generally recognised that their best interests lay with a British victory and chose sides accordingly, as did some blacks. The eventual triumph of the 'American patriots' hastened westwards expansion at the expense of **Native Americans**. It also, according to radical historian Howard Zinn, allowed revolutionary leaders to enrich themselves by taking over confiscated loyalist land and distributing some of it to small farmers in order to create a broad base of support for the new regime (p. 83), leaving poorer whites in much the same situation as before the war.

With the fall of Yorktown to the Americans in 1781 the war was effectively over for the British, although given that the states had taken until 1781 to finally adopt the Articles of Confederation, in many ways it is a wonder that they did win. The Articles, largely the work of John Dickinson, and regarded by many as the United States' first Constitution, bound the states together in a fairly loose alliance, creating a legislative body but not an executive one, nor an independent court system. At least 9 of the 13 states (i.e. two-thirds) had to agree for an important measure to be implemented, while all 13 had to agree for any amendment to be made to the Articles. The **unicameral** Congress, in which each state had one vote regardless of population, continued to have problems raising taxes, regulating trade, raising troops and making decisions to which all states would agree.

By the terms of the Treaty of Paris in 1783, Britain granted the US independence covering land from the southern border of Canada to the northern border of Florida, and as far west as the Mississippi. This quickly became a source of dispute between several of the states. Many Americans assumed that after the war the states would essentially continue to govern themselves, and that there would be no need to further centralise power. After all, had they not just fought a war against an over-mighty government. In 1783 all states had their own constitutions, designed to limit the power of executive branches, with legislatures usually elected annually, but by the end of the 1780s many state constitutions had been revised to create greater stability, often by reducing levels of popular participation.

In 1783 Congress actually moved itself to Princeton, New Jersey – to avoid the threats of army veterans eager for pay they were still owed – then to Annapolis, Maryland, before settling in New York in 1785. Delegates did not always attend regularly, which also undermined the Congress's position, and by 1786 it had become apparent to many that the states faced significant problems which only a revision of the Articles of Confederation could remedy. The difficulties in convincing Britain and Spain to actually adhere to the terms of the Treaty of Paris (the British held on to forts in the north-west and Spain closed off the Mississippi to American trade) also highlighted the diplomatic weakness of the states under the Articles, although a system was devised for organising land to the west. The post-war depression, which lasted from 1784 to 1787, exacerbated the problems of ensuring an adequate supply of money, and without the power to impose taxes, the **Confederation** could not pay off its debts. Financial issues were further complicated by different states dealing in different currencies.

Connecticut quarrelled with its neighbours over trade, Maryland and Virginia disputed ownership of the Potomac river, and Pennsylvania and Connecticut disputed the Wyoming valley, and Rhode Island infuriated other states by issuing a paper currency of its own. Perhaps the most alarming incident of post-war society came in 1786 with the revolt led by Daniel Shays, which aimed to put pressure on the Massachusetts state legislature to cancel debts. There was wide support, particularly from small farmers who owed money, and the revolt spread beyond Massachusetts, eventually being put down by a force of state militia financed by a group of wealthy merchants. The debtors Shays led even helped George Washington, a Virginia plantation owner, to overcome his doubts regarding the wisdom of a constitutional convention. Shays' Rebellion is often treated in isolation from previous acts of insurrection, but it is worth noting that the trend started with Bacon's rebellion in Virginia in 1676. By 1760 there had been 18 separate uprisings aimed at overthrowing colonial governments, as well as 6 black rebellions, and 40 serious riots (Zinn 1996: p. 59). Zinn contends that this rebellious energy had been channelled by the elites against the British during the war, but with the British gone the elites began to worry. The historian Charles Beard argued that other than minimising and repressing physical violence, the main purpose of any government is to make rules that decide property relations between members of society. There certainly seems to have been no popular clamour for a new constitution. M.J. Heale (1986) has even suggested that there was no overwhelming economic or military reason to abandon the Articles of Confederation and pointed out a number of successes of the Articles, arguing the states were far from disintegrating, as New York's Alexander Hamilton, for example, would have had people believe (Heale 1986: p. 42).

 ## Revising the Articles of Confederation

The Philadelphia Convention that met in May 1787 had officially been assembled to revise the Articles, but the representatives from Virginia, led by James Madison and Edmund Randolph, put forward proposals for a completely new constitution. The only state not represented at Philadelphia was Rhode Island, the legislature of which was so divided that members could not agree upon whom to send as delegates. The motives and intentions of the Founding Fathers were mixed and have been the source of much debate among historians ever since. Alan Brinkley (2000) has asserted that Madison and his contemporaries believed that sovereignty lay with the people, but the Constitution drawn up did not acknowledge women, blacks or Native Americans as the equals of white males. Edward Countryman believes the Founding Fathers 'sincerely believed in the dual **enlightenment** principles of representation and consent of the governed' (1999: p. 25), but they drew their ideas from British tradition and law as well as from such enlightened thinkers as Montesquieu and Locke.

Many have concentrated on the social make-up of the Convention and suggested that the members of it designed a constitution to suit themselves. Heale has talked of the elite's desire for a 'unified republic

Figure 2.2
George Washington at the Constitutional Convention in Philadelphia, 1787

which would span a continent . . . and command the respect of the world' and said that as 'men of high status they were cool towards the popular and democratic tendencies in state and local government', arguing that 'their actions can be construed as counter-revolutionary' (p. 43). He concludes that 'the Constitution was designed to reconcile hierarchy with democracy' and the fact that it was decided the President and **Senate** should be chosen by electoral colleges rather than by direct popular vote suggests he is correct.

The average age of the Founding Fathers was about 40 and the majority of the original 55 were lawyers. Most were rich, owning land, slaves and businesses, while half were also moneylenders, and 40 held government bonds. The concept of a strong federal government must have had its appeal. After all it would be able to set high tariffs, prevent the use of paper money to pay off debts, open up Indian lands to speculation, safeguard slavery and raise taxes to pay off bonds. Whatever their precise motives, at Philadelphia the Founding Fathers created a model for government based on a separation of powers between the three main branches of government and ensured that individuals could not serve in more than one branch simultaneously. They combined this with a series of checks and balances which included: a federal system (to protect the country from the tyranny of an over-mighty central government as well as the tyranny of the people); a **bicameral** Congress whose laws could be vetoed by a President, who in turn could be overruled by a two-thirds Congressional majority, and even impeached for serious offences; a mechanism for changing the Constitution, but which prevented whimsical changes being made to it; as well as various other devices such as making the President's cabinet and **Supreme Court** appointees subject to Senate approval, and stipulating that the President and members of both Houses of Congress would each serve for a different number of years. It was not immediately apparent that the Supreme Court would come to rule on the constitutionality of laws passed by Congress, but in practice this is what came to happen.

Despite what the Founding Fathers may have had in common as a social elite, the Constitution finally agreed upon was based on significant compromises. Agreement was eventually reached over: how large and small states would be represented in a bicameral Congress; the three-fifths compromise for the counting of slaves in each state's representation in elections; the regulation of trade by Congress and the safeguarding of slavery; the eventual termination of the slave trade; and the thorny issue of the power relationship between central and state government. For the time the compromises seemed to have resolved major stumbling blocks in the creation of the new government, but they were to be compromises which contained the seeds of future rivalries between North and South.

Once the Constitution had been written the agreement of sufficient number of states was required to make it work. Cleverly and confusingly the supporters of the Constitution called themselves the **Federalists**, although in many respects their opponents who emphasised states' rights would have fitted the description better. The so-called **Anti-Federalists** doubted the very legality of what the Founding Fathers had done, never mind what the Constitution actually contained. The Federalists got their act together faster and more effectively than their opponents, and men such as Alexander Hamilton talked of a permanent body being necessary to 'check the imprudence of democracy'; while Madison, in *The Federalist* (a political pamphlet promoting the merits of the Constitution), argued for strong government to keep down the factional disputes which arose from 'various and unequal distribution of property'.

The conventions that ratified the Constitution were elected by about 20 per cent of white men, hardly popular sovereignty in action. Colin Bonwick (1991) has also highlighted some rather dubious tactics pursued by the Federalists. They insisted that all states elected conventions to ratify the Constitution (state legislatures would probably have rejected it), which would take time and hence allow them, the Federalists, to put out more propaganda; and two Anti-Federalist delegates were forcibly held in their places to make a quorum to ensure the Pennsylvania legislature called a convention (Bonwick 1991: p. 226). The promise of a bill of rights (which would add ten amendments, essentially protecting various freedoms, guaranteeing certain legal rights and establishing the power relationship between centre and states) was enough to swing the vote in Massachusetts, although, according to Leonard Richards, delegates at the Massachusetts Convention were possibly bribed to vote for ratification of the Constitution. Jackson Turner Main has even suggested that the Anti-Federalists were in a slight majority in the country as a whole.

Zinn concludes that the Constitution was the work of an elite aiming to protect and preserve its own privileges, while conceding just enough in the way of rights and freedoms to just enough people to achieve popular backing (1996: p. 97).

 ## The emergence of party rivalries

It has been suggested that in many ways the First Congress, which assembled in 1789, can be seen as a continuation of the Philadelphia Convention as there were so many gaps in the Constitution which still had to be filled. Decisions on the number of Supreme Court judges, how the lower courts would be organised, and the creation of government departments, all had to be made, and a bill of rights (the first ten amendments) also had to be drafted. It is significant that the 10th Amendment, concerning the relationship between the central and state governments, was approved without the addition of the word 'expressly' before the word 'delegated' regarding the powers of the US (which would otherwise have severely restricted the federal government's scope for action), causing much debate in the years to come. The debate over the nature of the Constitution was to continue once it was in place, and the party system which emerged and became another element of the 'checks and balances', was essentially as a result of differences over the interpretation of the power of the federal government.

The Federalists were effectively under Hamilton's leadership as Washington tried to take a non-partisan stance, and were strongest in the commercial parts of the north-east as well as coastal Virginia and South Carolina. They believed in strong national government and a diverse commercial economy. From 1792 Anti-Federalists became Democratic-Republicans and were strongest in New York, inland areas of Virginia and rural parts of the South and West, and although Washington was again unopposed in the election of 1792, the Republicans ran Clinton as their Vice-Presidential candidate against Adams. They followed the views of Jefferson who envisaged small independent farmers living in a country with minimal government interference. As Secretary of the Treasury, Hamilton set up a Bank of the United States in 1791. Secretary of State Jefferson and Attorney-General Randolph took the view that the government did not have the power to charter one, but Washington favoured Hamilton's argument that the Constitution should be 'broadly construed' rather than strictly, drawing on the implied powers of the 10th Amendment. The government passed a tariff, agreed to pay a small group of bondholders, and raised taxes accordingly.

It was one such tax, the 'Whiskey Tax', that provoked small farmers in western Pennsylvania who made whiskey, because it was easier to transport and sell than grain, to take up arms in 1794. Hamilton led troops to put them down, but the heavy-handed treatment of the Whiskey Rebellion by Washington, who had raised a force of nearly 15,000 men, was greeted with grave misgivings by Jeffersonians. Divisions between the parties would continue over the Constitution and government power, Hamilton's financial policies, and foreign relations, particularly the pro-British stance taken by the government during the Napoleonic Wars. In Bonwick's view, by 1800 the party system appeared to have proved its worth, and with its development and vindication, completed the Revolution (1991: p. 251).

 Politics and constitutional disputes

John Adams pipped Jefferson to the Presidency in 1796 by only three electoral college votes, and the latter had to be satisfied with the Vice-Presidency. It was not until the 12th Amendment of 1804 that electors could cast separate votes for President and Vice-President and even this was to cause problems. In 1800 the plan that one Republican elector would cast one of his two votes for a Presidential candidate other than Aaron Burr, to ensure that Jefferson won, went wrong, and the two men tied on 73 votes each which meant that the House of Representatives, in which the Federalists held a majority, had to decide the outcome. After the 36th ballot Jefferson was elected, but he never forgave Burr.

Despite the 1st Amendment of the Constitution apparently safeguarding free speech, in 1798 the Sedition Act made it a crime to say or write anything 'false, scandalous and malicious' against the government with the intent to defame, or stir up popular hatreds against them. It was passed at the time of the French-supported Irish rebellion and the Supreme Court upheld it. The Alien Act of 1798 aimed to reduce immigration and even encourage some of those recently arrived to leave, though Adams did not actually deport any aliens. The Sedition Act was used in the arrest and conviction of ten men, most of them Republican newspaper editors who had dared to criticise some aspect of government policy, but Adams restrained Federalists from persecuting their opponents. It is significant that during 1798–9 Jefferson and Madison each wrote a set of resolutions (anonymously) for Kentucky and Virginia respectively which drew upon the ideas of John Locke and the 10th Amendment to argue that individual states had the right to nullify any law if they felt that the central government had exceeded its powers in creating it. The proposals did not win widespread appeal, but thirty years later John C. Calhoun was to advance a similar argument in defence of South Carolina's response to high tariffs.

Figure 2.3 **Thomas Jefferson**

There is a tendency to associate the states' rights issue with the Southern states in the build-up to Civil War, but it was a group of Federalists in Massachusetts (the Essex Junto) who talked of **secession** from the Union and forming a Northern **confederacy** in the early 1800s, fearing that as the country expanded westwards Federalist and New England influence would wane. They accordingly persuaded Aaron Burr to stand for governor of New York in 1804, possibly with his support for the state seceding. Hamilton and Burr exchanged insults, which culminated in Hamilton's death in a duel fought between the two and Burr's flight to avoid a murder charge. The War of 1812 against the British brought further calls from New England Federalists for a right of nullification and demands for amendments to the Constitution to protect north-eastern interests from the South and West, but by the time of the Treaty of Ghent in 1814 party hostilities had died down.

The so-called 'Era of Good Feelings' was about to begin with Monroe trying to bring unity to politics by appointing a mixture

Figure 2.4
Map illustrating the Missouri Compromise, 1820

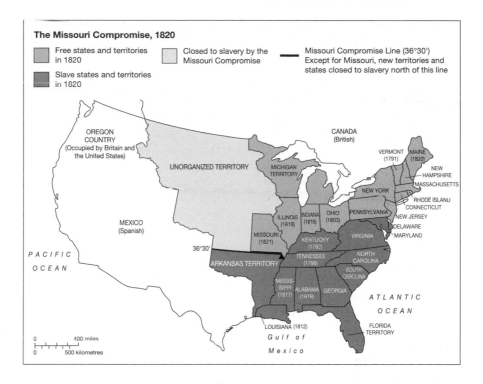

The Missouri Compromise, 1820

- Free states and territories in 1820
- Slave states and territories in 1820
- Closed to slavery by the Missouri Compromise
- Missouri Compromise Line (36°30') Except for Missouri, new territories and states closed to slavery north of this line

OREGON COUNTRY (Occupied by Britain and the United States)

CANADA (British)

UNORGANIZED TERRITORY

MICHIGAN TERRITORY

VERMONT (1791)
MAINE (1820)
NEW HAMPSHIRE
MASSACHUSETTS
NEW YORK
RHODE ISLAND
CONNECTICUT
NEW JERSEY
PENNSYLVANIA
DELAWARE
MARYLAND

MEXICO (Spanish)

ILLINOIS (1818)
INDIANA (1816)
OHIO (1803)

MISSOURI (1821)
KENTUCKY (1792)
VIRGINIA

PACIFIC OCEAN

36°30'

ARKANSAS TERRITORY
TENNESSEE (1796)
NORTH CAROLINA
SOUTH CAROLINA

MISSIS-SIPPI (1817)
ALABAMA (1819)
GEORGIA

ATLANTIC OCEAN

LOUISIANA (1812)
FLORIDA TERRITORY

Gulf of Mexico

0   400 miles
0   500 kilometres

of politicians from different sections and parties to his cabinet. Ironically in light of his subsequent stance, Calhoun introduced a bill into Congress which allowed use of government funds for internal improvements, but Madison vetoed it the day before Monroe took office on the grounds that Congress did not have the authority to do so. (In 1830 Andrew Jackson vetoed a proposed government subsidy to the Maysville Road in Kentucky on the grounds that the road lay entirely within that state and could therefore not be regarded as a part of 'interstate commerce'.) Monroe won the 1820 election without opposition in the wake of the rapid decline of the Federalists, but by the late 1820s the Republicans had begun to attract the same sort of criticisms that they had aimed at the Federalists in power in the 1790s over such issues as centralisation and expanded government scope.

The 1824 Presidential election saw Andrew Jackson win most votes in the country and electoral college, though not more than half. In the House of Representatives Henry Clay's supporters voted for the son of the second President, John Quincy Adams, who, once President, appointed Clay as his Secretary of State (a likely stepping stone to the Presidency). The so-called 'corrupt bargain' damaged Adams, and the Jacksonians in Congress blocked most of his legislation. By 1828 the US's second two-party system had emerged. The new parties had not originated in Washington as those of the 1790s had, but were essentially coalitions of state parties. They reflected a growing interest in national politics and by the 1840s turnout in national elections finally overtook that for state elections. Adams's supporters were known as the National Republicans (Whigs in the 1830s) and Jackson's as the Democratic Republicans (Democrats in the 1830s). The former were keen to preserve the economic nationalism of previous years, the latter demanded an assault on privilege and established wealth in favour of wider opportunities. The vitriolic campaign of 1828 included accusations of murderer thrown at Jackson over his execution of militia men in the War of 1812, and charges of bigamy against Jackson's wife who had apparently not been legally divorced from her first husband. She died within weeks of this attack. Although Jackson's victory was decisive, Adams won all of the north-east and much support in the mid-Atlantic region, strongly suggesting that not all voters wished to see the 'era of the common man' ushered in under Jackson.

'Jacksonian Democracy' is a term often applied to the 1820s and 1830s, but democracy was growing before Old Hickory's Presidency. The new states in the west had led the way in giving all white males the right to vote and hold office regardless of property or tax qualifications and older states followed suit fearing that people would be attracted to the west by its greater degree of democracy. In 1800 the people had chosen Presidential electors in only 6 of the 16 states but by 1828 Presidential electors were selected by popular vote in every state except South Carolina. In 1824 less than 27 per cent of adult white males had voted in the Presidential election, but in 1828 the figure rose to 58 per cent, and in 1840 it had increased to 80 per cent. It is worth noting however that in 1832 only 2 million *could* vote in a population of 13 million, and in reality Jackson's ideas of democracy and equality were narrowly confined to white male citizens in an effort to attacked entrenched privilege and vested interest. This extended to the permanent office-holders of the federal bureaucracy, but although he is often credited with establishing the 'spoils system', it should be remembered that Jackson did not remove more than 20 per cent of existing office-holders and in 1832 Jackson's supporters called a national convention to re-nominate him rather than keeping the process within the elite party machine.

Despite his reservations about government power, Jackson showed the strength of his belief in the importance of the Union during the Nullification Crisis, threatening to lead an army to South Carolina himself if the state refused to implement the law. His speech at the annual Democratic dinner in honour of Jefferson in 1830 proposed that the Federal Union must be preserved, in contrast to Calhoun's subtle toast to 'The Union, next to our liberty most dear'.

The Democrats in the 1830s continued to advocate limited federal government except where action might eliminate certain inequalities, and tended to support expansion, which they believed would widen opportunities. The Whigs were generally keener on government power and believed in an economic system including tariffs to protect domestic goods, internal improvement programmes and a national bank. They were wary of expansion and the instability it might bring. Both parties tended to say different things in different states to court favour. With this in mind the Whigs stood three candidates against Martin Van Buren in 1836, in a failed attempt to prevent any candidate from achieving a majority in the Presidential electoral college, and thereby pass on the task of choosing the President to the House of Representatives. In 1840 however, when the election was covered for the first time by the 'penny press', and both parties claimed to represent the 'common man', William Henry Harrison became the first Whig President – although he died after only a month in office, and was succeeded by John Tyler. Tyler was dumped by the Whigs before the 1844 election and he and a small group of Southern Whigs prepared to rejoin the Democrat Party. They believed among other things that the government ought to protect and possibly expand slavery and were also strong adherents to states' rights.

The breakdown in the US's second party system with the collapse of the Whigs in the 1850s had catastrophic implications, as it served as both a prelude to and significant factor in the build-up to Civil War. The new Republican Party, according to Eric Foner, 'gloried in . . . materialism, social fluidity, and the dominance of the self-made man – which 20 years earlier had been the source of widespread anxiety and fear in Jacksonian America' (Goodheart 1993: pp. 271–2). In 1854, the Republicans won enough seats to allow them to control the House of Representatives with their allies among the 'Know-Nothings', essentially an anti-Catholic, anti-foreign party. Following the pro-slavery result of the Dred Scott case, Republicans showed their contempt for the verdict of the Supreme Court and, by implication, the Constitution by claiming that when they won control of the Presidency they would 'pack' the Court with new members who might reach a different decision.

Sectional animosities had been smouldering for some years. The phenomenal expansion of the country (through the Louisiana Purchase of 1803, the acquisitions of Florida in 1819, Texas in 1845 and Oregon in 1846, and the vast territory bought in 1848 after the Mexican War) had raised the question of whether slavery would in turn expand. The Missouri Compromise of 1820 and the 1850 Compromise appeared to resolve differences at the time, but they were too deep-rooted to disappear so easily. With expansion Native Americans suffered, not at the hands of frontiersmen, according to Van Every, but from industrialisation and commerce, from the growth of population of railroads and cities, the rise in land values and the greed of businessmen – all sanctioned by the federal government. In 1860 the election of a Republican President, Abraham Lincoln, triggered the secession of a number of Southern states from the Union, and led to Civil War. Essentially, the North fought to preserve the Union, and it was only later that Lincoln decided to emancipate the slaves. Zinn has pointed out that the so-called 'war for liberty' also saw working people attacked by soldiers for striking, Indians massacred in Colorado and perhaps 30,000 political prisoners being held for criticising Lincoln's policies (1996: p. 228).

 ## Amendments to the Constitution

The first ten amendments essentially guaranteed the rights of citizens. The list was not intended to be exhaustive but free speech, freedom of the press and religion, protection of property, certain legal entitlements, the right to bear arms, and the relationship between the states and central government were clearly considered to be the most important issues not specifically covered by the Constitution.

The 11th Amendment (1798) stated that the judicial power of the US did not extend to a legal suit against a state. The 12th Amendment (1804) stated that electors were to vote by ballot for the President and Vice-President one of whom should not be from the same state as the elector. If no candidate had an overall majority, the Representatives were to choose from no more than the top three, votes would be made by states with each state having one vote, and the candidate requiring a majority of states to win.

Four years after the unsuccessful proposal of an amendment to prevent any future amendments giving Congress the power to abolish or interfere with slavery in any state, the 13th Amendment (1865) was passed which abolished slavery. This was followed by the 14th Amendment (1868) which guaranteed citizenship to all born or naturalised in the US, with any state failing to enact black suffrage to have its representation in the House of Representatives and electoral college cut proportionately. This was never enforced and it became inoperative with the passage of the 15th Amendment in 1870 which disqualified certain Confederate supporters from voting, and stated that the right to vote should not be denied on grounds of race, colour or previous condition of servitude.

 ## Judicial power

In 1801 the Federalist lame-duck Congress reduced the number of Supreme Court judges by one but increased significantly the number of federal judgeships as a whole. Before he left the Presidency, Adams quickly appointed Federalists to the new positions, in the so-called 'midnight appointments'. The 1801 Judiciary Act was repealed but this led to a challenge in the courts over whether Adams's 'midnight appointments' could take office. In 1796 the Supreme Court had exercised the power of judicial review for the first time by upholding the validity of a law passed by Congress, but in 1803 in Marbury v. Madison the Court, under Chief Justice John Marshall, declared an Act of Congress (the 1789 Judiciary Act) to be unconstitutional, which meant that the Court could not compel executive officials to appoint the judges.

In 1819, in McCulloch v. Maryland, Marshall confirmed the 'implied powers' of Congress by recognising the legality of the Bank of the United States despite great opposition to it in the South and West. In 1821, in Cohens v. Virginia, Marshall showed that the power of the Supreme Court to review legal decisions extended to state courts, asserting that the states had given up part of their sovereignty in ratifying the Constitution. Under Marshall's leadership from 1801 to 1835, the judiciary was established as a branch of government which was as important as the executive and legislature. The Supreme Court also supported the supremacy of the federal government over the states in regulating the economy for the good of the whole, and backed corporations and private enterprise.

Upon Marshall's death in 1835, Andrew Jackson appointed his ally, Roger B. Taney, as Supreme Justice; he subsequently diluted the economically nationalistic stance Marshall had tended to take. In 1837, in Charles River Bridge v. Warren Bridge, Taney ruled the object of government was to promote the general happiness and that overrode the possible breach of contract by Massachusetts regarding the building of a bridge.

Perhaps the most significant case heard by the Supreme Court before the Civil War was that of Dred Scott, the black slave who sued for his freedom on the grounds that he had been taken into a **free territory** by his master. The Court ruled that blacks were not citizens and therefore not entitled to a Court hearing, and that the Missouri Compromise of 1820 had in fact contravened the 5th Amendment against the seizure of property. This was the first time since 1803 that the Court had declared an Act of Congress unconstitutional, but the implications of the decision were far greater, for it implied that both the Republican Party's pledge to ban slavery from the western territories and Illinois Democrat Stephen Douglas's 'popular sovereignty' (whereby the inhabitants of territory voted on whether slavery should be allowed or not) were both unconstitutional. It also of course implied that no state had the right to exclude slavery. Taney and his judges had hoped to resolve the sectional crisis, but only served to intensify it by outraging anti-slavery campaigners in the North, as well as weakening the standing of the Supreme Court.

Despite there having been a civil war, apparently fought to resolve such issues, the Supreme Court still showed that after the war it could rule in favour of the states. In the 1873 Slaughterhouse case, New Orleans butchers claimed they had been deprived of their livelihood by a monopoly established by the state of Louisiana, which constituted an infringement their rights under the 14th Amendment, but judges decided that the rights of citizens should remain under state rather than federal control.

 ## Presidential powers

It was not the intention of the Founding Fathers that the President should be dominant within the governmental system established, but Article II did confer such powers on the incumbent as the making of treaties and the appointment of Supreme Court judges (both subject to the approval of the Senate), and made him commander-in-chief of the armed forces. The President was also to have the power of veto over legislation passed by Congress unless it achieved a two-thirds majority. Washington assumed the power to create a national bank and to introduce an excise tax. Congress acknowledged, reluctantly, the President's power to dismiss members of his cabinet.

Presidents following Washington tended to follow the precedents he had set, not seeking more than two terms in office and using their powers cautiously, although in 1803 Thomas Jefferson exceeded his powers by concluding the Louisiana Purchase with France which expanded the country by 827,000 square miles. The Senate later ratified the relevant treaty. Jefferson also used patronage to ensure that by the end of his second term virtually all federal posts were held by loyal supporters. He did cut government spending and scaled down the armed forces but, despite his reservations, the economy continued to become more diverse and commercialised.

Andrew Jackson who served from 1829 to 1837, despite wanting to reduce the scope of federal government, believed in strong leadership, and his introduction of the so-called 'spoils system' (to protect Americans from long-term office-holders) and reliance on an unofficial 'kitchen cabinet' gave him greater freedom than perhaps his predecessors had enjoyed, and pushed his powers to their limit. He used his Presidential veto more times than all previous Presidents put together. He saw off the Bank of the United States in 1836 although its demise left a gap which hindered the economic stability of the country. In the 1830s, in spite of a Supreme Court ruling, Jackson allowed the removal of the 'five civilised tribes' westwards, beyond the Mississippi, and in future years the federal government would break treaties made with other Indian tribes. By the 1830s Whigs were referring to Jackson as 'King Andrew I', despite the Democrats' supposed advocacy of limited federal government. Zinn chooses to remember 'Jackson the slaveholder, land speculator, executioner of dissident soldiers, exterminator of Indians' (1996: p. 129).

John Tyler became President in 1841 – following William Henry Harrison's death from pneumonia after making a long **inaugural speech** in the rain. Despite being a Whig, Tyler had been a Democrat, and once in power 'His Accidency' agreed to bills abolishing Van Buren's independent Treasury system and higher tariffs, refused to re-charter the Bank of the United States and vetoed internal improvement bills. As a result his own party dumped him. James K. Polk (1845–9) his successor, pursued a war with Mexico which resulted in the US acquiring vast new areas of territory. Under James Buchanan (1857–61) the Presidency was brought into disrepute. He was reluctant to intervene to alleviate the growing crisis and did little to check the drift towards war. He proved to be indecisive at vital moments, and seemed to lack understanding of the strength of feeling that existed on both sides, particularly the North.

Lincoln (1861–5), recently voted the greatest President in a survey of US History professors, exceeded his powers during the Civil War by sending men into battle without Congress declaring war (although he argued that because it was a domestic conflict he did not need to seek their permission), increased the size of the regular army without legal authority, and unilaterally declared a naval blockade of the South as well as suspending habeas corpus and imprisoning opponents, occupying Baltimore to stop border states seceding, turning Missouri and Maryland into an occupied state to safeguard Washington, and seizing Northern telegraph offices during the first three months of the war. Chief Justice Taney ruled that he had exceeded his powers in declaring the Emancipation Proclamation and there can be no doubt that had he survived the war he would have found himself at odds with the Radicals in his party who wished to control the process of Reconstruction. He did not however extend the powers of the President in any permanent way. Lincoln's ideas for Reconstruction (a process which in actual fact started during the war, although writers tend to opt for 1865 as a starting date) were more or less followed after his death by his successor Andrew Johnson, who was initially welcomed to the office by Radical Republicans. Johnson has the dubious honour of being the first President ever to be impeached by Congress. The charges brought against him were motivated purely by the wish for revenge on the part of those who believed he had wilfully obstructed Congressional attempts to introduce equal rights for blacks after the war and generally done his best to frustrate Radical Reconstruction. They were undoubtedly correct in their assessment, but Johnson had not exceeded his powers, and enough senators saw sense to prevent the impeachment finding him guilty.

 ## The constitutional impact of the Civil War and its aftermath

Eric Foner has argued that 'what was at stake in 1860, as in the entire sectional conflict, was the character of the nation's future' (Goodheart 1993: p. 274) adding that: 'In a sense, the Constitution and national political system had failed in the difficult task of creating a nation – only the Civil War itself would accomplish it' (p. 276). Shelby Foote has argued that any understanding of the US has to be based on an understanding of the Civil War, and that the war defined the US and its people (Burns 1989). Celia O'Leary has argued that what it meant to be an American remained undefined after the war, with regional differences persisting, class conflict increasing, mass immigration, the unresolved position of freed blacks, and continued bitterness in the South (1994).

What must be determined by anyone attempting to measure the impact of the war is what would have changed without it and what would not. The withdrawal of Southern Democrats from Congress in 1860 left the Republicans with a majority which they used to pass measures that could never have been passed had the Democrats stayed. The Homestead Act of 1862 put up 50 million acres of public land for sale in 160 acre lots, most of which were bought up by speculators. An additional 100 million acres was given by Congress to the railroads, and a national bank was also set up. The greatest impact the war made however was on the lives of four million black slaves who were set free by the 13th Amendment, and in that sense the war could be said to be truly revolutionary. The **rebel states** would not be readmitted to the Union unless they agreed to the 13th Amendment and that very fact highlights that slavery could not have been abolished constitutionally without the war.

The war resolved the questions over the nature of the Union and marked a triumph of federal over state power. After the war federal spending remained well above pre-war levels although national government continued to have little direct impact on most Americans. Having said that it is perhaps significant that the first ten amendments to the Constitution had attempted to limit the power of federal government while six of the next seven after the war empowered the government to act. The dominance of the North and capitalism was assured, with more tariff laws introduced postbellum, as well as a uniform currency and federal support for railroad construction.

Patrick O'Brien has suggested the interpretations of historians such as Beard, that the war marked a turning point in the economic life of the nation and represented the war as a triumph for free market capitalism over a feudal-type South, should be treated with care and feels that, in purely material terms, the Civil War did not pay (1988: p. 69), with both North and South suffering as a result. Several of those industrialists and financiers who emerged as 'robber barons' in later years took advantage of the opportunities created by the war and large-scale production was possibly accelerated, while a shortage of labour in the North stimulated a greater use of technology. Some argue that the major changes in agriculture, industry and transport had started before the war, and that although war may have been a catalyst for economic development it did not essentially change direction. Others have even argued that the war retarded economic growth. In the South there was industrial development and urban growth after the war, but it remained the poorest section of the US for another hundred years.

'Reconstruction', the term generally given to the period after the war has been debated hotly by historians with Dunning (1907) blaming a vindictive and power-seeking group of Northern Radical Republicans for hardships endured by the South. Du Bois (1935) saw Northern intentions as more altruistic in wanting to create a more democratic society in the South; and although Foner (1988) has said that Reconstruction can be judged a failure in terms of not securing for blacks' rights as citizens and free labourers, in many other ways the period brought great progress for blacks, including the holding of political office and economic advancement. Reconstruction also saw Presidential authority set against the power of Congress. Johnson vetoed the First Reconstruction Act because of the legal powers given to the military and Congress used a range of devices to block the testing of the Reconstruction Acts in the Supreme Court – there was even talk of the Radicals abolishing the Supreme Court altogether. The Tenure of Office Act passed in March 1867 was a ploy by Radicals to prevent the President from removing from office their ally in cabinet, Secretary of War Stanton, without the Senate's consent; and the Command of the Army Act prohibited the President from issuing military orders except through the commanding officer of the army and also from relieving him or assigning him elsewhere without Senate approval. Both laws appeared to violate the Constitution and Johnson sacked Stanton to enable a test case to be brought. Johnson's impeachment was an attempt by Congress to exceed its powers and its motives were essentially political, but even so he stood no chance of becoming President again.

The reassertion of power by Congress continued after the war, and it was not until Theodore Roosevelt in the early twentieth century that a more dominant President emerged. Dunning argued melodramatically that the single vote by which Johnson escaped conviction marked the margin by which the Presidency escaped destruction (not until 1926 did the Supreme Court declare the Tenure in Office Act unconstitutional). The seven Republicans who voted with the Democrats to acquit Johnson feared permanent damage to the Presidency, and that Benjamin Wade might succeed him. They effectively sacrificed their political careers to scupper the unscrupulous tactics of the Radicals.

By the end of Ulysses Grant's first term in office a number of 'Liberal Republicans' had come to oppose 'Grantism' and allied themselves with the Democrats to nominate Horace Greeley. In 1877, however, there was again a Republican in the White House, following an election marked by fraud and corrupt bargaining on both sides. 'The Compromise of 1877' ensured that Southern whites would restore their dominance in the region. By 1877, whites had reached what Maldwyn Jones has called a 'modus vivendi' at the expense of blacks who would be isolated and marginalised for decades to come (1995: p. 259).

National politics certainly changed course after the war. Prior to the war Southern slaveholders had held the Presidency for 49 years and the Supreme Court had always had a Southern majority. Following the war it was to be 100 years before a President came from a former rebel state, and over the next 50 years only 5 of the 26 Supreme Court judges were to be Southerners. Only two Democrat Presidents were elected in the 70 years up until 1930, although elections between 1876 and 1892 were very close. James McPherson (1990) calls this fundamental shift in the balance of political power between North and South a revolution, but it would have probably happened without the war, and the imminence of change was partly why the South left the Union in any case. What the war did was to remove the social and political system of the South and change the basis of its workforce and economic system.

In the first week of July 1877 in Baltimore, where all the liquid sewage ran through the streets, 139 babies died. When the railroad strikes of 1877 were over, a hundred people were dead and a thousand had been to jail. Economically the US was a less equal society than it had been in 1763, but the Union had survived, and the Constitution had evolved through amendment and interpretation during a period of dramatic changes, to produce a system of government which prohibited slavery and had attempted to guarantee equal political rights for African Americans.

Part 2: Essays

 The writing of the Constitution

1   Read the following Source and then answer the questions that follow.

An extract from Article I Section I of the US Constitution, 1787:

All legislative powers herein granted shall be vested in a Congress of the United States, which shall consist of a Senate and House of Representatives.

(a) Using the Source and your own knowledge explain briefly who would sit in Congress. (3)

(b) Outline the concept of the 'separation of powers' as applied by the Founding Fathers to the Constitution. (7)

(c) To what extent were the Founding Fathers primarily concerned with creating a federal government of limited power? (15)

(AQA)

(a) The Senate would be composed of two members from each state, ensuring that every state regardless of size had equality in at least one of the chambers of Congress, and senators initially would be indirectly elected. Those congressmen who were to sit in the House of Representatives were to be directly elected, and the bigger the population of a state the more members it was entitled to, thereby guaranteeing the bigger states greater say and voting power.

(b) The concept of the separation of powers as applied to the US Constitution was influenced by the writings of the political philosopher, Montesquieu, which were, ironically, based on his misunderstanding of the working of the British constitution. The powers refer to the three branches of government established by the Founding Fathers and the idea behind separation was that each branch would carry out a different function: the Executive (which was regarded with most suspicion by Americans) would carry out government; the Legislature would debate and pass laws; and the Judiciary, or at least a Supreme Court, would enforce the law, although the scope of its powers was vaguely defined.

The idea that no person should be a member of more than one branch of government at any one time was also part of the concept, with the one exception of the Vice-President who was entitled to sit in the Senate, but not to speak or cast a vote other than in the event of a tie. The separation was designed to ensure that too much power would not be allowed to accumulate in any branch of government or with any one individual. It could also be argued that the 10th Amendment to the Constitution which distinguished between state powers and federal powers was also an attempt to separate powers.

(c) The term 'limited power' needs to be considered carefully because limited power simply implies that there were rules created which restricted the scope of federal government, and it does not necessarily mean that federal government had little power. It is also worth considering the idea of limited power from two perspectives. If the 1787 Constitution is compared with the Articles of Confederation clearly the power at the centre had been increased massively at the expense of state sovereignty. For example under the new Constitution the federal government could levy taxes, regulate foreign and interstate trade and pass laws more easily than under the Articles, so if the word 'limited' is taken to mean reduced then clearly this was not the case in comparison with the Articles which had left the concept of state sovereignty firmly intact.

If one compares the power of federal government with that of the British government before the war however, then the system created by the Founding Fathers certainly did place limits on government power. It was limited by the separation of powers internally to ensure that no one branch of government or individual became too powerful. The powers of each chamber of the legislature were limited with respect to each other; and the frequency of elections, particularly for the House of Representatives, ensured that representatives could be replaced at regular intervals if necessary. The power of federal government was further limited by the Bill of Rights which outlined certain freedoms that could not be restricted or interfered with by the federal government, and of course the 10th Amendment firmly stated that states would broadly retain jurisdiction over areas not designated to federal government. The Bill of Rights was not of course originally intended by the Founding Fathers nor part of the original Constitution; neither did many envisage that the Supreme Court would also come to limit the power of government by ruling laws to be unconstitutional. It can however be argued that the Founding Fathers did intend to create a government of limited power – anything else in the wake of the war and the 'tyranny of King George' would have been unacceptable to the majority of Americans – but they also intended to create a government with just enough power to ensure that the country did not descend into petty squabbling and disunity, that would count for something on the international stage, and could pay off its debts.

2   Read the following Source and then answer the questions that follow.

> An extract from Richard Henry Lee's proposal to amend the new Constitution, September 1787:
>
> . . . it is submitted
>
> That the new Constitution proposed for the Government of the U. States be bottomed upon a declaration, or Bill of Rights . . .

(a) Using the Source and your own knowledge explain why Richard Henry Lee felt it necessary that a bill of rights be added to the Constitution. (3)

(b) How far were individual rights a consideration when writing the Constitution? (7)

(c) To what extent were eighteenth-century views of property rights and hereditary power challenged by the US Constitution? (15)

(AQA)

(a) Richard Henry Lee represented the fears of those who felt that the Constitution would give too much power to the federal government. The writers of the Constitution had presumed that, with such concepts as the 'separation of powers' and the checks and balances which had been built into the document, individual rights would be safeguarded against an over-mighty central government. Lee and others however wanted to ensure that certain rights, such as free speech and freedom from arbitrary arrest, would be guaranteed by the Constitution as well as getting a specific statement on where the jurisdiction/power of the federal government stopped, and that of the individual states applied.

(b) There is no doubt that the American Constitution of 1787 was the most democratic of its time, and there is thus a strong argument that individual rights were an important consideration in its framing. The precise influence of Enlightenment thinkers such as Locke and Rousseau is difficult to gauge, as is that of Thomas Paine, but certain extracts from the Constitution would indicate that individual rights were important. The fact that the right to stand for such offices as President or senator were not limited by wealth or property qualifications would suggest that individual rights were being taken seriously, but however progressive that may sound in theory, in reality it would not be possible for simply anyone to find the resources on which to base a campaign to become President. Other individual rights included protection from arbitrary arrest, the safeguarding of property, the right to vote for government representatives (although states would decide who could vote), and the enactment that citizens of each state would be entitled to all the rights extended to citizens of any other state. It was also decided that holding office would not be impeded by anyone's religious beliefs.

Individual rights outlined in the Constitution were of course essentially limited to white males. It was simply assumed that females, Native Americans and blacks were not part of the deal and it could not have worked if they had been. Black slaves were regarded as personal property, while free blacks were certainly not regarded as the equals of whites, even in the North, where very few were even permitted to vote. The fact that a bill of rights had to be promised before certain states would ratify suggests that the Founding Fathers had not gone far enough for many, and if the articles of the Constitution are examined, it would seem that the priorities as far as the Founding Fathers were concerned tended to be the relationships between the branches of government, how the members of the branches of government would be selected and the powers that the federal government would wield.

(c) It can be argued that contemporary views of hereditary power were shattered by the Founding Fathers, but in fact property rights were uppermost in the minds of those who wrote the Constitution, which was designed to safeguard the rights of property: to ensure that it would effectively be property owners who held influence in the new system even though in theory neither wealth nor property ownership were required to stand for office. The indirect voting for the President and the Senate was clearly an attempt to dilute the influence of popular forces; and although titles of nobility were barred by the Constitution that did not prevent the elites from handing down their huge estates and wealth to the next generations of their families or concentrating political power in their own hands.

Having said that, the fact that the new nation's head of state and members of the legislature would actually be elected was an astonishing step for the time in relation to other countries, although it might be argued that most of the states were more democratic than the new federal system established, with many of them having annually elected legislatures. It should also be remembered there had been discussions about Prince Henry of Prussia becoming monarch of the US, and there were some who felt that the President should be elected for life. In the end, with so much of the blame for the breakdown in relations between the states and Britain being put on George III and the need for a constitution that would be acceptable to the majority, it would have been very difficult to justify the creation of a King Washington for example. So there would be no hereditary monarch and nor would there be a hereditary upper chamber of the legislature resembling the House of Lords in Britain. But that did not mean that Congress would be filled with small farmers, mechanics and artisans.

It can actually be argued that the Constitution reinforced eighteenth-century views of property rights with its acknowledgement of slavery and bonded servitude, and safeguards on seizures of property. Madison asserted that Republican government was needed to maintain peace in a society riddled with factional disputes which arose from 'various and unequal distribution of property'. The Founding Fathers themselves were property owners and it made sense for them to create a system in which their interests would flourish. The rebellion led by Daniel Shays in 1786, which seemed to threaten the fabric of a social system based on property ownership, certainly made many think more seriously about revising the Articles of Confederation. In the new Constitution the electoral college voting systems for the President and the Senate were clearly devices by which popular feeling might be watered down and the real decision-making be left to people of more substance. In this way they managed, as Heale has put it, to 'reconcile hierarchy with democracy'.

It is also worth examining Article I Section 8 of the Constitution to gain an insight into what the Founding Fathers were concerned about: areas such as trade and finance, which a property-owning elite might be expected to prioritise. Gore Vidal's comment that 'the system established was the best sort of government for White Anglo-Saxon Protestant men of property to do business in' has probably proved to be correct.

3   Read the following Source and then answer the questions that follow.

> An extract taken from the Annapolis Convention of 1786:
>
> . . . there are important defects in the System of Federal Government . . . and . . . embarrassments which characterise the present state of our national affairs, foreign and domestic . . .

(a) Using the Source and your own knowledge summarise briefly the main defects in the Articles of Confederation to which the members of the Annapolis Convention referred. (3)

(b) To what extent was the Constitution based on practical considerations rather than principle? (7)

(c) 'The Founding Fathers wrote a Constitution that suited themselves.' Comment on this statement in light of the social positions and views of the men who framed the Constitution. (15)

(AQA)

(a) The members of the Annapolis Convention were concerned that the Articles of Confederation did not confer sufficient power on Congress to deal effectively with the problems that appeared to face the country at the end of the war. Such problems included 'domestic' ones such as paying off the country's debt, lack of a uniform currency, and the lack of an efficient way of ensuring law and order, and 'foreign' ones such as diplomatic status and defence. The war had highlighted the problems of raising taxes and soldiers in a situation where 9 of the 13 states needed to agree for major decisions to be passed, and unanimity was required to amend the Articles.

(b) Many of the issues with which the Founding Fathers were concerned were what could be described as practical issues rather than ones based on deeply felt principles or political philosophies. There is no doubt that writers such as Locke, Montesquieu, Rousseau and Paine influenced the men at Philadelphia to some degree, and that ideas concerning individual rights and democracy played their part, but in many ways the problems which perturbed the elites of the country were the lack of unity and uniformity, how to enforce law and order and weak diplomatic status. These concerns were the driving forces behind the actions of the men at Annapolis, who in 1786 voted to call a convention of state representatives at Philadelphia to redraft the Articles of Confederation.

With war over it had become apparent to some that the Articles of Confederation were insufficient to bind the states together in any meaningful way, although, following the Treaty of Paris, many could see no reason for the states to be bound more closely. The majority continued to identify more with their own states rather than their nation. But men who shared a national vision, such as Alexander Hamilton, found that they could not stand by while states imposed tariffs at different rates, unilaterally made wars and treaties with Indian tribes, set different requirements for naturalisation, disputed land ownership with each other, and issued a variety of currencies. Equally of concern to them were the problems at national level, with a Congress unable to pay off war debts, deal with the post-war depression, adequately defend the country or persuade the British and Spanish to honour the terms of the Treaty of Paris. Hamilton wrote: 'There is something . . . contemptible in the prospect of a number of petty states . . . fluctuating and unhappy at home, weak and insignificant by their dissensions in the eyes of other nations.' The rebellion of debtors in Massachusetts, led by Daniel Shays in 1786, raised additional fears about the security of loans and the potential for lawlessness among the better off such as Edmund Randolph, who saw 'the prospect of anarchy from the laxity of government'. Alex Waddan sees the economic dislocation of the period as the main factor prompting the creation of a stronger central government.

Article I Section 8 of the Constitution itself is really the best evidence for the hard-headed practicality of the Founding Fathers with regard to the day-to-day functioning of government. It covers the raising of tax, coining of money, standardisation of weights and measures, the establishment of post offices and patents for inventions and the raising of armies. It can also be argued that all the compromises made to secure the creation and ratification of the Constitution were examples of pragmatism. Anti-slavery principles were laid aside to ensure the support of Southern states regarding the three-fifths clause on counting slaves. South Carolina and Georgia (the only two states which had not banned the slave trade) were allowed to continue the importation of slaves for another 20 years. Smaller states were bought off by equal representation in the Senate. Northern commercial interest was assuaged by the simple majority in Congress needed to regulate trade, future migrants west were promised equal representation and a bill of rights was added to win over waverers; while it could be argued that women, Indians and slaves were all excluded on practical grounds.

(c) Edward Countryman has said: 'It was not the people who clamored for a Constitution, but rather a small, elite group of men who began the movement by writing letters to one another, essays in newspapers, and legal opinions.'

The best-known supporter of this line was Charles Beard who, in 1913, argued that the Founding Fathers were the spokesmen for an elite, keen to protect rights of property (including slaves and bonded servants). He argued that, apart from the repression of violence, the main purpose of any government is to make rules which determine the property relations of its citizens. Clinton Rossiter has called the 55 Founding Fathers 'an elite of an elite', and they certainly did not represent a microcosm of the population as a whole; their average age was around 40, with 13 owning plantations, 16 owning slaves, 30 possessing academic degrees at a time when few when to college, 13 being lawyers (although 36 had trained in law), 8 being merchants, 12 being state office-holders and 42 having served in Congress. Bonwick points out that no shopkeepers, artisans, or westerners, nor tenant farmers, served and there was only one small farmer. Rossiter, however, does not believe that the men were particularly self-interested, and maintains that 'devotion to the public good and concern for the national reputation' were the driving forces behind the document.

Having said that, 30 to 40 held financial interests in public securities which would surely appreciate in value with a more stable government and possibly half had money loaned out on interest. Rossiter argues that five of the largest holders of certificates of public debt voted against the Constitution and Forrest McDonald has shown that among the Founding Fathers and members of the ratifying Convention, ownership of depreciated paper had no significant influence on whether men voted for or against the Constitution. Nevertheless a new national government could vote for the taxation needed to pay off debts, and those holding securities could stop the use of devalued paper money by debtors. They could also stimulate manufacturing with tariffs on foreign goods, regulate trade and shipping, open up western lands for speculation and take action against Indians where necessary, and put down insurrections, as well as offering security against slave revolts and support to recapture runaways. For men of property who clearly favoured stability and prospects for future wealth these possibilities must have seemed most appealing, and in this light Howard Zinn's comments that the 'document becomes not simply the work of wise men trying to establish a decent and orderly society, but the work of certain groups trying to maintain their privileges, while giving just enough rights and liberties to enough of the people to ensure popular support' become compelling.

 The Constitution in practice

4   To what extent had the compromises agreed in the Constitution broken down by 1861? (60)

(OCR)

The main compromises made in the Constitution were between the large states and the small states, between North and South, between slave and free, and between those who favoured states' rights and those favouring more central power. By 1861 the compromises had largely been eroded by seemingly fundamental differences of opinion over such issues as slavery, or more accurately the expansion of slavery, and the power of the federal government over the states. These differences had increasingly been exacerbated by an exaggerated sense of a North–South divide which served to increase sectional tensions, and fuel rival conspiracy theories.

The so-called 'Great Compromise' between the large and small states in terms of Congressional representation seemed to survive the 70 years following the writing of the Constitution, but the question of how much power the federal government should wield became an issue from the very early days of the new nation. Within only ten years of the Constitution being framed, a party system which was essentially based around attitudes towards federal power had appeared in the US.

The Virginia and Kentucky Resolutions of 1798/9, written by Madison and Jefferson respectively, established a precedent for the argument that the states had formed a contract with the central government and whenever that central government exceeded the terms of the contract the states had the right to nullify the relevant laws. There was little support for this at the time, but when John Calhoun adopted a similar line regarding South Carolina's refusal to recognise a high tariff (Tariff of Abominations) set by Congress in 1828, it was only the lack of support from the other states that made his home state decide not to secede from the Union.

Slavery is often regarded as the major difference between North and South and yet the 'peculiar institution' (as Southerners called it) could be examined under a 'states' rights' or 'economy' heading alongside the tariff. That, of course, is to ignore the moral objections to slavery and the part it played in rival conspiracy theories as the country moved towards Civil War. To argue that the states' rights issue was paramount in the South's secession from the Union and slavery just happened to be one particular state right is to grossly oversimplify, for slavery was at the root of North/South differences and animosities, both real and imagined, and by 1860 it seemed that the future of slavery within the still expanding Union was exactly what could not be peaceably resolved. The Missouri Compromise of 1820 had maintained the equal ratio of slave to free states in the Senate and the northern boundary of slavery, and the 1850 Compromise also seemed to have resolved tensions, but the Kansas-Nebraska Act of 1854 brought up the future of slavery question once more, and this time it would not be avoided by discussion and deals. Prominent Republicans Seward and Lincoln stated that a house divided could not permanently endure, that the Union could not survive half free and half slave, and yet Lincoln stated he had no intention to interfere with slavery where it already existed. Southerners did not believe him, and they were right not to, for by 1862 he had broken his word and decided to free the slaves. As the debate on slavery became more a moral one, it could only be a matter of time before the issue, compromised on in 1787, came to a head. The future of the US was as a country without slavery – but it would take a war and the death of over half a million white men to achieve it.

5   To what extent was the 13th Amendment the most far-reaching amendment to the Constitution before 1877? (60)

(OCR)

In many respects the 13th and 15th Amendments to the Constitution during Reconstruction were the most far-reaching to date. They attempted to redress the most hypocritical elements of the Constitution, which had recognised slaves as property and permitted freed blacks to be treated as second-class citizens.

The 1st Amendment, regarding free speech, might be regarded as extremely important, and of course the fact that it was the first suggests that free speech was a priority – and yet it was a freedom of speech restricted to whites. The passage of the Alien and Sedition Acts in 1798 also demonstrated that a government with a will could seriously undermine that particular amendment.

The right to bear arms has had significant repercussions for life after the Revolution in the US although the wording of the 2nd Amendment clearly reflects the times in which the Constitution was written. Many would also argue that the 5th Amendment has gained a certain notoriety in high-profile legal cases when those on trial do not want to bear witness against themselves.

The relationship between the states, as defined in the 10th Amendment, was essential to the federal system itself. The fact that the wording of the amendment was 'The powers not delegated to the United States . . . are reserved to the States . . . or people' rather than 'The powers not "specifically" delegated . . .' has allowed the federal government a certain amount of room for manoeuvre and broad interpretation of its powers on occasions.

The 14th Amendment was superseded by the 15th, but the 15th was undermined by Southern laws which prevented blacks from voting for a range of reasons, thus getting around the wording of the amendment. It could be argued, of course, that in many ways the economic system in the South post-bellum came greatly to resemble that of slavery, given that blacks in large numbers stayed on the land they had worked as slaves and paid rent to white owners. Black vagrants also became liable to being hired out, but the important point was that slavery had been abolished, bringing massive legal, political, social and psychological changes for whites as well as blacks. The abolition of slavery fundamentally altered the path US society would take and must therefore be regarded as the most far-reaching amendment to the Constitution by 1877.

6   'The Constitution of 1787 contained the seeds of Civil War.' Discuss. (60)

(OCR)

Essay plan

Introduction: Give a broad outline of the areas to be covered in the answer, i.e. issues determined or unresolved by the Constitution which contained the potential for future disagreement, and other possible causes of the war which could not have been foreseen when the Constitution was written.

Para 1: The issue of states' rights versus federal powers, particularly the wording of the 10th Amendment, which allowed the federal government some scope for broad construction of the Constitution and would lead to much dispute.

Para 2: Linking to para 1, how the Constitution effectively regarded slaves as property, and did not determine that any law related to regulation of trade required a two-thirds majority in Congress, as many Southern states wished.

Para 3: The establishment of a Supreme Court of judges nominated by Presidents who tended to be supportive of the federal government, e.g. Dred Scott decision.

Para 4: The electoral college system of choosing a President allowed sectional candidates to win on a minority of the popular vote, e.g. Lincoln in 1860.

Para 5: The Senate having equal representation kept the issue of slavery smouldering– had the Senate's representation been based on population the South would have been eclipsed much earlier. This might have meant the Southern states seceding earlier and possibly being too strong for the Northern states to risk war.

Para 6: There being nothing in the Constitution about the legal right to secede, nor about expansion and how to deal with new territories. This could link to para 7.

Para 7: Arguments that other issues were at the root of the problem e.g. slavery (which pre-dated the Constitution), the expansion of slavery (which did not seem likely in 1787), war with Mexico, the rise in support for abolitionism in the North and the 'blundering politicians' of the 1850s.

Conclusion: The extent to which the Constitution contained the seeds of Civil War measured against other factors, with an attempt to determine what might be the major flaw of the document in relation to war.

7   To what extent was the President more influential in 1877 than in 1763? (60)

(OCR)

Essay plan

Introduction: Discuss briefly the difference between the legal power of the President, the role that individual personalities played in enhancing the scope of the position, and how earlier views of the President's role shifted over time.

Para 1: Examine the initial views of the role the President would play and Washington's interpretation of his own position.

Para 2: Assess whether the legal position of President changed in any way over the period.

Para 3: Determine whether the context of the times, such as war and Lincoln, and Reconstruction and Johnson, had an impact on the President's influence.

Para 4: Assess whether the personality of the President had an influence on the position, e.g. Washington, Jefferson, Jackson, Lincoln.

Para 5: Examine the idea that the Civil War was a watershed in terms of Presidential power, given that it was followed by **Congressional Reconstruction**, the impeachment of Johnson and the Presidency coming into disrepute under Grant.

Conclusion: The extent to which the President had become more influential by 1877. It may be possible to argue that although the Presidency had become more influential after Washington, its influence had been curtailed after the war.

PRACTICE QUESTIONS

8   How far were the differences between the two main parties in American politics between 1763 and 1877 based on contrasting views of the Constitution? (60)

(OCR)

Advice: *A strong grasp of the two-party system and the parties involved over the time period stated is clearly needed before attempting such a specialist question. The answer to this could also be approached in a fundamentally chronological way, starting off with the disputes between Federalists and Anti-Federalists during the ratification of the Constitution, which led on to the differences over the power of federal government during the 1790s and 1800s, and finishing with Democrat/Republican differences over the nature of the Union, slavery and states' rights. On the other hand a more thematic approach could be taken by concentrating paragraphs around key areas such as states' rights.*

9   'The Supreme Court played a crucial role in shaping the development of the US between 1763 and 1877.' Discuss. (60)

(OCR)

Advice: *In this answer, there should be a number of references to judicial review, and there must be good knowledge and understanding of: landmark decisions by the Supreme Court, such as McCulloch v. Maryland and Dred Scott; influential chief justices such as Marshall and Taney; and the general support the Supreme Court showed for federal government and business during the period. The question is a specialist one and really does require detailed knowledge and understanding.*

 The significance of the Civil War

10   How far do you agree that the Civil War was the key turning point in the development of the US from 1763 to 1877? (60)

(OCR)

The term 'key turning point' suggests the US took a significantly different path from the one it would have taken had the war not taken place. This contention is clearly open to debate, and it must be examined from economic and social as well as political perspectives. The abolition of slavery is perhaps the key to answering the question, in that had war not happened the prospects of gaining a two-thirds vote in Congress plus the support of three-quarters of the states were remote. Lincoln had expanded the powers of the Presidency during the war, but Johnson's impeachment and Grant's tainted terms in office saw a return to a less dominant Presidency. Lincoln talked of 'fundamental and astounding changes' resulting from the war, but he had little chance to speak with any real perspective and neither did those who spoke in revolutionary terms before the 1860s were over, although their initial reactions to the effects of the war should not be discounted.

Charles Beard took a Marxist line, seeing the war as a victory for capitalism over feudalism. Most now regard this view as a gross oversimplification but capitalism certainly flourished after the war. There is, however, a great deal of debate over the economic impact of the war. Some feel that the war may actually have retarded economic growth, while others feel it stimulated the use of technology and accelerated large-scale production and acted as a catalyst rather than fundamentally altering the course of the country's development.

In recent times, Shelby Foote has argued that the war defined the country although Celia O'Leary has said that what it meant to be American remained undefined with loyalties continuing to be diverse and regional differences persisting. There is certainly plenty of evidence that the United States remained very much a disunited society after the war, particularly during the 'Gilded Age', when the gap between the poorest and richest grew massively, and union action became increasingly violent in the face of unsympathetic employers, courts and government. It should be remembered that many Northerners had strongly resented Lincoln turning the conflict into a 'nigger war' while organisations of Confederate veterans refused to accept cultural defeat long after peace had been signed. Writers such as Degler and McPherson have to some extent sympathised with Foote and been happy to call the Civil War 'America's second revolution'.

Clearly the main results of the war were the triumph of the Union and the emancipation of black slaves. The Union existed before the war and so it could be argued that the war was fought to *prevent* change rather than to hasten it, but the war had determined what the nature of that Union would be in the long term, and certainly where states' rights would stand in relation to federal power, although for most people after the war it was still state governments which continued to play a greater part in their lives than Washington, despite greater taxation and involvement from the centre. The abolition of slavery was clearly a fundamental change in US society although it could be argued that blacks remained very much second-class citizens for decades after the war. Neither was the abolition of slavery simply a case of freeing four million black people – it had huge economic, social and political implications, particularly in the South which was hugely affected by the war. The war had devastated large areas of the region as well as fundamentally changing its social and economic systems. Southern incomes continued to fall after the war and agricultural production dropped significantly. The war confirmed the dominance of the Republican Party and by implication the North. After the war, a hundred years would pass before a Southerner became President again. And this pattern was repeated in other areas of national government, such as the Supreme Court where only five of the next 26 appointees would come from the South.

Part 3: Sources

1 The struggle to ratify the Constitution

■ **Source A: Extract from George Washington's letter accompanying the draft of the Constitution, 17 September 1787**

The friends of our country have long seen and desired, that the power of making war, peace and treaties, that of levying money and regulating commerce, and the correspondent executive and judicial authorities should be fully and effectually vested in the general government of the Union . . . Individuals entering into society, must give up a share of liberty to preserve the rest.

■ **Source B: Extract from a petition against ratification, presented to the Freemen of Pennsylvania, January 1788**

That the powers therein proposed to be granted to the government of the United States are too great, and that the proposed distribution of those powers are dangerous and inimical to liberty and equality amongst the people. That they esteem frequent elections and rotation in offices as the greatest bulwark of freedom. That they conceive standing armies in times of peace are not only expensive but dangerous to our liberty, and that a well-organised militia will be the proper security for our defence.

■ **Source C: Extract from speech by James Winthrop, Anti-Federalist of Massachusetts, 1787**

A few years ago, we fought for liberty . . . we placed the State Legislatures, in whom the people have a full and fair representation, between the Congress and the people . . . Now it is proposed to go into the contrary, and a more dangerous extreme – to remove all barriers, to give the new government free access to our pockets, and ample command of our persons, and that without providing for a genuine and fair representation of the people.

■ **Source D: 10th Federalist Paper by James Madison, 1788**

Among the numerous advantages promised by a well constructed Union, none deserves to be more accurately developed than its tendency to break and control the violence of faction . . . By a faction, I understand a number of citizens . . . of interest adverse to the rights of other citizens, or to the permanent and aggregate interests of the community . . . Liberty is to faction what air is to fire, an ailment without which it instantly expires. But it could not be less folly to abolish liberty, which is essential to political life . . . A rage for paper money, for an abolition of debts, for an equal division of property, or for any other improper or wicked project, will be less apt to pervade the whole body of the Union than a particular member of it . . .

OCR QUESTION FORMAT

The questions and answers that follow are based on the OCR style.

(a) Study Source A. From this Source and your own knowledge explain what Washington meant when he said that individuals 'must give up a share of liberty to preserve the rest'. (20)

(b) Study Sources B and C. How far does Source C support the views expressed in Source B that the Constitution gives too much power to the federal government? (40)

(c) Study all the Sources. Using all the Sources and your own knowledge explain the extent to which practicalities rather than idealistic political principles were the main motives of the Founding Fathers in writing the Constitution. (60)

(a) The historian Maldwyn Jones wrote *The Limits of Liberty*, in which he implied that in any society there must be rules (which by definition restrict individual freedom) in order to preserve a broader sort of freedom. John Locke advanced a similar argument – that one man's liberty stops at the point where it begins to interfere with another man's liberty. When Washington proposed that individuals must give up some freedom to preserve the rest he meant that, although the Constitution, in creating a central government with greater powers, may restrict some forms of freedom, it would be worth it for the wider benefits which society as a whole would gain, such as more ordered commerce, law and order, and greater diplomatic power.

(b) The petition of Source B is very direct in terms of its criticisms, stating that the powers 'to be granted to the government . . . are too great' and the 'distribution of those powers . . . dangerous and inimical to liberty and equality', as well as suggesting that more frequent elections are needed and standing armies may be a problem. James Winthrop in Source C also uses the word 'dangerous' when discussing government power, but is more specific than Source B in actually outlining which powers were too great, i.e. the power to tax and power over individuals. Source B clearly feels specifically that elections are not frequent enough, while Winthrop makes a more general comment regarding 'unfair representation of the people', which may not just be referring to frequency of elections. Overall, Source C supports broadly the ideas in Source B that government has too much power, and the representative system set up is unsatisfactory.

(c) Those men who met at Annapolis in 1786 and voted to call a convention to redraft the Articles of Confederation were essentially motivated by the lack of unity and status of the states, and also problems of law and order. States at that time imposed tariffs at different rates, issued diverse currencies, concluded their own treaties with Indian tribes and quarrelled with each other over territory. At a national level, Congress could not pay off war debts, do much to deal with the economic downturn or enforce the terms of the Treaty of Paris. Article I Section 8 of the Constitution covers issues such as raising taxes, coining money, standardising weights and measures, establishing post offices and raising armies, and gives an insight into what was on the minds of those at Philadelphia. Washington, in Source A, tends to reinforce the importance of practical issues by speaking of 'the power of making war, peace and treaties . . . levying money . . . regulating commerce . . . and . . . Individuals . . . [giving] up a share of liberty to preserve the rest'. It is also well known that Washington's whole attitude towards redrafting the Articles of Confederation was bordering on the apathetic until Shays' Rebellion of 1786 made him think again about the importance of preserving law and order. But his ideas of giving up some liberty 'to preserve the rest' went too far for some, and James Winthrop in Source C suggests that the new federal government held powers 'without providing for a genuine and fair representation of the people'.

It can be argued that every compromise made at the Philadelphia Convention on issues such as slavery and the representation of the large and small states, plus the decision to accept a bill of rights, confirms that a streak of ruthless pragmatism ran through the minds of those who were the driving forces behind the Constitutional settlement. Having said that, to argue the Founding Fathers were totally without idealism or principle would be misleading. The ideas of Locke, Rousseau, Montesquieu and Paine played their part. The 'separation of powers' was designed to ensure tyrannical government did not occur, the President and senators were to be elected indirectly by the people for four and six years respectively, while congressmen would be elected directly by the people (albeit a majority of white males) for two years at a time. These arrangements alone made the US the most democratic country in the world at the time, and if there were those who argued that the federal government had too much power, Federalists were quick to point out that law and order were often essential to preserving liberty. For the petitioners in Source B however the powers of the new government seemed 'dangerous and inimical' to the lofty principles of liberty and equality. The petitioners also complained of standing armies in peacetime, which was hardly surprising given that the standing army the British had left in America after the Seven Years War had proved expensive and ultimately been used against the colonists. Again this reflects that one of the priorities of the Founding Fathers was to keep an army on hand to protect the country and possibly to be used to maintain law and order. The speed and heavy-handedness with which the Whiskey Rebellion was put down during Washington's Presidency would doubtless have confirmed to the Founding Fathers they had been right to create safeguards against such disorder.

The motives of the Founding Fathers are portrayed in an even less favourable light by Madison in Source D. His views appear to be positively unprincipled with him openly stating that he sees one of the advantages of the new Constitution as being its capacity to impose law and order, to reduce faction and to prevent demands for 'paper money, for an abolition of debts, for an equal division of property'. Madison concedes the importance of liberty of a kind but in many respects this appears to be a liberty on his own terms rather than a genuinely principled definition of freedom. It is perhaps not surprising that many pushed for 10 Amendments to be added to the Constitution. By 1791 the Bill of Rights was clearly the part of the Constitution which was most strongly based on principled motives, and yet ironically it was the only part of the Constitution which had not been written at Philadephia by the Founding Fathers.

ADDITIONAL QUESTIONS IN THE OCR STYLE

(a) **Study Source B. From this Source and your own knowledge explain why the petitioners prefer a 'well-organised militia' to 'standing armies'.** (20)

(b) **Study Sources A and D. How far does Source D support Washington's view that a certain amount of liberty must be given up to preserve liberty on a broader scale?** (40)

(c) **Using all these Sources and your own knowledge explain the extent to which the new Constitution actually restricted the freedom of the American people.** (60)

2 The debate over the power of federal government

■ Source A: Extract from the 1st Amendment to the Constitution

Congress shall make no law respecting an establishment of religion, or prohibiting the free exercise thereof; or abridging the freedom of speech, or of the press; or of the right of the people peaceably to assemble, and to petition the Government for a redress of grievances.

■ Source B: The Sedition Act 1798

... That if any person shall write, print, utter or publish ... any false, scandalous and malicious writing ... against the government of the United States, or either house of the Congress ... or the President ... with intent to defame ... or to bring them ... into contempt or disrepute; or to excite against them ... the hatred of the good people of the United States ... then such person, being thereof convicted ... shall be punished by a fine not exceeding two thousand dollars, and by imprisonment not exceeding two years.

■ Source C: The Virginia Resolution 1798

... a spirit has in sundry instances, been manifested by the federal government, to enlarge its powers by forced constructions of the constitutional charter which defines them ... (which ... in the former articles of confederation were the less liable to be misconstrued) ... That the General Assembly doth particularly protest against the palpable and alarming infractions of the Constitution, in the two late cases of the 'Alien and Sedition Acts' ... the first of which exercises a power nowhere delegated to the federal government ... but on the contrary, [is] expressly and positively forbidden by one of the amendments.

■ Source D: The Kentucky Resolution 1799

... That if those who administer the general government be permitted to transgress the limits fixed by that compact [i.e. the Constitution], by a total disregard to the special delegations of power therein contained, annihilation of the state governments, and the erection upon their ruins, of a general consolidated government, will be the inevitable consequence: That the principle and construction contended for by sundry of the state legislatures, that the general government is the exclusive judge of the extent of the powers delegated to it, stop nothing short of despotism ... That the several states who formed that instrument, being sovereign and independent, have the unquestionable right to judge of its infraction; and that a nullification, by those sovereignties, of all unauthorised acts done under color of that instrument, is the rightful remedy ... that the said alien and sedition laws, are in their opinion, palpable violations of the said constitution ...

OCR QUESTION FORMAT

The questions and answers that follow are based on the OCR style.

(a) **Study Source D. From this Source and your own knowledge explain what is meant by the phrase 'nothing short of despotism'.** (20)

(b) **Study Sources C and D. How far do Sources C and D support the view that the federal government had attempted to enlarge its own powers?** (40)

(c) **Study all the Sources. Using all the Sources and your own knowledge explain the extent to which the broad constructionists of government power had won the battle against strict constructionists within 40 years of the Philadelphia Convention.** (60)

(a) The phrase 'nothing short of despotism' is used by Thomas Jefferson in the Kentucky Resolution to criticise the idea that it is for the federal government itself to determine the extent of its own powers. This document was written after the Supreme Court in 1796 had upheld the validity of a law passed by Congress, but before an act of Congress had ever been declared unconstitutional by the Court. The 10th Amendment had laid down the basis of the power relationship between states and centre but there were those who believed that the terms of the Constitution could be broadly construed to give the federal government greater scope where necessary. Jefferson was very much opposed to this interpretation of the Constitution and clearly used the term 'despotism' in an emotive way to galvanise feeling against the repressive Alien and Sedition Acts, which he regarded as unconstitutional, and to imply that the federal government had behaved in a tyrannical and oppressive way by supporting the passage of these laws.

(b) The Virginia Resolution (Source C) suggests that federal government had sought to 'enlarge its powers' by interpreting the role given to it by the Constitution too widely, and even goes further in its accusations by claiming it had acted illegally by passing the Alien Act, which Madison claimed to be directly contrary to one of the amendments. The Kentucky Resolution implies that 'those who administer the general government' had been allowed to overstep the limits laid down by the Constitution, and expresses grave concern that the federal government be regarded as 'the exclusive judge' of its own powers. Source D also uses the expression 'transgress the limits fixed by that compact' to suggest that the federal government has 'overstepped the mark'. Madison, in Source C, towards the end of the piece, addressed the Alien and Sedition Acts more specifically, which he believed to be examples of the government enlarging its powers and violating the Constitution. Both Sources could not be more condemning of federal government's attempts to enlarge its powers.

(c) The 10th Amendment, stating that the powers not delegated to the United States would be reserved to the states or people, was approved without the word 'expressly' preceding 'delegated'. This vagueness was significant for it led to much debate in years to come, but essentially it gave the federal government plenty of room for manoeuvre. It became an important element in the debate between those who felt that the powers granted to the federal government in the Constitution should be construed literally and strictly, and those who wanted to use a broader interpretation, effectively allowing the government greater powers than those specifically outlined. The first party system emerged as a result of the differences between broad and strict constructionists.

Hamilton led the Federalists arguing for broad construction and 'implied powers' for the government, with Washington trying to remain above it all; while the Anti-Federalists became known as the Democratic-Republicans and followed Jefferson's lead, campaigning for minimal state interference and championing states' rights. Under Hamilton the government created a Bank of the United States in 1791, raised taxes and passed a tariff act. Other actions that brought opposition from those who felt the government was exceeding its powers included the heavy-handed treatment of those involved in the Whiskey Rebellion in 1794, and also the pro-British policy pursued during the Napoleonic Wars. It was partly in response to opposition to this pro-British policy and the French-supported Irish Rebellion of 1798 that Congress passed the Alien Act in 1798, aiming to reduce immigration and encourage some recent arrivals to leave. On paper the terms of the Act appear to be potentially appallingly oppressive for they stated that, if the US was at war with or threatened by another nation, any citizen of that nation living in the US could be liable to arrest or removal from the country. However, in practice it was not used by Adams to deport anyone.

In the same year the Sedition Act was passed which appeared to encroach on such liberties as 'freedom of speech, or the press' by outlawing 'false, scandalous and malicious writing . . . against the government'. It was however upheld by the Supreme Court, and was used to arrest and convict ten men, most of whom were Republican newspaper editors. Although again, in practice, Adams restrained Federalists from persecuting opponents. Supporters of the Act could argue that the law simply clarified the 1st Amendment which had in any case never intended to allow complete freedom of speech.

Jefferson's idea of 'nullification' and that the states had the 'right to judge' the legality of any law, as expressed in Source D, had no constitutional basis. But neither did the American Revolution, which had been justified on the grounds that the British government had exceeded its powers coupled with various political theories of men such as John Locke. Madison's criticisms of the Alien and Sedition Acts as an attempt by the federal government to 'enlarge its powers' in Source C did not arouse much support across the country and neither did Jefferson's. Once in power, Jefferson himself realised that he could not always avoid a policy of minimal government interference, and, for example, he exceeded his powers as President in negotiating the Louisiana Purchase from France.

As early as 1796 the Supreme Court exercised judicial review by upholding a law which had been passed by Congress. This decision seemed to indicate that judges appointed by the President would always back the government line, but in another case in 1803, Marbury v. Madison, the Court declared the Judiciary Act of 1789 unconstitutional, and for the first time demonstrated how the judiciary could 'check and balance' the executive. This gave 'strict constructionists' some hope, but under the leadership of John Marshall the Supreme Court tended to back the supremacy of the federal government over the states and to sympathise with the idea of 'implied powers' which Hamilton had advocated so strongly. Indeed in 1819, in McCulloch v. Maryland, Marshall confirmed the 'implied powers' of Congress by giving recognition to the legality of the Bank of the United States; and in 1821, in Cohens v. Virginia, Marshall set a precedent for the Supreme Court to review legal decisions made in the state courts, arguing that the states had given up part of their sovereignty in ratifying the Constitution. By around 1830 the strict constructionists appeared to have lost the battle against those who wished to expand the role and powers of federal government.

ADDITIONAL QUESTIONS IN THE OCR STYLE

(a) **Study Source D. From this Source and your own knowledge explain how legitimate the doctrine of nullification was.** (20)

(b) **Study Sources C and D. How far does Source C support the view expressed in Source D that the Alien and Sedition Acts are unconstitutional?** (40)

(c) **Study all the Sources. Using all these Sources and your own knowledge assess the significance of the states' rights issue in the US between 1787 and 1860.** (60)

Part 4: Historical skills

 ### 1 Write your own constitution

In groups of two or three, put together a democratic constitution of your own. It should be loosely structured around a bill of rights, rules for elections, and the structures involved in creating an executive, a legislature and judiciary. Working in small groups will highlight the problems of reaching a consensus on a range of decisions where people may have widely differing views.

The exercise could be extended to allow a 'whole class constitution' to be produced.

 ### 2 A debate on the Constitution of 1787

Students should divided into two groups: one representing the Federalists who supported the new Constitution, the other the Anti-Federalists who had grave misgivings about many aspects of the document. Each group should work on a series of key points and rebuttals to enable a debate to take place over the potential merits and disadvantages of the document.

Sources and references

Anthony Bennett, 'The United States Supreme Court', *Politics Review*, April (2000).

Colin Bonwick, *The American Revolution*, Palgrave (1991).

Colin Bonwick, 'Thomas Jefferson – Pragmatist or Visionary?', *History Today*, April (1993).

Alan Brinkley, *The Unfinished Nation*, McGraw-Hill (2000).

Ken Burns, *The Civil War* (video), DD Video (1989).

Channel 4, 'Liberty', episode 4 (1997).

Simon Collinson, 'President or King?', *History Today*, November (2000).

Edward Countryman (ed.), *What did the Constitution Mean to Early Americans?*, Bedford/St Martin's (1999).

Eric Evans, *Liberal Democracies*, JMB (1990).

Eric Foner, *Politics and Ideology in the Age of the Civil War*, Oxford University Press (1980). Quoted in Lawrence Goodheart, Richard Brown and Stephen Rabe (eds), *Problems in American Civilisation*, D.C. Heath (1993).

M.J. Heale, *The American Revolution*, Methuen (1986).

Robert Hole, 'The American Declaration of Independence of 4th July 1776', *History Review*, March (2001).

James McPherson, *Battle Cry of Freedom*, Penguin (1990).

Maldwyn Jones, *The Limits of Liberty*, Oxford University Press (1983/1995).

Hamilton Jay Madison, '*The Federalist*, Phoenix Press (2000).

John M. Murrin, Paul E. Johnson, James M. McPherson *et al.*, *Liberty Equality Power*, Harcourt (2001).

Patrick O'Brien, *The Economic Effects of the American Civil War*, Macmillan (1988).

Celia O'Leary, 'Americans All: Reforging a National Brotherhood, 1876–1917', *History Today*, October (1994).

Thomas Paine, *Political Writings*, edited by Bruce Kuklick, Cambridge University Press (1989).

Jack Rakove, 'The Great Compromise', *History Today*, September (1989).

Leonard Richards, *Shays' Rebellion: The American Revolution's Final Battle*, University of Pennsylvania Press (2003).

Clinton Rossiter, *1787: The Grand Convention*, Norton (1987).

Matt Salusbury, 'The Dollar's Doleful Debut', *BBC History Magazine*, January (2002).

Alex Waddan, 'Presidents and Leadership', *Politics Review*, February (1998).

Alex Waddan, 'Reviewing the Constitution of the United States', *Politics Review*, February (1999).

Howard Zinn, *A People's History of the United States*, Longman (1996).

Chapter 3

The Origins of the American Civil War, 1840–1861

This chapter will examine the debates over slavery, states' rights and federal rights, and the sectional differences which gave rise to the secession of the Confederate states and the subsequent outbreak of the American Civil War.

 Historical background

Introduction
The problems of territorial expansion and
    attempts at compromise
Economic differences and the moral implications
    of slavery
States' rights and nationalism
Sectional divisions and conspiracy theories
Leadership: politicians and parties
Conclusion

 Sources

1   Understanding the Northern perspective
2   Understanding the Southern perspective

 Historical skills

1   Conspiracy everywhere
2   Who was most to blame?

 Essays

Expansion and slavery
Irresponsible agitators and blundering
    politicians
Motives for secession and fighting

Chronology

1820	Missouri Compromise
1831	First issue of *The Liberator* published
	Nat Turner Revolt
1832–3	Nullification Crisis
1836	Texas won independence from Mexico
1840	Whig William Harrison elected President
1841	Harrison died and Tyler became President
1844	Democrat James Polk elected President
1845	Congress agreed to annex Texas
1846	Beginning of Mexican War
	Wilmot Proviso
1847	Calhoun Doctrine (Platform of the South)
1848	End of Mexican War
	Treaty of Guadalupe Hidalgo
	Whig Zachary Taylor elected President
1850	Zachary Taylor died and replaced by Millard Fillmore
	Henry Clay's Compromise of 1850
	California admitted as a free state
1851–2	*Uncle Tom's Cabin* published
1852	Democrat Franklin Pierce elected President
1853	Gadsden Purchase
1854	Kansas-Nebraska Act passed (which led to 'Bleeding Kansas')
	Republican Party founded
	Ostend Manifesto
1856	'Bleeding Sumner'
	Pottawatomie Massacre'
	James Buchanan elected President
1857	Dred Scott decision by Supreme Court
	'Panic' of 1857
	Lecompton Constitution adopted in Kansas
1858	Lincoln–Douglas debates
1859	John Brown's raid on Harper's Ferry
	Execution of John Brown
1860	Lincoln elected President
	Secession of South Carolina
1861	Mississippi, Florida, Alabama, Georgia, Louisiana and Texas left the Union
	Kansas admitted as a free state
	Confederacy established and Jefferson Davis chosen as President
	Fort Sumter Crisis
	Second wave of secession: Virginia, Arkansas, North Carolina and Tennessee left the Union

Part 1: Historical background

 Introduction

Having been elected President of the Confederacy, in his inaugural speech of 1861, Jefferson Davis proclaimed it was 'the American idea that governments rest upon the consent of the governed', and added that it was 'the right of the people to alter or abolish governments whenever they become destructive of the ends for which they were established'. Although secession of Southern states from the Union did not necessarily have to lead to armed conflict, President Abraham Lincoln, and the majority of Northerners, felt so strongly that the precedent of states leaving the Union might lead to its ultimate disintegration, they were prepared to fight a war which left well over half a million dead – as many as were lost in all other wars the US has fought added together. By the time the war was over, the fight to preserve the Union had taken on a higher goal, and the victory of the North in 1865 ensured that nearly four million black slaves would be freed.

Prior to taking office in a letter of December 1860 to Alexander Stephens, future Vice-President of the Confederacy, Lincoln reasserted the public pledge he had made not to interfere with slavery where it already existed , but added: 'I suppose, however, this does not meet the case. You think slavery is right and ought to be extended, while we think it is wrong and ought to be restricted. That I suppose is the rub. It certainly is the only substantial difference between us.' In March 1861, Stephens himself seemed to confirm the importance of slavery by saying: 'African slavery . . . was the immediate cause of the late rupture.' South Carolina's declaration of the immediate causes of its secession argued that 'an increasing hostility on the part of the non-slaveholding States to the institution of slavery' had contributed in rendering the compact between the states invalid. It can be argued that slavery played a part in every pre-war crisis and the fact that the Confederate Constitution written in 1861, apart from differences in provisions for elections and the safeguarding of slavery, virtually replicated the document drafted at Philadelphia in 1787, would also suggest that the South's 'peculiar institution' was at the root of problems.

If slavery was however at the root of the decision of Southern states to secede following Lincoln's election as President, there was a certain illogicality to it. Given that the Republican Party which had nominated Lincoln had only existed since 1856, there was no guarantee that it would continue to be successful, and although Lincoln won the Presidency in 1860 (with less than 40 per cent of the popular vote) the Republicans did not have control of either House of Congress, and therefore could have done little in the short term to affect slavery. The Dred Scott decision made by the Supreme Court in 1857 had ruled that a slave taken into a so-called 'free territory' would still be classified a slave, which seemed to imply that Congress had no power whatever to prevent the expansion of slavery. The North feared the Supreme Court would next rule that the states could not exclude slavery. For slavery to be abolished, therefore, a Constitutional amendment would be required, i.e. a two-thirds majority in both Houses of Congress plus ratification by three-quarters of the states. In 1860, 15 of the 33 states in the Union (or 45 per cent) were slave states. At present 50 states make up the US, which raises the hypothetical absurdity that had those 15 states continued to uphold the existence of slavery, the 'peculiar institution' could still exist today. Unthinkable as this may be, the war did ultimately provide a solution to what, in Republican William Seward's words, appeared to be 'an irreconcilable conflict'.

To regard the protection of slavery as the main cause of Southern secession is one thing, but to see the abolition of slavery as the main reason Northerners went to war in 1861 is untenable. Lincoln knew that to declare the abolition of slavery as an initial war aim would be political suicide, and could well be the death knell of the Union if it provoked the four border slave states (none of which had voted for him as President in 1860) to secede as well, so instead he committed the North to war solely to preserve the Union. He had however argued that 'a house divided against itself' (on the issue of slavery) could not stand, and that he expected it to 'become all one thing, or all the other'. During the Lincoln–Douglas debates of the Illinois election campaign for the Senate in 1858, Stephen Douglas pointed out that Lincoln appeared to be ignoring the fact that 'the divided house' had stood since the 1780s, and, perhaps not surprisingly, the South refused to be reassured by his promise not to interfere with slavery where it already existed.

Slavery was also essentially what made the South the South, although some writers have even questioned whether the region should be described as a 'slaveholding society' given that only 25 per cent of white families owned any slaves at all, and in some towns slaves were hired out or required to simply yield a percentage of their earnings to their masters. There were in fact 'many Souths', and conditions varied considerably from state to state. Half the Southern slave owners owned five or fewer slaves and often worked side by side with them. And in 1832 the legislature of Virginia, the most powerful Southern state, voted by a surprisingly narrow margin, given the influence of slave owners, to retain slavery.

The problems of territorial expansion and attempts at compromise

Territorial expansion westwards lay at the root of the United States' problems leading up to the Civil War. As more land was acquired by the nation, and pioneers, potential settlers, prospectors, and those hoping to practise their religion free from persecution, continued to travel west, so more territories would apply to become new states in the Union. This in turn would raise the issue of whether these new states would be pro-slavery or free. Missouri was the first territory from the Louisiana Purchase of 1803 to apply for statehood, and the associated Missouri Compromise of 1820 highlights perfectly the dilemma expansion brought with it. At the time the slave states and free states were equally balanced in the Senate. If Missouri joined as a slave state it would tip the balance in favour of the South. Henry Clay's solution was to create a new free state called Maine out of part of Massachusetts, and to ban slavery in the Louisiana Purchase above a line of latitude 36° 30′.

Figure 3.1 **Stephen A. Douglas**

It may have appeared that, on balance, the North benefited more than the South from Henry Clay's '1850 Compromise' over the land acquired from Mexico, given that the free states gained a majority in the Senate with the admission of California, but the senators California returned were so 'dough-faced' that the balance was not, in reality, tipped against the South. Some historians have also argued that the new Fugitive Slave Law of 1850, which supposedly made it easier to recapture escaped slaves, proved very difficult to enforce. Although, according to Murrin *et al.*, 84 fugitives were actually returned to slavery with only 5 released in the first 15 months of the law's operation (2001: p. 375). Hardly any slaves were taken to New Mexico and Utah (part of the land acquired from Mexico), which made it unlikely that either territory would eventually become a slave state.

A further acquisition of land from Mexico in the Gadsden Purchase of 1854 aroused Northern suspicion and opposition to the possibility that a Southern transcontinental railroad might be built, and it was the drive to build a Northern transcontinental railroad which was to lead to an intensification of the crisis. In order to remove the objections to a northern route (that would run through unorganised territory guaranteed free soil by the Missouri Compromise of 1820), Illinois' Stephen Douglas promoted the passage of the Kansas-Nebraska Act, which proposed that the settlers in each area should vote along the lines of 'popular sovereignty' on whether they accepted slavery or not. All Southern members of the Democrat Party and nearly all Southern members of the Whig Party voted for the Kansas-Nebraska Act, while every Northern Whig voted against it, and Northern Democrats split down the middle. The new law instantly nullified the Missouri Compromise line, but, more importantly, precipitated the collapse of the Whig Party and led to the foundation of the Republican Party as well as widespread violence in Kansas. At a stroke, Douglas, who had underestimated the depth of Northern anti-slavery feeling, revived sectional hostilities, weakened his own Democrat Party and jeopardised his own future hopes of becoming President.

Economic differences and the moral implications of slavery

There were certainly differences between North and South economically, and it could be argued that slavery was at the root of those differences. There has been a tendency to assume that the South was economically backward compared to the North. Although this should not be exaggerated, it does seem that despite growth in the Southern economy, it did not really develop, and the region remained more reluctant than the North to embrace new technology. It is true that the North had greater diversity than the South, and between 1800 and 1860 the proportion of the Northern labour force engaged in agriculture fell from 70 per cent to 40 per cent, while the Southern proportion remained constant at approximately 80 per cent; also only approximately 10 per cent of Southerners lived in urban areas compared with 25 per cent of Northerners.

In the 1920s, progressive historians Charles and Mary Beard argued that the war was one fought between capitalism and feudalism – an expanding commercialised North fighting a static agrarian South for power – and that the North essentially fought for its own economic interests. Most Republican support however appears to have come from small farmers rather than big businessmen favouring further industrialisation, and the Republican Party was clearly divided on issues such as the tariff, the need for a national bank and nativism, as well as embracing a range of views on the position of blacks in society. Eric Foner has argued that 'free labour' lay at the heart of Republican ideology, perhaps confirming the economic motive; and in 1858 William Seward made a similar point, saying that the social systems of slave labour and free labour were incompatible. The North's belief in free labour however did not extend to free trade, and the tariff question continued to cause dissension.

Figure 3.2
Anti-slavery cartoon, 1839

The North's reluctance to allow the Confederacy to exist independently certainly made sense on economic grounds. The South provided 60 per cent of all US exports and it has been estimated that 15–20 per cent of the price of raw cotton went into the pockets of creditors, insurers, owners of warehouses and shipowners, most of whom were Northerners or British. An independent Confederacy could have put an end to a lucrative market for Northern products, reduced Northern control of Southern trade and stopped the free transit of Northern goods down the Mississippi.

To many Northerners slavery was simply an economic issue, but as time went on more came to see it as a moral issue. It would seem that from the 1830s, in the wake of increasing attacks on slavery from Northern abolitionists, Southerners decided to stop apologising for the existence of their 'peculiar institution' as a necessary evil, and actively started to justify slavery, comparing it favourably with 'wage slavery' in the North, and claiming that blacks were inferior. William Lloyd Garrison was the man who gave the flagging anti-slavery movement renewed impetus, and he demanded the immediate abolition of slavery. He set up his own newspaper in 1831 and the American Anti-Slavery Society in 1833, which had over a quarter of a million members within five years.

Abolitionism experienced divisions in its ranks during the years to come and, although never representing the majority view in the North, it did serve both to irritate the South and influence Northern opinion. Frederick Douglass's *Narrative*, describing his life as a slave in Maryland, published in 1845, and Harriet Beecher Stowe's *Uncle Tom's Cabin*, published in 1852, also undoubtedly raised the consciousness of many Northerners – the latter sold more than two million copies over the next ten years. Claims that it won thousands of converts to the anti-slavery cause are probably exaggerated, although Lincoln is reputed to have said to Stowe on meeting her in 1862: 'So you're the little woman who wrote the book that made this great war.' Millions of Northerners apparently moved closer to an anti-slavery position after the 1850 Compromise when armed slave catchers began to appear on their streets. Seizures of 'fugitives' who had lived for years in the North panicked thousands of blacks in the North to head for Canada, or to arm themselves, and there were several instances of violence where the authorities attempted to arrest or hold fugitives.

 ## States' rights and nationalism

Jefferson Davis claimed that the South had fought for states' rights rather than to save slavery, but it is difficult to avoid the conclusion that the state right of paramount importance to the South was the right to own slaves. Hugh Brogan notes that the states' rights doctrine had evolved out of the necessity to protect slavery (1985/1999: p. 317), but in 1832 South Carolina had threatened secession over the tariff, and as early as 1799 Thomas Jefferson had championed states' rights in the face of the draconian Alien and Sedition Acts. When the Supreme Court made its infamous decision regarding the status of black slave Dred Scott in 1857 it ruled that no slave could become free by virtue of simply living in a free territory. The implications of Dred Scott were that neither Congress nor an individual state could legally bar slavery from any land. This represented a major blow to the right of states to determine whether slavery should exist or not within its borders, but this defeat for states' rights was lost amid the rejoicing south of the Potomac.

In terms of nationalism there is a strong argument that the war *created* Southern nationalism rather than the other way round, but slavery was a vital element, in many ways actually defining the South. Maldwyn Jones asserts that 'secession challenged the ideological basis of American nationalism as the mass of Northerners had come to understand it . . . They had learned . . . to identify the Union with liberty and democracy and to feel that the maintenance of territorial integrity was the touchstone of the experiment in popular government begun in 1776' (1983/1995: p. 216). Little wonder that the Republican Party election slogan of 1856 – 'Free Soil, Free Labor, Free Men, Fremont' – went down well in the North. In 1861 Northern soldier Sullivan Ballou seemed to have little doubt about his cause, writing, before battle, in a letter to his wife: 'My love of country comes over me like a strong wind and bears me irresistibly

. . . to the battlefield' (Burns 1989). For General Robert E. Lee, who opposed slavery and secession, 'country' meant his home state of Virginia, and when Virginia decided to join the Confederacy so did he, rather than accept Lincoln's offer of command over Union forces.

In the 1940s/1950s, Bell Wiley argued that the letters of soldiers seemed to reveal that they were influenced by friends, pay, fear of future conscription, a sense of duty and a vaguely defined but strongly felt love of country, as well as a hostility towards those who seemed intent on destroying it. McPherson has suggested that ideological factors played a major part in sustaining the will of soldiers to fight. Contemporary Northern author Nathaniel Hawthorne summed up the confusion: 'We have gone to war, and we seem to have little, or, at least, a very misty idea of what we are fighting for . . . The Southern man will say, we fight for states' rights, liberty, and independence. The middle and Western states-man will avow that he fights for the Union; whilst our Northern and Eastern man will swear that, from the beginning, his only idea was liberty to the Blacks, and the annihilation of slavery' (Burns 1989).

 ## Sectional divisions and conspiracy theories

Recently historians have tended to stress what the North and South had in common, such as British descent, protestantism, language, legal system and political beliefs, rather than concentrate on their differences. Writers now generally accept that the 'conflict of cultures' theory has been exaggerated as a cause of the crisis, but there is no doubt that crude stereotyped depictions of North and South were widely accepted in the build-up to hostilities, and the conspiracy theories of 'slave power' versus 'black republicanism' gained more and more credibility as time went on.

It has also been argued that, despite having much in common, by about 1850 the two sections had become distinctly different. The South appears to have been a more violent region than the North to the

Figure 3.3 **Map illustrating slave and free states on the eve of the American Civil War**

extent that Southerners were somehow 'less civilised' than their Northern counterparts. Bryan Holden Reid, for example, has pointed to the 'casual attitude of the secessionists to the use of force' (1996: p. 399) and maintains that the South was the aggressive party relishing the prospect of war and deluding itself that the war would be won with ease (p. 384).

From the late 1830s the idea of the 'slave power' took hold in the North, with increasingly aggressive justifications of slavery by Southerners prompted by abolitionist attacks, which in turn gave abolitionists further evidence of a conspiracy of Southern slaveholders 'to foist slavery upon the nation, destroy civil liberty, extend slavery into the territories (possibly to whites), reopen the slave trade, control the policies of the federal government, and complete the formation of an aristocracy founded upon and fostered by a slave economy (Nye 1949: p. 20). Others point to sectional agitators, such as John Tyler and John Calhoun, both political outsiders whose careers had been blocked by the major parties, and who clearly stood to gain from such conspiracy theories and also from slavery becoming a national issue. There were even extremists who claimed that the Southern 'slave-ocracy' had been responsible for the deaths by poison of two Presidents and had tried to kill three others.

Further evidence that seemed to justify the existence of a conspiracy of slaveholders included:

* the Gag Rule, which prevented debates over slavery in Congress between 1836 and 1844;
* two-thirds of volunteer soldiers in the Mexican War had come from slave states, which could indicate that the war itself was fought for Southern interests, especially given that President Polk who went to war with Mexico seemed very reluctant to secure the whole of Oregon in the north-west;
* some expansionist Democrats had even wanted to take the whole of Mexico;
* various Southern-led expeditions to invade Cuba and Nicaragua in the 1850s;
* calls to reopen the African slave trade;
* the beating of Northern senator Charles Sumner by Southern congressman Preston Brooks in 1856, which gained the Republicans thousands of votes; and
* President Buchanan's acceptance of Kansas's pro-slavery Lecompton Constitution and the pressure he brought to bear on the Supreme Court over the Dred Scott decision.

In reality there was no conspiracy, although most white Southerners were united in supporting the institution of slavery, despite the fact that the vast majority of them did not own slaves. Nevertheless, according to Foner, it was the fear of 'slave power' that gave the Republicans the anti-aristocratic appeal which men like Seward had long wished for and was the 'ideological glue' of the party (1993: pp. 272–3).

On the other side of the coin, Southern leaders insisted that they had been forced out of the Union by a 'black republican' conspiracy that aimed to destroy slavery once and for all. In January 1831 the first edition of William Lloyd Garrison's abolitionist paper, *The Liberator*, came off the presses – and within only a few months 60 whites had been killed in Virginia in the Nat Turner slave revolt. Further abolitionist agitation and national events seemed to confirm Southern fears, and many historians have argued that John Brown's raid in 1859, which again raised the spectre of slave rebellion, was the single most important factor in causing the war. Having dominated the Presidency and membership of the Supreme Court until the 1850s, Southerners came to see themselves as constituting a permanent minority grouping, whose interests would be ignored or trampled on by a tyrannical Northern majority. The fact that the Republican-dominated Congress, in the absence of Southern Democrats during the war, took the opportunity to pass bills on proposals that they knew Southerners opposed, suggests that they may well have been right.

 Leadership: politicians and parties

In the 1940s, 'Revisionists' led by James Randall and Avery Craven claimed that politicians and agitators of both sides were unusually incompetent. Alan Nevins has declared that the 30th Congress, which met in

December 1847, contained a 'galaxy of talent' perhaps never equalled before or since – but within five years three of the stars, Clay, Calhoun and Webster, were dead. It could be argued that the slavery question had simply reached a point at which it demanded an answer, and politicians who were more ideologically committed than earlier generations were prepared to provide it.

Many have blamed Buchanan for escalating the conflict, and he certainly appears to have been reluctant to act decisively to prevent the 'general drift to war', and it was ultimately Buchanan's record as President that gave Lincoln his chance. In contrast to Buchanan's apparent ineptitude, the Republican Party proved itself rather adept at attracting all the different groups opposed to the Democrats. It offered such incentives as 160-acre homesteads, subsidies for a transcontinental railroad and higher tariffs, and managed to focus on republicanism rather than black slavery in the run-up to 1860. The Republicans also ensured that Seward, who had alienated the 'Know-Nothings', was not selected as Presidential candidate in 1860, but rather 'Honest Abe' Lincoln, who stood in contrast to rival candidates Douglas and Breckinridge, both tainted by their connections with the Buchanan administration. Nativists tended to regard the Democrats as the party of Catholics, while continued Democrat opposition to the tariff in the wake of the 1857 panic, and Southern opposition to homestead legislation and federal aid for a transcontinental railroad created many Republican voters.

Brogan seems to reiterate Foner's views on Tyler and Calhoun (1993) by arguing that in the 1850s: 'A new generation of sectional politicians was arising: of men, that is, who lacked a national following. Seward was one; Jefferson Davis . . . another' (1985/1989: p. 301). As well as these there were men such as John Brown; and if Stephen Douglas was not a sectional politician, it was certainly his desire to profit from a railroad and his support of the 'morally irresponsible' popular sovereignty and complete underestimation of Northern anti-slavery feeling, which had massive repercussions that included the demise of the Whig Party.

In the wake of the 1850 Compromise, Southern 'fire-eaters', angered by the admission of California and by various attempts by Northerners to frustrate the operation of the new Fugitive Slave Law, urged secession; but in some Southern states Constitutional Union parties appeared, winning the governorships of Georgia and Mississippi, the legislatures of Georgia and Alabama, and sending a number of congressman to Washington. This seemed to confirm to Northerners that threats of secession were bluff, but McPherson has described Southern unionism as 'a perishable commodity'(1990: p. 87). It should be noted however that as late as 1860 over half of Southern voters supported pro-Union candidates other than Lincoln.

In 1978 Michael Holt moved the debate away from the issue of slavery by arguing that the disintegration of the Whig-Democrat party structure was a major cause of the conflict and that, at other times during the century, the party system and the politicians operating within it managed to contain conflict and to find compromise. He asked why, if the conflict essentially revolved around slavery, all the slave states did not secede and suggested that the causes of sectional differences were not necessarily what caused armed conflict. He looked more to the party system itself rather than individuals, and also argued that distrust of politicians had reached an all-time high in the 1850s, with voters completely losing faith in the system amidst a sense of crisis across the whole country – which allowed leaders of Southern states to seize the initiative from prominent national politicians. Southern secession, according to Holt, was not just about rejecting Lincoln but about 'a belief that the system could not neutralise his threat' (1978: p. 6). Critics of Holt contended that the second party system (i.e. Democrats/Whigs) could only survive as long as it avoided sectional issues such as slavery. Holt examined at state level parties that had much more of an effect on the everyday lives of people than the 'flimsy national organisations that came together once every four years to contest the Presidency' (p. 14) and maintained that it was issues such as prohibitionism and nativism particularly in the North, based on local social tensions, that produced voter realignment in the 1850s rather than national issues such as slavery. To some extent this has been confirmed by others. Holt also asserted that the failure of the Whig-Democratic system to provide a genuine choice for voters meant that they looked elsewhere and that the system broke down out of consensus rather than conflict. There is however an example of slavery/expansion causing a serious rift before the 1850s – in 1848 following the Whig nomination of Zachary Taylor for the Presidency. This choice of someone who was a hero of the Mexican War and also a large slave owner prompted the 'Conscience Whigs' to leave and create a coalition with the Liberty Party and anti-slavery ('Barnburner') Democrats to form the Free Soil Party. As far back as 1820, of course, Congress had aligned itself sectionally over the admission of Missouri as a state.

Following the first wave of Southern states to secede, last ditch attempts at compromise in the Crittenden Plan failed largely because of Lincoln's refusal to budge, and in that sense, he too must bear a share of responsibility for the start of the war.

 Conclusion

It should be remembered that the causes of secession are not necessarily the same as the causes of the war itself, but the basis for conflict in the form of slavery had existed since the writing of the Constitution and the different meanings that Northerners and Southerners took from the American Revolution itself. Future expansion of the United States threatened to resurrect the slavery issue, and in the 1850s a succession of events raised tensions to an unprecedented level. It is difficult to get away from the idea that slavery was at the root of the problems the country faced. Where other factors are cited, they seem inextricably linked to slavery. If the war was fought for economic reasons then slavery was the key economic difference between the sections; if it was fought over states' rights, then the key right, as far as the South was concerned, was the right to own slaves and take them elsewhere; if the conspiracy theories polarised the sections and increased alienation then they were theories based on the future of slavery; if agitators stirred up emotions, they did so using the slavery issue.

Figure 3.4 **Campaign banner showing Abraham Lincoln and Hannibal Hamlin**

Part 2: Essays

 Expansion and slavery

1   Explain the reasons behind the 1850 Compromise and assess its consequences. (20)

(AQA)

Ralph Waldo Emerson prophetically announced that: 'The United States will conquer Mexico, but it will be as the man who swallows the arsenic which brings him down. Mexico will poison us.' It can be argued that this is exactly what happened, although the 1850 Compromise inspired by Henry Clay would have caused many to believe that Emerson's prediction of the country's demise was premature.

The Compromise of 1850 was a direct consequence of the war which the US fought with Mexico between 1846 and 1848, and can be seen as a further attempt to solve the problems created by expansion. The Treaty of Guadalupe Hidalgo signed by the two nations resulted in the US acquiring a vast amount of territory – Mexican land from the Rio Grande to the Pacific, 529,000 square miles to be exact – for $15 million which, once more, raised the question of how the new territory would be organised.

Many Northerners had denounced the war as a Southern war intended to expand slavery, and the enthusiasm for war in the South was certainly much stronger than in the North, with the South providing two-thirds of the volunteers who fought in Mexico. In 1846 and in 1847 the Wilmot Proviso was passed by the House of Representatives in an attempt to bar slavery from land which might be acquired from Mexico, but was defeated in the Senate. Supporters of the bill included anti-slavers and many western Democrats who felt that President James Polk was sacrificing their interests to the South and were furious at his failure to get the whole of Oregon from the British in Canada. Polk had also vetoed bills to use federal funds for improvements to western rivers and harbours. The shift in alignments marked an important step in the agricultural west's movement away from the plantation South towards the industrial North. Polk regarded the issue of slavery as an abstract one and, like many, felt that New Mexico and California were unsuited to slavery; but others disagreed: cotton was already grown in parts of New Mexico and slaves had worked in mines. The subsequent failure of slavery to take root in these areas however tends to support Polk's viewpoint, nonetheless the 1850 Compromise was intended to resolve the debate over slavery in those territories.

In February 1847, John C. Calhoun introduced into the Senate a series of resolutions known as the Platform of the South, which argued that territories were the common property of all states, and Congress had no right to stop people moving there with their property; in other words no territorial legislature could debar slavery. Popular sovereignty put forward by senator Lewis Cass and taken up by Stephen Douglas appeared to be a middle way, but the 1850 Compromise was to delay the discussion of Calhoun's argument until the Dred Scott case of 1857.

The gains of the war itself contributed to the need for some sort of settlement but it was the prospective admission of California which had seemed far off at the beginning of 1848, yet quickly became imminent with the discovery of gold in that year, which hastened the need for action. The subsequent gold rush which followed meant that California had a population of 100,000 by the end of 1849. The issue of statehood was pressing, and it seemed highly unlikely that California's constitution would uphold slavery. Other pressures that led to the Compromise included demands for the abolition of slavery in the District of Columbia, Southern pressure for a more effective Fugitive Slave Law and Texan claims on part of New Mexico.

President Taylor wanted California and New Mexico to frame their own constitutions to avoid Congress having to make a decision on slavery. However, by the end of 1849, a secessionist movement had developed in the South, which was especially strong in South Carolina and Mississippi. Taylor, a pro-Northern Southerner, urged the admission of New Mexico and California. The governor of Texas threatened to use force to uphold the claims of his state to Santa Fe and all the rest of New Mexico east of the Rio Grande, and a clash with the US army appeared imminent, with Southerners threatening to join the Texans. It was only Zachary Taylor's death from acute gastroenteritis on 9 July which broke the deadlock, for the new President, Millard Fillmore, was a New York Whig who sympathised with the Compromise and the South.

The 1850 Compromise was an attempt to appease both sections. The fact that the original omnibus bill which had included all measures was defeated and had subsequently to be divided into single bills is a clear indication of the divisions which some of the issues engendered.

Before assessing the consequences of the Compromise it is necessary first to outline the key measures: California was admitted as a free state; the south-west area between Texas and California was opened to popular sovereignty; a new Fugitive Slave Act, which allowed owners to arrest suspected runaways without a warrant and deny them the rights both to trial by jury and to give evidence on their own behalf; and heavy fines for anyone helping a slave to escape, with the federal government committing itself to support the return of runaways.

The 1850 Compromise in many ways failed in much of what it set out to achieve, although it could be argued that it isolated South Carolina (the only Southern state to actually vote in a convention to secede), and ensured that secession was delayed by ten years, which may ultimately have saved the Union. There is an argument that, had the Southern states seceded in 1850, they may well have done it successfully.

James McPherson has argued that California was admitted as a 'free soil' state, but in reality the courts tended to allow the 'sojourn' – for up to several years in some cases – of slave owners and slaves, and although the senators California voted in were Democrats they were 'dough-faced' (i.e. tended to sympathise with the South), which meant that the South did not get outvoted in the Senate. Following an 1842 Supreme Court ruling, the recapture of runaway slaves was deemed to be a federal responsibility, and the 'free soil' states passed laws to make life difficult for slave owners trying to recover their 'property'. The federal government wanted to give the impression that it would do all it could to enforce the new Act of 1850, and almost immediately a number of blacks were seized, provoking fear among black communities in the North and prompting thousands to flee north to Canada. Others armed themselves, and in September 1851 at the 'Battle of Christiana' (in Pennsylvania), a slave owner plus relatives and deputy marshals attempted to seize two fugitives who had been given refuge by Quakers. More than 20 armed blacks turned up resulting in the death of the slave owner and wounding of his son. Southerners demanded justice or they would secede. Fillmore wanted to be seen to act, although following prosecution, charges were dropped against several whites and blacks. In the meantime, at Syracuse, New York, a group of blacks and whites broke into a police station and rescued escaped slave William McHenry, who was subsequently smuggled to Canada. Only one black man was convicted for his part in the action and he died before he could appeal. Southern 'fire-eaters' burned with rage, but cotton prices were the highest they had been in ten years and the cotton yield was the highest ever, which tempered the calls for secession; and Constitutional Union Party candidates (a mixture of Democrats and Whigs), who opposed secession, won the governorships of Georgia and Mississippi, control of the legislatures of Georgia and Alabama, and won 14 out of 19 seats in the House of Representatives from these states. Many Northerners were thereby convinced that secessionist rhetoric had been mere talk intended to frighten the government into concessions. But this was a misjudgement for, as James McPherson has put it, 'Southern unionism . . . was a perishable commodity'.

The new Fugitive Slave Act was, according to McPherson, the 'most divisive legacy' of the Compromise. In the first 15 months of the new Fugitive Slave Act, 84 escapees were returned to slavery and only 5 released. The case of Margaret Garner who, when about to be captured by government officers in Ohio, killed her three-year-old child and attempted to kill the other three rather than having to return to captivity, brought home to many the harsh realities of life as a slave. Murrin suggests that, although most Northerners were not abolitionists, millions of them, shocked by the spectacle of 'slave catchers' on their streets, moved closer to an anti-slavery stance. Many fugitive slaves kept running when they reached the North, and did not stop until they reached Canada. By 1852 the number of runaways being returned South had dropped by a third since the first year of the law's operation.

There were, however, attempts made in the North to reassure the South, with Indiana and Iowa actually passing laws preventing the immigration of any blacks at all, but the most notorious incident had yet to come. In 1854, escaped slave Anthony Burns was arrested in Boston where abolitionists tried to release him – resulting in the death of a deputy marshal. President Pierce pulled out all the stops, spent over $100,000 (roughly $2 million today) and brought in troops to ensure Burns was returned to Virginia. Textile magnate Amos Lawrence said: 'we went to bed one night old fashioned, conservative, Compromise Union Whigs and waked up stark mad Abolitionists.' Not surprisingly Maldwyn Jones has described the Fugitive Slave Law as a 'hollow victory for the South' as it proved so difficult to enforce, while very few slaves were taken into New Mexico and Utah, which in reality made it unlikely that when it came to a vote the two areas would become slave states.

2 Outline the 'states' rights' versus 'federal rights' argument in the build-up to the war and assess the extent to which slavery was the most important states' right for Southerners? (20)

(AQA)

From the time that the Founding Fathers sat down together in Philadelphia to draft a constitution, one of the burning issues which had to be resolved was where power would lie. Many of the so-called Anti-Federalists who opposed the ratification of the Constitution argued that too much power had been given to the federal government at the expense of the states, which of course already had their own legislative assemblies and forms of government. Some Southerners argued that any Congressional law passed affecting trade would have to receive a two-thirds majority vote out of suspicion that the North would attempt to use Congress to its own economic advantage. Others lobbied so that the 10th Amendment would ensure that any powers not granted to the federal government in the Constitution would belong to the states. Clearly a compromise was reached, but the issue refused to go away in subsequent years.

In 1828 supporters of the Democrat Presidential candidate Andrew Jackson attempted to embarrass President John Quincy Adams who wanted a high tariff put on imports to stimulate Northern industry. Southerners resented having to pay more for their goods to subsidise Yankee businesses, and feared foreign retaliation against their cotton exports, the price of cotton in South Carolina having been low for some years. Jackson's supporters decided to support a high tariff on foreign manufactured goods in exchange for heavy rates on wool and flax which Northern mill owners needed, in the hope that North and South would combine to defeat the President. The flax- and wool-producing West however supported protection for its raw materials, and the North, although begrudgingly, was prepared to pay higher prices to maintain its virtual monopoly on manufactured goods. In the South, the new tariff was called the Tariff of Abominations. Vice-President Calhoun anonymously issued the South Carolina Exposition, which declared the Southern states had the right to declare a federal law void within their borders if they thought it unconstitutional. This 'nullification doctrine' (which had been proposed as early as 1798 by Thomas Jefferson in response to the Alien and Sedition Acts) was refuted by senator Daniel Webster who argued that the Constitution was not a compact between states but one between the people, and only the Supreme Court had the power to interpret it.

In 1832 a new tariff act reduced duties, but not by enough for South Carolina. Given that only months earlier the Nat Turner slave revolt in Virginia had resulted in the slaughter of many whites, that the North's population had been rising much faster than the South's, and that with abolitionism also gaining ground, the South felt threatened. Calhoun resigned the Vice-Presidency to fight for Southern rights in the Senate, and South Carolina called a convention, which declared the two tariff acts null and void and threatened to secede if the federal government tried to enforce them. Jackson promised he would personally invade South Carolina if necessary with the result that the state then recruited an army. Finally, Clay and Calhoun created a compromise to reduce tariffs over nine years.

Sectional Southern voting, bolstered by at least a half of the Northern Democrats, usually defeated attempts to raise tariffs, pass land grant measures (including a Homestead Act, which might open up the West to free soilers from the North and a Pacific Railroad Act), and award grants to states to set up agricultural and mechanical colleges. Defeating these measures may have helped economic problems, but in the 1850s the measures were perceived by Southerners as being particularly in Northern interests, and even when the Land College Grant and Homestead Acts were passed, Buchanan vetoed them. It could therefore be argued that it was actually self-interest which motivated Southern action, rather than any greater affinity for states' rights, especially as Southerners had rarely invoked the states' rights argument when there was a balance between free states and slave states in Congress, and they had dominated the Presidency and Supreme Court. It could in fact be argued that it was the prospect of being a permanent minority in a Union that had outlawed the expansion of slavery which gave rise to the states' rights cause, because, ironically, the Supreme Court's decision over Dred Scott, which was widely supported in the South, was an implied attack on the rights of states to determine whether or not slavery existed within their borders.

The North certainly seemed to identify more with the institutions of the Union, but again it can be contended that this was also born of self-interest, and that issues such as the Tariff, the Homestead Act and government aid for improvements were simply measures that the North wanted for its own benefit.

Post-war claims by Jefferson Davis that states' rights had been the main cause of the South's secession have been treated sceptically by many historians, but there is no doubt that one of the consequences of war was the increase of central power over the states. Davis, in retrospect, may well have been attempting to make the Southern cause seem more noble than it had been, but it can be argued that as far as Southerners were concerned the state right of prime importance was that of slavery.

As early as the 1820s John Calhoun had laid down the principle that the states had the right to nullify federal laws, but the issue which had prompted Calhoun to set out such an argument was that of the tariff, not slavery, and it was the tariff which in many ways was more of an issue until the 1850s, when 'Bleeding Kansas' played its fatal part in the polarisation of the sections.

When South Carolina declared the reasons for its secession it argued that the Republicans would wage a war on slavery until it was abolished, at which point the equal rights of the states would be lost and the federal government would have become the enemy of the Southern states. The significance of this is that it was not the tariff, nor land grants, named as the key issue, but slavery. Alexander Stephens, Vice-President of the Confederacy, argued that slavery just happened to be the issue over which supporters of states' rights and those who favoured a stronger central government clashed, but it was more fundamental than that. Had slavery not existed in the South before the 1860s, it is extremely difficult to imagine any war taking place. Slavery was what defined the South and that is what made it the most important state right. Debate over tariff levels had brought dissent in earlier years, but even that issue was related to slavery in the sense that the South's economy was more dependent on exports than the North's, and therefore the South feared the possibility that countries such as Britain would retaliate against high US tariffs by raising the duty on commodities such as cotton. The fact that the North was a more economically diverse and industrialising region than the South was also inextricably linked to slavery and a reliance on labour-intensive agricultural production in the South. Even opposition to homestead grants seemed to be based on the premise that the beneficiaries of the grants were more likely to come from the more populous free states, which would in turn ensure that the territories where they settled would have a majority of inhabitants who voted against slavery when it came to applying for statehood. In the light of these considerations, it would appear that slavery must be judged the most important states' right as far as Southerners were concerned.

3   How far was Southern nationalism the product of Northern attacks on slavery and to what extent were sectional differences responsible for the outbreak of war? (20)

(AQA)

It is probably fair to say that Southern nationalism or a distinct Southern consciousness did not really begin to emerge until the 1840s. Up until then all of the things which the two sections had in common seemed more significant, for example the same language, legal system and religious views. The year 1831 was in many ways significant, given that the Nat Turner slave revolt took place in Virginia, and William Lloyd Garrison published the first issue of his abolitionist paper *The Liberator*. The Nullification Crisis of 1832 saw South Carolina threatening to secede over a high tariff. Other Southern states were not prepared to go as far, but the appearance of the Free Soil Party, which won 14 per cent of the Northern vote in 1848, was a further cause for alarm as far as Southerners were concerned, because it marked the conspicuous entry into national politics of an issue which had hitherto only been an issue for abolitionist pressure groups to champion.

In the debates surrounding the 1850 Compromise, Seward ominously spoke of a 'higher law than the Constitution' in his attacks on slavery and the government quickly attempted to disclaim his speech, but he spoke for many in the North who were becoming convinced of the immorality of slavery. Attempts to enforce the 1850 Fugitive Slave Law, with notorious examples such as the Anthony Burns case, had enraged elements in the North and the subsequent resistance had in turn enraged the South. In the late spring of 1852 *Uncle Tom's Cabin* was published as a book, and sold 300,000 copies within a year in the US alone (the equivalent of about three million copies today). Within a decade it had sold two million in the US. The author of the book, Harriet Beecher Stowe, had based the novel on what she had seen of slavery in Kentucky, her brother's experiences working in New Orleans and accounts from runaway slaves; some Northerners, and not all Southerners, were portrayed in a bad light, but the South was appalled by the book, perhaps because of the truths it contained. Lincoln, upon meeting Stowe in 1862, apparently remarked to her: 'So you're the little woman who wrote the book that made this great war.'

During the 1850s, Frederick Law Olmstead, a Northern journalist, travelled through the South, and in three books argued that the institution of slavery had helped to create a society that lacked resourcefulness or economic initiative. It could be argued that, given the price of cotton, the South did not need to diversify as the North had. Historians differ over the extent to which investment in other areas such as railroads and mills would have made more profit, and there is also evidence to suggest that parts of the South had begun to industrialise. A further literary assault on the South appeared in 1857 with Hinton Rowan Helper's book called *The Impending Crisis of the South*, which portrayed the region as economically backward, with widespread illiteracy and poverty. The book made a huge impact in the North and Republicans distributed an abridged version of it during election campaigns.

By this time the South had become more assertive in its justifications of slavery and George Fitzhugh's *Cannibals All* in 1857 argued that the South was superior to the North, describing free labour under capitalism in the North as a sort of 'social cannibalism' in a society where the strong oppressed the weak.

Historian Ed Beares has argued that John Brown's raid on Harper's Ferry was the single most important cause of the war in the sense that the Southern militia system was immediately improved as a result, increasing the possibility of conflict. The wave of sympathy engendered in the North by Brown's eloquent defence of himself and his subsequent execution – church bells were rung on the day of his death and there were rumours that prominent Republicans had given covert support to Brown – convinced the South that slavery could not be protected in the Union. Brown's raid was clearly a short-term cause of the war, and it should be remembered that it was Lincoln's election which triggered secession, but there can be little doubt that Southern nationalism emerged as a response to perceived threats from the North. Fatally, it was to give many Southerners a false impression of their own abilities and the confidence to leave the Union.

The crucial issue here is to decide whether conflict caused sectional differences or vice versa. It is true to say that votes on the 1850 Compromise divided essentially along sectional rather than party lines, as had votes on other issues such as the tariff and land grants, which suggests that sectional differences existed before 1860. The fact that they had existed before 1860 however raises the question of why war did not break out prior to 1860.

Holt blames the breakdown of the party system for the failure to contain the issue of slavery, and yet there had always been a possibility that at some point the party system would be unable to contain an issue so potentially explosive. In December 1860, Lincoln suggested that views on slavery marked the only substantial difference between North and South, but there is evidence which might suggest otherwise. McPherson has argued that of the 143 important inventions patented between 1790 and 1860, 93 per cent came from the free states. Southern cotton accounted for something like 75 per cent of the world's supply, and the South provided 60 per cent of all American imports. Between 1800 and 1860 the percentage of the North's labour force working in agriculture dropped from 70 per cent to 40 per cent yet the Southern proportion remained constant at 80 per cent. Approximately 25 per cent of Northerners lived in urban areas, compared to just 10 per cent of Southerners, while 88 per cent of immigrants settled in the free states. There is also a view that Southerners tended to take the view that 'trade' was beneath a Southern gentleman. North and South tended to react in a sectional way towards the Tariff and Homestead Acts, having a Bank of the United States and improvement grants. Although these were not entirely sectional issues, given that Northern Democrats usually voted with the South against them, nonetheless they formed part of the sectional differences of importance that existed before the war.

In recent years, historians have come to take the view that sectional differences have been exaggerated. Brian Holden Reid concurs that slavery was 'central to the sense of cultural divergence between the North and South, even if this has been exaggerated'. It is, however, one thing for historians to look back in a detached way at events when what is important is what people thought *at the time*, and perceived sectional differences certainly gave impetus to the rival conspiracy theories, which in turn increased perceptions of sectional differences. The movement to reopen the African slave trade in the late 1850s; attempts to annex Cuba (1850 and 1851) with Southern volunteers, which had the tacit acknowledgement of the government (Pierce was determined to get Cuba but Spain would not sell); talk of seizing other islands and some parts of Mexico; the 1854 Gadsden Purchase from Mexico; and filibuster (freebooter or pirate) William Walker's expedition to Nicaragua in 1855, which raised Southern hopes for plantations in the area, all contributed to the sense that the South had different values.

It is reasonable to take the view that there were long-term, medium-term and short-term causes of the war. The long-term causes can be seen as expansion, the issue of slavery, economic differences between the sections, and states' rights; the medium-term causes include the rise of abolitionism, the emergence of rival conspiracy theories, and an exaggerated perception of regional differences; and the short-term causes include the individual roles of key people, issues such as Kansas-Nebraska, the Dred Scott case, John Brown's raid, Lincoln's election, and secession. Utilising this perspective, it is possible to argue that sectional differences were not as important as some of the long-term factors. But this ignores the fact that slavery was the most important sectional difference, and was what gave rise to other perceptions of diversity.

Edward Ranson and Andrew Hook are sceptical about an Old South of aristocratic and chivalrous planters in white mansions, elegant women and slaves singing in cotton fields, and trace this romanticised version of life to the 1830s and 1840s. They suggest that the South deliberately tried to create a distinct identity for itself, and point to the drawing of the Mason-Dixon line between Maryland and Pennsylvania in the 1760s to settle a boundary dispute, when nobody took the view that people north of it were in any way different from the people who happened to be living south of it. In reality the South was geographically diverse and consisted of 'many Souths', while its language, laws, religion and culture were hardly any different from those of the rest of the country, although from the 1830s Southerners decided to stop apologising for slavery and instead argued its merits. It is certainly possible to argue, as Paludan has suggested, that the North identified more closely with the country's democratic institutions.

Irresponsible agitators and blundering politicians

4   To what extent was James Buchanan responsible for the outbreak of war in 1861? (20)

(AQA)

In a recent survey of American History professors, Buchanan was voted the worst of all the men to have held the office of President. Paul Finkelman has claimed that his policies directly and indirectly encouraged and aided secession, although others have maintained that he could have done little to prevent secession given the circumstances and issues that arose.

Buchanan's victory in 1856 was sectional. He was the first President since John Quincy Adams not to win a majority of both Northern and Southern states. At the time of his election he was 65 and had been out of the country for three years, which left him out of touch and unable to understand the depth of Northern opposition to the expansion of slavery. Douglas, who had not been out of the country, also misunderstood the depth of Northern feeling. Buchanan however did not help the situation and right from the start of his Presidency he made some serious mistakes. Four of his cabinet were slaveholding Southerners, two others were pro-South and one member was against the anti-slavery movement. He valued the advice of personal friends above that of skilled politicians, and, most significantly, he did not choose Douglas, the most popular Democrat in the North, to be in his cabinet. The advisers to whom he listened outside his cabinet also tended to be slave owners.

Some have argued that Buchanan was the ultimate 'dough-face' (i.e. a Northerner with Southern beliefs) and he certainly saw nothing immoral in slavery. He appointed Robert Walker as governor of Kansas, who informed him that, despite a minority of settlers being pro-slavery, as a result of fraudulent elections a majority of the Lecompton legislature was pro-slavery. At first Buchanan backed Walker, and in the process undermined criticism of Dred Scott and the Kansas-Nebraska Act. Finkelman argues he could have brought Kansas in as a Democrat-supporting free state and perhaps ended the debate over slavery in the territories, but he failed to give Walker the support he needed. Walker resigned, and Buchanan refused to insist the pro-slavery Lecompton Constitution be put to a fair vote. This further convinced Northerners of a sectional conspiracy reaching the highest office.

David Potter noted that, by trying to bring Kansas in as a slave state, Buchanan failed to see how badly the Northern wing of the Democrat Party would be damaged, and what an awkward position it would put Northern Democrat congressmen in. Anti-slavery Republicans voted with Douglas and his Democratic allies. The House's vote against the admission of Kansas was a major loss for Buchanan's party and Presidency according to Finkelman. Buchanan persuaded Congress to pass the English Bill, which declared that if the people of Kansas voted for the Lecompton Constitution they would receive immediate statehood and 19 million acres of public lands; if they rejected it (which they did), Kansas would not be admitted until it had 90,000 settlers. The people of Kansas effectively voted to wait.

Had Buchanan managed to resolve Kansas, Stampp argues that the Republicans would have had no major issue on which to campaign. But they did have other issues and one of those was the corruption of Buchanan's administration: there was evidence in a Congressional report that the government had bribed congressmen to vote for the admission of Kansas under the Lecompton Constitution, as well as bribing judges to naturalise immigrants prematurely so they could vote in the crucial states of Pennsylvania and Indiana to help swing those states to Buchanan. Buchanan also tried to unseat Douglas through patronage and threats, but failed, and the Republicans won 109 seats in 1858 in the House of Representatives. The Republicans managed to exploit splits among the Democrat and Whig/'Know-Nothing' representatives and elect a Republican speaker, despite not having a majority in the House.

Within days of Buchanan's inauguration the long-awaited verdict of the Dred Scott case was announced. Chief Justice Roger Taney declared in March 1857 that Congress did not have the power to ban slavery from the territories. The fact that Buchanan had been informed of the Court's decision before it was announced contributed to the mistrust felt by many and confirmed the fears of those who believed in a 'slaveholders' conspiracy'. It also appears that Buchanan put a lot of improper pressure on Grier, one of the Northern Supreme Court judges, to support Taney's decision in order to avoid accusations of a sectional ruling. Buchanan's designs on Cuba and his tendency to turn a blind eye to the attempts by Southern filibusters to expand slavery by conquest (some say he even tacitly encouraged it) only served to increase the mistrust.

Buchanan's response to the economic panic that started in August 1857 following the collapse of many banks, was to tighten the money supply – exactly when more money was needed. Northerners blamed the panic on a low tariff and the blocking of a transcontinental railroad, internal improvements and the Homestead Bill. It is difficult to determine accurately the part each played but Buchanan's position on money and hostility to a national banking system showed a lack of leadership, and further alienated Northern support.

In 1860 some felt that support for Breckinridge would throw the election open to a decision of the House, where each state would have one vote for the top two electoral college candidates, believing Bell and Lincoln would split the North – which, in the event, Lincoln carried. By the time Buchanan had left office seven Southern states had seceded. He blamed Northern agitators and threats to slavery, and although he acknowledged secession as illegal he did nothing to prevent it.

Buchanan may not have been able to prevent war in the long term, but he clearly played a major role in the timing of the war, as did others who inhabited the White House. In the words of Finkelman: 'The blundering generation of Presidents from Fillmore to Buchanan set the stage for the war.'

Stampp sees the events of 1857 as crucial in preventing a peaceful solution, and blames Buchanan for pursuing policies that alienated Northerners. Nevins called Buchanan's actions in 1857–8 'one of the significant failures of American statesmanship'.

PRACTICE QUESTION

5   How far were 'irresponsible agitators and blundering politicians' to blame for the outbreak of the American Civil War? (20)

(AQA)

Advice: *The main focus of this answer should obviously be the role of individuals in the build-up to war. It is good form to start with individuals rather than examining longer-term causes first. You can always cover other factors later on in the essay. Men such as James Buchanan, Stephen Douglas, John Brown and Abraham Lincoln might all figure in your answer, and if you can write relevantly about the historiography, all well and good. A useful conclusion to the answer might be to consider whether you think the war would have broken out eventually, regardless of the individuals who played such a major role in the 1850s.*

 Motives for secession and fighting

6   How much truth was there in the Southern belief that a black republican conspiracy to abolish slavery existed and to what extent was the North responsible for the outbreak of Civil War? (20)

(AQA)

There was certainly opposition to slavery in the North. Particularly since the 1830s, abolitionists had mounted a consistent campaign against the evils of slavery from a moral standpoint. In the 1840s, many

Northern states blocked the recapture of runaway slaves, and in 1852 *Uncle Tom's Cabin* was very well received in the North. In the North, some objected to slavery because it represented unfair competition to the 'free labour' system outside the South; others were indifferent to the rights and wrongs of slavery as long as conflict could be avoided. But, step by step, a belief in the South took hold that there existed an organised conspiracy in the North, bent on the overthrow of slavery. And once that had taken hold, every little bit of evidence seemed to confirm its existence, just as many Northerners came to believe in a slaveholders' conspiracy to extend slavery, destroy civil liberties and take control of the federal government.

Although from the South, Chief Justice Taney had released his own slaves. Nonetheless, he felt that Southerners were under threat from the North, and wrote in a private letter 'the knife of the assassin is at their throats'. Whatever Taney's motives, the Dred Scott decision helped to strengthen the Republican Party, and gave ammunition to Seward and Lincoln to accuse Buchanan and Taney of collusion, which seemed to provide further evidence of a 'slave power' conspiracy.

The sympathetic reaction in the North to John Brown's execution seemed to provide further evidence of Northern collusion, and some Southerners even contested that the backing for the raid came from members of the Republican Party itself. Expressions of horror at Brown's raid from prominent Republicans such as Lincoln cut little ice in the South, and his subsequent Presidential victory on a sectional Northern vote said it all as far as Southerners were concerned. What more evidence could anyone want?

To a certain extent it is possible to sympathise with the South in the sense that the institution of slavery was clearly under threat, if not in the short term then certainly in the long term. Lincoln had stated that he expected the Union to become all slaveholding or all free, and there were no prizes for guessing which option he thought would happen. Most Northerners were certainly opposed to the expansion of slavery, be it on economic or moral grounds, but it was precisely the different motives for opposing the expansion of slavery and the varying attitudes towards interfering with slavery where it already existed that meant that in reality no Republican conspiracy existed.

Brian Holden Reid appears to have no doubt that the South was the aggressive party and solely to blame for the conflict, blaming the secessionists' casual attitude to, and over-reliance on force, with the South deluding itself that a war for independence could be easily won with foreign help and a little violence.

In January 1831 the first issue of William Lloyd Garrison's abolitionist paper, *The Liberator*, came off the presses; and, within months, 60 whites had been killed in Virginia in the Nat Turner revolt. Ranson and Hook have argued that: 'these two events electrified the South, and they did much to ensure that the spirit of sectional unity would continue to grow.' In other words, there was a perception that the revolt was linked to the rise of abolitionism in the North. They argue further that, until the 1830s, Southern spokesmen tended to apologise for slavery as a necessary evil, but as a result of abolitionist pressure Southerners became more assertive, arguing that slavery beat 'wage slavery' in the North, and blacks were inferior, citing numerous historical precedents.

In 1832, Garrison established the New England Anti-Slavery Society, and in 1833 the American Anti-Slavery Society was set up, having nearly 200,000 members by 1840. The Liberty Party stood at the 1840 elections but never campaigned for the outright abolition of slavery, wanting mainly to keep slavery out of the territories. In Prigg v. Pennsylvania (1842) the Supreme Court ruled that states did not have to help enforce the 1793 Fugitive Slave Law, and several Northern states passed personal liberty laws forbidding state officials from helping aid the return of runaways.

Foner said that the emergence of militant abolitionism, Nat Turner's rebellion, the Virginia debates on slavery, and the Nullification Crisis, presented attacks to slavery from within and outside the South. In response Southern society closed ranks in defence of slavery. It should be noted that the events within the South were also partly influenced by those outside it. Given the growth of pro-slavery arguments in the South in the 1830s and the Congressional Gag Rule, plus mob attacks on abolitionist printing presses, abolitionists could argue that, besides being morally wrong, slavery was incompatible with democratic values and concepts of freedom. In the South, the 'internal dynamic' of claim and counter-claim was exacerbated by agitators seeking to exploit sectional conflict for personal gain. Foner has pointed to John Tyler and John Calhoun, two of the so-called agitators, as political outsiders whose careers had been blocked by the major parties.

In 1852, *Uncle Tom's Cabin* shook the nation, and attitudes in both North and South were perhaps never quite the same again after its publication. Foner also points to the development of Republican ideology based on such areas as 'free labour', enterprise, glorifying the self-made man and materialism, and defined the South as backward and stagnant. The Whig Party had been regarded by many as the party of wealth and privilege, and the perpetuation of the 'slave power' conspiracy, described by Foner as 'the ideological glue of the Republican party', allowed the Republicans to portray themselves as anti-aristocratic. A strong argument can also be constructed for the North wanting to fight for economic reasons.

When the states of the Lower South decided to secede, the North could have chosen to let them go, and, in that sense, it was the North's decision to fight. Having said that, it could be argued that Southerners should have realised there was a good chance that the North *would* fight, although it is not entirely certain that they did, nor is it necessarily clear why Northerners valued the Union so highly, they were prepared to lay down their lives in vast numbers to preserve it. Stampp also argued that politicians and people in the South made a series of 'horrendous blunders' during 1860 and 1861, embarking 'irrationally and irresponsibly' on a war which was always likely to be disastrous.

7 **'Economic issues were at the root of the problems which led to Civil War.'**
   Discuss. (20)

                                                                                      (AQA)

Essay plan

Introduction: Indicate a line of argument showing that in some way economic causes could be at the root of problems, given that slavery can be viewed as an economic issue; or offer a broad outline of the economic issues which need to be examined, as well as other causes which should be considered.

Para 1: Marxist/Revisionist view of war as feudal South v. capitalist North, e.g. Charles Beard, and the arguments that this is oversimplistic, given the diversity of Republican supporters and other factors.

Para 2: Slavery as an economic issue to link into next para.

Para 3: Detail differences between North and South, particularly the tariff question, and other perceived differences linked to the economy.

Para 4: Examine how far the North depended on the South economically and whether the South overestimated its ability to survive economically in the long term.

Para 5: Discuss how far economic factors may have been exaggerated.

Paras 6/7: Assess the extent to which other factors played a part in the coming of war, such as slavery as a moral issue, individuals, sectional conspiracies, etc.

Conclusion: How far did economic issues in their own right cause the war, and how far did they link to other causes of the war?

8   **How far did the breakdown of the Democrat/Whig Party system in the 1850s precipitate the outbreak of war?** (20)

(AQA)

Essay plan

Introduction: A comment regarding the views of Michael Holt put forward in the 1970s.

Para 1: Further discussion of Holt's views related to the breakdown of the party system, and the counter theory that it was the issue of slavery that caused the breakdown.

Para 2: Assessment of the party system, and what the parties stood for.

Para 3: Examine why the Democrat/Whig system had been able to keep sectional animosity at bay for so long.

Para 4: Look at the impact of 'Know-Nothingism' and what caused the break-up of the Whigs, and also what the emergent Republican Party stood for.

Para 5: Examine other issues that contributed to war in the 1850s, e.g. Bleeding Kansas, Dred Scott and John Brown's raid.

Para 6: Assess the extent to which the creation of the Republican Party and Lincoln becoming President made war inevitable.

Para 6: Examine other factors that contributed to war and the views of historians who reject Holt's theory.

Conclusion: The role the breakdown of the Democrat/Whig system played, and how far the new Republican Party increased tensions in the build-up to war.

9   **Why did the Southern states secede from the Union and to what extent did secession make Civil War an inevitability?** (20)

(AQA)

The declarations of the causes of secession issued by the Southern states indicate that their prime reason for leaving the Union was to protect the institution of slavery.

Brian Holden Reid views the movement towards secession in a slightly wider context, maintaining that it was a reaction against a system that had allowed a sectional President, who was seen as a threat to the South, especially with regard to slavery, to come to power. Reid believes that an independent Confederacy would have attempted to extend its influence over the whole of the Caribbean basin, even if it may not have actively tried to expand slavery. The argument that the South fought to defend its own way of life, which essentially revolved around slave labour, believing that it could succeed economically without the North, and that it adopted secession as a sort of 'plan B', in the sense that other attempts to safeguard their demands had failed, suggests that secession was the work of a highly provincial, possibly insubstantial, excitable minority. David Potter also adheres to the idea that a secessionist minority, which seems to have been strong in the plantation districts, determinedly exploited discontent and confusion to achieve their own ends.

There was certainly a perception among Southerners that they would be better off without the North. An Alabama newspaper said of the Southerner: 'In Northern vessels his products are carried to market, his cotton is ginned with Northern gins, his sugar is crushed and preserved with Northern machinery, his rivers are navigated by Northern steamboats.' It has been estimated that some 15–20 per cent of the price of raw cotton went outside the South to Northern or British creditors, insurers, and shipping and ware-housing, and there was a strong sense that the North depended heavily on the South. The 'Panic' of 1857 which affected the South relatively lightly seemed to confirm to many Southerners that the North was weaker economically, but in the long term, of course, its diversity proved to be a greater strength.

Holt has argued that Southern conservatives who were against secession were poorly organised and often portrayed as unpatriotic, which tended to make them cautious of voicing their doubts. 'Immediatists' had won the day against 'Co-operationists' across the South, despite the fact that the Republicans did not control either House in Congress. He also argued that Southerners had lost faith in their congressmen by 1860, and local politicians rather than national figures took the lead in the secessionist movement. Whatever the motives behind secession there appears to have been a belief in the South that the North would not fight a war to preserve the Union.

Allowing the precedent of secession would mean that, at any point in the future when a state felt its interests no longer coincided with those of the other states in the Union, it could secede. Potentially this could mean the complete disintegration of the Union or a return to a loose confederation of states such as had existed under the Articles of Confederation. The Southern states which formed the Confederacy do not seem to have worried unduly that the Confederacy might in turn disintegrate itself, and the internal bickering which dogged the Southern war effort at times could well have ultimately manifested itself in a break-up of the Confederacy.

Southerners also tended to feel that if Northerners did want to fight they would quickly lose owing to superior military leadership and prowess in the South. There is evidence to suggest that there was some-thing of an inferiority complex in the North regarding Southern military ability, but this was not sufficiently strong to convince Northerners that a war could not be won, even given the problems of effectively having to invade the South and subdue it to win. It is easy with hindsight to assume that the North would win any war, but that was far from clear at the time, and the decision to fight was not one taken lightly by Lincoln and his cabinet. There were major worries over the position of the border states as well as that of the Upper South.

There seems little doubt that just as Northerners had assumed Southerners would never actually secede en masse, so Southerners believed that the North would not actually try to prevent secession. Northern affinity for the Union and what it stood for was severely underestimated by the South; and from a Northern viewpoint secession had to be stopped. Slavery may have been the main issue which led to Southern seces-sion, but the North did not initially go to war to abolish slavery.

10 How far was Abraham Lincoln responsible for the failure to find compromise in 1860–1? (20)

(AQA)

Lincoln's selection as Presidential candidate for the 1860 election over the more outspoken Seward was calculated to win over support of the 'Know-Nothings' and give the Republicans a better chance of winning Illinois, which was Lincoln's home state. Lincoln's victory in 1860 triggered the secession of South Carolina, which was soon followed by the other states from the Lower South.

Nevins and Potter have both argued that, as a party, the Republicans had refused to take warnings of secession seriously, which was a significant mistake, but secession had already happened by the time Lincoln took office. There was a tendency in the North to believe in a repressed Unionist majority in the South, which would at some point assert itself, but, as McPherson has argued, Southern Unionism was a 'perishable commodity'.

The seven three-hour Lincoln–Douglas debates during the election campaign for the Senate in Illinois, which centred on slavery, did allow Douglas to point out inconsistencies in Lincoln's stance, asking why the country could not endure half slave/half free, and highlighted the fact that Lincoln certainly did not believe in black equality with whites. If Lincoln had no intention of interfering in states where slavery already existed how did he expect to bring slavery to its ultimate extinction?

The best known of the attempts to create a last minute compromise came in the form of the Crittenden Plan, put together by a Senate 'Committee of Thirteen' which included Seward, Wade, Douglas, Jefferson Davis and John J. Crittenden (a slave-owning supporter of the Union). It proposed to guarantee slavery perpetually against future interference by the federal government and to prohibit slavery in all the territories north of the Missouri Compromise line (there was a precedent for an amendment that could not be overridden in Article V, which prohibits change in Senate representation); and federal compensation was to be paid to slave owners who failed to recover slaves under the Fugitive Slave Act, but Lincoln's opposition proved to be crucial. He was happy to accept compensation for slave owners and to guarantee slavery but he remained opposed to its extension. In December 1860, Congress, which no longer contained members from the Lower South, defeated the plan 25 to 23 in the Senate and 113 to 180 in the Representatives. A further convention, which met in Washington in February 1861 at the behest of Virginia, and produced only slight modifications of Crittenden's proposals, failed to win the interest of Congress.

Lincoln was resolved to preserve the Union when he assumed the Presidency in 1861. One has to wonder how possible compromise was, given that the Southern states wanted to be out of the Union and the Northern states wanted them to remain. By 1861 the Southern states seemed convinced that slavery was no longer safe in the Union. The only way in which Lincoln could have persuaded the Confederate states to come back would have been to renounce the pledge made in his election campaign to prevent the further expansion of slavery. Had he guessed a war would result in the deaths of over 600,000 people, he may have been more inclined to do just that.

Lincoln knew that if he relieved militarily the federal garrison at Fort Sumter in Charleston Harbor, under the command of Major Robert Anderson, he would be blamed for starting the war and could provoke the Upper South into secession. If he ordered Anderson to withdraw, as South Carolina wanted, it could divide Northern opinion and potentially his cabinet. He decided to stall. Seward advised him to give up Sumter, which would reduce the chances of the Upper South seceding and encourage Unionism in the South. General Winfield Scott assured Lincoln that reinforcing Sumter would be impossible. Only one person in Lincoln's cabinet, Montgomery Blair, advised Lincoln to hold Sumter regardless of the risk, but Lincoln agreed. Seward had leaked to the press that Sumter would be given up and the wave of public opposition that swept the North convinced Lincoln to stick to his guns. He won the cabinet over to the idea of resupplying Sumter – a calculated move which left the ball in the court of the Confederacy, where Jefferson Davis was under pressure to attack Sumter before enthusiasm for secession waned and to force the Upper South to make a choice.

Lincoln caused the war in the sense that he decided the South would not be allowed to secede, and he was prepared to use force of arms to ensure that they were brought back into the Union. Whether the South could realistically have expected the North to let it leave is open to debate. There is certainly evidence to suggest that many Southerners did not think the North would fight. Brian Holden Reid argued that the decision to fire on Fort Sumter was taken by overconfident Southerners who believed the North could be intimidated into meekly accepting secession, but Lincoln was made of sterner stuff.

PRACTICE QUESTION

11 Why did the American Civil War not break out earlier than 1861? (20)

(AQA)

Advice: *The answer to this question should probably concentrate on: the various compromises, such as that of 1850, which had effectively averted war, and the men who created them; the common ground shared by North and South; and the short-term triggers of war which occurred in the 1850s, such as the collapse of the Whig Party, Bleeding Kansas and John Brown's raid.*

Part 3: Sources

1 Understanding the Northern perspective

- **Source A: 'The True Remedy for the Fugitive Slave Bill', editorial from Frederick Douglass's paper, 9 June 1854**

A good revolver, a steady hand, and a determination to shoot down any man attempting to kidnap. Let every colored man make up his mind to this, and live by it, and if needs be, die by it. This will put an end to kidnapping and to slaveholding, too.

- **Source B: Abraham Lincoln from first Lincoln–Douglas Debate at Ottawa, Illinois, 21 August 1858**

. . . I have no purpose directly or indirectly to interfere with the institution of slavery in the States where it exists . . . I have no purpose to introduce political and social equality between the white and the black races . . . I, as well as Judge Douglas, am in favor of the race to which I belong, having the superior position . . . but . . . there is no reason in the world why the negro is not entitled to all the natural rights enumerated in the Declaration of Independence, the right to life, liberty and the pursuit of happiness . . . I agree . . . he is not my equal . . . perhaps not in moral or intellectual endowment.

- **Source C: *New York Courier and Enquirer*, 1 December 1860**

We love the Union, because at home and abroad, collectively and individually, it gives us character as a nation and as citizens of the Great Republic; because it gives us nationality as a People, renders us now the equal of the greatest European Power, and in another half century, will make us the greatest, richest, and most powerful people on the face of the earth.

- **Source D: *Trenton Gazette*, 3 January 1861**

The present attempt at a forcible dissolution of the Union, is the result of a conspiracy which has been brooded upon and actively conducted by ambitious men for nearly thirty years past . . . Their aim is to found a Southern Empire, which shall be composed of the Southern States, Mexico, Central America, and Cuba, of which the arch-conspirators are to be the rulers.

OCR QUESTION FORMAT

The questions and answers that follow are based on the OCR style.

(a) **Study Source A. From this Source and your own knowledge explain the term 'any man attempting to kidnap' in the context of the 1850 Fugitive Slave Act.** (20)

(b) **Study Sources A and B. How far does Lincoln's view on the issue of slavery in Source B differ from Douglass's perspective in Source A?** (40)

(c) **Study all the Sources. Using all these Sources and your own knowledge explain how far you agree with the view that the North went to war to abolish slavery.** (60)

(a) Frederick Douglass is referring to any slave owner (or anyone helping him) attempting to 'recapture' a runaway slave. He is suggesting that, in order to prevent Southerners from seizing escaped slaves, blacks should take up arms and resist. The 1850 Fugitive Slave Act had made it easier for Southern slaveholders to come North and capture runaway slaves, and the federal government had committed itself to support their actions. In some respects, Douglass's suggestions of 1854 had already been put into practice in a number of instances where both whites and blacks had used force of arms against slave owners, such as at the 'Battle of Christiana' in 1851 and the incident involving slave William McHenry at Syracuse.

(b) In Source A, Douglass clearly takes the view that men should resort to the use of force to intimidate slave owners attempting to reclaim their property by talking of a 'determination to shoot down any man attempting to kidnap', even though the Fugitive Slave Act of 1850 permitted slave owners to seize escaped slaves. He therefore condones the breaking of a law passed by Congress on the grounds of higher morality, i.e. that it is fundamentally wrong to own slaves. He is quite clearly against slaveholding where it already exists. Lincoln gives the impression in Source B that he is prepared to tolerate the continued existence of slavery where it already exists and goes on to argue that blacks are perhaps inferior in certain ways to whites 'in moral or intellectual endowment', which it may be assumed Douglass would have disagreed with. Lincoln in some ways contradicts himself because, having said that he does not intend to 'interfere with the institution of slavery in the States where it exists', he goes on to argue that negroes should be entitled to 'all the natural rights enumerated in the Declaration of Independence' which is clearly not possible if some blacks remain as slaves.

(c) The abolition of slavery was certainly not a stated reason for the North fighting in 1861. Lincoln preferred to keep war aims to the preservation of the Union, in a successful attempt to keep as many slaveholding states in the Union as possible. He was acutely aware that a declaration of intent to abolish slavery would probably result in the secession of the four border states whose loyalty was absolutely vital to Northern prospects of winning the war.

In Source A, Frederick Douglass certainly seems to suggest a strong intention to 'put an end to . . . slaveholding', and a readiness to use force to do so, but as an ex-slave himself that might be expected. Even by 1860, however, it is unlikely that Douglass spoke for a majority of white Northerners. In Source D, the *Trenton Gazette*, having seen South Carolina secede, blames a conspiracy based on slaveholding for the attempt to dissolve the Union. The newspaper does not state that the North must fight to abolish slavery, but it clearly implies that slavery is at the root of the country's problems, and therefore there may be an implication that slavery should not be allowed to expand.

In Source B, Lincoln explicitly says he has 'no purpose . . . to interfere with . . . slavery . . . where it exists', but it is also worth remembering that in 1858 Lincoln was standing in the Senate elections against Stephen Douglas, and he would not have wanted to alarm voters unnecessarily. Having said that, Lincoln consistently denied his intent to interfere with slavery, until of course he decided to do it for practical reasons. Had the war been won quickly by the North it is highly likely that slavery would not have been abolished when it was, and therefore it is probably true to say that Lincoln did not necessarily go to war to abolish slavery, but to preserve the Union, as he constantly reiterated.

The *New York Courier and Enquirer* in Source C does not mention the issue of slavery but merely outlines the advantages of the Union remaining intact, particularly looking to a future as the 'greatest, richest and most powerful people on the face of the earth'.

The key issue in the build-up to war, as far as most were concerned, was the expansion of slavery, not slavery itself, although Southerners felt that, in the long term, if new states would all be free states, they would become a permanent minority and increasingly marginalised within the Union. There was gross hypocrisy at the root of Northern policy: either slavery was disapproved of or it was not. The Republicans and Lincoln attempted to sit on the fence, which meant that abolitionists such as Douglass would never wholeheartedly support Lincoln. But Lincoln was a consummate pragmatist and judged public opinion perfectly. Northerners would not have embraced war against the South in the way that they did, had the abolition of slavery been a stated war aim at the outset. It can therefore be concluded that, although Lincoln may have wanted to abolish slavery from a personal perspective, the North as a whole did not go to war to abolish slavery.

ADDITIONAL QUESTIONS IN THE OCR STYLE

(a) **Study Source D. From this Source and your own knowledge explain the basis of the 'slaveholder conspiracy' which existed in the North by 1861.** (20)

(b) **Study Sources A and D. How far does Source A support the viewpoint put forward by the *Trenton Gazette* in Source D regarding a Southern conspiracy?** (40)

(c) **Study all the Sources. Using all these Sources and your own knowledge explain how far you agree that Southern states left the Union because of a 'black republican' conspiracy to abolish slavery in the North.** (60)

2 Understanding the Southern perspective

■ **Source A: Speech of John C. Calhoun, read by James Mason to the Senate, 4 March 1850**

What has caused this widely diffused and almost universal discontent? . . . One of the causes is, undoubtedly, to be traced to the long-continued agitation of the slave question on the part of the North, and the many aggressions which they have made on the rights of the South . . . There is another lying back of it . . . that may be regarded as the great and primary cause. This is to be found in the fact that the equilibrium between the two sections, in the Government as it stood when the constitution was ratified . . . has been destroyed. At that time, there was nearly a perfect equilibrium between the two . . . but as it now stands, one section has the exclusive power of controlling the Government, which leaves the other without any adequate means of protecting itself against its encroachments and oppression.

■ **Source B: Declaration of the Immediate Causes Which Induce and Justify the Secession of South Carolina from the Federal Union 1860**

A geographical line has been drawn across the Union, and all the States north of that line have united in the election of a man to the high office of President of the United States, whose opinions and purposes are hostile to slavery. He is to be entrusted with the administration of the common Government, because he has declared that that 'Government cannot endure permanently half slave, half free', and that the public mind must rest in the belief that slavery is in the course of ultimate extinction.

■ **Source C: Letter from Lincoln to Horace Greeley's *New York Tribune*, 22 August 1862**

If I could save the Union without freeing any slave, I would do it; and if I could save it by freeing all the slaves, I would do it; and if I could save it by freeing some and leaving others alone, I would also do that.

■ **Source D: Jefferson Davis, *The Rise and Fall of the Confederate Government* (vol. 1, pp. 77–85), New York, 1881**

The Southern States and Southern people have been sedulously represented as 'propagandists' of slavery, and the Northern as the defenders and champions of universal freedom . . . It was not the passage of the 'personal liberty laws', it was not the circulation of incendiary documents, it was not the raid of John Brown, it was not the operation of unjust and unequal tariff laws, nor all combined, that constituted the intolerable grievance, but it was the systematic and persistent struggle to deprive the Southern States of equality in the Union.

OCR QUESTION FORMAT

The questions and answers that follow are based on the OCR style.

(a) **Study Source A. From this Source and your own knowledge explain what Calhoun meant by the 'equilibrium between the two sections . . . has been destroyed'.** (20)

(b) **Study Sources B and C. How far does Source C bear out the fears surrounding Lincoln's election outlined in Source B by South Carolina?** (40)

(c) **Study all the Sources. Using all these Sources and your own knowledge explain how far you agree with the view that it was Northerners who were responsible for the outbreak of the war.** (60)

(a) Calhoun refers to the fact that when the Constitution was written, in 1787, the population and subsequent representation of Northern and Southern states in Congress was roughly equal, but that since then the North had outstripped the South in terms of population and had thus increased its representation over that of the South. The Missouri Compromise of 1820 had kept the balance or 'equilibrium' between the free and slave states in the Senate, but the Compromise of 1850 tipped the balance in favour of the free states. Even though historians have pointed out that newly admitted California senators tended in practice to be sympathetic to the South, as far as Calhoun was concerned, the writing was on the wall in that it could only be a matter of time before the Southern states constituted a permanent minority in the Union, given that new territories were likely to be settled by a majority of Northerners moving west.

(b) Lincoln's comments in Source C reveal him as the arch-pragmatist, and certainly not strongly opposed to slavery on any ideological grounds: this does not seem to bear out the fears, expressed by South Carolina, that he 'is hostile to slavery' or intended to abolish slavery in the long term. Lincoln clearly implies that his main priority is the preservation of the Union, and that he is prepared to 'save the Union' at almost any cost whether that means freeing slaves or not. Source C however does imply some sort of contradiction in Lincoln's stance, for if he believes the US cannot continue to exist half slave and half free, he must have believed at some point that slavery would be abolished. It is, then, perhaps not surprising that Southern states were *not* reassured by his promises. Nonetheless, at face value, Source C certainly does not back the view that Lincoln was staunchly committed to abolition.

(c) After the war, Jefferson Davis was understandably at pains to exonerate himself in his memoirs, and concentrated on states' rights and 'equality in the Union' (Source D), but he definitely blames the North for the war. In many ways his arguments echo those of Calhoun, in Source A, where he talks about the destruction of the equlibrium between the North and South. South Carolina's exposition in the aftermath of Lincoln's election seems to identify the Northern threat to slavery as the root cause of secession. This is linked to Calhoun and Davis's comments in the sense that if Calhoun and Davis were both concerned about the South being outvoted in Congress, or losing control of the Presidency, it was out of fear that the North would seek to pursue its sectional aims over those of the South. These included a higher tariff, the Homestead Act and possibly the abolition of slavery – and what was it that defined the major sectional difference between North and South if not the institution of slavery.

Lincoln's statement indicates he merely wished to 'save the Union', but it can be argued that statements he had made previously on slavery indicated that he was certainly in favour of stopping its expansion, and, as South Carolina argued, slavery was 'in the course of ultimate extinction'. In the short term, Lincoln's decision to uphold the Union and subsequently to invade the South was what caused the war, but perhaps an alternative course of action would have been unthinkable, given all that the United States had been through since 1776. It is of course fairly easy to construct an argument demonstrating that the preservation of the Union would probably have been to the disadvantage of the South. The South remains the poorest and most marginalised region of the US to this day. Whether successful secession could have benefited the South in the long term is unlikely, given that the basis of its economic wealth, cotton, would probably have suffered eventually from foreign competition, and also that as other countries increasingly disapproved of slavery they would refuse to trade with the South. Secession was a last-ditch attempt to prevent the inevitable: the expansion of the number of free states of the US, resulting in the South becoming a permanent minority and gradually losing its influence in all branches of federal government.

ADDITIONAL QUESTIONS IN THE OCR STYLE

(a) **Study Source A. From this Source and your own knowledge explain the 'slave question'.** (20)

(b) **Study Sources A and D. How far does Source A support the views expressed by Jefferson Davis in Source D regarding the main grievance of the South?** (40)

(c) **Study all the Sources. Using all these Sources and your own knowledge explain how far you agree that all the factors which contributed to the outbreak of war were in some way related to the issue of slavery.** (60)

Part 4: Historical skills

 ## 1 Conspiracy everywhere

Students should divide into Northerners and Southerners and then research the evidence for the rival conspiracy theories that played such a prominent role in the build-up to the war. This textbook contains many references to 'slave power' and 'black republican' conspiracies but further research will bring even more far-fetched theories. The exercise should allow students to empathise with those who believed in such conspiracies at the time.

 ## 2 Who was most to blame?

This exercise should focus on the roles of individuals rather than the wider factors. Students should concentrate on leading and influential figures in the build-up to the war, such as: John Calhoun, Henry Clay, Harriet Beecher Stowe, William Lloyd Garrison, Stephen Douglas, John Brown, John Tyler, James Buchanan, William Seward and Abraham Lincoln. They should, based on evidence, try to rank the men in order of their accountability for the outbreak of war.

Sources and references

Malcolm Bradbury and Howard Temperley (eds), *Introduction to American Studies*, Longman (1998).

Ken Burns, *The Civil War* (video), DD Video (1989).

Alan Brinkley, *The Unfinished Revolution*, McGraw-Hill (2000).

Hugh Brogan, *The Penguin History of the USA*, Penguin (1985/1999).

Henry Steele Commager, *The Blue and the Gray*, The Fairfax Press (1982).

Alan Farmer, *The Origins of the American Civil War 1846–1861*, Hodder & Stoughton (1996a).

Alan Farmer, *The American Civil War 1861–1865*, Hodder & Stoughton (1996b).

Alan Farmer and Vivienne Sanders, *American History 1860–1990*, Hodder & Stoughton (2002).

Paul Finkelman, 'James Buchanan', in Melvin Urofsky (ed.), *The American Presidents*, Garland Publishing (2000).

Eric Foner, *Politics and Ideology in the Age of the Civil War*, Oxford University Press (1980). Quoted in Lawrence Goodheart, Richard Brown and Stephen Rabe (eds), *Problems in American Civilisation*, D.C. Heath (1993).

Eric Foner, *Free Soil, Free Labor, Free Men*, Oxford University Press (1970). Quoted in Kenneth Stampp (ed.), *The Causes of the Civil War*, Touchstone (1991).

Susan-Mary Grant, 'For God and Country . . .', *History Today*, issue 50 (7), July (2000).

Michael Johnson (ed.), *Abraham Lincoln, Slavery, and the Civil War – Selected Writings and Speeches*, Bedford (2001).

Brian Holden Reid, *The Origins of the American Civil War*, Longman (1996).

Michael Holt, *The Political Crisis of the 1850s*, Norton (1978).

Maldwyn Jones, *The Limits of Liberty*, Oxford University Press (1983/1995).

James McPherson, *Battle Cry of Freedom*, Penguin (1990).

James McPherson, *For Cause and Comrades*, Oxford University Press (1997).

John M. Murrin, Paul E. Johnson, James M. McPherson *et al.*, *Liberty Equality Power*, Harcourt (2001).

Derrick Murphy, Kathryn Cooper and Mark Waldron, *United States 1776–1992*, Collins (2001).

Russel B. Nye, *Fettered Freedom*, Michigan State University Press (1949). Quoted in Kenneth Stampp (ed.), *The Causes of the Civil War*, Touchstone, Simon & Schuster (1991), p. 20.

Kenneth Stampp (ed.), *The Causes of the Civil War*, Touchstone, Simon & Schuster (1991).

Hugh Tulloch, *The Debate on the American Civil War Era*, Manchester University Press (1999).

Howard Zinn, *A People's History of the United States*, Longman (1996).

Chapter 4

The American Civil War, 1861–1865

This chapter will focus on the war itself through the analysis of strategy, leadership and other factors which contributed to the ultimate preservation of the Union.

 ## Historical background

The outbreak of war and the taking of sides
The advantages of each side and strategy
The eastern and western theatres, 1861–1862
Emancipation, Gettysburg and Vicksburg
The appointment of Grant, Lincoln's re-election
    and the end of the war
Why the North won

 ## Essays

Northern war aims and the advantages of both
    sides
Emancipation and the black contribution to the
    Northern war effort
The turning point in 1863 and the changes in
    warfare
Northern resources and Presidential leadership
Southern strategy and advantages, and military
    leadership

 ## Sources

1   Emancipation
2   Leadership during the war

 ## Historical skills

1   Songs of 'the Blue and the Gray'
2   Statistics on their side

Chronology

1861	Confederate States of America (CSA) formed
	Jefferson Davis became President of the Confederacy
	First shots of the war fired at Fort Sumter
	First Battle of Bull Run (Manassas)
1862	Union troops captured Forts Henry and Donaldson
	Battle of the *Merrimac* (*Virginia*) and the *Monitor*
	Battle of Shiloh
	Military draft in Confederacy
	Union captured New Orleans
	Stonewall Jackson's Shenandoah valley campaign
	Lee took command of the army of Northern Virginia
	McClellan's Peninsula campaign
	Second Battle of Bull Run
	Lee invaded Maryland
	Battle of Antietam
	Battle of Fredericksburg
1863	Emancipation Proclamation
	Conscription for the Union forces
	Battle of Chancellorsville
	Grant appointed commander-in-chief of Union forces
	Battle of Gettysburg
	Surrender of Vicksburg
	Anti-draft riots in New York City
	Attack on Fort Wagner
	Battle of Chickamauga
	Battle of Chattanooga
1864	Battle of the Wilderness
	Battle of Spotsylvania
	Fall of Atlanta
	Sherman's march to Savannah
	Lincoln re-elected as President
	Battle of Nashville
1865	Confederate evacuation of Richmond
	Lee surrendered to Grant at Appomattox
	Lincoln assassinated

Part 1: Historical background

 The outbreak of war and the taking of sides

The secession of seven states from the Lower South over the winter of 1860/1 was met with inactivity by **'lame duck'** President Buchanan as he saw out his term of office. By the time Lincoln took over in March, the 'rebel states' had sworn in Jefferson Davis as a provisional President. Southerners had already taken control of 11 forts and military installations in the Confederacy, when the news came through that Lincoln intended to send supplies to the US garrison in Fort Sumter, Charleston Harbor. On 12 April 1861 Confederate forces opened fire on the fort, claiming that, as South Carolina no longer belonged to the Union, US soldiers had no right to occupy the fort. Lincoln's determination to preserve the Union meant that he had little option other than to order a blockade of the Confederate coastline and the raising of an army of 75,000 men. His action provoked the secession in May of four more Southern states, including Virginia, a state which would prove vital to the South's war effort, and the consequent loss of Robert E. Lee, a man to whom Lincoln had offered high command in the Union army.

It was absolutely vital for Lincoln that no more of the slaveholding states seceded and it was with this in mind that Lincoln remarked: 'I hope to have God on my side but I must have Kentucky.' The position of Maryland was also crucial, for had it seceded Washington DC itself would have been left in 'enemy territory', so Lincoln acted quickly to ensure that secessionists there were suppressed. Fortunately for him the border slave states decided not to leave the Union, but it had been a close run thing, and ultimately perhaps affected the outcome of the war. Had the slave states of Maryland, Kentucky, Delaware and Missouri joined the Confederacy, its white population would have increased by 45 per cent and its manufacturing capacity by 80 per cent. Lincoln's decision not to make the war an anti-slavery war initially had paid off. In addition the Confederacy also contained areas of discontent, usually the more mountainous regions away from the plantations. The western uplands of Virginia actually seceded from the Confederacy to join the Union in June 1861 and form the state of West Virginia in 1863, and in fact Union regiments were raised from every Southern state except one.

 ## The advantages of each side and strategy

It is easy, with hindsight, to adopt the view that the result of the war was a foregone conclusion from the start, given the advantages the North possessed in terms of population and resources, but that was certainly not a widely held view at the time. The onus was on the North to defeat the South, which covered an area of 750,000 square miles. This meant not only having to win battles but also having to occupy territory. The South could therefore, as Jenkins (1997) has put it, 'win by not losing'. The South lacked obvious targets apart from Richmond, had interior lines of communication and a very long coastline, which would be difficult to blockade. The longer the South resisted the greater the chance of war weariness growing in the North. The South was defending its own territory and way of life and thus morale tended to be higher. There was also a belief, not just confined to the South, that Southerners would make better soldiers than Northerners. Given the existence of slave labour, a higher proportion of whites could be released (from agricultural production) to fight than in the North. Britain would continue to need Southern cotton, the sales of which could support the war effort, while France and Russia had no great desire to have to compete with an economically strong United States. British and French ships were expected to break the Northern blockade with ease.

Nevertheless, the North was greatly superior to the South in terms of resources (with an estimated 30:1 capacity over the South to produce munitions), but it was only in a long drawn-out war that such resources would give an advantage. The North produced 94 per cent of US pig iron, over 90 per cent of coal and firearms, 80 per cent of wheat and had twice as much railroad mileage

Figure 4.1 **General Robert E. Lee**

(which was also better integrated in terms of gauges). In terms of population, 22 million Northerners faced 9 million Southerners, nearly 4 million of whom were slaves and would not be used as soldiers. The North also kept control of the US navy and merchant navy, which allowed it to blockade the Southern coastline as part of the so-called 'anaconda strategy' of Winfield Scott, the first supreme commander of the Union forces. Scott proposed to send one army to split the Confederacy by taking control of the Mississippi, while another force would invade Tennessee in the west. A third would march on the Southern capital of Richmond in the east, and at the same time the Confederate coastline would be blockaded. This might however take time, and such a campaign of attrition could well lead to 'war weariness' in the North, which could be exploited by those seeking peace.

 ## The eastern and western theatres, 1861–1862

Lincoln demonstrated his own confidence early on in the war by ignoring the advice of Winfield Scott, and ordering an attack on Confederate forces in the east at the important railroad crossroads of Manassas in July 1861. He believed that the war could be ended if General Irvin McDowell could beat his Southern counterpart, Pierre Beauregard (the man who had commanded the Southern shelling of Fort Sumter), but in the first major battle of the war at Bull Run, Virginia (or Manassas to Southerners who preferred to name battles after the nearest inhabited place, rather than geographical feature as favoured by the North), the Confederates defeated the Union forces, following the despatch of 12,000 Confederate reinforcements by rail. McDowell's retreat back to Washington was hampered by civilians who had come to watch the battle and picnic nearby. This major blow to the Union cause prompted Lincoln to call up a further 500,000 recruits, pursue a policy of multiple offensives and intensify the naval blockade. On 10 August, at Wilson's Creek, Missouri, a Union force defeated secessionists attempting to lead their state out of the Union. General George McClellan in the meantime moved his force into western Virginia to help anti-secessionists who wished to remain in the Union.

In April 1862, Union ironclad and wooden boats under David Farragut helped to take New Orleans by coming from the south rather than the north as the Confederate high command had expected. This was the first major Union victory. New Orleans was the largest city in the South as well as the most important banking centre; and control of it prevented Confederate trade using the mouth of the Mississippi River. James A. Smith, a young seaman in the Union navy, wrote a letter to his parents in England on 9 July 1862 and optimistically reported, 'The war is very near ended' (unpublished diary).

In early 1862, General Ulysses S. Grant had begun a major campaign in the west to win control of the Tennessee and Cumberland rivers. Confederates had built a fort on each of the rivers, which held the key to Kentucky and western Tennessee, and also the Mississippi. Having taken Forts Henry and Donelson, in April he was taken by surprise at Shiloh, near the Tennessee-Mississippi boundary, by Beauregard and Albert Johnston (who was killed in the battle), and it was only after being reinforced by Don Carlos Buell that Grant was able to force a Confederate withdrawal. Nonetheless, Union forces subsequently controlled the upper and lower reaches of the Mississippi. Braxton Bragg invaded Kentucky and drew Buell's forces out of Tennessee but, following the Battle of Perryville in October 1862, Bragg retreated south to be slowly pursued by first Buell, and then his replacement William Rosecrans, who forced Bragg to retreat after the Battle of Murfreesboro (Stone's River) in December/January 1862/3.

In the eastern theatre, which certainly was given more emphasis by the South, General George McClellan who had spent the winter of 1861/2 training the army of the Potomac, made slow progress in his attempt to take Richmond. He moved west towards Richmond along a peninsula between the York and James rivers, and, by the end of May, was within five miles of the Southern capital. The Confederate government prepared to evacuate, having lost much of Tennessee and the Mississippi valley, as well as New Orleans. Joseph E. Johnston's Confederate forces attacked McClellan at Seven Pines (Fair Oaks). McClellan awaited the arrival of McDowell's army from the north and the Confederates withdrew to Richmond. A wounded

Johnston was replaced as commander by Robert E. Lee who, having recalled Thomas 'Stonewall' Jackson from his brilliant campaign occupying far superior numbers of Union troops in the Shenandoah valley, fought McClellan skilfully in a series of costly but indecisive actions in the Seven Days Battle during June and July 1862. McClellan subsequently would not advance on Richmond.

John Pope, took over command from McClellan and his army of Virginia, which had incorporated most of the army of the Potomac, and was ordered to move to Richmond, but he was defeated by Lee at the Second Battle of Bull Run (Manassas) in August 1862. Pope was replaced by McClellan who pursued Lee's invasion of Maryland in September, but, despite gaining information about Lee's positions and orders, he failed to inflict a decisive victory on the rebels with his numerically superior force at Antietam (called Sharpsburg in the South) in September 1862. Antietam did however prove critical in the sense that it prevented European recognition of the Confederacy and also prompted Lincoln to issue a preliminary Emancipation Proclamation that proposed to free all slaves in rebel states. This made it extremely unlikely that France or Britain would recognise the Confederacy in the future. Lincoln replaced McClellan for good with Ambrose Burnside in November, but he proved to be no better and was soundly defeated in December 1862 at Fredericksburg, Virginia, on the Rappahannock river.

 ## Emancipation, Gettysburg and Vicksburg

Emancipation was a calculated risk for Lincoln, and it was one which paid off. As well as giving the war a new and more noble cause, it opened up another source of recruitment and by the end of the war over 200,000 black troops had served in the Union armies. In the mid-terms of 1862, the Democrats nearly won control of the House of Representatives, but support for Lincoln returned in 1863. According to Philip Jenkins , '1863 proved to be the pivotal year of the war in which the South lost the strategic initiative'(1997: p. 142). Lincoln had made Joseph Hooker his new army commander but he was defeated at Chancellorsville in May 1863 by Lee. It may have been the Virginian's greatest victory but he did not destroy the Union army and he crucially lost 'Stonewall' Jackson, who died from wounds inflicted by his own troops when they failed to recognise him returning to the lines. Lee followed up Chancellorsville by invading the North, with his initial target being the rail junction at Harrisburg, which would allow him to cut Union supply lines from east to west, and might well contribute to greater war weariness in the North.

Figure 4.2
**Confederate soldiers
captured at Gettysburg**

When Hooker was refused his requested further reinforcements, he resigned, being replaced by George Meade. Meade fought Lee's army at Gettysburg in July 1863, where he held a defensive position and succeeded in fighting off Lee's attacks, although he did not follow Lee's retreating army. Nevertheless Gettysburg marked the last time that Confederate forces were able to threaten Northern territory seriously. On 4 July, the same day that Lee withdrew from Gettysburg, Union forces under Grant captured Vicksburg, the major Confederate stronghold on the Mississippi, which divided the eastern Confederate states from Arkansas, Louisiana and Texas. There followed a Union defeat for Rosecrans by Bragg at Chickamauga in September 1863 and he retreated to Chattanooga, to be replaced by George Thomas. Grant, Hooker and William Sherman at the Battle of Chattanooga in November, routed the forces of Bragg, who was duly replaced by Joseph E. Johnston. Northern troops had driven Confederates back into Georgia and taken control of most of eastern Tennessee as well as the Tennessee river. A fourth Confederate state was thereby cut off from the remaining seven.

 ## The appointment of Grant, Lincoln's re-election and the end of the war

In March 1864, Grant took over from Henry Halleck as commander of all Union armies. His strategy was for Sherman's army of the west, in Georgia, to destroy the remains of Johnston's Confederate army and their supplies, while he moved with George Meade's army of the Potomac against Richmond. On his way to Richmond, Grant fought the costly and indecisive Battle of the Wilderness (May 1864) and was then defeated by Lee at Spotsylvania Court House (also May 1864). Further losses were sustained at Cold Harbor in June where there were 6,000 Union casualties in a single hour. On 3 June, one young Union soldier, in his last diary entry, wrote simply: 'I was killed.' Grant failed to take the vital rail centre of Petersburg from Beauregard in the same month. During the Wilderness campaign, in the space of a month Grant lost 55,000 men – killed, wounded or captured – against Lee's 31,000. Shortly afterwards, by way of distraction, Jubal Early attacked the outskirts of Washington DC itself, but was turned round at the Battle of Fort Stevens on 12 July. In the meantime, Grant had changed his strategy and he besieged the vital railhead of Petersburg for nine months, eventually cutting off Richmond from the rest of the Confederacy. In the west, Sherman had advanced towards Atlanta but was defeated heavily by Johnston at Kennesaw Mountain in June 1864. Jefferson Davis rewarded Johnston's campaign, to the astonishment of his men, by replacing him as head of Confederate forces in the west by John Bell Hood, who eventually abandoned Atlanta, one of the key transportation centres of the Confederacy in September, boosting Lincoln's chances of re-election considerably.

Lincoln was re-elected in November 1864 as the candidate of the so-called Union Party, a loose alliance of Republicans and 'War Democrats'. George Thomas finished off Hood at Nashville in December while Sherman began a 300 mile march of destruction through Georgia. Having reached Savannah in December, he turned North wreaking further destruction through the Carolinas. By 1865 Union forces numbered perhaps one million while Confederate troops in the field totalled 200,000. Lee, having been made general-in-chief, had reinstated Johnston who took the realistic option by surrendering to Sherman in North Carolina in April 1865. In the east, Confederate forces evacuated Richmond and Petersburg in April 1865 and, having been prevented from meeting up with Johnston's men, Lee surrendered to Grant at Appomattox Court House on 9 April. On 14 April Lincoln was assassinated.

 ## Why the North won

The longer the war went on, the more it was likely that the North would win, provided of course that there was no foreign intervention on behalf of the South, that morale held up and that Lincoln got himself re-elected in 1864. There were times when war weariness in the North seriously threatened the outcome of the conflict, but ultimately victory was ensured by the North's greater numbers and resources, stronger economic and financial system and better intelligence system, as well as, eventually, the effects of Northern naval supremacy and the blockade. In addition, of course, it can be argued that Lincoln proved to be a better wartime leader than Jefferson Davis, and that the North pursued a more effective strategy than the South, with Davis following a vaguely defined 'offensive-defensive' strategy, and being unwilling to give up parts of the South that he might have been wise to.

Part 2: Essays

 Northern war aims and the advantages of both sides

1 **(a) What were the aims of the North at the beginning of the American Civil War?** (30)

(b) Assess the relative advantages held by each side in 1861. (60)

(OCR)

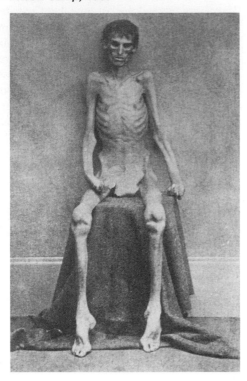

Figure 4.3 **Emaciated Union Army soldier after his release from Andersonville Prison Camp, 1865**

(a) In fairly broad terms, the North aimed to preserve the Union while the South aimed to win its independence. The extent to which the abolition of slavery was a war aim of the North at the outset is debatable. Brogan maintains it was always Lincoln's intention to abolish slavery, but he could not let this be known, at least not until he was in stronger position. One of the reasons he would not have felt sufficiently confident to do so was because there was a good chance that four slave states would not join the Confederacy, and Lincoln's main short-term aim was to ensure that the so-called 'border states' did not secede.

Lincoln said that hoped to have God on his side, but added that he must have Kentucky. Maryland too was vital, and it is likely it would have followed Virginia's decision to secede, making Washington untenable as the Northern capital, had Lincoln not made quick arrests and rapidly deployed troops. Missouri, Kentucky and Maryland would have increased the Confederacy's population by 45 per cent and its manufacturing capacity by 80 per cent. It is true that the 'border states' produced about as many soldiers for the South as the North during the war, but their real significance was geographical. The Ohio river was the key to the Mississippi, which was vital to the Northern war effort as it divided the Confederacy in two. The South did not appreciate its importance until too late. Lincoln had successfully created the impression that Richmond was his main aim, but he knew the South could survive without it. Nonetheless, Richmond was only about 100 miles from Washington and, if it could be captured, Southern morale might collapse. As well as being the political centre of the South, it was also a medical and manufacturing centre, and the primary supply depot for Confederate troops in the north-east.

Lincoln also realised that destroying the Confederate armies in the field rather than occupying large areas of the South was the key to finishing the war. Strategy initially revolved around the so-called 'anaconda plan', which aimed to starve the South into surrender with a coastal blockade and increase of military pressure on land and major rivers, but Lincoln, whether influenced by public opinion or the possibility of ending the war more quickly, ordered McDowell to advance into Virginia.

(b) The Confederacy aimed to exist independently from the Union, and did not have to totally defeat Union forces or occupy large areas of the North to achieve that. The North, however, did have to totally defeat Confederate armies and occupy large areas of the 750,000 square miles of Southern territory to win. This was not going to be easy. The mountains, rivers, wide streams, dense forest areas, swamps and marshes would be difficult to penetrate. In wet weather many roads in the South turned to mud. In Virginia, rivers flowing west to east formed natural defensive barriers for the South. The Shenandoah valley led away from Richmond but could be used by Confederates to strike into the North. In addition the South had interior lines of communication, familiar ground, a coastline extending 3,500 miles, over 20 major ports, plus 150 places where ships could unload which probably largely cancelled out the North's manpower advantage. The fact that Southerners were effectively fighting to defend their homes was almost certainly a stronger motivating factor than saving the Union was for Northerners. Southern white opinion was firmly committed to the war from the outset, but Northern opinion was more divided – although all Confederate states except South Carolina actually provided regiments to fight for the Union. There was also a feeling in both North and South that Southern boys might make better soldiers than their Yankee adversaries, but the majority of soldiers and officers in the regular army remained loyal to the Union.

If the South could hold out long enough there was a good chance that disillusion would grow in the North. Also, given that 75 per cent of Britain's raw cotton came from the South, there was a belief that the British navy would break the Union blockade, and there was also a feeling that economically the South might be better off than the North.

One of the main advantages held by the North lay in the size of its population. Immigrants to the US had tended to settle in the North and that continued to be true during the war. They were often met by recruitment officers when they got off the boat, and by the end of the war the Union army contained German brigades, Italian regiments, an Irish brigade, and at the First Battle of Bull Run there was even a Scottish regiment fighting in kilts. The North's population was 22.5 million, the South's 9 million, and that included nearly 4 million slaves who would not be fighting, although the fact that they could mainly work on the land meant that the South could actually enlist a higher proportion of its white male population than the North. The reality of it was however that the Confederacy had only 2 million men of military age against the North's 7 million, and that was not counting the hundreds of thousands of blacks in the North who might be allowed to serve.

The other key advantage the North possessed was the extent of its manufacturing capacity. It boasted 90 per cent of the country's industrial capacity and shipping, 80 per cent of its bank capital (most capital in the South was tied up in land and slaves leaving little for the purchase of bonds to finance the war), 75 per cent of its railroad mileage which was better integrated than the South's (although, once in the South, Union troops would become dependent on Southern railroads and have long lines of communication to protect), better rolling stock, and 75 per cent of its taxable wealth. In a long war, the North clearly looked the better bet. However, neither side expected it to be a long war.

 Emancipation and the black contribution to the Northern war effort

2   (a) **What contribution did blacks make to the Northern war effort after emancipation?** (30)

    (b) **Explain why Lincoln issued the Emancipation Proclamation when he did?** (60)

                                                          (OCR)

(a) Following the Emancipation Proclamation in 1863, slaves escaped from plantations in greater numbers than before, which certainly served to weaken the Confederate military effort, and over the next two years 100 regiments and 16 companies of US Colored Infantry, 11 regiments and 4 companies of US Colored Heavy Artillery, 10 batteries of the Colored Light Artillery, and 6 regiments of US Colored Cavalry were raised. By the end of the war 186,000 black soldiers and sailors (of whom 134,000 were recruited in slave states) had served in Union forces, and blacks came to make up 10 per cent of the total fighting force, although they comprised only 1 per cent of the North's population. Although 3,000 died on the battlefield, the black mortality rate was higher than the white overall due to the number of diseases caught from labouring long hours in insanitary conditions and lower levels of immunity. Generally, blacks were widely discriminated against, receiving poor quality training, weapons and medical aid, and more fatigue duties. Black soldiers also had a much harsher deal at the hands of the enemy. The Fort Pillow massacre of over 260 captured black soldiers in 1864 was not typical, but it did show that blacks could expect little sympathy at the hands of their erstwhile masters.

The first major action for black regiments was the attack on Port Hudson on the Mississippi in Louisiana in 1863 where they proved their bravery. In May and June at Milliken's Bend near Vicksburg, black regiments fought well, and in July the Massachusetts 54th led the attack on Fort Wagner in South Carolina, losing over half its men. In 1864, after Cold Harbor, Grant crossed the James river and moved against Petersburg. Union soldiers took Fort Harrison on 29 September where Medals of Honor were awarded to 14 black soldiers.

The impact of blacks on the Northern military effort can perhaps best be viewed in the light of Robert E. Lee's request that black slaves be allowed to fight for the South.

(b) According to Murrin *et al.* it was the military situation that determined the timing of the Emancipation Proclamation as well as its scope. Lincoln himself called it a military necessity, and took the view that, following the Confederate success at the Second Battle of Bull Run and subsequent invasion of Maryland, the Union could only win the war by making the abolition of slavery a war aim. He accepted Seward's advice to wait for a military victory before 'upping the stakes' of the war, rather than making it look like an act of desperation.

In March 1861, as part of an attempt to appeal to Unionist feeling in the Confederacy, and to dissuade the states of the Upper South and 'border region' from seceding, Lincoln reiterated that his main aim was to safeguard the Union rather than to safeguard or destroy slavery. Brogan and others however have implied that Lincoln was being less than honest when he said this, and that, in reality, slavery was the central issue of the war from the start but that Lincoln could not afford to admit this. In other words, he had always wanted to free the slaves but was not in a position to say so until the duration and casualty rate of the war had made emancipation and the possible enlistment of blacks acceptable to the majority of Northerners. This appears to make sense, given that great pains were taken to reassure the Northern public that it was essentially a method for winning the war. Even the issue of the initial draft of the Emancipation Proclamation could be regarded as a test of public opinion before it was formalised on 1 January 1863. Whatever Lincoln's personal motives may have been, he had a fair idea that making the abolition of slavery a major issue would isolate the South internationally, and end the possibility of formal recognition of the Confederacy by Britain.

As early as 1861 Congress had in fact passed the Confiscation Act, which declared that all slaves used for 'insurrectionary' purposes (i.e. helping the Confederate war effort) would be regarded as free. In the spring of 1862 slavery was abolished in the District of Columbia and the western territories, with compensation provided for owners. And in July 1862 the second Confiscation Act declared that the slaves of any whites who supported the Confederacy were free and also allowed Lincoln to employ blacks, including ex-slaves, as soldiers. There had also been unofficial attempts to liberate slaves such as that in 1861 by General Benjamin Butler who gave protection to runaway slaves in Virginia and refused to return them to slave owners saying they were 'contraband of war'. Butler immediately became a favourite with the Radical Republicans but Lincoln believed his actions contravened the Fugitive Slave Law, although a cabinet meeting agreed not to take action. Three months later Major General John C. Fremont, Union commander in St Louis, declared that all slaves owned by Confederates in Missouri were free. Lincoln asked him to free only those owned by men actively working for the Southern cause bringing it into line with the 1861 Confiscation Act, and sacked him when he refused to, infuriating Radicals who saw it as a way of reassuring the border states (which had been horrified by Fremont's actions). In addition, in 1862, Major General David Hunter, having begun to enlist black soldiers, announced that all slaves in Georgia, Florida and South Carolina were free. Lincoln told him to take back his declaration and to disband the 1st South Carolina Volunteers regiment (of African descent). Brigadier General Jim Lane in Kansas simply ignored the War Department and raised a black regiment, the First Kansas Colored Volunteers, in 1862 – though it was not officially recognised until 1863 by which time it had already fought.

With the growing casualty list many of the political leaders in the North also came to take the view that there should be a higher cause to the war in order to justify so many deaths. The increasing influence of the Radicals also put Lincoln under more pressure, while Horace Greeley had openly criticised Lincoln over his treatment of Hunter and for not making slavery the main issue of the war. There existed therefore a growing momentum to abolish slavery and Lincoln skilfully put himself at the head of it before it became active opposition to him. Nonetheless, had he acted earlier the loose and sometimes uneasy coalition between Republicans of different shades, Democrats and border states may well have collapsed. Once War Department solicitor William Whiting advised him that the President's war powers allowed him to emancipate the slaves under the commander-in-chief's power to confiscate enemy property, Lincoln was prepared to move.

On 22 September 1862, following the Battle of Antietam, which he chose to regard as a victory, Lincoln issued the Emancipation Proclamation: it stated that on 1 January 1863 all slaves would be declared free in the states still in rebellion – hence it did not apply to slaves in states or parts of states already under Union control and the border states. In other words it did not free a single slave at the time. The final draft of the Proclamation had removed a passage suggesting that the government was prepared to support slave rebellions in the South (due to pressure from conservatives in the cabinet) and Lincoln had also accepted a clause allowing former slaves to enlist in the Union army (under pressure from the Radicals) although in reality the War Department had sanctioned the recruitment of black troops in August 1862.

The decision to emancipate the slaves came when the war was not going well, and at the time of the first draft (conscription) in the North. Susan-Mary Grant argues that racist objections to blacks being armed could be countered by the argument that it was better for a black soldier to die than a white one. Nonetheless, the raising of black regiments resulted in a white backlash towards emancipation, and it was only once blacks started to prove themselves on the battlefield that attitudes started to change. Many Northern soldiers initially objected to Lincoln turning the conflict into 'a nigger war', and Grant argues that the Proclamation made the North's morale problem worse. Although McPherson has found evidence that more than twice as many of those soldiers expressing an opinion supported the measure as opposed it. Some Democrats warned that emancipation would lead to freed blacks coming to the North to take white jobs and, judging by the appalling level of violence directed against blacks, essentially by the Irish during the New York draft riots, many believed the warnings.

 ## The turning point in 1863 and the changes in warfare

3 (a) How far was 1863 the crucial year in determining the outcome of the war? (30)

(b) How far did warfare change during the American Civil War? (60)

(OCR)

(a) There is strong evidence, particularly in respect of the Battle of Gettysburg and the fall of Vicksburg, that 1863 was a crucial year in determining the outcome of the war, but stronger evidence still that it was not *the* crucial year, with key turning points taking place in 1861, 1862 and 1864.

It could be argued that 1861 was a key year in determining the outcome of the war in the sense that Lincoln managed to keep the loyalty of the border states. It is quite possible that had the Confederacy gained the extra manpower and industrial resources contained within those four states, as well as their crucial defensive topology, it could have won its independence.

It has been argued that in the summer 1862 the Second Battle of Bull Run followed by the invasion of Maryland and counter-offensives in the west brought the Confederacy to the peak of its power, and offered the realistic possibility of Confederate success, convincing Lincoln that slavery must become an aim of war. By the end of 1862 the Confederacy was on the back foot having lost much of Tennessee, New Orleans (its biggest city and most important port), Norfolk (the major port of Virginia), and having Charleston, Mobile and Savannah blockaded. In addition, the Battle of Antietam, despite being a drawn action, convinced Lincoln to go ahead with emancipation, effectively putting paid to Southern hopes that European aid for their cause might be forthcoming, and possibly preventing a Democrat victory in the November elections of 1862. This is why Alan Farmer has pinpointed Antietam as the key turning point of the war. It could of course be argued that Britain would not have given formal recognition to the Confederacy in any case, that Lincoln's powers as commander-in-chief would not have been limited by Democrat majorities in Congress, and that McClellan missed a great opportunity to follow through and destroy Lee's army after Antietam, thus allowing the South to fight again.

By 1863 Lee's army of northern Virginia was perhaps as effective a fighting force as any in history, but it was not invincible – and the Battle of Gettysburg was to shatter the myth that it was, giving a much needed boost to Northern morale. Gettysburg has however at times been overrated as a major turning point, although it did mark the 'high tide' of the Confederacy. Had Lee beaten Meade at Gettysburg, there could have been foreign recognition of the Confederacy and Lee's army could well have occupied key Northern cities, although it almost certainly lacked the manpower and ammunition to hold them for any length of time. Such a loss could well have led to the spread of defeatist sentiments in the North, and put Lincoln under great pressure to come to terms. Jones sees Gettysburg as decisive in that Lee was never able to take the offensive again. It should be remembered, however, that nearly another two years of fighting took place after Gettysburg, as did major draft riots, and a decline in the value of 'greenbacks' and government bonds in 1864, during which time Northern will could still have ebbed and Lincoln could still have lost the Presidential election. Meade was in no position to follow up Gettysburg and Lee remained in control of northern Virginia. From a strategic point of view Gettysburg was far less important than the Confederate loss of Vicksburg which also took place in July. The capture of Vicksburg and Port Hudson gave the Union control of the Mississippi and thus split the Confederacy in two. Maintaining control of the river would of course use up a lot of Northern troops, and some have argued that there was not a great deal of trade passing between those Confederate states west of the river and those east of it anyway. But Brogan has argued that following Gettysburg and Vicksburg the strategic initiative passed to the North, and if Northern morale held out it was only a matter of time before the North won – but that was a big 'if'.

In November, at the Battle of Chattanooga, Union forces drove Confederates back into Georgia and took control of the Tennessee river leaving four of the eleven states cut off from the rest. Murrin has argued that, over the winter of 1863/4, Southern morale suffered significantly, with desertions from the army increasing, inflation rising and greater criticism of Davis's leadership becoming apparent, and candidates opposed to Davis's aims came close to winning control of the Confederate Congress. Southern morale however did not break, leaving the possibilities that a war of attrition could still be fought and that impatience to end the war could result in Lincoln not being returned as President – and this came quite close to happening.

Following the Union triumphs of 1863 there was high expectation in the North that fairly soon Grant in Virginia and Sherman in Georgia would deliver the final blows to the South. However by the summer of 1864 severe Union casualties, particularly at Spotsylvania Court House and Cold Harbor, and lack of success in the east had increased the demand for peace negotiations in the North. There was a realistic chance Lincoln would not be re-elected. (In fact, Horace Greeley of the *New York Tribune* became involved in peace negotiations with Lincoln's approval.) However on 2 September Sherman captured Atlanta, which perhaps saved the election for Lincoln. Sherman's subsequent devastating 'March to the Sea', Sheridan's defeat of Early's army in the Shenandoah valley, and the wearing down of Lee's forces in the Wilderness made victory inevitable and the South lost the will to continue.

In many ways 1864 was the crucial year in determining the outcome of the war, for despite the Northern successes of 1863 the South was still in a position to carry on fighting. It was the campaigns of 1864 which crushed Southern military power and ultimately sealed the fate of the Confederacy. Defeat on the battlefield undermined the collective will of Southerners to fight on. Gettysburg and Vicksburg certainly contributed to the outcome of the war but did not make the defeat of the South inevitable; the campaigns of 1864 did.

(b) In order to answer this question thoroughly it is necessary to examine changes in military strategy and tactics, as well as the impact of technological innovation in weaponry.

The war has often been depicted as 'the first modern war' in the sense that it was mainly fought by mass citizen armies rather than by professional soldiers, and involved the 'mobilisation' of civilian populations in production of armaments and supplies. The use of certain types of weapons and technological innovations have also pointed to the conclusion that the war had much in common with the conflicts of the next 60 years. The apparent modernity of the war should not however be exaggerated because railroads (although on occasion proving vital as in the case of the 12,000 Confederate reinforcements moved to the First Battle of Bull Run) and telegraph wires could be put out of action and in reality communications on the battlefield continued to depend on horses to a great extent. There was also a tendency not to take advantage of new inventions like the breech-loading rifle, and so the muzzle-loading musket, albeit with a rifled barrel which improved range and accuracy, remained the basic weapon used by the infantry. Other innovations such as the Gatling gun, submarine and underwater mine were too basic to have any significant impact, but nevertheless warfare did change.

At the start of the war military thinking had largely failed to keep up with technological changes and one reason for the high casualty rate, particularly early on in the war, was that although weapons had changed tactics often had not. Strategically, generals tended to be affected by leaders from bygone eras. Joseph Johnston's 'concentration and manoeuvre' approach seems to have been influenced by Napoleon, Jomini and Frederick the Great. Lee was more adaptable, like Washington or Wellington. Cavalry leader Nathan Bedford Forrest unwittingly adopted Frederick the Great's strategy of avoiding major battles. Eighteenth-century and Napoleonic warfare had emphasised massed ranks and dense columns of infantry in tight formations, moving and firing shoulder-to-shoulder in volleys, and tended to put the onus on offence, with a bayonet attack expected to follow volleys of fire. Napoleon had used his artillery in conjunction with infantry attacks and similar tactics had been used successfully by US forces in the Mexican War at a time when the main infantry weapon was the single-shot muzzle-loading smooth-bore musket, with an effective range of about 80 yards and a maximum range of about 250 yards. Cannon fire could support infantry as artillerymen were fairly safe from enemy fire at 200 yards away, and bayonet charges worked because soldiers could cover 80 yards in the 20 or so seconds it took to reload. West Point Military Academy stressed the tactical offensive, and thus, certainly at the start of the war, most officers believed the tactical offensive of close-order infantry supported by artillery fire won battles. Few remembered the Duke of Wellington's acerbic comments regarding Napoleon's tactics at Waterloo, 'Damn me, the fellow's just a mere pounder after all', or his attention to defence, attributing Napoleon's defeat at Waterloo to his poor health. However, with the horrendous casualties sustained early on in the war, commanders gradually came to realise the advantages an entrenched defensive position offered. George McClellan had studied and witnessed the Crimean War and, despite having an army of 150,000 at his disposal, was acutely aware of the risks of frontal assaults. There were rare examples of head-on assaults paying off, such as the Union victories at Missionary Ridge and Cedar Creek, and Confederate victories at Chancellorsville and

Chickamauga, but infantry formations gradually became more like skirmish lines, taking advantage of cover to reload before rushing forward again, working in groups of two or three to load and shoot alternately. This sort of attack was much more difficult to control and there were some officers who persisted with close-order attacks. Loose-order tactics, despite being less costly, did not really move the advantage back to the 'tactical offensive' against trenches and breastworks, and it became generally accepted that an attacking force needed a 3:1 advantage to take an entrenched position. At Cold Harbor, in June 1864, Confederates constructed fortified trenches over a six-mile front with artillery support. On one day Grant lost nearly 6,000 killed and wounded, and most of these were lost within one hour. This changed the war in the east from one of manoeuvre to siege warfare.

Of casualties sustained in combat situations, about 80–90 per cent were inflicted by muskets and rifles (a muzzle-loading rifle could be fired two to three times a minute). Rifling the barrel of a musket increased its effective range four times to about 400–600 yards (it could kill at 1,000 yards). Few soldiers carried rifles before the 1850s, although some of the best-known soldiers of the Napoleonic Wars, the 95th Rifles, had carried them, effectively being used as skirmishers and snipers. The problems came from trying to ram a conical bullet, large enough to 'take' the rifling, down the muzzle, and after a few shots the build-up of powder residue had to be cleaned out of the grooves before it could be used again. In 1848 however a French officer, Claude Minie, produced a bullet both small enough to be simply dropped down a rifled barrel and the base of which expanded when fired thus filling the barrel, but it was expensive. James Burton produced a cheaper and better bullet.

Ironically, it had been Jefferson Davis who, while Secretary of War in 1855, made the decision to arm US soldiers with the .58 calibre Springfield rifled musket. This became the main infantry weapon of the war, along with the similar British .577 calibre Enfield rifle, which took the same bullet and was used more by the South (which had major difficulties producing its own). They were both muzzle-loading weapons and single-shot but the better types of bullet meant that a well-trained soldier could fire it three times a minute. Breech-loading rifles did exist in 1861 but were largely unreliable and even dangerous to the user. Progress in this area did make the single-shot Sharps carbine and rifle favoured weapons with Union cavalry and sharpshooter units and the development of metal cartridges (as opposed to paper-wrapped ones) allowed the Union to arm its cavalry and some infantry with repeaters by 1863, of which the seven-shot Spencer carbine was most successful. However, repeaters had a smaller powder charge and therefore shorter range than paper-cartridged Springfield and Enfield weapons and were also more prone to misfiring, so muzzle-loaders remained the main weapon used by infantry during the war.

In 1862 most Union regiments received new Springfields or Enfields while many Confederates were still using smooth-bores. This was one reason for the 2:1 ratio of Confederate to Union casualties in the Seven Days Battle. By 1863 virtually all infantrymen on both sides used rifles, making the bayonet redundant. This had a major effect on casualty figures and strengthened the tactical defensive, but even after the widespread adoption of rifled muskets generals continued to send close-order attacks with poor artillery support. Given that the artillery guns now had to fire over longer ranges as well as the unreliability of shells, artillery bombardments became less useful. Artillery guns were gradually rifled but as the terrain over which many battles were fought was rugged forest their effectiveness was still limited. Nonetheless, artillery could still be used effectively in defensive situations with grapeshot and canister against infantry. Rifled weapons also allowed sharpshooters to pick out enemy officers almost at will, with the result that they soon stopped riding horses and took to wearing uniforms like the privates. This partly explains why generals in the war stood a 50 per cent greater chance of being killed than ordinary soldiers. For example, in May 1864 General Sedgewick in order to reassure his men than they could not be hit by Confederate sharpshooters would not take cover. His final words before being shot dead were: 'They couldn't hit an elephant at this distance.'

The Civil War produced some legendary leaders of cavalry such as George Armstrong Custer for the Union, and Nathan Bedford Forrest and J.E.B. Stuart for the Confederacy, even though it witnessed the eclipse of the old-style cavalry charge and the sabre, as rifled weapons and explosive shells came to dominate the battlefield. Horsemen were, however, used successfully for scouting and reconnaissance, screening the movements of infantry, attacking the rear of an enemy, pursuing a retreat, and striking at weak points, although the Union was slow to appreciate how useful cavalry could be. Initially all Union cavalry were under the command of Brigadier-General Cooke who was a poor leader. In addition McClellan resented and distrusted the volunteer cavalry and would assign individual companies to infantry brigades where they served primarily as messengers and orderlies rather than for scouting and screening where they could have been much more effective. The poor use of cavalry probably cost McClellan the chance to destroy Lee at Antietam, for they could have been used to delay Hill's division from Harper's Ferry, giving Burnside more time to carry out his attack. On the bloodiest day of the war, McClellan's cavalry suffered only 12 casualties. Some have argued McClellan slowed down the development of cavalry by a year-and-a-half and allowed Stuart's cavalry to gain superiority in terms of morale and effectiveness. In desperation at Stuart's bold strikes Lincoln and his senior generals sought talented cavalry leaders regardless of previous rank or age, while foreign mercenaries also came to hold high rank, at least until March 1863 when the Battle of Kelly's Ford was fought. It took Hooker to appreciate the value of cavalry and to use them effectively. Having been let down, as he felt, by his cavalry commander Stoneman at Chancellorsville, he was replaced in May by Brigadier-General Alfred Pleasonton who was ordered to attack a Confederate cavalry force reported to be in the Culpepper area near the Rappahannock river. This led to the Battle of Brandy Station, the biggest cavalry battle of the war. At Brandy Station in June 1863 the myth of Stuart's cavalry was shattered and they came close to defeat, even though the Confederates finally won the encounter. Brigadier-General John Buford had skilfully used his cavalry as mobile infantry using their breech-loading carbines rather than employing the shock tactics of charge and sabre. The Battle of Brandy Station was effectively where the sabre became obsolete. Never again could Confederates simply write-off the Union cavalry. (It has been suggested that Stuart wanted to raid behind enemy lines to restore his reputation prior to Gettysburg, but it meant Lee lost contact with him and hence lost his scouting skills, leaving Lee unaware of Meade's closeness.)

One of the most enduring incidents of the war was the battle between the ironclad ships, the USS *Monitor* and CSS *Virginia* (*Merrimac*), on 9 March 1862, following which naval warfare was changed forever. By the end of the war, the Union had built or started 58 ships of the same class as the *Monitor*. Other innovations included marine torpedoes (mines) and even submarine warfare. The sinking of the *Housatonic*, a Union battleship, was carried out by the *Hunley*, a Confederate submarine, in February 1864, but the *Hunley* itself went down soon afterwards. Confederate torpedoes sank or badly damaged over 40 Northern ships. Brigadier-General Raines' land mines certainly slowed the Union advance up the peninsula but caused outrage on both sides. The gathering of more accurate military intelligence had been facilitated by Jack LaMountain's balloons which first appeared over Hampton Roads in the summer of 1861. In turn aerial reconnaissance by balloon led to camouflage and 'anti-aircraft' fire with Colonel Alexander of the CSA elevating his artillery. The widespread appearance of journalists and photographers on the battlefield was something new, as was the use of elaborate intelligence units.

PRACTICE QUESTIONS

4 (a) **Assess the significance of the fall of Vicksburg for the Confederate cause.** (30)

(b) **How important was the battle of Gettysburg to the outcome of the war?** (60)

(OCR)

Advice: *Both parts expect you to be able to assess the importance of two key events during the war. For Part (a) you will need to assess the importance of Vicksburg from both strategic and psychological perspectives, as well as measuring it against other issues; and for Part (b) it may be worth considering the argument that the significance of Gettysburg has been overstated, while again measuring it against other issues.*

5 **(a)** **How far did cavalry tactics change during the Civil War?** (30)

(b) **'Modern weapons, outdated tactics.' How valid is this verdict on the nature of warfare during the American Civil War?** (60)

(OCR)

Essay plan

Part (a)

Introduction: Indicate general line of argument to be followed, i.e. cavalry tactics appear to have changed significantly, with brief ideas as to why.

Para 1: Outline general cavalry tactics employed before the Civil War.

Para 2: Examine the factors that led to changes in tactics, e.g. rifles which could be fired more frequently, and strong defences.

Para 3: Outline how the use of cavalry changed, e.g. charges replaced by scouting, and cavalry fighting on foot. Also, contrast early success of Southern cavalry against McClellan's reluctance to employ his.

Conclusion: The extent to which cavalry tactics changed.

Part (b)

Introduction: Comment on quote with some degree of agreement/disagreement expressed.

Para 1: Examine influences on tactics going into the war, particularly Napoleonic.

Para 2: Consider tactics employed in the early stages of the war, and link to para 3.

Para 3: Assess the greater accuracy and efficiency of weapons used in the war and the implications they had for tactical changes. Remember to consider the limitations of such innovations as submarine warfare.

Para 4: Analyse how tactics changed or did not change during the war, e.g. increasing use of entrenched positions to counter increased firepower, and the resulting tendency to change attacking formations.

Conclusion: Try to avoid great generalisations on the modernity of weapons and the unwillingness to modify tactics before making a final decision on the quote.

 Northern resources and Presidential leadership

6 **(a)** **To what extent did the North win the war because of its superior resources and larger population?** (30)

(b) **To what extent was Abraham Lincoln a better wartime leader than Jefferson Davis?** (60)

(OCR)

(a) It is certainly true to say that the North had superior resources during the war and was able to out-produce the South substantially in terms of weapons, ammunition and supplies. It has been argued that the longer the war went on the better the chance the North had of winning because of its 'big battalions'. But Northern opinion was divided, volatile and impatient, and the longer the war went on the greater the chance of disillusion and war weariness setting in, which could seriously undermine the will of the North to fight on. Military historians will also point out that strategy, tactics and bad decisions in the heat of the moment on the battlefield were always likely to have as much impact on the outcome of the war as anything else.

Any neutral considering the war today, were it not for the issue of slavery, would probably side with the Confederacy, which was clearly the underdog. Eighty per cent of the nation's factories were in the North, along with the country's main supply of meat and grain, banking resources, and shipping and shipbuilding. Compared with the South, 15 times as much iron was produced in the North, 38 times as much coal and 27 times as much in woollen goods. On top of all that the North had a population of 22 million against about 9.5 million in the South, nearly 4 million of whom were slaves and so unlikely to fight. The North could therefore effectively be self-sufficient in war materials while the South had to rely heavily on Europe. It has however been argued that, because the South had so many slaves working, a higher proportion of men of military age were freed up to fight than in the North but at the end of the day the North could afford to lose more men than the South, and Grant knew it. It is worth noting that Lee actually lost more of his men per battle than any other general in the war, which must raise serious questions about Southern strategy and tactics. It is also significant that Chickamauga Creek was the only major battle at which Union troops were outnumbered by Confederate forces. It has been suggested that the South did have sufficient guns by the end of the war, but not enough men to use them. This is borne out by the decision to allow black slaves to fight in the Confederate army, although the plan never came into effect, and highlights the difference in population numbers between the sides. Brogan has argued: 'only Robert E. Lee's idea, of unrelenting brilliant battle, with the object of breaking the Northern will to go on fighting, offered any hope . . .' This again emphasises that the South was always up against numbers. By the end of the war one in three Southerners of military age had died as a result of the war. It was a wonder the South held out as long as it did, given that by the end of 1862 much of Tennessee had been lost, New Orleans, the major port, had gone, as had Norfolk, Virginia's major port, while the key ports of Charleston, Mobile and Savannah had been blockaded, the border states had remained loyal and no foreign countries had given support.

Several historians have concentrated on internal factors that they believe ultimately lost the South the war, rather than focusing on the North's resources. David Donald in 1995 argued that the South 'died of democracy', suggesting that Davis never managed to sufficiently centralise the war effort, or to override the selfish motives of certain Confederate states. Tulloch has suggested that the Confederacy might have collapsed from within, that Southern taxes and inflation were borne more heavily by the poor and that, as the war progressed, morale declined and soldiers became less inclined to fight a war for the rich. Gallagher has not detected a demoralised Southern army nor resentment among the poor for fighting a rich man's war, and McPherson is also convinced that it was military failure rather than low civilian morale which proved decisive. Brogan has suggested that the existence of 22,000 miles of railway allowed the North to move men and supplies very effectively and neutralised the South's interior lines of communications (there were only 9,000 miles of line in the South, which became a strategic weakness). It has been suggested that the South could have achieved independence had it not been for its inability to replace damaged track and rolling stock. As the war progressed it became very difficult to get food to soldiers and civilians while the Northern economy simply grew stronger.

Northern naval strength was also a crucial factor. In the South there was not a shipyard capable of building a modern warship at the start of the war. Confederate Naval Secretary Stephen R. Mallory realised that the outdated Union navy was vulnerable to far-ranging commerce raiders and ironclad rams, which might be purchased in Europe, thereby allowing cotton exports to continue. The Confederate Navy Department showed great ingenuity, for example using Southern engineers to build 'torpedoes' (mines). The CSS *Virginia* (or *Merrimac*), in its first outing at Hampton Roads, sank a Union boat with its ram and 11 guns while shells and shot bounced off its armour plating, although the Union's ironclad USS *Monitor* quickly appeared to neutralise its threat. However, the North could produce ram ships more quickly than and in larger numbers than South might get them in Europe. It was also difficult for Richmond to raise the money to buy ships from abroad (two commerce raiders which sank a number of US boats were built for the Confederacy in Liverpool in 1862). Davis did not seem to understand the importance of sea power and made a big mistake in not supporting his naval aides more than he did. Nor did Davis understand international politics, hoping that Britain would intervene in the war at a time when Britain was more concerned about France. At the time there was a surplus of cotton in Britain so the Southern strategy of keeping cotton did not work, when it could have been sold abroad and used to buy materials. The fact that external aid failed to materialise was crucial.

From an economic point of view, the South struggled. The Confederate Congress was slow to raise taxes and much capital was tied up in land and slaves, which meant there was little available to purchase war bonds. The Congress began a process of issuing Treasury notes that could be redeemed in gold or silver after the war, but the notes declined in value with each successive issue, and by early 1863 it cost $8 to buy what $1 would have bought at the beginning of the war. By the last year of the war the value of the Confederate dollar was only worth 2 per cent of its 1860 value or 1 US cent. Proportionately the Confederacy raised 60 per cent of its revenue by printing paper money, under 40 per cent through loans, and less than 10 per cent through taxes. The South increased its money supply by 60 per cent compared to the North's 13 per cent. Stanley Lebergott blames this disastrous financial policy on the planters who often seemed to be more concerned with maintaining profit margins and refused to switch production to food when urged to by the Confederate Congress. The North raised 66 per cent of is revenue through war bonds, about 20 per cent through taxes, 13 per cent by printing Treasury notes ('greenbacks'), which were legal tender rather than to be redeemed, and avoided the crippling inflation of the South. It has been argued, particularly by Douglas Ball, that the failure of the South could largely be attributed to its financial policies, but higher taxes could also have been counter-productive, as with the 10 per cent tax on agricultural produce, which resulted in many farmers hiding crops and animals, or refusing to plant. The Confederate government did direct production and distribution, playing a greater role than Lincoln in economic affairs (although greater intervention with the railroads, which were owned by more than 100 companies and operated different gauges, would have been useful). Controlled blockade-running however was remarkably successful, with runners having about a 75 per cent chance of getting through until the last month of the war. Blockade-running was responsible for bringing in 60 per cent of small arms, 30 per cent of lead, 75 per cent of saltpetre and most of the paper for cartridges.

By the winter of 1863 the South was suffering serious economic problems, the escape of slaves and occupation of some its prime agricultural areas. Much land had been converted to food production but the railroads were in a poor state and food was scarce. This problem was exacerbated by the April 1862 draft, which took many farmers aged 18–35 from the land, as they were unable to pay the cost of hiring a substitute. To have won the war, the South would have had to follow up early victories at Bull Run and Wilson's Creek with a decisive strike, but strategy was more defensively-minded at the time. Ultimately the loss of men, land and privations suffered by civilians could not be sustained and surrender negotiations were opened by Lee and Johnston before guerrilla action gained momentum. Ultimately military events were crucial and Grant in the east understood all too well that the North could afford to lose more men than the South.

(b) Maldwyn Jones has argued that 'Lincoln more than anyone . . . saved the Union', but, as President, he was initially hesitant and overestimated the strength of Southern Unionism, which he had expected to reassert itself following secession. In the first half of the war he failed to give his generals his full confidence and tended to intervene unhelpfully. Fortunately his political sense was far sharper and he knew when to act decisively in that sphere. Lincoln also had certain advantages over Davis in that he took control of a government system that had been functioning since the Constitution, whereas Davis had to start from nothing, although he did have the experience of cabinet office and greater military experience behind him.

Despite Lincoln's limited military service in the state militia, he proved to be the North's most important military commander according to Brinkley and eventually found a chief of staff in Grant who shared his belief that continual fighting and making enemy armies the target would pay off. He shaped a national strategy of unconditional surrender and although some of his choices of commanders were criticised on purely military grounds, they often made sense in terms of pacifying different parts of the North and factions in Congress. He certainly appeared to change his generals too frequently, but once he was convinced of Grant's abilities he stayed with him (Grant was his ninth general in charge). However, recent evidence suggests Lincoln offered the command of the Northern forces to Giuseppe Garibaldi, unifier of Italy, in 1862, demonstrating his lack of faith in American generals.

Davis had been to West Point, gained military experience in the Mexican War and been Secretary of War in the US government, all of which Brogan believes gave him a vastly inflated opinion of his own military abilities. For much of the war he planned strategy alone, not appreciating the need for a supreme military commander. His appointment of Lee was clearly a good one and he certainly gave freedom to the generals he trusted, but he has been accused of interfering too much with military affairs. His feuds with top generals Beauregard and Johnston undoubtedly damaged the war effort, as did his stubborn decisions to stick with the incompetent Braxton Bragg and Lucius Northrop. It has been suggested that the South mobilised with amazing speed at the start of the war, which has to be to Davis's credit. But another mark against Davis is the argument that the eastern theatre got the bulk of soldiers and munitions and that he failed to see the war would be won and lost in the west. Beauregard argued that Davis was too defensive, Johnston argued that he was too offensively-minded, while Davis blamed Johnston for the loss of Vicksburg – although others have since suggested that the ambiguous command structure in the west was really to blame, with Confederate armies organised into departments under different generals making coordination and cooperation difficult at times. On balance therefore it would seem that as a strategist and and as a day-to-day leader of military operations Lincoln was more effective.

In terms of their ability to lead and to communicate, Lincoln again seems to have had the edge on Davis. Lincoln could be ruthless: holding men without trial (over 13,000 arrests were made in the North during the war), taking action without Congressional approval such as sending troops into battle, increasing the size of the army, setting up a naval blockade, and even considering arresting Chief Justice Taney when he ruled the President had exceeded his power. As he gave the Gettysburg Address, his soldiers apparently guarded the polls at a state election in Delaware to ensure a Republican victory. It should also be remembered that the Emancipation Proclamation was of dubious legality, although it proved to be an inspired move. Davis's Vice-President, Stephens, thought Davis 'weak, timid, petulant, peevish, obstinate' and blamed him for virtually all that went wrong. Davis certainly failed to establish a good working relationship with many, and experienced a relatively high cabinet turnover, getting through four secretaries of state and six secretaries of war, although much of the turnover was due to criticism from Congress. To his credit, Davis did defend many of his colleagues and left cabinet members to get on with their jobs generally. Confederate government functioned fairly smoothly, although Davis found it hard to prioritise and delegate, was often indecisive and got bogged down in debate. His critics at the time called him despotic, but historians tend to argue that he should have used *more* power, as Lincoln did (David Donald arguing that the South 'died of democracy'), for example to nationalise the railroads, and that he was too lenient with press criticisms and opponents. He suspended habeas corpus only under Congressional authority, but he was behind the 1862 Conscription Act, and used martial law in areas under threat from invasion. He also urged high taxes on land, cotton and slaves, and towards the end of the war was prepared to support the recruitment of slaves into the Confederate army despite opposition.

Lincoln appears to have been better at communicating with people, and keeping factions together. The work of Chase in finance and Seward in foreign policy demonstrates that Lincoln picked better subordinates and knew how to delegate. He managed his cabinet well and listened to a range of viewpoints to ensure widespread support within the party. His political timing was superb. Davis showed a lack of humour and inflexibility, was proud and sensitive to criticism, although he was known for his honesty and loyalty, tending to stand by unpopular individuals and decisions. He also seems to have been a good public speaker.

Both leaders had problems with internal opponents. Lincoln had the Joint Committee on the Conduct of the War to hide behind where necessary, although he was usually happy to take the tough decisions. He was generally supported by Northern opinion, for example over the removal of McClellan and Buell. There was, however, dissension in the North over the aims of the war, from within the Republican ranks as well as from the Democrat 'Copperheads', who appeared to want peace as a priority. From Davis's point of view it is now contended that the very absence of political parties in the Confederate Congress was a problem for him because it meant that congressmen and governors could be much more independent, and not subject to party discipline, which could have created greater unity – as it did with the Republicans and Lincoln. In the North, the fact that opposition came from the Democrats meant that the Republicans became more unified, outwardly at least, and worked to discredit the Democrats. McPherson says that the South had no such institutionalised political structure to galvanise support for the war effort and discredit dissenters, but he concludes that internal divisions neutralised this factor. In the 1863 Congressional elections Southerners who had opposed secession in 1861 won votes, and of the 137 members, 40 per cent were new, many of them opposed to Davis. Of 26 senators in the new House, 12 were opponents, for a range of reasons: for example, states' rights, strategy, peace and returning to the Union. Davis became increasingly dependent on the support of congressmen from areas under Union control, many of which had not been able to hold elections in 1863. On balance it looks as if state obstructionism weakened the Southern military effort, and Frank Owsley has claimed that the Confederacy 'died of state rights'. Davis was certainly hampered by the individualism of the planter class, and particular problems with Vice-President Stephens as well as the governors of Georgia and North Carolina, who did not want to send troops to fight away from their states. However, most states were extremely loyal. Lincoln too had his problems. The New York City draft riots in July 1863 resulted in 1,000 people being killed or wounded, and serious opposition from the Democrats in 1864 meant that his popular majority of 400,000 in a poll of over 4 million was far from convincing. In addition, over 120,000 Northerners avoided the draft and 200,000 deserted.

David Potter, in 1960, pointed to Davis as the key reason the Confederacy lost, and others have suggested that had Lincoln led the South and Davis the North the result of the war could have been different, although that seems overstated. Robert E. Lee said no one could have led the South better than Davis, and historian Alan Farmer says it was the leadership of Davis that ensured the South held out as long as it did. Davis was probably the best man for the job in the South, but ultimately he was up against a consummate political leader who would rank among the greatest ever. On balance, Lincoln was a more effective wartime leader than Davis.

PRACTICE QUESTION

7 (a) **Why was it so important to Lincoln that the border states did not secede?** (30)

   (b) **'The South never stood a chance.' To what extent was the outcome of the war a foregone conclusion?** (60)

                                                                                            (OCR)

Advice: *Part (a) requires a good understanding of the geographical significance of the states, in terms of Washington and defence, as well as the importance of the states' populations and resources. A Part (b) answer should look at the chances the South had for victory, for example, striking quickly and winning a succession of early victories, or holding out over a long period of time in the hope that, in the North, war weariness would set in. The advantages held by the South should also be considered, particularly the idea that to win the war the North had to effectively conquer the South, whereas the South had only to not lose.*

Southern strategy and advantages, and military leadership

8 (a) **To what extent was the South's strategy flawed?** (30)

  (b) **'Robert E. Lee was the most able Confederate military leader of the Civil War.'**
  Discuss. (60)

(OCR)

(a) Davis may have been inclined to fight a guerrilla-type war but felt duty-bound to defend the whole of the Confederacy rather than sacrificing certain bits of it, which could certainly have weakened morale and resources. The South in general also tended to feel it could take on the Yankees and beat them in battle.

Davis's strategy has become known as 'offensive-defensive', although it was never clearly defined, and seemed to emerge over a period of time based on events. It was supposed to depend essentially on defence, but counter-attacks would be carried out where appropriate. In reality, Davis built up resources and supplies and took the initiative when the situation offered, and except for a few significant offensive actions his strategy effectively became one of passive and dispersed defence, ultimately weakening the Confederacy. The lack of a coordinated defensive strategy was a fatal weakness. Beauregard argued that Davis was too defensive, but given that the North had to militarily defeat the Confederate armies, conquer the geographical obstacles and occupy vast areas of the South to win the war, some have suggested that a defensive strategy of French General Antoine Jomini – 'the space and time defence' – would have worked. In other words, the South could actually have drawn Northern forces further South thus stretching Northern lines of communication which would then have been vulnerable to attack. In turn the Union would have been forced to deploy more troops to guard the supply lines, thereby reducing the strength of the main attacking army. In turn, the South would not have needed such large armies as the army of northern Virginia or the army of Tennessee to take on the reduced Northern forces. For example Sherman's dependence on the Western and Atlantic Railroad, which he initially guarded with 20,000 men, could have been exploited during his Atlanta campaign.

Johnston was certainly skilful enough to avoid being drawn into a major battle. At one point he asked Davis to place all available cavalry under Forrest's command so they could attack Sherman's communications. Lee later supported the plan but Davis refused to implement it, which may have helped save Atlanta or at least delayed its fall, with a resulting impact on Lincoln's re-election and the war. It is also contended that civilian morale in the South could have withstood allowing Northerners deeper into the South, although Davis was not prepared to take the risk. He seemed to regard Vicksburg of great symbolic importance for morale, and referred to it as 'the nail head that held the South's two halves together', but in reality there was relatively little trade between the western and eastern parts of the South, and the Union, once Vicksburg was taken, had to use huge numbers to keep control of the Mississippi. As it was, Grant's supply line was very nearly destroyed by Forrest and van Dorn in his advance on Vicksburg. Despite Davis valuing Vicksburg, he has been criticised for not seeing that the war would be won and lost in the west rather than the east, and for persisting in sending more troops and supplies the way of Lee. The fall of Kentucky gave the Union the Ohio river, which was of great strategic significance.

Johnston criticised Davis for being dangerously offensive and ultimately self-defeating. Grade McWhiney and Perry Jamieson have supported this view by arguing the Confederacy 'bled itself to death' in the first three years of the war, pointing out that in 8 of the first 12 big battles of the war the Confederate forces attacked, and lost 97,000 men, compared to 77,000 Northerners. They attribute this in part to the Celtic origins of many Southerners and the cultural tradition of the frontal charge. It is perhaps in the east where this criticism is best exemplified. Lee was convinced that only defeats inflicted against Northerners on their own land would increase the pressure on Lincoln sufficiently to let the South go, and he may have been right. Others have argued that Lee tended to think and fight as a Virginian first and foremost and did not fully appreciate the need to develop an overall strategy.

It could be argued that the South pursued the wrong strategy, placing too much faith on being able to defend the Mississippi river with large fortifications, and being too ambitious in attempting to invade the North, resulting in Antietam and Gettysburg, both of which came to be regarded not just as military victories but political victories for Lincoln. In addition, there seems to have been a confused command structure in the west, no detailed strategy for controlling Kentucky, as well as the failure to achieve a successful alliance with foreign nations, which meant that gradually Northern blockades reduced the South's seaborne trade to less than a third of its normal level.

(b) It has been argued that when Lee died in 1870 he was considered second to Jackson in terms of ability, but then former members of his staff set about raising his profile by criticising General Longstreet, particularly blaming him for not attacking at the hour Lee had specified at Gettysburg. Lee has since achieved an almost iconic status with Southerners and Northerners alike, but does his great and untarnished reputation stand up to scrutiny?

There are certainly a number of Confederate leaders who can give Lee a run for his money. Joseph Johnston, for example, was admired by his opponents more than by his own President. Grant said Johnston gave him 'more anxiety than any of the others' and Sherman described him as 'the most enterprising' of all the Southern generals. It has been suggested Johnston based his 'concentration and manoeuvre' strategy very much on the ideas of Napoleon, Jomini and Frederick the Great. Johnston believed that the Confederacy could not be defended everywhere against Union encroachments and that it was better to give ground where necessary and to concentrate forces to fight against the main Union armies. He would have given up Vicksburg for the sake of the Confederacy and used Pemberton's troops to fight with others. However, Davis was unwilling to do that. Johnston's critics have maintained that he was defensively-minded, but evidence suggests that he often did not have the numbers or the right position for a bolder strategy. While he was in Virginia he had actually asked Davis for more men so he could take the initiative and invade the North, but Davis's response to this request in October 1861 was to approve a number of partial operations against the North rather than an invasion. In April 1862, Johnston again raised the issue of a major offensive against the North, arguing that he could not compete with McClellan in terms of engineering and artillery.

Thomas J. Jackson earned his nickname 'Stonewall' following the refusal of his Virginia brigade to budge at the First Battle of Bull Run. His Shenandoah campaign showed great flare, as he managed to win four battles against three separate Union armies, which outnumbered him by two to one. His accidental death was a loss that could never be replaced, and Lee always thought that, had he had Jackson at Gettysburg, the outcome could have been different. Jackson, despite some rather odd personal habits, certainly possessed military genius, but his war was probably too short to fairly judge him against Lee.

Shelby Foote has championed the cause of Nathan Bedford Forrest, who he has described as 'a natural genius'. Sherman called him the most remarkable man the war produced, given that he rose from private to lieutenant-general, had 30 horses shot from under him and apparently killed 31 men in hand-to-hand combat. Forrest, as a commander of cavalry, however, cannot be compared to Lee fairly.

In the early part of the war, Lee earned the nicknames 'King of Spades' and 'Granny Lee' for his digging of entrenchments around Richmond. He also suffered setbacks in the east. Stuart Reid has praised Lee's defensive qualities, but doubted his attacking capabilities – calling Pickett's charge at Gettysburg 'a serious error' – and his ability to control his subordinates such as J.E.B. Stuart at Gettysburg.

Fuller and Liddell Hart have argued that Lee threw victory away by being too offensive and suffering excessive casualties, which could not be sustained, and for failing to adapt to new conditions. McWhiney and Jamieson have contended that the Confederacy bled itself to death in the first three years of the war by being too offensive. McPherson has also argued that, although Lee's daring won battles, it lost the war, as a more cautious approach could have been more successful. Foote suggests that, following a series of brilliant victories, Lee came to believe in his own invincibility and that of his army; and at Gettysburg that was his doom. He judges Pickett's charge a terrible mistake, with Lee overestimating his men, and declining the advice of Longstreet who warned against an attack. Lee has also been accused of limiting his vision to the eastern theatre where he concentrated resources at the expense of the west, which is ultimately where the war was lost. It should be remembered too that Lee had the highest losses of all army commanders with a 20 per cent casualty rate. However, he was working within a defective command structure, received poor intelligence and often had subordinates letting him down, particularly Jackson failing to carry out instructions. He also had his own problems: his son was held for ransom, and he had to contend with heart trouble.

McPherson feels that Lee deserves to be regarded as the best tactician of the war. He created the army of northern Virginia, the finest fighting force of the war. Gary Gallagher suggests Davis and Lee's offensive/defensive approach was the best option. Brogan has praised Lee's idea of 'unrelenting brilliant battle' as the only real hope the South had. Farmer feels Lee should be held in high regard and that without his leadership the South would have lost sooner. He boosted Southern morale and managed to damage Northern morale. It can also be argued that it was unlikely concentrating more resources in the west would have made much difference to the war's outcome. Lee won some brilliant victories against great odds, and for these alone he deserves to be regarded as the Confederacy's most able military leader.

9   (a) **Assess the extent of the geographical advantages the South had against Northern invasion.** (30)

      (b) **How far was the North better led militarily and politically than the South?** (60)

                                                                                 (OCR)

Essay plan

Part (a)

Introduction: Comment on the sheer size of the South, which would be difficult to occupy, but make the point that in the end Lincoln and Grant realised that destroying Confederate armies in the field was the key to victory.

Para 1: Analyse the significance of the extensive Southern coastline.

Para 2: Look at Southern rivers flowing west to east.

Para 3: Consider mountains, the Shenandoah valley leading away from Richmond, dense forests and swampy land.

Para 4: Consider the limitations of the geographical advantages and how the North might exploit geographical features, e.g. the significance of Ohio and Mississippi rivers.

Conclusion: How far geography worked in favour of the South.

Part (b)

Introduction: Discuss the extent to which political and military leadership were intertwined, given that the rival Presidents both took a leading role in military decision-making.

Para 1: Assess advantages Lincoln held over Davis from the outset.

Para 2: Examine the success that Lincoln and Davis had in military affairs.

> *Para 3: Consider the abilities of both men to inspire support and communicate, and how they dealt with opponents.*
>
> *Para 4: Look at generals in the field of both sides and consider the reputations of Lee, Johnston, Jackson and Stuart, for example, against those of Grant, Sherman, McClellan and Meade.*
>
> *Conclusion: This could be split in the sense that a verdict could be reached of superior Southern military leadership against better Northern political leadership, but it could be a verdict totally in favour of the North.*

Part 3: Sources

1 Emancipation

■ Source A: Lincoln speaking to Christian ministers from Chicago in September 1862

I admit that slavery is the root of the rebellion . . . I would also concede that emancipation would help us in Europe, and convince them that we are incited by something more than ambition . . . And then unquestionably it would weaken the rebels by drawing off their laborers . . . But I am not sure we could do much with the blacks. If we were to arm them, I fear that in a few weeks the arms would be in the hands of the rebels . . . I will mention another thing . . . There are fifty thousand bayonets in the Union armies from the Border Slave States. It would be a serious matter if, in consequence of a proclamation such as you desire, they should go over to the rebels.

■ Source B: *Blackwood's Edinburgh Magazine*, November 1862

With their armies baffled and beaten, and with the standards of the rebel army again within sight of Washington, the President has at length owned the impossibility of success in fair warfare, and seeks to paralyse the victorious armies of the South by letting loose upon their hearths and homes the lust and savagery of four million Negroes . . . henceforth it is a war of extermination. The North seeks to make of the South a desert – a wilderness of bloodshed and misery; for thus only, now, does it or can it hope to overcome the seceding Confederacy.

■ Source C: Abraham Lincoln's Emancipation Proclamation, 1 January 1863

That . . . all persons held as slaves within any State or designated part of a State, the people whereof shall then be in rebellion against the United States, shall be then, thenceforward, and forever free . . . [and] will be received into the armed service of the United States . . .

■ Source D: Letter to General US Grant from Abraham Lincoln, 9 August 1863

. . . Gen. Thomas has gone again to the Mississippi valley, with the view of raising colored troops . . . I believe it is a resource which, if vigorously applied now, will soon close the contest. It works doubly, weakening the enemy and strengthening us.

OCR QUESTION FORMAT

The questions and answers that follow are based on the OCR style.

(a) **Study Source C. From this Source and your own knowledge explain exactly which slaves would be freed by the Emancipation Proclamation.** (20)

(b) **Study Sources A and D. How far do Lincoln's sentiments in Source D agree with the views he expresses in Source A?** (40)

(c) **Study all the Sources. Using all these Sources and your own knowledge explain why Lincoln changed his attitude towards emancipation during the war.** (60)

(a) Lincoln's Emancipation Proclamation is very carefully worded. It refers to those slaves in parts of the South that were still in a state of rebellion on 1 January 1863. In other words, those slaves in parts of the South which had already been occupied by Northern troops would not be freed, and neither would those slaves in the four border states that had remained loyal to the Union from the start of the war. The Emancipation Proclamation therefore freed no slaves at all. It did, however, set out Lincoln's intent to free slaves in areas subsequently 'liberated'.

(b) In Source D Lincoln makes the point that the emancipation of slaves 'doubly' benefits the North, i.e. the loss of slaves weakens the enemy, and then, when the ex-slaves join the Union army, it also helps the North. This supports the views in Source A to a certain extent, but only as far as Lincoln thought that losing labourers would weaken the South. In Source A he does not really believe there will be a double benefit to the North, saying 'I am not sure we could do much with the blacks', and clearly does not feel they would make good soldiers.

(c) From the time that the states of the Lower South seceded Lincoln had to play things very cautiously. If he made the abolition of slavery an aim of war straight away, he could lose the Upper South, the border slave states, and also divide opinion in the North. As it was, the Upper South seceded anyway, but the fact that Lincoln did not make the abolition of slavery a war aim probably saved the Union and brought about the emancipation of slaves. Some historians have been convinced that Lincoln all along wanted to free the slaves but was simply waiting for the right moment. By September 1862 when he spoke to Christian ministers he was probably convinced that the abolition of slavery would happen, although his justification for the act outlined in Source A suggest that it was important to him people should think he wanted to free the slaves as a way of winning the war and saving the Union, rather than it becoming an aim in itself. He also, to a certain extent, was outlining why it would make sense at that time to free the slaves, to 'convince them' in Europe, and to 'weaken the rebels', but he still appears to be cautious, including the proviso that 'fifty thousand bayonets . . . from the Border Slave States' may be lost if slaves in the rebel states were freed.

Blackwood's Edinburgh Magazine (Source B) clearly viewed Lincoln's intention to let loose 'the lust and savagery of four million Negroes' in a very cynical and desperate light, suggesting that without freeing the slaves Lincoln's armies could well have been facing defeat. But it was especially to *avoid* the appearance of desperation that Lincoln waited until after Antietam, which he chose to regard as a Union victory, before issuing his proclamation. The Emancipation Proclamation of 1863 was so carefully worded ('slaves within any state . . . in rebellion against the United States') that it actually freed no slaves at all, and this reveals Lincoln as the great pragmatist. He did not intend to free slaves in the border states or the occupied states of the South, thereby ensuring continued loyalty from these areas. Source D reveals how Lincoln had come round to the idea of 'raising colored troops' for the Union army, and although initially reluctant to use them in combat situations, he gradually relented, and allowed black regiments to play their part in the winning of the war.

Lincoln could probably not have risked the Emancipation Proclamation earlier. He had to wait until war weariness and casualty rates in the North made the freeing of the slaves an acceptable aim for the majority of whites. Once that time had come, Lincoln could see the advantages of giving the Northern cause more impetus by adopting a nobler cause than simply safeguarding the Union.

ADDITIONAL QUESTIONS IN THE OCR STYLE

(a) **Study Source A. From this Source and your own knowledge explain why Lincoln was so concerned about the 'fifty thousand bayonets . . . from the Border Slave States'.** (20)

(b) **Study Sources B and D. How far does Source D support the motives ascribed to Lincoln in Source B?** (40)

(c) **Using these Sources and your own knowledge explain how far you support the view that Lincoln did not go to war to abolish slavery.** (60)

2 Leadership during the war

■ **Source A: Extracts from letters written by Abraham Lincoln to General George B. McClellan, October 1862**

You remember my speaking to you of what I called your over-cautiousness. Are you not over-cautious when you assume that you can not do what the enemy is constantly doing?

I have just read your despatch about sore tongued and fatigued horses. Will you pardon me for asking what the horses of your army have done since the battle of Antietam that fatigue anything?

■ **Source B: Abraham Lincoln's proclamation suspending the writ of habeas corpus, 24 September 1862**

. . . disloyal persons are not adequately restrained by the ordinary processes of law . . . from giving aid and comfort in various ways to the insurrection . . . therefore, be it ordered . . . That the Writ of Habeas Corpus is suspended in respect to all persons arrested . . .

■ **Source C: Order of Retaliation, 30 July 1863 (Abraham Lincoln's response to the Confederacy executing or selling into slavery captured black soldiers)**

It is . . . ordered that for every soldier of the United States killed in violation of the laws of war, a rebel soldier shall be executed.

■ **Source D: Letter from Abraham Lincoln to General U.S. Grant, 30 April 1864**

. . . I wish to express, in this way, my entire satisfaction with what you have done up to this time . . . The particulars of your plans I neither know, or seek to know . . . I wish not to obtrude any constraints or restraints upon you.

OCR QUESTION FORMAT

The questions and answers that follow are based on the OCR style.

(a) **Study Source B. From this Source and your own knowledge explain why the 'Writ of Habeas Corpus' was suspended by Lincoln in 1862.** (20)

(b) **Study Sources A and D. How far do Lincoln's sentiments expressed in Sources A and D appear to represent a contradiction in terms of how he dealt with senior army officers?** (40)

(c) **Study all the Sources. Using all the Sources and your own knowledge explain the extent to which Lincoln expanded the powers of the President during wartime.** (60)

(a) Lincoln, invoking his war powers as commander-in-chief, decided that the ordinary laws and courts were not effective enough against those who in some way aided and abetted the rebel cause. The problems of bringing charges that stuck are made apparent by his decision to suspend the right of habeas corpus (i.e. to be charged with an offence or released) 'in respect to all persons arrested', so that traitors to the Union could be held in prison indefinitely without being charged or brought to trial.

(b) In Source A Lincoln appears almost to be at his wit's end with McClellan, dropping unsubtle hints about what he believes his general should be doing, such as matching the movements of the enemy and not claiming that his horses are too tired. His use of the term 'over-cautiousness' is a clear criticism of an experienced officer, and his sceptical tone in the second paragraph suggests that he does not believe McClellan. Source D could not be more different than Source A in terms of Lincoln's manner. Rather than Lincoln appearing to be a meddler, he gives the impression of having absolute confidence in Grant, expressing his 'entire satisfaction' and not even wishing to know 'the particulars' of Grant's plans. He even adds that he does not wish to restrain his general in any way. Sources A and D certainly do suggest that Lincoln dealt with different officers in different ways.

(c) Lincoln was commander-in-chief during wartime, which by definition gave him greater powers than during peacetime. The extracts in Source A do not necessarily show that he expanded his powers, but do demonstrate his willingness to intervene in military affairs when, for example, he felt that McClellan's 'over-cautiousness' was an issue. He later dismissed McClellan when he was utterly convinced of his general's apparent reluctance to take the war to the South. In the same way Source D does not really give any indication that Lincoln had expanded his powers greatly other than confirming that although the war was fought on the ground by soldiers, he was still ultimately in charge, even when giving his backing to an officer. His expression that he did not 'seek to know' particulars of plans implies that he could have done if he had wished to.

There is no doubt that Lincoln took a broad view of his Presidential powers and took the view that saving the Union, even if it meant acting unconstitutionally at times, was worth it. He actually began to use his war powers in April 1861 before Congress had officially recognised a war existed. His belief that the ordinary legal process was not up to dealing with the wartime situation justified his use of martial law in the border states and his decision to suspend 'the writ of habeas corpus' (Source B). Thirteen thousand people were arrested under martial law during the war. He was later judged by the Supreme Court to have exceeded his powers, but it is clear he would never have taken such actions during peacetime. The Emancipation Proclamation and his rulings on Reconstruction were definitely dubious from a legal point of view, but victory in war vindicated him. Source C's threat that 'a rebel soldier shall be executed' for every Union soldier executed again demonstrates Lincoln using his 'war powers', as well as his ruthlessness.

There is no doubt that Lincoln expanded the powers of the Presidency during wartime, but he did not do it any permanent way, and when peace came, the powers of the President reverted back to normal as Congress gradually gained the ascendancy.

ADDITIONAL QUESTIONS IN THE OCR STYLE

(a) **Study Source A. From this Source and your own knowledge explain why in October 1862 Lincoln accused McClellan of being overcautious.** (20)

(b) **Study Sources B and C. How far do Sources B and C support the viewpoint that Lincoln was prepared to act ruthlessly when necessary?** (40)

(c) **Using all these Sources and your own knowledge explain the extent to which Lincoln was a better wartime leader than Jefferson Davis.** (60)

Part 4: Historical skills

 ## 1 Songs of 'the Blue and the Gray'

The following are extracts from popular Civil War songs. Students should examine the lyrics and discuss the sentiments behind them as a way of gaining an insight into the motivations of the men who fought.

'All Quiet along the Potomac'
(sung by both armies)

> 'All quiet along the Potomac,' they say,
> Except now and then a stray picket
> Is shot, as he walks on his beat to and fro,
> By a rifleman hid in the thicket.
> 'Tis nothing – a private or two now and
>   then
> Will not count in the news of the battle;
> Not an officer lost – only one of the men,
> Moaning out, all alone, the death-rattle . . .
>   Ethel Lynn Beers

'Maryland! My Maryland!'
(a marching song of the Confederacy)

> The despot's heel is on thy shore,
>   Maryland!
> His torch is at thy temple door,
>   Maryland!
> Avenge the patriotic gore
> That flecked the streets of Baltimore,
> And be the battle queen of yore,
> Maryland! Maryland!
>   James R. Randall

'The Battle Hymn of the Republic'
(Northern song)

> Mine eyes have seen the glory of the coming
>   of the Lord:
> He is tramping out the vintage where the
>   grapes of wrath are stored;
> He hath loosed the faithful lightning of his
>   terrible swift sword:
> His truth is marching on.
>   Julia Ward Howe

'Tenting Tonight'
(popular with both sides)

> We are tired of war on the old camp ground,
> Many are dead and gone, of the brave and
>   true
> Who've left their homes, others been
>   wounded long.
> Many are the hearts that are weary tonight,
> Wishing for the war to cease;
> Many are the hearts looking for the right
> To see the dawn of peace . . .
>   Walter Kittredge

'Weeping, Sad and Lonely'
(initially a Northern song but also adapted by the South)

> But our country called you, darling,
> Angels cheer your way:
> While our nation's sons are fighting,
> We can only pray.
> Nobly strike for God and liberty,
> Let all nations see
> How we love the starry banner
> Emblem of the tree.
> > Charles C. Sawyer

'Lorena'
(popular with both sides)

> The years creep slowly by, Lorena,
> The snow is on the grass again:
> The sun's low down the sky, Lorena,
> The frost gleams where the flowers have
> > been,
> But the heart throbs on as warmly now,
> As when the summer days were nigh;
> Oh, the sun can never dip so low,
> Adown affection's cloudless sky.
> The sun can never dip so low,
> Adown affection's cloudless sky.
> > H.D.L. Webster (?)

 ## 2 Statistics on their side

One of the key factors that helped to determine the outcome of the war was the advantage held by the North in population and resources. Use the following statistics to plot bar charts which show the advantages the North held in percentage terms over the South in the areas listed below.

For example, population and railroad mileage.

	North (%)	South (%)
Population	71	29
Railroad mileage	71	29
Farm acreage	65	35
Wheat production	80	20
Manufacturing output	92	8
Boots and shoes output	90	10
Firearm output	97	3
Cloth output	93	7
Cotton production	4	96
Coal production	97	3
Pig iron	94	6
Wealth produced	75	25
US army officers	67	33

Sources and references

Alan Brinkley, *The Unfinished Nation*, McGraw-Hill (2000).

Ken Burns, *The Civil War* (video), DD Video (1989).

Brian Collins, 'Why did the South Lose?', *History Today*, November (1988).

Henry Steel Commager, *The Blue and the Gray*, The Fairfax Press (1982).

Alan Farmer, *The American Civil War, 1861–1865*, Hodder & Stoughton (1996).

Alan Farmer and Vivienne Sanders, *American History, 1810–1990*, Hodder & Stoughton (2002).

Donald Gilmore, 'Revenge in Kansas, 1863', *History Today*, March (1993).

Susan-Mary Grant, 'Pride and Prejudice in the Civil War', *History Today*, September (1998).

Brian Holden Reid, 'Why the Confederacy Lost', *History Today*, November (1988).

Philip Jenkins, *A History of the United States*, Palgrave (1997).

Michael Johnson (ed.), *Abraham Lincoln, Slavery, and the Civil War – Selected Writings and Speeches*, Bedford (2001).

Maldwyn Jones, *The Limits of Liberty*, Oxford University Press (1983/1995).

James McPherson, *Battle Cry of Freedom*, Penguin (1990).

James McPherson, *For Cause and Comrades*, Oxford University Press (1997).

John M. Murrin, Paul E. Johnson, James M. McPherson *et al.*, *Liberty Equality Power*, Harcourt (2001).

Hugh Tulloch, *The Debate on the American Civil War Era*, Manchester University Press (1999).

Howard Zinn, *A People's History of the United States*, Longman (1996).

Chapter 5

Politics, Reform and Westwards Expansion, 1865–1919

This chapter will examine the post-war debate over individual rights, and the extent of state and federal power through the issues of Reconstruction, westwards expansion, industrialisation, urbanisation, immigration, the rise of labour, Populism, 'Gilded Age' politics and progressivism. (Note: the position of African Americans and the progress they made during the period is essentially covered in Chapter 10.)

 Historical background

Reconstruction
Westwards expansion
The 'Gilded Age' and Populism
Big business
The Progressive era and government
    intervention
Roosevelt, Taft and Wilson
Immigration
Organised labour

 Essays

Reconstruction
Big business
The West
Immigration and government intervention

Labour and Populism
Progressivism

 Sources

1   Big business and Progressivism
2   Immigration

 Historical skills

1   Robber barons or captains of industry?
2   The themes of Progressive legislation

Chronology

1865	Lincoln assassinated – Andrew Johnson became President
	Freedmen's Bureau established
1866	Civil Rights Bill passed by Congress and Freedmen's Bureau expanded over Johnson's veto
	National Labor Union founded by William Sylvis
1867	Congressional (Radical) Reconstruction began
1868	Impeachment of Andrew Johnson
	Ulysses Grant (Republican) elected President
1869	Transcontinental railroad completed
	Knights of Labor founded by Uriah Stephens
1870	Standard Oil founded by Rockefeller
1871	Ku Klux Klan Act passed
1872	Grant re-elected President
	Boss Tweed convicted
1873	Carnegie Steel founded
	Panic and depression
1877	Rutherford Hayes (Republican) became President following disputed election
	End of Reconstruction
	Desert Land Act
	National railroad strike
1880	James Garfield (Republican) elected President
1881	Federation of Trades and Labor Unions (FTLU) founded
	Garfield assassinated – Chester Arthur became President
1882	Chinese Exclusion Act
1883	Supreme Court upheld segregation
	Pendleton Act began reform of civil service
1884	Grover Cleveland (Democrat) elected President
1886	Haymarket bombing, Chicago
	American Federation of Labor founded out of the FTLU by Samuel Gompers and Adolph Strasser
1887	Interstate Commerce Act
1888	Benjamin Harrison (Republican) elected President
1890	Sherman Anti-Trust Act
	Sherman Silver Purchase Act
	McKinley Tariff
	Jacob Riis's *How the Other Half Lives* published
1892	Homestead Steel Strike
	Cleveland (Democrat) elected President
1893	Depression began
	Sherman Silver Purchase Act repealed
1894	Immigration Restriction League founded
	Pullman Strike
1896	William McKinley (Republican) elected President
1900	Galveston, Texas, created City Commission government
	Robert La Follette (Progressive) elected governor of Wisconsin

1901	McKinley assassinated – Theodore Roosevelt became President
1902	Ida Tarbell's exposé of Standard Oil
	Northern Securities Anti-Trust case
	Newlands Act
1903	Elkins Act
	Federal court dissolved Northern Securities Company
1904	Theodore Roosevelt (Republican) elected President
1905	Industrial Workers of the World (IWW) founded
	National Forest Service established
1906	Hepburn Railroad Regulation Act
	Pure Food and Drug Act
	Meat Inspection Act
1908	William Taft (Republican) elected President
1909	Payne-Aldrich Tariff
1911	Triangle Shirtwaist Factory Fire
1912	Wilson (Democrat) elected President
1913	16th Amendment income tax
	17th Amendment direct election of US senators
	Federal Reserve Act
1914	Ludlow Massacre
	Clayton Anti-Trust Act

Part 1: Historical background

 Reconstruction

Over 600,000 American men had died during the Civil War, a quarter of all (white) Southern men of military age had been killed or wounded, and, in 1865, the state of Mississippi had to spend 20 per cent of its revenue on the purchase of artificial limbs for Confederate veterans. War had ruined the Southern economy, and seen the national debt rise to $3 million. Approximately four million slaves had been freed, but many would die from disease and starvation in the months following freedom. In addition to all of these issues there remained the question of how and when the rebel states would be readmitted to the Union.

Lincoln's main aim under what has become known as 'Reconstruction' was to readmit the Confederate states to the Union as quickly as possible. As early as 1863 he issued a Proclamation of Amnesty and Reconstruction, which proposed to grant readmission to the states and amnesty to all Southerners except high civil and military leaders as long as 10 per cent of each state's voters swore an oath of allegiance to the US and recognised the ending of slavery. Lincoln also insisted that any legal confiscation of property in the South would be limited to the lifetimes of its owners and would not apply to their heirs. Many former slaveholders simply took the oath of allegiance and continued to own their land. In 1864 Louisiana drew up a new constitution prohibiting slavery, but did not grant blacks, who made up nearly half the population, the vote. When over 10 per cent of voters (based on number of votes cast in 1860) in Louisiana supported the new Constitution, Lincoln was happy to see it return the Union. Republican Radicals, however, who viewed Reconstruction as a Congressional function, persuaded Congress to reject Louisiana's readmission and refuse to admit its senators, seeking to delay Reconstruction until after the war when the President would be in a weaker position. Two of the Radicals, Benjamin Wade and Henry Davis, were behind the Wade-Davis Bill, which proposed to exclude anyone who had taken up arms or held high office for the Confederacy from either voting or standing for political office, and also required that 50 per cent of a state's voters take an 'Ironclad Oath', swearing that they had never supported secession voluntarily, before readmission. Lincoln vetoed the Bill in August 1864, but the stage was set for future conflict.

With the death of Lincoln, which for many Northerners suggested a conspiracy organised by the leaders of the South, Andrew Johnson became President. He had been the only Southern state senator to remain loyal to the Union, and many radicals were optimistic that he would be less tolerant than Lincoln towards the former rebel states. Their optimism was misplaced, and he continued in much the same vein as his predecessor, although Lincoln had favoured a limited suffrage for blacks, and had not intended to pardon as many ex-Confederates as Johnson set about doing. Johnson extended a general pardon to Confederates who would take the oath of allegiance, and dealt generously with personal requests for pardons from high office-holders (he pardoned about 15,000 ex-rebels, sometimes hundreds in a single day, and abandoned his intention to charge Southern officers and politicians with treason). In addition he recognised governments in Virginia, Louisiana, Arkansas and Tennessee, and indicated that the other seven states would be recognised if they withdrew their ordinances of secession, and ratified the 13th Amendment. The Southern states, in flagrant defiance of their position, refused to enfranchise blacks, and in both state and Congressional elections proceeded to vote for prominent ex-Confederates. Georgia chose Alexander Stephens, the former Vice-President of the Confederacy, as its senator. To compound the situation the Southern states introduced the so-called '**Black Codes**' aimed at keeping blacks in a subordinate position by restricting their legal, political, social and economic rights. Eric Foner (1984) found that violence against blacks 'reached staggering proportions' in some areas, for example estimating that in the Shreveport area of Louisiana over 2,000 blacks were killed in 1865. In December 1865 when Congress reassembled it refused to allow those who had been voted in by the Southern states to take their seats (with the backing of Northern opinion, which had turned against the South) and it set up a Joint Committee on Reconstruction to determine whether the Southern states were ready to rejoin the Union.

Many of the leading Radicals who had blocked the seating of Southern representatives, such as Charles Sumner and Thaddeus Stevens, had done so out of a genuine concern for black rights. Others such as Wade had done it more for reasons of political advantage realising that, following emancipation, blacks would count for five-fifths rather than three-fifths when calculating populations and hence the Southern states would be entitled to 15 extra seats in the House of Representatives. With the war over, there was a good chance that Northern and Southern Democrats would reunite, possibly leaving the Republicans as the smaller party (in 1864 the Democrats had won 45 per cent of the Northern vote). It was therefore imperative to disenfranchise as many ex-Confederates as possible and ensure that as many blacks as possible got the vote (it was assumed that blacks would vote Republican). There were certainly vested business interests who wished to see the continued Republican dominance of Congress, but Maldwyn Jones (1995) has argued that, despite Congress passing measures during the war of which Southerners disapproved, Northern businessmen were divided over tariff and currency policies, as were the Republicans. There was, therefore, a range of aims for Congressional Reconstruction which included:

- the readmission of the Southern states;
- the improvement of black rights (which some hoped would prevent an exodus of freed slaves to the North where they would come into direct competition with poor white workers);
- the maintenance of the Northern/Republican dominance of government;
- the economic rehabilitation of the South;
- and possibly an element of vindictiveness following the South's apparent reluctance to accept the verdict of war and the terms of their defeat. (Northerners never did 'hang Jeff Davis on a sour apple tree' as

the words to the song 'John Brown's Body' promised, although he was imprisoned for two years. In fact only one man was executed for his role in the war, Henry Wirz, who had been in charge of the notorious Andersonville prison camp.)

For the next three years Johnson was at loggerheads with Congress over the course Reconstruction should take, vetoing an extension to the lifetime of and expansion of the legal power of the Freedmen's Bureau (which had initially been set up in March 1865 to provide ex-slaves (and whites) with food, shelter, clothing, food, medical aid and education, and to find land on which some of them might settle) and also vetoing a Civil Rights Bill which promised full citizenship for blacks. Johnson argued that the former would unconstitutionally extend military rule during peacetime and the latter would infringe states' rights and should not be passed while 11 states were still not represented in Congress. His stance pushed many moderates into the hands of the Radicals, who were able to gain the two-thirds majority needed to repass the laws over Johnson's veto. It also enabled Congress to pass the 14th Amendment in 1868 giving blacks citizenship and penalising any state which refused to allow them to vote. Only Tennessee ratified, and was declared to be back in the Union. The other ten rejected it and were left outside the Union, although Delaware and Kentucky, slave states that had remained loyal to the Union during the war, also rejected it.

From 1867 (with the First (Military) Reconstruction Act, passed over Johnson's veto) to 1877 most of the South was controlled by Republican administrations and the military, while many Southern whites were disqualified from voting and office-holding, and many pardons granted by Johnson were withdrawn. Southern states refused to call conventions to draft new constitutions which would allow for black suffrage and the disqualification of ex-Confederates. Johnson tried to undermine 'Radical Reconstruction' by replacing military governors appointed by Congress with men more sympathetic to the South. He believed that Congress was going too far and feared that the federal system itself was under threat from centralising tendencies. Matters came to a head between Johnson and his Congress following the passage of two Acts in March 1867. The Tenure of Office Act forbade the President to remove civil office-holders without the approval of the Senate – a move designed to protect Stanton, Johnson's Secretary of War who was a staunch ally of the Radicals – and the Command of the Army Act prevented the President from issuing military orders except through the commanding general of the army, or from relieving the commanding general or assigning him elsewhere without the Senate's consent. Congress had already been at odds with the Supreme Court over the use of martial law in peacetime where civil courts were available, and it was highly likely that the Supreme Court would rule that the two new laws restricting the power of the President were unconstitutional. In this hope Johnson dismissed Stanton, but before the case could come to court, the House of Representatives voted to impeach Johnson for 'high crimes and misdemeanours in office', seemingly believing that this was the only way of getting their brand of Reconstruction through. In the end, 7 Republican senators (who effectively sacrificed their careers by doing so) voted with 12 Democrats for acquittal, fearing that Johnson's removal would permanently damage the Presidency, and that Benjamin Wade would probably succeed him. Johnson was never the same after the trial, and Congressional-style Reconstruction won the day. By June 1868, six of the former rebel states had been readmitted to the Union. Mississippi, Texas, Georgia and Virginia were not readmitted until 1870.

Ulysses Grant became President in the 1868 election but needed 700,000 black votes to win a popular majority of 300,000. Grant was unsuited to the Presidency and a poor judge of character when it came to choosing his political allies. His administration became tainted by scandal and corruption in high places, in a sense reflecting the corruption apparently endemic across the whole country, for example, in New York under 'Boss' William Tweed, who controlled the city's Democratic machine at Tammany Hall. Under Grant, Reconstruction continued to take its course. In the South, Southern collaborators ('**scalawags**') and Yankee financiers ('**carpet-baggers**') ran the show, but despite their denigrators and the countless accusations of waste, corruption and overspending, many were men of integrity who set up businesses, poor relief, fairer tax systems, expanded railroad building and founded schools. Nonetheless, this did not wash with the 'die-hards' who blamed the 50 per cent fall in the price of cotton between 1872 and 1877 and Southern poverty in general on the Radical regimes, and formed groups such as the 'Knights of the White Chamelia', 'the Red Shirts', 'the White League' and the '**Ku Klux Klan**' to intimidate blacks and white collaborators. Ultimately, the Republican regimes in the South during Reconstruction relied on the manipulation of the black vote, and the political will of Washington to back them, by use of military force if necessary. Grant took action in 1870–1 with three Force Acts, and by the end of 1871 the Klan had effectively been suppressed.

Gradually wartime hatreds faded and people took the view that Southern whites and blacks would eventually have to sort out their own problems. Some of the Radical Republicans died and the political will to enforce Reconstruction at the barrel of a gun waned, as other issues such as the scandal in Washington and the 'panic of 1873' came to the fore. In 1872 the Amnesty Act restored political rights to all but a few ex-Confederates, and the Freedmen's Bureau was allowed to lapse. White Southerners sensed the changing mood in the North and seized the initiative. In 1874 Democrats devised the Mississippi Plan to push the remaining scalawags into the Democrat party and prevent blacks from voting. White rifle clubs and semi-military groups marched openly, and politically active blacks were refused jobs, charged higher prices in shops and denied tenancies. Eric Foner (1984) sees Grant's failure to intervene in Mississippi as a milestone in the retreat from Reconstruction. Tennessee and Virginia were effectively back under Democrat control as early as 1869, and by 1876 whites had redeemed every state in the South except Louisiana, South Carolina and Florida, all three of which would play a key role in the controversial election of 1876.

The Presidential election of 1876 was marked by fraud on both sides, and the results were disputed in three states. A Congressional commission decided in a strictly partisan way to effectively award the election to Rutherford Hayes, the Republican governor of Ohio, rather than Samuel Tilden, the Democrat governor of New York. To avoid further trouble, Hayes (from then on known by opponents as 'His Accidency' or 'His Fraudulency') promised Tilden he would appoint a leading Southerner to his cabinet, deal sympathetically with Southern demands for railroad subsidies and remove the last federal troops from the South. With the removal of the military came the collapse of the last three Republican state governments in the South and Reconstruction was over.

To assess whether Reconstruction can be seen as a success, it is necessary to determine whether its aims were met and to view it from the different perspectives of those involved. Reconstruction was successful in that the Union was restored in a relatively peaceful manner, although some have argued that it left a more bitter legacy in sectional and racial terms than the war itself. Jones has said that by 1877 'reunion had been achieved, but not reconciliation' (1995: p. 259). Slavery was abolished, clearly a landmark in the progress of black Americans, but, Jones argues, a modus vivendi was reached by white Americans at the expense of blacks, with the North effectively abandoning the race problem to the South. During Reconstruction 2 blacks won seats in the Senate and 15 in the Representatives. Well over 600 sat on state legislatures – 'a stunning departure' in American politics according to Foner – but after 1877 numbers dwindled. By 1900 George White was the only black congressman left, while black rights were steadily eroded and segregation became the norm in the South. Ransom and Foner have stressed the major role blacks played during the process and how the foundations of a modern black community were laid with black churches and businesses being set up and blacks themselves becoming landowners, teachers and clergymen. They have also suggested that blacks made more progress economically than previously thought, and improved their living standards substantially in some cases. Education and health improved for all those living in the South to a certain extent. Brinkley (2000) has argued that the dramatic improvement in Southern education was perhaps the most important accomplishment of Reconstruction. The Freedmen's Bureau coordinated the spending of $17 million on setting up 100 hospitals and 4,000 schools, as well as establishing the first black institutions of higher education. By 1876 there were 70,000 blacks at school in the South compared to none in 1860, and there were 50,000 whites at school compared to 20,000 in 1860.

Dunning, writing in the early twentieth century, claimed the South had been cruelly oppressed during Reconstruction. This view is now regarded as grossly overstated, although such was the level of intimidation brought against the Supreme Court by Radical Republicans that in 1867 it refused to take two cases where Southern states were seeking injunctions against the enforcement of the Reconstruction Acts. In the 1950s and 1960s Stampp and John Hope Franklin depicted Reconstruction as lenient, with few Confederates imprisoned, only one executed, and with most recovering both their land and the vote. Farmer (1997) also sees Reconstruction as a success for Southern whites even though the South was to remain an impoverished region of the country, dependent almost entirely on cotton, with many Southerners, white and black alike, reduced to tenant farming. After 1877, the South came under the control of a powerful conservative elite, the 'Redeemers' or 'Bourbons', many of them from the planter class that had dominated the pre-war South, and, in the words of Foner, 'the dark night of injustice settled over the South' (1984: p. 612).

 ## Westwards expansion

The growth of the US had continued pretty much unabated since Jefferson's purchase of the Louisiana Territory in 1802. The West came to represent an important element in the American psyche, taking on mythical proportions, and seemingly symbolising some sort of American ethos. Walt Whitman called it 'the real genuine America', a place where democracy and equality thrived against a backdrop of harsh weather conditions and the threat from hostile Indians. Erasmus Beadle's Western dime novels, which were churned out from 1860 onwards, glorified the image of the West as did the paintings of Russell and Remington, emphasising rugged individualism and self-reliance, virtues which many wanted to be a reflection of American society as a whole. In the 1890s Frederick Jackson Turner, then a young historian, argued that the advancement of American settlement westwards explained American development, and that democracy was born on the frontier, confirming for many a belief that in some way the frontier had contributed to the values of liberty and equality held so dear by many Americans. Although no historian since has successfully argued that the frontier had no impact on American development, Turner's views have pretty much been discredited by those who have pointed to the importance of the east, the influence of European thinking on democracy, the roles of government and business in settling the West, the parts played by women, blacks, Native Americans, Chinese and Hispanics, and so on.

Between 1862 and 1900 the government gave out 80 million acres under the Homestead Act, but much of the land went to speculators, cattlemen, mining and lumber companies. The government failed to appreciate that many ordinary people could not afford to buy 160 acres, or that 160 acres was too small to make a living on the Great Plains, as well as the investment farmers had to make in tools, seeds and livestock. Further land grants (the 1873 Timber Culture Act, which allowed individuals to claim an extra 160 acres if they planted it with trees within ten years, and the 1877 Desert Land Act, which allowed settlers to buy an additional 640 acres provided the area was irrigated within two years) served to obstruct genuine settlement further. Colonising activities contributed far more to settlement than public land policy, with railroads advertising the benefits of life on the Plains and even offering temporary shelter and lessons in farming to those willing to go west. During the war alone the federal government gave over 100 million acres to the railroads, and between 1869 and 1893 five transcontinental railroads were built. Large numbers of Britons, Germans and Scandinavians moved from the eastern states but their departure tended to be more than offset by the numbers of immigrants coming into the US after the war, who invariably settled in the growing cities of the east. Inventions such as barbed wire, wells, windmills, better ploughs and reapers helped settlers overcome the adversities they faced, along with a government policy directed against the Indians.

Although the pioneers and settlers travelled from east to west, the mining frontier advanced from west to east, following the discovery of gold in California in 1848. The image of '49-er prospectors staking their claims and panning for gold was slowly replaced by that of the machinery of big business, as it came to appreciate the potential that certain minerals had. By the 1870s silver had taken over from gold as the main mineral mined, while copper mines provided the copper wire for light bulbs and telephones. In 1867, 35,000 cattle were shipped from the railhead of Abilene, Kansas; by 1871, 700,000 were passing through that same route, and other railheads had been established by the cattlemen and cowboys at Dodge City, Wichita and Laramie, while the development of the refrigerator car had also made a significant contribution. Cattle fattened on the Great Plains led to the end of the open range, as did the development of ranching and the railroads, and even the fencing-in of land by ranchers came to resemble the large-scale corporatism of American industry, and contributed to the destruction of the Plains Indians.

When gold was discovered in 1875 in the Black Hills of Dakota, one of the areas the government had recognised as an Indian reservation several years earlier, the government broke its promise. In 1876 General George Armstrong Custer was sent in to assess the strength of the Indians who had gathered in Montana under Sitting Bull and Crazy Horse. Custer split his force and attacked instead, and his command was wiped out at the Battle of the Little Big Horn. News reached Washington during the centennial celebrations. After that it could only be a matter of time before the Indians were brought to heel. In 1886 Geronimo's Apaches were defeated and then in 1890, at Wounded Knee Creek, 200 Indians, mostly women and children, were gunned down by the Seventh Cavalry, putting an end to any resistance. The railroads, electric telegraph, Winchester repeating rifle, destruction of millions of buffalo, white attitudes, disease, and government policy combined against the Native Americans, who were placed on **reservations** and taught white ways. In the 1870s and 1880s the Indian Rights Association and National Indian Defense Association persuaded the federal government to adopt a policy of breaking down tribal structures and assimilating the Indians. In 1887 the Dawes Act stated that Indians could become citizens if they renounced tribal ways, and it also broke up reservation land into smaller plots, which allowed land-grabbing by whites.

The 'Gilded Age' and Populism

The 'Gilded Age' is a term often applied in a negative way to the quarter century after the Civil War, and was taken from a novel by Mark Twain and Charles Warner(1873) that criticised the superficiality of economic growth and materialism. The period is often viewed as being very much in contrast to the 1890s, which saw the beginning of the so-called Progressive movement (when action started to be taken to address some of the problems America faced). During the 1870s and 1880s despite the romantic symbolism of the western frontier, the dominant themes within the US were urban growth and industrial expansion on a massive scale, both of which were largely fuelled by the millions of immigrants who entered the country during that period. The gap between rich and poor widened, social problems multiplied, the pressure on governments to intervene more directly in people's lives grew to an unprecedented level, and big business came to dominate politics, which was based on patronage rather than principle and was all about power, as well as the economy.

Johnson's impeachment was soon followed by Grant's Presidency, which was dogged by corruption. The most infamous scandal involved the Credit Mobilier company and the construction of the Union Pacific Railroad with the submission of false bills and the attempted bribery of congressmen in the hope of preventing an investigation taking place. Graft was also widespread in city politics with party bosses and party machines ruling the corrupt roost. Boss Tweed in New York defrauded taxpayers out of an estimated $50 million before being jailed for fraud in 1873, largely as a result of a prolonged campaign against him by celebrated cartoonist Thomas Nast.

In the five Presidential elections between 1876 and 1892 no more than 1 per cent of the popular vote separated the two leading candidates, except in 1892 when it was 3 per cent. Both parties tried to avoid taking a stand on the controversial issues of the day, with patronage becoming more important than principle to many in politics, but electoral turnout was higher than at any time in American history. During the period the government came to take greater responsibility for issues such as finance, immigration, women's rights and Populism. The assassination of President James Garfield in 1881 gave a final push for the reform of the civil service and in 1883 the Pendleton Act opened up some civil service jobs to competitive exams. In 1884 Grover Cleveland became the first Democrat President to be elected in 28 years. With a large surplus in the Treasury Cleveland vetoed a bill that would have granted $100,000 to help Texas farmers buy seed grain during a drought, arguing that such a move might weaken the national character, yet in the same year paid government bondholders at $28 above the $100 value of each bond, at a cost of $45 million.

The Presidential election of 1888 was the most corrupt in American history, with the Republicans outbidding their opponents to win majorities in both Houses of the so-called 'Billion Dollar Congress'. The government went on to pass the Dependent Pensions Bill and the McKinley Tariff Act (which was regarded as a payback to the financial backers of the party). By the Sherman Silver Purchase Act of 1890, the government agreed to buy up a certain amount of silver every month (which pleased miners) and to issue paper money (which had an inflationary effect and pleased western farmers). In addition public works were set up and subsidies were given to steamships. The most significant developments in the 1890 mid-terms were the loss by the Republicans of nearly half their seats in the House (the Tariff Act and the extravagance of Congress were blamed but there were other factors as well) and the election of nine new congressmen and two senators from the Alliance-Populists representing farmers. As early as 1867 the first national farmers' organisation, the National Grange of the Patrons of Husbandry (or Grangers), was set up. It had social and educational aims and worked with the major political parties. During 1873–4 the Grangers won control of 11 mid-western state legislatures, but lost strength with the return of prosperity in the late 1870s. Other farmers' groups joined the Greenback Labor Party, which won over a million votes and 14 seats in the 1878 Congressional elections with its call for inflation. Farmers were suffering from declining status and there was overproduction internationally; wheat farmers in particular were affected, as were cotton planters whose markets were mainly abroad. By the end of the 1880s farmers' organisations had formed the Southern Alliance (which called for loans in paper money from the Treasury) and the Northwest Farmers Alliance (which organised statewide parties) and in 1890 they had won a number of state legislatures, and had two senators and nine congressmen. The Southern Alliance was worried about splitting the South with a new party so it set out to control the Democrats, returning two state governors and 40 congressmen. The Northwest Alliance formed the People's Party (or Populists) in 1892, calling for low interest loans, a graduated progressive income tax, federal ownership of the hated railroads, direct election of senators, the free unlimited coinage of silver (the government kept the amount of money in circulation steady, but with the population growing this caused problems, particularly for those owing money), a shorter working day, immigration restrictions and the use of more democratic political tools, such as the secret ballot, initiative, referendum, recall and directive. They did well in the middle border and Rocky Mountain states, winning four of them, but only polled 9 per cent of the total vote, not doing particularly well in some of the old Granger states, where farmers had diversified, or in the South, where whites tended to stick with the Democrats.

Populism continued after the Panic of 1893 and subsequent unemployment. President Cleveland was convinced that the Depression had been caused by the Sherman Silver Purchase Act, which had allowed holders of silver certificates to exchange them for gold leading to a drain on Treasury gold reserves. In 1893 he secured its repeal with Republican support but this had little effect and it was a loan from the banks which ended the monetary crisis at the end of 1896. The 1896 election was dominated by the battle of the gold and silver standards. The Republicans, with William McKinley of Ohio, supported the 'hard money' gold standard and protective tariff while the Democrats put forward William Jennings Bryan of Nebraska campaigning for free silver. During the campaign he uttered the immortal words: 'You shall not crucify mankind upon a cross of gold.' Eastern bankers and industrialists funded the Republicans, while Bryan absorbed the Populist votes, but lost despite winning 22 out of 45 states. Urban workers realised inflation would cut their real wages and they would pay more for bread if wheat prices rose. Populism was the first organised political movement to identify and try to deal with some of the problems of industrialisation. In 1900 the country officially adopted the gold standard.

The 'Gilded Age' was not all bad, though, according to some. Robert Barrows identifies the 'reformist' historians as those who concentrate on the corruption of the political machines and heavily criticise city government; the 'functionalists' who believe the bosses met the basic vital needs of their constituents such as jobs, food and fuel; and the 'celebrationists' who regard municipal government during the period as a great success in solving such problems as water supply, sewage disposal, public health and transportation, and for providing parks and libraries. Nor was politics at a national level rotten through and through, for there were many men of integrity serving in the Senate, and also the frequent appearance of third parties such as the Granger movement.

The Republican Party remained the party of the Union. Its core support lay in New England and the upper mid-west, with the business community, many working men and better-off farmers. The Democrats remained strong among Southern whites, immigrants in the big Northern cities, Catholics, small farmers and a minority of businessmen. Parties tried to cover up the differences between them, but the Republicans continued to support an integrated economy, protective tariff and black progress (or at least paid it lip-service), and were sympathetic to Prohibition, Sabbatarianism, and immigration restrictions. The Democrats remained sympathetic to states' rights and tariff reduction, but unsympathetic to blacks.

Big business

The United States' vast supplies of natural resources, the railroads and mass production techniques, as well as government support, foreign capital, cheap immigrant labour and a hard work ethos, all contributed to the rapid growth of industrialisation after the war. With the expansion of industry came the emergence of a new business elite and class of weekly wage earners, and trusts, which were essentially large-scale combinations of nominally independent and apparently competing firms controlled by a board of trustees. They cut manufacturing costs, and allowed better coordination and specialisation, but also limited competition, resulting in near monopolies in certain areas and allowing trustees to accumulate vast amounts of wealth and political influence. In 1882 Standard Oil of Ohio created the first trust – albeit one which was based largely on intimidation and predatory pricing. Others followed, and fairly soon men such as Andrew Carnegie (steel), William Vanderbilt (railroads), John D. Rockefeller (oil) and J.P. Morgan (banking) were household names.

People soon 'grasped that businessmen who wanted to control raw materials, markets, workers and the legal system might also have greater power than ordinary citizens in local, state and federal government' (Milton Goldin, 1988). For example, by 1888 the Pennsylvania Railroad had gross receipts of $115 million and employed 100,000 men, while the entire state of Massachusetts had gross receipts of $7 million and employed 6,000 men. By 1890 railroad revenue was well over double that of the federal government. Thomas Edison promised New Jersey politicians $1,000 each in return for certain legislation which would be beneficial to him. J.P. Morgan, at his peak, sat on the boards of 48 corporations, and Rockefeller on 37. Eric Arnesen was happy to use the term 'robber baron' rather than 'captain of industry' when referring to the new breed of capitalist, and emphasised the poor condition of labour rather than the rise in real wages and reduction in hours; and Howard Zinn (1996) was equally scathing, highlighting the levels of bribery and corruption in high places associated with the building of the first transcontinental railroad. He emphasised the unscrupulous nature of J.P. Morgan who, during the Civil War, had sold defective rifles that tended to shoot off the thumbs of those using them, and had avoided military service himself by paying $300 to a substitute – as had John D. Rockefeller, Andrew Carnegie and Jay Gould.

Porter has stressed the positive contribution of new goods and services for consumers and claimed that big business never really threatened democracy or Republican values. By Andrew Carnegie's death in 1919, he had given away $350,695,653. Nevertheless the anti-trust movement was largely motivated by fears that the economic power accumulated by certain trusts threatened democracy and individualism. By the end of the century the term 'laissez-faire', which had once been associated with individual freedom, had come to stand for trusts and the associated loss of individual freedom, with competition stifled and workers de-humanised by their conditions.

 ## The Progressive era and government intervention

As early as the 1870s writers and journalists began to criticise big business. Henry Demarest Lloyd exposed the Standard Oil Company in 1881, in *The Atlantic Monthly*, and Jacob Riis in 1890 brought the slums of New York to national prominence in his book *How the Other Half Lives*. The term '**muckraking**' is often attributed to the November 1902 issue of *McClure's*, in which Ida Tarbell exposed Standard Oil. The article was followed by similar exposés in the magazine such as Lincoln Steffens's attacks on urban corruption. President Theodore Roosevelt disliked some of the sensationalist journalism associated with 'muckraking', but there could be no doubting the collective will to tackle the problems of an urbanised and industrialised society. Progressivism, which emerged in the 1890s, was never a unified movement. It encompassed such issues as: the prohibition of alcohol, the vote for women, reform of local government, the improvement of working conditions, child labour, regulation of the economy, public health and housing, and conservation. More than anything else, it was perhaps a moral movement which spread nationwide embracing politicians from all parties, mainly driven by middle-class urban dwellers who were generally well educated, sympathetic towards a redistribution of wealth, and concerned about trusts, concentrations of wealth, social problems, crime (during the 1880s the murder rate quadrupled and the prison population rose by a half), violent strikes, immigration and political corruption. Cynics such as George Mowry and Richard Hofstadter in the 1950s saw the movement as a privileged middle-class elite attempting to regain status in the wake of ground lost to big business leaders, rather than it being genuinely popular, and since then a whole range of interpretations have emerged.

Gabriel Kolko has argued that Progressivism actually helped to stabilise the capitalist system during a time of uncertainty. The Commission Plan first used in 1901 following a devastating flood in Galveston, Texas, gave trained experts power rather than professional politicians. Robert M. La Follette of Wisconsin was an outstanding Progressive state governor between 1900 and 1906, pioneering Progressive ideas, such as extending workers' rights, improving education, cleaning up politics, and widening the scope for public participation with the use of such devices as the referendum. Roosevelt dubbed Wisconsin 'the laboratory of democracy'. Perhaps not surprisingly the Senate's first socialist came from Wisconsin.

Progressivism gradually increased the pressure on federal government to intervene more directly in national life, although in many areas state and city government had beaten Washington to it. In 1869 Massachusetts was the first state to establish a supervisory railroad commission, and in 1871 'Granger laws' in Illinois set maximum rates for passengers and freight. However, unscrupulous businessmen could get round state laws. For example, during the so-called Erie Railroad Wars, Cornelius Vanderbilt started to buy shares in the Erie Railroad Company, his competitor, to drive it out of business. Daniel Drew, Jay Gould and Jim Fisk, shareholders in Erie, had 100,000 worthless stocks printed, which they sold to Vanderbilt. With their arrest imminent, Fisk, Gould and Drew travelled to New Jersey where New York laws did not apply to what they had done. From safety Gould bribed members of the New York state legislature to the tune of $1 million to pass a law making the sale of watered stock legal. As a result he, Drew and Fisk got away with $7 million.

During the 1880s hostility towards the railroads extended to a more general attack on trusts (monopolies or colluding companies). There were laws passed prohibiting trusts in 27 states and territories, but trusts often circumvented such laws by moving their headquarters to states where the laws were more lax. In 1886 the Supreme Court also decided that state intervention encroached on the exclusive power of Congress to regulate commerce. Neither did the states have the power to regulate trusts involved in interstate commerce, which of course made it very difficult to bring the railroads to book, but in 1887 Congress established an Interstate Commerce Commission (ICC) to regulate railroad abuses such as rebates and discriminatory charging. The early rulings of the ICC were constantly challenged and generally overturned by the Supreme Court. Nonetheless, it marked a step forward in government attempts to regulate big business, although some may argue it did virtually nothing to regulate the railroads. In 1888 both Republicans and Democrats promised action to curb the trusts, and in 1890 Congress passed the Sherman Anti-Trust Act aimed at breaking the monopolistic practices of trusts, although the wording of the measure left it open to wide interpretation by the courts and it even came to be used against unions deemed to be interfering with free trade.

 ## Roosevelt, Taft and Wilson

Theodore Roosevelt of New York was the first of three Progressive Presidents and, in taking over the office at the age of 42 following McKinley's assassination, he is still the youngest man to hold the office. He called the office of President 'a bully pulpit', and believed it was his duty to do whatever was in the national interest so long as there was nothing in the Constitution to stop him. He was cautious initially, as befitting someone who had not actually been elected to the office, although only a year after becoming President he intervened decisively in a miners' strike by threatening the mine owners with federal takeover of their mines unless they came to terms with the miners. In 1902 he used the moribund Sherman Anti-Trust Act to dissolve a railroad holding company – much to the amazement of J.P. Morgan who could not believe that Roosevelt had not been prepared to discuss the issue with him first. By the time Roosevelt had become President, trusts essentially monopolised vital commodities such as oil, beef and the railroads. His government developed a reputation for 'trust-busting', though often his rhetoric was more radical than his actions, and he certainly took the view that regulation was preferable to dissolving companies, acknowledging the importance of big business to the US. Hofstadter has called him a conservative from the start. Nevertheless in 1903 he persuaded Congress to set up a Bureau of Corporations to investigate the abuses of trusts, and his government used the Sherman Act against 44 corporations. In actual fact, *more* trusts were set up under Roosevelt than had been under McKinley, and Taft was to mount twice as many anti-trust suits in four years as Roosevelt had in seven.

Roosevelt's offer of a 'square deal' in 1904 won him election in his own right. His second term was less impressive in many ways, despite the passage of the Hepburn Act in 1906 (which allowed for stricter regulation of the railroads and extended the powers of the ICC), as well as the 1906 Meat Inspection Act (following the publication of Upton Sinclair's novel *The Jungle*, which highlighted the appalling conditions in the meat-packing industry) and the Pure Food and Drug Act, both of which were landmark measures in public health. The Newlands Act of 1902 allowed Roosevelt to permit land reclamation and dam building to help irrigate millions of acres of western land, and he used the 1891 Forest Reserve Act to protect 150 million acres of forest land. He also, perhaps dubiously, closed 85 million acres in Alaska and the northwest, which were rich in coal and oil, to public entry. Some of his actions brought Roosevelt into conflict with Congress, which tended to see conservation as a threat to private initiative. Before standing down in the face of big business reluctance to embrace greater reform and the rise of socialism (which wanted to vastly increase the role of the state), he had called for increased use of the eight-hour day, income tax, death duties, limitations on injunctions in strikes, federal supervision of the stock market and workmen's compensation laws – all measures designed to help the workforce.

William H. Taft of Ohio, who defeated Bryan for the Presidency in 1908, was more conservative than Roosevelt, but nonetheless GEC and US Steel were both prosecuted during his term in office. Other notable achievements included the Mann-Elkins Act, which extended the jurisdiction of the ICC, the establishment of a postal savings bank, the creation of a Department of Labor and Federal Children's Bureau, the approval of an eight-hour day for federal workers and safety legislation for miners, and support for the 16th Amendment for income tax, and the 17th Amendment for the direct election of senators. Following Taft's siding with the Old Guard conservative Republicans ('standpatters') over the role of the speaker of the House and the Tariff, the Progressives (or 'insurgents' as they would be called) lost faith in him. Taft annoyed many by signing the Payne-Aldrich Tariff Bill and a trade agreement with Canada, and the re-opening of water sites to public entry led to big Republican losses in the mid-terms of 1910, with the Democrats taking control of the House.

It seemed that Roosevelt had returned from his world tour in the nick of time, and in 1912 he stood as Presidential candidate for the Progressive Bull Moose party on a New Nationalism platform. The Democrats, under Woodrow Wilson of New Jersey, called for a 'New Freedom' and endorsed a similarly progressive set of policies. Taft was the official Republican candidate.

Following his election victory, which resulted from the splitting of the Republican vote, Wilson took a lead in legislative matters and used patronage to ensure the passage of such laws as the Underwood-Simmons Tariff Act in 1913, which cut duties. He created a more flexible currency and 12 Federal Reserve Banks, while the Federal Trade Commission Act established a commission to regulate and investigate business practices, and the Clayton Act of 1914 legislated against price discrimination which led to monopoly. Following Republican gains in 1914, Wilson went on to support long-term rural credit through Federal Land Banks, compensation for federal workers, child labour laws and eight-hour days for railway workers, effectively adopting Roosevelt's 'New Nationalism'. In 1919 the 19th Amendment, giving women the vote nationally, was passed – although women already had the vote in several states.

In many respects, however, with the coming of the First World War, Wilson's term in office saw a repression of freedoms. As well as the renaming of German-American terms during the war – e.g. sauerkraut became 'liberty cabbage' and hamburger 'liberty sandwich' – the Espionage, Sabotage and Sedition Acts passed in 1917–18 gave the government sweeping powers to curb dissent and marked the greatest curtailment of freedom since 1798. By the spring of 1918 the government had arrested 2,000 members of the left-wing Industrial Workers of the World which had opposed the war. Eugene Debs, President of the American Railway Union and Socialist Presidential candidate, was sentenced to ten years in prison for an anti-war speech. In the meantime the Committee on Public Information set up by Wilson encouraged people to report neighbours they suspected of being anti-war, spread tales of German atrocities and contributed to the wave of anti-German hysteria. Some German-Americans felt obliged to change their names in order to avoid hostility. Wilson also reluctantly signed a bill introducing a literacy test for immigrants in 1917 (see 'Immigration', Chapter 6).

None of the so-called 'Progressive Presidents' had solved the problems of monopoly, reduced inequality or removed 'boss rule' or political corruption. Social welfare still lagged well behind Europe and big business would make a comeback in the 1920s.

 ## Immigration

The sheer scale of immigration to the US during the nineteenth century was bound to cause problems. Waves of immigration tended to follow certain patterns. Before the Civil War the so-called 'old immigration' consisted of British, German and Irish immigrants, plus some Dutch, Swiss and Scandinavian immigrants, who tended to settle along the eastern seaboard and upper Mississippi valley. In the 1830s about 50,000 immigrants a year arrived, but by the 1850s those numbers had risen to 300,000. By 1860 New York had 200,000 Irish, who became the country's first slum dwellers and the target of the anti-Catholic nativism of the 'Know-Nothing' or American Party, which feared the loss of social unity, crime and poverty that foreigners seemed to bring with them. In 1858, for example, out of 17,000 arrests in a New York quarter, 14,500 were foreigners and of these 10,500 were Irish.

Immigrant communities were also linked to electoral violence and fraud. Catholicism was linked to the absolutist monarchies of Europe, and was felt to be incompatible with American values. Rumours of papal plots abounded. Millard Fillmore stood for the 'Know-Nothings' in the Presidential election of 1856 on a platform that aimed to keep Catholics out, limit their political influence and exclude 'undesirables'

Figure 5.1 **Pie-charts showing sources of immigration, 1860–1920**

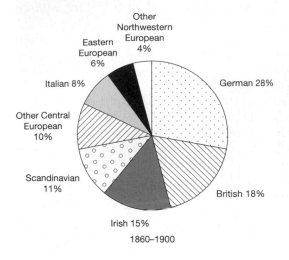

1860–1900

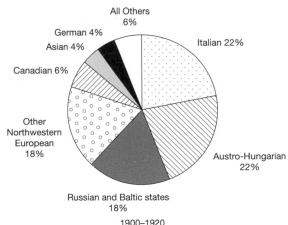

1900–1920

from entering the country. Support came in particular from native-born Protestant skilled workers and small businessmen – and in 1854 they won 104 Congressional seats out of 234. 'Know-Nothingism' was eclipsed in the 1850s by Republicanism.

The Civil War had been fought to preserve the Union and American values, but these seemed to be increasingly under threat as immigration grew again after the war. Between 1865 and 1915 over 26 million immigrants arrived, and, particularly after 1880, the so-called 'new immigration' came to be dominated by people from southern and eastern Europe: Italy, Austria-Hungary and Russia. By 1910 a third of the populations of the 12 largest cities were foreign-born, while another third were children of immigrants. These people tended to perform the least desirable jobs, working long hours in appalling conditions. The different customs, poverty and illiteracy, and the fact that many came from non-democratic countries, led to a second wave of nativism, which advocated a literacy test for immigrants in their own language. Cleveland, Taft and Wilson vetoed literacy tests on the grounds that they measured opportunity rather than ability, but Wilson capitulated in 1917 and the agitation of the Immigration Restriction League (set up in 1894 to keep 'lesser breeds' out) died down as a result. Unions also opposed immigration on the grounds that foreign workers tended to drive down wages, could be used to break strikes and generally contributed to keeping the union movement divided.

In 1882 the first restrictive immigration act was passed to ban paupers, convicts, criminals, lunatics, the Chinese, and anyone likely to be a public charge, but it made little impact on the numbers admitted. Immigrants became a convenient scapegoat for the problems brought by urbanisation and industrialisation, such as unemployment, strikes, crime and increasing welfare bills. In 1891 an immigration act was passed regarding dangerous and contagious diseases, and in 1906 a Gentlemen's Agreement gave the US the right to exclude the Japanese. In 1907, under pressure from the Immigration Restriction League and others, the Senate appointed the Dillingham Commission to study immigration patterns. In 1910–11 the Commission reported that since the 1880s immigrants had mainly been southern and eastern Europeans who were unsuited to life in the US and who were also considered to be inferior. The report recommended the use of literacy tests for immigrants in their own language.

Figure 5.2
Immigrants arriving in America around 1910

 Organised labour

In the 1840s less than 1 per cent of workers belonged to unions, which tended to develop far more slowly in the US than in Europe. Union growth was impeded by a number of factors:

- immigrants divided by culture, religion and language, who could be used by employers for lower pay and strike-breaking;
- a restriction of women's and black membership;
- labour spies;
- armed force;
- bias of law courts against unions, often regarded as un-American and even illegal;
- poor leadership;
- divided aims, e.g. middle-class leaders tended to aim for voting rights, free education and abolition of imprisonment for debt, whereas workers were more concerned with pay and conditions;
- fluctuating membership and low membership because workers often felt that jobs would be temporary;
- the Depression of the 1870s;
- divisions between skilled and unskilled workers (trade/labour); and
- the public reaction to violence during strikes.

In 1834, six craft societies united to a form a National Trades Union, which had some success before the Depression of the late 1830s brought about its collapse. In Massachusetts in 1842 a court ruled that trade unions were not in themselves criminal conspiracies, a ruling which other state courts often followed. State laws regarding shorter hours and child labour were often undermined by parents giving permission for children to work longer hours and also negotiating longer hours for themselves. In the 1860s, craft unions coalesced to form national organisations – the first attempt to combine different unions into a single body confederation. In 1866 William Sylvis, leader of the Iron Molders, founded the National Labor Union (NLU), which lasted for six years and included trade unions, farmers' groups and reform groups. However, the NLU began to spend more time on political issues such as currency reform and lost its way.

Many historians have glossed over the appalling conditions in which people worked during the second half of the nineteenth century, but not so Howard Zinn (1996). He has quoted the 1889 records of the ICC, which reveal that 22,000 railroad workers were killed or injured in that one year. He goes on to highlight that, in 1904, 27,000 workers were killed in manufacturing, transport and agriculture, while in 1914, 35,000 workers were killed in industrial accidents, with 700,000 injured.

The 1870s, with its increased mechanisation and reduced requirement for skilled workers, saw an increase in industrial conflict, which became more violent. The Molly Maguires, a secretive Irish organisation based in the Pennsylvania anthracite areas, went on strike, murdered mine superintendents, derailed rail cars and burned coal tips. The Pinkerton Detective Agency was called in, infiltrated the organisation and brought about the conviction and execution of 19 ringleaders in 1876. The Great Railroad Strike of 1877 affected the whole nation and resulted in about 100 deaths and 1,000 people being jailed. Approximately 100,000 workers had gone on strike, and the railroad companies did withdraw some wage cuts, however Hayes had to send in federal troops to restore order.

During the 1880s the dominant labour organisation was Terence Powderly's powerful Knights of Labor, which included farmers, capitalists, skilled and unskilled workers, blacks and whites, men and women. They waged several successful strikes and campaigned for an eight-hour day, equal pay for women and the end of child labour, paper money, income tax and the nationalisation of the railroads. It was perhaps the range of their aims, together with support coming from the more extreme Socialist Labor Party and anarchists, which led to its decline. The Haymarket Bomb of 1886 in Chicago and the subsequent execution of anarchist August Spies was certainly made the most of by anti-union forces.

The British-born Samuel Gompers' American Federation of Labor, set up in 1886, became the dominant labour organisation for more than a generation. It was a loose federation of national trade unions, except for the four railway brotherhoods. It concentrated more on bread-and-butter issues such as wages, hours and conditions. Gompers' seemingly moderate approach helped him to win wide acceptance, but for members of other unions life remained extremely tough.

In 1887 approximately 10,000 people went on strike for higher wages in Southern sugar plantations, resulting in the killing of over 30 blacks by the militia and white vigilantes. Four years later 15 leaders of an Arkansas cotton pickers' strike were killed.

In 1891 miners of the Tennessee Coal Mining Company were asked to sign an 'ironclad contract' pledging that they would not strike, they would agree to be paid in scrip (a form of payment in 'tokens', which had some sort of recognised financial value), and give up the right to check the weight of coal they had mined (by which they were paid). They refused to sign, and as a consequence were evicted from their houses and replaced by convicts. A thousand armed miners set the convicts free and the company gave up trying to force through these changes. However, when strikes became violent they usually lost public support, and this was something the unions could ill afford.

Such was the strength of the trusts, that even official government attempts to curb their power failed initially. Between 1890 and 1893 of the eight cases brought against corporations, the government lost seven and in 1895 in US v. E.C. Knight Company the Court even ruled that manufacturing was not strictly commerce and therefore did not come under the wording of the Sherman Act. With such bias in the law courts there is little wonder that unions struggled to make their mark.

One of the best-known strikes of the period was that of 1892 at Carnegie's Homestead Steel plant. Following a series of wage cuts, Andrew Carnegie and Henry Frick decided the Amalgamated Association of Iron and Steel Workers, which was affiliated to the American Federation of Labor (AFL), had to go. Three hundred 'Pinkertons' were brought in, three of whom were killed along with ten workers. The Pinkertons surrendered to the strikers, but the governor of Pennsylvania sent in an entire state National Guard of 8,000 to restore order. An attempt to assassinate Frick turned the public against the workers, and finally they drifted back to work.

In the same year as the Homestead Strike, Eugene Debs had formed the American Railway Union (ARU), with the aim of including all railway workers. In 1893 a third of the workers on Pullman rail cars were laid off and the rest had their wages cut by 30 per cent, though rents and prices in company stores were not cut. Within days workers were out on strike in 27 states and territories. Cleveland sent 2,000 troops to the Chicago area and a federal court injunction based on the Sherman Anti-Trust Act ruled the strike illegal. When the injunction was defied, Debs was arrested with others and imprisoned. The strike quickly collapsed with 34 having died during it.

In 1894 Jacob Coxey led a march of unemployed to Washington to demand the creation of jobs by the government and the printing of money and was arrested for trespass on the lawns of the Capitol.

In 1898 John Mitchell, a former miner and self-educated man, became President of the United Mine Workers of America, and went on to lead the Anthracite Coal Miners' Strike of 1902, successfully uniting immigrant groups in a campaign for better pay and conditions. Arbitrators awarded miners a 10 per cent wage increase and a nine-hour day. Roosevelt had also threatened intervention against the mine owners. In 1900 Mitchell joined fellow union leader Samuel Gompers and prominent businessmen, including Mark Hanna and J.P. Morgan, to form the American Civic Federation, which attempted to mediate and avoid conflict between employers and workers. However employers remained generally unsympathetic. Further violence seemed to indicate that employers and workers would never see eye-to-eye. The 1905 murder by bomb of Frank Steunenberg, ex-governor of Idaho, and the 1910 dynamiting of the 'LA Times' building (owned by a leading supporter of the open shop), which led to the charging of members of the Iron Workers Union, also gave unions a bad reputation with the general public.

Nevertheless in the period of prosperity following the Spanish-American War of 1898 union membership had grown rapidly, as had strike action. Employers formed the National Union of Manufacturers, which began an aggressive open shop campaign, and the American Antiboycott Association was set up in 1902 to fight unions in the courts. In 1905 in Lochner v. New York, the Supreme Court held that a law establishing a ten-hour day for bakers was an unjustified interference with the right of a worker to work as many hours as he chose, and in the 1907 Buck's Stove and Range Company Case a federal judge issued an injunction stopping the AFL from boycotting the goods of a company which had been unfair to workers. The 1908 Danbury hatters case saw the Supreme Court rule that secondary boycotts contravened the Sherman Act in restraint of trade, and the Court tended to block attempts to improve working conditions as violations of the 14th Amendment.

Both conditions and responses to industrial action remained appalling, even under so-called 'Progressive' Presidents. In 1911 the Triangle Shirtwaist Fire claimed the lives of 146 workers, mostly young women, and it emerged that the company had kept all its doors locked during working hours. The Colorado Coal Strike of 1913–14 was one of the most violent industrial conflicts in US history but seems to have had little or no coverage in most textbooks. The miners held out for 14 months in tents on the prairies with 66 dying in conflict. Between 1884 and 1912, 43,000 coal miners had been killed in accidents in the US, nearly 2,000 of these in Colorado mines where the death rate was twice the national average. 'Packed' coroners' juries almost always reached verdicts which absolved the coal companies from responsibility for their workers, most of whom were immigrants from eastern and southern Europe. The most notorious and horrific incident of the Colorado strike was the Ludlow Massacre of April 1914 at the mines of the Rockefeller-owned Colorado Fuel and Iron Company. The Rockefellers had hired the Baldwin Felts Detective Agency to help break the strike and the National Guard were also called in on behalf of the mine operators, intimidating miners and protecting strike-breakers. On 20 April, the miners' tents were machine-gunned and torched, with 26 killed, including 2 women and 11 children, who had suffocated in a pit dug under their tent. Following the incident miners went on the rampage and federal troops had to be sent in to restore order. Not one militia man or mine guard was indicted over the deaths. In 1915 a federal commission reported that between a third and a half of all American wage-earning families lived below the poverty line.

Figure 5.3
The Ludlow Massacre

By 1914 the AFL had over 2 million members, but this was only 11 per cent of the non-agricultural workforce in the US, although the much smaller Industrial Workers of the World ('Wobblies'), an anarcho-syndicalist union movement set up in 1905, gained as much coverage. The Wobblies were committed to fight capitalism and unite the workers of the world. They were hated and feared by employers for their 'free speech campaigns' and aggressive leadership of strikes, and they were to be the main victims of the anti-radical hysteria of the First World War and the 'Red Scare' of 1919.

Part 2: Essays

 Reconstruction

1   Why did white Southerners resent Reconstruction, and to what extent did they manage to undermine the process? (20)

(AQA)

In short, Reconstruction was essentially about the abolition of slavery and the attempts to enfranchise blacks and give them equality with whites. Southern whites who had been used to treating blacks as an inferior people were bound to be resentful, although the initial terms of Reconstruction laid down by Presidents Lincoln and Johnson did not seem too harsh as far as Southern whites were concerned, and resentment at that time was minimal.

Johnson quickly recognised the restored governments in Virginia, Louisiana, Arkansas and Tennessee, indicating he would recognise the other seven if they ratified the 13th Amendment, and held elections for state governments and Congress. He issued a general pardon to those who would take an oath of allegiance, and granted many individual requests for pardons. He even said voting qualifications should be left to the states. Southern voting for prominent ex-Confederates and the Black Codes designed by Southern states to keep blacks 'in their place' infuriated the North, and by 1867 **Presidential Reconstruction** had become Congressional or Radical Reconstruction, dominated by Radical Republicans such as Benjamin Wade and

Thaddeus Stevens. They were wholly committed not just to the emancipation of slaves but to equality for blacks, which included the right to vote and recognition as citizens. For Southern whites accustomed to viewing blacks as inferior this was to be a hard pill to swallow. In addition, the criteria for readmission to the Union were to be made tougher than Lincoln and Johnson had set out, and in 1867, as a result of the First (Military) Reconstruction Act, the South (apart from Tennessee) was divided up into five military districts and run by Union generals who were to ensure elections were conducted fairly. Opponents of the Act vented their frustrations by lynching hundreds of blacks despite the presence of Union soldiers.

Reconstruction Acts between 1867 and 1868 invalidated the state governments recognised by Lincoln and Johnson as well as a number of pardons. For another ten years the military and Republicans ran the South, while thousands of Southern whites were barred from voting and holding office. The Union League often marked ballots for blacks, falsely registered them and stuffed ballot boxes, giving rise to such later interpretations of Reconstruction as those given by Dunning, who labelled the period 'Black Reconstruction', regarding it as undemocratic and dominated by corrupt Radicals who were essentially agents of Northern capitalism. Historians Franklin and Stampp came to regard Reconstruction as lenient for whites in many respects.

It is interesting to note that Northern businessmen moving south after the war were often welcomed initially given the money they brought to invest, but soon became resented as 'carpet-baggers' out to make a profit from Southern misfortune. Southerners who collaborated with Republicans were dubbed 'scalawags' and suffered much abuse. The Southern economy remained in a poor state as blacks often chose to work less hard than they had done under slavery, and even the falling price of cotton in 1872 was blamed on Republican administrations. It is certainly true that the spending of local government increased and there was white resentment towards the work of the Freedmen's Bureau (although it did not exclusively help blacks). Great achievements were made, however, particularly in education, but even this was resented as it gave blacks 'ideas above their station' as far as whites were concerned.

There is no doubt that unscrupulous Northerners took advantage of conditions in the South, and men such as Wade were clearly motivated by the political advantages of enfranchising blacks, but equally there were many men of great integrity among the Republicans, and Thaddeus Stevens' commitment to the black cause was so deep that even in death he was buried in a black cemetery.

Southern whites resented the abolition of slavery in itself, and further resented the 14th Amendment which established that there would be: no compensation for loss of slaves; penalties for any state denying black suffrage; a disqualification of ex-Confederates from office; and black citizenship. The 15th Amendment, which effectively enforced black suffrage, was another much resented measure which also led to black voters outnumbering whites in five Southern states – although only in one state did blacks ever form a majority of the legislature. 'Blue-bellied' Union troops in the South remained as a visible reminder in some areas of the lost war and the dominance of the North over the South.

In many ways Reconstruction was undermined as much by the North as by Southern whites. Many in the North became disappointed with Republican manipulation of blacks and carpet-bag corruption, uneasy about the extent of federal intervention and the use of the military, and came to take the view that blacks at some point must fend for themselves. Animosities towards the South declined over time, while some of the Radicals died or mellowed. The 1872 Amnesty Act restored political rights to all but a few hundred ex-Confederates, and in the same year the Freedmen's Bureau was allowed to lapse. Political scandal in the North distracted attention away from the South, as did the economic depression of 1873. The Civil Rights Act of 1875 guaranteeing equal rights in public places was never enforced, and President Grant became increasingly reluctant to use the Force Acts. Southern Republicanism became divided over issues such as racism and economic and social policy, and its support from the North dwindled. Having said all that, Southern whites did their fair share of undermining as well.

The fact that the Confederacy had lost the war seemed to make little difference to many Southern whites, and from the early days of Reconstruction attempts were made to undermine its effectiveness, usually through intimidation and violence. In 1865, according to Foner, over 2,000 blacks were killed in the Shreveport area of Louisiana alone. Across the South, freedmen were routinely assaulted or murdered if they attempted to leave plantations, as fear of black uprisings haunted the South. The Black Codes were initially an attempt to keep blacks in their place by a series of spurious laws, ostensibly aimed at preserving law and order, but Northerners saw them for what they were and members of Congress acted quickly to override such measures.

Of the covert and less covert paramilitary organisations set up by Southern whites to undermine Reconstruction, the Ku Klux Klan was the best known, although other groups such as the Red Shirts and White League 'policed' elections. At its peak, the Klan had possibly over half a million members, but the Force Acts helped break the Klan during Grant's Presidency.

It was not long however before Southern whites, encouraged by the waning enthusiasm in the North in the 1870s, devised the Mississippi Plan (in 1874) to force all whites into the Democrat party and clubs, and to persuade blacks either not to vote or to vote Democrat. Blacks involved in politics were denied jobs and intimidated. Grant failed to intervene in Mississippi, and the South had effectively been redeemed.

The compromise made in the wake of the disputed 1876 Presidential election was at the expense of blacks in the South and signalled the end of Reconstruction. Southern whites began to consolidate the gains they had been making since the late 1860s in some areas. Alan Farmer ultimately sees Reconstruction as a success for Southern whites, which would imply that it was undermined to a great extent. The **'Jim Crow' laws** which followed soon after would ensure that blacks were treated as second-class citizens in the South for decades to come. Nonetheless, blacks had made great progress in education, church organisation and economic areas, and would continue to do so. After 1877 the ex-Confederate states came under the control of white Redeemers or Bourbons, and, according to Foner, a 'dark night of injustice settled over the South.'

 Big business

2   Assess the impact of big business on the US in the period 1865 to 1890. (20)

(AQA)

The term 'the Gilded Age', taken from a novel by Mark Twain and Charles Warner, has been used to ridicule the materialism and unequal economic growth of the 25 years following the Civil War, a time when the vast majority of people lived in poverty and squalor, while wealthy entrepreneurs amassed huge personal fortunes, when party machines and corruption dominated government and political life, and the power of big business came to threaten enterprise and even democracy. Big business had a huge impact on American life after the Civil War, and can be seen to have affected it in economic, social, political and psychological ways.

As far as the economy was concerned big business turned the US into the foremost industrial power in the world. Trusts, and concentrations of wealth and power, threatened competition with monopolistic practices, stifled individualism with increased mechanisation of production, and intimidated rivals out of the market with predatory pricing and other underhand methods. These ideas were the basis of the first trust formed in 1882, Standard Oil of Ohio. Trusts undoubtedly had a tendency to eliminate weaker competitors, but it could be argued that this created greater stability in the economy, in which companies could thrive without the additional worry about competition and pricing. It did however mean that the whole concept of the free market and competition became something of a sham, not that that worried the likes of the Rockefellers and Carnegies of the 'Gilded Age'. It could be contended that, as Carnegie gave away much of his fortune to worthy causes, the system benefited everyone. However, not all businessmen were so charitable, and the great steel magnate's philanthropic works certainly did not overshadow the unscrupulous dealings of those involved in such scandals as Credit Mobilier or the Erie Railroad.

As businesses grew and cities sprang up around them the social make-up of America began to change. A new business elite emerged alongside wage labourers, many of them immigrants, or the children of immigrants. The speed at which big business grew was too fast to have been achieved with social justice, and government at all levels could not keep up with the social problems that went with the rise of big business and the growth of the cities. Jacob Riis's exposé of the New York slums in 1890 came as a startling revelation to many, previously unaware of 'how the other half lived'. Municipal authorities did what they could to deal with the worst of the overcrowding, disease, poor sanitation, terrible working conditions and crime, which went hand-in-hand with urban growth, but it never seemed to be enough. For example in the first week of July 1877, 139 babies died in Baltimore, where liquid sewage ran through the streets. But it was not just city dwellers affected by the changing economy. The perception among farmers that their interests were being sacrificed to those of big business during the period also grew, and culminated in much successful political agitation, as their incomes fell in real terms and banks continued to foreclose on mortgages. Big business, of course, if it was to expand, needed a continuous supply of unskilled and cheap labour, and this in part came from the immigrants who had come to America before and after the war. In a way, therefore, it can be argued that business stimulated the growth in immigration after the war, and helped to create a more cosmopolitan society, which of course raised many problems of its own.

Politically, big business came to dominate politics, from the bosses at city level (such as William Tweed in New York) to the funding of candidates and even members of the cabinet at federal level. A contemporary magazine, *Forum (16)*, complained about the railway companies securing the nominations of their friends at political conventions and controlling state legislatures. And by 1890 railroad revenue was well over double that of federal government. Milton Goldin has argued that people came to realise that those who sought to control both markets and workers and the legal system might also seek greater political power. Porter has argued that the positive benefits outweighed the threat to democracy but Arnesen used the term 'robber baron' for the men who accumulated such power. The year 1888 held the most corrupt Presidential election in American history, with the Republicans outbidding rivals to win control of both Houses and the McKinley Tariff Act of 1890 was seen as payback time for the Republicans' financial backers. Little wonder that government and the Supreme Court supported big business.

The psychological impact of big business is harder to assess. By 1890 there were still more people living in rural areas than in the cities but the US was a long way from the republic of farmers that Thomas Jefferson had envisaged 100 years earlier. The official closing of the frontier in 1890 was another reason for Americans to question the long-term future. Despite the cities becoming the dominant influence in American society by the end of the nineteenth century, people still mythologised the West and the frontier, and longed for a time and a place (which had probably never existed) when individuals could make a difference.

Big business turned the US into the world's greatest industrial and, ultimately, political power. However, internally it shaped the country to value material progress above all else, and made it economically and socially unequal.

3   (a) **Account for the rapid rise of big business in the 1880s and 1890s.** (30)

    (b) **How far did the power of big business threaten democracy in the US in the period 1890 to 1914?** (60)

(OCR)

Essay plan

Part (a)

Introduction: Stress a range of factors involved and mention some of them.

Para 1: Consider long-term context, e.g. raw materials, laissez-faire government, large supply of cheap unskilled labour, . . .

Para 2: Consider the war as a possible catalyst in terms of large-scale production.

Para 3: Methods of businessmen, e.g. corruption and tendency towards creation of trusts; link to para 4.

Para 4: Look at the role of the railroads

Conclusion: Conclude with long-term and short-term factors, picking out the most significant.

Part (b)

Introduction: Give the line of argument you broadly intend to follow.

Para 1: Consider the amassing of wealth by a small group of people in society and the implications.

Para 2: Examine corruption on a local scale, e.g. city bosses such as William Tweed.

Para 3: Look at power of the railroads and bribery of federal government; perhaps consider the 1888 Presidential election.

Para 4: Examine the tendency of federal government to side with big business against unions.

Para 5: Consider the argument that big business did not threaten democracy greatly, citing the action taken to curb monopoly and influence, e.g. during the 'Progressive age'.

Conclusion: Weigh up extent to which big business threatened democracy.

 ## The West

4 What role did the government play in encouraging westward movement between 1865 and 1890? (20)

(AQA)

The traditional image of rugged individuals, pioneers and wagon trains blazing a trail westwards against the elements and the Indians owes as much to popular fiction, art and cinema as to anything else. That is not to say that the likes of Davy Crockett and Daniel Boone did not exist, but in reality most of the westwards expansion was much less romantic, and was heavily influenced by government intervention and big business, particularly the construction of the railroads and the spread of towns rather than homesteads.

As early as 1850 Congress granted nearly four million acres of public land to help finance the Illinois Central Railroad from Chicago to New Orleans and over the next ten years gave 18 million acres to the railroads. In 1869 the first transcontinental railroad was complete and by 1893 another four transcontinental lines had been built, facilitating settlement, creating new markets for western products, and generally stimulating growth. The government's generosity with public land was not confined to the railroads, and between 1862 and 1900 it gave out 80 million acres of land under the Homestead Act. Much was bought up by speculators, mining and lumber companies, and cattlemen, rather than individuals who often could not afford to buy 160 acres, which in any case was too small a plot by which to make a living on the Great Plains. Potential settlers also lacked the money for seeds, animals and equipment. Later land grants under the 1873 Timber Culture Act and 1877 Desert Land Act tended to further obstruct genuine settlement. The advertising campaigns and the colonising activities of the railroads contributed far more to settlement than the public land policy had, but the government's role was not just about land policy.

One of the key roles performed by the federal government to encourage westwards expansion was the gradual removal of the Plains Indians to reservations, but this was not to be without a fight. In the 1860s all Plains Indians were brought onto reservations in the Black Hills of Dakota and what would later become

Oklahoma. When gold was discovered in the Black Hills in 1875 the government broke its promise to guarantee the areas, and prospectors flooded in. Under the leadership of Sitting Bull and Crazy Horse, Native Americans gathered in Montana. The Seventh Cavalry under George Armstrong Custer was sent to assess the situation, but Custer exceeded his orders and, in 1876, at Little Big Horn, he and his command were wiped out. Nonetheless, the writing was on the wall for the Indians, and it was only a matter of time before superior numbers and resources prevailed. Sitting Bull surrendered in 1881, and in 1886 Geronimo's Apaches were defeated. Organised resistance seemed to be at an end, although there was to be one final chapter at Wounded Knee in 1890, where a Sioux band led by Big Foot on its way to a reservation was gunned down by the Seventh Cavalry, leaving 200 Indians including many women and children dead in the snow.

Government action had played a crucial role in the removal of the Plains tribes but other factors had also conspired against them: the railroads, the electric telegraph, the Winchester repeating rifle, the systematic destruction of the buffalo (over 12 million killed in the 20 years following the war), and white attitudes in general. The final insult to a once proud people was to attempt to convert them to white ways. The Indian Rights Association and National Indian Defense Association in the 1870s and 1880s persuaded the government to break down the tribal structure and to attempt to assimilate Indians. Youngsters were sent to boarding schools, while Indian religions were outlawed, and the 1887 Dawes Act broke up reservation land into individual plots, which allowed land-grabbing by whites. Given the widespread belief in John O'Sullivan's 'manifest destiny' of white Americans to overspread the continent, it is perhaps not surprising that the fate of the Indians was such.

The discovery of precious minerals such as gold, silver and copper (which came into its own with the advent of electricity) may not have been carried out by government, but the government usually helped to open up and expand mining following initial discoveries, and the lone prospector panning for gold was usually very quickly replaced by corporate intervention. Inventions also played their part in westwards expansion. The refrigerator car turned cattle drivers into ranchers, while barbed wire, wells, windmills and better ploughs all had an influence on people deciding to take their chances in the West.

 Immigration and government intervention

5 **(a)** **Assess the changing nature of immigration to the US after the Civil War and the impact it had on American society up to 1890.** (30)

   (b) **To what extent did federal intervention in social and economic areas increase during the years 1865 to 1919?** (60)

(OCR)

(a) Up until the Civil War immigrants to the US had essentially come from Britain, Germany and Ireland and were generally northern and western European in origin. The bulk of Irish immigrants were Catholics and hostility to them had arisen in the 1850s with the upsurge of nativism. In the years following the war however, the pattern of immigration shifted to the countries of southern and eastern Europe, and particularly after 1880 the cities of the east became even more diverse places than they had been before. Millions of immigrants from countries such as Italy, Austria-Hungary, Russia and China came into the country. Five times as many people (over 26 million) came into the country in the 50 years after the war as came in the 50 years before. The so-called 'new immigrants' came to the US for similar reasons to their predecessors, a mixture of religious and political persecution and economic hardship.

The sheer number of immigrants provided a willing and cheap workforce on which American economic prosperity could be based. The immigrants were prepared to work in terrible conditions and to put up with appallingly squalid living conditions. They were also useful when employers wanted to break strikes by existing workers, and were often brought in as blackleg labour, to the strong objections from the unions. A number of Presidents refused to bring in a literacy test for immigrants on the grounds that it measured opportunity rather than ability, and had it been enforced in the past would have excluded hundreds of thousands who had since made a valuable contribution to the economy.

White Anglo-Saxon Protestant America in the 1880s, typified by groups such as the anti-Catholic American Protective Association, made immigrants the scapegoats for the increase in strikes, unemployment, crime and welfare costs, which were in reality the products of industrialisation, urbanisation and a capitalist economy that exploited workers and peaked and troughed seemingly at will. The move towards greater violence in industrial disputes was also blamed on immigrants, with such incidents as the Haymarket Bomb, which implicated German anarchists, confirming suspicions. The 1882 Chinese Exclusion Act reflected a growing resentment on the west coast towards those from the Far East. The constant arrival of immigrants also provided corrupt political machines with willing supporters and voters who could be found jobs in return. The 'Boss' and 'Padrone' systems of the big cities demonstrated a negative impact of immigration, though it could be argued that those newly arrived in America were simply voting in their own interests – which is just what other Americans had always done.

In the short term immigration contributed enormously to American prosperity, became a significant part of the social problems in the US, prompting intervention by the federal government on a far greater scale in the next century, and generally undermined (perhaps permanently) the development of unions. Immigrants also contributed to a diverse and creative culture in the cities of the East.

(b) The period of Reconstruction saw government intervention on an unprecedented level, including the 13th, 14th and 15th Amendments to the Constitution, a series of laws regarding enforcement, the Freedmen's Bureau and the use of a military force of occupation; but by 1877 the experiment seemed to be over, and federal government once again took a back seat. Local governments in the states and the cities were often the first to take action to ensure fairness and better conditions, and it would take Washington a long time to acknowledge that certain issues required direct intervention.

As well as Reconstruction, which essentially applied to the South, the government gave a great deal of support to westwards expansion, granting land and money for internal improvements, encouraging the railroads, and using troops where necessary to put down the threat from Native Americans. In the country as a whole, government intervention can usefully be broken down into the areas of: economic regulation, labour/welfare/consumerism, the environment, finance and repression.

The setting up in 1887 of the Interstate Commerce Commission (ICC) was a landmark for government regulation of the economy, as it established a precedent for the monitoring of big business. Many have argued that it lacked effectiveness with its early rulings being constantly challenged and overturned but nevertheless it was the first independent regulatory agency, and in 1906 and 1910 respectively the Hepburn Act and the Mann-Elkins Act extended the ICC's powers and jurisdiction. Despite the fact that, in the 1880s, 27 states and territories mainly in the South and the West had passed laws prohibiting trusts, trusts often transferred their headquarters to states with more lenient laws such as New Jersey. Nor were states allowed to interfere with interstate commerce. In 1890 therefore the Sherman Anti-Trust Act was passed, ostensibly aimed at curbing the power of the trusts, but later used to penalise trade unions acting in restraint of trade, and frequently successfully challenged by the businesses it hoped to regulate. In fact in many respects the government remained more inclined to support big business than to restrict it, and this was demonstrated when federal troops were sent in to break the Pullman Strike of 1894, although governments argued that they were safeguarding the national interest in such cases. It could sometimes, however, work the other way, as in 1902 when Theodore Roosevelt threatened the mine owners with a federal takeover if they did not talk with the workers. He also resurrected the Sherman Act when he came to office and dissolved the vast Northern Securities Company of J.P. Morgan, as well as using the law against a further 44 corporations. His successor William Taft brought twice as many prosecutions as Roosevelt. Wilson never showed such enthusiasm, however. Nonetheless, during his Presidency the Federal Trade

Commission Act established a Commission to regulate and investigate business practices; and the Clayton Act of 1914 was passed against price discrimination that led to monopoly. The role of government with regard to business was very much one of regulation rather than suppression. At heart, even 'trust-buster' Roosevelt believed big business was good for America.

The period also saw major advances made regarding labour, welfare and consumer issues. The 1890 Dependent Pensions Bill doubled the number of pensioners, while in the same year Jacob Riis's exposé, *How the Other Half Lives*, brought about changes in attitudes towards poverty. The climate of Progressivism influenced landmark measures such as the 1906 Meat Inspection Act and Pure Food and Drug Act aimed at improving conditions of work and the quality of goods produced. The Department of Labor and Federal Children's Bureau were also set up under Taft along with post office savings banks. The 1916 first federal child labour law was created by the Keating-Owen Act, and under Wilson the first federal workmen's compensation laws to cover federal employees was established by the Kern-McGillicuddy Act. The Adamson Act regarding the railways was the first federal law to guarantee workers an eight-hour day.

One of Roosevelt's projects was to prevent private interests exploiting certain natural resources of the country by setting aside vast areas of land for the public. He utilised the 1891 Forest Reserve Act and Newlands Act of 1902 most effectively in spite of having to face quite a lot of opposition from members of Congress.

The government had in the past taken action over such issues as the currency, for example the Sherman Silver Purchase Act of 1890, and for decades of course the tariff had been one of the areas in which the federal government had regularly intervened, usually to raise duties, but in 1913 the Underwood-Simmons Act bucked the trend when it lowered rates. During Wilson's Presidency 12 Federal Reserve Banks were also set up by the government.

Federal government reaction to strike action had at times been repressive but during the First World War measures took on a more sinister tone. In 1917/18 the Espionage, Sabotage and Sedition Acts were passed, and a number of arrests of members of the Industrial Workers of the World (IWW) were made as a result. The Committee on Public Information spread tales of German atrocities and encouraged people to inform on neighbours acting suspiciously. In 1918 over 11,000 people were arrested for criticising either the government or the war effort.

There is no doubt that intervention by the federal government in social and economic areas increased significantly during the years 1865 to 1919. Reconstruction brought with it much activity and set a precedent for future intervention, but did not last beyond 1877. State and city governments often took the lead during the 'Gilded Age' in attempting to redress the economic and social problems the country was experiencing, but gradually, partly due to the influence of Progressivism, those in Washington came to take greater responsibility for the problems that had arisen during industrialisation. Welfare and labour rights still lagged behind Europe by the end of the First World War but great strides had been made in several areas, and precedents had been established for future intervention.

PRACTICE QUESTION

6 **How successfully did the federal government respond to the problems brought by industrialisation and urbanisation between 1870 and 1890?** (20)

(AQA)

Advice: *This question effectively focuses on the so-called 'Gilded Age'. Industrialisation and urbanisation went hand-in-hand in late nineteenth-century America, but brought different problems. It is important to note that the question only expects you to go up to 1890, which means that the impact of Progressivism cannot be included in the answer, and the question also specifies 'federal government' which means that city and state government responses cannot be included in their own right either. Problems could be themed under such headings as political, economic and social, while the general line of the answer should probably be that the federal government did not respond particularly successfully during the period: the violent nature of strikes and the publication of Jacob Riis's* How the Other Half Lives *bearing testament to that.*

7 How far did the power of government increase between 1865 and 1890? (20)

(AQA)

Essay plan

Introduction: Overview of whether power did in fact increase and whether it was permanent.

Para 1: Examine period of Reconstruction in terms of amendments to the Constitution and legislation, and assess whether Reconstruction resulted in a permanent shift in power given its ending in 1877.

Para 2: Examine legislation after 1877 and areas in which the government intervened.

Para 3: Assess whether the Supreme Court curbed the intentions of federal government in any way

Para 4: Analyse role that Presidents played during the period.

Para 5: Look at role played by government at a lower level and whether it suggests federal government was doing relatively little.

Conclusion: The extent to which the power of federal government changed.

PRACTICE QUESTION

8 'The US had become a more democratic country by 1890 than it had been in 1840.' Discuss. (20)

(AQA)

Advice: To answer this question well it is necessary at some point to define the term democracy by discussing such issues as liberty, equality, individual rights, etc. The question is a broad one and an answer could cover: the experiences of a range of groups in the US, including African Americans, women, Native Americans, ethnic groups such as Irish Catholics and the Chinese; Constitutional/legal definitions linked to democracy; the impact of big business on politics; the economic inequalities in the country; and the extension of government intervention.

 Labour and Populism

9 (a) What were the causes of Populism? (30)

(b) Account for the failure of the labour movement to achieve greater gains more quickly towards the end of the nineteenth century. (60)

(OCR)

(a) After the Civil War farmers in America suffered from declining status, but this was within an international context of overproduction that particularly hit wheat farmers and cotton planters because of their overseas markets. In 1867 the first national farmers' organisation, the National Grange of the Patrons of Husbandry, was set up with essentially social, cooperational and educational aims, although motivation gradually became more political.

The Granger movement raised issues linked to railroad regulation, which it clearly felt was not strong enough. Populists resented the emphasis placed on property rights, the unfairness of business monopoly, Social Darwinism and laissez-faire, and the uneven distribution of wealth in general. Farmers believed they were being sacrificed to keep the US on the gold standard as a result of the influence of London bankers, especially the Rothschilds (there was even an anti-Semitic element in later years).

The increased mechanisation of agriculture had led to great efficiency gains but also brought problems for independent farmers in terms of actually being able to afford machines and repairs. There had been a growth in specialisation of farm products, but most farmers had stuck to traditional crops, and often invested everything in monoculture. After the war there was an increase in agricultural exports, leaving farmers open to exploitation as markets came to depend on factors beyond their control, for example: business cycles, credit, transport, labour supply, price structure and government policies. As new agricultural lands became available, the price of land went up but crop prices fell, and the farmers had to mortgage property to put more land under cultivation. In the 1870s and 1880s there was unusually high rainfall which helped the farmers in the short term, but big business and bankers charged farmers very high interest on their mortgages, and when drought struck the mid-west in 1886 it was disastrous.

The fact that Populism actually manifested itself in three main groupings would suggest that motives varied from region to region, but in 1892 the Farmers' and Laborers' Union of America (from the southwest, with three million members by 1890), the Northwest Farmers' Alliance (from the mid-west, with two million members by 1890) and the Colored Farmers National Alliance (from the South and mid-west, with a membership of 1–1.5 million by 1890) held a joint convention, setting out a number of demands: the permanent union of all working classes; wealth for the workers; government ownership of rail; government ownership of all communications systems; a more flexible and fairer distribution of the national currency; low interest loans; free and unlimited coinage of silver; no more ownership of land by those who did not actually use it; the secret ballot, initiative, referendum, recall and directive; a shorter working day; and immigration restrictions. In short a platform that endorsed greater government intervention in the economy, major financial changes tending towards inflation, and a number of progressive political ideas that would enhance democracy within the country. Within 20 years some of the Populists' less radical demands became law: the secret ballot, a graduated income tax and the direct elections of senators.

(b) In broad terms the problems which held back the progress of the labour movement in the United States consisted of: internal divisions and the problems of unifying labour; general opposition from the government, the courts and employers; and the widespread perception that unions were somehow un-American.

Immigration, which provided such a huge number of workers for the economy, kept wages down. Workers from abroad were often unskilled, which diluted their bargaining power, while religious, language and cultural divisions tended to work against those from different national and ethnic groups coming together to form unions. Workers also often felt that jobs would be temporary. Immigrants and blacks both tended to be unpopular among longer-established groups because they were often used by employers to break strikes. Immigrants were not the only group which found it difficult to either set up or join unions. Women were often refused membership, as were blacks, and skilled unions would not admit unskilled labourers. There were, however, despite the sheer size and diversity of the workforce, attempts to form national unions through confederations of different unions. In 1866 William Sylvis founded the National Labor Union, but unfortunately most of its leaders were more concerned with long-term political, economic and social reform than the immediate problems of the workers, and the movement lasted for only six years. Leadership could often be a problem in terms of individual personalities and also aims. Middle-class leaders tended to prioritise voting rights and free education, and the abolition of imprisonment for debt, over the bread-and-butter issues that were important to workers. Nor did the economic situation help, with membership declining steeply during the Depression of the 1870s.

In the 1880s Terence Powderly's Knights of Labor became the dominant labour organisation incorporating blacks, farmers, skilled and unskilled workers, and women. By 1886 it embraced 700,000 working people, but it had also attracted too many radical allies such as the Socialist Labor Party and various anarchist groups. By 1890 membership of the Knights of Labor had declined to 100,000, and within a few years it had ceased to function. In 1886 the American Federation of Labor was set up by Samuel Gompers and it was able to fill the gap left by the Knights. It was a loose federation of national trade unions (excepting the four railway brotherhoods), but it was less political than the Knights, concentrating on skilled workers and sticking to wages, hours and conditions, accepting the existing economic system and rejecting ideas for a separate Labor Party.

A major reason for the slow progress of unions in the late nineteenth century was that the employers were invariably hostile to unions and equally invariably the authorities sided with the employers, and this seems to have been particularly the case in the US. In the 1870s Pinkerton detectives were called in by mine owners in Pennsylvania to infiltrate 'the Molly Maguires', a militant secretive labour organisation, resulting in the execution of nine ringleaders in 1876 following a campaign of violence against the mine companies.

In the Great Railroad Strike of 1877, 25 men were killed in a fight with the state militia, and federal troops were eventually sent in. In 1887 a strike for higher wages on a Louisiana sugar plantation led to the massacre of over 100 blacks by the militia and white vigilantes. Four years later 15 leaders of an Arkansas cotton pickers' strike were killed, including 9 lynched after they had been arrested. And during the 1894 Pullman Strike, federal troops were sent to Chicago and a federal injunction was taken out (based on the Sherman Anti-Trust Act) forbidding the union to continue its strike.

Presidents remained generally unsympathetic towards labour until the 1900s and public attitudes were adversely influenced by the violence connected to strikes. There might often be support initially when strikes started peacefully, but once violence crept in public support tended to shift away from the strikers: for example, during the Homestead Steel Strike, especially after the attempt by an anarchist to kill plant manager Henry Frick. The Haymarket Bomb of 1886 was also linked to labour agitation. Union membership remained extremely low in comparison to countries such as Great Britain during the same period, and the ethos prevailed that there was somehow something un-American about joining a union, something that went against the grain of 'rugged individualism' and self-sufficiency.

 Progressivism

10 (a) Explain the origins of Progressivism. (30)

(b) To what extent did Roosevelt prove to be a more progressive President than Taft or Wilson? (60)

(OCR)

(a) Prior to the 1950s most historians agreed that Progressivism was a movement by the people to curb the power of special interest groups, but during that decade writers argued that Progressive leaders certainly in some areas tended to be from a privileged elite who were suffering either a loss of economic or psychological status against the rise of big business. Gabriel Kolko in the 1960s argued that Progressivism was actually used by business leaders to protect themselves against competition, while others saw it as businesses and the professional middle classes wanting to bring order and efficiency to the political and economic life of the country. In 1981 Richard McCormick argued that during the Progressive era pressure groups came to the fore as political parties went into decline. Ultimately Progressivism was very diverse, which is why it has attracted a range of interpretations.

Back in 1881 Henry Demarest Lloyd exposed Standard Oil in *The Atlantic Monthly*, and this can be seen as a sign of a growing collective will to tackle the problems of an urbanised and industrialised society which included: corruption in politics, Prohibition, votes for women, local government reform, working conditions, child labour, regulation of the economy, public health, housing, crime (in the 1880s the murder rate quadrupled) and conservation.

It certainly seems that Progressivism originated with mainly well-educated middle-class urban dwellers and crossed party boundaries. Progressives saw the problems of trusts and monopolistic practices, but recoiled from violent strikes, and had concerns about the impact of immigration, which they may have felt damaged the cohesion of society. It seems likely that they saw issues in moral terms rather than in a cynical light connected to loss of status in a changing world. Particular stimuli, such as Jacob Riis's *How the Other Half Lives*, played their part in inspiring Progressivism, but the movement was diverse and had a number of motives behind it, which were not always obviously connected.

(b) In 1902 miners strike arbitrators awarded strikers a 10 per cent wage increase and a nine-hour day. Theodore Roosevelt threatened government intervention if the mine owners did not come to terms. In the same year he shocked the business world by using the Sherman Anti-Trust Act to dissolve J.P. Morgan's Northern Securities holding company. In spite of this, Roosevelt's rhetoric was often more radical than his actions, and he preferred regulation to trust-busting essentially believing that big business was in the national interest. Accordingly in 1903 he set up the Bureau of Corporations to investigate trust abuses, and proceeded to use the Sherman Act against 44 corporations – although more trusts were actually set up under Roosevelt than had been under McKinley. However, Taft's 'trust-busting' credentials are, on paper at least, more impressive than Roosevelt's. He pursued twice as many anti-trust suits in four years as his predecessor had in seven. In addition, Roosevelt's second term was in some ways less impressive than his first, but the Hepburn Act allowed for greater railroad regulation and extended the powers of the ICC. The Meat Inspection Act and Pure Food and Drug Act were also landmark measures. The Newlands Act of 1902 permitted land reclamation and the irrigation of millions of acres of western land, while the 1891 Forest Reserve Act was used to protect 150 million acres of forest land. Before standing down as President he called for a more widespread eight-hour day, income tax, death duties, a limit on the use of injunctions in strikes, federal supervision of the stock market and workmen's compensation laws. Roosevelt was certainly not against capitalism but he did see the social problems such a system brought with it. He also remained acutely worried about the rise of socialism in the face of the reluctance of big business to reform itself, and the implications this might have for society. Having said that, some of Roosevelt's actions were genuinely progressive.

Taft, although effectively nominated by Roosevelt as his successor, was altogether a more conservative figure, but nonetheless included GEC and US Steel among his prosecutions. During his leadership the Republicans split on the tariff and other issues, with the conservatives (or 'standpatters') favoured by Taft taking on the insurgents (or Progressives) who were against a high tariff. Despite such internal acrimony, the 1910 Mann-Elkins Act extended the jurisdiction of the ICC, and post office savings banks, a Department of Labor and Federal Children's Bureau, an eight-hour day for federal workers, safety legislation for miners, the 16th Amendment for income tax and 17th Amendment for the direct election of senators were all established. Ultimately, however, Taft sided with the old guard which controlled the party machine, and annoyed many by signing the Payne-Aldrich Tariff Bill, and reopening water sites to public entry, which undermined his Progressive credentials. They also led to big Republican losses in the mid-terms of 1910.

Among the measures passed during Wilson's administration were the 1913 Underwood-Simmons Tariff Act, which actually, and unusually, cut duties, the creation of a more flexible currency, as well as the creation of 12 Federal Reserve Banks, the Federal Trade Commission Act, which established a commission to regulate and investigate business practices, and the 1914 Clayton Act against price discrimination that led to monopoly. By the autumn of 1914 Wilson seemed to think the reforms of the 'New Freedom' were basically completed. Subsequently he did not support female suffrage, he condoned reimposition of segregation in the agencies of the federal government in contrast to Roosevelt, and he refused further reforms as either being unnecessary or unconstitutional. In the 1914 Congressional elections the Democrats suffered major losses, and by the end of 1915 a second set of reforms was on its way. The fact that Wilson needed the stimulus of electoral defeats to prompt him into further action raises a question mark about his progressive nature. He also seemed to lose interest in the Clayton Act and did little to protect it from conservative attack. Neither did he really pursue monopolies with any great zest. Wilson's repressive nature was revealed during the First World War after his narrow re-election in 1916; and his refusal to help the National Association for the Advancement of Colored People (NAACP) in its campaign against lynching also shows him in a bad light, even though he did push through the first federal laws regarding workmen's compensation and child labour, an eight-hour day for railway workers, and he also encouraged female suffrage campaigners.

On balance Roosevelt was probably the most progressive President of the three, and he stood out on environmental issues. Taft sided with the conservatives ultimately, and Wilson's failure to back certain causes or to push for further reform until he realised votes were at stake, must go against him. However Progressive the three Presidents were, they did not solve the problem of monopoly, reduce inequality, remove 'boss rule' or political corruption, nor did they raise social welfare to European levels, and big business would make a big comeback during the less idealistic 1920s.

PRACTICE ESSAY

11 (a) **How far was President Wilson a reluctant Progressive?** (30)

  (b) **'In practice more conservative than in theory.' Discuss this view of Progressivism.** (60)

(OCR)

Advice: *For Part (a) a balanced answer is required that weighs up the evidence suggesting Wilson was whole-heartedly committed to Progressive reform against his apparent waning enthusiasm for reform by the autumn of 1914. For Part (b) a very good understanding of the issues linked to Progressivism is needed as well as a grasp of the historiography. The motives of Progressives need to be understood, as well as the essential reluctance of 'Progressive Presidents' to interfere with big business.*

Part 3: Sources

1 Big business and Progressivism

■ **Source A: F.B. Tracy, 'Why the Farmers Revolted', *Forum* 16 (October 1893), pp. 242–3**

Nothing has done more to injure the [western] region than these freight rates . . . The extortionate character of the freight rates has been recognised by all parties . . . Another fact which has incited the farmer against corporations is the bold and unblushing participation of the railways in politics. At every political convention their emissaries are present with blandishments and passes and other practical arguments to secure the nomination of their friends . . . By these means, the railroads have secured an iron grip upon legislatures . . .

■ **Source B: Robert La Follette, 1908**

1898 was the beginning of great industrial organization . . . Within a period of three years following, 149 such reorganizations were effected with total stock and bond capitalization of $3,784,000,000 . . . The success of these [re-]organizations led quickly on to a consolidation of combined industries, until a mere handful of men controlled the industrial production of the country . . .

No student of the economic changes in recent years can escape the conclusion that the railroads, telegraphs, shipping, cable, telephone, traction, express, mining, iron, steel, coal, oil, gas, electric light, cotton, copper, sugar, tobacco, agricultural implements and the food products are completely controlled and mainly owned by these hundred men ... With this enormous concentration of business it is possible to create, artificially, periods of prosperity and periods of panic. Prices can be lowered or advanced at the will of the 'System'.

■ Source C: Theodore Roosevelt

The effort to restore competition as it was sixty years ago, and to trust for justice solely to this proposed restoration of competition, is just as foolish as if we should go back to the flintlocks of Washington's continentals as a substitute for modern weapons of precision ... Our purpose should be, not to strangle business as an incident of strangling combinations, but to regulate big corporations in a thoroughgoing and effective fashion, so as to help legitimate business as an incident to thoroughly and completely safeguarding the interests of the people as a whole.

■ Source D: Ruling of the Supreme Court on Eugene Debs and the Pullman Strike, David Brewer, 1895

It is obvious that while it is not the province of the government to interfere in any mere matter of private controversy between individuals, or to use its great powers to enforce the rights of one against another, yet, whenever the wrongs complained of are such as affect the public at large, and are in respect of matters which by the Constitution are entrusted to the care of the nation, and concerning which the nation owes the duty to all the citizens of securing to them their common rights, then the mere fact that the government has no pecuniary interest in the controversy is not sufficient to exclude it from the courts or prevent it from taking measures therein to fully discharge those constitutional duties.

The national government, given by the Constitution power to regulate interstate commerce, has by express statute assumed jurisdiction over such commerce when carried upon railroads. It is charged, therefore, with the duty of keeping those highways of interstate commerce free from obstruction, for it has always been recognized as one of the powers and duties of a government to remove obstructions from the highways under its control.

OCR QUESTION FORMAT

The questions and answers that follow are based on the OCR style.

(a) **Study Source C. From this Source and your own knowledge explain what Roosevelt means when he says he wants to 'regulate big business'.** (20)

(b) **Study Sources C and D. How far does the view of the Supreme Court in Source D support Roosevelt's views on the regulation of big business in Source C?** (40)

(c) **Study all the Sources. Using all these Sources and your own knowledge explain how far you agree that all branches of federal government were generally supportive of big business in the late nineteenth and early twentieth centuries.** (60)

(a) Roosevelt means that he believes federal government should monitor and generally 'keep an eye' on the practices of trusts and corporations, rather than simply allowing the 'free market' to operate. He sees regulation as a way of making business fairer and 'completely safeguarding the interests of the people as a whole', without stifling business, which he broadly thinks is in everyone's interest. He feels that regulation is the way forward rather than attempting to turn back the clock and likens it to exchanging effective modern weapons for the outdated 'flintlocks of Washington's continentals.'

(b) The Supreme Court verdict in Source C supports Roosevelt's views that big business should be regulated rather than 'strangled' in the sense that it does not believe the government should 'interfere in any mere controversy between individuals', and also asserts that 'whenever the wrongs complained of . . . affect the public at large' the government effectively has a duty to act in the public interest even though there may be no financial advantage to be gained by the government. It upholds the government's right to 'regulate interstate commerce', but goes further than Roosevelt by also advocating the government's right to act against strikes (i.e. against the workers as well) if the interest of the public as a whole is threatened, as was judged the case in the Pullman Strike.

(c) Theodore Roosevelt developed the reputation of being a 'trust-buster' but in reality his rhetoric often spoke louder than his actions. In other words he tended only to prosecute big business when it seemed to be acting in a detrimental way, creating monopolies, stifling competition, or acting against the general interests of society. He was certainly not against big business per se and emphasises in Source C how he does not wish to 'strangle business', but to safeguard the interests of the people as a whole by preventing abuses from taking place within the system.

Roosevelt's predecessors in the White House had taken a much more non-interventionist line regarding big business, but Roosevelt could see divisions emerging within society if government did not remedy problems, the rise of socialism being something that concerned him in particular. Source A provides evidence of opposition from the farmers towards the railroads over such issues as the 'extortionate character of the freight rates' and the 'unblushing participation of the railways in politics'. Source B highlights progressive concerns about the economic power concentrated with 'a mere handful of men'. Roosevelt obviously shared the same concerns when he prosecuted Morgan's great Northern Securities holding company. The fact that Roosevelt was behaving differently from his predecessors is illustrated by Morgan's shock that the President had not contacted him for a friendly chat 'to sort things out' prior to prosecution.

If anything, the Supreme Court was more conservative than even the Presidents in protecting the rights of big business. Early prosecutions using the Sherman Anti-Trust Act and the Interstate Commerce Act were thrown out by the Supreme Court, but Roosevelt's resurrection of the Sherman Act proved successful, with 44 corporations prosecuted. It is worth noting however that more trusts were set up during Roosevelt's time in office than had been under McKinley who was regarded as something of a 'corporate lapdog', emphasising the point that even Roosevelt was broadly supportive of big business. The Supreme Court's decision in Source D to grant an injunction against the Pullman Strike demonstrates judicial determination not to allow the unions to hold the country to ransom or to obstruct 'interstate commerce', and this tended to be supported by Presidential decisions to send in troops to put down such conflicts as the Great Railroad Strike of 1877 and the Pullman Strike in 1894.

As far as Congress was concerned there was generally a sympathy with big business, with the election of 1888 regarded as the most corrupt in American history. The Republicans effectively outbid the Democrats to win control of both Houses of the 'Billion Dollar Congress'; the passage of the McKinley Tariff Act, which raised duties to an extremely high level as well as extending the number of products covered, was regarded as a payback for the industrialists who had bankrolled the party. It was little wonder, then, that anti-business laws were few and far between.

Broadly speaking all branches of federal government were generally supportive of big business in the late nineteenth and early twentieth centuries, although their consciences had been stirred during the 1890s, and Progressive reforms over the next 20 years or so alleviated some of the worst problems big business brought with it. Even so, the odds remained heavily stacked in favour of business and heavily stacked against the workers.

ADDITIONAL QUESTIONS IN THE OCR STYLE

(a) **Study Source D. Explain the term 'interstate commerce' as used in Source D.** (20)

(b) **Study Sources A and B. How far does Source A support the fears expressed about big business in Source B?** (40)

(c) **Study all the Sources. Using all these Sources and your own knowledge explain the extent to which big business threatened liberty and democratic institutions in the US in the late nineteenth and early twentieth centuries.** (60)

2 Immigration

■ **Source A: Francis A. Walker, 'Restriction of Immigration',** *Atlantic Monthly* **June, vol . 77, no. 464 (1896), pp. 822–3**

The question today is, not of preventing the wards of our almshouses, our insane asylums, and our jails from being stuffed to repletion by new arrivals from Europe; but of protecting the American rate of wages, the American standard of living, and the quality of American citizenship from degradation through the . . . peasants from the countries of eastern and southern Europe.

■ **Source B: John Mitchell,** *Immigration and the Living Wage* **(1913)**

Formerly, the great majority of immigrants came from England, Ireland, Germany, and the Scandinavian countries, from countries, in other words, where conditions of life and labour were, to some extent, comparable to those of the United States. At the present time, the source of immigration shifted from northern and western to eastern and southern Europe, and from men with a higher to men with a lower standard of living. The illiteracy of the immigrant has become more pronounced. This illiteracy, amounting in some cases to sixty-five to seventy-five per cent, debars the newly arrived immigrant from many trades, makes it more difficult for him to adapt himself to American conditions and American manners of thought, and renders it almost inevitable that he fall into the hands of the sweater and exploiter. The practically unrestricted immigration of the present day is an injustice both to the American workingman, whether native or foreign-born, and to the newly landed immigrant himself. As a result of this practically unrestricted and unregulated immigration, the congestion of our large cities is so intense as to create abnormally unhealthy conditions. The average immigrant from eastern and southern Europe brings with him from eight to ten dollars, which is about the railroad fare from New York to Pittsburgh and is hardly sufficient to support him for two weeks. It is inevitable, also, that he remain where he lands and take the work offered him on the spot.

■ **Source C: Dr Charles Benedict Davenport,** *Heredity in Relation to Eugenics* **(1911)**

. . . the population of the United States will, on account of the great influx of blood from South-eastern Europe, rapidly become darker in pigmentation, smaller in stature, more mercurial, more attached to music and art, [and] more given to crimes of larceny, kidnapping, assault, murder, rape and sex-immorality . . . [and] the ratio of insanity in the population will rapidly increase.

■ **Source D: President Cleveland objecting to the literacy clause of the proposed Immigration Act (March 1897)**

A radical departure from our national policy relating to immigrants is here presented. Heretofore we have welcomed all who come to us from other lands except those whose moral condition or history threatened danger to our national welfare and safety. We have encouraged those coming from foreign countries to cast their lot with us and join in the development of our vast domain, securing in return a share in the blessings of American citizenship.

A century's stupendous growth, largely due to the assimilation and thrift of millions of sturdy and patriotic adopted citizens attests the success of this generous and free-handed policy which, while guarding the people's interests, exacts from our immigrants only physical soundness and moral soundness and a willingness and ability to work.

OCR QUESTION FORMAT

The questions and answers that follow are based on the OCR style.

(a) **Study Source B. From this Source and your own knowledge explain why immigrants from 'eastern and southern Europe' appear to be a problem.** (20)

(b) **Study Sources A and B. How far does Source A support the fears expressed in Source B?** (40)

(c) **Study all the Sources. Using all these Sources and your own knowledge explain how far immigration in the late nineteenth and early twentieth centuries posed a serious problem for the US federal government.** (60)

(a) John Mitchell, leader of the mineworkers, initially suggests that the earlier immigrants came from places such as England, Ireland, Germany and Scandinavia, 'where conditions of life and labour were, to some extent' like those in the United States. The implication of this statement becomes apparent when he goes on to discuss the poorer and less literate immigrants from eastern and southern Europe, who because they are unable to read or write cannot do certain jobs, will find it 'more difficult to adapt . . . to American conditions and . . . manners' and could well find themselves exploited. In other words the new immigrants themselves will face problems. Mitchell however then goes on to point out the problem immigration poses to workers already living in America as well as the new immigrants, by citing the overcrowding and 'abnormally unhealthy conditions' in the cities. Finally he seems to come back to the new immigrants specifically, worrying that most are so poor they will simply ending up taking the first jobs they can get. As a union leader himself, Mitchell would also have been acutely aware of how difficult it was to organise workers from a diversity of cultural backgrounds, and how the constant stream of immigration had a downward effect on wages, with new arrivals being prepared to work for low wages and to break strikes.

Although Mitchell does refer to the poverty of the immigrants, their illiteracy, and difficulties fitting in, there is certainly no overt reference to any sort of racial inferiority, or linking of immigrants to crime, which was made by many at the time.

(b) In Source A, one suspects that Francis Walker, by drawing attention to the fact that he does not believe the main question is to do with new immigrants becoming a welfare burden, is actually intending to draw attention to exactly that issue. He does however go on to suggest that the real issue is 'protecting the American rate of wages . . . standard of living . . . and quality of American citizenship from degradation through . . . peasants' from eastern and southern Europe. He therefore does not support Mitchell to any great extent, because Mitchell actually appears more genuinely concerned for the immigrants than people already living in America.

Walker is clearly most worried about the impact the immigrants will have on others, and whereas Walker suggests that poverty is not the main question, Mitchell obviously believes that the fact that 'the average immigrant brings . . . from eight to ten dollars' is a problem. Terms Walker uses such as 'degradation' regarding citizenship, and 'peasants', have overtones of racial superiority, which are not present in Mitchell's piece at all. Walker's sentiment only really support Mitchell's fears in the sense that he fears for standards of living. Mitchell's concerns about congestion in the cities is clearly linked to living standards.

(c) Immigration posed a problem for federal government in many respects, and many related issues are covered in the Sources. The sheer scale of immigration was a problem in itself with something like 26 million immigrants arriving between 1865 and 1915, mainly crowding into cities that were already struggling to cope with the problems of industrialisation and urbanisation. John Mitchell in Source B highlights the 'congestion' in the cities and 'abnormally unhealthy conditions'. These problems of squalor in living and working conditions were undoubtedly a result of the pace of industrialisation but immigration made the situation worse, and hastened the Progressive reforms of the early nineteenth century. Some of the worst working conditions tended to be in occupations where immigrants formed the bulk of the workforce such as in the Colorado coalfields and urban garment factories.

One of the main problems faced by government was nativist and racist sentiment felt towards immigrants by those Americans who had lived in the US for a longer period. Francis Walker in Source A alludes to this with his talk of 'degradation' of citizenship, while in Source C Davenport uses racially-charged language to suggest that new immigrants will bring with them a tendency to 'larceny, kidnapping, assault, murder, rape and sex-immorality' as well increasing 'insanity in the population'. He also refers specifically to a rapid change in skin pigment of the people. Incidents such as the Haymarket Bomb, which was linked to German anarchists, did give the government cause for concern, as did rising crime rates in the cities in areas of immigrant population, but as stated above, these could be regarded as problems linked to industrialisation rather than immigration specifically. However the government did bow to nativist pressure at times, passing such measures as the 1882 Chinese Exclusion Act, and setting up commissions in response to groups such as the Immigration Restriction League, but Presidents Cleveland, Taft and Wilson all vetoed literacy tests for new arrivals.

In other respects the federal government recognised the benefits that immigrants brought. Cleveland in Source D clearly felt that American prosperity had been largely based on the 'assimilation and thrift of millions' of immigrants, and although men like John Mitchell might have concerns about immigrants holding back the labour movement and keeping down wages, federal government would have had no such qualms. The fact that huge numbers continued to pour in, despite various Immigration Acts putting slight restrictions on those arriving during the period, suggests that the federal government did not really view immigration as a serious problem, and in many ways regarded it as a great benefit.

ADDITIONAL QUESTIONS IN THE OCR STYLE

(a) **Study Source A. From this Source and your own knowledge explain why Walker in Source A feared that immigrants would endanger American wages, the standard of living and quality of citizenship.** (20)

(b) **Study Sources C and D. How far does Source D contradict the views expressed in Source C?** (40)

(c) **Study all the Sources. Using all these Sources and your own knowledge explain how far supporters of immigration restriction were motivated by nativist and racist sentiment.** (60)

Part 4: Historical skills

 ## 1 Robber barons or captains of industry?

Using the Spartacus Educational website and any other sources you wish, one half of the group puts together evidence that businessmen in late nineteenth-century America were 'robber barons' who feathered their own nests using unscrupulous methods, while the other half looks for evidence that they deserved the title 'captains of industry' for their enterprise and the benefits they brought to the country. Some of the men worthy of investigation include: Andrew Carnegie, Henry Ford, William Vanderbilt, J.P. Morgan, John D. Rockefeller and William Tweed.

 ## 2 The themes of Progressive legislation

When writing an essay a straight chronological approach to events rarely works, and it is often far more effective to adopt a thematic approach. Using the chronology at the start of this chapter, and taking the Progressive laws from 1890 onwards, try to construct a series of themes or categories under which all the reforms could be organised. This could be displayed as a spider diagram using different colours for different types of legislation.

Sources and references

Alan Brinkley, *The Unfinished Nation*, McGraw-Hill (2000).

Vincent P. De Santis, *The Shaping of Modern America 1977–1920*, Harlan Davidson (2000).

Charles W. Eagles, *America, A Narrative History*, Norton (1999).

Alan Farmer, *Reconstruction and the Results of the American Civil War 1865–1877*, Hodder & Stoughton (1997).

Alan Farmer and Vivienne Sanders, *American History, 1860–1990*, Hodder & Stoughton (2002).

Eric Foner, *Reconstruction – America's Unfinished Revolution 1863–1877*, Harper & Row (1984).

Glenda Gilmore (ed.), *Who Were the Progressives?*, Bedford (2002).

Milton Goldin, 'The Gospel of Andrew Carnegie', *History Today*, June (1988).

Lewis L. Gould, *America in the Progressive Era 1890–1914*, Longman (2001).

Maldwyn Jones, *The Limits of Liberty*, Oxford University Press (1983/1995).

John M. Murrin, Paul E. Johnson, James M. McPherson *et al.*, *Liberty Equality Power*, Harcourt (2001).

Celia O'Leary, 'Americans All: Reforging a National Brotherhood, 1876–1917', *History Today*, October (1994).

David Paterson, Susan Willoughby, Doug Willoughby, *Civil Rights in the USA 1863–1980*, Heinemann (2001).

Hugh Tulloch, *The Debate on the American Civil War Era*, Manchester University Press (1999).

Margaret Walsh, 'New Horizons for the American West', *History Today*, March (1994).

Margaret Walsh, 'Frederick Jackson Turner and the American Frontier' (n.d.).

Howard Zinn, *A People's History of the United States*, Longman (1996).

Chapter 6

Boom and Bust: Economy and Society, 1919–1933

This chapter will assess the impact of the Bolshevik Revolution on the US and the economic, social and political development of the nation through the 'boom and bust' years of the 1920s.

 Historical background

Introduction
The 'Red Scare' of 1919
Sacco and Vanzetti
The Ku Klux Klan
The 'Monkey Trial'
Immigration
Prohibition and organised crime
Politics in the 1920s
The boom of the 1920s
The 'crash' and causes of the
    Great Depression
The Depression and attempts to deal
    with it

Prohibition
Causes of the Depression

 Sources

1   Society in the 1920s
2   Boom and bust

 Historical skills

1   Report on immigration
2   Were Sacco and Vanzetti guilty?

 Essays

The boom
Xenophobia and racism

Chronology

1919	18th Amendment ratified (Prohibition)
	Police strike in Boston
	Race riots in Chicago and other cities
	Steel strike
	Volstead Act over Wilson's veto enforcing 18th Amendment
1920	19th Amendment ratified (Female suffrage)
	Palmer Raids and the 'Red Scare'
	Sacco and Vanzetti convicted of murder
	Harding elected President
1921	Emergency Quota (Immigration Restriction) Act
1922	Fordney-McCumber Tariff Act
1923	Harding died in office – Calvin Coolidge became President
1924	Coolidge elected President in own right
	Immigration Restriction Act
1925	Scopes Trial
1926	Revenue Act cut taxes
1927	Sacco and Vanzetti executed
1928	Herbert Hoover elected President
1929	Wall Street crash on 'Black Tuesday'
	Agricultural Marketing Act
1930	Hawley-Smoot Tariff Act
	Drought began in Dust Bowl
1931	Reconstruction Finance Corporation established
	Bonus Army marched on Washington
1932	Franklin D. Roosevelt elected President

Part 1: Historical background

 Introduction

Despite America's late entry to the First World War, it lost 112,000 men, and although this number was relatively low compared with those of other countries involved it had a huge psychological effect on the country, and seemed to confirm to many that America should have remained neutral. The war had also brought about restrictions of American liberties, with the Espionage Act of 1917 and Sedition Act of 1918 basically stopping public criticism of government. Washington had also stirred up anti-German feeling to dangerous levels, and with it came a patriotism that had further implications for free speech. There can be little doubt that some of the less pleasant trends of the 1920s, such as xenophobia, emphasis on '100 per cent Americanism', and an almost paranoid fear of left-wing ideas were partly a result of the war and the feelings it engendered. Race riots also increased between 1917 and 1919, partly as a result of hundreds of thousands of blacks moving to Northern cities during the war, and, as unemployment increased after the war, tensions between whites and blacks and immigrants simmered.

Contemporaries liked to refer to the 1920s as 'the New Era', an age in which the US was becoming a modern nation. To a large extent this was true, but as well as being a decade of materialistic gain, it was also a period of disillusion, intolerance and inequality.

The 'Red Scare' of 1919

During the war there was much hostility shown towards the German-Americans, and with the Bolshevik Revolution of 1917, a xenophobic mood was set for the immediate post-war years. There was great suspicion of the motives of American communists and socialists, many of whom were foreign-born, and when in 1919 industrial unrest (which included a police strike in Boston and a walkout of 100,000 workers in Seattle for five days) tainted by violence broke out across the country fears multiplied. In April, a number of bombs in the mail of prominent capitalists such as J.D. Rockefeller and J.P. Morgan Jr and senior government officials were discovered. In June bombs exploded in eight cities, including one outside the home of Attorney-General Mitchell Palmer – which gave him the perfect excuse to further his Presidential ambitions by authorising a series of raids on left-wing groups. During the so-called 'Palmer Raids' in December 1919 and January 1920 the Justice Department (depending on the historian and source) arrested between 1,000 and 10,000 people who were held without trial, and uncovered the paltry sum of three pistols. Over 500 radicals were deported to Russia, and in New York five elected members of the State Assembly were disqualified from taking their seats because they were socialists. A number of explosions took place soon after, including one at the House of Morgan Bank on Wall Street, which killed 30 people. In November 1920 one million people voted for Eugene Debs' Socialist Party. Also in 1920 Andrea Salsedo, an anarchist, was arrested, held for eight weeks, and not permitted contact with his family or a lawyer. His body was subsequently found 14 floors below where he had been held by the FBI. The verdict was suicide. Many of his associates began to carry guns as result, including two men, Nicola Sacco and Bartolomeo Vanzetti.

 Sacco and Vanzetti

During a raid in South Braintree, Massachusetts, a paymaster and factory guard were murdered and $15,000 stolen. Two Italian immigrants Nicola Sacco and Bartolomeo Vanzetti, anarchists and draft dodgers, were arrested despite very little evidence against them. The trial judge made it fairly clear what he thought of the two men and in July 1921 they were sentenced to death. Much debate over their guilt followed during the subsequent years with many claiming the trial had been a travesty, until in August 1927, amid international outcry, they were both electrocuted.

 The Ku Klux Klan

The mood of post-war America was also reflected in the resurgence of the Ku Klux Klan (KKK), as 'Wasp' (white Anglo-Saxon Protestant) small-town mentality attempted to reassert itself. The Chicago race riots of July 1919, which left 23 blacks and 15 whites dead and 537 people wounded, had been sparked off by a black teenager drifting towards a 'whites only' beach on Lake Michigan. Similar but smaller riots broke out in at least 20 other cities and rural towns. What made these riots different from previous episodes of large-scale rioting, such as the Atlanta riot of 1906 and the Springfield riot of 1908, was that blacks fought back and whites were killed and injured in significant numbers. It was in this sort of atmosphere that the new Klan began to thrive. Founded in 1915 in Georgia by William Simmons, who was inspired by D.W. Griffith's heroic portrayal of the earlier Klan in the film 'Birth of a Nation', the new Klan was not so much directed at blacks but Catholics, Jews and foreigners in general. It also tended to be anti-'immoral' values such as drinking alcohol, sexual promiscuity and dancing. Membership increased dramatically following the appointment of two full-time recruitment officers in 1920, and by 1925 had soared to between two and five million (depending on the historian), having rapidly outgrown its Southern origins and expanded to Northern cities. In areas such as Oklahoma and Oregon, the KKK infiltrated state assemblies; Hugo Black,

Figure 6.1 *Ku Klux Klan, c.1920*

later a Supreme Court justice, had been a Klan member, as was a governor of Alabama. It is estimated that in the early 1920s Klan support helped to elect 16 US senators, and in 1924 the Klan claimed to control 24 of the country's 48 state legislatures. It also managed to block the nomination of Al Smith at the Democratic Convention essentially because he was a Catholic.

Those welcomed as members had to be white, native-born men with essentially Christian views. Typically, they were lower middle-class clerical workers, small businessmen and blue-collar workers, although they did represent a cross-section of communities. The Klan's tendency to simply be against things rather than putting forward a more positive set of policies or ideas restricted its growth. From 1925 it faced increasing criticism in the press and membership plummeted. In 1925 David Stephenson, Grand Dragon of the Indiana Klan, was found guilty of rape and murder in the second degree having kidnapped a secretary who subsequently committed suicide. He revealed details of corruption at high levels in the organisation which caused further damage, while the attempts of Imperial Wizard Hiram Wesley Evans to turn the Klan into a sort of social club further undermined its standing. Government acts to restrict immigration removed one of the Klan's main grievances and the onset of the Depression tended to reduce tensions between different groups in society. By 1930 it is estimated that the Klan had only about 45,000 members.

 ## The 'Monkey Trial'

In Dayton, Tennessee, in the summer of 1925, John Thomas Scopes, a 24-year-old teacher, was tried for violating the state's anti-evolution law. The American Civil Liberties Union had offered free legal counsel to any Tennessee teacher who was willing to defy the law so that a test case could be brought. Many

Figure 6.2 *Jury of the Scopes 'Monkey Trial'*

Americans were fundamentalist Protestants who regarded the creation of the world in seven days by God set down in the Bible as literally true, and rejected the Darwinian theory of evolution. In 1925 Tennessee had banned any teaching which contradicted the Bible. William Jennings Bryan led the prosecution of Scopes, who was found guilty and fined, although Bryan's reputation was damaged by the brilliant defence mounted by Clarence Darrow, and he died of a heart condition and exhaustion days after the trial. The trial received national coverage and the cause of fundamentalism was damaged greatly by the trial. Scopes went back to teaching evolution without hindrance.

 ## Immigration

The First World War had engendered anti-German and anti-Austrian feeling and the Russian Revolution of 1917 had caused increased suspicion of foreigners. The atmosphere of the 'Red Scare' and recession of 1920–1 also created antipathy towards immigrants, particularly those coming from Asia. Nativists argued that the 1917 literacy test had failed to protect the US and new measures were called for, particularly by 'Waspish' rural and small-town communities. Politicians and journalists warned of national decline and racial degeneration as 'new immigrants' flooded unchecked into the country.

In 1921 the Emergency Quota Act limited the number of immmigrants to 357,000 per year, and set quotas for national groups at 3 per cent of the number of the residents from those countries living in the US in 1910. The year 1910 was chosen in order to limit the number of 'new immigrants', although exceptions were made for artists, actors, singers, lecturers, nurses and other professionals. Essentially there was an attempt to keep out the unskilled. Immigrants from French Canada and Latin America continued to enter in great numbers. The National Origins Act (Johnson-Reid Act) of 1924 reduced the number of immigrants to 165,000 per year, and cut national quotas. Eastern European quotas were lowered to 2 per cent of the 1890 figure (affecting those from southern and eastern Europe), Asians were excluded completely, greatly offending the existing Chinese and Japanese communities. Mexicans were not included as they provided a vital labour source for California. The Act came into permanent force in 1929 and set a limit of 150,000 with each nationality set a figure based on its population of 1920. In reality about 85 per cent of the quota was allocated to countries from northern and western Europe. The legislation of the 1920s thereby marked a significant break with past attitudes towards immigration.

 ## Prohibition and organised crime

About half of the states were actually 'dry' by 1917, and it is possible to see temperance campaigners as a part of a wider movement that included anti-evolutionists and those who disapproved of relaxed sexual morality. Once America had declared war on Germany, pressure for a national ban on the production and consumption of alcohol grew. In particular the largely Protestant middle-class Anti-Saloon League was critical of morality in the big cities. Its members argued that it was morally wrong to drink while men died in Europe, as well as it being against the will of God. On practical grounds it was important for the country to conserve important grains such as barley, while it could be argued that the efficiency of workers and the armed forces would also be improved. Social workers had major worries about the effects of alcoholism, while others saw Prohibition as a way of getting at brewers of German origin.

Given that the liquor industry was the seventh largest in the country and also that Prohibition marked a very far-reaching restriction of personal freedom it still seems amazing that Prohibition was ever passed. The issue was to split the Democrats into the 'drys' from the rural South and West, and the 'wets' in the urban North and East, but in January 1920 the 18th Amendment came into effect. Despite the hundreds of thousands prosecuted for alcohol-related offences, Prohibition proved to be extremely difficult to enforce effectively given the money available. The geographical area of the US, its long borders with Canada and

Mexico, and 29,000 kilometres of coastline, all of which had to be policed, added to the problems. There were only 1,500 government agents employed to deal with Prohibition, some of whom would have been susceptible to bribery. The ban was unpopular with the richest in society who resented the impingement on their freedom, and working-class immigrants tended to be another group particularly opposed. Even President Harding had alcoholic drinks delivered to the White House.

One of the unforeseen consequences of Prohibition was the rise of organised crime. The high participation of Italians, Irish and Jews in bootlegging and gangster activity reinforced the view that anyone from those ethnic backgrounds was a threat to law and morality. Chicago was the ideal place for the distribution of alcohol as it was near the Canadian border and had very good road and rail links. Al Capone became the chief racketeer there, employing 1,000 men to protect his trafficking of alcohol. By 1927 his annual income was estimated at $60,000 million. Hundreds of gang murders took place, but there were very few convictions. Other sorts of crime increased as well. The St Valentine's Day Massacre of 1929 was the most notorious incident in all of the violence, but when Capone was eventually convicted in 1931 it was for evasion of income tax. Nor did Prohibition actually reduce the amount of drinking in the country. By 1929 there were 32,000 speakeasies in New York, twice the number of saloons before Prohibition. By 1927 drink-driving offences had risen by 467 per cent while deaths from alcoholism were up 600 per cent up on the 1920 figure. The Depression meant most people had little money to spend on liquor, and consumption began to drop only when bad times came.

 ## Politics in the 1920s

Democrat candidate James Cox of Ohio and his running mate Franklin Delano Roosevelt made membership of the League of Nations their key issue in the election of 1920. The census of 1920 indicated that for the first time more people lived in urban areas than elsewhere, and this election was the first time that women had voted on a national scale. The League was rejected by the Republicans and people generally at that time seemed weary of idealism and reform, and more concerned about rising prices and strikes. Warren Harding the Republican candidate, also from Ohio, was strengthened by his running mate Calvin Coolidge who had, as governor of Massachusetts, helped to stop the strike by Boston police. The Republicans favoured higher tariffs, low taxes, the restriction of immigration and aid to farmers, but Harding was kept away from speech making as far as possible during the campaign. He did however manage to coin the slogan 'Let us return to normalcy', and, whatever it meant, it seemed to suit the mood of the country. His victory was by a greater margin than any previous candidate had achieved and it marked a move away from Progressivism back to laissez-faire. The Republicans would retain control of the executive and generally Congress as well until 1933 when Roosevelt himself became President.

Over the years, Harding has been the butt of much criticism from historians, who have picked on his intellectual shallowness on major issues and his parochial view of politics and contrasted it with the high-mindedness of Wilson, but he was far from being a reactionary bigot. Nonetheless, he certainly made some poor choices of men to serve in his cabinet, bringing to Washington a number of friends from his home state, hence their nickname 'the Ohio Gang'. As well as giving some of them cabinet office, he also socialised with them. Several of 'the Ohio Gang' became implicated in financial scandals, including Albert Fall, the first US cabinet member to be convicted on a criminal charge, and sent to jail for accepting bribes in office. Harding did, however, make some very good appointments to his cabinet such as Mellon, Hughes, Wallace and Hoover. He also commuted the prison sentence of socialist leader Eugene V. Debs, supported calls for an eight-hour day in the steel industry, vetoed a soldiers' bonus bill in 1922, and supported arms limitation at the Washington Conference on Naval Disarmament (also in 1922). There is little evidence to suggest that he was implicated in the underhand activities of the 'Ohio Gang' but the worry its members caused him probably contributed to his death from a coronary thrombosis in August 1923. His successor

Calvin Coolidge was a man of impeccable moral standards, and this limited the damage done to the Republicans by Harding's Presidency.

In January 1924 Coolidge made a speech saying 'the chief business of the American people is business'. He believed in minimal government and was keen to balance the budget, cut taxes and ensure credit was available. These ideas seemed to appeal to the nation, although a new Progressive Party emerged with Robert La Follette as its candidate, standing on a platform that opposed monopolies. and supported tariff reduction and government control of the railways. It polled 4.8 million votes.

In February 1925 the Revenue Act cut the maximum surtax (tax on the rich) payable from 40 per cent to 20 per cent and led to spending and investment. Historians have traditionally picked up on these sorts of policies and Coolidge's narrow approach, but in 1998 Robert Ferrell (*The Presidency of Calvin Coolidge*) described Coolidge as idealistic and hard working with a strong sense of public service; and it should be remembered that, in his speech of 1924, he argued for more schools and the growth of liberties. He was comfortably re-elected in his own right in 1924, although, given certain health concerns, he chose not to stand again. When 'Silent Cal' died in 1933, Dorothy Parker quipped 'How can they tell?'.

Hoover was chosen as the Republican candidate in 1928, and based his campaign on continuing Coolidge's policies, proposing more tax cuts, continuing with tariff protection, and maintaining Prohibition, although he was regarded as the more progressive member of the Harding/Coolidge administrations. The Democrats were split over issues such as Prohibition and immigration. Al Smith was chosen as their candidate. He was a Catholic from New York and anti-Prohibition, but a 'human progressive' according to Traynor (2001). He polled 15 million votes, almost double Davis's 8 million in 1924 and beat Hoover in the 12 biggest cities of the country (cities which the Republicans had won in 1924), but Hoover won comfortably overall. He promised 'a chicken in every pot and two cars in every garage', words that would return to haunt him.

 ## The boom of the 1920s

The basis of the boom in the 1920s had been laid in earlier times. The sheer size of the population gave the US vast numbers of workers as well as potential consumers. The transcontinental railroads had created a good transport infrastructure, and raw materials such as coal and oil were in plentiful supply. The prevailing work ethic and belief in rugged individualism fostered an entrepreneurial spirit that bordered on the religious. Had Calvin Coolidge not once said that 'The man who builds a factory builds a temple'? Large corporations in the meantime brought economies of scale, better integration and increased stability to business.

War had given many businesses the opportunity to supply food and munitions, and to enter new export markets that had hitherto been supplied mainly by Germany and Britain, as well as bankrupting rivals. Banks also profited from loans to the Allies at the end of the war in Europe, and following a brief recession in 1921–2 Harding's appointment of Andrew Mellon to the Treasury and various other government measures, the economy began to prosper, with more jobs becoming available and the standard of living improving for most. Industrial output increased by over a third with new production methods and types of management, and by 1929, the year of the Wall Street crash, the US made about 46 per cent of the world's industrial goods. Buying on credit or hire purchase (in 1921 the credit extended by the US Federal Reserve Bank was $45.3 billion, by 1929 $73 billion), or paying by instalment, combined with low taxation allowed many more people to purchase the consumer goods being churned out by improved business methods and new industries. Alfred Sloan, who later became President of General Motors, set up the first consumer credit agency in 1919. During the boom between 1922 and 1929 gross national product rose from $74 billion to $104 billion, output increased by about 40 per cent, while income per head per year grew from $672 to $857. New advertising methods, especially on the radio, proved to be very effective. In 1920, people owned 60,000 radios in the US; by 1929 this figure was 10 million. There was also a huge growth in department stores from 312 in 1920 to 1,395 by 1929, and chain stores also appeared. Standard clothing sizes had been introduced during the war for the production of military uniforms, and led to mass-produced ready-to-wear clothing in the shops in the 1920s. The emergence of the first mass consumer society was taking place.

Three new industries led the boom: electricity, motor vehicles and related goods, and chemicals. In 1914, 30 per cent of US factories were powered by electricity but by 1929 this had risen to 70 per cent. Electricity began to be used to power homes, making possible the use of new time-saving devices such as cookers, vacuum cleaners, washing machines and refrigerators, which stimulated production further. In 1921 there were 5,000 refrigerators a year produced, but by 1930 there were one million. In 1920, the first radio broadcasting station, KDKA, was set up.

Between 1909 and 1928, 15 million (a million a year produced in the 1920s) Model T cars were produced from Henry Ford's 'moving assembly line' (introduced in 1913, it cut the time to make a car from 12.5 hours to 1.5 hours and had done away with the idea of labourers building the whole car). For the first time cars came within the price range of ordinary workers, it being possible to buy a Model T for less than 3 months' wages for the average worker by 1925. Tasks in the factories however became duller and more repetitive for workers and discipline was tightened as competition increased and targets had to be reached. Labour turnover was high, which is why Ford doubled pay, cut the working day to eight hours and introduced profit-sharing. The factory completed at River Rouge, Michigan, employed about 80,000 workers (many of whom were taken on in the spring and laid off in the autumn each year) and was the biggest factory complex in the world. Ford's Protection Department employed security men who intimidated and assaulted union organisers, and it was not until 1941 that Ford officially recognised any labour union representing the employees in pay bargaining. These sorts of attitude were not uncommon among employers and tended to be supported by the courts. 'Yellow dog' contracts by which workers pledged not to strike were also backed by legal judgements. 'Welfare capitalism', such as Ford espoused, only helped a relatively small number of workers, and most workers got wage increases proportionately lower than the rate of growth of the economy. The employers' campaign for the 'open shop' was in reality an attempt to weaken the power of the bigger unions.

The motor industry in turn stimulated demand for other products, and by the mid-1920s was using 96 per cent of the nation's oil, 75 per cent of its plate glass, 65 per cent of its leather, 80 per cent of its rubber and 20 per cent of its steel. John Traynor (2001) says that the increase in road building (for which the government took responsibility, building an average of 10,000 miles of road per year in the 1920s), the movement to the cities, growth of the suburbs, and the building of skyscrapers can all be linked to changes Ford had brought.

Presidents Harding, Coolidge and Hoover were happy to take much of the credit for the boom in prosperity until the crash of October 1929. The Republican Party's attitude towards business certainly encouraged investment, stimulated production and contributed to consumer confidence, while technological innovation and the scientific management methods of experts such as Frederick Taylor contributed to high levels of production. Between 1921 and 1933 the Treasury and the Departments of Agriculture and Commerce were staffed by very capable men. Andrew Mellon, the second richest man in the country, served at the Treasury in the 1920s, supporting high tariffs, low taxes and big business in general. The high tariffs of the Fordney-McCumber Act of 1922 brought money to the government, which allowed it to regularly reduce taxes, and thereby stimulate consumer purchasing in the 1920s. As Secretary of Commerce, Herbert Hoover helped to modernise industry and extended the role of his department.

Despite the appearance of general prosperity and the rise in average wages during the 1920s, the US remained a country of extremes. Prohibition remained a divisive issue, racism continued, and crime became organised and more violent. American confidence was, however, reflected in other areas. The arts flourished, with authors such as Ernest Hemingway and F. Scott Fitzgerald and poets such as Robert Frost and T.S. Eliot emerging. Jazz made a significant impact, and in 1927 the first full-length talking picture, *The Jazz Singer*, appeared. Aviation burgeoned, with Lindbergh's flight across the Atlantic in 1927, and by 1930 nearly half a million passengers and a growing proportion of mail were being carried by plane in the US. By 1929 there were also over 400 skyscrapers (buildings over 20 storeys high) in the country, and in 1931 the Empire State Building became the tallest building in the world, providing office space for 25,000 people.

 ## The 'crash' and causes of the Great Depression

The stock market crash of October 1929 and the Depression that followed have inspired a number of explanations from economists and historians, but there can be little doubt that the economy had been fundamentally unsound. In 1963 Milton Friedman and Anna Schwartz put forward the 'monetary' interpretation of the Depression, i.e. that it was caused by the drastic contraction of the currency resulting from bad decisions made by the Federal Reserve Board, which raised interest rates when it should have lowered them. The 'spending' interpretation tends to be supported by Keynesian economists such as Peter Temin who has argued that, although the contraction of the currency may have made the Depression worse, it was a drop in investment and consumer spending which came first and helped to cause the contraction.

There does seem, however, to be a consensus of opinion that one of the key underlying causes of the Depression was that too few people had shared in the prosperity of the period. The boom in business did not bring higher living standards for all and certain industries such as textiles and coal mining actually went into decline. The lack of employment law made it difficult for some workers to do anything to improve pay and conditions for themselves, and union membership fell from 5.1 million in 1921 to under 3 million in 1929, by which time the wealthiest 5 per cent of American families received 30 per cent of the country's total family income, and the poorest 40 per cent of families got 12.5 per cent. Of families at the top end of the scale, 0.1 per cent received an income equivalent to that of 42 per cent of families at the bottom. The share of national income that went to the poorest 60 per cent fell by almost 13 per cent between 1918 and 1929, while the share that went to the wealthiest 20 per cent rose by over 10 per cent. Conditions as well as pay also remained poor for many, with 25,000 workers killed a year in their jobs, and 100,000 permanently disabled in accidents at work during the 1920s.

Working-class women, African Americans, Native Americans, the elderly and the rural poor all remained untouched by the rise in prosperity, as did the new unskilled immigrants in the big cities. The number of women in work continued to increase but pay remained low and their jobs were usually menial. Many blacks had moved North during the period 1916–20, attracted by higher wages in the armaments

Figure 6.3
Boom and bust cartoon

factories and driven away by harsh conditions in the South. In Northern cities, however, blacks tended to fill unskilled low-paid jobs, live in slums areas and suffer hostility from whites. Native Americans had lost their land and culture in the previous century, and many resided in poor conditions on reservations where incidents of alcoholism, crime and infant death rate were all high. Particularly poor areas in the 1920s included the textile towns of New England, the Appalachian region of West Virginia and Kentucky, and the rural South in general.

It should be remembered that in the 1920s one-third of the workforce was still in agriculture, but per capita farm income fell to one-third of the national average. Farmers had accumulated huge new debts during the First World War as they tried to take advantage of wartime price rises, but in the 1920s these debts became a crippling burden. Prices went down as demand from Europe fell while fertilisers and machinery remained expensive. Increasing competition from Canada and Argentina did not help but over-production was the main problem, with farmers increasingly having to sell food at less than it cost to produce. In the South the boll weevil destroyed the cotton crop, the Fordney-McCumber Tariff Act of 1922 had the effect of closing many foreign markets to US farmers, and Prohibition cut the demand for grain from brewers and distillers. In 1924 alone about 600,000 farmers lost their farms, and during the decade as a whole about 13 million acres of cultivated land were abandoned. Farmers put pressure on politicians and a series of Acts were passed between 1921 and 1927 to relieve some of the problems they faced. However, in 1927–8 Coolidge gave a stark reminder of the Republican mindset by vetoing the McNary-Haugen Bill, by which the government would have bought surplus produce at a guaranteed price to sell on the world market, on the grounds that it would lead to overproduction and create a large bureaucracy of officials. The crash of 1929 meant Americans were unable to pay the prices for food they had been doing, and with the Depression hitting worldwide there was no market abroad. Dairy farmers and fruit and vegetable growers profited as city markets had grown, but farming in general was in serious decline.

Industrial workers fared better than others in the 1920s, with hours falling, real wages going up by 26 per cent and unemployment going down to 4.2 per cent by 1928. Working conditions did improve and 'company unions' developed, though many employers remained hostile towards unions and it was not unusual for strike-breakers to be brought in and for deaths to occur during industrial disputes. In 1922, following the killing of two strikers by two guards at the Southern Illinois Coal Company, 19 strike-breakers were killed, leading to public hostility towards the unions.

In 1929 it was reckoned that 12 million families were below the poverty line, and by 1930 this figure had risen to 16 million families (about 70 million people). The maldistribution of income meant that by 1929 earlier rates of consumption could not be sustained. It is also worth noting that 70 per cent of dividend income from shares went to the richest 1 per cent of the population.

Alan Brinkley (2000) has pointed to the lack of diversification in the economy in the 1920s as a major problem, with prosperity effectively based on a limited number of industries such as cars (which employed 7 per cent of all manufacturing wage earners) and construction. When they went into decline so did the economy as a whole. The year 1927 is now seen to be when problems began to manifest themselves, but were ignored. Sales of cars fell, the rise in industrial wages slowed down and fewer new houses were built.

Feverish stock market speculation has often been regarded as a major cause of the crash, and in 1928 the Federal Reserve Board raised interest rates to try to limit the purchase of shares, and warned banks not to lend money for speculation on the stock market. For a long time the explanation of the speculative mania which seized people in 1928 and 1929 was that people were enticed to borrow and credit was easy to obtain for the purchase of shares 'on margin', but this now seems far too simplistic and ignores the fact that in times before and since the same preconditions have existed without there being a ruinous crash. J.K. Galbraith has suggested that the hyper-confident mood of the people was what was important. Another problem appears to have been that share prices continued to rise, regardless of the performance of the companies, and this helped to maintain an illusion of prosperity.

Some say that the crash took money out of the system and led to the Depression, but Farmer and Sanders have pointed out that the US actually survived the crash in many respects, and business activity did not begin to decline significantly until the middle of 1930. In fact, few Americans were directly affected by the crash. By April 1930 share prices had regained 20 per cent of the losses of the previous autumn, and it was in 1931–2 that the really disastrous falls took place. Nevertheless it is the autumn of 1929 which gains most attention.

On 24 October 1929 (Black Thursday) 13 million shares were sold and prices plummeted. On 29 October (Black Tuesday) 16.5 million shares were sold. By November the price of shares had fallen by a third. Most agree that speculation on the stock market had run out of control. The increase in share values over the preceding years had made them more attractive to a wider public and by early 1929 at least one million people (not a huge proportion of the population) held them, but the value of shares could not continue to grow. Many investors had bought shares 'on margin', i.e. borrowed money (up to 75 per cent), which did not help stability, and when demand began to slow down there was a realisation that many shares had been overvalued. As soon as doubt set in, people started to get rid of their shares. Between 1930 and 1933 depositors lost $2.5 billion in savings from banks that closed their doors or went bankrupt, which partly contributed to the money supply contracting by about a third, and consequently affected purchasing. The country's banking structure was fundamentally unsound. David Kennedy has said: 'American banks were rotten even in good times.' The US had over 30,000 independent banks, many of which were poorly managed, with limited capital, overly-dependent on the local economy and susceptible to sudden withdrawals by many people if there was a 'run'. The Federal Reserve Board, which supervised the banking system, had limited powers but even so did not do enough to help banks in difficulties and its failure to help prevent the New York City Bank from closing its doors in December 1930 is often seen as a key event. Brinkley (2000) has also added that corporate structure was unsound as well as the banking system.

Another issue which must be considered when looking at the causes of the Depression is what was happening *outside* the US. American loans had helped many countries in Europe during and after the war, but high US tariffs made it difficult for those countries to sell their products in the US and therefore pay back the loans. They also began to retaliate against high American tariffs, and overproduction worldwide meant US markets began to diminish. In early 1931, when it looked as if the US might pull out of the Depression, banking collapses in Germany and Austria (countries in which US banks held a large stake) contributed to further decline, and following Britain's decision to leave the gold standard in September 1931 over 500 US banks collapsed in a month.

Galbraith has suggested that there was a 'poor state of economic intelligence' (1975: pp. 199–200) in the country with economists at the time 'almost uniquely perverse' (p. 200) in advising the need for balanced budgets and fearing going off the gold standard and risking inflation. Hoover himself cut government spending in 1931 as there was less tax being collected, and put up taxes in 1932 which made things worse. He also decided not to leave the gold standard, and raised import duties to the highest levels in US history, which simply led to retaliation by other countries.

 ## The Depression and attempts to deal with it

The downward spiral of the economy continued for three years. Trade fell from $10 billion in 1929 to $3 billion in 1932, and output fell by half. By the autumn of 1931 unemployment stood at 8 million, by 1932 it was at least 13 million (25 per cent of the workforce), with 1–2 million people travelling the country looking for work (hobos). Industrial production was cut by half between 1929 and 1932, and real earnings fell by a third between 1929 and 1933. Five thousand banks went out of business during 1929/30, and nine million people lost all their savings. At the beginning of 1929 Ford employed 120,000 workers at his Detroit factory, but by August 1931 it was only 37,000. The impact on nearly all classes and areas was equally bad, although Robert McElvaine argues the majority of the rich were 'quite comfortable' over the period. Thousands of farms were repossessed, wheat prices fell by nearly two-thirds in three years, as did cotton between 1929 and 1932, and from 1930 a large area of the Great Plains began to suffer from one of the worst droughts in history, the 'Dust Bowl' region stretching from Texas north into the Dakotas. The fact that there was no dole meant that millions became reliant on soup kitchens and private charities. The suicide rate went up 14 per cent during 1929–32, and the number of marriages fell by 10 per cent. There were 110 reported deaths from starvation during the Depression, but poor diet and malnutrition hastened the deaths of many others, and infant mortality rose as well. In 1935 it was estimated that 20 million people were not getting enough to eat. 'Hooverville' shanties of the unemployed on the edges of major towns and cities became a feature a life in the 1930s.

Michael Bernstein, in 1987, suggested that the reason the Depression lasted for so long was that 1929 was too late for the motor and construction industries to help resolve it, and too soon for newly emerging industries such as aviation, petrochemicals/plastics, aluminium and electrical to be able to help. Given this analysis, one wonders what the government could have done, but Herbert Hoover has taken much criticism for his role.

Hoover was ironically the most able of the three post-war Republican Presidents. He had been elected President in 1928, and was in favour of minimal government intervention in the economy, tax cuts, balanced budgets and low interest. He was highly regarded by many, having come from a poor background and risen to millionaire status, which had shaped his belief in 'rugged individualism'. Hoover's initial response to the fall in share prices was to hold meetings with the leaders of industry to convince them to continue with investment and to maintain targets for production and wage levels. He also encouraged local officials to spend more on public works. He had organised famine relief during the war and was a compassionate man, but his political and economic beliefs favoured private initiatives and voluntary projects to get America back on its feet rather than government intervention. In April 1929, he pressed Congress to help farmers, which led to tariff protection and the setting up of a Federal Farm Board to provide financial help, but he also took the view that the United States' problems, to a large extent, lay with external factors such as over-production, political unrest and financial crises. Having taken credit for the boom, he took criticism for the crash and it eventually became unsafe for him to campaign on the streets, although levels of violence during the Depression were remarkably low.

In November 1929 Hoover persuaded railroad directors to continue with building railways, and local politicians to increase spending on public works – but it would never be enough. He did establish, in October 1930, the Emergency Committee for Employment to coordinate voluntary relief agencies, and in 1931 he persuaded the largest bankers to set up the National Credit Corporation to lend money to smaller banks to make loans to businesses. He also cut taxes. The Hawley-Smoot Tariff Act of 1930, however, accelerated decline abroad and at home, as other governments retaliated.

In December 1931 Hoover asked Congress to create an Emergency Reconstruction Finance Corporation (RFC) to permit huge loans to insurance companies, railroads and banks to promote fresh investment that might spark recovery. The organisation was headed by Charles Dawes, but many businesses were too scared to borrow, so much of the money went to large businesses in an attempt to restore confidence, and to those who promised to pay for themselves. The RFC never had enough money to make a real difference and it did not even spend what it had.

Recent interpretations of Hoover have been less harsh than those of his contemporaries. Robert McElvaine has used the term 'progressive individualism' rather than 'rugged individualism' as a more accurate description of his beliefs, as Hoover opposed large concentrations of wealth and believed the poor and needy should be cared for by their own communities; but even he concedes that Hoover's response of voluntary charity combined with local and state relief was totally inadequate and his attempt to pursue a middle way between direct intervention and laissez-faire was ineffective. In 1952 Hoover's memoirs blamed the First World War as the primary cause of the Depression. He worked tirelessly and intervened more than any of his predecessors, nearly doubling the federal public works expenditure in three years, and in 1932 taking the federal budget $2.7 billion into the red, the largest peacetime deficit in US history, thus paving the way for the New Deal. It should be said that, at the time, the Democrats had little to offer as an alternative.

Early in 1932, with an election looming, Hoover intervened more decisively. Congress provided $2 billion to fund the RFC, and in February he signed the Glass-Steagall Act allocating $750 million of government gold reserves for loans to private businesses. In July he also signed legislation authorising the RFC to give $2 billion to state and local governments for public works programmes, and to help people who could not pay off their mortgages, but all these measures still failed to alleviate the problems. Hoover needed state governments to keep up spending, farmers to cut production, employers not to lay off any workers, reform and regulation of banks and economy, as well as financiers to invest money in private enterprises and bankers to give consumers credit, but people had 'lost confidence in their economy, in themselves and in the ability of Republican politicians to lead them out of the Depression' (2000: p. 90).

In the late spring of 1932, 22,000 First World War veterans helped by communist activists marched on Washington, demanding payment of a veterans' bonus approved by Congress in 1924 but not scheduled to be paid until 1944. The Senate defeated the bill to pay them off and in July Hoover approved a plan to evict the 'Bonus Marchers' who had stayed on in the Anacosta Flats area. Under the command of General Douglas MacArthur (who greatly exceeded Hoover's orders) and Colonel Dwight D. Eisenhower, 700 armed soldiers led by Major George Patton attacked, resulting in the deaths of two veterans and a baby, and a thousand people injured by gas. This was the final blow for Hoover.

The Depression was more psychologically damaging for the US than for any other country because of the relative prosperity of the 1920s, although the collapse was not as complete as in Germany. Galbraith has pronounced that 'the rejection of both fiscal [tax and expenditure] and monetary policy amounted precisely to a rejection of all affirmative government economic policy . . . a triumph of dogma over thought. The consequences were profound' (1975: p. 202).

Franklin D. Roosevelt's campaign differed little from that of the Republicans and he did not outline in detail what his New Deal meant, although he did call for an end to Prohibition. Following Hoover's 'lame duck' period in office until March, during which time the economy got worse, the 20th Amendment was passed which cut the interval to two-and-a-half months between election and inauguration of a new President.

Part 2: Essays

 The boom

1 What were the causes of the economic boom during the 1920s and to what extent did all Americans share in the prosperity of the 1920s? (45)

(OCR)

There were certain preconditions which allowed the United States to create an economic boom in the 1920s, namely: a large population which provided both workers and consumers; an excellent transport infrastructure based on a number of transcontinental railroads, to which the government added a further 100,000 miles of road in the 1920s; and plentiful supplies of raw materials such as coal and oil. American attitudes favoured individualism and hard work and tended to work against the interests of unions, while government remained sympathetic towards employers and allowed the growth of large corporations, bringing economies of scale and greater integration. The importance of business to the US was summed up by President Calvin Coolidge whose comments included 'the chief business of the American people is business' and 'the man who builds a factory builds a temple'. A number of other factors contributed to the boom including: the war; new production methods and management techniques; the lead given by particular industries; the expansion of money available; the development of a mass consumer market; and Republican policies in government.

The First World War had stimulated the growth of businesses, particularly those involved in the supply of food and munitions, while the weakened capacity of countries such as Britain and Germany to trade had been exploited by the US, which was able to enter new export markets. At the end of the war, US banks made profits from loans to Allied powers, and this also helped to create a platform for further growth.

Widespread consumer credit, such as that introduced in 1919 by Alfred Sloan, facilitated the boom in spending and helped to create a mass consumer market, while rising wages among industrial workers and low taxation helped to maintain it. New production methods, the development of the assembly line by men such as Henry Ford, scientific management techniques influenced by men such as Frederick Taylor, and improved marketing such as that of Chrysler, all contributed to the increase of industrial output by a third. GNP rose from $74 billion in 1922 to $104 billion by 1929. The automobile industry in particular led the way, and stimulated other industries, such as oil, rubber and glass to follow. John Traynor has said that Henry Ford 'probably did more than any other individual to transform America into a modern, urban society'. The growth of other new industries such as chemicals, electricity (particularly regarding the development of domestic appliances) and synthetic textiles also had a great impact.

The Republicans, who monopolised the Presidency for the 1920s as well as Congress for most of the decade, encouraged investment and stimulated production. High tariffs such as those set by the Fordney-McCumber Act helped protect domestic production from foreign competition as well as increasing the money government had in its budget, which in turn meant that taxes could be lowered, thereby leading to an increase in consumer spending. The government also took responsibility for the building of roads.

If any factors can be singled out as more important than others they are possibly innovation in production methods and the expansion of credit on a mass scale, as the other factors had all been present well before the 1920s in America.

Industrial workers broadly benefited from the prosperity of the 1920s, with a decline of working hours, real wages going up by 26 per cent and unemployment declining to 4.2 per cent by 1928. Some businessmen believed that higher wages would increase production, and more was done on safety and recreational facilities. However, many groups did not share in the general prosperity and, during the decade, the top 5 per cent of American families received 30 per cent of total family income, while the poorest 40 per cent had 12.5 per cent of national income.

Certain industries were hit worse than others. Textiles went into decline in parts of New England, as did coal mining and farming more generally. Per capita farm income was only a third of the national average in the 1920s, and measures such as the McFadden Banking Act of 1927 to improve the availability of loans had little effect overall. Given that a third of the nation's workforce was employed in agriculture this had major implications. Parts of the Appalachians and regions of the Great Lakes lacked modern amenities and living conditions were barely at subsistence levels. Migrant farmworkers, particularly Mexican immigrants in California, experienced extremely poor living conditions and low pay. The rural South, with its 8.5 million tenant and sharecropper families (3 million of whom were African Americans), depending on landlords for housing, tools, loans and land, remained very poor.

For women (particularly those from the working class) the quality of employment opportunities did not improve, nor did pay. Work remained menial, and few worked in the professions except for teaching and nursing. The number of electrical domestic goods on sale did take some of the drudgery out of housework, and the wider use of birth control cut the birth rate to 21.3 per cent in 1930 from 27.7 per cent in 1920. African Americans, in the years from 1916 onwards, moved to the North in greater numbers but were limited to the low-paid, least-skilled occupations, and also suffered resentment from Northern whites. Indians lived on reservations, where crime and alcoholism, high infant death rate and low life expectancy were endemic.

By 1930 there were at least 16 million families, embracing about 70 million people, below the poverty line. The richest 1 per cent of the population received 70 per cent of dividend income from shares, and 25,000 people a year died in accidents at work. The share of national income that went to the poorest 60 per cent had fallen by almost 13 per cent between 1918 and 1929, which meant that most people were earning less proportionately by the end of the decade than they had at the start. It can be fairly confidently concluded that only a minority of Americans shared in the prosperity of the 1920s.

2   Account for the popularity of the Republican Party in the 1920s. (45)

(OCR)

> *Essay plan*
>
> *Introduction: Background-type introduction describing the election successes of Republican Presidents Harding, Coolidge and Hoover, and possibly including a brief comment that Republican policies as well as factors over which they had limited control combined to help them dominate the Presidency.*
>
> *Para 1: Assessment of popularity of Republicans based on scale of election victories in terms of the popular vote and electoral college numbers.*
>
> *Para 2: Explain context of post-war United States – anti-foreign, inward-looking, intolerant and wanting to move away from the government intervention that had marked the Progressive era.*
>
> *Para 3: Assessment of how Republican policies seemed to suit the public mood.*
>
> *Para 4: Analysis of the success of Republican Presidents in office particularly the apparent economic prosperity.*
>
> *Para 5: The 1924 election and the impact of a third candidate of significance which split the anti-Republican vote.*
>
> *Para 6: Examine what the Democrats had to offer during the 1920s and the candidates they put forward. It may also be worth considering the argument that Roosevelt had little new to offer in 1932 other than fresh faces in charge.*
>
> *Conclusion: Decision on whether the Republicans' popularity was essentially down to their own policies, the mood of the country at the time or the weakness of the Democrats.*

 Xenophobia and racism

3   To what extent were Americans xenophobic, anti-left and generally intolerant in the ten years after the First World War? (20)

(AQA)

In the First World War, 112,000 US troops died, although this is a relatively small number when compared with the losses of countries in Europe. It nonetheless made a big psychological impact on Americans. Many Americans had wanted neutrality, however government propaganda had stirred up anti-German feeling, and jingoism. Government intervention had also limited free speech. The Russian Revolution of 1917, the subsequent 'Red Scare' and rise of communist and socialist movements in the US (many of which were led by foreign-born men), the industrial unrest of 1919 (which included a five-day general strike in Seattle), and the Boston police strike, all raised fears of impending revolution and saw the growth of xenophobia and anti-left feeling.

The attempted assassination of Attorney-General Mitchell Palmer prompted the Palmer Raids on left-wing organisations, resulting in nearly 10,000 arrests, the discovery of only three pistols and over 500 deportations to Russia. In addition the New York legislature excluded elected socialist members. A number of explosions and bomb attacks, including one on Wall Street killing 30 people, seemed to confirm that America had been right to take the threat from the left and foreigners seriously, as did the one million votes cast for Debs' Socialist Party in the 1920 elections. The conviction for murder of Italian-born anarchists Sacco and Vanzetti, based on extremely flimsy evidence and heavily influenced by a judge who made no pretence to be neutral in the case, seemed to confirm the mood of the nation, although there were plenty who protested in the strongest terms to try to save these two men.

As well as anti-foreign and anti-left feeling in the country, interracial tension peaked as well after the war. Many blacks had moved to the North during the war in search of better jobs and greater tolerance, but were not necessarily able to find either. There were 25 race riots in the last six months of 1919 alone, and in Chicago 38 people were killed and over 500 injured, after a black teenager had inadvertently drifted towards a 'whites only' beach on Lake Michigan. The resurgence of the Ku Klux Klan also peaked during the years following the war, with its members taking an intolerant line on sexual morality, dancing and drinking alcohol, as well as being against blacks, Jews, foreigners and Catholics. By 1925 membership had risen above two million and included men from all social groups. The government, to a certain extent, shared the fears of small-town America, and in the 1920s broke with the past by introducing a series of Quota Acts to restrict the numbers of immigrants entering the country from southern and eastern Europe and Asia. This legislation contributed in part to the rapid decline of the Klan in the second half of the decade.

The mood of intolerance was further reflected in the 'Monkey Trial' of 1925 in which the state of Tennessee prosecuted a biology teacher who had taught students about Darwinian theories of evolution rather than sticking to the biblical version of creation. Prohibition in itself, which provided a backdrop to the decade, could be said to have been a further indicator of intolerance with its restriction of civil liberties. Republican governments during the period were generally short on idealism, and although there was a flourishing of the arts, particularly literature, as well as the development of greater rights for women and the emergence of a confident and flamboyant culture in many respects, the ten years following the war were years of unprecedented xenophobia and intolerance towards anything or anyone seeming less than '100 per cent American'.

4 Account for the popularity of the Ku Klux Klan in the 1920s. (20)

(AQA)

The post-war period in the US was characterised by intolerance, racial bigotry and suspicion of foreigners and immigrants from certain countries. It was in this atmosphere that a revived Ku Klux Klan thrived for a short period of time.

In 1915 William Simmons, inspired by the epic film 'Birth of a Nation', in which the original Klan was portrayed in heroic and romantic terms, resurrected the organisation. At first the popularity of the new Klan was low, but when professional promoters Elizabeth Tyler and Edward Clarke were employed to boost recruitment, its popularity soared and spread from the South to the states of the mid-west. Some estimates have put membership at between four and five million by 1924.

Klan popularity was based on the reaction of conservative rural and small-town America towards the changes taking place in society during the early 1920s. It appealed particularly to white middle-class Protestant men squeezed between the big corporations and growing radicalism of the trade unions, but it does seem to have gained support from a cross-section of whites. The bizarre costumes and ceremonies that were all part of the secretive rituals of the Klan must have had an appeal for some, but those who joined the Klan tended to be moved by other issues. They shared common fears about the growth and influence of the cities, declining social morals, an increasingly assertive black population, Jews, Catholics, 'racially inferior' immigrants, emancipated women, jazz, smoking, gambling, more independent teenagers, and anyone who did not measure up to their idea of 'one hundred per cent Americanism'. Some of the Klan's appeal also lay in its claims that it would sort out political corruption and crime, and the fact that the Klan actually took control of government in several states such as Indiana and Colorado, must also have given the impression that being involved with the Klan could change things. In Utah, for example, Klan support emerged from resentment towards the Mormons who held a great deal of economic and political influence in the state.

In many respects the appeal of the Klan was negative in that it is easier to define what the Klan was against rather than what it stood for. Quite what was meant by 'one hundred per cent Americanism' has never been exactly clear but the sheer range of things they were against was bound to strike a chord with a number of people.

PRACTICE QUESTION

5   Account for the decline of the Ku Klux Klan. (20)

(AQA)

Advice: The answer to this could adopt a two-pronged approach, examining internal factors in the downfall of the Klan (such as their essential negativity, violence and scandal at the top of the organisation) and external influences such as government action on immigration and the impact of the Depression). In a conclusion, it might be worth weighing up whether one or two factors in particular were more important than others.

 Prohibition

6   Explain the reasons behind Prohibition and determine the extent to which it could be said to have been a failure. (20)

(AQA)

About 65 per cent of the country had already banned alcohol before Prohibition on a national scale went into effect, so in many respects the amendment to the Constitution was simply an extension of what was already happening in most states. There were of course a number of factors behind the movement towards Prohibition, including practical, moral and religious ones.

From a practical point of view, it made sense to conserve grain during the war effort, and in addition it could be argued that workers and soldiers would be more efficient in carrying out their duties without the temptation of drink. It was also felt that banning alcohol would solve many social problems of the time such as poor health and crime, specifically domestic violence, which in turn would cut the number of people in prisons as well as reduce poverty, and thereby reduce taxes.

Groups such as the American Temperance Society argued that it was morally wrong to drink, especially while men were dying in Europe. The Anti-Saloon League called the beer of German brewers in Milwaukee 'Kaiser brew' and portrayed the campaign against alcohol in nationalistic anti-German terms.

The Women's Christian Temperance Union believed that drinking alcohol went against God's will, and others felt that Prohibition would somehow help to clean up corruption in politics and help Americanise immigrants among whom drinking tended to reach relatively higher levels.

Behr has suggested that temperance campaigners received disproportionate media coverage because of the shortage of newsworthy items at the time in isolationist America.

In order to ascertain the extent to which Prohibition was a failure it is necessary to examine the aims of those who passed the 18th Amendment and Volstead Act. The main aim was obviously to stop the consumption of alcohol, but it was hoped that this would in turn lead, in the long term, to a reduction in crime, prostitution and sexual promiscuity, and an improvement in health. In the short term, Prohibition did help to conserve grain for the war effort.

Initially liquor consumption and arrests for drunkenness declined, with alcohol being too expensive for most, and the drinking of hard liquor falling by 50 per cent. It did not take long, however, for drinking to increase to pre-Prohibition levels. Protest drinkers drank more than they would have in order to express their discontent with the law and what they saw as an infringement of their liberty. Lee has referred to this as drinking 'with a sense of high purpose'. The 1920s were an era of change, and non-conformity and drink became a part of that. Vogue drinking was not necessarily related to Prohibition but probably more to changing social values. There was also a tendency during the 1920s for greater amounts of hard liquor to be drunk, as it was easier to smuggle and therefore cheaper. Thornton has suggested that Prohibition of alcohol also led drinkers to switch to substances such as opium, marijuana and cocaine. By 1929 there were 32,000 speakeasies in New York, twice the number of saloons before Prohibition.

Crime, both directly and indirectly related to drinking, also soared. Prohibition was simply too difficult to enforce from the outset, given the resources the government was prepared to expend. Not enough agents were employed (never above 3,000) nor were they sufficiently well paid to resist the temptations of bribery. The country's huge landed borders with Canada and Mexico as well as 29,000 kilometres of coastline contributed to about 95 per cent of smuggled liquor actually getting into the US. The police were either diverted from their enforcement of other laws – half the police in Chicago were apparently on the payroll of notorious gangster Al Capone – or simply stopped enforcing Prohibition, as did the New York State Police from 1923. Arrests in the country for drunk and disorderly conduct rose by 41 per cent and arrests for drink-driving increased by 81 per cent during Prohibition (Thornton). In 1932 alone there were 44,678 jail sentences for alcohol-related crime, by which time prisons were full to bursting. In the large cities the murder rate rose from 5.6 per 100,000 to nearly 10 during Prohibition. Bowen says there were over 400 gang-related murders a year in Chicago alone. Crime never returned to pre-Prohibition levels and the whole system was brought into disrepute with hundreds of government agents and thousands of policemen taking bribes, juries being got to, gangsters such as Capone, O'Bannion and Moran flouting the law, and millions of ordinary people being turned into lawbreakers. In addition the government lost huge amounts of revenue from beer and yet more money had to be spent on prisons. Respect for the government and the Constitution declined, as the measure had never been supported by the public, the rich and working-class immigrant communities being particularly resentful.

If anything 'the noble experiment' had made worse the very problems it had been intended to solve. From a health point of view there were no standards for illegally-made alcohol and deaths from poisoned liquor rose from 1,064 in 1920 to 4,154 in 1925. In 1932 teetotaller John D. Rockefeller admitted that drinking had generally increased, while crime grew hugely, becoming better organised and more violent. The banning of alcohol also made thousands officially unemployed, while hypocrisy could be seen at the highest level, with Harding having alcohol smuggled into the White House and his Attorney-General, Harry Daughtery, accepting bribes from bootleggers. LaGuardia and Wenburn, who argue Prohibition was a success, have looked at data for the first two or three years, e.g. the death rate from alcoholism had been cut by 80 per cent in 1921 from pre-war levels, and alcohol-related crime also dropped markedly. They also attribute the rise in crime subsequently to changing social norms and lower standards of policing, but overwhelmingly the evidence seems to suggest that Prohibition failed to achieve all of its major aims. The only other developed country to attempt Prohibition at this time, Finland, also abandoned it after a decade.

PRACTICE QUESTION

7   How far was Prohibition responsible for the rise in organised crime? (20)

(AQA)

Advice: *In order to answer this question effectively you will need to do more than simply produce figures to show that organised crime increased during the 1920s. There has to be evidence to link cause and effect, which means that it is important to concentrate specifically on organised crime related to alcohol before examining the wider increase in organised crime.*

Causes of the Depression

8   How far was the main cause of the Depression in the US overproduction, and to what extent has Herbert Hoover been unfairly criticised for his role in dealing with the Depression? (45)

(OCR)

Historians tend to agree on which factors caused the Depression but they usually differ on emphasis. Overproduction was certainly an issue in the run-up to the Depression but had wealth during the 1920s been more equitably distributed, consumer demand could have been sustained for a longer period. Over 70 per cent of dividend income went to the richest 1 per cent of the population. There was, however, a worldwide problem with overproduction, particularly overproduction of food, and this had been an issue since the early 1920s, although it was not until 1929 that a drastic fall in domestic demand took place. Foreign markets had already disappeared by this time. The reluctance of Republican administrations to intervene sufficiently to aid farmers and the tendency of many farmers not to diversify in terms of what they produced made problems worse. Alan Brinkley has pointed to a lack of diversification in the economy as a whole, citing the particular dependence on the motor industry. When it went into decline, so did many industries linked to it such as oil, rubber, glass, steel and leather.

There were also clearly fundamental weaknesses in the banking system with over 30,000 independent banks at the start of the 1920s, many of them small with limited capital, and not necessarily well managed. They often made purely speculative loans, and were vulnerable to sudden large-scale withdrawals or runs. Five thousand banks collapsed between 1923 and 1930. The US had lent a great deal of money to Latin America and Europe after the war, and when Germany, for example, experienced economic problems it had a knock-on effect. Protective tariffs had also made it difficult for countries recovering from the effects of war to export to the US. Some have criticised the role of the Federal Reserve Board, which acted as a kind of regulatory body for the banking system. In 1928 it raised interest rates to try to reduce stock market speculation. Monetarists have argued that this contributed to a contraction in the money supply, which had disastrous results, although Keynesians have argued that the drop in consumer spending came first and that is what led to a contraction in the money supply.

Sustained prosperity could only be based on new consumers or further investment from existing shareholders on the stock market, but as demand slowed many realised they had bought shares at inflated prices. Sufficient production only becomes overproduction when there is a slowdown in people buying. Sustained consumer purchasing would only have been possible if more people had genuinely shared in the prosperity of the 1920s, and the fact that this was not the case meant that at some point overproduction was inevitable. There was a limit to the number of people who could afford a car or a fridge unless real wages rose for more workers. A vast secondhand car market also gave consumers a cheaper alternative to a newly manufactured model as the economy faltered. At root, therefore, the unequal distribution of income was probably the main cause of the Depression.

Hoover was the most able of the three post-war Republican Presidents, but he was elected to continue similar policies, i.e. minimal government intervention in the economy, tax cuts, balanced budgets and maintaining low interest rates. In addition, his own background as a self-made millionaire reinforced his views that individuals thrived when the government pursued a laissez-faire policy. At the time of his election, he appeared to have good reason for promising 'a chicken in every pot' and 'a car in every garage', but things soon began to go wrong.

Galbraith has suggested that Hoover was badly advised at the time by economists, calling them 'almost uniquely perverse' in their arguments that budgets must be balanced and their fears of the inflationary consequences of leaving the gold standard. To an extent, even with this advice, Hoover believed that the causes of the Depression lay outside the US with issues such as overproduction and instability in other countries. In his memoirs he blamed the First World War for the problems. Given that he felt the causes of Depression were beyond his control, it is likely he felt that the solution to it was also. Michael Bernstein has in a sense supported this line by arguing that the Depression went on for so long because it came too late for the motor and construction industries to help, and too soon for emerging industries such as aviation and electrics to help. This suggests that there was a limit to what any President could have done.

Hoover, however, did not simply sit by waiting for the economy to right itself. As a response to the crash, by the end of November Hoover had met with railroad presidents urging them not to stop investment in planned track building, asked business leaders to continue with investment plans and to maintain wage levels and targets, and encouraged mayors and governors to increase spending on public works. His commitment to a balanced budget and belief in voluntarism rather than federal intervention, however, was strong. He also believed that the problems were more psychological than economic, and in the winter of 1930/1 relief payments were halved and many desperate families taken off the relief rolls. The Hawley-Smoot Tariff Act of 1930 raised duties in the hope that American industry would be further protected from competition, but other countries retaliated by making it more difficult for American exports. A thousand economists petitioned Hoover not to sign the Bill – but he did. Brogan calls it the most unaccountable action of his career. In October 1930 Hoover set up an Emergency Committee for Employment to coordinate voluntary relief agencies, typifying his faith in voluntary action. There was no dole in the US and millions became dependent on soup kitchens and private charity for their survival.

Had Hoover *increased* government spending in 1931 there could have been improvements, but instead he cut spending on the grounds that less tax was being collected, and then put up taxes in 1932 making things worse. In June 1931, Hoover proposed a one-year moratorium on all intergovernmental debts, thus stemming the tide for a short time, but within months the downward spiral continued. It was not until the winter of 1931/2 that he modified the voluntary approach slightly. Hoover's most significant move came in December 1931 when he set up an Emergency Reconstruction Finance Corporation to authorise huge loans to insurance companies, railroads and banks to try to stimulate new investment. But many did not want to borrow, much of the money went to large clients, and the purpose of the venture was essentially to restore confidence rather than actually to help needy groups. Early in 1932 Hoover signed the Glass-Steagall Act allocating $750 million of gold reserves for loans to private businesses.

Nothing Hoover did was enough. In 1983 Robert McElvaine called Hoover 'a man of principle' and argued that he was more compassionate than many have portrayed him, believing not in 'rugged individualism' but in 'progressive individualism', i.e. communities of 'socially responsible individuals' helping the unemployed, but even McElvaine regards Hoover's 'voluntary charity, local and state relief' as wholly inadequate. He did however intervene more than his predecessors, doubling public works expenditure in three years and in 1932 taking the federal budget $2.7 billion into the red, the largest peacetime deficit in US history. It should also be said that the Democrats had little to offer as an alternative, and Franklin D. Roosevelt's New Deal remained vague and short on detail. In this light, Hoover probably has been judged too harshly, but for the millions living lives of desperation, not knowing where the next meal was coming from, for the hundreds of thousands of hobos and 'Hooverville' dwellers much more could have been done.

Hoover was a product of his times, a prisoner to his party's policies, and a slave to an American ethos which valued individual initiative and rejected government intervention. Nevertheless he must take a great share of responsibility for failing to take more direct action to alleviate the worst effects of the Depression. He was simply not a politician – he was an engineer and a superbly efficient bureaucrat – and this meant he lacked Roosevelt's infectious style and skilled communication.

8   'The main cause of the Depression was that too many Americans did not share in the prosperity of the 1920s.' Discuss. (45)

Essay plan

Introduction: Indicate main line of argument but also mention other possibly significant factors.

Para 1: Examine the groups who did share in the prosperity of the times, e.g. businessmen and urban workers.

Para 2: Look at the groups who did not share in the prosperity of the period, such as farmers and African Americans, and produce some sort of statistical evidence to show how those at the top benefited much more than those at the bottom.

Para 3: Consider the argument that had prosperity been more widely distributed consumer spending could have been sustained long enough to avoid serious depression and link to para 4.

Para 4: Discuss the idea that prosperity was too dependent on a limited number of industries, e.g. car manufacturing and construction.

Para 5: Consider other factors that may have contributed to the downturn, such as: the banking system; the international situation; overproduction; and lack of government intervention.

Conclusion: Should probably decide that the maldistribution of wealth was a major cause of problems.

Part 3: Sources

1 Society in the 1920s

■   **Source A: Butler Act, Tennessee state law**

Be it Enacted, by the General Assembly of the State of Tennessee, that it shall be unlawful for any teacher in any of the universities, normals, and all other public schools in the State, which are supported in whole or in part by the public school funds of the State, to teach the theory that denies the story of the divine creation of man as taught in the Bible, and to teach instead that man has descended from a lower order of animals.

■   **Source B: Clarence Darrow, defence lawyer in the 'Monkey Trial'**

Here we find to-day as brazen and as bold an attempt to destroy learning as was made in the Middle Ages and the open difference is we have not provided that malefactors shall be burned at the stake. But there is time for that, your Honor. We have to approach these things gradually . . . If to-day you can take a thing like evolution and make it a crime to teach it in the public school . . . at the next session you may ban books and newspapers . . . Ignorance and fanaticism are ever busy and need feeding. Always they are anxious and gloating for more.

■   **Source C: Frederick L. Allen writing about Prohibition and Al Capone in 1931**

It is said that he had discovered that there was big money in the newly outlawed liquor business. He was fired with the hope of gaining control of the whole bootlegging and speakeasy operations in the city of

Chicago. Within three years it was said that he had seven hundred men at his disposal, many of them experts in the use of the Thompson sub-machine gun. As the profits rolled in, the new 'King of Chicago' learned to manage politics and politicians and had installed his own mayor in office. There were over 500 gang murders in all, but few of the murderers were arrested. Careful planning, money for bribes, intimidation of witnesses and the refusal of any gangster to testify against any other met that danger.

■ **Source D: F. Scott Fitzgerald, *Tales of the Jazz Age* (1922)**

The parties were bigger – the pace was faster – the shows were broader – the buildings were higher – the morals were looser – and the liquor was cheaper.

■ **Source E: Walter Lippmann, 'The Causes of Political Indifference Today', *Atlantic Monthly*, 139, no. 2, February (1927), pp. 265–7**

The questions which really engage the emotions of the masses . . . manifest themselves in the controversies over prohibition, the Ku Klux Klan, Romanism, Fundamentalism, immigration. These, rather than the tariff, taxation, credit and corporate control, are the issues which divide the American people . . . These questions . . . arise out of the great migration of the last fifty years, out of the growth of cities . . . Prohibition, the Ku Klux Klan, Fundamentalism, and xenophobia are an extreme but authentic expression of the politics, the social outlook, and the religion of the older American village civilization making its last stand against what looks to it like an alien invasion. The alien invasion is in fact the new America produced by the growth and prosperity of America.

EDEXCEL QUESTION FORMAT

The questions and answers that follow are based on the Edexcel style.

(a) **Study Sources C and D. What can you learn from Sources C and D about Prohibition?** (6)

(b) **Use your own knowledge to explain why Prohibition failed.** (10)

(c) **Study Sources C and E. Assess the value of these two Sources to a historian studying American society in the 1920s.** (10)

(d) **Study Sources A and B. Does Darrow (Source B) agree with the views expressed in Source A. Explain your answer by reference to both Sources.** (10)

(e) **Study Sources A and E and use your own knowledge. Do you agree with the view that the US was an intolerant society in the 1920s? Explain your answer by reference to these two Sources and your own knowledge.** (24)

(a) Source C suggests that although officially alcohol had been banned, the supply and drinking of it continued anyway, except that the government did not collect any taxes from the sales, and the control of the liquor business fell into the hands of gangsters who became powerful enough to effectively run cities. One of the aims of those who campaigned for Prohibition was to cut crime. Source C, by focusing on the most notorious gangster of the period, seems to suggest that crime actually got worse – with Al Capone having possibly 'seven hundred men at his disposal' and managing to install 'his own mayor in office.' Source D also implies that some of the aims of 'the noble experiment' were not met. One of the aims of the temperance lobby had been to improve moral values in the US as well as stopping the consumption of alcohol. Scott Fitzgerald's comments that 'the morals were looser – the liquor was cheaper' seem to confirm that, if anything, Prohibition was counter-productive. Both Sources C and D therefore support the view that Prohibition failed to achieve its aims.

(b) Prohibition failed for a number of reasons, but mainly because large numbers of Americans did not want to stop drinking. It could be argued that certain pressure groups such as the Anti-Saloon League had come to exert a disproportionate influence on government policy. Others saw the amendment to the Constitution as an infringement of personal liberty, and, for many, alcohol became part and parcel of the new culture of the 'Jazz Age'. If one adds to that a reluctance on the part of government to actually spend enough money on ensuring that Prohibition was enforced, then it is possible to see why it failed.

The number of agents to enforce the laws was never above 3,000 for the whole country – there were 32,000 speakeasies in New York alone. The police in many areas gave up on alcohol when they saw it pulling resources away from dealing with more serious crime. Many police officers and politicians also ended up on the payroll of gangsters and bootleggers, which had a corrosive effect on law and order and the political system generally. Given the huge landed and coastal borders of the US, the prevention of smuggled liquor would always have been difficult to enforce, and by 1932 it had become apparent that it would only be a matter of time before Prohibition was repealed.

(c) It could be said that Source C concentrates only on the situation in one city of the US. Given that even today Chicago is the murder capital of the country, and that in the 1920s its proximity to the Canadian border and good transport links made it an ideal location for bootlegging, it could be argued that Chicago was far from typical of the country as a whole. Evidence would definitely suggest that bootlegging and illegal drinking went on at a higher rate in the cities, particularly those with larger proportions of immigrants. Source C, however, does accurately reflect the reality of Capone's rule in Chicago and as such does give the historian a good insight into the rise of organised crime that took place during the 1920s as well as reactions to Prohibition.

Source E also concentrates on negative aspects of society, suggesting that people did not care about serious political issues such as 'the tariff, taxation, credit and corporate control' but were more concerned with emotive issues arising from immigration such as xenophobia and the influence of Roman Catholics, and Prohibition. This sheds light on a number of issues which arose during the 1920s. Lippmann also gives historians an idea of other trends during the period such as 'growth and prosperity', and clearly reflects the tensions between what he calls 'the older American village civilization', and 'the new America'.

Used together, the Sources give the historian a very good idea of some of the major issues that dominated the 1920s, although neither Source necessarily gives an overview of society, much detail, or covers other issues during the period such as the Wall Street crash, the emergence of mass consumerism, or the changes in culture and social habits during the 'Roaring Twenties'.

(d) Source A, from a Tennessee law, states that it is illegal 'to teach the theory' of evolution in schools and insists that the biblical story of creation must be adhered to. Clarence Darrow who was the defence lawyer in the 'Monkey Trial' disagrees most strongly with Source A, calling it 'an attempt to destroy learning' and suggesting that it may be the thin end of the wedge in the sense that censorship of teachers may extend to 'books and newspapers'. He also, for good measure, implies that those supporting the Tennessee law are ignorant and fanatical.

(e) In many respects the US was definitely an intolerant society in the 1920s. Some of the intolerance was a hangover from the First World War and a reaction to the events in Russia in 1917, when anti-foreign propaganda had been stirred up to high levels. In particular the Bolshevik Revolution aroused fears of the political left and the many foreigners and immigrants associated with such movements. The results of the Palmer Raids confirmed that Americans had grossly overreacted to what was in reality a non-existent 'red menace', and the treatment of anarchists Sacco and Vanzetti suggested that popular feeling as well as that in government circles was xenophobic.

The meteoric rise of the Ku Klux Klan in the 1920s also suggests that many 'old stock' Americans were intolerant of the 'new America' built on the cities, the growth of industry, and immigration from southern and eastern Europe and Asia. The government's introduction of Quota Acts seemed to officially sanction racist sentiment. Source E confirms how the Klan built up its strength by indicating that issues such as 'Romanism, Fundamentalism, [and] immigration' were what stirred people up. Throughout the period there was also a great deal of anti-black feeling in the US.

Source E also touches on the moral backlash to the more relaxed morals of the post-war period by mentioning Prohibition. Despite the good intentions of its backers, it too reflected an intolerance of a kind, and a willingness to intervene in people's personal lives. Source A shows that there was even a reluctance to embrace decades-old scientific thinking in favour of a rigidly literal interpretation of 'the story of the divine creation of man as taught in the Bible'.

In other respects, however, America led the way in culture, with writers such as Scott Fitzgerald and Hemingway making their mark, and jazz music becoming extremely popular. In business, too, new methods of production were embraced by men like Ford, and mass consumerism developed, suggesting that some people were quite prepared to embrace new ideas. America then, as now, remained an extremely diverse society, but in many respects the US in the 1920s was an intolerant society.

ADDITIONAL QUESTIONS IN THE EDEXCEL STYLE

(a) **Study Sources A and B. What can you learn from Sources A and B about American society in the 1920s?** (6)

(b) **Use your own knowledge to explain why the Ku Klux Klan became so popular in the early 1920s.** (10)

(c) **Study Sources A and D. Assess the value of these two Sources to a historian studying US society in the 1920s.** (10)

(d) **Study Sources C and E. Does Source C agree with Source E that the cities contained the roots of major social problems in the US? Explain your answer by reference to both Sources.** (10)

(e) **Study Sources C and D. Do you agree that Prohibition caused more problems than it was intended to solve? Explain your answer by reference to these two Sources and your own knowledge.** (24)

2 Boom and bust

■ Source A: Hoover's 'New York City speech', 1928

When the Republican party came into full power . . . it freed and stimulated enterprise, it restored the Government to its position as an umpire instead of a player in the economic game . . . projection of government in business . . . would impair the very basis of liberty and freedom . . . The very essence of equality of opportunity and of American individualism is that there shall be no domination by any group or combination in this Republic, whether it be business or political. On the contrary, it demands economic justice as well as political and social justice. It is no system of laissez faire . . . We are nearer today to the ideal of the abolition of poverty and fear from the lives of men and women than ever before in any land . . .

■ Source B: Robert La Follette's Progressive Party platform, 1924

Through control of government, monopoly has steadily extended its absolute dominion to every basic industry. In violation of law, monopoly has crushed competition, stifled private initiative and independent enterprise, and without fear of punishment now exacts extortionate profits upon every necessity of life consumed by the public. The equality of opportunity proclaimed by the Declaration of Independence . . . has been displaced by special privilege for the few . . . The people know monopoly has its representatives in the halls of Congress, on the Federal bench, and in the executive departments . . . a total of more than 600,000 or 26 percent of all farmers . . . have virtually been bankrupted since 1920 in . . . fifteen states alone . . . the direct and logical result of the policies . . . which protected with exorbitant tariffs the industrial magnates, but depressed the prices of the farmers' products . . .

Source C: average monthly earnings of US workers in 1929

Farmers in South Carolina	$129
Town workers in South Carolina	$412
Town workers in New York	$881
Fruit farmers in California	$1,246

■ **Source D: selected share prices in cents, *The Wall Street Journal*, 1928**

	March 1928	*Sept 1928*
Montgomery Ward	132	466
Union Carbide and Carbon	145	413
Westinghouse	92	313
Anaconda Copper	54	162
Woolworth	181	251

■ **Source E: income distribution before the Great Depression, 1929**

	Share of income (%)
Wealthiest fifth	52
Second wealthiest fifth	19
Middle fifth	14
Second poorest fifth	10
Poorest fifth	5

EDEXCEL QUESTION FORMAT

The questions and answers that follow are based on the Edexcel style.

(a) **Study Sources C and E. What can you learn from Sources C and E about the distribution of wealth in the US by 1929?** (6)

(b) **Use your own knowledge to explain why share prices rose so much in 1928.** (10)

(c) **Study Sources A and D. Assess the value of these two Sources to a historian studying the 'boom' of the 1920s.** (10)

(d) **Study Sources A and B. Does Source B agree with Source A that there was 'no domination by any group or combination' of government or the economy in 1920s America? Explain your answer by reference to both sources.** (10)

(e) **Study Sources B and E. Do you agree that the maldistribution of wealth in the US during the 1920s was a major factor in causing the Great Depression? Explain your answer by reference to these two sources and your own knowledge.** (24)

(a) Both Sources would suggest that certain groups in society did not earn as much as others. Source C indicates the variations in wage rates in different parts of the country for different jobs, and implies that even within certain jobs wages could vary enormously: for example, fruit farmers in California clearly out-earning farmers in South Carolina. The figures for town dwellers also suggest that Northern cities paid better than Southern ones. Source E does not give as much detail as Source C but in some ways it makes more of an impact because it clearly shows that the wealthiest fifth of the country earned more than half of the country's income, and that the poorest fifth only earned a twentieth.

(b) Share prices rose quickly during the late 1920s, essentially because of the confidence of share buyers. Share prices effectively lost touch with reality and often did not bear any relation to the actual performance of companies during the period, which is why, when confidence dipped, the results were disastrous for some. Buying on margin combined with the increase in the number of loans from banks meant that more people could afford to buy more shares, but it was the optimism of the period buoyed by great increases in industrial production and consumer spending which really caused the rise of share prices.

(c) Source A is taken from a 1928 speech by Herbert Hoover, the Republican Presidential candidate and previously Secretary of Commerce. He clearly has political points to be made regarding the role of his party in shaping the economic prosperity of the period, saying that it 'freed and stimulated enterprise' and safeguarded 'economic justice'. In short, he seems to be claiming the credit for the boom. Given that the speech is designed to spread a political message it must be used cautiously but that does not mean necessarily that Republican administrations did not have an effect on prosperity. As a set of statistics Source D is possibly more reliable than Hoover, but in some ways is more limited than Source A. However, by showing a huge rise in share prices in 1928, it does seem to confirm the impression given in Hoover's speech – that the economy of the country was booming. What neither Source really shows is whether the whole population was benefiting from the boom.

(d) Source A depicts the government as a neutral 'umpire' maintaining liberty and opportunity by ensuring that there is 'no domination by any group or combination' of the economy or politics, and helping to stimulate enterprise. Source B utterly refutes this by stating firmly that industrial monopolies dominated American society, and had 'crushed competition' and 'stifled private initiative' as well as replacing equality of opportunity by 'special privilege for the few'. La Follette goes on to say that monopoly has bought the support of politicians, and cites as evidence the tariffs to protect industrial magnates, while government has done little to help the farmers.

(e) There appears to be strong evidence that maldistribution of wealth in the US contributed greatly to the Depression, but other factors such as the lack of diversification in the economy, the unsound banking system, the reluctance of the Republican administration to intervene, and also the impact of the international situation must also be considered.

La Follette in Source B highlights the plight of the farmers, citing the fact that '26% of all farmers' in 15 states had been virtually bankrupted, and the government, by implication, had been reluctant to help. Given that a third of all American workers were employed in the agricultural sector any decline in farming would have serious effects. Throughout the 1920s the majority of farmers struggled, as did other groups such as miners, cloth workers, women, blacks, new unskilled immigrants and those in the South generally. With the poorest fifth of the population receiving only 5 per cent of the country's total income (Source E) it is hardly surprising that the consumer spending required to sustain prosperity did not materialise. Those people at the bottom could barely afford their food and rent, never mind fridges, vacuum cleaners and cars, while the 20 per cent at the top of society earning 52 per cent of its income did not need great numbers of fridges or cars for their families.

The slowdown in spending can be seen to be a result of the maldistribution of income, and as the number of cars being sold dropped, along with other consumer products, employers laid off workers or made them part-time, and this further reduced the money supply. As optimism began to falter so did confidence in the stock market and the banking system, which was under-regulated and according to David Kennedy 'rotten even in good times'. When the government did intervene it put up tariffs, leading to retaliation abroad and further restricting markets for American goods. There is no doubt that overproduction and other problems in different parts of the world had their impact and set the context for a slowdown, but a wider distribution of income away from the very rich and possibly some of the urban workers would have perhaps allowed the momentum of economic growth to have been maintained.

ADDITIONAL QUESTIONS IN THE EDEXCEL STYLE

(a) **Study Sources A and B. What can you learn from Sources A and B about the way the US economy worked in the 1920s?** (6)

(b) **Use your own knowledge to explain why all American workers did not share in the prosperity of the 1920s.** (10)

(c) **Study Sources A and B. Assess the value of these two Sources to a historian studying the approach of governments to the economy in the 1920s.** (10)

(d) **Study Sources C and E. Does Source C support the evidence in Source E that income was distributed unfairly? Explain your answer by reference to both Sources.** (10)

(e) **Study Sources A and B. Do you agree that Republican policies in the 1920s contributed significantly to prosperity? Explain your answer by reference to these two Sources and your own knowledge.** (24)

Part 4: Historical skills

 ## 1 Report on immigration

You have been asked to compile a report on the nature and impact of immigration on the US in the years since the Civil War. You should cover such areas as the national origins of immigrants, contributions to the economy and how they feature in crime statistics (particularly in the big cities) and union activity. Information ought to be presented in tables and graphs as well as prose. Textbooks and Internet sources such as Spartacus Educational could be used for research.

 ## 2 Were Sacco and Vanzetti guilty?

Imagine that you have been asked to prepare an appeal against the guilty verdicts passed on Sacco and Vanzetti. Examine the evidence on website http://www.law.umkc.edu/faculty/projects/ftrials/ftrials.htm (The Sacco and Vanzetti Trial – Famous Trials – UMKC School of Law) as a starting point and attempt to highlight any inconsistencies in evidence or any behaviour by the judge likely to influence the verdict of the jury.

Sources and references

Alan Brinkley, *The Unfinished Nation*, McGraw-Hill (2000).

Charles Eagles, *America: a Narrative History*, Norton (1999).

Alan Farmer and Vivienne Sanders, *American History, 1860–1990*, Hodder & Stoughton (2000).

J.K. Galbraith, *The Great Crash 1929*, Penguin (1975).

Maldwyn Jones, *The Limits of Liberty*, Oxford University Press (1983/1995).

John M. Murrin, Paul E. Johnson, James M. McPherson *et al.*, *Liberty Equality Power*, Harcourt (2001).

Spartacus Educational www.spartacus.schoolnet.co.uk.

John Traynor, *Mastering Modern United States History*, Palgrave (2001).

John Traynor, 'Prohibition and Organised Crime in the USA', *Modern History Review*, November (2002).

Clive Webb, 'The Ku Klux Klan', *Modern History Review*, April (2002).

Doug Willoughby and Susan Willoughby, *The USA 1917–45*, Heinemann (2000).

Howard Zinn, *A People's History of the United States*, Longman (1996).

Chapter 7

Franklin D. Roosevelt and the New Deal, 1933–1941

This chapter focuses upon the federal government's response to the Great Depression, assessing the aims and success of the measures introduced, and draws particular attention to criticisms aimed at the administration of Franklin Delano Roosevelt (FDR).

 Historical background

Franklin Delano Roosevelt
The aims and nature of the New Deal
Financial reforms
Providing relief
Industrial recovery and reforms
Agriculture
Regional development
Critics of the New Deal
The Supreme Court and the New Deal
The decline of the New Deal

 Sources

1   The agricultural crisis
2   Views from within the administration

 Historical skills

1   'Alphabet agencies' task
2   Using art as historical sources

 Essays

The policies of the New Deal
Problems for the New Deal
The results of the New Deal

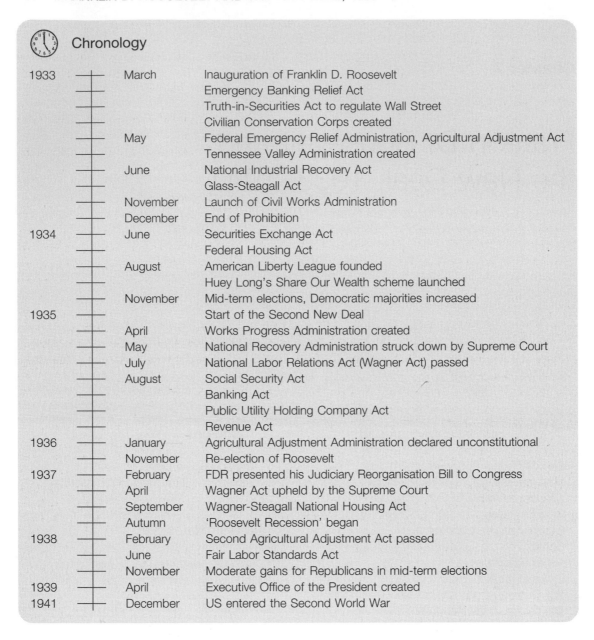

Chronology

1933	March	Inauguration of Franklin D. Roosevelt
		Emergency Banking Relief Act
		Truth-in-Securities Act to regulate Wall Street
		Civilian Conservation Corps created
	May	Federal Emergency Relief Administration, Agricultural Adjustment Act
		Tennessee Valley Administration created
	June	National Industrial Recovery Act
		Glass-Steagall Act
	November	Launch of Civil Works Administration
	December	End of Prohibition
1934	June	Securities Exchange Act
		Federal Housing Act
	August	American Liberty League founded
		Huey Long's Share Our Wealth scheme launched
	November	Mid-term elections, Democratic majorities increased
1935		Start of the Second New Deal
	April	Works Progress Administration created
	May	National Recovery Administration struck down by Supreme Court
	July	National Labor Relations Act (Wagner Act) passed
	August	Social Security Act
		Banking Act
		Public Utility Holding Company Act
		Revenue Act
1936	January	Agricultural Adjustment Administration declared unconstitutional
	November	Re-election of Roosevelt
1937	February	FDR presented his Judiciary Reorganisation Bill to Congress
	April	Wagner Act upheld by the Supreme Court
	September	Wagner-Steagall National Housing Act
	Autumn	'Roosevelt Recession' began
1938	February	Second Agricultural Adjustment Act passed
	June	Fair Labor Standards Act
	November	Moderate gains for Republicans in mid-term elections
1939	April	Executive Office of the President created
1941	December	US entered the Second World War

Part 1: Historical background

Franklin Delano Roosevelt

The man who was inaugurated as the 32nd President of the United States on 4 March 1933 was to become one of the most eminent holders of that office. Franklin Delano Roosevelt, or FDR as he is known, stands alongside Washington and Lincoln as a saviour and shaper of his nation. In common with these illustrious predecessors Roosevelt faced problems of an overwhelming magnitude. The man who would lead his country through to the closing months of the Second World War had to first do battle against the economic collapse that had begun in mid-1929 and had since brought the nation to its knees.

In the early years of the 1930s the economic and social situation in the US worsened. Manufacturing output and investment fell as people put purchases of goods such as cars and refrigerators on hold. By 1933 unemployment officially stood at 25 per cent. In addition, many of those with work suffered a reduction in hours and wages. Agriculture, as well as industry, was in crisis as farms produced more to pay off debts only to see the prices for their produce fall still further. As deflation became entrenched, people queued to withdraw their money from banks and from Saving and Loans schemes. This contributed significantly to waves of bank collapses throughout the early 1930s. The nation was in a dire state and as the final weeks of Hoover's 'lame duck' period dragged on there seemed no way out of the crisis. People and business alike turned to President-elect Roosevelt.

Franklin Delano Roosevelt was born in 1882 to a wealthy New York family of Dutch descent. Inspired by the example of his cousin, Theodore Roosevelt, he first worked as a lawyer before entering politics at an early age, rising to the level of state governor by 1928. He quickly rose to prominence within the Democratic Party, acquiring a reputation as an independently minded reformer. As governor he took an interventionist stance in New York in response to the Wall Street crash and the ensuing Great Depression, striving more than most to ensure the provision of relief to the needy. He inspired loyalty from those who worked alongside him and generated faith among the people he served. Appealing for wide support for his efforts to tackle the Depression, he famously told the nation during his first inaugural address 'the only thing we have to fear is fear itself'. He was giving notice that his administration would not shirk the responsibilities it had assumed and would provide bold leadership. This charismatic man, who made a point of standing, despite having lost almost all use of his legs through polio, was the antithesis of the insipid Hoover. America believed him.

 ## The aims and nature of the New Deal

When FDR accepted his party's nomination to be the Democratic candidate in the 1932 Presidential elections he had given a victory speech in which he spoke of his ambitions for the nation, including a 'new deal for the American people'. The phrase stuck and now stands as the epithet to 1930s America. Everyone knew the name New Deal, but no one was really sure what it amounted to. In his inaugural address, little in the way of specifics was divulged as the new President pledged that putting people to work was his priority.

In short the New Deal was a series of measures to stabilise business and prompt economic recovery while providing relief to those who were suffering. Reforms were also an integral part of FDR's plans as he sought to restore confidence in the nation's financial institutions and ensure that some of the more obvious mistakes of the 1920s could not be repeated. The New Deal should not be thought of as a coherent, carefully thought out programme. To an extent the steps that FDR took were simply reactions to events. Some pieces of legislation contradicted others, while some were deemed by the courts to be unconstitutional and therefore unlawful. Nor should the programme be viewed as being exclusively the work of President Roosevelt. He assembled a talented group of advisers, the so called 'Brains Trust', that on occasion pressured him to act on issues in which he had little desire to become involved. Furthermore, there are examples of notable New Deal legislation that originated in Congress rather than the White House. Augmenting this pressure were conservative opponents, who favoured less government intervention, and radicals, who favoured more fundamental reforms. It is clear that a full understanding of the New Deal needs to take into account wider aspects of American polity and society in the 1930s.

The torrent of legislation that was the New Deal has been categorised by historians who endeavour to ascribe boundaries to measures that were almost certainly not conceptualised as distinct entities. The period is commonly split into two. The First New Deal ran from 1933 to 1934 and introduced policies primarily

Figure 7.1
Migratory Mexican field worker's home, California

designed to provide relief to the millions suffering the effects of the Depression and promote economic recovery. Owing to various factors, including a lack of recovery and growing opposition, there was a shift of emphasis in 1935 when a more radical Second New Deal began. This wave of legislation brought in a more coherent set of permanent reforms that included significant implications for business and labour and created a national system of benefits for the first time in the US. While bearing this apparent change of direction in mind it is arguably easier to comprehend the New Deal as a whole by examining it thematically, taking in how it impacted upon America sector by sector.

 ## Financial reforms

Dire necessity dictated that Roosevelt's first actions after his inauguration were to try to rescue the banking system. To forestall more closures, a 'bank holiday' was declared while options were considered. The resulting Emergency Banking Bill set the trend as the first of many executive-initiated reforms as it was swiftly passed by a willing Congress. The Act gave support to stronger and, as critics pointed out, larger banks and closed those most at risk. Roosevelt gave a radio address soon after to convince worried citizens. He explained the steps to be taken and said: 'I can assure you that it is safer to keep your money in a reopened bank than under the mattress.' His actions succeeded in their intentions as banking was stabilised.

Further legislation in the first 'Hundred Days' of his administration guaranteed bank deposits and during the Second New Deal control over the banking system was centralised. Action was also taken to devalue the US dollar and to restore credibility to Wall Street. In sum, Roosevelt's banking and financial reforms sought to strengthen the existing order within US capital by introducing more controlled systems and ridding it of some of its flaws.

 ## Providing relief

Roosevelt had demonstrated his compassion for the needy when he was governor of New York. Once in the White House his team quickly set about accommodating within America's closely held ethos of individualism the notion that the state had a responsibility to directly intervene on behalf of the less fortunate. Action fell broadly into two categories: work relief and social security.

The Federal Emergency Relief Administration (FERA), established in May 1933, was the first instance of the US federal government providing money to those out of work. It distributed money to states, which would then be matched by them and passed on to the unemployed. There were problems encountered in the administering of such a vast project as the federal apparatus in the states simply did not exist and the amounts given were usually small. But FERA no doubt saved many from starvation and represents a watershed in the relationship between the government and the people. The New Deal saw the establishment of the American welfare state when the Social Security Act of 1935 was passed. It was a piece of legislation that would have an impact in the long term, providing pensions and unemployment benefit based on contributions from both employees and employers. It excluded several groups at the bottom of society, for example domestic servants and agricultural labourers, and sidestepped the issue of health insurance. Yet credit must be given to this Act because it broke new ground and laid the foundations of the modern American welfare system.

Creating government agencies to provide work was considered preferable to handing out dole. In November 1933 the head of FERA, Harry Hopkins, created a work relief programme, the Civil Works Administration, (CWA) which placed an emphasis on providing manual

Figure 7.2 **Cartoon illustrating how the Depression affected farms**

labour. Another early example of such a scheme was the Civilian Conservation Corps (CCC). It provided employment for young men carrying out work such as planting trees and draining marshland in exchange for a meagre wage, most of which was sent directly to their families. The Public Works Administration (PWA) kept the construction industry going and attempted to stimulate the economy through the building of schools, dams, bridges, etc. with a $3.3 billion budget. During the Second New Deal in 1935 the Works Progress Administration (WPA) built on earlier efforts at providing work relief. It eventually employed an average of 2.1 million men during its eight-year life in the construction of public projects such as schools and bridges. Its wage levels were adjusted to reflect local economic conditions, so that Northern workers got more than Southern workers. One of the principles behind all work relief schemes was to bypass the giving of handouts, which people often found demeaning, yet avoiding paying people so much that they would be deterred from taking a 'proper' job.

 Industrial recovery and reforms

The cornerstone of the early New Deal was the National Industrial Recovery Act (NIRA). This ambitious measure, passed on 16 June 1933 (the last of FDR's 'Hundred Days'), attempted to promote recovery and reconcile the interests of business and labour. To counteract deflation anti-trust laws were suspended, which meant that manufacturers could now join together and agree prices. In return for this potentially monopolistic, pro-business reform manufacturers had to accept a series of regulatory codes. These codes had a positive impact upon wages, hours and conditions, for example child labour was banned. But all too often the codes were drawn up by big business in their own favour.

Workers were given the right to freely organise themselves into unions under Section 7(a) of NIRA. However, the legislation was difficult to enforce. Unions rightly claimed that the right of 'collective bargaining' was insufficient in the face of business hostility. Although NIRA marked a new beginning in US industrial relations, it ultimately failed to promote industrial recovery with its Public Works Administration programmes. In May 1935 the Supreme Court declared NIRA unconstitutional and therefore void.

The rights of labour were reasserted and strengthened in the 'Second Hundred Days', when the National Labor Relations Act was passed in July 1935. This legislation had started life on Capitol Hill; Roosevelt himself was reluctant to become embroiled in labour legislation and only threw his weight behind senator Robert Wagner's bill once it became clear that the Supreme Court would strike down NIRA. This time the right to collective bargaining was to be guaranteed with enforcement mechanisms and the National Labor Relations Board (NLRB) was set up to oversee labour–industry relations. This was an interventionist measure that strengthened labour and promoted a healthier economy by reducing the number of industrial disputes in the following years. The 'Wagner Act', upheld by the Supreme Court in 1937, is remembered as one of the landmarks of the New Deal years.

Some business leaders supported Roosevelt's attempts to reform relations between industry, government and labour. However, many resented the intrusion into their affairs and became critical of FDR. The Public Utility Holding Company Act provided another cause for complaint for some in the 'Second Hundred Days'. A small number of giant companies had come to dominate the provision of power in many regions, avoiding regulation in the process. Roosevelt's determined stance resulted in the eventual reorganisation of the sector. The issue was fought bitterly but, like other New Deal legislation, it ultimately sought to strengthen business by clamping down on its worst excesses.

 ## Agriculture

Already weak in the 1920s, farming had been badly hit by the Depression. At the heart of the problem lay overproduction. The Agricultural Adjustment Act of 1933 attempted to arrest the decline in farm prices by curtailing production. Farmers were paid to reduce the amounts of cotton, corn and pigs they produced by a system of subsidies that stabilised farm income. The Act proved more popular with farmers, and particularly landlords, than with the public – who objected to the slaughter of six million piglets in times of economic hardship. Throughout the mid-1930s, more and more land was taken out of production and prices slowly rose. This was partly a direct consequence of the administration's policies as well as the effects of a severe drought and the lower value of the dollar. The gains brought by the Agricultural Adjustment Administration (AAA) along with other legislation concerning electrification, conservation and the refinancing of mortgages went a long way to countering the effects of the Depression, drought and subsequent dust storms of 1934 to 1935. The Act became another major New Deal casualty of the Supreme Court when it was declared unconstitutional in January 1936. However, another Agricultural Adjustment Administration was established in 1938, which gave farming a long lasting presence in Washington DC.

 ## Regional development

One of the major successes of the New Deal was an attempt to develop one of the poorest regions of the nation, the Tennessee valley, which covers 40,000 square miles across seven states. Drawing inspiration from the Progressives of the previous decade, the power of the Tennessee river was to be harnessed to bring cheap electricity to the region. The Tennessee Valley Authority (TVA), established in May 1933, organised the construction of 20 dams and the formation of cooperatives, welfare and educational programmes in an area where only one in fifty farms had electricity. The administration had to battle against privately owned energy companies who saw it as an encroachment upon their domain. Ultimately the scheme did more than provide power and create jobs. It encouraged further investment from industrialists thus advancing the economic development of this poor area.

Nature augmented economic problems in 1934 and 1935 when a severe drought hit the central states of the US. Although somewhat fortuitous for the government's drive to reduce production in agriculture, the drought and accompanying dust storms caused severe hardship for countless thousands of farm families. Newly established federal agencies such as the AAA, CCC and the Soil Conservation Service (SCS) provided much needed aid and modernisation for rural America but could not pretend to be an instant panacea. There was a wave of migration from the 'Dust Bowl' as people headed west in search of work. The federal government was successful in reducing the number of farm foreclosures and did strive to improve conditions for migrant workers through the Resettlement Administration (RA), however the artistic works of contemporaries such as Woody Guthrie, Dorothea Lange and John Steinbeck stand as testament to the enduring suffering of millions of Americans during the 1930s.

 ## Critics of the New Deal

Once the immediate threat of collapse had been removed cracks began to appear in Roosevelt's broad support. The mid-1930s saw various attacks upon the New Deal from both within politics and from popular movements throughout the nation. Roosevelt was criticised from both left and right – accused of being both a fascist and a communist.

In terms of membership, the 1930s represented the heyday of American **communism**. Communists criticised the New Deal as a capitalist tool and certainly FDR's main mission was to save capitalism in the United States. Apart from the formation of Farmer-Labor parties in parts of the mid-west, little organised headway was made towards public ownership of resources. There simply was not enough support in the country for such dogma. The workers and the unemployed stood by Roosevelt. After all, he had given them unions and relief, and his anti-elitist rhetoric appealed directly to them.

The flamboyant Louisiana senator, Huey Long, launched his radical Share Our Wealth scheme after he became disillusioned with Roosevelt following the First New Deal. He proposed placing limits on wages and inheritances for the extremely rich, which would then be shared out more evenly. With a claimed five million supporters nationwide talk of a third party campaign in the 1936 Presidential elections seemed credible. But Long was killed in Baton Rouge in September 1935, apparently by one of his own bodyguards during a scuffle with an opponent. It can be argued that Roosevelt's Revenue Tax Act of 1935, which increased the higher rates of income tax, was designed to undercut the appeal of Long's plan.

Another fanciful idea to end the Depression was Dr Francis Townsend's Pension Plan. This amounted to giving the retired a $200 monthly pension on condition that it would be spent within the month, thus boosting consumption and production and increasing the number of jobs available. Townsend's prescription was understandably popular with the aged but was totally unworkable in practice. However, the influence of this popular left-wing idea can be seen in the Social Security Act of the Second New Deal, which introduced a national system of pensions for the first time in the United States.

Left-wing critics lacked the electoral base from which to pose a serious threat to Roosevelt's continuation in office, but they demonstrated that there was mass discontent throughout the nation, among young and old, farmer and factory worker. The popularity of these critics' ideas showed Roosevelt that the public desired more far-reaching action. In 1935 the Second New Deal was launched in response to the continuing economic stagnation as well as to head off his critics. It brought a change of emphasis as legislation encompassing ideas that had been widely supported, such as progressive taxation and social security, was passed.

Criticism also came from the right. The Liberty League was a group of wealthy businessmen and conservatives from both major political parties who launched vitriolic attacks against FDR accusing him of bringing communism to the US. The business community had begun to turn against the New Deal after the initial

'Hundred Days'. Section 7(a) of NIRA appalled many who were simply not willing to contemplate the unionisation of the workforce. Many on the right believed in limited government and so it was inevitable that FDR's interventionist administration would not enjoy their support. However right-wing groups and politicians had less of an impact than the left until Roosevelt's second administration began in 1937.

 ## The Supreme Court and the New Deal

The New Deal's most effective opponent proved to be the Supreme Court. Since 1803 it had assumed the right to judge void any Act of Congress that it considered contravened the Constitution. In 1935 the Court unanimously declared NIRA to be unconstitutional. The justices ruled that the federal government had no business intervening in intra-state trade as outlined in Article 1 Section 8 of the Constitution. All NIRA codes were therefore void as this major piece of New Deal legislation floundered. A divided Court declared the Agricultural Adjustment Act unconstitutional the following year.

FDR signalled his intent after his second inauguration when he presented Congress with his Judiciary Reorganisation Bill. It amounted to a crude attempt to 'pack' the Supreme Court with sympathetic justices. Roosevelt may have been able to claim that the Supreme Court was standing in the way of much needed reform, for which he had an impressive mandate, but he had misjudged America's sentiments towards its institutions. The bill was defeated in July 1937. However, the Supreme Court, with a nod to reality, was beginning to uphold New Deal legislation. Although Roosevelt had been defeated, his ideas won the day. The Supreme Court had sanctioned the extension of the President's powers into the realms of regulating the economy.

 ## The decline of the New Deal

For Roosevelt an unforeseen and unfortunate by-product of the Supreme Court battle was the strengthening of opposition to himself and the New Deal. Conservative Southern Democrats joined a bolstered Republican Party in checking the power of the executive. For the President a series of problems ensued and the reforming impetus withered. Many critics blamed a downturn in the economy in 1937 on Roosevelt's desire to balance the budget. It had coincided with a rapid reduction in the WPA's expenditure and was consequently dubbed the 'Roosevelt Recession'. Unemployment had risen by four million before Roosevelt requested more funding for relief programmes.

Further discontent followed with his attempt to reorganise the workings of the White House. The Executive Office of the President was eventually created in 1939, much to the chagrin of Congress. The midterm elections of 1938 saw the failure of an attempted purge of Democratic Conservatives by Roosevelt and the Republicans made modest gains in both the Senate and the House of Representatives. The wind had been taken from the sails of domestic policy and the New Deal was over. At the same time events in Europe and the Pacific began to loom ominously on the horizon. By the end of the New Deal, America had not yet risen from the ashes of its spectacular economic collapse, beginning almost a decade before. Massive arms sales to Britain and its own entry into the war finally brought a long awaited recovery to the US.

Today historians contest the nature of the New Deal and its impact on America. The weaknesses of various pieces of legislation are easy to identify and the absence of an economic recovery in the 1930s all too obvious. Some regard the period as a missed opportunity for more radical change and highlight the conservatism of many reforms. However, this runs the risk of misinterpreting Roosevelt's aims and downplaying the significance of the New Deal. The achievements of both are concrete enough and the steps taken resulted in the strengthening of the American systems of democracy and capitalism. He had told America at his first inauguration in March 1933: 'This great nation will endure as it has endured, will revive and will prosper.' It did, and Franklin Roosevelt and the New Deal had played their parts.

Part 2: Essays

 The policies of the New Deal

1 **How effective were New Deal reforms of the banking and financial sectors in achieving their aims?** (20)

(AQA)

Financial reforms were an integral part of the New Deal. They were required to set the institutions of US capital on a firmer footing and to prevent a repeat of mistakes made during the 1920s, which had been largely responsible for the spectacular stock market collapse. Consequently, throughout the years of the New Deal, Roosevelt's administration made several notable changes to America's financial systems.

The immediate priority was to take action to halt the alarming rate of closure of the nation's banks. The system appeared to be on the verge of collapse with bank after bank closing as people rushed to withdraw their savings. A 'bank holiday' was declared in order to providing breathing space as FDR and his team considered their options. A mere five days after the inauguration, the Emergency Banking Bill sailed through a specially reconvened Congress. Solvent banks were to be backed by the federal government, which itself extended its powers to control the banking system, whereas the weakest banks were not allowed to reopen.

Roosevelt addressed the nation on the radio three days later in the first of his 'fireside chats'. In his confident yet friendly manner he assured Americans that their savings were now safe. He went on to explain the reforms and ask for the people's help in rectifying the situation. The run on the banks quickly halted as people deposited their savings just as their President had requested. The banking system had been stabilised in a matter of days. So how had FDR accomplished this? After all the proposals were hardly new – by and large they had been adopted from Hoover's administration. Roosevelt had simply introduced a balanced measure that was enough to convince the people without alarming the business community. The unequivocal success of this first piece of New Deal legislation also illustrates the faith that FDR was able to inspire among the American people. It is difficult to imagine Hoover being successful with a similar ploy.

There were two other notable forays into banking reform for the New Deal. The Glass-Steagall Act, which was passed on FDR's 100th day in office, was designed to prevent a recurrence of some of the problems of the 1920s by, for example, banning stock market speculation by commercial banks. Furthermore, it insured bank deposits of up to $2,500 for individual investors. This Act can also be considered successful in achieving its goals as, together with the Emergency Banking Relief Act, it restored confidence in US banking. Just three months earlier that same banking system had been close to a collapse. During the Second New Deal the Banking Act of August 1935 effectively gave the federal government control over banking. The Federal Reserve Board was revamped and given responsibility for certain decisions such as setting the bank rate and the appointment of key personnel. In effect the US now had a central banking system that would be run from Washington DC.

It was felt that Wall Street also needed to be reformed. The Securities Act of 1933 stipulated that realistic information must be given to investors on share issues. This was intended to remove the threat of wild over-speculation in the stock markets, which had contributed to the Wall Street crash. The Securities Act of 1934 set up the Securities and Exchange Commission (SEC) under Joseph P. Kennedy: this acted as a scrutiniser of Wall Street and proved to be effective at its job. The measure helped Wall Street regain some credibility – as well as helping FDR's administration earn a totally unwarranted anti-business reputation.

Other financial measures included taking the US off the gold standard in April 1933. Freeing the US from international constraints regarding the value of the dollar would make it easier to manipulate its level. FDR's actions had the effect of devaluing the US dollar and undoubtedly were contributory factors behind a modest increase in prices. The price to pay for this was the wrecking of the International Economic Conference in London in July 1933. The US was taking an isolationist stance in its efforts to climb out of the Depression and neglecting its responsibilities to its trading partners.

These financial reforms removed a number of problems, which had become all too apparent in the 1920s when boom had led to bust. As a result banking was rescued and the stock exchanges re-acquired some much needed credibility. Roosevelt had not taken any particularly radical steps and was criticised by some who wished him to go further and, for example, nationalise the banks. In fact he relied upon advice from the banking sector when proposals were being drafted. This indicates that his aim was to preserve the existing system by removing its flaws rather than to fundamentally change it. Therefore the reforms should be seen as a success given that they encouraged a restoration of confidence in the banking and financial systems of the US. They were not intended to bring about an economic recovery from the depths of the Depression in which the US was languishing. Direct intervention in industry and agriculture were required for that task.

2   (a) Explain the motives behind the passage of the National Industrial Recovery Act. (7)

(b) Why was there so much opposition to NIRA? (18)

(Edexcel)

The National Industrial Recovery Act, passed on 16 June 1933, was the centrepiece of Roosevelt's first frantic period of legislating known as the 'Hundred Days'. It is seen as a pro-business reform with important concessions given to labour. The Act consisted of two parts. Firstly, the National Recovery Administration (NRA) was intended to promote industrial recovery through the restructuring of business relations via a series of regulatory codes. These codes of conduct were at the heart of NIRA. There were to be separate codes for each industry that regulated competition, wages and conditions, and workers were guaranteed the right to have input into them. They therefore introduced a cooperative relationship between companies by the removal of the destructive practice of competitive pricing. With prices maintained or increased, business could produce a profit, which would then be reinvested. The second element was the establishment of the Public Works Administration, which would provide work through construction programmes and consequently increase consumer purchasing power. The aim of both parts was to provide a much needed shot in the arm for the beleaguered American economy. An examination of the inspiration behind and the intentions of those who drafted the legislation will shed light on why it was passed.

Stabilising banking and the other financial reforms had been necessary but would not result in increasing employment. Direct action was needed and Roosevelt's administration was coming under pressure from Congress, which had its own plans to affect a recovery. Action had to be taken quickly therefore to pre-empt Congressional moves. Added to this pressure were the voices of advisers from within Roosevelt's 'Brains Trust'. Several notable New Deal advisers were among those who blamed competition between businesses for the Depression. One of the main provisions of the resulting Act therefore ensured anti-trust laws were to be overlooked if industry implemented other codes. The codes would benefit business by regulating prices as well as workers through agreements on wages and conditions. The scrapping of the anti-trust laws removed a perceived obstacle to industrial expansion. This was a change that had been pushed for by several business leaders since the early 1920s and had found fresh impetus after the head of General Electric, Gerard Swope, proposed a similar move to prompt recovery in 1931.

Historians of the left, for example Radosh, have pointed out that the NRA had a strong corporate background and was passed in the interests of business. He claims the conservative origins of the reforms were camouflaged to a degree by the inclusion of seemingly radical measures. One of these measures was Title II of NIRA, which set up a Public Works Administration. Public construction programmes were appropriated $3.3 billion over two years to relieve unemployment and economic stagnation. Although the Public

Works Administration was part of NIRA, it was separated and handed to the conscientious Harold Ickes to run. It pumped money into worthwhile projects and in turn it was hoped that the economy would benefit, as workers saw their purchasing power increase and once more became consumers.

From the perspective of the left the PWA was launched for other than philanthropic purposes. 'To the hungry and unemployed, it symbolised a direct concern by the government for their plight. Its effects were limited and it did not interfere with private business prerogatives' (Radosh). From this standpoint the PWA was little more than a sop to the people to disguise the pro-business measure from which it was derived.

The part of NIRA that is most often focused upon is Section 7(a), which allowed workers to freely organise into unions. Radical critics of the New Deal claim that Section 7(a) was also a concession to labour in return for the acceptance of the codes of conduct that allowed business to regulate itself. Furthermore, it was conceptualised as being in the long-term interests of business anyway. Unionisation was a way for business to institutionalise their conflict with labour within the existing corporate system, thus forestalling the development of any more serious opposition. In 1926 the leading moderate, Gerard Swope, had tried to convince other industrialists of the need for unionisation, explaining that the outcome would be 'the difference between an organisation with which we could work on a businesslike basis and one that would be a source of endless difficulties' (Radosh).

However this can be seen as an overly cynical view of the NRA and its codes. The historian Anthony Badger has written that the impetus for business self-regulation came from smaller companies who stood to gain more than big business through the reduction in competition. Some labour leaders too had been supportive of such measures, seeing the destructive effects of competition as a danger to jobs within their industries. The inspiration behind Section 7(a) had actually come from the United Mine Workers, which had proposed the acceptance of codes of self-regulation in their industry in return for guaranteed rights of collective bargaining (Badger). The apportionment of influence behind the legislation can be debated but it is undisputable that the aim of NIRA was to promote economic recovery.

(b) The National Recovery Administration Act was vast in its scope, incorporating hastily drawn up codes of conduct for many different industries and $3.3 billion of funding for a Public Works Administration. The aim was to promote industrial recovery. There were differing views about the best way to achieve this goal and so it is no surprise to find that the Act provoked criticism. The most contentious opposition came from small businesses, larger industries and organised labour. This central piece of the First New Deal, which had attempted to please all, ended up pleasing no one during its two-year lifespan.

Many small firms felt aggrieved that the process of writing the codes of conduct was dominated by big business. Government officials commonly left industries to draw up the codes themselves due to a lack of knowledge and time. The resulting codes did not significantly aid economic recovery but it was felt they had resulted in tilting the playing field even more in the favour of big business. Codes covering restrictions on levels of production together with the overlooking of anti-trust measures were a licence for larger corporations to operate the NRA to their own advantage at the expense of smaller companies, which were squeezed out (Badger). Opposition also came from several senators who supported the position of the small businessman. They were against the suspension of anti-trust legislation and wished to see the full restoration of market conditions.

NIRA was responsible for the alienation of the traditional business community from Roosevelt's administration by early 1934. This appears odd, as the Act had given business the power to regulate itself. But the rich resented government-imposed reform of an economy that they were used to running. Big business resented the concessions that they had to make to labour, with the exception of some of the more far-sighted employers who saw that it was in their benefit to have more stable relations (Brogan). A prime example of opposition to NIRA was Henry Ford, who objected to the automobile code's intrusion and refused to sign up (though he did follow its hours and wages provisions). The sheer volume of the codes and the related bureaucracy confirmed business in its disdain for NIRA. As Badger has pointed out, it was a test case sponsored by US Steel that brought the NRA codes down in 1935 in Schechter Poultry Co. v. The United States.

As well as causing consternation among employers, employees were not content with the NRA either. Organised labour felt let down because they did not receive enough protection under Section 7(a) of NIRA. It ultimately lacked a way of being enforced properly and therefore proved to be of little value to organised labour. Senator Robert Wagner of New York was prominent in highlighting the problem. He introduced what became the National Labor Relations Act in 1935 in response to the inadequacy of Section 7(a), which incidentally he had helped to draft. He said it had had limited success, leading mostly to the formation of 'sham unions' dominated by employers (Polenberg). It was his Act two years later, not NIRA, which would finally ensure workers the freedom to form effective unions. Wagner also pointed to the inability of the National Labor Relations Board, set up in August 1933 to oversee disputes, to enforce its decisions and he sought to strengthen the Board as part of his bill. The codes had few friends, but despite their numerous shortcomings they had brought some benefits including the abolition of child labour and sweatshops, and the introduction of hours and wages agreements.

The Public Works Administration was spared the opposition that the NRA had attracted. It was a well run and creative agency responsible for the building of countless bridges, dams, highways and public buildings. It was good for the construction industry but ultimately was not substantial enough to spark economic recovery. Furthermore, funds were allocated slowly as its diligent head, Harold Ickes, endeavoured to fund only useful projects. Roosevelt himself remained unconvinced about the wisdom of a government spending its way out of recession. This helps explain why the actual investment in the PWA was under a third of the figure that some politicians had suggested was necessary to make a real impact. The PWA may have created many jobs but failed to bring a recovery and so did little to counter the criticisms of NIRA.

It was the regulatory side of NIRA that attracted most criticism, which came from all sides and for widely differing reasons. The recovery that NIRA had promised was not forthcoming, arguably illustrating the belief that politicians cannot command and conquer the economy, unlike other policy areas. The NRA helped in reducing unemployment to 14 per cent and did promote a small amount of growth but such was the extent of opposition that it was almost a relief for all concerned when the Supreme Court found the codes unconstitutional.

PRACTICE QUESTION

3   **To what extent did the New Deal fail to solve the problems of rural America in the 1930s?** (20)

(AQA)

4   (a) **To what extent is the claim that the New Deal failed African Americans a valid assertion?** (7)

(b) **How successful were the steps taken to provide for the destitute?** (18)

(Edexcel)

(a) The answer commonly given is that Roosevelt's administration took little, if any, action that would improve life for the most disadvantaged groups in America, and unfortunately they were the ones who needed help the most. Blacks were affected terribly by the Depression; they were usually the first workers to be laid off and the last to be hired. Poor whites took over jobs traditionally done by blacks forcing even more into further depths of poverty.

The reforms of the New Deal that were designed to give help to people directly were overwhelmingly aimed at white men, to the detriment of ethnic minorities. Welfare programmes marginalised blacks and sometimes neglected them totally. For example, the 1935 Social Security Act did not cover farm labourers and servants, both jobs in which many blacks worked. Furthermore, the New Deal spurned the opportunity to pass civil rights laws. In fact, Roosevelt refused to lend his support to an anti-lynching bill in 1934 and the NRA codes permitted unequal wages. This could indicate that he was not in favour of advancing the position of African Americans.

But it was political realities rather than a lack of ideals that most probably prevented action. Roosevelt was extremely reluctant to offend Southern Democrats, who had thus far been loyal supporters. The South was a conservative region with social relationships that had changed little since the time of Reconstruction. Roosevelt knew that any threat to Southern culture would be resented and could well signal the end of his 'New Deal coalition', which was needed to get reforms through Congress. Rather than jeopardise the New Deal the administration consequently paid scant attention to the plight of blacks.

This view, that goes some way to exonerating the administration, is supported by several significant gestures that signalled the slow advancement of black people. An unprecedented number of blacks were employed within Roosevelt's administration, which virtually eliminates claims of racial hostility. Leading 'New Dealers' Harry Hopkins and Harold Ickes strove to ensure that blacks were not excluded from relief programmes; and black men and Hispanic people were allowed onto CCC and WPA schemes. However there was prejudice in the allocation of work and in the provision of dole, where it was not uncommon for blacks to receive substantially less than whites. And, above all, there was the extraordinary First Lady, Eleanor Roosevelt. She had a high profile and used it to campaign publicly for greater racial equality.

Blacks benefited from the drives to unionise, which were a product of the New Deal era, and from demographic shifts as more moved northwards and into the cities where they had more chance of being able to vote. The black vote, where it existed, overwhelmingly switched allegiance from Republican to Democrat, the obvious inference being that they saw Roosevelt as a friend to their race. Although the issue of race had been largely ignored there was an unintended consequence on the civil rights issue. The federal government had shown itself willing and able to intervene in hitherto untouched areas of American life for the benefit of the disadvantaged. The example set during the 1930s gave hope as black leaders began to believe that governmental action on race relations was a possibility for the future.

(b) With industrial production halved and an estimated quarter of the workforce out of work, vast numbers of families were in a dire situation. There was no direct assistance available from the state for the unemployed. President Hoover had maintained that providing relief was the business of charities and at best state and local governments. Meagre charity payments of around $2 per week were grossly inadequate for a family's needs and indeed were non-existent in many rural areas. For millions the early 1930s was a time of vagrancy, migration, scavenging, breadlines and malnutrition. Roosevelt shared Hoover's concern with balancing the federal budget, but was prepared to intervene on a much wider scale than his predecessor, even though Hoover had gone further than his own predecessors would have done. New Deal reforms aimed to provide a safety net for the destitute until economic recovery brought full employment.

The FERA represented a significant break with the past as the federal government assumed the responsibility of providing the unemployed with dole. Because there was not the capacity in the federal bureaucracy to deal with the administration of relief on such a large scale, the government had to rely on state apparatus. There was a certain degree of enmity between the two levels of government, notably in parts of the mid-west and the South. Governors strove to balance state budgets and 'reliefers' were often regarded as scroungers. Consequently, there were problems in setting the level of dole and ensuring it was distributed. The head of FERA, Harry Hopkins, may have spent an impressive $5 million in the first two hours of business but the amounts given by FERA were inadequate when compared to normal working wages. Furthermore, FERA helped the unemployed but it overlooked those whose hours and wages had been reduced, who were also suffering the effects of the Depression. While noting that FERA was less than perfect it is more important to acknowledge the precedent that had been set and to admire the will to provide for the destitute in times of great need.

Reform of a long-term nature came in the summer of 1935 in the Second New Deal when the landmark Social Security Act was passed. It made provisions for pensions and unemployment benefit based fully on contributions from both employees and employers. Roosevelt was arguably convinced of the need for such a measure in the wake of the widespread popularity of alternative schemes being proposed by others. It was not without its problems, however. Certain groups were excluded from the scheme and the amounts to be paid were modest. The most notable omission was health insurance. This put the US system at odds with similar schemes being developed in Europe and consequently bequeathed to the future an issue the country still wrestles with today. The President was simply not interested in implementing a health insurance scheme. It has been argued that this was because he did not want to antagonise conservative critics and the influential American Medical Association, which was against such a measure. This issue notwithstanding, Roosevelt was proud of the Social Security Act of 1935. It represented the foundation of the American welfare state and was something that could be built upon by future administrations. Nevertheless, an inclusive health care system, national in scope and funded through taxation, is commonly regarded as an integral element of an advanced industrialised nation. The case against Roosevelt is that the failure of the US to reach this pinnacle of nationhood is due to his failure to seize the initiative when the opportunity presented itself.

Valiant attempts to provide work were devised by the federal government throughout the decade. Work relief had less stigma attached to it than collecting relief payments and helped restore self-pride for the millions involved. Despite critics' jibes of creating merely 'leaf-raking' jobs the 'alphabet agencies' irrefutably undertook many useful projects. The Civilian Conservation Corps provided emergency employment mainly, though not exclusively, for young white men. It eventually employed 2.5 million men on a temporary basis. The Public Works Administration (itself an offshoot of the National Recovery Administration) helped the construction industry and attempted to stimulate the economy through the building of schools, dams, bridges and other public projects with a $3.3 billion budget. The Civil Works Administration generously gave $400 million of PWA money in emergency relief to the unemployed during the harsh winter of 1933/4 before being dissolved in March 1934. The plethora of agencies and the overlap of their remits is a reflection of the haphazard nature of the First New Deal and illustrates a hurriedness that was born out of a genuine concern for people's plight.

During the Second New Deal in 1935 the relief programme was consolidated with the Social Security Act and a new public works scheme. The Works Progress Administration (WPA) built ambitiously upon earlier efforts at providing work relief. Roosevelt personally favoured this move away from direct relief to work relief and requested $4.8 billion from Congress. It eventually kept an average of 2.1 million men in employment during its eight-year life in the construction of public projects such as schools and bridges.

Its funding was limited and consequently it could never hope to provide work for all those who needed it. Nevertheless it made a significant contribution to improving the lives of millions of families as well as transforming the infrastructure of cities and towns. The agency had a wide-ranging scope, even going so far as to create work for unemployed musicians and actors through ventures like the Federal Theater Project. Roosevelt, who had grown increasingly convinced of the need to balance the federal budget, significantly reduced WPA spending in 1937. It was expanded once more in 1938 in response to a severe economic downturn. This decision to reawaken work relief programmes in the face of renewed economic problems illustrates that they were considered to have a positive impact upon the economy and in providing a level of relief to the destitute.

Further to providing relief through work and the dole, the New Deal also gave aid to families and farmers in order that they could retain their homes and farms. The Home Owners' Loan Corporation established in June 1933 had refinanced over one million mortgages by the end of FDR's first term. The Federal Housing Administration (FHA) of 1934 helped both the construction industry and middle-class families by insuring mortgages. This led to the growth of suburban housing, but neglected the poor in the inner cities. When compared to intervention by European governments, New Deal housing reforms appear pitiful.

But such criticism needs to be considered alongside an understanding of the differing histories and values in the new world and the old. Farmers received assistance through a variety of measures. The Farm Credit Administration provided much needed mortgage relief and the Frazier-Lemke Farm Mortgage Act of June 1933 enabled some to regain land they had lost through foreclosure. Efforts such as these were successful to an extent in their aims: 75 per cent of farmers retained their land and continued to farm. However this still left one in four dispossessed and out of work.

When viewed from a European perspective, the American system of welfare that was introduced appears limited in its scope. The New Deal has been criticised for failing to introduce more far-reaching reforms at a time when there was scope for a lot more to be done. However, it is important to bear in mind the greater emphasis placed upon individualism in America, and thus recognise the clear break with the past that occurred as the state took some degree of responsibility for the destitute. The 'alphabet agencies' were a noble endeavour and were quite bold in their intent, especially if one considers the efforts made to support artists and the emphasis on conservation. And, while acknowledging the faults of the welfare state, credit should be given where it is due for the willingness to take the first step.

PRACTICE QUESTION

5   **To what extent can the First New Deal be regarded as a failure in dealing with the effects of the Depression?** (20)

(AQA)

 Problems for the New Deal

6   (a) **How effective was right-wing opposition to the New Deal?** (7)

   (b) **Assess the impact of left-wing and populist critics of the New Deal.** (18)

(Edexcel)

(a) It is commonly claimed that left-wing critics were of greater concern to Roosevelt than those of the right. But while the left succeeded in capturing the imagination of millions throughout America, it was a conservative coalition that reined in the New Deal as the 1930s drew to a close.

Initially Roosevelt enjoyed widespread support from both sides of the ideological spectrum during the passage of the First New Deal. Farming and business benefited from legislation that propped up prices and stimulated the economy, and therefore raised few objections to the measures introduced. Republicans in Congress, outnumbered by 311 to 116 in the House of Representatives and by 60 to 35 in the Senate, could provide little more than token resistance at best. In fact one sector of the party, the progressive wing, stood fully behind the President on the majority of early New Deal legislation.

This climate of cooperation changed in 1934 as the impact of the first wave of reforms was felt. Farmers remained individualist in nature, despite benefiting immensely from government credit and price fixing. They objected vociferously to measures that helped the urban poor as the New Deal entered its second phase. Opposition from agricultural regions was to have political ramifications later on as representatives from these areas, many of them Democrat, turned their backs on Roosevelt.

Opposition from business was even more explicit. The business community overwhelmingly believed in limited government and objected to what they saw as interference from Washington DC. Their loathing of Roosevelt probably owed more to these instincts than to a rational analysis of political and economic realities and the content of the New Deal legislation. There can be no doubt that many of the steps taken by the administration were to the benefit of business. Banking had been rescued, Wall Street had been cleansed and NIRA had allowed big business to draw up codes to regulate themselves. The Acts that introduced responsible unionism were intended to stabilise industrial relations and were accepted by some of the more far-sighted as an inevitable progression. By 1935 however, many businessmen were hostile to the New Deal.

A group of wealthy business leaders and conservatives from both parties formed the American Liberty League in August 1934. Individually they had supported the early New Deal reforms but they were soon united in their claims that Roosevelt and his radical advisers were anti-business. The League's aims, as stated in a nationwide radio address by its President, were to save the American system of government, which the New Deal had 'sought to destroy' and to resist Roosevelt's attempts to set up a '**totalitarian** government'. For all their money and vitriolic rhetoric, the American Liberty League was only able to enlist 125,000 members. In comparison to the numbers attracted to more populist movements on the left, the American Liberty League was not significant. For Roosevelt it proved to be more of an irritation than a real worry.

It was in Congress itself where conservative opposition finally made headway. After a poor campaign for the White House in 1936, the Republicans closed ranks in their opposition to the increase in power of the federal government and Roosevelt's clumsy proposal to reform the Supreme Court. The party moved rightwards and fared better in the 1938 mid-terms gaining eight seats in the Senate and 80 more in the House. They found common ground amongst Southern Democrats, who were extremely wary of the impact that the New Deal might have on the Southern way of life. It was a wish to defend tradition that brought them together in opposition to Roosevelt. This bipartisan alliance was very powerful on key Congressional committees and in vetoing legislation from 1938 onwards. It proved very effective in stymieing domestic reforms and helped shape US politics for the next 50 years.

(b) By the end of 1934 there had been a partial recovery from the depths of the Great Depression. Farm prices were stabilised, falling industrial production had been halted and millions throughout the nation had been helped by the myriad of 'alphabet agencies' that Roosevelt's administration had established. But 11 million people were still unemployed and millions more, including the elderly and agricultural labourers, felt overlooked by New Deal legislation. Unsurprisingly interest groups sprang up, left-wing politics gained more relevance and populist speakers with quick-fix solutions to the nation's problems were able to attract many a sympathetic ear. An examination of the left-wing critics of Roosevelt sheds light on the short-comings of the New Deal and serves to illustrate the plight of millions of Americans during the mid-1930s. It also reveals that, although Roosevelt was untouchable at the ballot box, it does not necessarily follow that his critics had no influence whatsoever on public policy.

Communists and socialists suffered from a lack of support from workers as well as from the under-cutting of their appeal by the reforms of the New Deal. The 1930s may have represented the heyday of American communism in terms of the number of members but, as Anthony Badger has pointed out, it should be noted that turnover was high and only a dedicated core remained members for any length of time. Furthermore in terms of votes the left fared unimpressively, failing to eclipse the level of support for Eugene Debs a generation before. Arguably the high water mark for the left in the 1930s came in 1934 when a known socialist, Upton Sinclair, managed to become the Democratic gubernatorial nominee in California. His plan to 'End Poverty in California' (EPIC) using socialist remedies proved immensely popular and he was only narrowly defeated following a Republican smear campaign that deliberately mis-represented his aims and leanings.

Historians of the New Left, notably Howard Zinn, have highlighted grass-roots discontent across America that resulted in a heightened sense of self-reliance and occasional violent clashes. People organ-ised themselves to prevent evictions and to protect the rights of the unemployed. Miners in Pennsylvania sold millions of tonnes of 'bootleg' coal and from 1934 to 1938 a wave of labour disputes, encompassing new 'sit down' strikes, rocked the establishment. The lowest ebb of such activity was the 'Memorial Day Massacre' in Chicago in 1937 when police fired into a picket line of steel workers killing ten people. Zinn claims that the government moved towards giving unions legal status in order to channel workers' energy into negotiations, union meetings and elections. While there is no doubt an element of truth in this, it would be an exaggeration to imply that communism posed a serious threat in the United States. Workers remained loyal to Roosevelt – they did not want extremist solutions. The centre ground and the American ideals of freedom and individualism were simply too well entrenched. Roosevelt also proved to be immensely popular with the poor, as evidenced by the thousands of grateful letters that found their way to the White House each month.

More worrying for FDR and arguably more influential were the series of popular movements headed by charismatic 'demagogues', which culminated in a third party challenge for the Presidency in 1936. These populists had initially been supportive of Roosevelt but seized upon the shortcomings of the First New Deal from 1934 onwards. They offered seemingly simple remedies of dubious merit aimed right at the heartland of America.

The Townsend Old Age Pension Plan quickly rose to national prominence in late 1934. Dr Francis Townsend of California had a popular yet ludicrous panacea for the Great Depression. His idea was to give everyone aged over sixty $200 a month if they retired from work and spent all the money before the next instalment came along. This attracted half a million members into Townsend Clubs. In his thorough analysis of the New Deal's Social Security Act, first published in 1936, Paul Douglas pointed out that the arithmetic behind Townsend's plan was startling: it would require spending half the national income on pensions alone. At the same time a plan for comprehensive unemployment insurance was also attracting support. This left-wing proposal was introduced into Congress in 1934, and again in 1935, by a socialist Farmer-Labor Party congressman from Minnesota, Ernest Lundeen. It is impossible to consider Roosevelt's own Social Security Act, introduced in the Second New Deal, without the consideration that his restricted measure was in part a response to the popularity of the more radical Townsend Plan and Lundeen Bill.

Public opinion was important to Roosevelt and he did pay attention to his critics, especially those with mass appeal. With an audience of millions, radio priest Charles Coughlin preached his own economic programme throughout the mid-1930s. Coughlin's ideas lacked any depth and the man himself drifted into anti-Semitism as his influence declined. Although Roosevelt did meet with Coughlin on occasion it was only for the purpose of calming the turbulent priest. Coughlin and his National Union for Social Justice had no discernible impact upon policies.

The greatest populist threat came in the form of Louisiana's charismatic senator Huey Long. He had an impressive record of reform in his state, which he ran in a dictatorial style. His public programmes had brought many benefits to the infrastructure of Louisiana and to its people. Citing the grossly uneven distribution of the nation's wealth as the cause of the nation's woes, he launched his Share Our Wealth scheme in February 1934. Long's proposal of using the tax system to redistribute wealth and bring the Depression to an end had an oversimplified and irresistible quality. Coupled with his proven record and effective use of radio, he built up a nationwide following of millions. A poll by the Democratic Party in 1935 estimated that Long might receive 10 per cent of the vote if he stood as a third party candidate the following year. This could deprive the Democrats of enough votes to allow the Republicans back into the White House. Owing to his untimely death in September 1935 Long's potential was to remain pure speculation. However, the 'Kingfish' of Louisiana lived long enough to see his bitter opponent, Roosevelt, undermine him by introducing a series of tax reforms in the Second New Deal. Roosevelt's Revenue Act, which called for a modest increase in income tax, was begrudgingly dismissed as a sell-out by Long.

The similarity in the timing and nature of Long's plan and Roosevelt's actions cannot be explained away by coincidence. Historian Albert Fried has written that Roosevelt had not been greatly concerned by Long's embryonic election campaign. This may be an accurate assertion but it does not automatically follow that left-wing critics made no impact. The popularity of such movements demonstrated to FDR the size of the discontent across the nation, with people favouring a radicalisation of the New Deal. This discontent was a significant factor behind the more socially democratic reforms of the Second New Deal as the pragmatic President moved to appropriate the liberal left.

7   (a) **Why did Roosevelt attempt to 'pack' the Supreme Court in 1937?** (45)

   (b) **Explain why FDR's 'Court-packing' plan failed and assess the impact the controversy had on the New Deal.** (45)

(OCR)

(a) The most stubborn obstacle in the path of the New Deal was not Congress, which seemed content with the enhanced role of the Presidency; rather it was the Supreme Court. One of the functions of this body is to interpret and safeguard the US Constitution. The power of judicial review, that is the power of the Court to declare actions of the other branches of government unconstitutional or indeed to confirm constitutionality, was asserted in 1803. This power has been used sparingly except for in the mid-1930s when a conservative-dominated Court struck down no fewer than 11 federal laws.

In retrospect it is little surprise that there was a rift between the executive and judiciary. The programmes of the New Deal were important departures and saw the government enter hitherto uncharted territory. The Court was bound to question the constitutionality of Acts of Congress that meddled in intra-state commerce and allowed the federal government to regulate the economy. The Court had consistently ruled that this was the domain of the individual states and not the federal government. One should bear in mind the prominent role of the debate over states' rights versus federal rights at Philadelphia in 1787 and in the ensuing ratification saga. The US Constitution had placed limitations upon the powers to be wielded by the various actors in government. And here was Franklin Roosevelt pushing the boundaries of that sacred document to its extremes.

Furthermore the make-up of the Court in the 1930s helps explain the sudden upsurge in judicial review of acts of Congress. Chief Justice Hughes and four other conservatives (the 'Four Horsemen of Conservatism') ensured that the Court remained stuck in the past. The laissez-faire attitude held by the majority of the nine justices set the Supreme Court at odds with the other branches of government and public opinion, which had clearly demonstrated a desire for legislative intervention for the common good. So the ethos of the Court taken together with the nature of New Deal ensured a collision was nigh on inevitable.

It was not long in coming. Two pieces of legislation crucial to the New Deal were struck down during FDR's first term in office. In May 1935 the Court unanimously declared the National Recovery Administration unconstitutional. Schechter Poultry Co. v. The United States was a case concerning a firm of New York butchers prosecuted for selling diseased meat. This was in contravention of an NRA code, which had been regulating commerce and industry since 1933. The Schechter brothers appealed on the grounds that the federal government had no right interfering in a matter of internal state trade. The Court concurred stating that the NRA codes contravened Article 1 Section 8 of the Constitution, which under the existing interpretation allowed the federal government to regulate commerce between states but not within a state. The Court also declared NIRA unconstitutional on the grounds that Congress had delegated too much power to the executive without giving guidelines on the use of such powers. In other words, the US had shifted from having a Congress-centred government towards a President-centred government and the Supreme Court disapproved.

Presumably the Schechter brothers cared little who they were prosecuted by, be it the United States or New York State. The 'Sick Chicken' case, as it became known, was anything but a trivial matter: in fact it was a test case, financed by industry, in order to challenge the regulation of commerce brought in by the New Deal. The following year saw the Agricultural Amendment Act struck down by a divided Court. United States v. Butler concluded with a controversial decision resting on the constitutionality of certain taxation laws. (Taxes had been raised from the food processing industry in order to provide subsidies to farmers who agreed to limit their production.) These landmark cases, together with several lower profile ones struck at the very heart of the New Deal. An angry Roosevelt knew he needed to deal with this obstacle before pushing ahead with further reforms. Indeed the Court still had to rule on legislation from the Second New Deal, thus imperilling the National Labor Relations Act and the Social Security Act.

Roosevelt claimed, with considerable justification, that the Supreme Court was out of step with the rest of the nation. There had been no deaths or retirements on the Supreme Court during his first term and so FDR had not had the opportunity to make any appointments of his own. He faced a Court that apparently cared little for public opinion and political realities. They were preventing him from doing things that needed to be done and that he had been elected to do. The Court, for its part, felt that it was performing its duty to safeguard America's carefully crafted system of checks and balances.

Roosevelt's mandate was renewed in the autumn of 1936 with an overwhelming victory that saw him carry all the states in the Union except for Vermont and Maine. He made his move against the Court shortly after his second inauguration (now in January following the passage of the 20th Amendment) when he presented his Judiciary Reorganisation Bill to Congress. For every judge over the age of 70, the President wanted the power to appoint another in the name of efficiency. It was a blatant attempt to secure a more sympathetic Court and unsurprisingly was criticised as merely a crude 'Court-packing plan'. It was one of most significant political miscalculations that Roosevelt made. The bill was defeated in the Senate by 70 votes to 20 after a shrewdly fought conservative campaign. The scale of Roosevelt's error is brought sharply into focus if one considers the apportionment of seats in the Senate. The Democrats had 76 to the Republicans' 16.

The President had presumably felt that introducing such a measure was the most effective way of protecting reforms that were both needed and desired. The only other feasible way of constraining the Supreme Court would have been through Constitutional amendment but this method would have required more time and greater support in order to succeed. Rather than alter the Constitution itself Roosevelt felt it better to alter the body charged with interpreting the document.

A clash between the President and the judiciary was virtually unavoidable given the differing ethos of the New Deal and the Supreme Court. However it should be noted that the build-up to the collision had been many years in coming. The Court's reactionary interpretation of the commerce clause of the Constitution had been a point of friction between the two branches of government at various points throughout preceding decades. The battle was long overdue by the time it finally arrived, brought on by the federal government needing to become more interventionist in the face of the Great Depression.

(b) The defeat of the Judiciary Reorganisation Bill in July 1937 is considered to be a humiliation for President Roosevelt. However the episode did yield some positive consequences for the administration. Generally speaking, the controversy had a two-fold effect upon the New Deal. Firstly, it prompted the Supreme Court to be more sympathetic to Roosevelt's reforms and, secondly, it helped apply the brakes to the most frenzied period of legislative activity the United States has ever seen.

There were several reasons why Roosevelt's plan failed. Prominent among these was Roosevelt's taking Congress for granted. During his first term, Congress had shown itself more than willing to cooperate with the President, content to pass his proposals with little debate. As time wore on and the emergency was assumed to be under control, Congress became less amenable. In the Second New Deal, reforms on business and income tax produced hesitation and dissent. Following the elections of 1936 the Democrats held even larger majorities in both Houses. FDR assumed that after such an overwhelming vote of confidence in himself and his administration's policies Congress would continue to bend to his whim.

However, he unveiled his plan just days after he had taken Congress aback with his proposal to re-organise and strengthen the running of the White House. Furthermore, Roosevelt had made his decision on Court reform without consulting Congressional leaders. He displayed an overly presumptuous attitude towards fellow Democrats in assuming that they would toe the party line. In the vast and diverse US, party unity is somewhat looser than it is in a more homogenous, unitary state such as Britain. Congressional opponents from both parties, buoyed by their worst suspicions of Roosevelt's dictatorial ambitions apparently gaining substance, formed the National Committee to Uphold Constitutional Government. It ran a shrewd campaign to persuade wavering senators to stand up to Roosevelt.

The President, fresh from electoral triumph, miscalculated the public's mood too. Although he had received 60.8 per cent of the vote only months earlier, he neglected to consider the strong affection that Americans have for their institutions, including the Supreme Court. He could not carry the public with him on this issue. It seemed a less urgent matter than agricultural subsidies or labour rights and appeared as a blatant attack on the work of the Founding Fathers. Consequently Roosevelt received little support from interest groups even though they would have benefited from the bill.

The justices themselves reacted wisely to the affront. The Chief Justice made a strong case against Roosevelt's claim that they were proving inefficient owing to old age. One of the conservatives announced his retirement in May 1937 allowing Roosevelt his first Supreme Court nomination. But most tellingly of all, the Court changed tack and began to uphold New Deal legislation when one of the five conservative justices switched sides.

This occurred while the bill was still under debate and thus took away the impetus behind the reform. This 'switch in time that saved nine' saw the Court uphold types of legislation that it had rejected only weeks before. Crucially it upheld the National Labor Relations Act (Wagner Act) and the Social Security Act. It was no surprise when the Senate heavily defeated the Judiciary Reform Bill.

Roosevelt had lost the battle but it can be claimed that he won the wider war over the role of government in the United States. The Supreme Court's reinterpretation of the commerce clause gave powers to the federal government that previously it could only wish for. Acts that concerned workers' rights, the regulation of the economy and the formation of a welfare state were now safe under the Constitution. It represented a monumental breakthrough, dragging the national government into the modern age. This fundamental change, all too often downplayed, was forced through by Franklin Roosevelt's determination to protect the New Deal. Unfortunately for him there was a price to be paid.

As mentioned above, emerging opposition in Congress was a significant factor behind the defeat. The progressive wing of the Republican Party that had been sympathetic to FDR found itself reunited with more conservative colleagues over the issue. Conservatively inclined Democrats joined them. Emboldened by their victory over the popular President and having received renewed mandates from the people in 1938, Roosevelt's carte blanche from Congress was rescinded. The controversy served to strengthen existing scepticism and opposition to Roosevelt, aided and abetted by a period of industrial unrest and renewed recession. The compliance of Congress was now a thing of the past. It gave little away as the New Deal ground to a halt and attention turned outward to the Pacific and Europe.

8   How supportive of the New Deal were the people and institutions of the United States? (20)

(AQA)

Essay plan

Introduction: State that levels of support for the New Deal varied between different groups and changed over time.

Para 1: Broadly speaking, Roosevelt enjoyed the consistent support of the vast majority of American citizens. Election results and the thousands of letters that flooded the White House each week provide evidence for this.

Para 2: Business and financial institutions were supportive during the 'Hundred Days' but this changed as they began to view government regulation as a threat.

Para 3: Congress willingly gave its support to the First and Second New Deals but Republicans and some Democrats effectively opposed FDR in the latter half of the 1930s.

Para 4: *The Supreme Court proved to be the least supportive institution. Examine the make-up of the Court and explain its switch in 1937.*

Para 5: *An examination of groups that opposed the New Deal serves to illustrate the true level of support it had. Outline criticisms from both left- and right-wing groups and individuals.*

Conclusion: *The people, and consequently their representatives in Congress, were largely supportive of the measures taken to alleviate the effects of the Depression. A consistent source of opposition came from conservative groups, business leaders and Republicans. Identify the common ground between their opinions and use this to show why the New Deal stands as one the most remarkable periods of legislation in the US.*

 The results of the New Deal

9 **(a) Why was there a Second New Deal in 1935?** (7)

   (b) Did Roosevelt change direction in 1935? (18)

(Edexcel)

(a) The major legislating phase of the New Deal can be said to have lasted around 1,000 days, although some commentators have proposed a six-year period for the New Deal (Brogan) and a 'Third New Deal' in 1938 has been suggested (Clements). Of these 1,000 days, two periods of intense activity stand out. The initial 'Hundred Days' following Roosevelt's inauguration in March 1933 saw the passage of 14 significant pieces of legislation. The pace slackened after 16 June 1933, but important Acts concerning financial reforms were passed in 1934. This period is usually spoken of as the First New Deal.

A 'Second Hundred Days' of frantic law-making arrived in spring 1935. At least seven major Acts were passed during this period, usually termed the Second New Deal. Whether or not it represented a change of direction for Roosevelt's administration is open for debate. The very notion of a Second New Deal has been played down by some who highlight the continuity with past measures and point out that several of the reforms of 1935 had long been in preparation (Jones). But in terms of the number of important Acts passed, it is appropriate to claim there was a renewed momentum to legislate in early 1935.

There were numerous reasons behind this. The continuing economic crisis was a significant factor in prompting further action from the White House. Although unemployment had been reduced a little, the hoped-for economic recovery had failed to materialise. Work relief measures were collated and extended under the Works Progress Administration as it became clear that unemployment was going to be a long-term problem. The business community had removed their support for the New Deal after the first year and the President resented their perceived ingratitude towards his administration. Roosevelt was facing a drawn-out struggle against the Depression as well as being the object of criticism from both left and right. In this light it is hardly surprising that he kept Congress in session throughout the summer and demanded they accept major pieces of legislation.

Political realities played a role in furthering the New Deal. The President was facing re-election in autumn 1936, but the jostling for position begins many months earlier in the US. The increasing popularity of radical demagogues augmented his will to act. Roosevelt's modest increase in progressive taxation was in part intended to forestall Huey Long's crusade and the Social Security Act surely owes a modicum of debt to the appeal of the Townsend Plan.

The Supreme Court unwittingly added to the legislative impetus. Its invalidation of New Deal legislation necessitated the formulation of replacement measures. For example, the striking down of the National Industrial Recovery Act prompted senator Wagner to introduce the National Labor Relations Bill. The 'Wagner Act' also owes a debt to the inadequacies of the initial Section 7(a) of NIRA and to the growing demands of organised labour.

Pressure from within Congress is another factor to consider. The mid-term elections in 1934 had seen gains made by liberals in both Houses. Senators Wagner and La Follette were to the fore of those demanding action from the White House and from the legislature itself. Roosevelt had broken the convention of Congress's domination of proposing legislation with the First New Deal. He knew that if he failed to act, they would.

(b) A second period of legislating began with the enlargement of work relief programmes in spring 1935. The pace intensified during the summer, following the striking down of the NRA, and a raft of legislation was passed, including a rise in income tax and the strengthening of the rights of trade unions. This Second New Deal is commonly held to be more radical than its predecessor. In terms of timing it follows the breakdown of Roosevelt's relations with the business and finance sector, which had for the most part turned against the President by the end of his first year in office. In appearance the Second New Deal was certainly more populist and less orientated to the demands of larger corporations. However, to state that there was a change of direction in 1935 somewhat exaggerates the situation. An examination of the major laws that were enacted at this time shows that there was in many respects a strong element of continuity between the First and Second New Deal.

The Works Progress Administration was established under the Emergency Relief Appropriation Act of April 1935. It consolidated and significantly extended work relief programmes that had been started during the First New Deal. With an initial investment of $4.8 billion and a wide-ranging scope, including providing work for many artists and young people, it represented the most substantial of all the 'alphabet agencies' for many millions of Americans. The WPA is best viewed as a natural progression from earlier efforts rather than a radical departure. It was the ongoing economic depression that had made further action necessary not a change in thinking. Work relief was not enough to increase demand sufficiently to produce a recovery, but would continue to be pivotal in helping millions to endure the hard times.

The Social Security Act of August 1935 laid the basis for the American welfare state, for better or worse. A federally administered system of pensions and a limited unemployment insurance scheme were established. Both schemes were to be based on contributions from workers and employers. The Act also provided assistance to those who were unable to work through no fault of their own, for example, people with injuries or disabilities. The Act should not be considered a truly radical measure due to its limited scope and the millions it excluded from coverage, but for its time and place it certainly represented a public-minded reform.

The Revenue Act (or Wealth Tax Act) incorporated modest reforms of the taxation system. A progressive income tax was introduced on large companies and the highest rate of personal income tax was increased to 79 per cent. This would raise money to help pay for New Deal reforms and had the added bonus of undermining the appeal of Huey Long and his Share Our Wealth campaign. Critics labelled it the 'Soak-the-Rich Act' but it must be stated that the new taxes raised relatively modest amounts. A major redistribution of the nation's wealth was certainly not on Roosevelt's agenda.

The Banking Act of August 1935 centralised the US banking system. The power the Presidency held over key institutions in banking was significantly increased, as the Federal Reserve Board became the focal point for monetary policy. Although conservatives saw it as an attack on the banking sector, the Act was hardly a change of direction: in many ways it was a progression from earlier financial reforms. Furthermore, creating a centralised banking system was an overdue necessity rather than an attack on established interests.

The Public Utility Holding Company Act aimed to break up powerful monopolies in the energy sector. The provision of power had come to be dominated by a few gigantic companies that owned a myriad of smaller companies. Roosevelt felt that the best way of dealing with these companies was simply to liquidate them. It signalled a return to trust-busting in an attempt to regulate the industry. This Act can be viewed as a change of direction from the First New Deal, which had more or less encouraged larger companies to engage in monopolistic practices under NIRA.

The National Labor Relations Act was designed to strengthen the rights of workers by guaranteeing collective bargaining and strengthening the National Labor Relations Board, which was to oversee relations between industry and unions. The Act is correctly regarded as one of the most prominent pieces of legislation from the New Deal era but its origins actually owed more to labour sympathisers in Congress than the initially reluctant President. The 'Wagner Act' was a pro-labour reform and can therefore be viewed as leaning towards the left of the political spectrum. However, it does not represent an abrupt change of direction by Roosevelt. The Act was born out of the weaknesses of NIRA and NIRA's invalidation by the Supreme Court and is therefore better viewed as part of the ongoing process of stabilising business–labour relations.

When taken en masse the legislation of the Second New Deal was more radical in the sense that it overtly favoured the people and represented an end to conciliation with business. However it did not represent a definite break with the past, as there were elements of consistency running from 1933 into 1935. It is better to describe the Second New Deal as a change of emphasis as Roosevelt and his advisers sought to build upon the First New Deal by introducing more permanent reforms.

10 To what extent did the Second New Deal bring fundamental change to the US? (20)

(AQA)

Essay plan

Introduction: State why the legislation of the Second New Deal was deemed necessary in light of all the measures passed in 1933. It can be ascertained that the Second New Deal was intended to bring about more permanent reforms than the somewhat incoherent and reactive First New Deal.

Para 1: Examine the Wagner Act and show that it represents a more fundamental reform of labour relations than the moves made under NIRA.

Para 2: The Social Security Act certainly represents fundamental change but criticism can be offered as health insurance was omitted. State that the federal government had already assumed responsibility for the welfare of the people during 1933.

Para 3: The consolidation of work relief efforts under the WPA cannot be taken as a fundamental change as it was intended to be ad hoc in nature. The TVA, however, did bring long-lasting change to rural America.

Para 4: Examine the changes brought to the financial sector by the Banking Act.

Para 5: The scope and size of the federal government was greatly increased during the mid-1930s. The creation of the Executive Office of the President illustrates this growth.

Conclusion: Acknowledge that left-wing historians have pointed to the conservative nature of some of FDR's reforms but the Second New Deal must be said to have fundamentally altered political, social and economic realities.

11 To what extent was the New Deal conservative? (20)

(AQA)

The New Deal aroused the contemporary opposition of conservatives, who felt it was too radical, as well as the opposition of radicals, who felt it was too conservative. The benefit of hindsight has not resulted in the ending of this debate, although a majority of historians would concur that one of Roosevelt's primary goals was to preserve and strengthen capitalism by reforming it. In the opinion of historians of the New Left, for example Barton J. Bernstein and Howard Zinn, the New Deal had a minimal impact on the US. They claim the reforms were meant to reaffirm the dominance of larger corporations and to forestall changes of a more radical nature occurring. These historians have provided the most damning critique of the New Deal and offered a significant insight into its conservative nature. However, their suggestions are tantamount to saying that the New Deal was a cynical exercise in hoodwinking the public while reaffirming the status of capitalism and have proved contentious as they overstate the radical will of the era and downplay the significance of the changes made.

More recent analyses have challenged this 'corporate liberal' view and have, for example, highlighted the extent of opposition to the New Deal from the very interests that are claimed to have been its intended beneficiaries. However there remains a consensus that the essence of the New Deal was conservative. The aim was not to challenge the capitalist system, rather to support it. But to simply describe the New Deal as conservative is not enough. In what ways was it conservative? Could it have been more radical?

An examination of the New Deal does reveal a strong vein of conservatism running throughout. Many pieces of legislation undoubtedly bolstered established interests: Wall Street, larger banks and giant corporations were strengthened and NIRA effectively allowed business to regulate itself. The AAA worked to the advantage of larger farmers and did little for tenant farmers and labourers. The gains made by the average person pale in comparison to those made by big business. There was no significant redistribution of wealth, thus leaving one of the causes of the Depression intact. The provision of unemployment relief was welcome but woefully insufficient. The welfare state that was established was essentially conservative, especially when compared to those in other industrial nations. Many groups were omitted and the issue of health care was avoided; and racial and gender discrimination went virtually unchecked. All of which serve to illustrate a conservative social agenda.

This leads to the question why the New Deal was not more radical in nature. Firstly, Roosevelt himself was not a radical. He was lukewarm at best on labour reform, seemingly indifferent towards health care provision and reluctant to engage in civil rights matters. He can certainly be described as a fiscal conservative. It was only when faced with a dramatic downturn in the economy in 1937 following spending cuts that Roosevelt finally chose to ignore the counsel of his more conservative advisers and revert to deficit spending. Roosevelt's conservative approach to spending led to his continuing hesitancy to fully embrace the approach favoured by those influenced by the British economist Keynes. Many of the limitations of the New Deal can be linked to this fiscal conservatism.

As well as self-imposed constraints, there were limitations placed on the ambitions of the New Deal by external factors. The reforms themselves cannot be isolated from their context – they had to exist within the realities of 1930s America. The administration lacked the apparatus and expertise that would have been necessary in order to conceive and implement much more radical reforms. It is little surprise that the New Deal relied upon businesses and farmers to regulate their own sectors: there was no other choice. The federal government also had to take into account the power of the individual states and local officials who were relied on to administer New Deal projects. Added to these considerations were the hurriedness with which the administration had to act and the realities of working with conservatives in Congress. Lastly, the American people did not want radical change – they wanted jobs and greater security within the existing system. Taken in this light a pertinent question raises itself: could the New Deal have been more radical if Roosevelt had wished it to be?

The acknowledgement of the conservative ethos at the heart of the New Deal has led many critics to imply that little was achieved. Such a conclusion would be wrong: the New Deal undeniably had a great impact upon the United States. The overall aim was to preserve the existing system, but, in doing so, many measures broke new ground, brought changes and aroused considerable opposition from conservatives. The federal government's authority to regulate and legislate was moved forward and the degree to which it impacted upon the everyday lives of individuals increased significantly. The financial system was rescued and stabilised and deficit spending was cautiously advanced. There was unprecedented movement towards a limited welfare state with the introduction of relief programmes and social security. Workers were empowered as 'responsible' trade unions were established and their voice came to be represented in a strengthened Democratic coalition. The infrastructure of the United States received unparalleled investment as public works and electrification programmes transformed America. Can all these changes be the work of a conservative administration?

Politically, socially and economically the New Deal clearly changed the US to a degree that no other administration can claim to equal. Many changes alarmed conservatives and the business community and brought significant gains to liberal causes. Roosevelt's intent was to uphold the capitalist system and therefore to state that the overall objective was conservative is accurate. However, it has to be recognised that there was neither the impetus nor the opportunity to demolish capitalism and the changes the New Deal brought are better described as liberal, not conservative.

12 To what extent was the New Deal successful in fulfilling its goals in the 1930s? (20)
(AQA)

By comparing the intended results of New Deal legislation to its actual results a measure of success can be determined. The overall aims were to underwrite the systems of capital, finance and democracy and restore people's faith in them. The New Deal was a battle fought on many fronts as the sheer scale of the Depression necessitated action across all areas of policy. Assessments of three broad areas – bringing economic recovery, reforming America's economic and social systems, and providing relief for the people – reveal the New Deal to be at least a partial success, though its successes need to be qualified by reference to their shortcomings and the failure of the New Deal to bring economic recovery must be affirmed.

The National Industrial Recovery Act represented the major attempt of the New Deal to stimulate the economy into recovery. But the National Recovery Administration pleased no one, not even the larger corporations who came to dominate the code authorities. Badger has asserted: 'The NRA only restored modest profitability to American business, if it restored any at all'. It did not deliver what it had been conceptualised for and can be regarded as an eminent New Deal failure.

NIRA's spending programmes also proved inadequate to produce a full recovery. Roosevelt remained unconvinced by Keynesian economic theory and was therefore reluctant to incur large spending deficits in a 'no-holds-barred' attempt to promote recovery. The Public Works Administration and the later Works Progress Administration were simply allocated too little to achieve this end. Yet it seems that this was no surprise for the New Dealers, who had envisaged a full-scale recovery coming from renewed confidence in the private sector rather than from massive public spending. Perhaps the best that can be said of NIRA's codes and programme of work relief is that they stopped the economic situation getting worse and laid the foundation for a full recovery once demand significantly increased with the outbreak of war.

Agricultural reforms were intended to help fuel an increase in consumption and undoubtedly did lead to the creation of jobs. Although the impact on the American economy was positive, again it was not enough to prompt a full recovery from such depths. This does not mean that the administration's agricultural policies were a total failure. On the contrary, the problem of overproduction was quickly solved and agricultural prices had doubled by 1937 (Brogan). New Deal policies were largely responsible for the turnaround in fortunes but there are criticisms to bear in mind. The reforms tended to work in favour of larger farmers and rural poverty and discrimination persisted. However, the positives outweigh the negatives and, as Alan Brinkley has written: 'the agricultural economy as a whole emerged from the 1930s much more stable and prosperous than it had been in many years.'

The numerous banking and financial measures of the New Deal were largely successful in achieving their aim of ridding the capitalist systems of a number of their worst excesses. Public confidence returned and the nation was better protected from the possibility of a recurrence of the devastating collapse of the stock markets and banks. Political reforms can also be judged a success, notwithstanding the defeat of the Judiciary Reorganisation Bill. Roosevelt established the modern Presidency and made Washington DC a true capital city.

The various relief programmes also deserve credit despite their many faults. When making an historical judgement it is important to consider events and actions in their full context. New Deal measures to provide work and dole payments deserve to be considered in light of what had come before rather than lamented as a missed opportunity to usher in more radical reforms. Furthermore, the limitations on Roosevelt, such as a lack of state machinery to administer welfare payments, the system of federalism and the speed in which he had to act, should be remembered when passing judgement. It is almost too easy to criticise the shortcomings of the 'alphabet agencies' rather than to focus on their actual achievements. Their contribution was to help millions of families struggle through until prosperity returned. Failure would have been to let them suffer without spending billions in aid. The American people responded with genuine affection for their President as well as with votes.

The electoral success of the New Deal can be safely judged overwhelming. Gaining re-election is something that typically comes to the fore in Presidential thinking and activity during the latter half of a first term. The contemporary judgement from the millions who endured the Great Depression was unequivocal. The New Deal had helped them to cope in the most desperate of times. Roosevelt was easily returned to power in 1936 in an election that was a virtual referendum on the New Deal. Franklin Roosevelt eventually won four Presidential elections (the 22nd Amendment was not passed until 1951) and occupied the White House until his death on 12 April 1945.

Amid the successes and failures, judgement inevitably draws upon one's opinions of the role of the state in a modern industrialised nation. Notably the New Deal failed to bring economic recovery and by 1939 there remained nine million unemployed. But weighed against this apparent failure it should be borne in mind that prior to FDR the federal government's role in economic affairs was negligible by comparison, a point which illustrates just how much had been achieved. Furthermore, bare facts can be presented in differing ways. It can be said with equal truth that from 1933 to 1939 unemployment was halved, a period in which the population increased by around eight million. To a significant extent it becomes a matter of interpretation. Is the glass half full because unemployment was halved or half empty because full employment was not restored? When all is said and done, it would be appropriate to claim the New Deal a noble endeavour and a partial success. It had transformed America and bequeathed many positive achievements to the nation.

Part 3: Sources

1 The agricultural crisis

■ **Source A: Henry A. Wallace (Secretary of Agriculture, 1933–40), extract from a speech delivered by radio, 10 March 1933**

The problem is clearly revealed. During the few years just preceding 1929, we were selling in foreign markets the product of roughly sixty million acres of land. The value of those exports this past fiscal year was sixty percent below that of 1929. We must reopen those markets, restore domestic markets, and bring about rising prices generally; or we must provide an orderly retreat for the surplus acreage, or both.

For twelve years American agriculture has suffered, and suffered cruelly. This has been largely because the government could not, or would not, formulate the policies that would enable the United States to act as a nation should which is owed money by other nations.

■ **Source B: Extract from an address by Roosevelt to Farm Groups, 14 May 1935**

... a plan for the adjustment of totals in our major crops, so that from year to year production and consumption would be kept in reasonable balance with each other, to the end that reasonable prices would be paid to farmers for their crops and unwieldy surpluses would not depress our markets and upset the balance. We are now at the beginning of the third year of carrying out this policy. You know the results thus far attained. You know the present price of cotton, of wheat, of tobacco, of corn, of hogs and of other ham products today. Further comment on the successful partial attainment of our objective up to this time is unnecessary on my part. You know.

■ **Source C: Mr Justice Roberts delivered the opinion of the Court, United States v. Butler, 6 January 1936**

... another principle embedded in our Constitution prohibits the enforcement of the Agricultural Adjustment Act. The act invades the reserved rights of the states. It is a statutory plan to regulate and control agricultural production, a matter beyond the powers delegated to the federal government. The tax, the appropriation of the funds raised, and the direction for their disbursement, are but parts of the plan They are but means to an unconstitutional end.

■ **Source D: Mr Justice Stone dissenting, United States v. Butler, 6 January 1936**

... the only check upon our own exercise of power is our own sense of self-restraint. For the removal of unwise laws from the statute books appeal lies, not to the courts, but to the ballot and to the processes of democratic government. Of the assertion that the payments to farmers are coercive, it is enough to say that no such contention is pressed by the taxpayer, and no such consequences were to be anticipated or appear to have resulted from the administration of the act.

OCR QUESTION FORMAT

The questions and answers that follow are based on the OCR style.

(a) Using Sources A and B and your own knowledge assess the impact of the First New Deal on the agricultural crisis. (15)

(b) Using Sources C and D and your own knowledge explain why the Supreme Court struck down the Agricultural Administration Act. (30)

(a) [Advice: *You will have to use your wider knowledge to be able to assess if Roosevelt was justified in stating that a partial though significant recovery was under way in the agricultural sector. It is important to examine also the shortcomings of the First New Deal within rural communities.*]

Less than a week after the inauguration Henry Wallace, the Secretary of Agriculture throughout the New Deal, identified overproduction as the major problem facing US agriculture. The depression in both foreign and domestic markets had exacerbated this problem. The net result of overproduction was falling prices. In Source A, Wallace states quite categorically that the reluctance of previous governments to take appropriate action to remedy the situation had led to much suffering in the sector. He was thus giving notice that the new administration was prepared to take an interventionist stance in response to the crisis.

Reviving the fortunes of agriculture was clearly a priority during the early New Deal era. Indeed Roosevelt and several of his advisers considered recovery in this sector vital to stimulating the economy as a whole. With in excess of 40 per cent of the population living in rural areas it is not difficult to see why the New Deal focused upon the agricultural economy from the outset. In Source B, Roosevelt, speaking in 1935 to a group of farmers, claims that his administration's policies had had a beneficial impact upon the agricultural sector. The government had introduced production controls in order to solve the problem of overproduction. The effect of keeping production in balance with consumption was an increase in prices.

The medicine administered had not been easy to take. It involved reductions in farmed acreage and the slaughter of livestock. This solution was skilfully administered by a system of self-regulation, with, for example, farmers checking on other farmers' fields. Subsidies helped them through this transition and, as the President claims in the Source, prices certainly did increase as a result. It must be stated that for many small farmers and agricultural labourers the New Deal was too little too late and that the government's task was aided by the drought and dust storms of 1934 and 1935. Countless thousands of families lost their livelihoods and became migrants in search of work. Loans and mortgage aid did help to stem the tide to a degree and together with the production controls of the AAA Roosevelt was justified in claiming a measure of success by May 1935.

(b) [Advice: *Both Sources C and D are from Supreme Court justices and concern the case United States v. Butler, which resulted in a declaration that the AAA was incompatible with the Constitution. The views given are the majority decision, which rules against the Act, and the dissenting view, which serves as a defence of it. The wider context of the decision, namely the conservative nature of the Court, must be mentioned in order to gain the higher grades.*]

By the time it was declared unconstitutional, the AAA had significantly improved the lives of a proportion of farmers. Prices had risen by over 60 per cent on average, which was a result of production controls plus a severe drought that affected the South particularly badly. Farmers who owned the land they farmed gained the most from the regulations that had been introduced, but the situation of tenant farmers and labourers remained dire. As the Sources show, the Supreme Court struck down the Agricultural Adjustment Act with the United States v. Butler decision in January 1936. There was a split between the conservative and liberal elements in the Court, the former prevailing in a 6–3 decision. Sources C and D illustrate both viewpoints and clearly show that there was a considerable gulf between the two.

A particular point of contention was a tax that had been levied on the food processing industry. It had been necessary for the government to raise this tax so they could pay subsidies to farmers who had reduced their production in order to facilitate price increases. In Source C, Mr Justice Roberts outlines the majority opinion of the Supreme Court. He states that the federal government had encroached on the powers of the individual states by assuming powers that had been guaranteed to the states in the Constitution. He is saying that the federal government did not have the authority to regulate and control production as the right to do this was not granted to the government specifically and therefore this right belonged to the states. The production controls and the food processing tax were therefore an unconstitutional act on the part of Congress, which had willingly passed this bill and numerous others that had emanated from Roosevelt's White House during the 'Hundred Days'.

The Supreme Court was able to overturn the AAA and other reforms because it had an in-built conservative majority. The justices, who are appointed by Presidents as and when there are vacancies, are not unbiased actors on the political stage. They have their own beliefs and policy preferences and can and do bring these to bear on public policy. Mr Justice Stone gives the minority opinion in Source D. He makes an appeal for what he sees as common sense to prevail in the matter. In his dissent he puts the case that the Supreme Court should endeavour to take into account the views of the people and those of the government that they have elected.

Mr Justice Stone paints an image of an unresponsive Court that was both out of touch with the people and modern economic realities. This concurred with the thoughts of many Democrats, including Roosevelt himself. The President's victory in 1932 had been emphatic enough and his landslide in 1936 served only to reiterate and strengthen his mandate from the people. The message from the nation to Washington DC could hardly have been clearer. Roosevelt had been elected to take action to rescue the country from its plight and it appeared undemocratic that the partisan Supreme Court was willing to block the type of legislation for which he had twice been given a resounding mandate.

On the part of the justices, they felt that it was their task to uphold the Constitution and to give in on the AAA would be to invite further transgressions by Congress against the work of the Founding Fathers. But they had gone further than simply wishing to interpret the Constitution too literally. They were handicapping the ability of the United States to recover from the Depression. The Founding Fathers had bequeathed to the nation a brief (6,000 words) framework document that clearly invited future generations to fill in the details for themselves. The American economy had changed drastically from the time when the US was a collection of thirteen largely rural seaboard states consisting of some 4 million people. Its modern industrial economy required a degree of regulation from government, but the Supreme Court stood in the way. In retrospect the Supreme Court had failed to change with the times. In all of American history it has only very rarely gone against current public opinion for long; the 1930s being the classic example of an out-of-step Court.

ALTERNATIVE QUESTIONS IN THE OCR STYLE

(a) Study Sources A and B. How did the Roosevelt administration attempt to solve the problem of overproduction in the agricultural sector? (15)

(b) Using the Sources and your own knowledge explain why a collision between Roosevelt and the Supreme Court was seemingly unavoidable. (30)

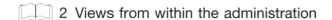 2 Views from within the administration

■ Source A: Roosevelt's first inaugural address, March 1933

In such a spirit on my part and on yours we face our common difficulties. They concern, thank God, only material things. Values have shrunken to fantastic levels; taxes have risen; our ability to pay has fallen; government of all kinds is faced by serious curtailment of income; the means of exchange are frozen in the currents of trade; the withered leaves of industrial enterprise lie on every side; farmers find no markets for their produce; the savings of many years in thousands of families are gone.

More important, a host of unemployed citizens face the grim problem of existence, and an equally great number toil with little return. Only a foolish optimist can deny the dark realities of the moment.

■ Source B: Roosevelt's State of the Union message, January 1935

We have undertaken a new order of things, yet we progress to it under the framework and in the spirit and intent of the American Constitution. We have proceeded throughout the Nation a measurable distance on the road toward this new order. Materially, I can report to you substantial benefits to our agricultural population, increased industrial activity, and profits to our merchants. Of equal moment, there is evident restoration of that spirit of confidence and faith which marks the American character. Let him who, for speculative profit or partisan purpose, without just warrant would seek to disturb or dispel this assurance, take heed before he assumes responsibility for any which slows our onward steps.

■ **Source C: Frances Perkins, national radio address delivered 25 February 1935**

The process of recovery is not a simple one. We cannot be satisfied merely with makeshift arrangements which will tide us over the present emergencies. We must devise plans that will not merely alleviate the ills of today, but will prevent, as far as it is humanly possible to do so, their recurrence in the future. The task of recovery is inseparable from the fundamental task of social reconstruction.

Our program deals with safeguards against unemployment, with old-age security, with maternal aid and aid to crippled and dependent children and public health services. Another major subject, health insurance, is dealt with briefly in the report of the Committee on Economic Security, but without any definite recommendations.

■ **Source D: Roosevelt's second inaugural address, January 1937**

But here is the challenge to our democracy. In this nation I see tens of millions of its citizens, a substantial part of its whole population, who at this very moment are denied the greater part of what the very lowest standards of today call the necessities of life. I see millions of families trying to live on incomes so meagre that the pall of family disaster hangs over them day by day; I see millions whose daily lives in city and on farm continue under conditions labelled indecent by a so-called polite society half a century ago; I see millions denied education, recreation, and the opportunity to better their lot and the lot of their children; I see millions lacking the means to buy the products of farm and factory and by their poverty denying work and productiveness to many other millions; I see one-third of a nation ill-housed, ill-clad, ill-nourished.

It is not in despair that I paint you that picture. I paint it for you in hope because the Nation, seeing and understanding the injustice in it, proposes to paint it out. We are determined to make every American citizen the subject of his country's interest and concern; and we will never regard any faithful law abiding group within our borders as superfluous. The test of our progress is not whether we add more to the abundance of those who have much; it is whether we provide enough for those who have too little.

OCR QUESTION FORMAT

The questions and answers that follow are based on the OCR style.

(a) **Using Sources A and D assess if Roosevelt is acknowledging the failure of his first administration in overcoming the dark realities of the Depression.** (15)

(b) **Using Sources A to D and your own knowledge explain the opposition that the New Deal faced.** (30)

(a) [Advice: *FDR cited the problems he aimed to tackle at his first inauguration, including the issue of poverty, and yet in 1937 the newly re-elected President highlighted enduring poverty in the US. However, rather than being an admission of failure, FDR was probably more mindful of the growing criticisms of those on the right and was therefore restating the importance of cooperation in his renewed appeal to the nation.*]

On the surface Roosevelt's second inaugural address appears to contain a tacit admission of failure. Problems that are identified in Source A, namely the plight of farmers and the high level of unemployment, are evident in Source D, which draws attention to enduring social problems in cities and on farms. Much had been achieved but a real recovery remained beyond the horizon. Both Sources evoke vivid images of suffering and Source D acknowledges their stubborn presence four years on from his first inaugural address. However Roosevelt's words do not contain any admission of shortcomings on his administration's part. It is likely that Roosevelt's intention was to draw attention to the scale of the task that remained and garner support.

Implicitly Roosevelt may well have been criticising the Supreme Court's blocking of his administration's attempts to tackle the problems of the Depression. The Court had declared major pieces of legislation unconstitutional and seemed destined to continue its obstruction. In Source D both farming and industry are specified as pressing concerns. The Court had struck down the NRA and the AAA, which were seen as pivotal measures in the attempt to improve living standards and bring about economic recovery. Given Roosevelt's resounding success of 1936 and the nature of inaugural addresses, the President was spelling out the social conditions that he had an impressive mandate to improve.

(b) [Advice: *The sources state the nature and size of the task facing Roosevelt's administration in the 1930s. Given the severity of the Depression and the watershed nature of the New Deal, opposition from various quarters was to be expected.*]

All four sources contain appeals from within the administration for support for the task of bringing relief, recovery and reform to the United States. All Presidents require support from the people, Congress, Supreme Court and business if they wish to successfully enact and execute major legislative initiatives. In the months following Roosevelt's first inauguration he was successful in commanding a reforming coalition ranging from business interests to the population as a whole. The 'withered leaves of industrial enterprise' and drop in share values to which the President alluded were all too evident and it is understandable why FDR initially enjoyed broad support.

Source B, taken from FDR's 1935 State of the Union message, condemns business and Republicans, including the Supreme Court, who were standing in the way of progress. During the course of 1934 a proportion of the business community grew to resent the degree of control they were ceding to the government. Such is the benefit of hindsight, it may be pointed out that they seemingly disregarded the inherent conservatism of the New Deal. FDR was certainly more a friend of capitalism than a foe. Source D is from 1937, the year when FDR attempted to reform the Supreme Court due to its striking down of major New Deal measures. By presenting himself as the champion of the needy, Roosevelt inferred that the Court was the enemy of democracy, not his administration.

Source C is an explanation of the Social Security Bill of 1935 and provides an eloquent justification for this fundamental measure. In her radio address, Frances Perkins acknowledged that health insurance was a 'major subject' and was obviously under consideration by some in the administration, but the bill that was drafted contained no attempt to introduce such a scheme. The President knew all too well that he would face fierce opposition from private medical interests and his reluctance to act was pivotal in this glaring omission of the New Deal.

The New Deal faced opposition from various quarters as the Sources imply. This opposition was successful in reining in the New Deal and preventing it from going further than some in the administration would have liked. Unmentioned in the Sources are the voices of radicals who criticised the effectiveness of the New Deal and campaigned for greater state intervention to provide relief to the people. However, by and large, the American people supported FDR and it was this fact that aided him in controlling Congress and in winning his argument with the Supreme Court.

ALTERNATIVE QUESTIONS IN THE OCR STYLE

(a) **Using Sources A and B show how the First New Deal tackled economic depression in the industrial and agricultural sectors.** (15)

(b) **Study Sources C and D. Explain the passage of the landmark Social Security Act of 1935.** (30)

Part 4: Historical skills

 ### 1 'Alphabet agencies' task

A source of difficulty for students of the New Deal is learning the names and remits of the numerous federal initiatives that have become known as 'alphabet agencies'. This group task should ease this problem and provide points for discussion.

1 Give the full names for the following agencies
2 Arrange them into appropriate groupings
3 Agree upon the most and least successful agencies from the list

AAA CCC CWA FERA FHA NLRB NRA PWA RA SCS SEC TVA WPA

2 Using art as historical sources

What insight do the following sources offer about the experience of the Depression for the people of rural America?

Lots of folks back east, they say, leaving home
    most every day,
Beating the hot old dusty way to the California
    line.
Across the desert sands they roll, getting out of
    that old dust bowl
They think they're going to a sugar bowl, but
    here is what they find.
Now the police at the point of entry say,
You're number fourteen thousand for today.

Woody Guthrie
'Do Re Mi'

The dawn came, but no day. In the gray sky a red sun appeared, a dim red circle that gave little light, like dusk; and as that day advanced, the dusk slipped back toward darkness, and the wind cried and whimpered over the fallen corn.

Men and women huddled in their houses, and they tied handkerchiefs over their noses when they went out, and wore goggles to protect their eyes.

The Grapes of Wrath,
John Steinbeck, 1939

Sources and references

Anthony Badger, *The New Deal – The Depression Years, 1933–1940*, Macmillan (1989).

Alan Brinkley, *The Unfinished Nation*, McGraw-Hill (2000).

Hugh Brogan, *The Penguin History of the USA*, Penguin (1985/1999).

Peter Clements, *Prosperity, Depression and the New Deal*, Hodder & Stoughton (2001).

Paul Douglas, *Social Security in the United States: An Analysis and Appraisal of the Federal Social Security Act*, Beard Books (1936).

Albert Fried, *FDR and his Enemies*, St Martin's Press (1999).

R. Garson and S. Kidd (eds), *The Roosevelt Years*, Edinburgh University Press (1999).

M.J. Heale, *Franklin D. Roosevelt*, Taylor & Francis (1999).

Maldwyn Jones, *The Limits of Liberty*, Oxford University Press (1983/1995).

R.D. Polenberg, *The Era of Franklin D. Roosevelt 1933–1945*, Palgrave (2000).

R. Radosh and M. Rothbard (eds), *A History of Leviathan*, Ditton (1972).

Howard Zinn, *A People's History of the United States*, Longman (1996).

Chapter 8

Foreign Policy, 1890–1941

This chapter will consider a period that includes two world wars. With the closing of the frontier in 1890 the United States began to devote more energy to its influence overseas. By present standards US foreign policy at the turn of the century seems limited and unsophisticated, but a growing interest in world politics, peacemaking and naval power all set the tone for US foreign policy through the twentieth century. The US did not enter the First World War until 1917, by which time illusions of a quick and glamorous victory were long gone. US intervention proved successful but at great human and economic cost. This contributed to an upsurge of isolationism in the 1920s and 1930s, deepened by the impact of the Great Depression but eroded by the rise of aggressive dictatorships in Europe and Asia. When the Japanese attacked Pearl Harbor in 1941 the nature of the attack was a shock, but US foreign policy was already moving towards war.

 Historical background

The emergence of the US as a world power, 1890–1914
The impact of the First World War upon US foreign policy, 1914–1920
A more conservative foreign policy, 1921–1936
The US's road to war, 1937–1941

 Essays

US foreign policy in the 1890s
Theodore Roosevelt's foreign policy
Causes of US intervention in the First World War
The US and the Treaty of Versailles

Isolationism in the 1920s and 1930s
The abandonment of isolationism in 1941

 Sources

1   The causes of the Spanish-American War
2   Arguments for neutrality in the First World War

 Historical skills

1   Assessing US Presidents in foreign policy
2   The extent of change in US foreign policy 1890–1941

Chronology

1898	April–August	Spanish-American War
	July	US annexation of Hawaii
	December	Treaty of Paris gave the US control of Puerto Rico, Guam and the Philippines
1899		'Open Door' policy announced for China
1900		Boxer Rebellion in China
1902		Platt Amendment established US protection over Cuba
1903	November	Panama Canal Treaty gave the US power to build the Panama Canal (started 1906, completed 1914)
1904		Roosevelt Corollary to the Monroe Doctrine
1905	September	Treaty of Portsmouth marked end of the Russo-Japanese War
1906		Algerciras Conference
1913	February	General Huerta seized power in Mexico, leading to civil war until 1917 (Carranza victorious)
1914		Outbreak of the First World War in Europe. US declared neutrality
1915	May	*Lusitania* was sunk by a German U-boat killing 128 Americans
1916	Jan.–Feb.	Colonel Edward House's second peace mission to Europe
	July	British blacklisting of US and Latin American firms dealing with Germany
1917	January	US severed diplomatic relations with Germany
	February	'Zimmerman Telegram' revealed
	April	US declared war on Germany
1918	January	Wilson announced his 'Fourteen Points' peace plan
	November	End of First World War with Allies and US victorious
1919	Jan.–June	Paris Peace Conference
		Signing of Treaty of Versailles included provision for a League of Nations
1920		Treaty of Versailles finally rejected by the US Senate
1921	August	US signed separate peace treaties with Germany, Austria and Hungary
	November	Washington Conference convened to limit naval power (until February 1922)
1924	April	Dawes Plan introduced to help German recovery
1928	August	Kellogg-Briand Pact in Paris renounced war
1929	June	Young Plan reduced German reparations
	October	Wall Street crash
1930	Jan.–April	London Conference set new naval limits accepted by US, Britain and Japan
1931	September	Japanese occupation of Manchuria, minor US protest
1933		US officially recognised the USSR
1935	August	Pittman Resolution limited Presidential power to apply sanctions
	August	First Neutrality Act
1936	February	Second Neutrality Act
1937	May	Third Neutrality Act
	July	Japanese invasion of China

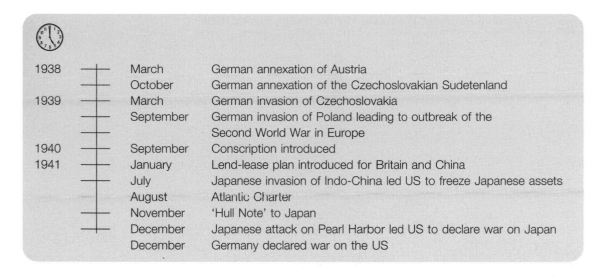

1938		March	German annexation of Austria
		October	German annexation of the Czechoslovakian Sudetenland
1939		March	German invasion of Czechoslovakia
		September	German invasion of Poland leading to outbreak of the Second World War in Europe
1940		September	Conscription introduced
1941		January	Lend-lease plan introduced for Britain and China
		July	Japanese invasion of Indo-China led US to freeze Japanese assets
		August	Atlantic Charter
		November	'Hull Note' to Japan
		December	Japanese attack on Pearl Harbor led US to declare war on Japan
		December	Germany declared war on the US

Part 1: Historical background

 The emergence of the US as a world power, 1890–1914

The end of the frontier in 1890 coincided with, but only partly caused, a growing attention by the US government to foreign policy. Before the 1890s the US had no distinct foreign policy other than an adherence to the 1823 **Monroe Doctrine** (that pronounced all of the Americas to be within the US sphere of interest) and a wish to support US economic investment abroad. The latter point combined with westward expansion in the late nineteenth century to produce a growing US interest in the Pacific. There was territorial expansion (Alaska and Midway) but growing economic domination of independent states such as Hawaii was more typical of US activity. This was accompanied by a Christian missionary zeal and a wish to bring civilised US attitudes to less enlightened parts of the world. As a result, US visitors, traders and settlers were to be found all over the Pacific, the Caribbean and Latin America. While the government had no specific foreign policy to regulate this, in the 1880s it began to build a modern navy to protect US interests. The 1880s and 1890s saw European powers seeking to build up huge colonial empires, most notably in the 'scramble for Africa', where the interior was hurriedly carved up between the colonial powers, but also in the Far East, where a weak and disunited China was forced to accept European trade interests. The US was not willing to allow a potential major trading partner fall under complete European domination, and declared itself hostile to European-style colonial expansion (having formerly been a set of British colonies itself). Presidents Harrison (1889–93) and Cleveland (1893–7) contrasted US tolerance and freedom to European empire-building. It was in the Caribbean, however, that US world power status, and its own colonial empire, was established in the 1890s. Cuba had long been a Spanish colony but had been open to US trade. However, a native uprising led to brutal Spanish suppression and commitment of troops to the island. US sympathy was with the uprising and a chain of provocative events in early 1898 led to President McKinley declaring war on Spain. The war itself was brief and showed the limits of US military might. However, Spain was unable to maintain the war and agreed to a peace deal that made Cuba independent and thus likely to fall even more under US influence. More significantly, the US received the Philippines, Guam and Puerto Rico. When added to existing territorial possessions and the US annexation of Hawaii in 1898 and American Samoa in 1900, the US entered the twentieth century as a Great Power comparable to the major European empires.

Figure 8.1 **Theodore Roosevelt surrounded by his 'Rough Riders', 1898**

The expansion of US control and influence brought with it new responsibilities and problems. In 1900 US soldiers were fighting in both the Philippines, to crush a nationalist uprising there, and in China, where the 'Boxer' rebellion by Chinese nationalists attacked US and European interests there. These were some of the issues faced by Theodore Roosevelt, who served as President 1901–9. His aggressive manner and favourite foreign policy saying 'speak softly and carry a **big stick**' have given him an image as a forceful, expansionist maker of foreign policy. In reality he was more conservative and cautious than this image suggests, and did not lead his country into any new wars. However the US asserted itself more in foreign policy under Roosevelt than it had done before. Roosevelt added his own 'Corollary' to the Monroe Doctrine, justifying pre-emptive action in the name of good government, but in effect to protect US interests in the Americas. He also built up and paraded the modern US navy. The showpiece achievement of the Roosevelt Presidency, the Panama Canal, was begun in controversial circumstances, with the US backing a Panamanian secession from Colombia in order to secure permission to build the canal. Roosevelt also intervened in Cuba when a 1906 rebellion there threatened US interests, in the Dominican Republic when it was threatened by European powers trying to collect debts, and he refereed a dispute between Venezuela and Britain. Elsewhere Roosevelt built a reputation as peacemaker, helping Japan and Russia to reach a post-war settlement in 1905 and chairing an international conference at Algeciras in 1906 to settle a dispute over Morocco. One effect of this was to establish a tradition of Presidential leadership in US foreign policy, which was not always maintained in the decades afterwards but was more apparent in the second half of the twentieth century.

Roosevelt's successor, William Taft (President 1909–13), was a product of Roosevelt's foreign policy, serving first as governor of the Philippines and then as Secretary of War. Taft was less inclined to intervene directly in world affairs than Roosevelt had been, preferring a 'dollar diplomacy' approach that encouraged US business investment abroad. However, he still intervened militarily in Nicaragua when a rebellion there threatened US business interests. This deepened anti-US feeling in Central America and left problems for his successor, Woodrow Wilson (1913–21) to deal with. Wilson is best known for his decision to enter the First World War and his work at the Paris Peace Conference after the war. In Central America, however, he took an interventionist approach, establishing US protectorates over Haiti and the Dominican Republic, and opposing the new dictator of Mexico, General Huerta. This led to the destabilisation of Mexico and attacks on US citizens, resulting in over 10,000 US troops operating in Mexico by 1916. Wilson's desire to 'teach the South American republics to elect good men' reflected the overbearing and interventionist approach of US foreign policy in the Americas at this time.

 ## The impact of the First World War upon US foreign policy, 1914–1920

Although the US did not enter the First World War until 1917, the outbreak of hostilities in August 1914 forced Wilson to make some uncomfortable decisions. While he privately supported the Allies, he was aware of the divide in US public opinion over the war and he also recognised that the US was remote from the causes and theatre of conflict. His initial request that the US remain completely neutral and impartial could not be sustained for long. By 1915 the war was clearly not going to end quickly and US trade interests were suffering from the naval blockades imposed by Britain and Germany against each other. Trade with Britain and France was the more practicable option, but both powers were unable to buy US goods without credit and Germany was using U-boats to sink merchant shipping. With business interests warning of economic recession in the US, Wilson authorised US loans to the Allies and pressured Germany into stopping its U-boat campaign. Real US neutrality had ended, therefore, by 1915.

Wilson now looked at ways to bring the World War to a peaceful end. Attempts to mediate between the Allies and the Central Powers failed during 1915 and 1916, but Wilson developed his own ideas of open diplomacy, national self-determination, general disarmament and a just peace without victory during the war. This was to lead to his **Fourteen Points** peace programme, proposed at the start of 1918. In the meantime, fears that the Allies might be defeated, continued submarine attacks and the discovery of a German offer of an anti-American alliance to Mexico led to a US declaration of war against the Central Powers in April 1917. It was hoped that this would accelerate the end of the war and give the US the chance to shape the post-war peace.

The US was not ready for war in 1917, but exceeded foreign expectations by training and equipping over two million soldiers in time for them to play a part on the Western Front in Europe. The US expeditionary forces to Europe were desperately needed. Russia underwent communist revolution in November 1917 and subsequently pulled out of the war, allowing Germany to launch a strong assault on the Western Front in early 1918. Despite this, Wilson refused to send US troops piecemeal to be integrated into existing Allied commands, reminding Britain and France that the US had entered the war as an 'Associated' not 'Allied' power. US troops really began to make their presence felt in a successful first encounter against a major German force in early June 1918, and thereafter there was a rapid flow of trained and equipped US soldiers into France. This helped the Allied counter-offensive of July 1918 to become a decisive success.

Equally significant was the intervention of the US navy in the war. The Allies had lost nearly a million tons of shipping in April 1917 alone. The US introduced and provided protection for convoys of merchant shipping, and began to lay a barrage of sea mines in the North Sea to catch German U-boats. An Emergency Fleet Corporation, set up in April 1917, rapidly built up US naval strength, more than outweighing the losses to U-boats. The results were dramatically successful; U-boat attacks fell by two-thirds within six months and no US troop ships were lost at all in 1918.

Within the US a Committee on Public Information was established in April 1917 to secure public support for the US intervention in the war. Public speakers, posters and pamphlets were used to justify the intervention. Civil liberties were undermined by the 1917 Espionage Act and the 1918 Sedition Act. These gave the government the power to suppress active opposition to the war effort and led to the imprisonment of approximately 1,500 people. Steps were taken to regulate war industries, food and fuel production and distribution, railways and merchant shipping. Tax increases raised over $11 billion and the sale of government bonds over $20 million. These domestic initiatives far outreached those from any previous wars. With approximately 115,000 US soldiers killed in action or through disease the war had an unprecedented impact on the US and helped to generate anti-war feeling and **isolationism** after 1918.

Despite Wilson's efforts to create a just and lasting peace settlement after the war, the Paris Peace Conference led to a harsh and punitive Treaty of Versailles against Germany. The most 'Wilsonian' aspect of the Treaty was the creation of a League of Nations. American membership was rejected by the US Senate despite a substantial level of public support. This set the tone for a relatively isolationist foreign policy in the 1920s and contributed to the defeat of Wilson's preferred successor, the Democratic candidate James Cox.

 A more conservative foreign policy, 1921–1936

Both the new President, Warren Harding (1921–3) and his successor Calvin Coolidge (1923–9) took little personal interest in foreign policy beyond a pledge to keep the US out of the League of Nations. However, the Secretary of State up to 1925, Charles Hughes, pursued an active foreign policy. This included an international conference in Washington during 1921–2 to negotiate a disarmament treaty and establish Great Power rights in the Far East and the Pacific. The conference was, at least temporarily, a success and enabled the US to reduce its defence budget in the 1920s. It was decided that the US and Britain would have naval parity. Japan would be allowed to build its navy up to 60 per cent of the US's naval strength; and France and Italy would each be allowed to build to one-third of the US's naval strength. The **'Open Door'** policy towards China, sought by the US since the 1890s, was agreed upon. The US also involved itself in European problems by introducing the **Dawes Plan** in 1924: essentially a massive US loan to help Germany to economic recovery and recommence reparation payments. The Harding government also reduced US commitments in Latin America, recognising General Obregon's Mexican government in 1923 in return for compensation for land seized in the 1910s and guarantees of US oil and mineral business holdings. The piecemeal withdrawal of US troops from the Dominican Republic and Nicaragua began in 1924. All of this reflected the US's wish to avoid military commitments and instead seek peaceful diplomatic solutions to problems. As this was similar to the aims of the League of Nations, it was perhaps unsurprising that by 1924 the US was sending delegates and observers to League conferences on world economic issues. The appointment of Frank Kellogg as Secretary of State in 1925 led, however, to a more assertive policy in Latin America in defence of US business interests, which grew from $1.26 billion in 1920 to $3.52 billion by 1928. A rebellion in Nicaragua in 1927 led to the US despatching 5,000 marines to protect the Diaz government, and when a new government in Mexico under Calles tried to place 50-year lease limits on US business holdings, Kellogg successfully threatened military intervention. A Pan-American conference in Havana in 1928 saw strong criticism of the US and a US refusal to guarantee non-intervention in the future. In contrast, a pact between Kellogg and French Foreign Minister Briand in 1928, expressing a common wish to renounce war, was signed by most major powers. However, the pact contained no binding terms and was little more than a joint statement. The failure of the Geneva Conference the previous year, which attempted to set further limitations on the Great Powers' navies, showed that diplomacy could not solve all problems.

Figure 8.2 **Map to show the war in the Pacific**

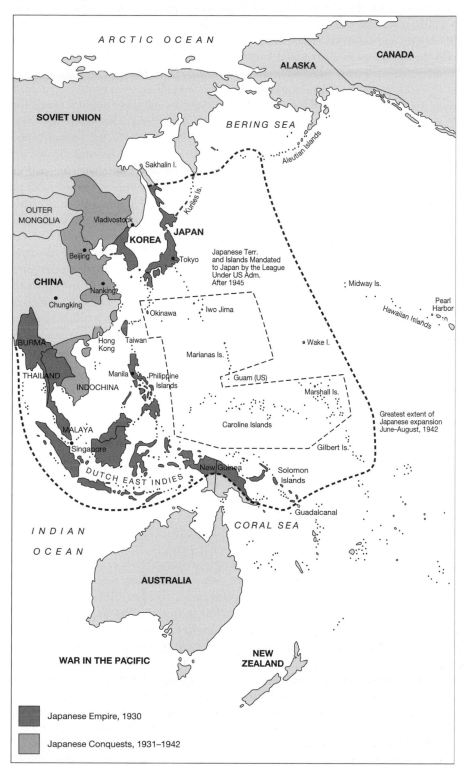

WAR IN THE PACIFIC

Japanese Empire, 1930

Japanese Conquests, 1931–1942

This was proved especially true as new President Herbert Hoover (1929–33) found his attempts at diplomatic solutions undermined by the worldwide Great Depression. Initially his foreign policy was successful as the 1929 Young Plan reduced and rescheduled German reparation payments, and the US reached agreement with Britain and Japan on naval limits at the 1930 London Conference. However, as the Depression took hold the Great Powers looked to domestic solutions and trade barriers, and the 1932 World Disarmament Conference at Geneva failed to reach lasting agreement. More ominously, in 1931 Japan broke the agreed 'Open Door' in China by occupying Manchuria and disregarded protests by the US and the League of Nations. In the US, however, the Depression overshadowed all other political issues and Hoover lost the 1932 election heavily. The Democrat victory made Franklin D. Roosevelt President (1933–45). His most famous foreign policy achievement was to lead the US to victory in the Second World War; however in his first Presidential term he was preoccupied with economic recovery and did not yet take an internationalist approach to foreign policy. At the 1933 World Economic Conference in London, the US refused to cooperate with other world powers on exchange rates. A series of trade agreements during 1934–6 eventually led to improved cooperation, but this was designed to aid US economic recovery rather than marking a turning point in US foreign policy. The US took no effective action (and neither, to be fair, did Britain or France) against Japanese aggression in China or Italian aggression in Abyssinia. Even in Mexico, where anti-US leader Cardenas began to confiscate US business holdings from 1934 onwards, Roosevelt opted for peaceful negotiation rather than military intervention. Popular and Congressional opposition to war and support for isolation was at its peak by the mid-1930s and a series of Neutrality Acts, designed to prevent the US from being sucked into war as it had been in 1917, were passed during 1935–7. By the end of 1936, with Italy victorious over Abyssinia, Germany rearming and remilitarising the Rhineland, and the Spanish civil war under way, war in Europe looked more likely than at any point since 1919. However the US's foreign policy was even less focused on world power politics than it had been in the 1920s.

 ## The US's road to war, 1937–1941

The period 1937–41 saw the US first gradually, and then dramatically, pulled into world conflict. An internationalist foreign policy evolved in response to the aggression of Japan and Germany. Japan's full-scale invasion of China in July 1937 was far more significant than their occupation of Manchuria in 1931. US interests were now directly threatened and Roosevelt sent an extra 1,200 marines to Shanghai to increase US military presence in China to 3,200. He also began to educate US public opinion against neutrality, but did not yet feel that collective action against Japan was possible. As a result the US refused to support a League of Nations initiative against Japan, and even considered withdrawing from China altogether when US gunboat *Panay* was sunk by Japan in December 1937. In Europe Germany began to extend its borders in 1938, but Britain and France chose a policy of **appeasement** rather than military resistance. Roosevelt was dubious about this policy but did not try to intervene. Appeasement failed in 1939, and Germany's invasion of Poland triggered the outbreak of the Second World War in Europe. The US looked on with concern, but did not take resolute action. Instead the US defence budget was increased, an open plea to Germany and Italy to cease aggression was brushed aside and the US embargo on arms sales was lifted, but only to allow the Allies to pay up front and transport US arms themselves – a 'cash and carry' principle. The US therefore took a more neutral stance in the first months of the Second World War than in the corresponding months of the First World War, even though in the second war it was much clearer which side was the aggressor.

The year 1940 saw a tremendous sequence of German victories in Europe, leaving France defeated and the British Empire in serious danger. War between the Allies and Axis was one thing, the likelihood of comprehensive victory for the Axis powers was more serious and a direct threat to US interests. The US was especially concerned that French, Dutch and British colonies in the Far East were now vulnerable to Japanese attack. Further defence budget increases, tougher economic sanctions against Japan and an arms deal with Britain all followed. By the middle of 1941 the US had passed a '**lend-lease**' bill to provide more arms to Britain and had occupied Iceland for strategic reasons. A Japanese attack on southern Indo-China in July 1941 started the countdown to US intervention. Japanese domination of the Far East was now a genuine possibility. Germany had launched an invasion of the USSR in the previous month with considerable success, and began to attack US destroyers in the Atlantic during September and October. Final attempts at diplomatic agreement between Japan and the US failed in November, making war inevitable in Japan's eyes. Japan then launched a pre-emptive attack at the US naval base in Hawaii, Pearl Harbor, in December. The US immediately declared war in response and Germany in turn declared war on the US a few days later. The US, therefore, did not enter the Second World War at a time of its choosing and it was to be nearly a year before it was able to make an impact on the outcome of the war. As with Britain and France, US foreign policy in the 1930s represented a failure. The Second World War was only won nearly four years after US entry to the war, and at tremendous cost.

Part 2: Essays

 US foreign policy in the 1890s

1   From McKinley's 'war' message to Congress, 1898:

> . . . The present condition of affairs in Cuba is a constant menace to our peace . . . and compel us to keep on a semi-war footing with a nation with which we are at peace . . .

(a) Explain the Monroe Doctrine in relation to US foreign policy. (3)

(b) Explain the significance of the Spanish-American War. (7)

(c) Explain why US foreign policy changed in the 1890s? (15)

(AQA format)

(a) The Monroe Doctrine was named after President James Monroe, but was essentially put together by John Quincy Adams in the 1820s. It claimed that all of the Americas came within the sphere of interest of the US. This belief would contribute to US intervention in several areas of the Caribbean, Pacific, Central and South America during the nineteenth and twentieth centuries, including the Spanish-American War in Cuba in 1898. The Doctrine also asserted that the US would not interfere in any of the internal concerns of the European powers.

(b) By modern standards, the Spanish-American War was a minor conflict. Nor was it a turning point in US foreign policy. However, it did encapsulate US foreign policy direction and the US victory had consequences well beyond Cuba, the venue for the war.

President McKinley had said the previous year he wished to avoid 'wars of conquest'. However the outbreak of war in 1898 reflected the influences in the US that could now push the country into war. Cuba was only 90 miles from Florida and US businesses had invested heavily in Cuban sugar plantations. Ironically a US-imposed tariff on foreign sugar in 1892 had indirectly caused the 1895 Cuban uprising. Spain deployed nearly 200,000 troops to Cuba over the following three years, and ruthlessly suppressed the uprising. The US press, especially newspapers owned by press barons Hearst and Pulitzer, reported Spanish atrocities in detail, stirring up public opinion against Spain. Two events in February 1898 heightened press outrage:

firstly, the sinking of US battleship *Maine* in Havana harbour with 260 crew lost, then the publication of a leaked letter written to the US by the Spanish ambassador, de Lome, which sneered at McKinley. Congress responded to popular feeling by approving $50 million in military spending. McKinley, under pressure from press, public opinion, Congress and his own party colleagues, went with the flow and intervened in Cuba. This inevitably led to a Spanish declaration of war in April 1898.

The nature of the war had an impact on US military development. At a cost of approximately $250 million and nearly 5,500 lives (mostly from disease) the war was won by August. The army effort grabbed press headlines but it made little impact, being literally bogged down and suffering from malaria, yellow fever and unsuitable clothing. The real success story for the US was its navy. A swift attack on the Spanish Pacific fleet at Manila Bay in May was successful and made a hero of US Pacific fleet commander Dewey. This was followed by a decisive US naval victory off Santiago, Cuba in July, leaving Spain unable to pursue the war further, and raising the status of the emergent US navy as a formidable force.

Dewey was not the only hero in the war. Theodore Roosevelt, a relatively junior government figure as Under-Secretary for the navy before 1898, led a volunteer cavalry unit nicknamed the **'Rough Riders'**. This unit was a scratch mixture of different occupations and delighted the press, especially its involvement at the Battle of San Juan Hill in July 1898. Roosevelt, exhilarated by the war ('I killed a Spaniard with my own hands', he boasted afterwards) and elected governor of New York on the strength of his war record shortly afterwards, rose to become Republican Vice-President, and then, following the assassination of McKinley, President by the end of 1901. His interventionist approach led to a more active US foreign policy during the early twentieth century. His rise to the Presidency was at least accelerated by, and possibly caused by, his role in the war.

The outcome of the war expanded the US's global influence, but also brought new problems with its new responsibilities. The Treaty of Paris in December 1898 saw Spain confirm Cuba's independence, the granting of Puerto Rico and Guam to the US and the 'sale' of the formerly Spanish Philippines to the US for $20 million. The US had also annexed Hawaii for security reasons during the war. Cuba quickly fell under greater US influence. By the 1920s three-quarters of Cuban imports came from the US, and four-fifths of Cuban exports went to the US. The US position was affected, however, by the civil wars, revolutions and growing Cuban resentment of US influence that led ultimately to the ascendancy of Castro in the 1950s. In the shorter term, the Philippines proved even more problematic. A pro-independence uprising and guerrilla warfare campaign there resulted in 70,000 US troops deployed at a cost of $200 million to fight an ultimately successful but uncomfortable war from 1899 to 1902. The US had, despite some opposition to imperialism at home, emerged as a global world power. The Spanish-American War was one of several factors that caused this. World power status gave the US some difficult foreign policy dilemmas in the decades that followed.

(c) The closing of the frontier in 1890 is generally seen as a turning point for US foreign policy. With westward expansion complete, US expansionist tendencies would inevitably show a greater interest in affairs beyond the boundaries of the US, especially the Pacific where the US now had a long western seaboard. The result of this was a more proactive and interventionist foreign policy from the 1890s onwards. However, most US foreign policy initiatives in the 1890s were based either on longer-term economic expansion or reactions to the initiatives of other powers.

Before the 1890s the United States, outside its own geographical sphere, limited itself to minor territorial acquisitions in the Pacific, for example Alaska and the Midway Islands in 1867, and the operation of the 1823 Monroe Doctrine in the Caribbean, Central and South America. However, its expansion of economic interests was rapid. US farming and manufacturing output were exceeding domestic demand by about 10 per cent by the late 1800s. This led to an interest in opening up foreign markets and increasing influence in world trade. For example, in Hawaii the first US missionaries had arrived in 1819. This was followed by **economic colonialism** and by 1885 Hawaiian sugar production was worth $8.4 million.

By 1892 about 21 per cent of the population were white settlers from the US or Europe, and they owned about two-thirds of Hawaiian property, including all the sugar farms. Once this economic dominance was threatened in the 1890s, the US soon acted to bring Hawaii under their control. This economic expansion did not automatically lead the US to seek a colonial empire, but it did lead to a more assertive foreign policy. President Cleveland explained this well during his first term in office in 1886 when he referred to 'our close and manifest interest in the commerce of the Pacific Ocean' as reason to keep a close eye on Hawaii.

It is harder to measure the psychological factors that influenced the US in overseas expansion. However there was a surge of interest in 'Social Darwinism' during the 1880s and 1890s, a theory that the fittest races and creeds would eventually triumph over inferiors. This seemed to fit well with US ideals and success up to that point, and provided a racist rationale for the white, largely Protestant United States to become dominant in world affairs. One writer, John Fiske, predicted 'a world covered with cheerful homesteads blessed with a sabbath of perpetual peace' as an outcome of Social Darwinism. Coupled with this was a religious and moral belief that the US could act as a Christian and civilising influence in less enlightened parts of the world. Josiah Strong's *Our Country* (1885) called the US the 'workshop of the world' and also equated US expansion with the spread of Christianity. These opinions cannot be directly linked to US foreign policy in the 1890s, but they were flying around intellectual circles at the time and were likely to have influenced government thinking. More concrete evidence is found in the development of the US navy. Construction of steel warships began in 1883, and by 1900 the US had the third strongest navy in the world. Captain Alfred Mahan (naval strategist and author of *The Influence of Sea Power upon History*, 1890) argued that naval expansion was needed to support economic expansion, if not necessarily territorial expansion. The 1893 Chicago World Fair had a 30-acre showpiece display depicting the US navy's new 'Great White Fleet', attracting thousands of visitors. However this navy would be used in future, it did reflect, and encourage, a growing interest in US foreign affairs.

The changing economic, social and political situation within the US, all greater priorities to successive Presidents than foreign affairs, pushed US foreign policy to a more assertive level. Industrial output rose rapidly between the 1860s and early 1880s, bringing with it social transition. Republican congressman John Kasson warned in 1881: 'we must turn our eyes abroad, or they will look inward upon discontent.' Economic depression during 1882–6 did not lead to a reorientation of foreign policy. However, the 1890s saw a sharper and deeper depression. Unemployment in the manufacturing and transport sectors rose from 4 per cent in 1892 to 16.7 per cent in 1894. This led to a sense of panic during 1893 and 1894. Approximately 160,000 miners went on strike, thousands of unemployed marched on Washington, riots broke out in Californian cities and federal troops were used to quell industrial unrest in Chicago. The *New York Tribune* warned of 'a nondescript socialism as dangerous and revolutionary as it is imbecile and grotesque'. The political consensus was that the depression was caused by overproduction and that the US would have to do more to open up world markets for its products. The Republicans won control of Congress in 1894, then the Presidency in 1896. This resulted in a ruling political and economic elite (including much of the press) all agreed that active foreign policy would serve economic recovery. Even so, the new Republican President, McKinley, warned (and meant it) in 1897 'we must avoid the temptation of territorial aggression'. Events outside the US, though, overrode his warning.

The US, having established economic influence in the world, found this influence under threat in the 1890s. In Hawaii the accession of Queen Liliuokalani in 1891 led to attempts to reduce the influence of foreign settlers and traders. This led to unrest in Hawaii and, eventually, US annexation in 1898 as a means of securing its economic position. In South America resentment of US influence was growing – for example in 1891 an angry mob attacked US sailors in Chile, and the US's successful demand of an official apology after threatening war made relations worse. At the same time European powers were extending their imperial influence. Germany and Britain both competed with the US for trade with Samoa, leading to a fragile tri-power agreement in 1889, and Britain tried to forcibly assert control over a disputed border territory between British Guiana and independent Venezuela, where gold had been discovered. A US threat of war was needed to persuade Britain to agree to independent arbitration, which ruled in their favour anyway. Most significant of all was unrest in Spanish-ruled Cuba followed by ruthless Spanish attempts to reassert control. This escalated into the 1898 Spanish-American War, marking a new aggression in US foreign policy.

US economic expansion was always likely to be followed by a more active government interest in foreign affairs. The quickening pace of world events by the 1890s combined with domestic discontent, changing US foreign policy in response to these factors. However, this was still far short of the more pro-active foreign policies that developed in the twentieth century.

 Theodore Roosevelt's foreign policy

2   Theodore Roosevelt:

'Speak softly and carry a big stick'

(a)   Explain the 'Roosevelt Corollary' in relation to US foreign policy. (3)

(b)   Explain the motivation behind Theodore Roosevelt's policy in Latin America and the Far East. (7)

(c)   Explain how far Theodore Roosevelt's foreign policy was a failure. (15)

(AQA)

(a)   The **'Roosevelt Corollary'** of 1904 was a more assertive version of the Monroe Doctrine, by which the US would seek to oppose any attempt at European imperialism in the Americas, taking pre-emptive action if necessary, even if it meant intervening in the domestic affairs of its neighbours in certain cases. The Corollary was first put into action with regard to the Dominican Republic, and was basically a response to the expansion of European empires in the late nineteenth and early twentieth centuries. It reflected Roosevelt's 'big stick' approach to foreign relations, and was marked by an increase in the size of the US navy.

(b)   Roosevelt's bombastic manner and hands-on approach to foreign policy (the first US President to visit a foreign country while in office), plus his support for the 1898 war with Spain and the 1917 entry to the First World War, give an initial impression of an aggressive, ambitious maker of foreign policy. In reality his motives were more conservative and contradictory; his favourite saying 'speak softly and carry a big stick' in itself shows some inconsistency in his approach to foreign policy. This is less of a reflection on Roosevelt than on the transitional nature of world affairs during his Presidency. Problems in Latin America and the Far East were especially complex.

Unsurprisingly in the aftermath of the Spanish-American War, Roosevelt saw the Caribbean as very important. He paid special attention to the building of a canal in Panama, negotiating agreement from Britain and protecting a Panamanian independence uprising when it became clear that Colombia, Panama's previous rulers, would not grant the US the land it wanted for the canal. Roosevelt's motives for building the canal were strategic as well as economic, providing a link between US Caribbean and Pacific interests.

In 1904 Roosevelt added what became known as the 'Roosevelt Corollary' to the Monroe Doctrine: the US demanded that European powers would not extend their influence in the Americas, and also asserted that US pre-emptive action would be taken if appropriate to defend its interests. This reflected Roosevelt's concern at European imperialism. For example, when the Dominican Republic failed to repay its loans from Europe, and European warships arrived to collect the debts, Roosevelt persuaded US creditors to take over the debts in order to prevent further European intervention. However, when Venezuela also defaulted on its loans, and Germany and Britain then blockaded Venezuela, Roosevelt told the German ambassador:

'If any South American state misbehaves toward any European country, let the European country spank it.' The US subsequently persuaded Venezuela to submit to international arbitration on the matter, but Roosevelt's comment shows that he would not take the Monroe Doctrine so far as to encourage Latin American defaulting on loans.

In the Far East Roosevelt was mainly concerned to prevent any one power from becoming dominant. The US itself was not powerful enough to dominate, but had already established significant economic influence in the Far East, especially China, whose huge potential market seemed an ideal outlet for US exports. However, China was unstable and restless (for example the 1900 Boxer rising) and the US 'Open Door' policy introduced in 1899 was already failing. Japan seemed the best counterbalance to European ambitions to dominate China. This, coupled with Roosevelt's dislike of Russia's expansionism and anti-Semitism, led to a pro-Japanese policy, especially over the 1904–5 Russo-Japanese War. However, after Japan won the war the US became concerned about the growth of Japanese power, and tried to encourage a peace that kept China free of control by either power. Roosevelt tended to put security and strategic aims ahead of business and economic aims, allowing Japan to take control of Korea in the face of US business interests there, although he also tried to shore up the unsuccessful America-China Development Company when its railway project in China was collapsing.

In both the Far East and Latin America Roosevelt had a common motive, to stop any one world power from gaining the ascendancy over others. This motivated other areas of his foreign policy and, later, led to the US's steps to intervention in both world wars.

(c) In 1907 Roosevelt sent the 'Great White Fleet' (the US navy), which had doubled in size and budget during his Presidency, on a world tour to demonstrate US strength and purpose, and deter rival powers from acting in the face of US interests. This was typical of his 'big stick' foreign policy, which was more ambitious and proactive than that of any previous President. There is no doubt that Roosevelt failed to achieve some of his foreign policy aims, but this does not mean his policies should be judged as failures in terms of the world situation and the constraints Roosevelt worked under.

The most enduring success of Roosevelt's foreign policy was the building of the Panama Canal. He had supported the canal idea since the 1890s and was quick to prepare the ground once he came to power. He successfully won Britain's support in return for a promise that the canal would be open to all shipping. The following year, in 1902, a treaty with Colombia was drawn up for the US to purchase a 99-year lease on a strip of land across Panama for $10 million, plus an annual payment of $250,000 starting nine years after the lease began. This was a bargain price and it was no great surprise that the Colombian Senate refused to ratify it. The plan survived, however, due to a Panamanian nationalist uprising in November 1903. The US immediately sent naval support to the nationalists and, before the new Panama government could assess the treaty properly, secured the canal land on the same terms previously offered to Colombia. This was a tremendous success for the US, so much so that Roosevelt, when discussing the canal with a re-election campaign manager in 1904, claimed: 'We have not a stronger card.' By the end of his Presidency in 1909, the building of the canal was well under way (built cheaply by West Indian workers on 60-hour weeks at 10 cents per hour), and it was eventually completed in 1914.

Elsewhere in the Americas Roosevelt was constrained by anti-US feeling, political instability and the threat of European interference. He was able to defuse the loan defaulting crises in the Dominican Republic and Venezuela, US creditors taking over Dominican threats and Venezuela agreeing to submit to the International Court at the Hague. The 'Roosevelt Corollary' was a success during Roosevelt's own Presidency. It should be noted though that he did not have to deal with any European interference on the same scale as Spain in Cuba in the 1890s. Nor did his policy win the US friends in Latin America. His successors, Taft and Wilson, both had to deal with the consequences of Latin American resentment. Unrest in Nicaragua, Haiti, the Dominican Republic and, worst of all, Mexico provided the US with foreign policy headaches during the 1910s.

In the Far East, by contrast, Roosevelt was less successful but deserves more credit given the worsening situation there. China was at the heart of the problem, with European powers grabbing trade concessions and the control of key ports there. Forces within China (especially the Boxers) destabilised the weak, disunited state further, making a US/China alliance impractical. And Japan, an emerging Great Power, was extending its influence over its neighbour. The US's 'Open Door' policy, designed to encourage free trade and stop further infiltration of China by rival powers, had already failed. Its architect, Secretary of State Hay, said in 1900 'our public opinion will not permit us to interfere with an army to prevent others from robbing her [China]. Besides, we have no army'. This summed up the problems well: indifference within the United States itself, a lack of US military power in the Far East, and the inference that rival powers could not be trusted (or trust each other) not to exploit China. Roosevelt's chosen option was to support Japan, and initially this seemed to work well. A secret agreement in 1905 saw the US and Japan pledge not to interfere in Korea and the Philippines respectively. The Russo-Japanese War of 1904–5 also brought an initially pleasing outcome for the US. To the delight of the US, Japan started the war with a surprise naval attack on the Russian fleet at Port Arthur (the same tactic used at Pearl Harbor 37 years later), and further Japanese victories destroyed the Russian naval threat in the Far East. Roosevelt's main aim now was to prevent Japan from achieving further dominance, and he brokered a peace in 1905 that saw neither side take any Chinese territory. This success was undone by a secret Russo-Japanese agreement in 1907 to dismember Manchuria and much of northern China between them in the future. It is hard to see how Roosevelt could have done more at the time, but he did seem to underestimate Japanese strength and ambition. Future Presidents would also fail to block Japanese ambition, which eventually pulled the US into the Second World War.

Roosevelt was more successful in his foreign policy towards Europe, although this was of less significance than his failure in East Asia. He wanted to see the balance of European power kept. He was on friendly terms with the German Kaiser Wilhelm II and regarded Britain as a declining power. This led to attempts at peacemaking diplomacy, designed to avoid a major European war that might leave one power dominant. Friendly terms with Britain were secured in 1903 after negotiations on a disputed border between Alaska and Canada were settled amicably. Roosevelt then offered to intervene when Germany disputed France's position in Morocco. The resulting 1906 Algeciras Conference was a success. Germany climbed down from the dispute and all the Great Powers accepted Roosevelt's proposals for international regulation of trade, banking and peacekeeping in Morocco. This did not prevent, but perhaps delayed, the eventual outbreak of European war. As a follow-up, at Roosevelt's suggestion, an international peace conference was held at the Hague in 1907. This was an attempt to codify international law and attracted representatives from 44 states, but it failed to agree on arms control. The Algeciras Conference thus represented the peak of Roosevelt's foreign policy towards Europe.

Theodore Roosevelt received the Nobel Peace Prize in 1906, and there was certainly no lack of effort in his foreign policy. Ultimately he did not increase US security or the chances of world peace. He did however set US foreign policy on its twentieth-century course, with the US acting as a 'Great Power' for the first time and trying to lead international diplomacy. His foreign policy cannot be regarded as a complete failure.

 Causes of US intervention in the First World War

PRACTICE QUESTIONS

3 (a) **How far was the Zimmerman telegram the most important short-term reason for the US's entry into the First World War?** (30)

(b) **To what extent were economic reasons the main cause of the US's entry into the First World War?** (60)

(OCR)

Advice: *To answer these questions effectively it is necessary to consider a range of factors including: public opinion and support for the Allies in the US at various times leading up to 1917: the impact of U-boat action against shipping (e.g. sinking of the Lusitania); attitudes towards the safeguarding of democracy; economic factors and the influence of the* **'merchants of death'**; *the February revolution in Russia; and the Zimmerman telegram.*

 The US and the Treaty of Versailles

4   **(a)   Explain the US's attitude to the Treaty of Versailles.** (30)

   (b)   Why and to what extent did the US pursue a policy of isolationism in the 1920s and 1930s? (60)

(OCR)

(a)   Wilson, elected President of the United States, had brought his country into the First World War with the intention of helping shape the post-war peace. He devised a coherent peace settlement and was present at discussions in Paris where a modified version of the settlement, including a planned League of Nations, was drawn up. Most of Congress, including the Senate, wanted some kind of settlement and League of Nations, even if not quite in the form drawn up in Paris. Public opinion in the US was also favourable. Despite this, for reasons which are not immediately obvious, the Treaty was rejected by the Senate. The US refused to join the League of Nations and thus appeared to isolate itself from world affairs during the 1920s and 1930s. This is not easily explained, but the simplistic notion that the US's rejection of the Treaty was caused by a wave of post-war isolationism is misleading.

Even though the US did want to participate in some kind of post-war settlement, there was already a feeling that US participation in the war had been a mistake and that US citizens had been killed without justification. Criticism of munitions manufacturers did not yet reach the levels of the 1930s, but there were accusations of profiteers growing rich from the war at the expense of human lives. A post-war settlement including a League of Nations would be satisfactory as long as the US was not bound by its decisions to intervene in Europe again. Senator Henry Cabot Lodge, who led opposition to the Treaty of Versailles, struck a key note when he said in 1919: 'the hard practical demand is, are you ready to put your soldiers and sailors at the disposition of other nations?' Lodge himself favoured some kind of League but for many the memory of the First World War was still too immediate to proceed without caution.

Wilson's original 'Fourteen Points' proposal for a peace settlement was the starting point for discussions at the 1919 Paris Peace Conference. However, the Treaty of Versailles that emerged seemed more designed to punish Germany than to create lasting and harmonious peace. Proposals for a League of Nations survived, but were surrounded by other issues such as the confiscation of German territory (including all colonies), demands for heavy reparations, forced disarmament and placing the blame for starting the war firmly upon Germany. French leader Clemenceau and, to a lesser extent, British leader Lloyd George, demanded particular clauses and concessions from Germany. As Wilson's vision for peace was general rather than specific, his plan was gradually undermined and unpicked by the other two leaders. The treaty became seen as a 'winner's peace', with Germany given no opportunity to negotiate and Japan allowed to keep its de facto control of the Shantung province in China. Furthermore, Wilson seems to have represented US interests poorly. John Maynard Keynes (part of the British delegation at Paris) was unimpressed by Wilson's performance and said: 'there can seldom have been a statesman of the first rank more incompetent than the President in the agilities of the council chamber.' Wilson was prepared to accept the treaty's harsher terms as he felt that a League of Nations would be able to modify these terms peacefully in time. This optimistic view was not universally shared in the US, though. To idealists, the League of Nations would be tainted by its association with a selfish and vindictive peace.

Despite this, the harshness of the Treaty of Versailles did not cause most concern in the US where, after all, in public opinion Germany had been the enemy for the previous two years. The main worry was the potential of the League of Nations to force binding commitments upon its members. Opposition in the Senate began months before all of the treaty's terms were decided, and once the treaty was signed, its individual flaws were used as a weapon against joining the League. As a result of the 1918 Congressional elections, the Republicans had a 49/47 majority in the Senate, where a two-thirds majority is required in order to ratify a treaty. Only 14 of these Republican senators were '**Irreconcilables**', determined to reject any form of League of Nations. The rest were 'strong' or 'mild' '**Reservationists**', seeking opt-outs for the US from some of the League's more binding commitments, but not opposed to the principle of a League. The Republican Senate majority leader, Henry Cabot Lodge, was a 'strong Reservationist' and, like most of his fellow Republicans, he was also motivated by a personal dislike of Wilson. Lodge, wishing to keep the support of both the Irreconciliables and the mild Reservationists in his party, embarked upon delaying tactics to prevent the treaty from being ratified quickly. A 'Round Robin' resolution was signed by 39 Republican senators in February 1919, refusing to support the League of Nations if its provisions went against the Monroe Doctrine. This complicated and slowed negotiations in Paris. Lodge then spent two weeks of Senate time painstakingly reading every word of the treaty (some 200 pages long) out loud. Following this, a series of reservations were tabled in the Senate, including Congress's right to withdraw the US from the League at any time, no League control over US military commitments, precedence for the Monroe Doctrine, and so on, totalling fourteen reservations in all.

As a result the treaty was not put to the vote in the Senate until November 1919. Ratification with the reservations was rejected 55/39, and ratification without reservations was rejected 53–38, with a few abstentions in either vote. Lodge had successfully mustered the support of virtually all Republicans and a few Democrats against ratification without reservations; and ratification with reservations was rejected by most Democrats and a few 'Irreconciliable' Republicans. The result was no ratification due to the lack of consensus over reservations. However, the treaty would be presented for ratification again, and next time it would be a choice of either the treaty with reservations or no treaty at all. In theory this would have led to ratification.

Ironically, however, it was Wilson himself who played a key role in the US rejection of the treaty. He asked the Democrat senators to vote against ratification with reservations when the Senate voted again in March 1920. The Senate voted 49–35 in favour this time, but this was seven votes short of the two-thirds majority needed for ratification. This was mainly due to a number of Democrat senators showing loyalty to Wilson at the expense of the treaty. To understand this we need to look at Wilson's motives and mismanagement of the Senate. Having chosen to personally lead the US delegation to Paris (and appointing no leading Republicans to his delegation), Wilson felt his own reputation was tied up with the Treaty of Versailles in its Paris form. A few minor compromises might be acceptable but one clause that Wilson would not compromise on was Article 10 of the League of Nations, which provided for the use of collective force against violation of sovereignty or territorial integrity. This, however, was the clause that worried Reservationists the most. Rather than seek a deal on the issue Wilson first bluntly rejected criticisms, saying in June 1919: 'We ought to either go in or stay out. To stay out would be fatal.' He then attempted to appeal to public opinion over the head of the Senate with a whistle-stop lecture tour during September, but the decision in reality lay with the Senate. However Wilson hated Senate majority leader Lodge as much as Lodge hated him, and Wilson feared that a treaty ratified with reservations would be seen as a Lodge achievement, not a Wilson achievement.

Our understanding of the US Senate's rejection of the treaty is clouded by the illness suffered by Wilson during 1919 and early 1920. His ill health had weakened his role at the Paris Peace Conference, and his lecture tour resulted in a major stroke in October 1919. This left him isolated from day-to-day politics for three months, but he refused to relinquish the Presidency and allowed his wife effectively to control his decisions. When Secretary of State Lansing tried to govern in Wilson's absence, Mrs Wilson persuaded her husband to dismiss him. It was in this context that Wilson refused to negotiate any deal on the Treaty of Versailles before the second Senate vote in March 1920. He planned instead to run again for the Presidency and treat the election as a popular referendum on US membership of the League of Nations. This was unrealistic judgement. However, there is no evidence of Wilson preparing to compromise with the Republicans in the Senate before his stroke. The identification of Republican opposition with the leadership of Lodge probably did more to cause Wilson's stubborn approach than his illness.

It was a peculiar chain of circumstances, then, that led to the US's rejection of the Treaty of Versailles. (The US would eventually sign a separate peace treaty with Germany under President Harding.) The fear of binding military commitment was the main sticking point, but, in the event, the League never demanded this level of commitment. As all of the League's leading members bypassed the League and used more traditional diplomatic methods when it suited them, the US's refusal to join arguably made little difference to US foreign policy or world peace generally. Successive Presidents after Wilson showed no interest in reconsidering US membership of the League. This contrasts with the US's commitment to the United Nations after the Second World War, suggesting that the lack of threat to the US after the First World War (unlike the Second World War) meant that the arguments for accepting the treaty and joining the League were not urgent or strong enough when placed alongside the arguments against.

Isolationism in the 1920s and 1930s

(b) 'Isolationism' refers to the refusal of the United States to join the League of Nations in the 1920s or enter binding alliances to counter the threat of the dictators in the 1930s. Compared to the post-1941 period, the US was certainly isolated in the 1920s and 1930s; however there was still plenty of interest in world affairs and various conferences and treaties. The US was never *truly* isolationist, just *relatively* so during this period. Isolationism deepened in the 1930s as new reasons for avoiding commitments elsewhere emerged – in particular the impact of the Great Depression.

Isolationism towards Europe grew out of the US's geographical remoteness and lack of regular dealings with European powers before the First World War. With the exception of the Algeciras Conference, the US only took an interest in European involvement in the Americas, the Pacific and East Asia, and only entered the war in 1917 after provocation from German unrestricted submarine warfare. The impact of the war upon the US, while economically beneficial, did carry a heavy human cost compared to previous US conflicts. Involvement in the war was viewed as a mistake during the 1920s and 1930s, and although the US came close to joining the League of Nations in 1920, once the decision was made not to join, public opinion was galvanised into hostility to the League. From its own perspective, the US seemed better placed away from 'Old World' squabbling, the creation of the League was linked to a vindictive and punitive treaty and the French occupation of the Ruhr in 1923 seemed to confirm that European powers had not learned to settle problems peacefully after the war. While the US kept an eye on the League and even had an agent in Geneva to communicate the US's views to League officials, public opinion opposed involvement. Joseph C. Grew, US ambassador to Switzerland, tried to steer clear of the League's headquarters and was horrified when, calling in briefly to pick up a friend in September 1922, he was caught by a *Chicago Tribune* reporter, suspecting secret US government dealings with the League. Grew was relieved when the story was not printed, but his alarm shows the unacceptability of the League to the US.

Successive Republican Presidents in the 1920s maintained this isolated approach and Harding's election victory in 1920 seemed to confirm public hostility to the League. Harding said in March 1921 the US was 'confident of our ability to work out our own destiny'. Republican foreign policy in the 1920s has been described as 'conservative internationalism'. The US did deal with other powers and seek international agreements, but on its own terms and in areas of its own interests only. The Monroe Doctrine remained a guiding principle, with US activity in Latin America continuing throughout the 1920s, but interest in

European affairs fell away. President Coolidge defined this approach to foreign policy accurately in 1925, stating: 'We can best serve our country and most successfully discharge our obligations to humanity by continuing to be openly and candidly, intensely and scrupulously, American.' This approach expressed itself in a rather half-hearted global policy in the 1920s. The Washington Treaty of 1922 saw the five largest naval powers agree limits on battleship tonnage, while the 1928 Kellogg-Briand Pact to condemn war was eventually signed by 62 states. The 1924 Dawes Plan and 1929 Young Plan, arranged by Hoover as Secretary of Commerce and then President, showed US involvement in the German reparations issue. However, the Washington Treaty did not stop the building of heavy cruisers and submarines, and was obsolete by the 1930s. The Kellogg-Briand Pact has to be offset by the US's failure to join the World Court in the Hague (ratification of membership failed as the Senate, then individual states of the US, tried to attach an endless stream of reservations). And the reparations plans were motivated by US economic interests; Britain and France needed German reparations in order to pay off US loans from the First World War. A general suspicion of international commitments and a succession of Presidents more concerned with domestic issues led to a rather languid foreign policy in the 1920s.

The Great Depression of the early 1930s led to a surge in isolationism and renewed suspicion of foreign commitments. By 1931 the Depression was so deep and apparently unstoppable that foreign concerns became insignificant compared to domestic problems. Even Roosevelt's election victory over Hoover in 1932 was accompanied by a promise that the US would concentrate on domestic solutions to domestic problems, rather than blaming the worldwide depression and looking for international solutions. This attitude was demonstrated at the World Economic Conference in London in June 1933: the US delegates did not even agree among themselves as to what they wanted from the conference, and a proposed return to fixed exchange rates based on the gold standard was rejected by the US, dooming the conference to failure.

Public opinion, substantially pro-isolation in the 1920s, now became vehemently so, crossing all social and political boundaries: isolationism was led by pacifist groups such as the Women's International League for Peace and Freedom and the Council for the Prevention of War; there was intellectual support blaming US involvement in the First World War upon greedy munitions manufacturers; famous individuals such as Albert Einstein and Charles Lindbergh promoted isolationism; and the Hearst newspaper group led press hostility to foreign affairs. An opinion poll from April 1937 suggested that 64 per cent saw involvement in the First World War as a mistake. This widespread attitude has been called 'insulationist' rather than truly isolationist, but it was still far in excess of attitudes in the early 1920s. Additionally, all European states, except Finland, defaulted on their war debts to the US in the early 1930s and US trade interests in Europe nose-dived at the same time.

Congress now passed a series of laws to maintain isolationism and avoid a repeat of the First World War involvement. The Nye Committee investigated the munitions industry during 1934–6 and condemned it for encouraging intervention in the last war. Meanwhile the 1934 Johnson Amendment forbade the sale of bonds for any European power that had previously defaulted on US loans. This was followed by the 1935 Pittman Resolution that forbade US Presidents from applying sanctions that discriminated in favour of victims of aggression. Then a series of Neutrality Acts from 1935 to 1937 banned arms exports to belligerents, war loans or credits, and US citizens travelling on belligerent ships, with the same restrictions to apply to civil wars as well as wars between countries. The 1938 Ludlow Amendment was only 21 votes short of a House of Representatives two-thirds majority: had it been passed the President would not have been able to declare war without holding a popular referendum first. This showed how isolationism was moving towards an extreme. Even as late as November 1939, when the menace of the dictators was clear to all, Congress was only willing to partially step down from its neutrality stance. Arms exports would be allowed but only on a 'cash and carry' basis; buyers would pay up front and make their own transport arrangements. This showed that isolationism lingered even after the Second World War had begun.

Roosevelt, newly elected President in 1933, had a track record as a Wilsonian internationalist. He was conscious of the threat of the dictators in the 1930s well before US public opinion seemed to be. However, even his attitudes were influenced by the 1930s Great Depression and he steered clear of foreign policy debate in the 1932 and 1936 elections, except to make bland statements such as 'I hate war' and to describe trade with belligerent powers as 'fool's gold'. Roosevelt seems to have stepped away from internationalism during the early 1930s, combining an understandable preoccupation with economic recovery, a wish to go with the tide of public opinion (he referred to it as a 'very large and perhaps increasing school of thought' in September 1935) and a personal tendency to put off binding decisions in foreign policy. He was also unimpressed by Britain's 'imperial preference' approach at the Ottawa Conference, where the British Empire put up external trade barriers against US trade. The League of Nations seemed to be losing authority in the early 1930s as first Japan, then Germany (and later Italy) all rejected the League, and a study of Japan's invasion of Manchuria suggested there was little the US could do about it with or without the League's help. Even existing US agreements seemed to be failing, the Washington and London naval agreements expiring in 1936 after both Japan and Britain had rejected renewal proposals. By 1937 Roosevelt was trying to educate public opinion into recognising the threat of the dictators, but concluded that the US was not ready to accept binding commitments in foreign policy just yet. The President's rhetoric became more internationalist over the following two years, gradually winning some public support as Japan pursued its invasion of China, but when war broke out Europe in 1939 US neutrality was no surprise.

In conclusion, the reasons for US 'isolationism' did change during the 1920s and 1930s, but always seemed to be underpinned by the belief that the US had no part to play in 'Old World' diplomatic intrigue. Such intrigue had led to the tragic First World War. As was the case in the European democracies, the effects of world war and then the Great Depression led to an upsurge of pacifism and distrust of binding international commitments. The US was not the only country to reject the League of Nations or fail to face up to the threat of the dictators during this period and in many respects the US was no more isolated or neutral than some other major powers. It was its refusal to join the League and the wave of 1930s neutralism that gave the US an isolationist image between the world wars.

 ## The abandonment of isolationism in 1941

5 Why did the US abandon isolationism in 1941? (45)

(OCR)

The United States had no option but to enter the Second World War in December 1941. First Japan, without declaring war, launched a surprise attack upon the US naval base at Pearl Harbor, then Germany declared war on the US a few days later. This gives the image of a supine, neutral US dragged into world war against its will. In reality isolationism was always an overstatement of the US position in world affairs, and the whole of 1941, not just December, saw growing US involvement in the war. This was caused not just by the aggressive nature of Japan and Germany demonstrated before 1939, but also by the way the war had progressed up to 1941.

President Roosevelt, who led the US into the war, had also presided over an isolationist US during the 1930s. His instincts were internationalist, though, and he felt warm personal ties to Britain and France since his experience of the First World War. By 1939 Germany, Italy and Japan, the Axis powers, had already shown their aggressive ambitions. Developments such as the German annexation of Austria and the Czechoslovakian Sudetenland, the Italian conquest of Abyssinia, and the Japanese invasion of China demonstrated this aggression. They also showed the failure of the League of Nations, and Britain and France's policy of appeasement, to deal with this aggression. With fascists apparently winning the Spanish Civil War, and all dictatorships building up formidable military power, Roosevelt recognised that by 1939 the US faced a dangerous world. This was confirmed in April 1939 when Germany contemptuously rejected the US's request for assurance that 31 named countries would not be attacked in the next ten years. So, despite public opposition to war running at around 80 per cent from 1939 to late 1941, Roosevelt warned Congress in January 1939 to pay close attention to international developments, then allowed the sale of thousands of US aeroplanes to France and warned Japan that, unless they ceased aggression against China, the US would cancel their trade treaties with Japan in January 1940. The US was beginning to play power politics again before the Second World War broke out in Europe.

Despite Roosevelt's pointed references in January 1940 to ostriches sticking their heads in the sand, the US was still unlikely to intervene while the existing balance of power existed in Europe. Arms were sold to Britain and France, but only on a 'cash and carry' basis; the Allies had to pay up front and transport the arms from the US themselves. The dramatic German success in 1940 changed that. With Poland conquered the previous autumn, Germany then had overrun Denmark, Norway, Holland, Belgium, Luxembourg and, most significantly, France by June 1940 – and France had been seen as the European country most likely to defeat Germany. This success was complemented by an effective German U-boat campaign. By the summer, the British Empire seemed very vulnerable to German and Japanese attack. Elsewhere in Europe, Germany had the friendship of Italy, Spain and the USSR, which had signed a ten-year non-aggression pact with Germany in August 1939 and had then gone on to invade eastern Poland and attack Finland during 1939–40. The European balance of power had clearly failed to regulate itself without US involvement. The balance of power in Southeast Asia was, as a result, also threatened, where French, Dutch and British colonies were Japanese targets. US security seemed to be dangerously undermined. If the British Empire was to fall, then US security would be shattered. With this in mind, and encouraged by election victory in 1940 despite 'warmonger' accusations from his opponents, Roosevelt persuaded Congress to reluctantly introduce conscription in September 1940 and then a 'lend-lease' scheme in January 1941, allowing Britain to receive US military aid on credit. A Presidential radio broadcast in December 1940 outlined Roosevelt's wish for the US to become the 'arsenal of democracy', providing munitions to the Allies. The US was now showing a similar level of pro-Allied commitment to that of 1915–16, possibly greater.

It was US relations with Japan, however, that really pulled it away from isolationism. Rivalry over East Asia and the Pacific had existed since the late nineteenth century. Mutual tensions had generally been settled through diplomacy, for example the 1922 Washington Treaty. However, the 1930s saw a surge in Japanese imperial expansion, motivated partly by a lack of raw materials and land, its overpopulation and a loss of world markets due to the worldwide Great Depression. Less than 5 per cent of US foreign investments were in China but the market there had massive potential. This, coupled with US territorial possessions in the Pacific (notably the Philippines) made a future clash of interests likely. Japan certainly perceived this to be so, and the US ambassador Joseph Grew said in May 1933: 'the Japanese fighting forces consider the United States as their potential enemy.' However, before 1937 war seemed unlikely.

The US built up its naval strength during the 1930s but did not break any treaty doing so. The Japanese conquest of Manchuria led to US trade there tripling between 1932 and 1940, showing the lack of disruption this caused to US/Japanese relations. Even the full Japanese invasion of China in 1937 did not lead to any determined US response or even a show of naval strength. When a US gunboat was bombed and sunk off the Chinese coast, the Japanese offer of an apology and reparations was accepted. And the 1934 Tydings-McDuffie Act, which promised independence for the Philippines in twelve years, suggested that the US was looking to reduce, rather than increase, its involvement in the western Pacific. As with Europe, it was the changing picture in 1940 that proved to be a turning point in US foreign policy.

By the end of 1940, the US had imposed embargoes on trade and credit with Japan. These included aeroplanes and aviation parts, aviation and motor fuel and lubricants, followed by a total embargo and the freezing of Japanese assets in the US in July 1941. These economic sanctions hit Japan hard, its lack of raw materials making it dependent on US exports for its own war effort. Despite this, there were still hopes of lasting peace between the US and Japan. Between January and June 1941, Secretary of State Hull embarked on a series of talks with the Japanese ambassador to the US, Nomura. The Japanese decision not to join in Germany's invasion of the USSR in May 1941 was also a promising sign that Japanese expansion might have limits, and might be deterred by the US threat. However the Japanese invasion of southern Indo-China (a French colony) in July 1941, and the stiffening of US sanctions as a result, was a point of no return. Control of Indo-China would put Japan in a position to control the whole of Southeast Asia and the western Pacific. It would also isolate Britain from its empire resources in Asia. The US, having seen Germany win dominance of Europe the previous year, could not see Japan achieve a similar level of dominance in East Asia. The Japanese, for their part, by a process of 'circular reasoning' now coveted the Dutch East Indies for its oil resources, even though a Japanese invasion would be almost certain to provoke a US declaration of war. As the oil would be needed to win a war against the US, this justified such an invasion. Japan made an arguably token attempt to avert war in November 1941 by offering to withdraw from southern Indo-China if the US lifted its economic sanctions against Japan. This proved to be the final peace initiative before war broke out.

The Japanese initiative was weak in any case, but its failure can be partly explained by the more resolute attitude shown by the US during 1941. The US still wanted to avoid war but, learning lessons from the failure of appeasement in the 1930s, refused to compromise with Japanese aggression. Roosevelt identified the US's future prospects more and more closely with the survival of the British Empire. The alternative seemed to be an isolated US in an Axis-dominated world. Secretary of War Stimson had (inaccurately) calculated that defeat for Britain would leave the Axis with naval superiority of seven to one and resulting dominance of world trade. A secret meeting between Roosevelt and Churchill off the Newfoundland coast led to the joint signing of the Atlantic Charter, where both agreed on shared principles and condemnation of Nazi tyranny, and agreed to work closely together in the future, for example in sending aid to the USSR. Any lingering US neutrality was further undermined by German U-boat attacks on US destroyers *Greer*, *Kearny* and *Reuben James* during September and October. There were now parallels with the First World War in early 1917, with Germany apparently winning the war and US ships under attack. In this context, the strong US response to the Japanese offer in November 1941 was unsurprising. The US reply (the 'Hull Note') demanded that Japan withdraw from China as well as Indo-China before sanctions would be lifted. With a more hardline government freshly installed in Japan, this reply was inevitably rejected. Japan now concentrated on making a surprise attack on the US at Pearl Harbor, leaving no time for any further diplomatic initiatives. The nature of the attack silenced any remaining isolationism in the US and made the declaration of war against Japan a formality. The US did not declare war on Germany immediately but Hitler saved Roosevelt the trouble of persuading Congress to extend the war further by declaring war himself on the US a week later.

The US's abandonment of isolation and entry into the Second World War in 1941 was mainly a reaction to the power and aggression of others. Support for neutrality lingered for some time after the nature of the aggressive states had revealed itself. Isolationism seemed to have served the US well when power elsewhere in the world was either balanced or tipped in favour of states friendly towards the US. By 1941 this was no longer the case. Nor was it the case in the late 1940s when the US, faced with the emergence of the USSR as an unfriendly superpower, opted not to return to inter-war isolationism but instead to retain its presence in Europe and East Asia. US foreign policy changed for the most fundamental reason – the future security of the United States.

Part 3: Sources

📖 1 The causes of the Spanish-American War

■ **Source A: Senator Henry Cabot Lodge (March 1895)**

It is not the policy of the United States to enter, as England has done, upon the general acquisition of distant possessions in all parts of the world. Our government is not adapted to such a policy, and we have no need of it, for we have an ample field at home; but at the same time it must be remembered that while in the United States themselves we hold the citadel of our power and greatness as a nation, there are outworks essential to the defence of that citadel which must neither be neglected nor abandoned.

■ **Source B: President Grover Cleveland (December 1896)**

The spectacle of the utter ruin of an adjoining country, by nature one of the most fertile and charming on the globe, would engage the serious attention of the government and people of the United States in any circumstances. In point of fact, they have a concern with it which is by no means of a wholly sentimental or philanthropic character. It lies so near to us as to be hardly separated from our territory. Our actual pecuniary interest in it is second only to that of the people and government of Spain.

■ **Source C: President William McKinley (December 1897)**

The story of Cuba for many years has been one of unrest, growing discontent, an effort toward a larger enjoyment of liberty and self-control, of organised resistance to the mother country, of depression after distress and warfare and of ineffectual settlement to be followed by renewed revolt. For no ending period ... has the condition of Cuba or the policy of Cuba not caused concern to the United States ... If it shall hereafter appear to be a duty imposed by our obligations to ourselves, to civilisation and humanity, to intervene with force, it shall be without fault on our part and only because the necessity for such action will be so clear as to command the support and approval of the civilised world.

AQA QUESTION FORMAT

The questions and answers that follow are based on the AQA style.

(a) **Study Source A. Using your own knowledge explain what steps the US had taken to acquire overseas territory by the 1890s.** (3)

(b) **Study Sources A and B and use your own knowledge to support your answer. Explain the role of economic factors in US foreign expansion by the end of the nineteenth century.** (7)

(c) **Study sources A, B and C and use your own knowledge. How important was Spain's treatment of Cuban rebels in causing the Spanish-American War in 1898?** (15)

(a) US expansion before the 1890s mainly consisted of pushing its frontier westwards. It consciously rejected the British style of empire, namely 'the general acquisition of distant possessions in all parts of the world'. However one point not mentioned in the Source was that the US had acquired the 'distant possessions' of Alaska and Midway in 1867. The Source also fails to mention the economic colonialism taking place in the Americas and the Pacific, for example Hawaii where US businesses controlled sugar production. When Lodge referred to 'outworks essential to the defence of that citadel' he had US economic fortunes in mind. While the US had acquired little overseas territory by 1895, this was no longer the case by 1900.

(b) Economic factors were central to US foreign expansion in the late nineteenth century. In Source B Cleveland is honest enough to say that US alarm at Spain's repression of Cuba in 1896 is 'by no means of a wholly sentimental or philanthropic character', but there is also a 'pecuniary interest'. Once you cut through the moral outrage and the vacuous assurance that this would merit 'serious attention . . . in any circumstances', the economic concerns are clear. There is also significant reference to the strategic importance of Cuba, as 'it lies so near' to the US, echoing Lodge's warning in Source A that 'there are outworks necessary to the defence of that citadel which must neither be neglected nor abandoned'. It is likely that Cuba was in Lodge's mind too. We can therefore establish from the Sources alone that economic factors, while very important, were not the only considerations for the US.

In fact the US, having been born out of a successful attempt to throw off British domination, had been motivated from a wish to prevent European encroachment upon US interests throughout the nineteenth century. A second defeat of Britain in war in 1812 was followed by the 1823 Monroe Doctrine, which declared all of the Americas (North, Central and South) to be a US sphere of interest and not for further European expansion. This doctrine was in practice extended to include much of the Pacific. The most significant US foreign expansion came in 1898 when the Treaty of Paris gave the US control of Puerto Rico, Guam and the Philippines, all former Spanish colonies. This was a consequence of the US's efforts to remove Spanish influence in and around the Americas, more a strategic than an economic decision.

It is also worth mentioning the surge of interest in Social Darwinism that, in theory, made it the US's destiny to dominate its continent and the surrounding oceans. The growing US navy was nicknamed the 'Great White Fleet' in 1893 and the tone of Lodge's pronouncement in Source A, of 'our power and greatness as a nation', implies a similar level of confidence and ambition that could lead to territorial expansion.

However, the US clearly stood to benefit economically from any foreign expansion as it would open up new markets for trade. An obvious example of economic factors causing US foreign expansion can be found in the case of Hawaii. Since 1819, US settlers had carved out a share of the Hawaiian economy and by 1892 they controlled about two-thirds of all property there. When Queen Liliuokalani tried to reduce US economic influence, the US simply annexed Hawaii on the pretext that law and order was breaking down. Economic factors seemed still to be predominant in US foreign expansion by the end of the nineteenth century, and would remain a strong influence in the twentieth century.

(c) Successive US Presidents in the 1890s made clear their outrage at Spain's treatment of Cuba. In Source B Cleveland bemoans 'the spectacle of the utter ruin of an adjoining country', while in Source C McKinley contemplates 'a duty imposed by our obligations . . . to civilisation and humanity, to intervene with force'. Both statements were made in the aftermath of the 1895 Cuban uprising and are likely to refer specifically to the Spanish suppression of the rebellion in the years that followed as well as more general distaste for the way that Spain had ruled Cuba before 1895. Spain was certainly brutal in its suppression of the revolt, and its deployment of nearly 200,000 troops to Cuba over the next three years was accompanied by stories of violent atrocities against the Cuban population. Violent repression of colonial uprisings was nothing new but was now taking place 'so near to us as to be hardly separated from our territory' (Source B). Much of the US press picked up on the repression and reported atrocities in detail, provoking anti-Spanish outrage among the US population. This could not be ignored by the US government and was a major factor in causing the 1898 war.

The way in which Spain chose to deal with the rebellion – with utter intolerance rather than attempting to find a compromise or peaceful solution – helps to explain why war broke out in 1898. Spain was in no mood to bow to US pressure over Cuba. Spanish repression continued through 1896 and 1897 into 1898 in the face of US protests; and a leaked letter, written by the Spanish ambassador to the US, de Lome, seemed to indicate Spanish contempt for the US President McKinley. McKinley himself was scathing about Spanish rule in Cuba, as indicated in his accusations in Source C of 'distress and warfare and of ineffectual settlement', and his implication that Spain was not part of 'the civilised world'. He had also pledged support for Cuban independence in his 1896 election campaign. Such comments would have enraged Spain and made war hard to avoid. De Lome's letter continued this process, especially as it was angrily paraded in the US press in February 1898.

It was not only the nature of Spain's treatment of Cuban rebels but also the proximity of Cuba to the US and the aims of US foreign policy that prompted US intervention. When Lodge spoke of 'outworks essential to the defence of that citadel' (Source A) he would have had Cuba, less than one hundred miles from Florida, in mind. While the US might not seek 'the general acquisition of distant possessions in all parts of the world' (Source A), Cuba could hardly be considered distant. The US had already annexed Midway and Alaska in recent decades and was soon to take full control of Hawaii. US foreign policy adhered to the 1823 Monroe Doctrine and considered the Americas to be their business, not that of European powers. At a time when other European powers were looking to expand their empires (for example the 'scramble for Africa') the US was especially determined not to allow an increase in European influence in the Caribbean, not even from an incumbent colonial power such as Spain.

While the factors above contributed to the outbreak of war, a specific development in February 1898 triggered the conflict. The US battleship *Maine* was blown up by a mine in Havana harbour resulting in 260 deaths. Whether the mine was planted by the Spanish or by Cuban rebels is unproven but the US press blamed Spain and encouraged public opinion to demand action. Congress was caught up in the mood of the time and approved an extra $50 million on national defence, and McKinley, conscious of the imminent mid-term elections and wishing to prove his own backbone, authorised US military intervention in April 1898. This made war inevitable; it was likely to break out in 1898 in any case and the sinking of the *Maine* increased this likelihood.

The US had a special economic and strategic interest in Cuba. In 1898, as in the 1962 missile crisis, it would not tolerate any developments there that were harmful to US interests. Colonial repression of native populations might be acceptable (and did take place without response from the US) in Africa or Asia, but not in 'Uncle Sam's backyard'.

ADDITIONAL QUESTIONS

(a) **Study Source B. Using your own knowledge explain President Cleveland's reference to 'the spectacle of the utter ruin of an adjoining country.'** (3)

(b) **Study Sources B and C. What factors led to the US intervention in Cuba in April 1898? Use your own knowledge to support your answer.** (7)

(c) **Study Sources A, B and C and use your own knowledge. To what extent did the US assert its influence over the Americas between 1890 and 1914?** (15)

(AQA)

2 Arguments for neutrality in the First World War

■ Source A: President Woodrow Wilson, August 1914

The people of the United States are drawn from many nations, and chiefly from the nations now at war. It is natural and inevitable that there should be the utmost variety of sympathy and desire among them with regards to the issues and circumstances of the conflict. Some will wish one nation, others another, to succeed in the momentous struggle. It will be easy to excite passion and difficult to allay it. . . . Such divisions among us would be fatal to our peace of mind and might seriously stand in the way of the proper performance of our duty as the one great nation at peace, the one people holding itself ready to play a part of impartial mediation and speak the counsels of peace and accommodation, not as a partisan but as a friend.

■ **Source B: Theodore Roosevelt, September 1914**

All of us on this continent ought to appreciate how fortunate we are that we of the Western world have been free from the working of the causes which have produced the bitter and vindictive hatred among the great military powers of the Old World. We owe this immunity primarily to the policies grouped together under the title of the Monroe Doctrine. . . . Neutrality may be of prime necessity in order to preserve our own interests, to maintain peace in so much of the world as is not affected by the war; and to conserve our influence for helping towards the re-establishment of general peace when the time comes.

■ **Source C: Senator George W. Norris (April 1917)**

No close student of recent history will deny that both Great Britain and Germany have, on numerous occasions since the beginning of the war, flagrantly violated in the most serious manner the rights of neutral vessels and neutral nations under existing international law, as recognised up to the beginning of this war by the civilised world. . . . Our government has officially declared both of them to be illegal and has officially protested against both of them. The only difference is that in the case of Germany we have persisted in our protest, while in the case of England we have submitted.

AQA QUESTION FORMAT

The questions and answers that follow are based on the AQA style.

(a) **Study Source B and use your own knowledge. Explain what was meant by the Monroe Doctrine.** (3)

(b) **Study Sources A and B and use your own knowledge. Why did the US choose neutrality when war broke out in Europe in August 1914?** (7)

(c) **Study Sources A, B and C and use your own knowledge. Explain why, despite arguments for neutrality and both Great Britain and Germany breaching international law, the US entered the war on the side of the Allies in April 1917.** (15)

(a) The Monroe Doctrine, presented by President James Monroe to Congress in 1823, was a declaration that the Americas were in the US sphere of interest and that any attempts by European powers to increase their colonial empires there would be resisted. This had been a specific response to Spain's attempts to win back its South American colonies but was retained and consistently followed over the next century. Source B shows Roosevelt upholding the doctrine as late as 1914. He praises the doctrine for keeping the US 'free from . . . the bitter and vindictive hatred among the great military powers of the Old World', i.e. the outbreak of the First World War in Europe. Here we see a fresh interpretation of the doctrine; as Europe is outside the US sphere of interest the US should take a neutral stance.

(b) There would have been logic behind any US decision to enter the war in 1914. The US economy relied heavily upon European trade and many US citizens were of European ancestry. Woodrow Wilson noted: 'The people of the United States are drawn from many nations, and chiefly from the nations now at war . . . it would be easy to excite passion' (Source A). The US could not ignore what was happening in Europe and even supporters of neutrality such as Theodore Roosevelt saw the need 'to conserve our influence' in European affairs (Source B).

Despite this, Europe was 3,000 miles away and Roosevelt's contrasting of 'the Western world' with 'the Old World' would have met with popular agreement in 1914 America. He mentions the 'Monroe Doctrine' and its implication that the US should only concern itself with the Americas and not Europe. European power politics and empire- and alliance-building disgusted Roosevelt who saw them as 'the causes which have produced this bitter and vindictive hatred'. There did not seem to be any justification for the war, instead it was a European malaise – and neutrality seemed the best way to keep it from spreading to the Americas. This seemed to be supported by US public opinion at the time.

While the majority of US citizens who felt a preference were inclined to support the Allies, there were many German immigrants, Irish Americans (who resented Britain) and Jewish Americans (including refugees from persecution in Russia) in the US. Woodrow Wilson acknowledged it as 'natural and inevitable that there should be the utmost variety of sympathy ... some will wish one nation, others another, to succeed in the momentous conflict'. Intervention in the war might lead to 'divisions among us' that 'would be fatal to our peace of mind'. Anti-war demonstrations, violent disagreements and riots were all possible consequences of taking sides.

It was also unclear how long the war would last for, and any US intervention on one side or the other would take several months to have any effect. Not only might the US support the losing side, it would lose the credibility needed 'for helping towards the re-establishment of general peace when the time comes' (Source B). The idea of the US as 'the one great nation at peace, the one people holding itself ready to play a part of impartial mediation and speak the counsels of peace and accommodation' (Source A) was close to the President's heart and was reflected in his 'Fourteen Points' peace initiative in 1918. Neutrality certainly seemed to be the most attractive option in 1914, at least for the time being.

(c) The benefits of neutrality were undermined by 1917. Senator Norris (Source C) refers to the behaviour of Great Britain and Germany, two leading participants in the First World War. Both had 'flagrantly violated in the most serious manner the rights of neutral vessels and neutral nations' on 'numerous occasions since the beginning of the war', two-and-a-half years earlier. US hopes of maintaining its trade with Germany and Austria-Hungary had been confounded by British naval power in the Atlantic, which used a 'stop and search' policy to blockade the transportation of goods to the Central Powers. The German high seas fleet never won control of the seas but German U-boats were able to disrupt trade between the US and Britain and France by attacking shipping. US ships and citizens were affected as Germany introduced unrestricted submarine warfare in 1915 and again in 1917. The longer war continued, the longer US trade would be disrupted.

Norris does make it clear, however, that both sides had broken 'international law' and that the US 'government has officially declared both of them to be illegal and has officially protested against both of them'. The US could not ignore the continued conflict, but any intervention in the war would have to be on one side or the other. There were long-standing arguments to remain impartial, Woodrow Wilson warning of 'divisions among us' (Source A) and Theodore Roosevelt of 'the need to preserve our own interests'. These statements had been made in 1914 however. In private Wilson admitted weeks later that 'England is fighting our fight' and, despite promising continued neutrality in his 1916 re-election campaign, he told his navy Secretary: 'Any little German lieutenant can put us into the war at any time by some calculated outrage.' Roosevelt, having initially supported neutrality, spent much of the next three years campaigning for the US to enter the war.

As the war dragged through 1915 and 1916, US intervention became more likely. US bankers in 1915 warned of economic recession and the government's response, given the blockade on its trade with the Central Powers, was to increase its trade with the Allies. This gave the US a vested interest in Allied victory. In any case Wilson believed that a victory for the Central Powers could lead to German domination of Europe and thus a threat to the US's world position. An Allied victory seemed more likely to keep the status quo. Germany, furious with the US's trade with the Allies, introduced unrestricted submarine warfare – in the eyes of the US this was a 'flagrant violation' (Source C). At the same time, Britain maintained its naval blockade but also took careful diplomatic steps to encourage US trade and warned that the Allies depended on the US to avoid defeat in the war. In 1916 the British Foreign Secretary Grey proposed a ceasefire and a retreat to August 1914 positions in Europe, knowing this would be rejected by Germany. The result was that Wilson, keen to see an end to the war, saw Germany as the more belligerent and intractable power.

This increasing US alignment with the Allies helps to explain Norris's complaint in Source C 'that in the case of Germany we have persisted in our protest, while in the case of England we have submitted'. His comment was accurate and reflected that true US neutrality had ended before April 1917. As long as the war continued, US intervention on the side of the Allies was becoming increasingly likely: that this intervention came in April 1917 can be explained by the reintroduction of unrestricted submarine warfare by Germany in January 1917. The US immediately broke off diplomatic relations and a spate of attacks on US merchant shipping in March 1917 provoked public fury, as had the publication of the 'Zimmerman Telegram' in the previous month. Norris was right to say that 'no close student of recent history will deny that both Great Britain and Germany' had disrupted US trade in violation of 'international law'. However, most US citizens had not studied recent history as closely as Norris, it seemed to be Germans rather than Britons killing Americans in the Atlantic, and the German Foreign Minister who was trying to provoke a Mexican attack on the US – in violation of the 'Monroe Doctrine' that Roosevelt valued so highly (Source B). For different reasons it was intervention in the war on the side of the Allies that seemed 'of prime necessity in order to preserve our own interests'.

ADDITIONAL QUESTIONS

(a) **Study Source C and use your own knowledge. Explain what senator Norris meant by 'both Great Britain and Germany have . . . flagrantly violated . . . international law'.** (3)

(b) **Study Sources A and B and use your own knowledge. What steps did Woodrow Wilson take to carry out 'our duty . . . to play a part of impartial mediation' during 1914–19?** (7)

(c) **Study Sources A, B and C and use your own knowledge. Explain why the US remained neutral in The First World War for so long.** (15)

Part 4: Historical skills

 1 Assessing US Presidents in foreign policy

Using the information in this chapter and the further reading, attempt an assessment of one or more of the following US Presidents in foreign policy:

- Theodore Roosevelt
- Woodrow Wilson
- Franklin D. Roosevelt

Draw up a list of their successes and failures. Which was the most successful of the three?

[After reading the next chapter you could also try making the same assessment for Truman, Eisenhower, Kennedy, Nixon and Reagan. Who do you think was the most successful twentieth-century US President for foreign policy? This would work well as a class 'balloon debate'. Each President should be represented by one member of the class who gives a speech explaining why not they, but one of the others should be thrown out of a hot air balloon. This should lead to both Presidential strengths and weaknesses being considered.]

2 The extent of change in US foreign policy, 1890–1941

Draw up a table with two headings: (i) continuity and (ii) change. Taking 1890 as your starting point, choose one of the following foreign policy areas and list the evidence of continuity or change during this period:

* US involvement in Latin America
* US involvement in the Far East
* US involvement in Europe
* US participation in international diplomacy

Sources and references

C.J. Bartlett, *The Rise and Fall of the Pax Americana*, Elek (1974).

Peter Brett, *The USA and the World, 1917–45*, Hodder & Stoughton (1997).

Richard D. Challener (ed.), *From Isolation to Containment 1921–1952*, Edward Arnold (1970).

Akira Iriye, *The Globalising of America 1913–1945*, Cambridge University Press (1993).

Walter LaFeber, *The American Search for Opportunity 1865–1913*, Cambridge University Press (1993).

Patrick Renshaw, *America in the Era of the Two World Wars 1910–1945*, Longman (1996).

Arnold S. Rice and John A. Krout, *United States History from 1865*, 20th edition, Harper Collins (1991).

Robert D. Schulzinger, *US Diplomacy since 1900*, 5th edition, Oxford University Press (2002).

John Traynor, *Mastering Modern United States History*, Palgrave (2001).

Chapter 9

Foreign Policy, 1941–2001

Second World War to Détente

This chapter will consider a period when US foreign policy took on greater significance in the minds of politicians and the public than ever before. For the first time since the eighteenth century the United States felt directly threatened by foreign powers, first Japan and then, for a far longer period, the USSR. A succession of US Presidents placed foreign policy at the top of their priorities, finally abandoned any notion of isolation in favour of an interventionist world view, spent escalating amounts on new military technology, and sent troops into unlikely places to fight the perceived enemy – communism. For the public, a growing fear of communism and nuclear war evolved into a more critical approach to US foreign policy.

 Historical background

From the Second World War to the Cold War,
    1941–1945
The Cold War develops and spreads,
    1945–1952
Brinkmanship, 1952–1964
Defeat and détente, 1965–1980
The end of the Cold War, 1980–2001

The Cold War in Vietnam and Southeast Asia
Public opinion and the Vietnam War
The end and legacy of the Cold War

 Sources

1   The causes of the Cold War
2   Public opinion and the Vietnam War

 Essays

The origins and beginnings of the Cold War
The development of the Cold War in the 1950s
    and early 1960s
The Cuban missile crisis

 Historical skills

1   Investigating Cold War case studies
2   The Cold War and US culture

Chronology

1941	December	Japanese attack on US at Pearl Harbor led to declaration of war, followed by German declaration of war on the US
1943	November	Tehran Conference
1944	June	US/British 'D-Day' landings in Normandy
1945	February	Yalta Conference
1945	April	Roosevelt died
	May	Victory in Europe after Germany's surrender
	July	Potsdam Conference
	August	Atomic bombs exploded over Hiroshima and Nagasaki. Japan's surrender followed
1947	March	Truman Doctrine announced to Congress
	June	Marshall Plan announced to Congress
	July	National Security Act created Department of Defense, NSC and CIA
1948	June	Start of Berlin blockade (ended April 1949)
1949	May	North Atlantic Treaty Organisation (NATO) formed
	September	USSR exploded its first atomic bomb
	October	China declared itself a communist People's Republic
1950	February	Senator McCarthy made first accusations of communist infiltration (continued until 1954)
	June	Start of Korean War (ended July 1953)
1954	July	Geneva Accords divided Vietnam at the 17th parallel
		US supported the government in South Vietnam thereafter
	September	South East Asia Treaty Organisation (SEATO) formed
1955	May	Warsaw Pact formed
1956	November	USSR crushed Hungarian revolution
1957	October	Sputnik satellite (first space satellite) launched by USSR
1958	August	Taiwan Straits crisis (August–October)
1961	April	CIA-backed Bay of Pigs invasion of Cuba failed
	August	Berlin Wall erected
1962	October	Cuban missile crisis
1963	November	Kennedy assassinated
1964	August	Gulf of Tonkin Resolution gave Johnson power to proceed with the Vietnam War without needing support from Congress
1965	March	US ground troops arrived in Vietnam
1968	February	Tet Offensive in Vietnam
1972	February	Nixon made first US Presidential visit to China
	May	SALT I agreement with USSR
1973	January	Paris agreements ended Vietnam War and US involvement
1975	August	Helsinki agreements accepted status quo in Europe
1979	June	SALT II agreement with USSR (later rejected by Congress)
	December	USSR invaded Afghanistan
1983	March	Strategic Defense Initiative (SDI or 'Star Wars') announced
1986	October	Reykjavik Summit – disarmament talks stalled over SDI
1987	December	INF Treaty between US and USSR
1988	February	Soviet withdrawal from Afghanistan announced

1989		November	Fall of Berlin Wall heralded collapse of communism in Eastern Europe
1991			Operation Desert Storm launched against Iraq (February),
		December	Gorbachev resigned and communism ended in the USSR
1993			US intervention in Somalia
1997			US signed Kyoto Accord (rescinded in 2001)
2001		September	September 11 tragedy: Al Qaeda terrorist attack on New York (leading indirectly to the US-led invasion of Iraq in 2003)

Part 1: Historical background

 ### From the Second World War to the Cold War, 1941–1945

The Japanese attack on Pearl Harbor in December 1941 was not completely unexpected. The US government had been expecting some kind of attack for the previous two weeks, and all US commanders in the Pacific had been put on alert. However, Pearl Harbor was under defended due to measures taken to protect other bases. More than 180 US planes, 7 battleships and several other naval vessels were sunk or badly damaged. However, the audacity of the Japanese attack draws attention away from its limited effectiveness and US fighting power in the Pacific remained largely intact. A US declaration of war unsurprisingly followed; more of a surprise was the German and Italian declaration of war against the US a few days later, although Japan, Italy and Germany had been allies since 1937. The US had tremendous resources to fight the world war, but it took some time for the War Production Board, a government agency set up to oversee key industries, to mobilise these resources. Within two years, however, US output was enough to give the Allies a decisive advantage against the Axis powers.

The first priority for the US was the Pacific, where Japan initially conquered most of Southeast Asia and the Philippines. The US did not inflict a defeat upon Japan until the Battle of Midway in June 1942, but further victories followed, and by June 1944 the US was launching successful air attacks on Japan itself. In Europe Roosevelt promised Stalin he would open a 'second front' by the end of 1942, but was persuaded by Churchill to first regain Allied control of North Africa. An invasion of Italy followed in July 1943, which brought down Mussolini's government, but was slowed down by German forces moving into the north of the country. By 1943 the US air force was participating in bombing raids on Germany and in June 1944 a land offensive in northern France ('D-day') began. A German counter-offensive in late 1944 held up US and British troops, and is one reason why much of central as well as Eastern Europe was under Soviet control by May 1945.

The partnership of the US, USSR and Britain during 1941–5 was known as 'The Grand Alliance'. The Tehran conference in November 1943 was a success and relations between Roosevelt and Stalin were cordial. Roosevelt was re-elected in the 1944 Presidential election and the Yalta Conference of February 1945 was another exercise in goodwill, including an agreement to set up the United Nations. The issue of post-war Europe was not resolved properly, however, with Germany (and Berlin) split into four military occupation zones and no decision beyond that made. Roosevelt died in April and Truman, his successor, was less accommodating to Stalin. More decisions on Europe were made at Potsdam in July, but the conference lacked goodwill. The US 'Manhattan Project', a secret programme set up in 1939 to develop an atom bomb, was now complete. Two atom bombs were dropped on Japan in August, forcing immediate Japanese surrender: the war had been won, but already there were obstacles to post-war peace.

The Cold War develops and spreads, 1945–1952

The second half of 1945 and early part of 1946 were characterised by increasing frustration and anger for the Truman government as the USSR entrenched itself in Eastern Europe and refused to hold genuinely free elections. Stalin imposed communist governments upon Poland, Hungary, Bulgaria, Romania, Albania and, soon afterwards, Czechoslovakia and East Germany. Despite these actions, the USSR, for all its oddities, had been a strong ally during the Second World War and it was widely thought that the US should now concern itself with domestic affairs and reduce its military commitment to Europe. Congress was prepared to criticise the USSR, but reluctant to make America put its money where its mouth was. For this reason, when Churchill toured the US in 1946 and warned of Soviet aggression, it was not initially well received. Churchill warned that an '**Iron Curtain**' had descended upon Europe, with all countries to the east of the 'Curtain' subject to repression and control by the USSR. Truman was inclined to agree and was hostile in dealings with the USSR's foreign minister, Molotov. The USSR was unmoved, however, and when Greece looked under threat in 1947, Truman decided to act. What followed set the tone for US foreign policy for the next 40 years. Truman declared that the world faced a conflict between freedom and repression, and that the US must protect freedom wherever it was challenged. This '**Truman Doctrine**' led initially to US aid for Greece and Turkey, granted by Congress after a struggle. Many billions of dollars worth of US financial and military aid would be poured into other countries in the decades to come. The Truman Doctrine introduced the theory of '**containment**': The US might not be able to overthrow existing communist governments, but it could work to prevent communist revolutions elsewhere.

Closely following the Truman Doctrine was the '**Marshall Plan**', a programme of economic aid to rebuild war-torn Europe. Congress only agreed to grant this financial aid (and far less than Marshall had proposed) after the USSR imposed control over Czechoslovakia in early 1948. The USSR then refused to allow countries under its influence to accept the Marshall Plan. This was used by Truman as evidence of Soviet repression, and stirred up public opinion against the USSR. It was around this time that the term 'Cold War' was used to describe the hostile superpower relations. In June 1948 the USSR, angry at the presence of Western Allied troops in West Berlin (the USSR occupied all territory east and miles west of Berlin, except in the city itself), cut off land communications with the west in an attempt to bring all Berlin under Soviet control. Truman refused to give in and authorised an airlift of supplies to West Berlin. This action helped him to a narrow re-election victory at home and the USSR eventually climbed down. The result was a divided Germany and a divided Berlin for 40 years. Truman secured the US's commitment to Western Europe through the formation of the **North Atlantic Treaty Organization** (NATO) in 1949. The USSR's response was to reveal it had developed its own atom bomb, and it later went on to form the **Warsaw Pact**, a military alliance designed to counter NATO. The Cold War had frozen into a permanent stand-off in Europe.

At home anti-communist opinion was starting to get out of hand. Truman had previously encouraged this. However, the early 1950s saw an increasing number of accusations and investigations against government figures, educators, artists and scientists who were suspected of having spied for and spread communism. Alger Hiss, a former leading civil servant, was found guilty in January 1950 and senator Joseph McCarthy then proceeded to lead witch-hunts against anyone suspected of leanings towards the left. Leading figures in the

Figure 9.1 **The Marshall Plan helping Western Europe**

Truman government, Marshall and Acheson, found themselves under scrutiny. A Security Act was passed, against Truman's wishes, to clamp down on troublemakers and the labour movement was purged of communists.

The Truman Doctrine of 'containment' also met its first test outside Europe in 1950. China had been 'lost' to communism the previous year, as McCarthy and others angrily pointed out. After a four-year civil war, Chairman Mao's communists had defeated Chiang Kai-Shek's nationalists, who had been forced to retreat to Taiwan. The US refused to recognise the new communist government and supported Chiang instead. Then, in June 1950, communist North Korea invaded the non-communist South. A policy of containment required the US to protect South Korea, and once United Nations blessing had been sought (with the USSR conveniently absent in protest against the UN's refusal to recognise Mao's government), US troops intervened. South Korea was quickly liberated but, on the advice of General MacArthur, Truman decided to conquer North Korea as well. China then intervened and the war settled into a long and destructive stalemate. The US had extended the Cold War to East Asia as well as Europe, and would pay the price in later decades.

 Brinkmanship, 1952–1964

Truman, under fire for the Korean War stalemate and worn down by McCarthyite suspicion, decided not to seek re-election in 1952. His nominated successor, Adlai Stevenson, was defeated by the Republican candidate and former Second World War General Dwight 'Ike' Eisenhower. Eisenhower argued that containment was not enough: the US should aim for '**roll-back**' and 'liberation' of states from communist control. In reality, Eisenhower mainly followed a policy of containment but did use the **Central Intelligence Agency** (CIA) to initiate regime change in Iran (1953) and Guatemala (1954). In each case the CIA provided financial and military support for domestic uprisings. Eisenhower's '**New Look**' at defence spending reduced conventional arms but increased nuclear spending. Secretary of State John Foster Dulles made most public pronouncements on foreign policy. He used the phrase 'massive retaliation' as a warning to the USSR not to spread communism. Dulles is associated with the policy of '**brinkmanship**' – pushing the USSR to the brink of nuclear war if necessary. He never had the chance to do this with the USSR but took a tough – and successful – line when China threatened Taiwan and its offshore islands of Quemsoy, Matsu and the Tachens in 1953 and 1958. However the 1950s saw the US increasingly alarmed as the USSR first crushed an anti-communist uprising in Hungary in 1956, then launched the first ever space satellite, the Sputnik, in 1957. The rockets that launched space satellites had the potential to become devastating military weapons. The 1960s were to see the US take the space race much more seriously.

One of Eisenhower's first priorities had been to bring the Korean War to a satisfactory end, which he eventually did in July 1953. The US remained involved in East Asian affairs, however, partly due to a wish to build up Japan as a secure non-communist ally, partly through a fear of newly communist China, and partly through a concern not to see ex-colonial states in Southeast Asia slip into communism. Eisenhower believed in the '**domino theory**', that if one state turned communist, others nearby would follow one by one. The French were forced to abandon their colony of Indo-China (or Vietnam) in 1954. North Vietnam had already turned communist; the US stepped in and, at a conference in Geneva, ensured that South Vietnam would stay separate and non-communist. In the tradition of NATO, the US set up the **South East Asia Treaty Organization** (SEATO), an ultimately unsuccessful attempt to make the non-communist states in Southeast Asia work together. The US also poured aid and, later, military force into South Vietnam.

Eisenhower had proved a popular President, and is now thought to have had a greater level of expertise and control over foreign affairs than was thought at the time. He was re-elected by a landslide in 1956 but was not eligible to run in 1960. His Vice-President, Richard Nixon, lost narrowly to the Democrat John F. Kennedy. Kennedy was assassinated in 1963 and has been elevated to legendary status since, but in fact his foreign policy record was patchy. Kennedy had been interested in foreign affairs since observing the failure of appeasement in Britain in the 1930s, and was determined to pursue the Cold War with vigour. His first year was overshadowed by a failed CIA attempt to overthrow Castro's communist regime in Cuba, another stand-off over Berlin, and he had trouble asserting himself against his opposite number, the older and more experienced Khrushchev. In 1962, however, when the USSR tried to base nuclear missiles in Cuba, Kennedy stood firm and demanded that the missiles be removed. The world was brought to the brink of nuclear war but Khrushchev was persuaded to back down and Kennedy was successful. The nuclear arms race, and Cuba, remained foreign policy concerns but attention switched back first to Europe, where Kennedy made a famously defiant speech next to the Berlin Wall in 1963, and then to South Vietnam, where communist agitation was growing. The number of US 'Green Beret' military advisers in South Vietnam swelled to 16,000. Then, to worldwide horror, Kennedy was assassinated in November 1963. His successor, Lyndon B. Johnson, was determined to carry on Kennedy's work, in particular to stop communist insurrection in South Vietnam. After a supposed attack on the US navy by North Vietnam, Johnson launched air strikes against the North, which would later be followed by the arrival of US troops. Nuclear war had been averted, but the Vietnam War was about to begin.

 ## Defeat and détente 1965–1980

Johnson, encouraged by a landslide election victory in 1964, launched the ground war in South Vietnam in 1965. He was confident of a quick and easy victory. However, the war was to drag on for nearly ten years and end in unquestionable defeat for the United States. This rocked US confidence and overshadowed all other aspects of foreign policy. More and more US troops and bombs were thrown into Vietnam in an attempt to destroy the '**Viet Cong**', a communist guerrilla army attempting to seize control of South Vietnam. It was a hard war to evaluate. The US was not trying to conquer new territory, just to clear Viet Cong forces out of South Vietnam. As these forces were dissipated throughout the country, were not easily identifiable as communists, and only engaged US troops at times of their choosing, it became a frustrating operation. The US certainly killed large numbers of Viet Cong but did not ever know how many soldiers they were facing, so victory never seemed close. The Viet Cong also inflicted some bloody defeats upon the US and, in February 1968, rose up all over South Vietnam to attack US forces. This operation, known as the 'Tet Offensive', was a break from normal Viet Cong tactics and did not, in military terms, succeed for them. However, the psychological impact on the US was enormous. It appeared to be losing against an

Figure 9.2

National Security Council during the Cuban missile crisis

Figure 9.3 **Map to show the Iron Curtain**

The Iron Curtain

ICELAND
1949

NETHERLANDS
1949

CANADA
1949

USA
1949

NORWAY
1949

FINLAND

SWEDEN

DENMARK
1949

SOVIET UNION

IRISH REPUBLIC

GREAT
BRITAIN
1949

BELGIUM
1949

LUXEMBOURG
1949

FRANCE
1949

EAST

POLAND

WEST
GERMANY
1955

CZECHOSLOVAKIA

AUSTRIA

HUNGARY

SWITZERLAND

ITALY
1949

ROMANIA

PORTUGAL
1949

YUGOSLAVIA

SPAIN

BULGARIA

GREECE
1952

TURKEY
1952

NATO countries with date of membership

Warsaw Pact countries in 1955

Neutral countries

The 'Iron Curtain'

enemy it barely respected, an impression sometimes reinforced by the way television reported the war. North Vietnam was certainly receiving aid from China and the USSR, and passing it on to the Viet Cong, but it was Viet Cong tactics that the US struggled to deal with. At home, as US casualties rose, vocal protest against the war intensified. Public opinion as a whole was turning against the war and public demonstrations reached dangerous levels during 1969–70. One demonstration in Washington attracted 500,000 people, and at one point the President was trapped in the White House, protected by troops against the angry mob. In 1970 The National Guard's shooting of four student protesters at Kent State University, Ohio, raised public anger still further.

Johnson, devastated by the failures in Vietnam, decided not to seek re-election in 1968. His Vice-President, Humphrey, was narrowly defeated by the Republican candidate Richard Nixon, who promised to look for ways to end the Vietnam War. This was not easy. Just pulling the troops out would immediately lead to North Vietnam conquering the South, and send signals to China and the USSR that the US was too weak to resist communist expansion. North Vietnam refused to negotiate a compromise deal, so Nixon adopted a policy called **'Vietnamization'**. This would involve a gradual withdrawal of US troops over a few years. In their place, South Vietnamese troops would be trained and equipped to resist the Viet Cong. The withdrawal took place but US bombing continued, spreading to Cambodia and Laos, where the Viet Cong had bases, in 1970. Nixon's approach generated furious protest in the US but he was re-elected by a landslide margin in 1972 and, in January 1973, signed the Paris agreements that pulled US troops out of Vietnam. Congress acted quickly to stop future Presidents from sending troops back in without their authorisation, and when North Vietnam invaded the South in 1975, refused to intervene. US policy had resulted in communist control, not just of the whole of Vietnam, but also Cambodia and Laos.

Johnson, rather than Nixon, has attracted most blame for the Vietnam defeat. Nixon became more notorious for the Watergate scandal. However, Nixon showed some skill and had some success in foreign policy. A policy of **détente** towards the USSR bore fruit in a 1969 treaty to stop the proliferation of nuclear weapons. This was followed by the first SALT (**Strategic Arms Limitations Talks**) agreement in 1972. Even more impressively, Nixon started negotiations with China, making his first visit there in February 1972, and leading to more cordial relations thereafter. When Nixon resigned in 1974, his Vice-President, Gerald Ford, succeeded him. Meetings at Vladivostock and Helsinki followed, marking a thaw in relations with the USSR. However, Ford's successor, Jimmy Carter (elected in 1976) had more difficulties with détente. A second SALT agreement with the USSR was rejected by Congress, and the Soviet invasion of Afghanistan in 1979 led to outrage in the United States. Détente seemed to have been taken too far and the USSR seemed to be taking advantage of US weakness. Carter tried to take a tougher line but his own reputation was further damaged by a crisis in Iran, where US citizens were taken hostage. Attempts to rescue them failed and Carter seemed weak. He lost the 1980 election to Ronald Reagan, a conservative Republican who was critical of détente and determined to strengthen the US's world position.

 ## The end of the Cold War, 1980–2001

Reagan immediately showed his foreign policy colours. Defence and CIA budgets were increased rapidly and attention was paid to more sophisticated and accurate offensive and defensive weapons, including the cruise missile and the **Strategic Defense Initiative** (SDI). This attracted controversy in both Europe and the US itself, where economic problems and fear of nuclear holocaust made Reagan's nuclear spending seem reckless. Reagan's aggressive rhetoric, referring to the USSR as an 'evil empire' at one point, also attracted criticism. US intervention in Lebanon, Grenada and Nicaragua led to Congress cutting off funding for Reagan's foreign policy intrigues. Reagan then authorised the sale of arms to Iran and used the proceeds to fund illegally the Nicaraguan Contras, a scandal that almost brought him down in 1986. The bombing of Libya in April 1986, which was an attempt at regime change after a terrorist attack on US servicemen, reflected the President's strong approach to foreign affairs.

Alongside this, though, Reagan was trying to initiate talks with the USSR. The President's genuine horror at nuclear weapons saw fruitless attempts at agreements with the USSR. A turning point came with the appointment of Gorbachev as Soviet leader in 1985. He was conscious of the USSR's economic weakness and sought ways of reducing military spending. Meetings at Geneva in 1985 and Reykjavik in 1986 saw disagreement about the future of SDI but enough understanding was reached to lead to the December 1987 INF Treaty in Washington, a major breakthrough in nuclear arms reduction. The USSR then announced cuts in conventional forces in Europe and this led on to the collapse of communism in Eastern Europe as unpopular governments, no longer protected by Soviet military force, were thrown out.

Reagan had served two terms and was not eligible for re-election in 1988. His Vice-President, George Bush, was elected instead and was more suspicious of the USSR than Reagan had eventually been. This did not delay negotiations for long and events overtook US foreign policy as communism collapsed, first in Eastern Europe, then in the USSR itself in 1991. This had a destabilising effect in the former USSR, and the establishment of a secure relationship was one of the challenges facing US foreign policy after 1991. Meanwhile the end of the Cold War seemed evident in the two superpowers' consensus on Iraq's invasion of Kuwait in 1990. The US led a successful UN liberation of Kuwait in 1991 and finished the year as the world's only superpower. The Cold War was won, but this was to pose US foreign policy difficult questions in the years to come.

Through the 1990s, US foreign policy was reappraised and, while Congress cut defence spending by 25 per cent and talked of a more unilateral approach to foreign policy, the Clinton administration (1993–2001) declared its commitment to active engagement in world affairs. Clinton was instinctively liberal and, in agreement with his Secretaries of State Warren Christopher and Madeline Albright, supported and promoted democracy across the globe. Immediately he ran into problems. The US led UN intervention in Somalia in 1993, which, after abandoning its peacekeeping brief and attempting to arrest one troublesome clan leader, saw eighteen marines killed and all US troops evacuated by the end of the year. Thereafter the US was reluctant to intervene in Africa and Clinton refused to send troops to Liberia or Rwanda despite the humanitarian atrocities being committed there. Relations between the US and the UN, rarely in total harmony, cooled and by 1996 the US was failing to pay $1.4 billion owed to the UN.

More successful were US attempts to reorientate NATO, an organisation that had lost direction since the end of the Cold War. Central and Eastern European states, newly free of communist rule, were encouraged to apply for NATO membership and thus stabilise Europe, without aggravating Russian hostility. A sign of NATO's new role was its intervention in the former Yugoslavia, working alongside the UN to enforce peace. The US was also successful, in a period of economic boom, in strengthening its worldwide economic influence. Canada and Mexico were brought together into the North American Free Trade Association (NAFTA) in 1994, China was encouraged to embrace the global economy and the US successfully blocked a Japanese initiative to create an Asian Monetary Fund in 1998, which would have undermined the US-dominated IMF.

Clinton's Presidential successor, George W. Bush, initially spoke of a wish to build on Clinton's internationalism. This was quickly forgotten as a more aggressive and unilateral foreign policy was implemented. The US withdrew from the 1997 Kyoto Treaty, which had sought to reduce world pollution and began, to the consternation of Russia, China and fellow NATO members, to develop a 'son of Star Wars' National Missile Defense initiative (NMD). The September 11 atrocity in 2001 shocked the US, but won worldwide sympathy and popularised Bush's Presidency. However, it was not long before support for Bush's foreign policy would fade outside the US. The UN Security Council and many NATO members would refuse to support the 2003 US invasion of Iraq, the US was voted off UN panels on drug control and human rights and the long-term future direction of US involvement in world affairs would seem less clear than at any time since the 1930s.

Part 2: Essays

 The origins and beginnings of the Cold War

1   From Truman's speech to Congress in March 1947:

> I believe that it must be the policy of the United States to support free peoples who are resisting attempted subjugation by armed minorities or by outside pressures.

(a) Explain the Truman Doctrine in relation to US foreign policy. (3)

(b) What were the causes of the Cold War? (7)

(c) To what extent was Truman's foreign policy a success? (15)

(AQA)

(a) The Truman Doctrine, outlined in 1947, is essentially another term for the policy of 'containment'. It pledged the US to 'support free peoples who are resisting attempted aggression by armed minorities or outside pressure' and was initially applied to aid sent to the governments of Greece and Turkey, helping both countries to fend off threats from communism. The doctrine served as the basis of US foreign policy for the next thirty years.

(b) The Cold War did not begin suddenly. Relations between the US and the USSR had experienced strains long before the Second World War, the wartime alliance between the two was based on common enemies rather than genuine friendship, and a series of events and pronouncements made by both sides saw a decline in relations between 1945 and 1949. The years 1946 and 1947 are most commonly identified as the point where 'Cold War' became an accurate description of US–Soviet relations. However, historians have suggested 1945, 1943 and even 1917 as starting points.

As well as disputing when the Cold War began, there is disagreement on why it began. There is a temptation to try to apportion blame, which clouds the truth. Both the US and the USSR saw themselves as the innocent party reacting in self-defence (and the defence of others) against the aggressive expansionism of the other superpower. In the 1960s, US foreign policy became subject to widespread public criticism in the West and this led to accusations that the US had overreacted to Soviet expansion after 1945, thus causing a Cold War. More recently, historians have argued that a harmonious settlement to the Second World War in Europe was never likely to occur and Stalin is again considered partly to blame for this.

There seemed to be a fundamental conflict of ideology between the US, the most powerful capitalist state, and the USSR, the only major communist state in 1945. This difference in ideology framed much of the rhetoric and propaganda used by each side against the other during the Cold War. This does not mean it *caused* the Cold War. However, the US was uncomfortable with the communist USSR from the start. Although US troops had been sent to Russia in 1918 in an attempt to help depose the new communist government, the US did not grant diplomatic recognition to the USSR until 1933, and then only in an attempt to increase its international trade which was suffering from the Great Depression at the time. Not only was the USSR communist, it was also totalitarian. The US wanted open markets to trade with, and the USSR's state control of its economy meant that US consumer goods could not tap into the USSR's economic potential. In the 1920s, the USSR had invited some foreign investment and the US responded to the tune of $60 million. After 1928 the USSR was less inviting to foreign investment – to the US's dismay. For the US, by 1945 the memory of the Great Depression was still fresh, and the USSR's subsequent refusal to open Eastern Europe to US trade was intolerable. The period 1917–41 was not, for the most part, a 'Cold War' but the difficulties of that period contributed to misunderstandings after 1945.

Because the US and USSR were allies during 1941–5, and the propaganda machines of both states were praising each other at this time, this can lead to an assumption that the dramatic decline in relations *after* the Second World War caused the Cold War. However, the world war made several important contributions. Both the US and the USSR were forced into the war by sudden, unexpected (and, in retrospect, rather embarrassing) attacks by Japan and Germany respectively in 1941. The US realised its geographical position no longer made it secure from attack and was determined not to be caught off guard again; and the USSR had now been invaded twice in less than thirty years and was determined not to allow a strong, unfriendly Germany to rise up again. Both the US and the USSR had observed and learned lessons from the failed policy of appeasement in the 1930s. By 1943, it seemed that the Allies were bound to win the Second World War, although it would not happen quickly. This turned minds to the state of Europe after the war. Stalin seems to have realised by 1944 that his main aim should be to occupy and control as much territory as possible.

The result of the war in Europe was not just the defeat of Germany but the creation of a huge geopolitical and economic vacuum in Central and Eastern Europe. This made the expansion of Soviet influence possible as well as desirable for the USSR. The US, as a global economic power, wanted a European economic recovery based upon free trade, which would require US involvement in European affairs after the world war. In this context, the failure of the US and its allies to open a second front in Western Europe against Nazi Germany before 1944 meant that an opportunity to keep Central and at least some of Eastern Europe from Soviet control had been lost. This, coupled with Roosevelt's belief that binding decisions were best left until a United Nations was set up after the world war, meant that the conferences at Tehran (1943), Yalta and Potsdam (1945) failed to reach meaningful agreement on the future of Europe.

What followed after Potsdam was a series of high-profile developments that fuelled a Cold War, which brings the roles of the leaders of the USSR and US under the spotlight. Stalin, the unquestioned dictator of the USSR, baffled and angered the US with his attitude. If Stalin had chosen not to dominate Eastern Europe after the Second World War, the Cold War would probably not have developed. However, Stalin had never trusted the West and felt that Soviet security lay in territorial occupation, not international agreements. His Foreign Minister, Molotov, later admitted 'my task was to expand the borders of the fatherland as much as possible', Stalin has been portrayed as a 'Red Emperor' with imperialist aims in the tradition of Ivan the Terrible and Peter the Great. He has also been portrayed as reckless, paranoid and unstable. However, his foreign policy after 1945 seems to be carefully designed, even cautious at times. He was certainly an opportunist, though, and was not prepared to see the USSR relinquish its opportunity to control over Eastern Europe having sacrificed so much to defeat Germany. To the US this seemed unfathomable so, regardless of Stalin's true aims, he was perceived as dangerous and untrustworthy.

The US's wartime President, Roosevelt, died in 1945 and was replaced by Truman. As this was soon followed by the Cold War, it is tempting to suggest that Truman himself must have been a factor. The image of Truman is as a no-nonsense, tough-talking President who, as well as authorising the use of the atom bomb against Japan, also spoke fiercely against the USSR (which he certainly did once the Cold War was under way). He has been criticised for his lack of delegation, hasty decision-making, lack of foreign policy experience and for masking personal insecurity by presenting a tough front. Looking closer, we find evidence of Truman's antipathy towards the USSR. In 1941 he said 'if Russia is winning we ought to help Germany and that way let them kill as many as possible', although he admitted he would ultimately prefer the defeat of Nazi Germany. The day after becoming President in 1945 he declared: 'We must stand up to the Russians.' However, these comments were made in private to government insiders, and were not for public consumption. Truman did not reverse Roosevelt's foreign policy of accommodating the USSR's wishes for nearly a year. During that time it became apparent that, while Roosevelt's public reputation after his death was sky-high, his foreign policy had proved to be a mess and could not be sustained. Truman complained in December 1945, 'I'm tired of babying the Soviets', and thereafter US rhetoric against the USSR was more aggressive. Truman thus presided over the developing Cold War, and although he arguably missed opportunities for reconciliation with the USSR, more often he had little option but to act the way he did.

The events of 1945 onwards collectively cooled US–Soviet relations to a point of 'Cold War', and we need to assess whether any particular event had special significance in causing the Cold War. The US's refusal to share the atom bomb with the USSR was hardly surprising, and both sides knew that the USSR would be able to develop its own within five to ten years, possibly less. The USSR's refusal to ease its grip on Eastern Europe is more significant and has been pinpointed as the cradle of the Cold War. While the US was initially prepared to accept this in return for promises of democratic elections in the occupied states, by 1947 it was denouncing it fiercely and condemning the USSR's refusal to allow Marshall Aid into Eastern Europe. The year before, however, the USSR's refusal to pull its troops out of northern Iran had led to a strong US response and had led to a Soviet withdrawal after several months. This episode was significant as, not only did diplomatic tempers spill over with the Soviet delegation storming out of a UN meeting, but also the US had threatened force and had faced the USSR down. This was to set the tone of US foreign policy in the future.

The year 1946 was also a significant year for words. Winston Churchill's famous 'Iron Curtain' speech in March 1946 did not directly cause a change in US foreign policy, but it did anger the USSR, which was more hostile in its own rhetoric thereafter. Also, Kennan's 8,000-word **long telegram** provided the basis for the US's future policy of 'containment' against communism. Arguably the Cold War was under way by 1946.

In conclusion, the causes of the Cold War seem to lie in the perceptions both sides had of each other. Neither the US nor the USSR were *primarily* driven by ideology, however each believed that the other was, and developed their response accordingly. This mutual suspicion was present long before the *start* of the Second World War. However, the course of the war left both superpowers deeply involved in European and world affairs, and the effects and results of the war meant that urgent questions were raised for which no mutually acceptable solution could be found. Both sides could have acted differently at times during 1945–9, but to blame either seems to lose sight of the real causes of the Cold War.

(c) Truman was a potential disaster for American foreign policy. With a new world order emerging, the new American President in 1945 had no experience of running foreign affairs and said of his appointment: 'I felt like the moon, the stars, and all of the planets had fallen on me.' He had been Vice-President for only a year, he had never been part of Roosevelt's inner circle, and had been kept in ignorance of developments as significant as the Manhattan Project. Nonetheless as President he was determined to be, and was, the man in charge. He has to be judged on his record, not his lack of experience. By 1952 although he had suffered several foreign policy difficulties, in the longer term he can be seen as a success.

Roosevelt was a tough act to follow, not just because of his record as President but also the problems he bequeathed to Truman. The wartime Grand Alliance was already in decay and the recent Yalta Conference had fudged the issue of post-war Europe and the future of Germany in particular. Truman found that Roosevelt's foreign policy simply could not be continued; new situations required new thinking. Truman was also constrained by public opinion which, initially, demanded a removal of commitment to Europe once the war was over, a Congress under Republican control from 1946 onwards, and economic problems such as inflation, meat shortages and labour strikes by late 1946. The greatest constraint of all was the USSR's seizing of the initiative in Europe as they refused, in effect, to relinquish control of Soviet-occupied territories. Stalin's intentions for Europe are still debated, at the time they looked like expansionism and repression. Truman had to respond to that.

The most infamous early Truman decision was to use the atom bomb against Japan. The moral debate has raged ever since, but as a short-term military initiative it was a success; Japan surrendered within a week. Truman's decision not to share the atom bomb with the USSR upheld a decision made by Roosevelt in 1944, and gave the US a temporary, but useful, advantage. Truman arguably overplayed this. His instincts were to take a tough line with the USSR – only his second meeting with Soviet Foreign Minister Molotov saw previous cordiality vanish and Molotov complain: 'I have never been talked to like that in my life.' Truman's reply was brief and not conciliatory. He was willing to give-and-take, but believed that the US should be able to get 85 per cent of what it wanted. As a result, the Potsdam Conference did not solve the problem of Europe. Later in 1945 Truman's adviser Henry Stimson suggested that more open negotiations were needed without 'this weapon rather ostentatiously on our hip'. Truman refused and, to the USSR's irritation, continued to boast of the bomb. In reality the US's atomic bombs were too few and too small at this stage to be an ultimate sanction against the USSR; Stalin knew this, and in any case had developed his own atomic bomb by 1949. An opportunity to reach a satisfactory settlement had perhaps been lost because of Truman's approach.

Another Truman adviser, Clark Clifford, noted that 'in times of crisis the American citizen tends to back up his President'. By late 1946 the crisis seemed to be receding, or at least freezing into stalemate with no major new developments. The US had fought two world wars in Europe without much thanks, and Truman could not afford to restore conscription or halt post-war demobilisation – from eight million to one million men under arms within two years. The year 1947 was a frustrating one, with communism still a threat in Greece and China, and the USSR tightening its grip over Eastern Europe. Truman played up the communist threat and persuaded Congress to spend $400 million to protect Greece and Turkey. He was risking the loss of public support for his plans to 'contain' communism. However, his resolute response to the Berlin blockade in 1948 strengthened anti-communist feeling, and Truman's popularity, helping to explain his narrow victory in the 1948 Presidential election. Within a year the European situation had frozen into a static, but, as a result, more stable balance, which Truman consolidated by creating NATO in 1949. The US had avoided defeat in the Cold War in Europe, for which Truman deserves some credit. However, Mao's communist victory in China in 1949 reflected badly on Truman's administration, which had arguably failed to provide sufficient backing for the defeated nationalist government. Furthermore, his anticommunist rhetoric encouraged McCarthyism in 1950, with unpleasant domestic consequences.

Truman's activation of containment policy in Korea in June 1950 also won popular support and was an initial success. Typically, he acted quickly and decisively. North Korea's attack on the South was interpreted as USSR opportunism, but the USSR, and China, did not intervene when US troops rapidly cleared the North Korean forces out of the South. It was MacArthur's idea, not Truman's, to continue the war by crossing the 38th parallel and invading the North, but Truman still has to take responsibility. The opportunity to defeat communism in Korea was too tempting. The gamble almost succeeded, as did the later gamble of removing MacArthur from command, but China soon carried out its threat to intervene and US forces were forced back south. It was now difficult for the US to end the war and avoid perceived defeat, and this unhappy stalemate led to Truman's decision not to seek re-election in 1952.

The unfinished Korean War was one legacy left by Truman for his successor, Eisenhower, to deal with. However, there were other more positive legacies. By 1952, the US had given Western Europe security, even rearming West Germany, had made a peace treaty with Japan giving the US useful military bases on the other side of the Pacific, and had also developed a thermonuclear bomb, once again giving the it a lead in nuclear arms. As Ambrose points out, his government's achievements were breathtaking. The Cold War was partly caused by Truman's approach to foreign policy, and he certainly framed the terms in which it would be conducted, costing billions of dollars and tens of thousands of lives. However, if we put his achievements in the context of 1945 problems, and set against the missed opportunities the denial of opportunities to the USSR, his record stands up well.

PRACTICE QUESTIONS

2 (a) What impact did the Truman Doctrine have upon superpower relations? (10)

(b) What other factors led to the formation of NATO in 1949? (20)

(Edexcel format without sources)

Advice: *To answer these questions you should include the following points:*

- *Immediate consequence of the Truman Doctrine – intervention in Greece and Turkey;*
- *the USSR felt threatened – increased hostility;*
- *The US introduced policy of 'containment' – extended Cold War beyond Europe to Korea, Vietnam, etc. Basis of US foreign policy for decades thereafter;*
- *NATO set up as a consequence of continued Soviet military power and control in Eastern Europe – deterrent to Soviet westwards expansion;*
- *NATO combined with Marshall Aid to cement good relations between US and Western Europe – US needed European support if it was to pursue containment against the USSR;*
- *NATO was a means of securing West Germany as part of democratic Western Europe.*

 The development of the Cold War in the 1950s and early 1960s

3 How successful was US intervention in Korea between 1950 and 1953? (30)

(Edexcel)

By autumn 1950 the US intervention in Korea seemed to have been completely successful, with its original aims apparently achieved. South Korea was again free from communist control and the USSR and

China, faced with US determination, had not intervened. Congress had adopted the defence spending plan proposed by the **National Security Council (NSC)**, and Truman's credibility seemed to be restored. Yet three years later Dean Acheson referred to the Korean War as: 'The greatest disaster which occurred to the Truman administration. It did more to destroy and undermine American foreign policy than anything I know about.' Although this could be seen as an overstatement.

The decision to cross the 38th parallel and invade North Korea led to Chinese intervention on the side of the North. Mao apparently spent 60 hours pacing up and down before deciding to intervene (and the USSR apparently would not have intervened even if China had not), so it was a close decision, but China had publicly and clearly warned beforehand that it would do so. As a result the war became a stalemate, dragging on through to 1953 with an estimated 34,000 US combat deaths; not many perhaps when compared to estimates of 1 million Chinese and 3.5 million Korean deaths, but still too many for what was meant to be a small, peripheral war for the US. It was hard to end the war, given the refusal of both North and South to conciliate and the fear that China might overrun South Korea if the US pulled out. Although by 1953 the original aim to keep South Korea free of communism was achieved, the war was judged as a draw at best, even a defeat for the US.

The escalation of the war also broadened the Cold War with relations between the US and China souring, and not improving until the 1970s: a path that was not inevitable before the Korean War. A.T. Steel's cynical remark that '700 million potential customers had turned into the apparition of 700 million dangerous adversaries' perhaps overstates the consequences of the Korean War, but it drove China, at least temporarily, into the USSR's camp and led to increased US commitment to East Asia. The US now had to protect Japan, Taiwan and Indo-China, leading eventually to the Vietnam War.

Truman's domestic position, weak before June 1950 but strengthened by the original success of the Korean intervention, fell away again. McCarthyism raged at home, not caused, but fuelled by the lack of victory in Korea. Truman's decision to dismiss General MacArthur in 1951 was unpopular at home, causing Truman's popularity to fall to an estimated 24 per cent and influencing his decision not to stand for re-election in 1952. Truman's Democrat party lost control of the Presidency anyway, with Stevenson defeated by the Republican (and military general), Eisenhower. One of Eisenhower's election promises was to 'go to Korea'.

In the longer term, the US intervention in Korea was seen in a more positive light, mainly because of what did *not* happen as a consequence. South Korea was not lost to the communists, and a study by military historian Stanley Sandler shows that US forces were more effective and better organised in Korea than was thought at the time. The Korean War tested the boundaries of the Cold War in what was, for all but the Koreans, a peripheral arena. The war did not spread outside Korea and nuclear weapons, despite MacArthur's wishes, were not used, nor is there convincing evidence of the accusation made at the time that the US was using bacteriological weapons. The US showed restraint, but also showed itself ready to fight communist expansion. The USSR also showed restraint by avoiding direct involvement and not trying to apply pressure in Europe while US eyes were elsewhere. Neither side could go into future conflicts and expect to win easy, complete victories. A useful note of caution entered Cold War diplomacy as a result.

However, the type of Cold War created by the Korean War had drawbacks. The US was frozen into a single global vision where communism had to be opposed regardless of the regional circumstances. This meant an escalating and more permanent commitment to East Asia. This meant a huge defence budget for decades to come, an apparently unlimited nuclear arms race and a constant, wearing vigilance and anxiety for the US. The Cold War would not now thaw in a hurry.

The Cuban missile crisis

4 (a) What were the immediate causes of the Cuban missile crisis? (30)

(b) Assess the significance of the Cuban missile crisis with regard to world peace. (60)

(OCR)

(a) Lack of understanding lay at the heart of the Cuban missile crisis. Neither Kennedy nor Khrushchev knew just how far the other could be pushed. Both leaders made moves during the crisis without full knowledge of what the other side had already done. Neither seemed fully in control, or to understand the stakes with which they were playing.

J.F. Kennedy is viewed today as one of the greatest US Presidents. But in autumn 1962, his reputation was not yet secured. The first full year of his foreign policy had been disappointing. A CIA-backed invasion of Cuba at the Bay of Pigs in 1961, authorised by Kennedy against the advice of his Joint Chiefs of Staff, had been a humiliating failure, with all invaders either killed or captured. It took 20 months, and a ransom of $53 million (paid in food and medical supplies) to secure the return of the prisoners. The US saw Castro's regime as communist, and his seizure of US-owned property in Cuba, coupled with trade negotiations with the USSR, seemed to confirm this. Kennedy did not give up and identified the removal of Castro as the government's top priority. Trade embargoes were set up, the CIA was eager to try again and 'Operation Mongoose', a plan to destabilise Cuba, included plans to invade Cuba again in late 1962.

Castro was well aware of US hostility, and made sure that Khrushchev was also aware of the danger to Cuba. The circumstances at the time made Khrushchev determined to help his new ally. Under pressure at home due to failing economic policies, criticised by China for weakness, conscious of a US advantage in nuclear missiles and, above all, aware of US missiles stationed in Turkey in 1961 (but not aware that Kennedy had already ordered their removal), Khrushchev decided to look for a prestigious victory by transporting nuclear warheads to Cuba. His advisers were keen, Andropov seeing Cuba as the 'soft underbelly of the Americans'. Such a move would help to protect Castro. And from what he had seen so far, Khrushchev believed the young US President could be pushed – he had no contingency plan worked out if Kennedy pushed back.

Kennedy had come off worse against Khrushchev so far, and it had infuriated him. The Bay of Pigs fiasco had been followed by an unsatisfactory meeting at Vienna, where a bullish Khrushchev had proved unaccommodating. Kennedy had also been powerless to stop the Berlin Wall (although he had kept West Berlin from communist control) and Khrushchev was demanding a solution to the Berlin question by the end of the year. The exchanges descended to crude shows of strength, each side pointedly 'testing' nuclear warheads, and Kennedy's assessment of Khrushchev by the end of 1961 seemed to fit Hollywood better than Washington: 'If Khrushchev wants to rub my nose in the dirt, it's all over. That son of a bitch won't pay attention to words. He has to see you move.' Dean Rusk suggested that the USSR might be preparing to use Cuba to force the West out of Berlin. It was thought that private words with Khrushchev would be no use – action was needed.

When the news came through of missile bases appearing in Cuba, and of suspected nuclear warheads being shipped across the Atlantic, the US responded immediately. Kennedy imposed an 800-mile blockade around Cuba, set up **EXCOM** (a special committee to plan the US response), and demanded that the USSR pull its military presence out of Cuba. The US navy took matters further, ignoring a Kennedy request to reduce the blockade from 800 miles to 500 miles, and forcing USSR submarines to the surface. Egged on by Castro, the USSR shot down an American U2 spy plane flying over Cuba. EXCOM members proposed an air strike, not knowing that nine short-range nuclear missiles were already installed in Cuba. This brought the US right to the brink of nuclear war. Kennedy's younger brother, Robert, asked for a day's delay, and used the time to reassure the Soviet ambassador that US missiles would be withdrawn from Turkey. This was enough to persuade Khrushchev to withdraw, just in time.

Khrushchev later wrote in horror of his consultation with his military commanders over the Cuban missile crisis. To a man they urged war, fired by determination to defeat the US, unappreciative of the consequences of nuclear war. Such ignorance and posturing was present on both sides, and nearly destroyed the world.

(b) The peaceful outcome of the crisis was a tremendous turning point in the Cold War. Both leaders claimed victory of course, but both were out of office within two years (one assassinated, one 'resigned'). However, the legacy of the crisis lasted longer than either leader.

Kennedy had come through a serious test successfully. His prestige at home was enhanced, and left him better able to assert his control over foreign affairs. Never again would a Presidential aide be sent packing from a military operations centre, his leader's orders rejected by a confident armed force. Nor would the US air force trespass in Siberia, escorting a stray U2 spy plane, against the express orders of the President. Kennedy took the Cold War away from military control, and US military action in the face of the USSR would from now be less aggressive and provocative.

This was the theory. In reality, Kennedy continued to stir trouble abroad, encouraging the CIA in Cuba, continuing to build up a nuclear weapons stockpile, falling out with French President, de Gaulle, over NATO issues, and above all increasing the US military presence in South Vietnam. Cold War conflict did not end, it merely transferred the venue to Southeast Asia and Africa. However, there were signs of a growing détente with the USSR. US missiles in Turkey were removed promptly (although secretly, to protect Kennedy's prestige at the expense of Khrushchev's), a superpower leader's 'hotline' teletype link was set up, and a Partial Test Ban Agreement in August 1963 ended US, USSR and British (but not French or Chinese) nuclear tests in space, the atmosphere and under water. This indirectly paved the way for arms control agreements in later years.

Khrushchev lost prestige as a result of the crisis. His role has been cast in a more favourable light since the end of the Cold War, but this was not seen at the time. He attempted to use the crisis as a springboard for détente, and readily acquiesced in the agreements referred to above. However, other Soviet leaders viewed the US as dangerously confident and demanded that the USSR be militarily strengthened. Khrushchev was forced to resign as leader in October 1964. His perceived defeat over Cuba was only one of several reasons for this, but it was certainly a contributory factor. Thereafter the USSR raised its military spending, but continued to pursue détente with the US. This was mainly due to growing fears of China, which had developed its own atom bomb and was making aggressive noises against both the USSR and US.

By the mid-1960s the US was also fearful of China, and the legacy of the Cuban missile crisis compounded this. While more cautious about nuclear brinkmanship, the US felt more confident about its use of conventional military power, and believed that problems could be resolved without escalating out of control. All of these factors did not add up to an explanation of the US's military intervention in Vietnam – however they made it more likely. The Cuban missile crisis made future nuclear war less likely, but it did not prevent future war.

PRACTICE QUESTION

5 (a) **What were the aims of Kennedy's foreign policy?** (30)

(b) **How successful was Kennedy's foreign policy?** (60)

(OCR)

Advice: *To answer these questions you should include the following points:*

• *Kennedy was critical of Eisenhower's inflexibility and called for a 'flexible response' to Cold War problems, e.g. he developed the '***Green Berets***' for work in the Third World.*

• *Strongly anti-appeasement and determined not to give ground to the USSR.*

- *Series of failures in 1961 – Bay of Pigs, Vienna meeting with Khrushchev, Berlin Wall.*
- *Cuban missile crisis seen as a success for Kennedy but closer investigation shows it to have been a near disaster.*
- *Success in 1963, e.g. Nuclear Test Ban Treaty, record cut short by assassination.*
- *Increased US involvement in Vietnam. Plans to reverse this cut short by assassination, therefore played a part in causing Vietnam War.*

 ## The Cold War in Vietnam and Southeast Asia

6 Why did Presidents escalate US involvement in Vietnam from the 1950s onwards? (30)

(Edexcel)

Vietnam was the US's worst nightmare during the Cold War. It found itself increasingly committed to a war it was unlikely to win. The experience of Korea during 1950–3 might have deterred the US from committing itself to Vietnam, and at almost every stage escalation was *not* the only option in Vietnam. However, a series of carefully considered decisions saw over half a million US troops in Vietnam, and unprecedented use of bombing, by the late 1960s. A lack of understanding of Vietnam's individual circumstances lay at the root of US decision-making.

During the Second World War, Vietnam (then called Indo-China) was invaded by Japan, and resistance against the invader was led by Ho Chi Minh. Ho was a nationalist as much as a communist. After the war, the former colonial ruler of Indo-China, France, returned and tried to reassert its control. Ho however kept control of North Vietnam and France was close to losing control of South Vietnam by 1954. A French withdrawal would lead to Ho's forces taking over the South.

The US found itself committing money and advisers to propping up South Vietnam after the French withdrawal in 1954 – just one plank of the its 'containment' policy. The US had already been meeting two-thirds of the cost of the French occupation of South Vietnam before 1954. As with Korea, it was felt a line had to be drawn against communist expansion to avoid a domino effect in Southeast Asia. John F. Kennedy referred to South Vietnam in 1956 as 'the finger in the dike'. Japan's economic recovery would be undermined if Southeast Asia turned communist. To this end, the US initiated the formation of SEATO and installed Ngo Dinh Diem, who had been in exile in the US, as head of the South Vietnam government. Diem would be bolstered by US economic and military aid, but direct involvement by US troops or bombers was not envisaged at this stage. The US did not foresee what might happen.

Although Johnson is the President most associated with escalation of US involvement in Vietnam, Kennedy's Presidency saw significant change. This was partly caused by instability in Southeast Asia. Diem, a member of the colonial elite, French-speaking and Catholic, was repressive and increasingly unpopular in the predominantly peasant, Buddhist South Vietnam. In 1959 North Vietnam began to infiltrate the South by sending in communist agents who in turn recruited and organised South Vietnamese communists into a guerrilla army, called the 'National Liberation Front' or 'Viet Cong'. By 1960, neighbouring Laos was in danger of falling to communist control, the Viet Cong had begun to fight in South Vietnam, and the newly elected President Kennedy was strongly anti-appeasement – making greater US intervention likely. It was an opportunity to demonstrate his doctrine of 'flexible response', and try out his elite 'Green Berets', a counter-insurgency force set up to stamp out communist insurrection in the Third World.

The temptation to intervene directly in Vietnam was increased by Kennedy's foreign policy record during 1961. Disappointments in Cuba, Laos and Berlin left Kennedy in need of a victory somewhere. South Vietnam could not be lost. A Presidential task force was sent to investigate the problems in the South, and they returned to recommend more support for Diem. As a result, during 1961–3 the number of US military 'advisers' in South Vietnam rose from 400 to 16,000. Still the US involvement in Vietnam seemed under control. However, in November 1963 Diem was thrown out of power and assassinated. The new government was weak and unable to control the Viet Cong. Kennedy himself was assassinated a few weeks later, just when US policy towards Vietnam was in turmoil. The new President was quick to declare 'Lyndon Johnson is not going down as the President who lost Vietnam'. This statement reflected not only the sense of Vietnam's strategic importance in the context of the Cold War, but also the fear of defeat in the 1964 election – public opinion at this stage still supported containment. Johnson's opponent in the election was to be Barry Goldwater, a conservative Republican who was already criticising Johnson over Vietnam. Johnson was therefore under pressure to act quickly.

The determination to avoid defeat in Vietnam goes some way towards explaining Johnson's escalation of US involvement from 1964 onwards. It does not, however, explain why this escalation was so great and so rapid. In August 1964, supposed attacks by North Vietnamese torpedo boats on US destroyers in the Gulf of Tonkin (a single bullet hole was the only tangible evidence) led to Congress passing a resolution giving Johnson a free hand to send US military forces to Vietnam. This resolution, in force until 1970, meant that Johnson could, crucially, escalate US involvement as quickly as he wanted without having to persuade Congress. A North Vietnamese attack on a US army barracks at Pleiku in March 1965 provided a further motive to escalate involvement. US bombers attacked North Vietnam bases, supplies and territory. US troop numbers in South Vietnam increased from 50,000 in early 1965 to 535,000 by 1968. Why did Johnson make such a massive commitment?

One answer to this question is overconfidence. Johnson, in a typically brash and forthright statement, called North Vietnam a 'raggedy-ass little fourth rate country'. The US air force claimed it could defeat Ho within a month, and Johnson accepted this simplistic view, believing 'America wins the wars that she undertakes'. The enemy was consistently underestimated. All the time it was argued that just a few more troops, helicopters and bombing campaigns would tip the balance. In 1966, McNamara said that victory was 'just around the corner'. Only with the 1968 Tet Offensive did the US lose its confidence. Johnson clearly misjudged the situation before 1968, but so did public opinion. Arguably, the whole direction and illusion of the US's foreign policy led to this moment. The US viewed the conflict in purely Cold War terms and failed to recognise the specific situation in Vietnam. And overconfidence did not just come from Johnson: even long after the event, Ronald Reagan claimed that the US would have won in Vietnam, if they had just committed greater military force . . .

Johnson's successor, Nixon, recognised that the US was unlikely to win in Vietnam. However, outright withdrawal was not desirable, yet. Nixon's solution was to 'Vietnamise' the conflict, building up South Vietnamese forces and gradually withdrawing US forces. However, he escalated US bombing, extending it into Cambodia and Laos to try to clear out the communists. This reflected the growing strength of the Viet Cong, the inadequacies of the South Vietnamese army (on one occasion they were helicoptered in to attack a communist camp and had to be helicoptered out again in humiliating retreat within minutes), and Nixon's desperation to negotiate a respectable settlement in the face of North Vietnam's stubborn refusal to reach a compromise. A united, communist, but neutral Vietnam might have been achieved years earlier, but Nixon, like Johnson, Kennedy and Eisenhower before him, could not see beyond the Cold War view of communism as monolithic and the need for containment. This view led to escalation, a lengthy and traumatic conflict, and ultimately defeat.

 ## Public opinion and the Vietnam War

7   (a) **Assess the nature and extent of public opinion regarding the Vietnam War.** (30)

    (b) **To what extent was public opinion the main reason for US failure in Vietnam?** (60)

(OCR)

(a) In November 1969 President Nixon made a televised speech where he referred to the '**great silent majority**'. While a vocal minority were protesting, the majority of American people did not support their protests and were instead supportive of Nixon's Vietnam policy. One of the best-known aspects of the Vietnam War is the storm of public protest, especially among students, during the late 1960s and early 1970s. This certainly affected US foreign policy. However, the majority voice was not really silent. During the 1960s and early 1970s, US public opinion was regularly and thoroughly researched through opinion polls. Both Johnson and Nixon kept a close eye on these.

Ever since the late 1940s, public opinion had been supportive of the US's Cold War policy of containment. If a President lost popularity on this issue, it was usually because they were seen as too weak, rather than too strong. Public opinion did eventually turn against the Vietnam War, but not straight away. A poll in May 1964 suggested that only 37 per cent of people were following developments in Vietnam, the rest showed no real interest in what was happening there – this partly reflected Johnson's low-key, secretive approach to the build-up of US involvement. By February 1965, shortly before US ground troops were sent to Vietnam, 40 per cent wanted to maintain existing policy, a further 13 per cent wanted greater commitment, 23 per cent wanted peace negotiations and 24 per cent were not sure. This showed a strong majority of those with an opinion supporting US involvement in Vietnam. The 24 per cent 'not sure' figure fell to 4 per cent in April 1965, when ground troops had been sent in, while peace negotiations now attracted 31 per cent support. This does not suggest a huge adverse reaction to Johnson's decision to send in the troops.

Vocal protest began in earnest in 1965. Colleges and universities held 'teach-ins' as a protest against the war. A demonstration in Washington DC in April attracted 15,000 protesters, followed by a series of 'Vietnam Summer' protests and, in October, a march on the Pentagon. Despite this public opinion seemed to rally around Johnson. When asked if the Vietnam war was a mistake, during 1966 only 30–40 per cent said 'yes'. Johnson's Presidential approval rating stayed over 50 per cent until June 1967. This suggests that the vocal protests gave a misleading impression of public opinion at first, but gradually public opinion did turn. Johnson warned his aides in October 1967 'we've got to do something about public opinion'.

The Tet Offensive in March 1968 accelerated the growth of public opposition to the war, with public opinion clearly influenced by their perceptions of what had gone on. Although Tet was a military failure for the Viet Cong, the public's impression was that they were confident and undefeated. Meanwhile, images of shot suspects and burning villages (one US army lieutenant said 'We had to destroy the town to save it') appeared on television screens. Johnson's approval rating plummeted to 35 per cent and, after almost losing the New Hampshire Primary, he declared he would not seek re-election and that he would try to negotiate peace in Vietnam. In 1967, 52 per cent of those polled saw themselves as '**hawks**' (supporters of military action in Vietnam), while only 35 per cent were '**doves**'. By 1969 only 31 per cent were hawks and 55 per cent were doves.

Nixon's promises to find an honourable end to the war, and the gradual removal of US troops from Vietnam, gave him a higher approval rating than Johnson had finished with, but anti-war protests continued and, if anything, intensified, Nixon admitting in 1969 'we are torn by division', and in November 1969 an estimated 500,000 people demonstrated in Washington. When Nixon sent troops into Cambodia in April 1970, university students then went on strike, with four students killed at Kent State University, Ohio, by the National Guard. The extent of vocal protest can be partly explained by the fashion of the times – 1960s US youths were protesting before Vietnam and civil rights became high-profile issues – but, set against this, another fashion of the times was to loyally support the President in fighting the Cold War. The level of protest reached at the end of the 1960s was unprecedented in Cold War US. Nixon retained enough support to win a second term in 1972, but his decision to bomb Hanoi in December 1972 saw his approval rating slump to 43 per cent.

Vocal protest raised public awareness of Vietnam: over 500,000 American young men sent into an atrocious and destructive war which the US did not seem to be winning, eventually turned public opinion against its Presidents. When George Bush announced on television that US troops were fighting Iraq in 1991, one of the first things he said was 'this will not be another Vietnam'. This was addressed to 'the silent majority'.

(b) Public opinion did not *cause* US failure in Vietnam, although it did put constraints upon Johnson's and Nixon's attempts to end the war successfully. However there were greater constraints working upon them.

Johnson did not prepare public opinion for a major war in Vietnam. Expecting an easy victory, the escalation of forces was not loudly publicised. Even once the scale of the war was clear to all, public opinion did not worry Johnson until late 1967. It was not so much the initial act of war in Vietnam that upset public opinion, but the way the war went on without success for years. As Nixon said, 'Public opinion will not continue to support a war that drags on without tangible signs of progress.' When public hostility became intolerable after the Tet Offensive, Johnson did not pull US troops out of Vietnam. Instead, he decided not to seek re-election that year. His successor, Nixon, knew that he would not be forced to end the war immediately. However, he also knew that public opinion would not tolerate any substantial escalation of US forces in Vietnam. As the existing level of forces was not enough to win the war, he would have to look for a way to end the war 'with honour', and try to appease public opinion by reducing the number of US troops in Vietnam. A plan, code-named 'Duck Hook' – to force North Vietnam to make peace by threatening massive retaliation if they did not – was quietly shelved after a spate of anti-war demonstrations in autumn 1969. Although public opinion would not now let the US win the war, the US had failed to win the war before public opinion became a constraint.

Vietnam was not a suitable country in which to fight a war of containment. Left to its own devices after the Second World War, the whole of Vietnam would have turned communist. The North was not just the core of Vietnamese communism, it was also the core of Vietnamese nationalism. South Vietnam had no such sense of purpose, its only purpose being negative – to keep out communism. The South Vietnamese, mostly Buddhist peasants, never had a really popular regime to support. Ngo Dinh Diem, a French-speaking Catholic, who had been in exile in the US and who was closer to the old colonial elite than the population at large, had replaced the earlier French colonial rule. Diem did not ever offer the strong, nationalist leadership presented by Ho Chi Minh. Diem also refused to hold democratic elections. By the early 1960s Buddhist monks were making suicide protests against Diem's regime, and when he was overthrown, a strong, popular government was never found to replace him. The US was disappointed by, but should not have been surprised at, the reluctant and lacklustre attitude of South Vietnamese soldiers and civilians when caught up in military conflict. Who were they fighting for? If the war was to be won, it would have to be won by US force.

The US expected a quick and easy victory. Although Johnson sent large numbers of troops to Vietnam, they were only deployed piecemeal, reflecting US confidence. The French had been driven out of Vietnam, but the US had a higher opinion of themselves militarily than of the French. Despite the fact that Viet Cong forces would have to be rooted out before an attack on the North could successfully be carried out, the army was prepared to fight a conventional war – this was inappropriate. The Viet Cong fought using guerrilla tactics, and were usually able to dictate when and where they would engage the enemy. The Tet Offensive is a good example of this even though it failed; it also caused support for the war in the US to fall away further. The US commander, General William Westmoreland, adopted a policy of attrition: to 'search and destroy' communist enclaves – but this proved to be like 'chasing the wind. North Vietnam received ample aid from the USSR and other communist states, including anti-aircraft weapons and some fighters and light bombers. Despite this, the US enjoyed air dominance, and had some successes, such as the 1968 Khe Sang campaign. However, air power was overrated, overused and limited by the thick jungle covering much of the country. Attempts at defoliation were ineffective; attempts to attack Viet Cong supply lines failed miserably; and as the US pushed more and more troops into the conflict during 1965–8, North Vietnam used the secret 'Ho Chi Minh Trail' to pour soldiers and supplies into the South, matching US increases.

If a military victory was beyond US abilities, could a political victory be achieved by negotiation? North Vietnam was stubborn, despite encouragement by the USSR to make peace. It demanded control of South

Vietnam and the unconditional removal of US troops, which was not acceptable to the US. Johnson spoke of negotiation but never took it seriously, a military victory seeming preferable. Johnson's lack of political understanding of Vietnam made him over-optimistic that the North would have to give in. He also over-estimated the South's support for US involvement with his policy of 'nation building' doing nothing to win South Vietnamese hearts and minds. Johnson's views were, however, shared by many Americans. There was, in senator Fulbright's words (1966), an 'arrogance of power' evident in the US's political approach.

Eventually, in 1973, a peace deal was negotiated and US troops finally left Vietnam. Less than two years later, North Vietnam broke the treaty (South Vietnam had technically breached the treaty already, but not to the same extent) and overran the South. This confirmed US intervention in Vietnam as a failure. Since the end of the war, there have been attempts to re-evaluate the causes of defeat. Reagan blamed timidity in US politics for the defeat. Kissinger claimed that Congress, by passing the War Powers Act in 1973, undermined the President's power to act if North Vietnam broke the agreement, so that when the North invaded the South, President Ford was not in a position to prevent it. Nixon had apparently promised aid to South Vietnam if the treaty was broken, but he was now out of office as a result of the Watergate scandal. Kissinger suggested that, had Nixon still been in office, North Vietnam would not have dared to break the treaty. This seems an optimistic suggestion!

Ultimately, the vocal expression of hostile public opinion was a feature, but certainly not a cause, of the US's slide to defeat in Vietnam. It was a war that, with hindsight, the US did not need to fight and would probably not have fought if it could have foreseen the consequences. There was plenty of govern-ment discussion of the consequences of not fighting, but a lack of understanding of the actual situation in Vietnam. Additionally, we should acknowledge that, regardless of by what means and even with substan-tial Soviet backing, North Vietnam won a dramatic victory apparently against all odds. The war had always appeared to be one that the US should be able to win, but, because of North Vietnamese tactics and resilience, in reality it was not.

PRACTICE QUESTIONS

8   (a)   **Assess the impact of the Tet Offensive on the Vietnam War.** (30)

   (b)   **Why did Nixon find it so hard to end the Vietnam War?** (60)

(OCR)

Advice: *To answer these questions you need to include the following points:*

* *The Tet Offensive was a military failure but psychological success for the Viet Cong.*
* *US public opinion was already becoming dubious about the Vietnam War but the Tet Offensive was a turning point; there were strong public protests and disillusionment thereafter.*
* *Johnson (already heavily criticised) was put under so much pressure he decided not to run as President again. Nixon decided Vietnam War could not be won.*
* *Nixon felt it impossible to just pull out of Vietnam – could cause a 'domino effect' in Southeast Asia and encourage USSR and China to spread communism elsewhere.*
* *Nixon weakened by public opposition to the Vietnam War at home – could not strengthen the US negotiating position against North Vietnam.*
* *North Vietnam believed US would not fight indefinitely and refused to compromise – made negotiations difficult.*

The end and legacy of the Cold War

9 **(a) How important was Ronald Reagan in ending the Cold War?** (10)

(b) Why and to what extent was the policy of détente unsuccessful in the 1970s? (20)

(Edexcel format without Sources)

(a) The Cold War could only end either with the collapse of one of the US or USSR, or because both sides wanted to end it. Of the two leaders in the mid-1980s, Gorbachev seemed the more enlightened and willing to make concessions. However, this was partly a reflection of desperate economic problems in the USSR. While Reagan had run up a massive national debt, there was no such desperation on the US's side to end hostilities. Nonetheless he negotiated successfully with Gorbachev. As a result of this, Reagan has been given credit for building up US military strength until the USSR could not compete, and then negotiating from this position of strength a solution acceptable to both sides.

Reagan was elected on his record as a conservative Republican, calling for a tougher line in the Cold War and criticising Carter's weakness in foreign policy. He claimed that the USSR had forged ahead in the arms race since 1973 as the US cut defence spending. In the light of the USSR's invasion of Afghanistan in 1979, this seemed a valid approach. The 1981 defence budget was set at $184 billion, compared to $134 billion in the previous year. Reagan declared that $1.6 trillion would be spent on defence over the next five years. In fact he never spent more than 6.5 per cent of US GNP on defence, compared to Eisenhower's average 10.4 per cent during 1954–9, and the Kennedy/Johnson average of 9.3 per cent during 1960–4. Carter had planned, if elected, a substantial increase in defence spending for the early 1980s. Reagan's defence plans were not so extreme in this context, but the increase in spending, combined with Reagan's Cold War rhetoric (he called the USSR an 'evil empire' in 1983), US interference in Central American politics and a revival of anti-nuclear protest in Europe and the US, hardly suggested a President looking to end the Cold War.

Reagan was always interested in negotiation, however, and he had written to Brezhnev in 1981, Andropov in 1983 and Chernenko in 1984. In January 1984 he made a public call for reduced nuclear arsenals and a better understanding with the USSR. The three Soviet leaders, noting the huge US military build-up, were unimpressed with Reagan's proposals to reduce nuclear stockpiles. There was no sign of the USSR becoming conciliatory in the face of US strength. Gorbachev showed much more interest, but was this could have been due to US strength, the collapsing USSR economy, or Gorbachev's own belief that the Cold War was out of date?

Reagan and Gorbachev met four times between 1985 and 1988. A key member of Reagan's staff was the Secretary of State George Shultz, a skilled negotiator and diplomat. However, Reagan, using his tough reputation as a credibility base, took the lead in negotiations, dealing directly with Gorbachev, even 'off the cuff'. The Reykjavik summit in 1986 was a failure as the two sides failed to agree on the future of the US SDI initiative, but it set a precedent for open and creative talks. This led on to the INF Treaty in December 1987, which seemed to formally thaw the Cold War with concrete plans to reduce armaments. The thawing process continued with exchange visits to Moscow and New York in 1988. Although no US President had dealt with such a helpful Soviet leader as Gorbachev before, Reagan deserves credit for seeing the opportunity, understanding the weakness of the USSR's position and encouraging negotiations. In 1990, though, the US magazine *Time* named Mikhael Gorbachev, not Ronald Reagan, as their 'Man of the Decade'.

(b) 'Détente' was the name given to a supposed policy of greater understanding and more direct, peaceful negotiation to settle quarrels between the US and USSR. In theory it had operated since 1963, on the basis that there had been no stand-off to the extent of the 1962 Cuban missile crisis, and that there had been a few agreements regulating nuclear testing and the arms race. This did not, however, provide a strong base on which détente could build in the 1970s. The US, who were the main initiators of détente, saw it as an alternative to military force as a way of containing the USSR; surely the Soviets would see the value of settling quarrels peacefully? The USSR, for their part, saw détente as a sign that the US was no longer able to maintain military superiority: its willingness to seek peaceful negotiation was a recognition that the USSR was now an equal power and deserved more respectful treatment. Détente was never a state of true cordiality and was largely seen as an opportunity for the USSR to strengthen its world position while the US was relatively weak. A lack of consensus and mutual understanding about the purpose of détente lay at the centre of its failure.

Détente operated in three main theatres: Europe, the Third World and the superpower arms race. Détente was most successful over the issue of Europe, significantly because the USSR was looking for recognition of its existing level of control there, rather than an extension of its control. The Germany and Berlin questions were settled at their status quo in 1970 and 1972 respectively. The 1973 Helsinki Conference (which led to the 1975 Helsinki Agreements) saw the West recognise the existing governments in Eastern Europe. In return, the USSR agreed to uphold human rights in its areas of influence – a vague promise which was never enforced properly by the West – and to work more openly with the US to defuse international crises. In theory this was a success for détente, although it only confirmed an existing situation rather than resolved it.

The Soviet promise to work more openly with the US was quickly thrown into doubt over the 1973 Yom Kippur War. As Soviet military advisers were pulled out of Egypt a month before that country's attack on Israel, this left the US suspicious that the USSR had known about, and chosen to keep secret the planned surprise attack by its ally (Egypt) on the US's ally (Israel). This reflected a continuing Soviet interest in expanding its influence in the Third World. The USSR also successfully intervened in Angola in 1976, Ethiopia in 1977 and Yemen in 1979, prior to its most significant expansionist move of the 1970s, the 1979 invasion of Afghanistan. This was perhaps a response to individual opportunities that arose, rather than a grand plan for Third World supremacy, but it infuriated the US and undermined hopes for détente.

The most high-profile achievements of détente were the two SALT agreements. They certainly set a useful precedent: that nuclear arms control could be agreed through top-level talks. SALT I in 1972 limited ABM installations to two sites per superpower. As ABMs were used to destroy incoming missiles, this limitation in theory preserved '**mutually assured destruction**' as a valid deterrent against nuclear attack. There were also limits placed on ICBMs and SLBMs; however the most significant new advances in nuclear weapons technology, especially MIRVs, were left out of SALT I. With long-range bombers also left out, SALT I soon became irrelevant, only restricting forms of nuclear weapons which would eventually become obsolete in the face of new technology. SALT II tried to limit bombers and MIRVs; however, this 1979 agreement was rejected by the US Senate after an untimely revelation that a Soviet combat brigade was secretly operating in Cuba (it had in fact been there since 1962) inflamed US political opinion. This showed the difficulties behind achieving really substantial arms control in the context of mutual suspicion.

While the USSR was always dubious about good superpower relations, in the US there was a lack of really committed pursuit of détente by successive Presidents. Nixon's foreign policy priorities were the conclusion of the war in Vietnam and also better relations with China; both were achieved and the latter was a success in its own right. However, the USSR was displeased and threatened by news of US/Chinese détente, and US hopes of '**linkage**' – combining positive encouragement coupled with threatening pressure to persuade the USSR to negotiate – proved a failure from the start. Ford's Presidency (1974–6) seemed to hold more promise for détente. The 1974 Vladivostok Agreement set guidelines for SALT II negotiations, and the Helsinki Agreements were signed in 1975. However, communist advances in Vietnam, Laos, Cambodia and Angola made 1975 a bad year for US foreign policy. This ran alongside economic decline in the US; GNP fell, inflation rose to 11 per cent and unemployment to 9 per cent. The result was political division within the US with Ford coming under attack from conservative Republicans, including Ronald Reagan. Under pressure, Ford banned the word 'détente' in US foreign policy and demoted its chief supporter, Henry Kissinger. The year 1976 was an election year, and by early 1977 the USSR was dealing with the US's third President within four years. This lack of continuity undermined détente in a similar manner to the succession of Soviet leaders in the early to mid-1980s.

The third US President of the 1970s, Carter, has received the harshest criticism of the three for his foreign policy. Even those historians who lean to the left struggle to judge his policy more highly than 'incoherent' or 'waffle'. Détente was already struggling by 1977, and would probably have failed regardless of Carter. However, his lack of experience and leadership in foreign policy managed to irritate but not intimidate the USSR. His advisers, Secretary of State Vance and National Security Adviser Brzezinski, were for and against détente respectively. Carter's idealistic attachment to human rights did not fit well with the realities of superpower politics, leading to USSR anger at the President's campaign in support of Soviet dissident Andrei Sakharov. Carter also disregarded the Vladivostok Agreement and unsuccessfully tried to restart SALT II talks on a new basis. Vance then breached confidentiality and gave the press details of the US proposals. At the same time, Carter's low profile over the Ethiopia question in 1977 gave an impression of US weakness, while a more experienced politician might have successfully pushed SALT II through Congress in 1979. Even before the Soviet invasion of Afghanistan in the same year, Carter was abandoning détente and pursuing a tougher line, which was continued and intensified by Reagan in the early 1980s.

In conclusion, détente was always unlikely to succeed, and US problems with Vietnam, the economy and uncertain leadership accelerated and increased the extent of its failure. By 1980 the nuclear arms race had continued its momentum and the Soviet invasion of Afghanistan made superpower relations as bad as they had been at any time since the early 1960s. The improvement in superpower relations in the 1980s came on a totally different basis to the attempts at détente in the 1970s. Détente was a failure.

PRACTICE QUESTIONS

10 (a) Explain the causes of the 1991 Gulf War. (10)

(b) What impact did the end of the Cold War have upon US foreign policy to 1991? (20)
(Edexcel format without Sources)

Advice: *To answer this question you should include the following points:*

- *Iraq invasion of Kuwait was blatant aggression but previous invasion of Iran had not led to a similar US-led response.*
- *Economic factors – Kuwait was oil-rich. Saudi Arabia and UAE were also oil-rich and vulnerable to Iraqi attack.*
- *Opportunity for US to work with USSR within the UN and help cement end of the Cold War.*
- *Bush keen to 'kick the Vietnam syndrome' and demonstrate US resolve.*
- *End of the Cold War left US dominant as main world superpower.*
- *Role of NATO thrown into question – US keen to keep going in case of new Russian threat.*
- *Spotlight thrown onto non-superpower dangers, e.g. Middle East.*

Part 3: Sources

📖 1 The causes of the Cold War

- **Source A: Telegram sent from George Kennan, chargé d'affaires at the US Embassy in Moscow, to the US State Department in February 1946**

We have here a political force committed fanatically to the belief that with the US there can be no permanent modus vivendi [acceptance of each others' way of life], that it is desirable and necessary that the internal harmony of our society be disrupted, our traditional way of life be destroyed, the international authority of our state be broken, if Soviet power is to be secure. . . . We must see that our public is educated to the realities of Russian situation . . . World communism is like malignant parasite which feeds only on diseased tissue.

- **Source B: Telegram sent from Nikolai Novikov, Soviet Ambassador to Washington, to Molotov in September 1946**

There has been a decline in the influence on foreign policy of those who follow Roosevelt's course for co-operation among peace-loving countries. . . . Obvious indications of the US effort to establish world dominance are also to be found in the increase in military potential in peacetime . . . The present policy of the American government with regard to the USSR is also directed at limiting or dislodging the influence of the Soviet Union from neighbouring countries. In implementing this policy in former enemy or Allied countries adjacent to the USSR, the United States attempts, at various international conferences or directly in these countries themselves, to support reactionary forces with the purpose of creating obstacles to the process of democratisation of these countries. In so doing, it also attempts to secure positions for the penetration of American capital into their economies.

- **Source C: James B. Reston writing in *Harper's Magazine*, August 1947**

Negotiating with the Russians is like playing tennis on a court without lines or umpire. If the indefatigable Mr Molotov hits one into the net (as he often does) and cries 'good,' there is nothing you can do about it except argue. If you call in the French, the British and the Chinese, and they all say, sorry, it went into the net, Mr Molotov is not only adamant but angry. . . . If he is in a bad mood, or if the Politburo feels that they need the point badly, Mr Molotov will veto the others; if not, Mr Molotov will 'compromise'; he will agree to play the point over. . . . It complicates the process. The European Advisory Commission, which was established long before the end of the war to co-ordinate the post-war policies of the Big Three, met over 500 times and accomplished virtually nothing. . . . We and the Russians start with different objectives and mentalities, are suspicious of the objectives of each other, and adopt totally different methods of negotiation.

- **Source D: Letter sent from Henry A. Wallace, former Vice-President, to President Truman, July 1946**

I have been increasingly concerned about the trend of international affairs since the end of the war, and I am even more troubled by the apparently growing feeling among the American people that another war is coming and the only way that we can head it off is to arm ourselves to the teeth. . . . We should make an effort to counteract the irrational fear of Russia which is being systematically built up in the American people by certain individuals and publications. . . . We should not act as if we too felt that we were threatened in today's world. We are by far the most powerful nation in the world, the only allied nation which came out of the war without devastation and much stronger than before the war. Any talk on our part about the need for strengthening our defences further is bound to appear hypocritical to other nations.

■ **Source E: Clark Clifford, former Special Counsel to President Truman, explaining in a 1996 interview why Truman launched the Marshall Plan in 1948**

Part of the president's attitude toward the Soviet Union was we must begin not only to strengthen ourselves, but to strengthen our historic allies. . . . Now at the end of the Second World War the Soviets were very powerful militarily; they'd come through the war well. . . . We used to talk about the fact that the Soviets could, if they chose, send their army westward across Europe and they could march unimpeded to the British Channel. Nobody could stop them. France was bled dry, Italy was out of the picture, nobody there to do it. And he thought that it wasn't enough just for us to strengthen our defences, but that we should begin to tell the rest of the world what this danger was, and help build them up so that they could be a force to align themselves with us and defend the world.

EDEXCEL QUESTION FORMAT

The questions and answers that follow are based on the Edexcel style.

(a) **Using your own knowledge and the evidence of Sources B, D and E, why did the US and USSR fail to reach a satisfactory settlement in Europe between the end of the Second World War and 1949?** (10)

(b) **'The Cold War was not wholly caused by either the US or USSR, but more by a mutual misunderstanding of each other's intentions.' Using your own knowledge and the evidence from all five sources, explain how far you would agree with this interpretation.** (20)

(a) At the end of the Second World War the USSR controlled almost all European territory east of a line running roughly down the centre of Germany. The US, Britain and France occupied the western part of Germany and were dominant in the rest of Western Europe. Agreements at Yalta and Potsdam in 1945 failed to resolve exactly what shape post-war Europe would take. Instead both sides ensured that their own political and economic systems would operate either side of the divide. As early as 1946 Churchill had warned that an 'Iron Curtain' had descended across Europe.

Source B reflects Soviet suspicion of the West, referring to 'the US effort to establish world dominance'. Stalin shook off US criticism and established communist regimes in 'neighbouring countries', Poland, Bulgaria, Hungary Romania and Czechoslovakia all falling victim during 1946–8. Stalin also opposed the reunification of Germany and tried, with the 1948 Berlin blockade, to drive the Western Allies out of West Berlin. Novikov's reference to US 'attempts to secure positions for the penetration of American capital' in Eastern Europe explains why Stalin refused Marshall Aid for the states under his control in 1948. This fear of US economic expansionism made Stalin determined not to give up control of his territories.

Source D recognises Stalin's point of view. Wallace acknowledged that the US was 'by far the most powerful nation in the world' and saw the 'hypocritical' side of playing up the Soviet threat. At this stage the US was the only power with atomic weapons and Truman, baffled by Soviet lack of cooperation and the lack of a resolution of the European problem, was aiming aggressive rhetoric at the USSR. Wallace's concern that an 'irrational fear of Russia' was 'being systematically built up in the American people' was well founded, and by 1947 Truman himself was one of the 'certain individuals' to encourage this view. His 'Truman Doctrine', announced in 1947, spoke of the conflict in terms of good versus evil, making compromise less likely.

Despite the US's general strength, it had pulled most of its troops out of Europe by 1948, and the USSR had vast superiority in conventional military forces in Europe. Clifford's view in Source E that 'the Soviets could, if they chose, send their army westward through Europe' and that, in Western Europe, 'nobody could stop them' explains why the US launched the Marshall Plan in 1948 and why, a year later, NATO was formed. The US did not just fear a Soviet invasion of Western Europe but also that the West, economically weak and uncertain after the war, might suffer internal communist revolutions. There was even a secret plan to intervene in France if the government system there collapsed. The USSR, however, saw all these as offensive and expansionist developments and any lingering hopes that a settlement be reached, and Germany be reunified, were finally ended. Germany, Berlin and Europe were rigidly divided into West and East, an arrangement that would last for 40 years.

(b) The US and USSR had fought on the same side in the Second World War, and therefore had developed some understanding of each other. Relations were never very cordial, however, and the two superpowers soon disagreed on the problem of post-war Europe. They also had deep-seated ideological differences, capitalism versus communism. These differences did not only help cause the Cold War, they have also influenced historical interpretations of why the Cold War started.

In the late 1940s, both sides squarely blamed each other. Sources A, B, C and E are full of angry language about the situation. Kennan (Source A), from his vantage point in Moscow, was in no doubt: the Soviets were 'fanatics', seeking the 'destruction' of the US way of life and communism was described as a 'malignant parasite' – extraordinary words from a diplomat. At this stage, February 1946, Soviet dominance of Eastern Europe was still taking shape and Stalin was insisting that he would ensure democratic elections and free government in the Soviet-occupied states. The USSR's definition of democracy and freedom seemed different to that of the US though. Kennan's interpretation of Soviet intentions coloured Truman's judgement, and his policies during 1947–9 reflected US distrust of the USSR. The US pledged support for Greece and Turkey, refused to pull out of West Berlin and kept the monopoly over the atom bomb. The USSR's approach to diplomacy did not reassure Truman. Reston's bemused assessment of Soviet Foreign Minister, Molotov, suggests that the USSR could be blamed for encouraging the US to suspect Soviet intentions. The tennis analogy reflects that well-established rules (for the US at least) were being broken. However, Reston admitted that there were problems on both sides, with 'different objectives and mentalities', and 'totally different methods of negotiation', meaning that both sides were 'suspicious of . . . each other'. This would support the 'mutual misunderstanding' interpretation in the question.

One of the key characteristics of the Cold War was that it went beyond Europe. It was not limited to any one venue or issue but became a worldwide struggle to prevent each other from gaining the upper hand. By the 1950s and 1960s, the Cold War was being fought in Korea, Southeast Asia, Africa and Central America. Novikov's (Source B) main concern was the question of Europe but, like Kennan before him, he did not hesitate to couch the issue in world terms, referring to 'the US effort to establish world dominance', and called US pressure in Europe 'the present policy of the American government' rather than the limits of its ambition. The USSR's assumption that the US had plans for economic domination seemed borne out by their plans for German and Japanese recovery based on capitalism and their intervention in Greece, Turkey and, in 1950, Korea. The Truman doctrine policy of 'containment' was, in Soviet eyes, an active denial of people's rights to turn to communism. The firm rhetoric from Truman himself and, as Wallace (Source D) noted, from 'certain individuals and publications' did suggest an 'irrational fear of Russia' and generated a concern in the USSR, as well as the US, that 'another war is coming'.

By the 1960s, a 'revisionist' interpretation of the causes of the Cold War was emerging with a greater likelihood of criticism of the US's role (see for example LaFeber). The Truman Doctrine, for example, began to be seen in a more cynical context as an attempt by the President to mobilise public opinion in support for US economic investment in Europe, which of course would have to be backed up by military security. Part of this took the form of the Marshall Plan, which Truman had assumed would be unacceptable to the USSR from the start. Clifford (Source D) places the Marshall Plan in the context of US security against Soviet domination of Europe, rather than as humanitarian aid. However, Clifford also notes that 'the Soviets were very powerful militarily', and his reference to the need to 'defend the world' reflects 'post-revisionist' interpretations, such as those by Hyland and Gaddis, that Stalin had no intention of working towards good relations and saw US capitalism, as Novikov suggested, as an implacable enemy.

This leads to a conclusion that neither side was free of responsibility for causing the Cold War. Both, justifiably, saw each other as a threat, although each posed a threat partly because they thought the other was a threat. The 'mutual misunderstanding' was evident in the rhetoric shown in the sources and the diplomatic failures of the late 1940s. This lack of understanding shaped the Cold War, and was to lead to world crises such as Berlin and Cuba. The difficulty in settling the European question after the Second World War hastened the beginning of the Cold War. The ideological differences gave identity to each side. These factors did not provide the prime cause, though. This lay in the emergence of two superpowers, both with strong national identities and aspirations, finding themselves in a dominant world position after 1945.

ADDITIONAL QUESTIONS IN THE EDEXCEL FORMAT

(a) **Using your own knowledge and the evidence of Sources B and E, assess the impact of the Second World War's outcome upon Europe.** (10)

(b) **'The wartime Grand Alliance was doomed to crumble after the death of Roosevelt and the accession of Truman.' Using your own knowledge and the evidence from all five Sources, explain how far you would agree with this interpretation.** (20)

2 Public opinion and the Vietnam War

■ **Source A: Eleanor Bockman, a middle-aged Atlanta housewife who took part in the October 1969 Moratorium Protest and was interviewed at the time**

I think people are thoroughly tired of the war. I think that some middle-class whites are just beginning to realise the depth of poverty in this country. Older people see the emptiness, the burden of the war. Younger people see it as a great waste of talent and life. Everybody knows that there is no answer now to the Vietnam War, but we've got to let Nixon know.

■ **Source B: Television address by President Nixon, November 1969**

I would like to address a word, if I may, to the young people of this nation who are particularly concerned, and I understand why they are concerned, about this war. I respect your idealism. I share your concern for peace. I want peace as much as you do. . . . I want to end [the war] so that the energy and dedication of you, our young people, now too often directed into bitter hatred against those responsible for the war, can be turned to the great challenges of peace, a better life for all Americans, a better life for all people on this Earth. . . . And so tonight – to you, the great silent majority of my fellow Americans, I ask for your support.

■ **Source C: Rennie Davis, anti-war protest leader, recalling anti-Vietnam War protests in a 1996 interview**

The large protests that I co-ordinated – there were about 150 national organisations – were united fundamentally around a commitment to non-violence. It didn't mean that there weren't elements within the movement that felt more aggressive means were essential to take, but relative to all the major mobilisations and to anything that represented a real coming together of people and forces, non-violence was an absolute bedrock to the American movement. . . . I viewed myself, quite honestly, as a patriot, and I viewed myself as supporting American GIs, and my way of supporting them was to get them out of that senseless war . . .

The capacity of the United States to wage war kind of indiscriminately anywhere in the world, without the American public looking over their shoulders very carefully, I think has been changed forever.

AQA QUESTION FORMAT

The questions and answers that follow are based on the AQA style.

(a) **Study Source A and use your own knowledge. How valid are the reasons given by Eleanor Bockman for the widespread popular protests against the Vietnam War?** (10)

(b) **Study Source C and use your own knowledge. How reliable is Source C as evidence of the nature of anti-Vietnam War protests in the US between 1967 and 1970?** (10)

(c) **Consult Sources A, B and C and use your own knowledge. 'The strength of public opinion against the war forced the US to abandon hopes of victory in Vietnam.' Assess the validity of this statement.** (20)

(a) Bockman's first reason, that 'people are thoroughly tired of the war', seems valid. By October 1969 the ground war in Vietnam had been going on for four-and-a-half years, longer than the US's involvement in Korea or either of the world wars. Public protest was relatively muted for the first two years, growing in prominence during 1967 and then escalating after the 1968 Tet Offensive. Public opinion as a whole turned against the war after Tet, and the 1969 Moratorium Protest was noticeable for its broad appeal, involving new sections of society that had not protested before, including many 'older people' and 'middle-class whites' – as Bockman said. The 'waste of talent and life' was evident to the US public as over 500,000 US troops had been involved in Vietnam and casualties were close to 40,000 by 1969. Television images of the war, especially the My Lai massacre, and the lack of an end in sight generated despondency in the US, hence the references to 'emptiness' and 'no answer now'. The reference to 'poverty' hints at a broader cause of dissatisfaction, the economic and social conditions in the US, problems apparently left unsolved despite Johnson's 'Great Society' promises, while billions of dollars were poured into the Vietnam War. Bockman's final reason, 'we've got to let Nixon know', reflected the blame attached to the Presidency for the Vietnam War. Nixon's predecessor Johnson had started the ground war and a 'credibility gap' had subsequently opened up – the public stopped trusting their President. Nixon had promised to end the war but there was no sign of this, other than the announcement of some troop withdrawals and reduction in bombing, by October 1969. All of the reasons given by Bockman are relevant.

However, there are other reasons for the popular protests not mentioned by Bockman. The war, and poverty, were not the only factors leading to protest. There was a trend in the 1960s towards vocal protest, especially among the young. The civil rights campaign also brought active protest into popular political culture. The late 1960s saw a 'flower power' hippy movement, which found anti-Vietnam War protest an important focus for anti-establishment and anti-war attitudes. Finally, most controversial was the use of conscription for the Vietnam War, arguably a breach of human rights; burning draft cards was a popular form of protest.

(b) Source C makes three main points about the nature of anti-Vietnam War protests. First, the protests were widespread and popular. Davis claims there to have been 'about 150 national organisations'. Second, the protests were, in the main, peaceful and committed to 'non-violence', although he admits to 'elements in the movement' who supported 'more aggressive means.' Third, the protests to some extent had patriotic rather than purely pacifist motives behind them, Davis saying 'I viewed myself, quite honestly, as a patriot'. All of these points taken together cast the anti-Vietnam War protests in a very inclusive and populist light, not the work of an extreme minority against the true wishes of 'the great silent majority' referred to by Nixon in Source B.

The authorship of the Source would lead us to expect bias and therefore a lack of reliability. Rennie Davis was not a neutral observer but a leading figure in the 1960s protests, who was controversially imprisoned for his role in protests in Chicago in 1968. He clearly opposed the war passionately as he did not just participate in, he 'co-ordinated' protests. It would therefore be expected that he strongly supported the protests and would emphasise their popularity. Although he was speaking in 1996, many years after the end of the protests and the war, he would still have an eye on history's assessment of the protests, and his own role, since the 1960s. The issue of patriotism is pertinent as conservative assessments of the Vietnam War since its end (such as that by Ronald Reagan, for example) viewed it as a patriotic and just struggle, lost due to a lack of will within the US, implicitly blaming the anti-war protests. There is a lack of proper reference to the more aggressive aspects of the protests. This all points towards Source C being unreliable evidence.

However, much of the content of Source C is supported by the other Sources as well as our knowledge of anti-Vietnam War protests. Davis calls the war 'senseless' and the protests 'a real coming together of people'. Eleanor Bockman spoke of the 'emptiness' of the war and suggested that people of different ages and social groups were brought together by opposition to the war. Certainly the 1969 Moratorium Protest was supported by millions across the US. The number and popularity of different protests during 1968–70 (perhaps less so in 1967) again supports Davis's assessment that the protests were well supported. And Nixon's television address (Source B) seems to bear out Davis's comment on how US foreign policy makers would have to pay closer attention to public opinion thereafter. Davis also admits that there were some 'aggressive means' although he underplays the real extent of violence and militancy. On this basis, then, the content of Source C is fairly reliable. However, it does not cover all issues relating to the nature of anti-Vietnam War protests, for example the sharing of the anti-war message with wider human rights and even revolutionary causes.

(c) Even before his election in 1968 Nixon believed that complete victory was not possible. The best policy, in his view, was to gradually withdraw US involvement from Vietnam and seek an honourable compromise peace with North Vietnam. Given the sheer economic and military might of the US, this seems at first sight an extraordinary statement, and hostile public opinion might be one explanation why Nixon felt he could not bring the full extent of US power to the war. There are, however, other contributory factors.

Source A supports the view that public opinion was strongly against the war. Bockman's statement 'we've got to let Nixon know' suggests that this public opinion had not yet influenced Nixon. In fact Nixon was already well aware of public hostility to the war, as Johnson had been before him. Johnson had decided not to seek re-election in 1968 due to public dismay at how the Vietnam War was progressing (the Tet Offensive especially upset public opinion) and Nixon had already begun his 'Vietnamization' programme, withdrawing US troops piecemeal from Vietnam, before October 1969. Source B does provide evidence that Nixon was very conscious of public opinion, although he did claim that 'the great silent majority' supported his gradual approach to ending the war.

Although Nixon implied that only a minority actively opposed his continuation of the Vietnam War, Source C suggests that anti-war protests were in fact very widespread and were organised to the extent that 'about 150 national organisations' actively campaigned to stop the war. This was not enough to force the US to pull out of Vietnam immediately, nor did it prevent Nixon from broadening and intensifying the bombing campaigns against the Viet Cong during 1970–1. However, it did make an increase in the number of US ground troops politically impossible. This, together with the failure of Nixon's 'Vietnamization' policy (the South Vietnamese troops were never strong enough to defeat the Viet Cong alone) forced the US to abandon victory hopes.

This all contrasts with the optimistic mood of the US government in 1965 when ground troops were first sent in. It was only after the war had dragged on for two or three years that anti-war protests really became a factor against victory. Political and military miscalculations prevented victory in the first two years. After that the sense of war weariness, indicated in Source A ('people are thoroughly tired of the war') and Source C ('get them out of that senseless war'), took hold and undermined the continuation of the war. The nature of the war also made it hard to pursue: the US was not capturing territory but attempting to clear areas of Viet Cong infiltration. There was plenty of violence and bloodshed but little evidence, other than dead Vietnamese, of any military progress. From this came a feeling of 'waste' (Source A) and 'senseless war' (Source C). Nixon himself admitted (or pretended to admit): 'I understand why they [young people] are concerned about this war.' From 1967 onwards, victory became increasingly unlikely, in part due to public opinion against the war.

There were other reasons, not mentioned in any of the Sources, which help to explain why the US had to abandon hopes of victory in Vietnam. The 'military miscalculations' mentioned earlier included ineffective deployment of the air force and ground troops, for example the troops were unused to guerrilla warfare and General Westmoreland's 'search and destroy' policy lacked the subtlety needed to outwit the Viet Cong. It also must not be assumed that it was up to the US to win or lose the war. The Viet Cong and their suppliers, North Vietnam, were well organised and tenacious. Soviet equipment and supplies were deployed effectively – the only exception being the 1968 Tet Offensive, but even this was a psychological masterstroke against a faltering US. Finally, North Vietnam's refusal to negotiate a compromise settlement before 1973, by which time Nixon was really desperate to end the war, made an advantageous solution to the war impossible for the US.

ADDITIONAL QUESTIONS IN THE AQA FORMAT

(a) **Study Source C and use your own knowledge. How valid are the reasons given in Source C for public support of anti-war protests?** (10)

(b) **Study Source B and use your own knowledge. How reliable is Source B as evidence of Nixon's conduct of the Vietnam War during 1969–72?** (10)

(c) **Consult Sources A, B and C and use your own knowledge. 'Anti-Vietnam War protests were mostly the work of a radical minority and not representative of US public opinion as a whole.' Assess the validity of this statement.** (20)

Part 4: Historical skills

 ## 1 Investigating Cold War case studies

Choose one or more of the following events of the Cold War. Undertake further research on it and then, either individually or in pairs, produce two short written descriptions of the event, one showing the US's perspective, and the other showing the USSR's perspective:

- the Marshall Plan, 1948;
- the Berlin blockade, 1948;
- the US intervention in Korea, 1950;
- the Hungarian uprising, 1956;
- the building of the Berlin Wall, 1961;

- the Cuban missile crisis, 1962;
- the 'Christmas bombing' of Hanoi, 1972;
- the Soviet invasion of Afghanistan, 1979;
- the Reykjavik Summit, 1986.

2 The Cold War and US culture

Use the Internet or other resources to find out more about US culture in the Cold War. This could include the following:

- Films – Hollywood sci-fi films (e.g. *Invasion of the Body Snatchers*) as 1950s allegories for the communist threat; Vietnam films (e.g. *The Green Berets*, *Apocalypse Now*) as indicators of different political interpretations of the Vietnam War.
- Sport – the Fischer/Spassky chess world championship in 1972; the boycotted Moscow Olympics in 1980.

Sources and references

Stephen E. Ambrose and Douglas G. Brinkley, *Rise to Globalism*, 8th edition, Penguin (1997).

S.J. Ball, *The Cold War*, Arnold (1998).

Mark S. Byrnes, *The Truman Years 1945–1953*, Pearson (2000).

David A. Deese (ed.), *The New Politics of American Foreign Policy*, St Martin's Press (1994).

J.P.D. Dunbabin, *The Cold War*, Pearson (1994).

Niall Ferguson, *Colossus: The Rise and Fall of the American Empire*, Penguin (2004).

T.G. Fraser and Donette Murray, *America and the World since 1945*, Palgrave (2002).

John L. Gaddis, *The Long Peace: Inquiries into the History of the Cold War*, Oxford University Press (1987).

John L. Gaddis, *We Now Know: Rethinking Cold War History*, Oxford University Press (1997).

Fraser J. Harbutt, *The Cold War Era*, Blackwell (2002).

William G. Hyland, *The Cold War: Fifty Years of Conflict*, Times Books (1991).

Michael Kort, *The Columbia Guide to the Cold War*, Columbia University Press (1998).

Walter LaFeber, *America, Russia and the Cold War, 1945–2000*, 9th edition, McGraw-Hill (2002).

Martin McCauley, *Russia, America and the Cold War 1949–1991*, Pearson (1998).

John W. Mason, *The Cold War 1945–1991*, Routledge (1996).

David Mervin, *The President of the United States*, Harvester Wheatsheaf (1993).

Richard Sobel, *The Impact of Public Opinion on US Foreign Policy Since Vietnam*, Oxford University Press (2001).

Robert D. Schulzinger, *US Diplomacy Since 1900*, 5th edition, Oxford University Press (2002).

John Traynor, *Mastering Modern United States History*, Palgrave (2001).

There are also numerous excellent web sites available. Two good starting points are:

www.americanpresident.org
www.cnn.com/SPECIALS/cold.war

Chapter 10

Civil Rights, 1863–2001

This chapter will look at the struggle for civil rights in the United States between 1863 and 2001. African Americans will provide the primary focus, but other groups such as Native Americans, Hispanic Americans, Japanese Americans and Chinese Americans will also be considered.

 ## Historical background

Introduction
The Civil War, 1861–1865
Reconstruction, 1865–1877
Race relations and civil rights, 1877–1917
The inter-war years, 1919–1941
The impact of the Second World War,
    1941–1945
The beginnings of the civil rights movement,
    1945–1960
Civil rights, 1960–1968
American race relations, 1968–2001
Conclusion

 ## Essays

Reconstruction and after
African Americans and Native Americans
Booker T. Washington and W.E.B. Du Bois
Civil rights in the 1950s and 1960s

 ## Sources

1   Responses to Plessy v. Ferguson
2   Responses to Brown v. Board of
    Education

 ## Historical skills

1   Role play: a television debate on whether
    to make Martin Luther King's birthday a
    national holiday in the US
2   Using numbers: analysis of the average
    income of persons with earned income,
    by race and sex
3   Mind maps
4   Hot seating: assuming a role and answering
    questions

Chronology

1863	Emancipation Proclamation
1866	Freedmen's Bureau established
	Civil War ended
1866	Civil Rights Act
	The Thirteenth Amendment to the Constitution abolished slavery
	Reconstruction Act
1868	The Fourteenth Amendment to the Constitution granted citizenship to all persons born in the US
1869	Fifteenth Amendment to the Constitution protected citizens' right to vote
1872	Civil Rights Act of 1866 found to be unconstitutional
1875	Civil Rights Act
1877	End of Reconstruction
1881	The First Jim Crow Law passed in Tennessee
1882	The Chinese Exclusion Act
1887	The Dawes Act gave Native Americans land if they renounced tribal allegiance
1896	Plessy v. Ferguson established 'separate but equal'
1909	National Association for the Advancement of Colored People (NAACP) founded
1919	Riots in 'Red Summer'
1920	The Nineteenth Amendment gave women the vote
1921	Quota Act
1924	National Origins Act – all Native Americans given rights of citizenship
1934	Indian Reorganization Act
1942	Congress of Racial Equality (CORE) founded
1943	Riots in Harlem, Detroit and Alabama
1948	US armed forces desegregated
1954	Brown v. Board of Education, Topeka, Kansas
1955	Segregation on interstate transport banned
	Montgomery Bus Boycott began
1957	Civil Rights Act
	Central High School, Little Rock, Arkansas: integration stopped by riots
1960	Student Non-violent Co-ordinating Committee launched
1961	Freedom Rides organised by CORE
1963	Demonstrations in Birmingham, Alabama
	March on Washington
1964	Martin Luther King Jr won Nobel Peace Prize
	Civil Rights Act
	Riots in New York, Philadelphia and Chicago
1965	Malcolm X assassinated
	Voting Rights Act
	Rise of Black Power
	Riots in Watts district of Los Angeles
1967	National Organization of Women set up
	Loving v. Virginia
	Riots in Chicago, Detroit and Cambridge, Maryland
	Martin Luther King assassinated

Chronology

1967	Civil Rights Act
	American Indian Movement founded
1974	Indian Self Development Act
1977	*Roots* broadcast to an estimated audience of 130 million television viewers
1982	The birthday of Martin Luther King Jr declared a national holiday
1984	Jesse Jackson ran for Democratic nomination for President
1988	Civil Rights Restoration Act
1991	Rodney King incident
1992	LA Riots left 55 dead
1995	Supreme Court attacked desegregation in schools
	Louis Farrakhan's Million Man March on Washington DC

Part 1: Historical background

 Introduction

Civil rights are those rights that citizens are entitled to expect in a free society. They include the right to vote, the right to equality of opportunity and the right to receive the protection of the law. However, for the majority of Americans their history is a history of the struggle to achieve civil rights. It could be argued that in the 'Land of the Free' only white, Protestant males of North European origin, who spoke English and possessed capital were truly free to enjoy their civil rights. All other groups were disadvantaged and had to fight institutional racism and sexism in order to achieve their freedom.

At the outbreak of the Civil War, most African Americans were slaves, Native Americans had been moved from their homelands, the majority of **Hispanic Americans** were trapped in low-paid employment, recent immigrants from Europe were living in eastern ghettos, Chinese Americans were the victims of racist attacks, and many women contented themselves with a supporting role for their families. All these groups were kept socially, politically and economically inferior to the American elite.

The Civil War was a catalyst for change, and from 1863 to 1870 American society changed considerably. At this time great strides were made by African Americans in their quest for civil rights but, as the century progressed, many of these gains were eroded and by the outbreak of the Second World War millions of Americans were still denied social, political and economic equality. However, things did eventually improve and the civil rights movement of the 1950s and 1960s is widely regarded as a success. Consequently, by the 1970s the majority of Americans enjoyed their legal and political rights to a greater extent than any of their ancestors. Whether they had all their civil rights, though, is a matter for debate.

 The Civil War, 1861–1865

The Civil War was not fought to free slaves. When it began Lincoln had no intention of emancipating African Americans. His attitude is reflected in the fact that the first Confiscation Act (1861) recognised slaves as property but did not give them freedom. His views can also be seen in his actions and words. In 1861 and 1862 he dismissed three Union commanding officers for trying to free slaves and late in 1862 he said: 'If I could save the Union without freeing any slave, I would do it . . . .' However, as losses increased and the need for more soldiers intensified, and this was coupled with both a fear of foreign intervention on behalf of the South and Lincoln's desire to strengthen his own position, the war to preserve the Union became regarded as a war to end slavery.

The Emancipation Proclamation took effect from 1 January 1863. The Union could now use African American soldiers in its ranks while also gaining the propaganda issue it required to keep the South isolated. However, many white soldiers would not fight alongside black soldiers so African American regiments were formed. These regiments were put into situations where they suffered heavy losses, black soldiers were paid less than white soldiers, and if they were captured they were not treated as prisoners of war. In addition to this, the recruitment of former slaves was bitterly resented by immigrants from Europe, leading to riots in Northern cities. In the summer of 1863, for example, over 1,000 people were killed or injured in a riot in New York. It can be seen, then, that although the slaves were now free, there was still a great deal of racism in the US and that equality had not yet been achieved.

 ## Reconstruction, 1865–1877

By the end of the war, the Confederate states were ruined and the new President, Andrew Johnson, was faced with the problems of how to restore unity to the United States while also determining the future and status of several million freed slaves. Between 1865 and 1867 he embarked upon a process of Presidential Reconstruction but he was regarded as being too sympathetic to the former Confederates and soon lost the support of his Party.

Most of the newly elected Southern assemblies refused to ratify the 13th Amendment while also refusing to give the vote to even a proportion of freed slaves. In addition to this, they introduced Black Codes which withheld African American rights to vote, serve on a jury, give evidence against a white person, carry arms, or marry a white person. African Americans had heavier penalties imposed on them if they broke the law, they were forced to enter labour contracts with their former employers and, if they remained unemployed, they could be hired out to plantation owners as a punishment for vagrancy.

Radicals in the Republican Party pushed for change. They supported the work of the Freedmen's Bureau and overrode Johnson's veto of the Civil Rights Act of 1866. They secured the 14th Amendment, which stated that all persons born or naturalised in the United States were citizens, while declaring that any state that denied the vote to any male citizen would have its representatives in Congress reduced. This was a direct attack on the Black Codes.

A period of Congressional Reconstruction followed. A series of Reconstruction Acts was passed between 1867 and 1868, which invalidated state governments who had refused to ratify the 14th Amendment. This was supported by the 15th Amendment (1870), which was intended to ensure that African Americans were given the vote throughout the US and the Civil Rights Act (1875) which aimed to prohibit segregation in public places (except schools).

However, the Civil Rights Act was never enforced, the 15th Amendment did not preclude the imposition of voting qualifications, and there was no guarantee that former slaves or their descendants could hold office. African Americans suffered attacks from the Ku Klux Klan, the police and recent immigrants from Europe. In addition to this, thousands of African Americans remained in the poverty trap, many were illiterate and few owned land.

In 1877 federal troops were removed from the South and the policies of Reconstruction, which were already weakened, were finally abandoned. African Americans in the South were now at the mercy of state legislatures who were allowed to pursue policies of segregation and discrimination unimpeded by federal intervention.

Race relations and civil rights, 1877–1917

African Americans

By 1877 African Americans had 'stood for a brief moment in the sun'. They had tasted freedom, re-established the family unit and seen their churches become important social and political institutions. They had gained some civil rights, but these were beginning to be eroded.

In 1883 the Supreme Court declared that the Civil Rights Act (1875) was unconstitutional. In 1890 a bill to provide federal supervision of elections in the South to stop African Americans being intimidated was blocked. During the 1890s loopholes in the interpretation of the 15th Amendment were exploited, 'Jim Crow' laws were introduced and African Americans continued to suffer violence while also being kept in a state of poverty.

As a result of this, the number of African Americans registered to vote fell considerably and, with the Supreme Court's decision in Plessy v. Ferguson, the notion of **'separate but equal'** became firmly established in the South.

In the North, where increasing numbers of Southern African Americans had migrated, things were little better. African Americans suffered discrimination, often lived in ghettoes, were excluded from skilled employment and trade union membership and endured high infant mortality rates.

Despite this, men such as W.E.B. Du Bois were working to change things. Du Bois demanded full civil rights, the end of segregation, the extension of the franchise, and equality of opportunity in all aspects of life and work. He became involved in the first civil rights movement when he joined forces with other activists in the National Association for the Advancement of Colored People (NAACP). He edited the NAACP's magazine, *The Crisis*, and through it he campaigned against lynching, 'Jim Crow' laws and sexual inequality.

Native Americans

By 1877 most Native Americans were forced to live on reservations, they were dependent on the white man's generosity, denied the annual payments that they had been promised in return for their land, and deprived of the rights and liberties of US citizens.

Figure 10.1
Public hanging in Kentucky

The Dawes Act (1887) divided up reservation land and allocated sections of it to the head of each Native American family. It also gave Native Americans the full protection of federal law. However, Native Americans were still forced to live on the poorest land and they suffered hunger, disease and hardship. They were often treated with contempt and they were segregated from the rest of the population. In addition to this, their children were sent away to boarding schools as the US government attempted to destroy their culture.

Chinese Americans

Chinese Americans were deprived of their civil rights. They suffered discrimination and hatred and they were often made scapegoats in times of unemployment and unrest. They were forced to live in their own areas of cities, particularly in western states, and they were not allowed to become naturalised. In 1882 Congress passed the Chinese Exclusion Act which banned Chinese immigration for ten years. Chinese Americans suffered a great deal as a result of their lack of civil rights.

Hispanic Americans

As the US acquired land from Mexico, many Hispanic Americans took their place in American society. Some of these were wealthy landowners and they were readily accepted in the social circles of white Americans. However, many poorer, dark-skinned Hispanics became itinerant agricultural labourers and were denied their civil rights. Later, other Hispanic workers came from Mexico, Puerto Rico and Cuba. Many of these people were short-term seasonal workers who were easily repatriated at times of racial tension. Very few of them gained the rights and privileges enjoyed by other US citizens.

European Americans

As the US continued to industrialise, many immigrants came from Europe. They were frequently illiterate and lacked bargaining power. Many of them worked long hours in dangerous conditions for low pay, however, there were no barriers to European Americans becoming American citizens. Nonetheless, because many of these new immigrants came from southern and eastern Europe, they did face discrimination and intimidation and the government did little to guarantee their civil rights.

Conclusion

By 1917 interracial violence and hostility were commonplace. All ethnic minorities endured poverty and discrimination and there was no political will to address the issue of civil rights.

 The inter-war years, 1919–1941

African Americans and Native Americans who fought in the First World War gained a glimpse of greater equality, but, when they returned home, white resentment at competition for jobs and housing led to race riots in twenty-five American cities and towns in 1919. In addition to this, German Americans faced hostility that lasted for some time after the war, and African Americans, Catholics, Jews, trade union members, and anyone suspected of subversion became victims of the reformed Ku Klux Klan.

On 1 January 1920, 6,000 'aliens' were rounded up and imprisoned or expelled from the US and, in the same year, Prohibition came into force. Opponents of the ban on the production, transportation and consumption of alcohol argued that it was an infringement of civil rights, but Prohibition was regarded by many as an attack on the foreign immigrants who were blamed for the vice, crime and drunkenness that took place in the US. It was certainly fuelled by anti-German feeling as the wealth and political influence of many German brewers was resented. Prohibition definitely showed that the federal government and the courts were now more willing to extend their power over ordinary citizens, and their actions could also be seen as an attack on civil rights.

Other examples of institutionalised racism can be found in the Quota Act (1921) and the National Origins Act (1924). Limitations were placed on the number of southern and eastern Europeans who were allowed to enter the country and, after 1924, Asian immigrants were excluded completely.

However, there were some gains during this period: Native Americans were given rights of citizenship (1924) and the 19th Amendment (1919) gave women the vote. The '**Harlem Renaissance**' produced talented musicians, such as Louis Armstrong and 'Duke' Ellington, and writers, such as Langston Hughes, who challenged racism and championed freedom and equality.

Despite divisions among some African Americans, there was an increased awareness of cultural identity and the rights to which they were entitled. During the Depression black workers began to join trade unions, which was an important step in the quest for civil rights. It gave African Americans both an increased awareness of their rights and greater confidence to pursue them. African Americans influenced the New Deal through the '**black cabinet**', and the NAACP continued to encourage ordinary African Americans to organise and assert themselves, to use the courts to challenge discrimination, and to fight against inequality in education provisions and funding. At this time the African American vote, where it existed, switched decisively from the Republicans to the Democrats.

 The impact of the Second World War, 1941–1945

African Americans

The Second World War increased African American consciousness. Black soldiers were seen as equal on the front line, but at military parades, in church services, transportation and in the canteens they were segregated from white soldiers. In addition to this, the irony of fighting the racism of the Nazis while African Americans were suffering similar treatment in the Southern states was not lost on the black troops. As a result of this, the African American press began to campaign for 'Double V' : victory against racism at home and abroad.

As the war progressed, the demand for labour gave black workers greater bargaining power and the membership of the NAACP increased from 50,000 to 450,000. A. Philip Randolph's proposed march on Washington led to the establishment of the Fair Employment Practices Commission and James Farmer established the Congress of Racial Equality which used non-violent tactics such as sit-ins in order to challenge segregation.

However, the majority of African Americans still lived in poverty and suffered racism and discrimination. There was considerable racial tension, illustrated by the race riots in Detroit and Harlem in the summer of 1943, but there was increased awareness and activism. These were both drawn upon as the campaign for civil rights matured after the War.

Native Americans

Native Americans played a significant part in the Second World War. Navajo soldiers, for example, used their own language as a radio code in the war in the Pacific. The Japanese were never able to decipher it.

In 1944 the National Congress of American Indians (NCAI) was formed. It intended to launch a series of legal cases to establish rights such as equal educational opportunity. However, the main aim of most Native Americans was to improve their standard of living and maintain their distinctive identity.

Japanese Americans

The war led to a direct attack on the civil rights of Japanese Americans, particularly on the west coast. Japanese assets on the US mainland were frozen, a curfew was imposed against them and in March 1942 over 100,000 Japanese Americans were interned in 'relocation camps'.

Hispanic Americans

During the war many Mexicans were encouraged to provide the US with cheap labour. They were not allowed to vote and they were denied basic civil rights. In addition to this, they were the victims of riots in Los Angeles.

Conclusion

The Second World War increased the awareness of civil rights issues for a number of groups. African American organisations were now using a 'combination of co-operation, coercion and confrontation when dealing with whites' (Sanders 2000) and the federal government was beginning to act in a way that benefited African Americans. The seeds had been sown for future civil rights developments.

 The beginnings of the civil rights movement, 1945–1960

After the war, many African American troops returned home looking for an end to segregation. The NAACP began challenging the 'separate but equal' doctrine of Plessy v. Ferguson, the number of African Americans registered to vote increased and a number of states adopted fair employment practices. President Truman set up the Committee on Civil Rights in 1946, which established civil rights as a moral issue and he ended discrimination in the US military.

However, Southern racism, the continuation of attacks by the Ku Klux Klan, anti-communist feeling and the issue of states' rights all restricted progress until Brown v. Board of Education (1954), the Montgomery Bus Boycott (1956) and Little Rock (1957).

In Brown v. Board of Education, Topeka, the Supreme Court led by Earl Warren found that African Americans should be given an equal educational chance and that segregation should end in schools. However, no time scale was set and nothing was done to set standards in schools. In addition to this, President Eisenhower failed to take any meaningful action to enforce the verdict and the Southern Manifesto was drafted to fight the judgement. Despite this, a legal precedent had been set and many places outside the Deep South began to integrate.

The Montgomery Bus Boycott began with the prosecution of Rosa Parks, who had refused to give up her bus seat for a white man. To coincide with her trial African Americans boycotted buses in Montgomery demanding a more polite service from the white bus drivers, the employment of black drivers and the end of black passengers standing when the bus was not full. When these demands were refused, the boycotters began to insist on total integration. As the protest continued and a legal and constitutional challenge took place, the Supreme Court eventually confirmed that bus segregation was unconstitutional (1956).

The boycott was significant because it showed the African American community could be encouraged to take action for themselves. It illustrated that solidarity and discipline were virtues that could lead to success and it was a sustained mass protest involving all sections of the black community. It introduced a new leader, Martin Luther King, a new organisation, the Southern Christian Leadership Conference (SCLC), and a new philosophy, non-violent protest. It drew the attention of the North to segregation in the South and it raised the question of federal response to segregation. In short, it was a vital event in the history of civil rights in America.

On 3 September 1957, nine African American students had attempted to take their places at Central High School, Little Rock, Arkansas. The governor of Arkansas ordered the National Guard to bar their way, as he had no intention of complying with the Brown v. Board of Education verdict. Eventually, Eisenhower intervened and used the National Guard to escort the children into school. They remained there for a year. This was significant because the President had used his federal authority to uphold the Brown verdict.

 ## Civil rights, 1960–1968

The year 1960 saw the launch of the Student Non-Violent Co-ordinating Committee (SNCC) and the revival of the Congress of Racial Equality. It also saw a dramatic increase in non-violent protest. On 1 February a sit-in took place in a branch of Woolworth's in Greensboro, North Carolina. It proved to be a successful way of protesting against segregation and it was imitated throughout the US. It also led to a shift in public opinion as television showed peaceful African American students being arrested by the police while the violent acts of white people opposed to the sit-ins were ignored by the police. Viewers could draw their own conclusions.

In 1961 CORE organised freedom rides with the intention of creating a crisis. A group of integrated passengers planned to take an interstate bus trip from the North to the South in order to test whether Southern states could impose segregation on interstate journeys. They hoped that if they were allowed to continue to travel together, then segregation would have received another blow. However, they also knew that if they were attacked then media attention would force the federal government to act. They got their wish in Birmingham, Alabama, where they were attacked and then interviewed. Following this, an injunction was brought against those who had been attacking the freedom riders. Federal Marshals were sent to Montgomery and Robert Kennedy, the US Attorney-General, organised the desegregation of all interstate travel.

Educational segregation was also challenged in Alabama, and also, most notably, by James Meredith in Mississippi. Protests led by Martin Luther King campaigned for desegregation in public places while also attempting to get more African American people to register to vote. However, more careful planning and coordination were still needed.

The campaigning, marches and speeches of 1963–5 saw the high point of the civil rights movement. Militant non-violent campaigns such as the ones in Birmingham and Selma, Alabama, were successful. The march on Washington emphasised the peaceful and multiracial nature of the movement, and the passing of civil rights legislation, such as the 1964 Civil Rights Act and the 1965 Voting Rights Act, also made it a time of tangible success. Two successive Presidents, John F. Kennedy and Lyndon B. Johnson, were regarded as being committed to the movement's aims and Martin Luther King's reputation was at its height. However, probably most importantly, public opinion was moving even further towards racial equality and the issue of civil rights in America had become an international news story.

By the close of 1965, though, there were clear signs of tension and division in the movement. The SNCC were becoming increasingly critical of Martin Luther King and

Figure 10.2 **Muhammad Ali addresses the Black Muslim Annual Convention, 1968**

the SCLC, and despite the political and legal gains made by some African Americans, many black people were concerned about the lack of social and economic reform that had taken place. In this climate the idea of Black Power and the views of Malcolm X became increasingly popular. As a result of this, and the riots that took place in the long hot summers of 1965, 1966 and 1967, some of the sympathy that the movement had gained from liberal whites and the federal government began to decline.

By the time of King's death in April 1968 the civil rights movement was weakened and divided. Segregation remained in public places in some parts of Mississippi, Alabama, Georgia and South Carolina, and black voter registration remained lower than white. However, more African Americans were registered to vote, segregation had largely disappeared in public places (with certain exceptions in parts of the Deep South), more transport systems and some schools were integrated, African Americans were rising to high office in many careers, 'Red Power' and 'Brown Power' had been inspired by the Black Power movement, and the principle of equal rights and opportunities had been accepted by the majority of the American public.

 ## American race relations, 1968–2001

With the death of Martin Luther King, the civil rights movement lost the sense of being a national movement. 'Jim Crow' had been destroyed but the problems of inner-city deprivation, drug abuse, rural poverty, job discrimination and segregated schools remained. These problems, which were shared with other groups, particularly Native Americans and Hispanic Americans, could only be tackled by increased participation in politics and federal intervention: Presidential policies and local activism were both vital in this period.

African American organisations such as the NAACP influenced politics in the US throughout the 1970s and 1980s, while the work of black politicians, such as Jesse Jackson, served as an example of how much progress had been made by African Americans in the field of politics. However, by 1992 African Americans were still suffering racism and discrimination. The tension that this caused manifested itself in the riots that erupted in South Central Los Angeles following the exoneration, by a white jury, of four white police officers who had been filmed beating an African American named Rodney King. The 55 deaths, 2,100 injuries and 9,000 arrests symbolised how much there was that still needed to be addressed in American society.

Clinton promoted many blacks to high office, but failed in his attempts to push through health legislation which would have helped ethnic groups, and by November 1999 there were, once again, no black senators in Congress. By the end of the 1990s, high schools were still holding segregated graduation parties, and there were nearly 800,000 black men in American prisons, compared with just over 600,000 in higher education. Calls for financial compensation for blacks for the years of slavery largely fell on deaf ears; and, in 1999, the killing of black West African immigrant Amadou Diallo by four police officers, who fired 41 bullets at him as he reached

Figure 10.3 **Black athletes giving the Black Power salute during the Olympic Games, 1968**

for his wallet, and the subsequent Bruce Springsteen song 'American Skin', showed that racial issues could still be explosive. At the 2000 Presidential election, 90 per cent of the black vote went to the Democrat candidate Al Gore, along with 62 per cent of the 'Latino' vote.

Conclusion

It can be seen, then, that despite over 100 years of struggle, civil rights remains a pertinent issue.

The gradual rise of the civil rights movement showed that American ideas of democracy and equality of opportunity could not be withheld by the traditional elite forever. Against huge odds, and with enormous courage, civil rights protesters did force the federal government to protect their right to vote and to be treated equally in the workplace and in education. However, deep-rooted attitudes have taken longer to change and African Americans and other minority groups in the United States still continue to encounter many economic and social problems in their everyday lives: only the consent of the traditional elite or a revolution can change this situation.

Part 2: Essays

 Reconstruction and after

1   What were the aims of Reconstruction and how far were they achieved? (20)

(AQA)

The Civil War, by its very nature, radically altered the United States. The loss of life, the destruction of property, the creation of resentment, the emancipation of the slaves, and the defeat of the South, all created the opportunity for further change. This change needed to be managed and Reconstruction is the term used to describe this process. It can be argued that the principal aim for all of those who were involved in Reconstruction was to manage the inevitable rebuilding of the United States that the Civil War had necessitated.

The war had been fought to preserve the Union, so the peace also needed to ensure this. However, it had also led to the emancipation of several million slaves and those involved in Reconstruction needed to consider how to deal with this situation. These were difficult issues and the possible approaches to Reconstruction as well as the specific aims of the individuals involved would be quite different.

Most Northern politicians wanted to restore the Union and ensure loyalty to the United States. They wanted the US to function as one political and economic force, to which all the individual states contributed. They also wanted to ensure that they would still be elected and so maintain their positions of power. These politicians therefore might alter their stance to suit the electorate they needed to appeal to.

Other politicians though might be more principled. The Radical Republicans were committed to securing the vote for freedmen while also punishing the former Confederate states for secession. They wanted to ban all ex-Confederates from politics and imprison all civil and military leaders. Men such as Thaddeus Stevens campaigned for the immediate extension of civil rights to African Americans and the work of Radical Republicans in Congress led to the establishment of the Freedmen's Bureau, the Civil Rights Act of 1866 and the 14th and 15th Amendments to the Constitution.

Moderate Republicans though were determined to limit the rights given to former slaves, and President Johnson even attempted to veto the Civil Rights Act. His aims were very different to those of the radical wing of his party. Johnson was willing to grant a pardon to almost all Southerners who were willing to swear an oath of allegiance to the Union. If they did this, and agreed to the ratification of the 13th

Amendment, they were allowed to vote and stand for election to the state assemblies. They were to have all their property, except slaves, restored to them and consequently many rich Southern plantation owners, politicians and army officers were able to maintain their positions of power. It can be seen, then, that Johnson's aim was to preserve the Union by refusing to further alienate the South. He certainly had little regard for ensuring that African Americans were granted their civil rights and he was also reluctant to seek retribution for secession. His attitude probably helped to preserve the Union but it did little to help former slaves.

Reconstruction did manage the change precipitated by the Civil War because it preserved the Union. However, although some former Confederates were punished and some gains were made by African Americans, these were both short-lived. Johnson pardoned approximately 13,000 former Confederates, he abandoned the intention to charge with treason and punish Southern politicians and army officers, he allowed rich planters to continue to hold office, and he failed to force newly elected state assemblies to ratify the 13th Amendment. He also allowed the state legislatures to introduce Black Codes, which denied African Americans the right to vote, serve on a jury, give evidence against a white person, carry arms or marry a white person.

Congress attempted to destroy the Black Codes through the Freedmen's Bureau, the Civil Rights Act of 1866 and the 14th and 15th Amendments but the gains these provided were soon eroded. The aim of allowing all freedmen the right to vote was never fully realised. There were a number of reasons for this: the lack of Presidential commitment to equality for African Americans; the avoidance of the implementation of the 14th and 15th Amendments to the Constitution; the way the Supreme Court upheld states' rights over those of the federal government; the development of sharecropping; and the violence and intimidation suffered by many African Americans at the hands of white racists, such as the Ku Klux Klan; these all contributed to the fact that African Americans did not made the social, economic and political gains Reconstruction could have provided.

In conclusion, the aims of Reconstruction depended upon individual circumstances: Radical Republicans wanted to punish the South and ensure that African Americans were given the right to vote and hold office; more moderate Republicans, including President Johnson, wanted to preserve the Union by giving African Americans *some* rights and by pardoning civil and military leaders from the South who appeared to be loyal to the United States; former slaves wanted to preserve their freedom and gain their civil rights, such as education for their children; and the Southern elite wanted to maintain their position of power.

How far these aims were achieved depended upon the expectations of the individuals involved. However, the high ideals of the Radical Republicans and the hopes of many African Americans were not fully realised in their lifetime. It would take a further hundred years of struggle before this was the case.

PRACTICE QUESTION

2 How much progress did African Americans make between 1865 and 1890? (20)

(AQA)

In order to assess the progress of blacks over the period 1865–90, it makes sense to break down the 25-year period into two sections in order to increase the scope for analysis. During Reconstruction up to 1877 the position of blacks changed in many ways, often for the better, but the following 13 years or so saw a gradual reduction in many of the gains made. In order to answer the question effectively, political (e.g. voting, office-holding), economic (e.g. land-owning, wages, types of jobs), social (e.g. education, family, churches, segregation) and legal factors (e.g. rights to marry, give evidence in court, serve on juries) should be taken into consideration, with evidence and statistics to back up points made.

African Americans and Native Americans

3   To what extent did the African American struggle for civil rights influence the campaign for civil rights for Native Americans? (60)

(OCR)

During the first half of the twentieth century, Native Americans were among the poorest and most neglected of all the people who lived in the United States. They had been deprived of vast areas of their lands and offered financial inducements to move into urban areas. Many white Americans regarded them as worthless and treated their culture with contempt, some attempted to educate them by sending their children away to boarding schools, and others attempted to convert them to Christianity. All these actions contributed to the destruction of their tribal bonds and led to many Native Americans enduring discrimination and racial abuse while also living in appalling urban conditions.

It was this situation that led to many of them joining the civil rights movement, and demanding compensation for the loss of their reservation land and also, among other things, demanding the right to be known as Native Americans. Their struggle can be seen as one that was both linked to and influenced by the African American campaign for civil rights.

The Dawes Act of 1887 had given Native Americans some rights of citizenship, including the protection of the law and the requirement to pay taxes. As a reward for their efforts during the First World War, their rights as citizens had been guaranteed in 1924. In addition to this, Hoover increased federal spending on Native Americans during the Depression and Roosevelt later looked to help them as part of the New Deal. In 1934 the Indian Reorganization Act was passed: it recognised and preserved traditional Native American culture and the right of the Native Americans to control their reservations. Loans were provided to encourage Native Americans to develop businesses and also to increase their educational opportunities. However, few prospered as independent farmers and even fewer were integrated into the mainstream of American society. Alcoholism and illiteracy were rife and many white Americans had a negative image based upon the 'cowboy and Indian' stereotype. Comparisons can be drawn with the situation that many African Americans found themselves in at this time. However, neither group had an organised campaign for civil rights until the Second World War.

Native Americans did have their own racial consciousness, and this can been seen by the Iroquois tribe independently declaring war on the Germans in 1942, but the campaigning of African Americans during the Second World War certainly influenced the actions of Native Americans. In 1944, Native Americans formed the National Congress of American Indians (NCAI). It intended to launch a series of legal cases to establish rights such as equal education opportunities. Its style of campaigning was obviously influenced by the National Association for the Advancement of Colored People (NAACP). This organisation had shown that Roosevelt would respond with positive action when he was put under pressure by organised groups such as this. The first real link between the campaigns of the Native Americans and African Americans for civil rights had now been made. During the 1950s and the 1960s the NCAI remained the main lobbying group for Native Americans. It recruited members from all tribes, in a similar way to how the NAACP had members from the North and South and from urban and rural areas; and women were well represented in both organisations. Many of its demands were peculiar to the needs of Native Americans but comparisons can be drawn with African American organisations as both groups concerned themselves with issues such as voter registration and better health and educational services.

The NCAI had made only limited progress with its campaigns concerning reservation issues, fishing rights and education by the mid-1960s, and some younger Native Americans became very critical of the organisation. Their criticisms were very similar to those of the younger African Americans who were impatient with the NAACP, and, in a move very reminiscent of the establishment of the Student Non-violent Co-ordinating Committee (SNCC), they established the National Indian Youth Council. The parallels between the two movements were now becoming more apparent.

In 1968, the Native Americans' equivalent of a sit-in, a fish-in, took place; and land was also recovered by legal action in New York and Massachusetts. However, many younger Native Americans were now moving to live in towns where, in common with African Americans, they continued to face poverty and discrimination. Disease, alcoholism and illiteracy were still all major problems and life expectancy, at 44 years, was 20 years lower than the US average. Suicide rates among the young were also well above the national average, and poor housing, unemployment and low pay all contributed to 300 Native Americans joining the Poor People's Campaign in 1968.

Black Power influences also became apparent by 1968. The establishment of the American Indian Movement (AIM) with its more militant 'Red Power' approach to their situation reflected this. The rejection of racial integration by Black Power was similar to Native American feelings about maintaining their distinctive lifestyle and a similar attitude towards the words 'Negro' and 'Indian,' which referred to the slave and colonial past were also apparent. At this time the terms African American and Native American began to be used.

However, many Native Americans, in common with some African Americans, disliked the new militancy, and divisions began to appear in their movement. Difficulties remained for both groups, although sympathetic legislation was passed throughout the 1970s. There was still little change in the traditional elite and it was still mainly white men with money who held power. At times when the US economy hit difficulties, it was still the minority groups, such as the African Americans and Native Americans, who suffered the most. Both groups had made gains but both African Americans and Native Americans still suffered hardship.

In conclusion, the African American struggle for civil rights certainly influenced the campaign for civil rights for Native Americans. However, the similarities in their movements owed more to the similarities of their situations than to one group leading the other in a certain way: both groups had to use whatever means were available to them in order to improve their situation. The ways in which they developed reflected the society in which they had to operate.

 ## Booker T. Washington and W.E.B. Du Bois

4   (a) Was Booker T. Washington's approach to civil rights ultimately more successful than that of William Du Bois? (30)

(b) How far did the methods advocated by Booker T. Washington and W.E.B. Du Bois regarding African American civil rights differ? (60)

(OCR)

(a) Washington's approach of 'accommodationism' is regarded by some historians as a success. He created Tuskegee Institute, founded the National Negro Business League, impressed many whites with his achievements and moderation, and won important recognition, if inconsistent support, from Presidents and other politicians. In addition to this, he had increased African American self-confidence by demonstrating that a former slave could become an internationally respected figure. He promoted black and white cooperation, yet campaigned secretly against segregation and disenfranchisement. Those who regard his approach as a success feel that he could have done little more at the time – the late nineteenth and early twentieth centuries – in the struggle for civil rights.

Du Bois' approach of vociferous campaigning has also been thought of as successful. He was prominent in establishing probably the most important African American organisation, the National Association for the Advancement of Colored people. He edited *The Crisis* which was read by thousands of Americans, both black and white, and he influenced the Harlem Renaissance. He never compromised by working too closely with white people and his actions and his philosophy certainly influenced the civil rights movement of the 1960s.

It can be agreed then that both men were successful, but it is usually Washington who is regarded as the more influential. This is because his approach was regarded as having more chance of consolidating African American gains in the United States. Du Bois' frequent changes of mind, his intellectual elitism, his associations with communism and his often unrealistic and uncompromising approach have led to his contribution being undervalued.

During the period 1900–15, however, when both Washington and Du Bois were active, the political will to address the issue of civil rights did not exist. The 'Black Codes' were still operational in the South and many Northern African Americans lived in poverty. Consequently, it could be argued that neither Washington nor Du Bois were ultimately successful.

(b) Both Booker T. Washington and W.E.B. Du Bois wanted equality for African Americans. They had worked together for the repeal of railroad segregation laws in Tennessee and for a New York Conference to discuss voting rights, but, as a result of their very different backgrounds, they advocated very different methods in order to achieve their aim.

Washington was a former slave who was put in charge of the Tuskegee Negro Normal Institute in Alabama in 1888. This school provided academic education but it concentrated most of its efforts on providing young African American boys with practical skills in areas such as farming and carpentry. It gained a national reputation and attracted the support of a number of white benefactors. He also founded the National Negro Business League to help support the setting up and running of African American businesses: it would appear that he was more interested in helping African Americans to show that they were responsible and reliable rather than achieving their political rights.

White politicians and businessmen approved of Washington's views. By developing practical skills and encouraging African Americans to gain respect, he seemed to be accepting segregation and the notion that black people were an inferior race who had no political role in the US.

His views were not this simplistic, but he certainly prepared to reassure and conciliate whites while quietly campaigning against segregation and discrimination through the law courts. He was a pragmatist who had to coexist with whites. He believed that African Americans would be given equality if they were peaceful, reasonable and made it apparent that they meant white people no harm. He wanted African Americans to concentrate on improving their economic position and appeared to favour 'separate but equal'. Washington was highly regarded by Presidents Theodore Roosevelt and William Taft but he was unable to use his influence to stop lynching or enable African Americans to exercise their right to vote. To his critics he was regarded as 'the greatest white man's nigger in the world', someone who was more interested in attracting money to his educational establishment rather than advancing the course of civil rights. He was dismissed as an 'Uncle Tom' who achieved very little.

Du Bois was probably Washington's most influential critic. He had been born a free man in the North, gained degrees from Harvard and Berlin and became a Professor of Sociology at Atlanta University. His elitist Northern African American background was very different to Washington's upbringing and helped to explain the differences in their methods.

Although he won the support of many liberal white people, Du Bois' approach was far more aggressive than Washington's. He demanded full civil rights, an end to segregation, the extension of the franchise and equality of opportunity in all aspects of life. He set up the Niagra Movement, which campaigned to gain the rights and freedoms white Americans enjoyed for all African Americans. He later joined the National Association for the Advancement of Colored People, and edited its magazine, *The Crisis*. He used this to campaign against lynching, 'Jim Crow' laws and sexual inequality. The magazine had a wide readership and helped in the campaigns against the racist film *Birth of a Nation*, and 'Grandfather' clauses that were used to disenfranchise African Americans in the South. He asserted that blacks were a chosen people with special cultural and spiritual strengths and he can be regarded as an inspiration to both the civil rights and Black Power movements of the 1960s.

It can be seen, then, that the methods employed by Washington and Du Bois were different. However, both were a response to the situations in which they found themselves. Washington's methods of 'accommodationism' was the result of the fact that he was a former slave from the South, whereas Du Bois' more radical approach was the direct consequence of his background. As a well-educated freeborn African American from the North his preconceptions were very different to those of Washington.

 Civil rights in the 1950s and 1960s

5 (a) What methods did Martin Luther King use in his civil rights campaigning? (15)

(b) How important was Martin Luther King in securing civil rights for African Americans in the period 1956–68? (15)

(Edexcel)

(a) After the Montgomery Bus Boycott had brought him to national prominence, King realised that he would need the help of experienced campaigners if full civil rights were to be achieved. So, with Bayard Rustin, who was black, and Stanley Levison, who was white, he set up the Southern Christian Leadership Conference (SCLC). It was a direct campaigning organisation, but as a result of their communist sympathies Rustin and Levison were unable to play a leading public part in its activities. Consequently, King was portrayed as the major player in its achievements.

King and the SCLC did not initiate the sit-ins and freedom rides of 1960–1. However, King was asked to address gatherings of students and he used the changing situation to develop the civil rights movement. King maintained non-violent protest as the mood of the country became more sympathetic to his aims, and this allowed him to keep the moral high ground and force a response from federal government in order to achieve a Civil Rights Act. Consequently, his actions were designed to achieve this aim and this led to criticism from others within the African American community.

One prominent critic was Malcolm X. He saw the white supporters of King's movement as hypocrites and the black leaders as deceived men. He was extremely critical of Martin Luther King and rejected the idea of integration. His ideas appealed to those who regarded King as a member of the African American elite and Malcolm X served as an inspiration to the Black Power movement, especially in the North. Many of those who accepted his views certainly had little regard for the influence of Martin Luther King.

(b) Martin Luther King is a controversial figure. His contemporaries and historians hold very different opinions about his importance to the civil rights movement. To some he was a communist who initiated violence and disorder in American cities, yet to others he was merely an '**Uncle Tom**'. Many admired him and felt that he was the most important figure in the civil rights movement. Others, such as Claybourne Carson, felt that the African American struggle would have developed in a similar way whether or not he had been a part of it. However, it is clear that his contribution to the civil rights movement cannot be ignored. From 1957–64, King had no major rival for overall leadership of the civil rights movement. He was a great orator who could communicate effectively with Southern blacks, Northern whites or the federal government when required to do so. He helped to keep civil rights on the political agenda and gave the movement status and respectability. In 1966 King attempted to enhance his reputation in the Northern ghettos by campaigning against poor housing and lack of employment opportunities in Chicago. However, his position was weakened as he appeared to be outmanoeuvred by Mayor Daley. This was compounded as white racists attacked African American demonstrators in larger numbers than had previously attacked black campaigners in the South. Additionally, King's lack of experience of African American life in the North was glaringly obvious. His reputation was further damaged when he denounced the Vietnam War in January 1967. He had now lost the support of many African Americans in the North, those who supported the ideals of Black Power, some moderate whites, the federal government and those who argued that only by working closely with the President and Congress would their aims be achieved. King was no longer the leader of a united movement.

However, it could be argued that he never had been. The civil rights movement had always had many factions and often King could be said to be one of those being led rather than the leader. Nonetheless, the results were frequently satisfactory to him. His involvement gained national and international attention and sometimes led to reform. At other times, though, his aims and methods were neither successful nor admirable. His patience was criticised by people such as Stokely Carmichael, and he managed to do too little in the view of 'Black Power' activists while many whites thought he was doing too much. He was a moderate leader with limited organisational skills, but he had a great ability to inspire others, and it can be argued that he made a significant contribution to the civil rights movement.

By the time of his death much had been achieved: segregation had been destroyed, African Americans were politically active and there was a greater self-confidence among black people in America. King's ability to inspire, his oratory skills and the media focus he brought to the movement all contributed to this. However, there were others who played important roles too.

There would have been no civil rights legislation without the political will to support it and the actions of Johnson's and Kennedy's governments were vitally important to the success of the movement. In addition to this, the actions of white extremists hardened public opinion against their stance and increased support for the civil rights movement. The actions of white extremists were reported in the media, which also played an important part in the success of the movement, hardening public opinion and increasing support. Television and newspapers showed the violence and racism of Southern whites and contrasted it with the peaceful protests of the African Americans. Audiences and readers were able to draw their own conclusions.

Many African Americans apart from King also played their part. Thousands of people educated others, protested and inspired. Organisations such as NAACP, CORE, SNCC and local churches all contributed to the struggle. Many famous, and not so famous, people helped to secure civil rights for African Americans in this period. Without their contribution, King would not have been able to achieve anything.

In conclusion, Martin Luther King was important in securing civil rights for African Americans in the period 1956–68 but he was fundamentally a figurehead. His actions were important as they brought media attention, government intervention, support from liberal whites, and direction to the actions of many African Americans, but without the contribution of a number of people and organisations African Americans would not have achieved their civil rights at this time. The movement rather than the individual was the most important factor.

PRACTICE QUESTION

6 (a) **Assess the significance of the Montgomery Bus Boycott in the campaign for civil rights.** (30)

   (b) **How important was the assassination of John F. Kennedy in securing civil rights for African Americans?** (60)

(OCR)

Advice: *Both parts of this question expect you to assess the importance of two key events during the campaign for civil rights. For Part (a), you will need to assess the importance of the Montgomery Bus Boycott from both strategic and psychological perspectives, in addition to measuring it against other events. For Part (b), you will also need to assess the significance of John F. Kennedy's assassination when compared with other events. For this question, it is important to consider the impact of the legislation that was passed in the wave of sympathy that accompanied Kennedy's death and how far changes to the law actually affected the lives of African Americans.*

Part 3: Sources

📖 1 Responses to Plessy v. Ferguson

■ **Source A: *Michigan Law Journal* (1896)**

In the Supreme Court of the United States was decided lately the case of Plessy v. Ferguson. In this case the question at issue was whether or not an act was constitutional which directed separate coaches and accommodations to be provided on railway trains for white people and colored people and which made a passenger liable to fine or imprisonment who insisted on occupying a coach or compartment other than the one set apart for his race. The act has been held constitutional and not contrary to the Constitution Amendment 14. The opinion is by Justice Brown and a distinction is made between laws interfering with the political equality of the two races and those requiring their separation in schools, theatres, etc. The opinion shows that acts under the second class have been in many cases held constitutional.

■ **Source B: Booker T. Washington: 'Who is Permanently Hurt?' (June 1896)**

The United States Supreme Court has recently handed down a decision declaring the separate coach law, or 'Jim Crow' car law constitutional. What does this mean? Simply that the separation of colored and white passengers as now practiced in certain Southern States, is lawful and constitutional. This separation may be good law, but it is not good common sense. The difference in the color of the skin is a matter for which nature is responsible. If the Supreme Court can say that it is lawful to compel all persons with black skins to ride in one car and all with white skins to ride in another, why may it not say that it is lawful to put all yellow people in one car and all white people, whose skin is sun burnt, in another car. Nature has given both their color; or why cannot the courts go further and decide that all men with bald heads must ride in one car and all with red hair still in another. Nature is responsible for all these conditions.

But the colored people do not complain so much of the separation, as of the fact that the accommodations, with almost no exceptions, are not equal, still the same price is charged the colored passengers as is charged the white people.

Now the point of all this article is not to make a complaint against the white man or the 'Jim Crow Car' law, but it is simply to say that such an unjust law inures the white man, and inconveniences the Negro. No race can wrong another race simply because it has the power to do so, without being permanently injured in morals, and its ideas of justice. The Negro can endure the temporary inconvenience, but the injury to the white man is permanent. It is the one who inflicts the wrong that is hurt, rather than the one on whom the wrong is inflicted. It is for the white man to save himself from this degradation that I plead.

If a white man steals a Negro's ballot, it is the white man who is permanently injured. Physical death comes to the Negro lynched – death of the morals – death of the soul – comes to the white man who perpetrates the lynching.

■ **Source C: Extract from the *New York Evening Journal* (May 1896)**

In justification of this law it is urged that while many colored people are less objectionable than many of the white race to first-class passengers, the majority of them are not only objectionable, but their presence in the same cars with the whites is a source of constant disorder. Hence it is simply a police regulation which any State has a perfect right to sanction. Of course, this decision does not interfere with the colored passengers' right to demand safe and comfortable accommodations, nor prevent them from suing for damages in the event of injury of person or loss of property.

■ **Source D: Extract from Charles W. Chesnutt's speech c.1911**

But to my mind the most important and far reaching decision of the Supreme Court upon the question of civil rights is that in the case of Plessy vs. Ferguson, a case which came up from Louisiana in 1895. The opinion is a clear and definite approval of the recognition by State laws, of color distinctions, something which had theretofore been avoided in civil rights cases. It establishes racial caste in the United States as firmly as though it were established by act of Congress. The Court cited the passage quoted by me from a former decision:

'The Fourteenth Amendment was ordained to secure equal rights to all persons, and extends its protection to races and classes, and prohibits any State legislation which has the effect of denying to any race or class, or to any individual, the equal protection of the laws, and made the rights of the two races exactly the same.'

And then the Court stabbed in the back, and to death, this ideal presentment of rights and threw its bleeding corpse to the Negro.

AQA QUESTION FORMAT

The questions and answers that follow are based on the revised AQA style.

(a) **Study Sources A and C and use your own knowledge. Account for the differences in the way in which the Plessy v. Ferguson decision was reported in the *Michigan Law Journal* and the *New York Evening Journal*.** (10)

(b) **Study Sources A, B, C and D and use your own knowledge. How significant was the Plessy v. Ferguson decision for African Americans?** (20)

(a) The *Michigan Law Journal* reports the Plessy v. Ferguson decision in a concise factual manner. It refers to the fact that both black and white people could be punished for 'occupying a coach or compartment other than the one set apart for his race' and it makes it clear that Justice Brown made a distinction between laws that prevented political equality and those that established segregation in public places. The *Michigan Law Journal* reports that an Act which directed separate coaches on railway trains was constitutional and that it did not contravene the 14th Amendment. The report does not pass any judgement on the decision.

The *New York Evening Journal* explains that the Plessy v. Ferguson decision was made because African American passengers were both objectionable to first-class passengers and that their presence would be 'a source of constant disorder'. This justification of the decision assumes that all first-class passengers were white and it implies that any disorder that resulted from allowing black and white passengers to travel together would be the fault of the African Americans. It reports that the judgement was 'simply a police regulation' which suggests that it was a perfectly logical decision. The journalist adds that any state had 'a perfect right to sanction' it. This is clearly an attempt to justify the decision as one that upheld the natural right of individual states of the Union to make judgements on matters such as this. The extract also upholds the 'separate but equal' notion by stating that the decision did not interfere with the rights of African Americans who chose to travel on the railway. The article is obviously an attempt to justify the decision.

The differences between the two articles stem from the fact that they were intended for different audiences. The readers of the *Michigan Law Journal* would have been educated people with an interest in law and who would have been expected to form their own opinions about the decision. The *New York Evening Journal* would have had a wider readership but they would still have been essentially white. Many of them would have been recent immigrants from Europe who would have seen African Americans as a threat to employment opportunities. The article would have been intended to appeal to their prejudices.

(b) On 18 May 1896 the United States Supreme Court ruled that a Louisiana law mandating 'separate but equal' accommodations for 'whites' and 'coloreds' on interstate railroads did not violate the constitutional rights of Homer Plessy, who, with one-eighth African blood, was a 'colored' person under state law. The Court's decision permitted a legal system of racial segregation in the US until the ruling of Brown v. Board of Education almost 60 years later.

The Plessy v. Ferguson decision is often regarded as the beginning of 'Jim Crow' but it came about because Plessy was continuing an existing struggle against segregation. Similar actions had preceded this protest and many more followed. Consequently, it should be seen as part of an existing struggle against 'separate but equal' that continued into the twentieth century. It should also be noted that the 1875 Civil Rights Act, which banned racial discrimination in public places and civil areas such as jury service, had effectively been nullified in 1883 by the Supreme Court on the grounds that it went further than the 14th Amendment (which aimed at stopping discrimination by states and not by individuals or private companies). In other words 'separate but equal' was already a fact of life by 1896, and 'Plessy' can simply be said to have reinforced the existing situation. However, Waldo Martin Jr has pointed out that 'Plessy' 'legitimized the culture of Jim Crow', and 'was the most widely cited precedent for the legality of Jim Crow' until it was overturned in 1954. The fact that the Court determined 'separate but equal' to be 'held constitutional' (Source A) therefore can be said to have influenced the lives of African Americans for over half a century.

Booker T. Washington in Source B acknowledges that 'the separation of . . . passengers as . . . practiced in certain Southern states' was lawful and constitutional. In other words it did not actually change anything in practice, although he anticipates that 'separate but equal' would in effect mean 'separate but unequal'. He argues that whites perpetrating such injustice would ultimately be the ones who were 'permanently injured'. The next 50 years would suggest that his assessment was overly optimistic, but this moral argument against Plessy would form part of the basis for the civil rights movement in the latter part of the twentieth century. The *New York Evening Journal* in Source C naively implies that 'separate but equal' will not affect the facilities blacks will have by suggesting that it did not 'interefere with the colored passengers' right to demand safe and comfortable accommodations'. These arguments were used for almost a hundred years so both Sources highlight the long-term impact of the decision.

Finally, in Source D, Chesnutt confirms that it was the first time that the Jim Crow laws had been recognised and legitimised by this branch of the federal government. He feels Plessy undermined completely the 14th Amendment, saying the idea of equality had been 'stabbed in the back, and to death' and left to the Negro to deal with. He clearly believes that 'Plessy v. Ferguson' was 'the most important and far-reaching decision of the Supreme Court upon the question of civil rights'. To him it was this decision that firmly established the 'racial caste' that African Americans would have to fight to overcome throughout the twentieth century.

Plessy v. Ferguson was certainly a very important decision in the struggle for civil rights, and shaped that struggle for the next 50 years or so. It also played a part in the formation of the NAACP in 1909.

ADDITIONAL QUESTIONS IN THE AQA STYLE

(a) **Study Source C and use your own knowledge. How useful is Source C in showing the 'white reaction' to Plessy?** (10)

(b) **Study all the Sources and use your own knowledge. Account for the different reactions to Plessy v. Ferguson.** (20)

2 Responses to Brown v. Board of Education

■ **Source A: *Post and Times Herald* (Washington DC), 'Emancipation' (18 May 1954)**

The Supreme Court's resolution yesterday of the school segregation cases affords all Americans an occasion for pride and gratification. The decision will prove, we are sure – whatever transient difficulties it may create and whatever irritations it may arouse – a profoundly healthy and healing one. It will serve – and speedily – to close an ancient wound too long allowed to fester. It will bring to an end a painful disparity between American principles and American practices. It will help to refurbish American prestige in a world which looks to this land for moral inspiration and restore the faith of Americans themselves in their own great values and traditions.

■ **Source B: *Daily News* (Jackson, Mississippi), 'Bloodstains on White Marble Steps' (18 May 1954)**

. . . Human blood may stain Southern soil in many places because of this decision but the dark red stains of that blood will be on the marble steps of the United States Supreme Court building.

White and Negro children in the same schools will lead to miscegenation. Miscegenation leads to mixed marriages and mixed marriages lead to mongrelization of the human race.

■ **Source C: *Herald* (Boston), 'Equality Redefined' (18 May 1954)**

The Supreme Court's history-making decision against racial segregation in the public schools proves more than anything else that the Constitution is still a live and growing document.

. . . The segregation ruling is frankly expedient. It recognizes the growing national feeling that the separation of Negro (or other minority) children from the majority race at school age is an abuse of the democratic process and the democratic principle. But it is also the culmination of a series of judicial opinions which circumspectly prepared the way for change.

■ **Source D: *Times* (Los Angeles), 'The Segregation Decision' (19 May 1954)**

. . . We may be sure that the present decision on segregation is not going to lead to civil war, but we may be almost as certain that it will provoke a social and political revolution. Yet it is hard at this point to see how the court could have come to any other conclusion.

Enforcement of the decision looms as a tremendous problem for the court. Apparently it will require pressure on, or coercion of, virtually the whole white populations of the States where segregation has been law and custom.

. . . The confusion of change in some areas could work to the disadvantage of at least one school genera-tion, Negro and white, unless mutual restraint and understanding are joined in resolving the issue.

AQA QUESTION FORMAT

The questions and answers that follow are based on the AQA style.

(a) **Study Sources B and C and use your own knowledge. Account for the differences in the way in which the Brown v. Board of Education decision was reported in the *Daily News* and the *Boston Herald*?** (10)

(b) **Study all the Sources and use your own knowledge. How significant was the Brown v. Board of Education decision for African Americans?** (20)

(a) The *Daily News* is a Mississippi newspaper. In other words, it might be expected to reflect the predom-inant views held by people in the 'Deep South' where segregation was a way of life. The apocalyptic terms used in the article such as 'human blood may stain Southern soil . . . because of this decision' reflect deep opposition to the Brown decision, in suggesting that violence may result. The fear of white and black mixing together is also overtly reflected in such racist comments as 'mixed marriages lead to mongrelization of the human race'. The *Boston Herald* appears to be more supportive of the Brown decision and as it is a New England newspaper this is not in itself surprising, but in actual fact the wording of the article tends to focus more on the 'growing national feeling' against segregation and the ruling being 'expedient' rather than actually praising the judgement on its merits. The Source also suggests that the decision was not entirely unexpected given the context of a 'culmination of a series of judicial opinions which circumspectly prepared the way for change'.

(b) The most important short-term consequence of Brown was probably the momentum it gave to the civil rights movement in the 1950s and 1960s and to Black Power. The decision applied specifically to ending segregation in education but it implied that segregation in any form was illegal. Within a year of Brown more than 500 school districts in the North and Upper South desegregated. Conservatives tended to see Brown as a restriction of states' rights by the federal government, while 'blacks and their progressive allies', according to Martin have seen the decision as a 'necessary step towards squaring America's treatment of blacks within the American creed: a simple matter of justice and morality'. Brown struck a great blow for equality, despite Eisenhower's opposition to it, and his reluctance to use federal power to enforce desegregation until Little Rock. The Brown judgement failed to set target dates for the implementation of desegregation, and even Brown II set no dates, which in part encouraged the setting up of White Citizens Councils particularly in the Deep South to oppose desegregation. So although Brown ended school segregation in theory, in practice it was less effective, particularly in certain parts of the country. The *Los Angeles Times* in Source D may have been slightly premature in hailing 'a social and political revolution' but does anticipate the problems of coercing 'virtually the whole white popula-tions' of Southern states. The *Washington Post* (Source A) takes a very positive approach regarding the judgement in describing it as 'an occasion for pride and gratification' and essentially sums up the views of black Americans. It is perhaps overly optimistic in its discussion of only 'transient difficulties' on the road to healing wounds, particularly given that separate white and black colleges and universities still exist in Southern states today. The *Daily News'* vision of 'blood . . . on the marble steps' (Source B) in a sense anticipated the violence to come, exaggerated the impact desegregation would have in practice, but in many ways reflected the views of those such as Herman Talmadge, the governor of Georgia, who said that his state would 'not tolerate the mixing of the races in the public schools', and effectively encouraged the terror campaigns of the Ku Klux Klan. The *Boston Herald* (Source C) sees the decision as bolstering 'the democratic process . . . and principle'. At elementary and secondary schools, desegregation in the South appears to have worked relatively well. In 1964, 98 per cent of blacks in the South were still attending segregated schools, but by 1997 only 33 per cent were. Ironically by the 1990s, most racially segregated schools appeared to be in the North and West. The Brown ruling gave great heart to the civil rights movement, and, in the short term, forced the federal government to take action to enforce desegregation, but in practice has perhaps proved to be less important in terms of school segregation, than it has as a symbol of justice and equality for blacks.

ADDITIONAL QUESTIONS IN THE AQA STYLE

(a) Use Source B and your own knowledge. How useful is Source B as a reflection of white opinion towards Brown? (10)

(b) Use all the Sources and your own knowledge. Account for the different reactions to the Brown decision. (20)

Part 4: Historical skills

 1 Role play: a television debate on whether to make Martin Luther King's birthday a national holiday in the US

The aims of this activity are to allow you to develop your research, listening and public speaking skills. You will also be given the opportunity to assess the wide-ranging opinions on the importance of Martin Luther King.

The year is 1981. Stevie Wonder has just had a hit single with 'Happy Birthday' a song requesting that King's birthday becomes a national holiday and there has been a great deal of coverage about this issue in the media. Each of you should represent one of the characters from the list below. How you decide who is allocated which character is up to you. You should think about your character's opinion of King and what you think about the advantages and disadvantages of making his birthday a national holiday. You should prepare a brief talk which expresses your views and deals with any points you think might be raised by people with different ideas to your own. After each of you has had your say, there should be time for a general discussion. You should also be prepared to take questions from people who have observed your discussion.

The people who should be represented at your debate are:

1   a white Southern Democratic congressman who was elected as a result of the African American vote;
2   a former NAACP activist who had been on the March on Washington;
3   a Republican congressman who is not reliant on the African American vote;
4   a poor African American agricultural labourer from South Carolina;
5   a young African American male from the west coast;
6   a poor white female from Georgia;
7   a well educated secret member of the Ku Klux Klan;
8   an African American Muslim;
9   a white Protestant clergyman from Boston;

10   an African American television executive from New York;
11   a white 'liberal';
12   a Native American who had been part of the 'Red Power' movement.

After the debate write a report in which you summarise the arguments and highlight the conclusions reached.

 2 Using numbers: analysis of the average income of persons with earned income, by race and sex

It is always useful to be able to use numbers and statistics and to show that you understand the different ways in which numerical information can be deployed.

Use the figures opposite to complete the following tasks.

1   What is the average wage for each group in the period 1967–91?
2   What does this lead you to believe?
3   Construct a graph to show all the information contained in the table.
4   What conclusions can you draw from you graph?
5   How useful are these figures in assessing the impact of the civil rights movement on the lives of African Americans in the US?

 3 Mind maps

Many students find the construction of mind maps a helpful way to revise and to plan essay answers. Choose any person whom you have read about in this chapter and write their name in the middle of a sheet of paper. Then add, leading into their name, any events or people who influenced them. Then add, leading from their name, any events or people that they influenced. Look for connections between all the people and events that you write down.

 4 Hot seating: assuming a role and answering questions

Each student is given or selects the name of one person covered in this chapter. The student then carries out extra research on their chosen person. The others in the group plan questions to ask the student in the 'hot seat' once they have completed their research. When they are ready they sit at the front of the class and assume the persona of the person they have researched. The others in the group then ask them questions in the style of a formal question-and-answer session. The person in the 'hot seat' should remain in character throughout the activity.

   Alternatively, each student could assume the role of an expert on a particular topic, issue or period studied in this chapter. They should carry out extra research on their chosen area and the others in the group should ask them questions when they are in the 'hot seat'.

   This is a particularly useful exercise for deepening knowledge and understanding of a particular person, topic, issue or period.

	Average income of persons with earned income, by race and sex (1991)					
	Male			Female		
	Black ($)	White ($)	B/W (%)	Black ($)	White ($)	B/W (%)
1991	12,962	21,395	60.6	8,816	10,721	82.2
1990	13,409	22,061	60.8	8,678	10,751	80.7
1989	13,850	22,916	60.4	8,650	10,777	80.3
1988	13,866	22,979	60.3	8,461	10,480	80.7
1987	13,449	22,666	59.3	8,331	10,199	81.7
1986	13,630	22,443	59.9	8,160	9,643	84.6
1985	13,630	21,659	62.9	7,945	9,312	85.3
1984	12,385	21,586	57.4	8,080	9,109	88.7
1983	12,335	21,092	58.5	7,615	8,912	85.4
1982	12,591	21,011	59.9	7,498	8,501	88.2
1981	12,851	21,611	59.5	7,412	8,343	88.8
1980	13,254	22,057	60.1	7,580	8,187	92.6
1979	14,019	22,648	61.9	7,358	8,085	91.0
1978	13,844	23,110	59.9	7,480	8,307	90.0
1977	13,560	22,850	59.3	7,446	8,622	86.4
1976	13,719	22,785	60.2	7,791	8,268	94.2
1975	13,475	22,538	59.8	7,530	8,288	90.9
1974	14,397	23,235	62.0	7,385	8,180	90.3
1973	14,754	24,392	60.5	7,352	8,146	90.3
1972	14,519	23,970	60.6	7,497	8,025	93.4
1971	13,639	22,870	59.6	6,778	7,736	87.6
1970	13,709	23,121	59.3	6,803	7,473	91.0
1969	13,603	23,386	58.2	6,361	7,543	84.3
1968	13,432	22,641	59.3	5,957	7,511	79.3
1968	12,554	21,935	57.2	5,478	6,960	78.7

Sources and references

Peter Carroll and David Noble, *The Free and the Unfree*, Penguin (1989).

W.E.B. Du Bois, *The Souls of Black Folk*, Bedford Books (1997).

Waldo E. Martin Jr, *Brown v. Board of Education*, Bedford/St Martin's (1998).

David Paterson, Susan Willoughby and Doug Willoughby, *Civil Rights in the USA 1863–1980*, Heinemann (2001).

Vivienne Sanders, *Race Relations in the USA since 1900*, Hodder & Stoughton (2000).

Brook Thomas, *Plessy v. Ferguson – A Brief History With Documents*, Bedford Books (1997).

Chapter 11

Domestic Policy from Kennedy to Bush, 1961–2001

This chapter examines the changing role of the federal government in political, economic and social affairs since 1961.

 ## Historical background

The Democrats' 'New Frontier' and 'Great Society'
The zenith of Presidential imperialism
A resurgent Congress and a humbler Presidency
The triumph of style over substance
'It's the economy, Stupid'
The return of the right

 ## Essays

The aims and impact of the 'New Frontier'
Explaining the legislative impact of Lyndon Johnson

The causes and consequences of Watergate
The problems that beset Gerald Ford
Was Jimmy Carter a Presidential failure?
The style and substance of President Reagan
The domestic failure of George Bush
Trends in the balance of power, 1960–1992

 ## Historical skills

1 Extracts from Ronald Reagan's speeches
2 Research questions on domestic issues, 1960–1992

Chronology

1961	January	Inauguration of John F. Kennedy
1962	April	Battle with US Steel
1963	November	Assassination of JFK and swearing in of Lyndon Johnson
1964		Launch of the 'Great Society'
	November	Election of President Johnson
1968		Assassinations of Martin Luther King and Robert Kennedy
		Nixon victory in Presidential elections
1972		Beginning of the Watergate scandal
1973		Gerald Ford replaced Spiro Agnew as Vice-President
1974	August	Resignation of Richard Nixon and accession of Ford
1977	January	Jimmy Carter became 39th President
1978	September	Camp David peace summit
1979	November	Beginning of hostage crisis in Tehran
	December	Soviet invasion of Afghanistan
1980	April	Hostage rescue attempt
	June	Energy Security Act
1981	January	Inauguration of Ronald Reagan
		Freeing of American hostages
		Economic Recovery Tax Act
		Omnibus Budget and Reconstruction Act
1984		Defeat of Walter Mondale
1987		Iran-Contra hearings
1989		George Bush inaugurated
1992		Race riots in Los Angeles
	November	Bush defeated by Democrat Bill Clinton
1994		Republicans gained control of Congress
1995		Temporary shutdown of federal government
1999		Clinton survived impeachment hearings before the Senate
2000		Controversial election victory of George W. Bush

Part 1: Historical background

 ## The Democrats' 'New Frontier' and 'Great Society'

The Cold War was to dominate US foreign policy from the end of the Second World War until the collapse of the Soviet Union. During this era the battle between capitalism and communism often overshadowed and affected events at home. However, domestic history throughout this period is an area rich in issues, events, ideologies and personalities, an examination of which not only sheds light upon the present-day United States, but also gives a greater insight into the twentieth century's great ideological struggle and America's ultimate victory.

For America, the 1950s was a time of consumer and cultural confidence, and self-contentment. But during the latter years of the Eisenhower Presidency, the US experienced a period of introspection and alarm as a generation of young people registered their discontentment with mainstream culture and

Figure 11.1

John F. Kennedy with Soviet leader Nikita Khrushchev in Vienna, 1961

the Soviet Union seemingly moved ahead in areas of technology. This national sense of drift was to define the elections of 1960 when the incumbent Vice-President, Richard Nixon, faced John F. Kennedy in the battle for the White House.

Kennedy was a young senator from Massachusetts who belonged to a wealthy and politically powerful family. He was also a Catholic, an issue that he succinctly neutralised in the Presidential campaign by simply asking whether the fact that he was baptised should automatically exclude him from being given the opportunity to serve as President. Kennedy's energy and charisma, coupled with the shrewd political awareness of his team and himself, saw him win the nomination of the Democratic Party over a more powerful senator, Lyndon Baines Johnson of Texas. Kennedy strengthened his hand by inviting Johnson to join with him, thus presenting a more appealing ticket of the young, Catholic Northerner combined with a more established, Protestant Southerner.

He focused his campaign on getting the country moving again, calling for a new sense of national purpose to meet the challenges that lay ahead. He claimed America was standing on the edge of a 'New Frontier' and presented himself as the person to take the nation forward. By shaping the agenda in such a way, he was able to use his relative youth to his advantage. The difference between the candidates was especially stark during televised debates when a rather gaunt Nixon appeared unfavourably alongside the vigour and charm of the young challenger. It is illustrative of the impact of television upon politics that Nixon was deemed to have won the live debates by radio audiences. In November 1960, Kennedy defeated Nixon by the narrowest of margins, owing his victory to a superbly run campaign and, so some have claimed, electoral manipulation by his father and the Mafia.

The new President delivered an eloquent and inspirational inaugural address that signalled the torch had been passed on to a new generation. The speech alluded overwhelmingly to foreign affairs and the Cold War in particular with little attention being devoted to domestic matters. This stood somewhat at odds with his acceptance speech in which he had spoken of the New Frontier, though it is for his role as foreign policy leader that he is best remembered. On social policy, Kennedy showed himself to be sympathetic yet cautious on civil rights, but committed to improving education and reducing poverty. Regarding the economy, he actively courted the support of the business community and has been described by economists Seymour Harris and Walter Heller as the first modern economist in the American Presidency. Domestically JFK is commonly judged to have achieved only a rather modest amount of success during his 2 years and 10 months in office. As the first President to be born in the twentieth century, Kennedy and his glamorous wife ushered in a new era in Washington that is often referred to as 'Camelot'. He was looking ahead to a more productive second term having laid the groundwork in the three years since his election. Following his assassination in November 1963, it was left to his successor to capitalise on the genuine wave of sympathy, and attempt to realise the vision that Kennedy had laid out.

Fortunately for America, the man whom Kennedy had asked to be his running mate was considered to be a capable and suitable replacement. Vice-President Lyndon Baines Johnson was sworn in while aboard Air Force One as it left Dallas on 22 November 1963. The Texan had entered politics after being inspired by Franklin Roosevelt's New Deal of the 1930s. He had served in the House of Representatives before moving to the Senate, where he held the position of Majority Leader throughout the 1950s. In stark contrast with his predecessor, he had a modest background and a crude, sometimes threatening style as he twisted arms to get measures through Congress.

His undoubted political skills, coupled with the nation's grief, enabled Johnson not only to realise some of JFK's initiatives, but also to go further and leave his own mark, the 'Great Society'. The mid-1960s was a period of intense legislating and investment in social programmes that rivalled, and some would say surpassed, the New Deal. President Johnson's first State of the Union address in January 1964 left no one in any doubt as to what his priorities were when he launched 'an unconditional war on poverty in America'. The ensuing Economic Opportunity Act led to the establishment of a range of initiatives, from the launching of a domestic version of the Peace Corps and work training programmes to giving loans to rural and small businesses. He then pushed through a more ambitious Civil Rights Bill than the one to which Kennedy had finally committed himself, before winning the White House in his own right in November 1964.

The elections were a crushing defeat for the Republicans. Arizona senator Barry Goldwater ran a very conservative campaign, criticising civil rights measures and other liberal legislation as an attack on individual rights while suggesting that Johnson was timid in foreign affairs and that the use of nuclear weapons was not all that bad an idea. Johnson won an impressive 61 per cent of the popular vote and was able to claim a clear mandate for his own programme, the Great Society.

Johnson's aim was to give people a 'hand-up' (as opposed to 'hand-out') in helping themselves out of poverty. Medical cover for the elderly and low-waged was guaranteed by the state and the introduction of the Food Stamp programme aimed to reduce malnutrition. Houses were built, cities were remodelled and local citizens were encouraged to participate in community-based projects. Federal aid was provided to elementary and secondary schools and pre-school was promoted through the 'Head Start' programme.

Economic growth helped fund this massive increase in government spending, but America's ever increasing involvement in Vietnam and the economic problems of the late 1960s took their toll on the Great Society as well as the President himself. Millions had been helped out of poverty but America was gripped by a sense of disillusionment. Civil rights riots, student protests, anti-war campaigns and a burgeoning counter-culture provided the backdrop to the latter half of the 1960s. President Johnson looked on bewildered by what he saw and taken aback by the apparent ingratitude of the people he had served for so long and so well.

He retreated inside the White House, showed signs of paranoia and even quit drinking, much to the concern of his aides. But he could not escape as crowds outside the White House constantly chanted: 'Hey, hey LBJ. How many kids did you kill today?'. His nerves frayed, particularly by Vietnam, Johnson chose not to stand for re-election in 1968. His Presidency was bookended by the assassinations of John Kennedy and Robert Kennedy, the latter being slain during the ensuing Democratic primaries. It was a tragic start and end to a Presidential career that had accomplished a considerable amount. Scholars have since tended to concentrate on Johnson's unique style and on the social tensions that opened up over civil rights and Vietnam to the detriment of his actual achievements.

 The zenith of Presidential imperialism

The elections of 1968 saw the Republicans gain control of the White House. Richard Nixon had been Vice-President under Eisenhower in the 1950s before withdrawing from political life following defeats in the

Presidential election of 1960 and the 1962 California gubernatorial election. During the mid-1960s Vietnam, social unrest and economic difficulties had strained the relationship between the people and the Presidency. Trust became an important factor as the people sought a President who would act more in accordance with their wishes. Nixon represented a link with more peaceful and prosperous times and seemed to be the person most able to capitalise on the Democrats' problems and the nation's worries. He narrowly defeated Democrat Hubert Humphrey in a race that saw the right-wing governor of Alabama, George Wallace, carry five states in the Deep South. The year 1968 had been a tortuous one for America and it now looked forward to a period of normalcy.

Nixon's major objectives were to bring 'peace with honour' in Vietnam and to reduce the role of the federal government at home. The economy did not perform well as the war dragged on and the Democratic-controlled Congress continued to spend. The price of oil multiplied due to problems in the Middle East and this had a significant impact domestically. Both unemployment and inflation rose and, furthermore, the US was now running a trade deficit. Nixon was to find more success with social policy. The President's preference for promoting local solutions to problems bore fruit in education where the swift reduction in segregated schooling was startling. Women's rights were advanced by the 1972 Equal Rights Amendment and the 1973 Supreme Court decision in Roe v. Wade, which safeguarded the right to a safe and legal abortion.

Facing a Democratic Congress that was prepared to override his veto, Nixon became more active on foreign policy. He pursued a policy of gradual withdrawal from Vietnam, which would give South Vietnam time to learn to rely upon itself. But several high-profile military ventures, such as incursions into Cambodia and Laos and an escalation in the use of air power early in 1972 gave the impression of an expansion of US involvement. To the public this was a clear transgression of campaign pledges and Nixon faced protests similar to those that had plagued his predecessor. In May 1970 campus riots left four dead in Ohio and Nixon showed his insensitivity by later denouncing young radicals as 'bums'.

Nixon was comfortably re-elected in 1972 but was forced to resign midway through his second term because of the Watergate scandal. He had faced George McGovern of the Democrats, who ran a liberal campaign encompassing an anti-war stance that Nixon had found easy to portray as a sign of weakness. But the victory had left behind the seeds of his own destruction, as a group of men, who had been detained while attempting to place surveillance equipment inside the headquarters of the Democratic Party (in the Watergate building in Washington DC), were brought to trial. In the ensuing investigations it became apparent that a trail of dirty tricks led directly to the White House. Nixon resigned on 9 August 1974 knowing that he would not survive impeachment hearings. His incumbency had resulted in a considerable easing in Cold War tensions but his greatest legacy was the destruction of the already shaken faith that the American people had in the office of President.

 ## A resurgent Congress and a humbler Presidency

Nixon's original Vice-President, Spiro Agnew, had been forced to resign after revelations of tax fraud and the Republican Congressional leader Gerald Ford had taken his place. Now the competent mid-westerner found himself in the White House although he had never stood for national office. His short administration was hindered by his pardoning of Richard Nixon and an eagerly assertive Congress and media. Ford managed to halt the decline of the Presidency in the eyes of the people as he adopted a humbler approach than the apparent imperialism of the Johnson and Nixon years, but he was rejected by the electorate in 1976.

Jimmy Carter was to continue the redemption of the White House that Ford had begun. Like his predecessor, Carter knew that America was in no mood for a slick politician as President, so he toned down the ceremony of the office and introduced a more frugal administration. The **imperial Presidency** was dead and finally a line could be drawn under the trauma of the previous ten years. Carter was an uncharismatic President who eschewed the backslapping and vote trading of Washington DC. The former farmer-turned-

Figure 11.2 **Elvis Presley with President Richard Nixon, 1971**

governor of Georgia instead brought with him a moral and ethical style that helped restore the people's faith in their leader.

He found success in foreign affairs, continuing the thaw in the Cold War and brokering peace at Camp David between the Egyptians and Israelis. Domestically he is recalled for his mishandling of Congress because of his reluctance to play the game in the way Washington was accustomed to. Though thwarted on tax and welfare reform and seeing his energy proposals blocked and amended, he nevertheless enjoyed a remarkably high and consistent success rate with a Democratic, though less controllable Congress.

The economy did not fare particularly well under Carter. The oil crisis of the 1970s fuelled inflation and interest rates and it transpired that there was little the White House could do to ease the situation. But Carter managed to reduce the federal budget deficit in the face of Democratic spending expectations and cut the domestic consumption of oil. Advancing the environment as a political issue and overcoming racial discrimination appeared almost as dear to him as running a tight ship. But his White House was not immune to controversy. The Director of the Office of Management and Budget, Bert Lance, was investigated for improper conduct in his previous career and the President's brother's business links with the Libyan government were scrutinised, thus staining the ethical image that the Carter administration strove to project. Feuds among his staff were not unheard of and he once felt compelled to sack half his cabinet.

Carter can be portrayed as a bungler who reacted to events rather than shaped them. An ongoing hostage crisis at the American embassy in Iran took its toll and the people rejected him after only one term. Alternatively, however, it might be said that his Presidency was good for America in the long term, and that Carter was a victim of his own success. By 1980 Carter's fireside chats and low-key administration seemed old and the people grew tired of the humbler Presidency. Their faith in the office largely restored, they were once more ready to accept a stronger more traditional type of leader to steer them through domestic and international waters.

The 1970s had not been a successful decade for America. The oil shock, Watergate, the losing of the Vietnam War, the hostage crisis and the Soviet invasion of Afghanistan had all had a detrimental effect on the American economy, political system and society. The nation had been made to realise that there were limits to its power internationally and domestically. These limitations were echoed in the Presidency, where an emboldened Congress, a more intrusive media and a jaded public had brought the executive branch of government to heel.

 ## The triumph of style over substance

But the 1980s was a new and different decade. America was ready for a change and the New Right seized its opportunity in the 1980 Presidential elections. Ronald Reagan, a former B-movie actor who had become governor of California, won a landslide victory in the electoral college in November 1980. His undoubted communication skills and ease in front of the cameras were used to full effect in putting across his simple black-and-white choices to America. Reagan entered the White House with a bold agenda and strong team around him. His Presidency was characterised by reductions in taxation, welfare programmes and the role of the federal government. Concurrently defence spending and the federal budget deficit rocketed.

Reagan became the first President since Eisenhower to serve a full two terms in office. His masterful 1984 re-election campaign proclaimed that it was 'Morning in America' and more good times were on the way. He easily defeated the Democrat challenger, Walter Mondale, carrying all but one of the fifty states. But Reagan's second term did not live up to the promise laid out by the hugely popular and seemingly invincible 'Great Communicator'. Those around him, such as Chief of Staff, Donald Regan, were vying for power and creating intrigue, and the National Security Adviser, John Poindexter, authorised an illegal triangle of selling arms to the Iranians in return for their influence in the Middle East, with the funds from the arms deals being covertly directed towards Nicaraguan rebels.

Following a recession in 1982 and 1983 the economy appeared to benefit from Reagan's policies. When coupled with the restoration of national pride following an incursion into Grenada and the successful Los Angeles Olympic Games, his re-election was a foregone conclusion. But by 1987, the economy was in trouble again, entering a period that saw the sharpest falls on Wall Street since the 1930s. A staggering tenfold increase in the national debt resulted in the haemorrhaging of tax dollars to pay the interest alone – and a strong dollar had led to rising interest rates and a fivefold increase in America's trade deficit. It would all have seemed terribly familiar to Reagan had he possessed the intellectual curiosity to engage in an analysis of the state of the nation. He had come to Washington on the back of Carter's supposed poor economic record and problems with Iran and now he too was in a not-dissimilar situation. The redeeming factor of Reagan's two-term Presidency was the final thawing of the Cold War, which followed his colossal arms build-up and the coming to power of Mikhail Gorbachev in the Soviet Union.

'It's the economy, Stupid'

Ronald Reagan was always going to be a hard act to follow. He had been an incredibly popular President with much of his appeal coming from his charm and a never-ending supply of folksy anecdotes and sound bites. But his deputy and successor, George Bush, lacked the charisma that had served Reagan so well. Foreign policy was to the fore of the Bush administration, which was not altogether surprising given that he had served as the senior American representative to the UN under Nixon and Director of the CIA under Ford. His one term in the White House from 1989 to 1993 oversaw the end of the Cold War and the expulsion of Iraq from Kuwait. Issues at home held less appeal and he failed to produce any major initiatives of his own. During the 1988 elections Bush had defeated an equally uninspiring Democratic challenger, Michael Dukakis, with a promise of a 'kinder, gentler America', which was taken to mean a more socially aware continuation of Reagan's policies. He had also promised not to raise taxes but found himself unable to deliver on both accounts.

Though strong and successful on the international stage, Bush proved to be ineffective on domestic policy. There were reforms concerning pollution, banking and an increase in the minimum wage, but his initiatives fell far short of addressing America's increasing economic and social problems. With Congress in the hands of the Democrats, it is understandable why Bush sought to make his mark on foreign policy but it was on domestic issues that action was required. Ultimately it was the economy more than any other factor that undermined his credibility and led to his eventual defeat. In 1991, with America in the middle of a depression, Bush realised that the federal budget deficit had to be reduced and so he raised taxes and cut back on government spending. There was an absence of any feel good factor under Bush: the economy was out of sorts and the President was not able to fill the void with illusions the way Reagan had. The gulf between the American Dream and stark reality had grown too wide and by 1992 the people were ready to endorse a Democrat candidate who promised to tackle the social and economic problems that had been avoided for too long.

It is probably too soon to comment on how history will judge the Clinton years. His stewardship of the economy was indisputably a success with most commentators highlighting the huge budget surplus and years of growth during his two terms in office. Spending on social programmes such as Medicare and educational benefits were increased in keeping with campaign pledges, however the administration failed to deliver on promises of a national heath insurance scheme during the first term. Throughout his Presidency Clinton was dogged by allegations concerning his personal morality as well as determined opposition from Congress, most notably in 1995 when the Republicans, under the maverick leadership of Newt Gingrich, engaged in a battle with the President that resulted in the temporary shutdown of the federal government. Despite his successes and personal popularity both at home and abroad the consensus of early verdicts balance the above with the spectacle of his impeachment and a feeling of missed opportunity.

 ## The return of the right

The incumbent Vice-President, Al Gore, distanced himself from Clinton throughout the 2000 election campaign and was narrowly defeated by George W. Bush. In the most controversial election in the nation's history, the failed oilman and governor of Texas had to rely on the Supreme Court for his eventual victory, due to a contested result in Florida, a state where another son of former President George Bush is governor. Generally considered to be a political lightweight, Bush has adopted a cabinet style of governing, relying on trusted advisers, several of whom played a part in earlier Republican administrations. He has taken the economy from record surplus to record deficit, after pushing Reaganesque tax cuts through Congress.

The terrorist attacks of September 11, 2001 precipitated a more hawkish foreign policy with the Truman Doctrine of protecting freedom seemingly having been superseded by the 'Bush Doctrine', the pre-emptive strike. Such was the shock of '9/11' to a country which, in stark contrast to Europe, the twentieth century had left unscarred by the ravages of war, that there followed arguable violations of civil liberties via the Patriot Act, intended to protect the homeland by enhancing the powers of the state.

Figure 11.3 **President Clinton with former Presidents George Bush, Ronald Reagan, Jimmy Carter and Gerald Ford at the funeral of Richard Nixon, 1994**

Given the nature of his election victory and a finely balanced Congress, Bush could hardly claim a convincing mandate for the right-wing agenda he set out to enact. The fact that the religious right, which had appropriated the Republican Party in the 1980s, had one of its own in the White House was illustrated by Bush's immediate moves to restrict the accessibility of family planning services. Some fear that Roe v. Wade, the 1973 ruling that guaranteed the right to abortion, may now be threatened. Issues that divide present-day America – abortion, gun-control, gay rights and health care – strike at the core of the nation for they are in many ways simply contemporary manifestations of the sort of moral and political issues that the Founding Fathers sought to resolve in establishing the United States of America.

Part 2: Essays

 ### The aims and impact of the 'New Frontier'

1 **What was the meaning of Kennedy's 'New Frontier' and to what extent did he succeed in delivering on his promises?** (20)

(AQA)

From the outset it must be said that domestic issues were not a priority for President Kennedy. Given that the executive branch is freer to decide on foreign matters, it is understandable that numerous Presidents have tended to concentrate more on external issues as they find their legislative path on the domestic front blocked by America's carefully crafted system of checks and balances. But during election season, it is on domestic policy that a Presidential candidate must make their mark and John F. Kennedy certainly accomplished this.

As a Presidential hopeful, Kennedy captured the imagination of many Americans with his vision of the future. In November 1959, before the Democratic Party of Wisconsin, he depicted the Eisenhower reign as 'the years the locusts have eaten' and made political capital of the notion that the Soviets had moved ahead of the United States. He continued: 'It is not too late . . . I think we can close the gap and pull ahead. But to do this we must put an end to this depression of our national spirit – we must put all these dull, gray years behind us and take on the rendezvous with destiny that is assigned us. We must regain the American purpose and promise.' This was the genesis of what would become known as the 'New Frontier'.

As the Primary season advanced, Kennedy honed his rhetoric and his concepts before finally winning the nomination of his party at the Democratic National Convention in July 1960 in Los Angeles. In his acceptance speech, he told his audience that they stood on the edge of a New Frontier, a new decade of hopes and threats. He gave a greater insight into his vision for a programme of legislation when he said: 'The New Frontier is here whether we seek it or not: unconquered pockets of ignorance and prejudice, unanswered questions of poverty and surplus.' He claimed that the New Frontier encompassed many areas, including an expanding and ageing population, education, demographic movements, science and space and even leisure time. These were the challenges that he laid out and he stated that the nation must accept and tackle them with no uncertain commitment.

During the campaign Kennedy reiterated that the New Frontier was not an offer to America but a challenge that required courage and conviction from the people and politicians alike. But was the New Frontier anything more than a campaign 'sound bite'? His eloquent and optimistic inaugural address on 20 January 1961 focused exclusively on America's position on the world stage and one could be forgiven for asking where were the civil rights pledges and the promises to tackle poverty? But still his challenge of the New Frontier was implicit in his most famous line: 'Ask not what your country can do for you – ask what you can do for your country.'

During the 1,000 days of Kennedy's 'Camelot', the Cold War and its related space race were arguably of paramount concern but the young President showed that he was willing to address the domestic challenges that he had highlighted. Education bills, notable civil rights gestures, raising the question of the provision of health care, an anti-poverty drive and the Apollo programme all illustrate that he did not simply forsake his campaign messages for the glamour of foreign policy. History has tended to castigate President Kennedy as a domestic failure, a chief executive who had poor relations with Capitol Hill and achieved little of note. However, upon closer inspection this verdict would appear to be too harsh.

Economic policy is arguably the key factor in determining the success of an administration. While acknowledging that politicians are to a significant extent constrained by the economic cycle and events beyond their control, it would be a fallacy to suggest that they have an unimportant role in economic affairs. It has fallen to the President to steer the nation through the economic tides via, for example, the manipulation of spending and borrowing and by promoting confidence in the economy.

Economists Seymour Harris and Walter Heller have described Kennedy as the first modern economist in the American Presidency. His landmark Commencement Address at Yale University in June 1962 certainly illustrated that he was prepared to discard old myths and approach the management of the economy in a careful and dispassionate way. The President questioned existing methods of measuring the federal budget and public debt and argued that the economy could be managed scientifically as opposed to ideologically. He went on to stress: 'What is at stake in our economic decisions today is not some grand warfare of rival ideologies but the practical management of a modern economy.' This willingness to embrace the future without the baggage of the past can be regarded as a bold and considered move by the young President.

Relations with the business community were for the most part constructive. Businessmen were naturally suspicious of the incoming administration after eight years of Republican control of the executive branch. Throughout the campaign and during his brief tenure in office, Kennedy sought the support of business by reiterating that he was a friend of capitalism who wished to 'serve it as well as it has served us'. He stressed the importance of economic growth to his dream of taking America forward. Following recessions in 1958 and 1960 the public and business were prepared to listen to his ideas. An early example of his willingness to support business was the offering of tax breaks to companies that modernised or actively looked for new ventures. There was a recovery, the so-called Kennedy 'boom' of spring 1961 that ushered in a long cycle of prosperity. In his thorough analysis of Kennedy's economic policies Jim Heath stated that Kennedy's early policies were effective in helping to bring prosperity. Accordingly Kennedy should be credited for the part he played in this.

Not all went well for JFK with the business community however. In April 1962 a battle of wills took place with the steel industry when the President intervened in wage and price structures. For the good of the economy as a whole, it was necessary to keep down the price of this basic commodity. This involved asking the unions to keep their wage increase requests to a modest level, a task in which Kennedy was successful. But the mighty US Steel refused to keep its side of the bargain and increased prices, much to the President's anger. He utilised every weapon at his disposal, for example, ordering the federal government only to deal with steel companies that had maintained prices at their present level, and was quickly able to force the giant corporation to back down.

In the realm of social policy, Kennedy faced stiff opposition but still managed to win some rounds with Congress and also paved the way for his successor's Great Society programme. Hugh Brogan has claimed it is a myth that Kennedy was uninterested in domestic politics and inadequate in his dealings with Congress. He paints a picture of a man who cared about the less fortunate and was prepared to address urgent social issues. Kennedy was instrumental in tackling the problem of poverty, pushing for a 25 per cent rise in the minimum wage in 1961 and issuing executive orders to speed up the distribution of food to the poor. The American historian, Arthur Schlesinger, has also praised Kennedy's domestic actions, for example his proposal of tax cuts in 1963 to help reduce unemployment. He portrays the Kennedy brothers as people who cared deeply about social injustice and who were moved to fight continually for the dispossessed with various executive programmes.

The President's reluctance to take significant action on civil rights appears to contradict this image. But Kennedy was cautious on this sensitive issue because he needed to keep Southern support within Congress, rather than through indifference. If he had been too active, Southern conservatives would have made the legislative process even more difficult for him, possibly leading to the blocking of measures that would prove beneficial to the plight of African Americans, such as the increase in the minimum wage.

An area of social policy to which Kennedy was deeply committed was education. The education system was facing a crisis due to a lack of investment. Shortages of teachers and facilities were all too evident during these 'baby boom' years and once more it fell to the federal government to rectify the situation. Improved education was an integral part of the New Frontier and Kennedy wasted little time in addressing the issue. He proposed giving financial aid to the states to help to pay for education but felt that, due to his religion and the close scrutiny of his critics, who were keen to seize upon any transgression of the separation between church and state, religious schools could not benefit from the funding. After being defeated in the House with his education initiatives in both 1961 and 1962, a more moderate version that focused exclusively upon further education was accepted in 1963.

Other victories on the domestic front included the establishment of the Peace Corps, a volunteer organisation for young people who were prepared to accept their President's challenge to ask what they could do for their country. Advancements in the treatment of the mentally ill were inspired by his eldest sister's plight and he furthered the case for the setting-up of a federally backed medical insurance scheme that would be of great benefit to the elderly. And of course it was during his Presidency that the United States committed itself to going to the moon, thus boosting the nation's pride, previously dented by the Soviet Union's initial lead in the space race.

Accordingly it appears just to conclude that Kennedy actually deserves a verdict of 'reasonably successful' for his achievements at home during his short time in office. Progress towards his New Frontier was made though there was still a lot of work to be done. By his own admission, foreign policy was Kennedy's priority and it follows that greater focus on domestic issues would have been possible. As Kennedy himself remarked to Nixon: ' Who gives a damn if the minimum wage is $1.15 or $1.25 compared to something like Cuba.' Above all, it should be borne in mind that the constitutional position of the Presidency allows for a much greater degree of freedom in the sphere of foreign policy than domestic policy, where the executive branch must contend with the powerful forces on Capitol Hill and the powers that are retained by the individual states.

Kennedy had his problems with Congress but these were not due to a lack of interest or poor political manoeuvring. He held a very slim mandate from the American people and had to contend with established conservative elements in Congress. Kennedy did in fact take on and defeat the powerful House Committee on Rules, which had threatened to stand in the way of any progressive proposals and was well placed to do just that. It is another example of a Kennedy domestic victory that was hard fought for and was to pay dividends later for Lyndon Johnson. It is clear that a major reason why he was not able to fully realise his domestic vision was due to opposition from Congress, a situation he hoped would improve following the elections of 1964. It was with this in mind that he decided to undertake a tour of two populous states, Florida and Texas, during which he was assassinated in Dallas in November 1963.

 ## Explaining the legislative impact of Lyndon Johnson

2   Account for the passage of the raft of liberal legislation between 1964 and 1966. (20)

(AQA)

Arguably the greatest period of progressive law-making in US history was ushered in by the unexpected accession of Lyndon Johnson. His Great Society programme had the best of intentions: to break the cycle of poverty in which many millions of Americans were seemingly trapped. Although Johnson never considered a significant redistribution of the nation's wealth by increasing progressive taxation and building a European-style welfare state, his measures went beyond those of the New Deal, Fair Deal and New Frontier in their depth. Given America's individualist ethic, federal system and the 'harmonious system of mutual frustration' that is Washington DC, it was quite an achievement.

Johnson's personal background gave him first-hand knowledge of poverty and also the iron will to tackle it, which his well-heeled predecessors had lacked. He came from rural west Texas, the son of a local politician with whom he often travelled when he was attending to constituents' needs. He held a succession of menial jobs, including that of shoeshine boy before graduating from teachers' college in 1930. His upbringing and experiences in teaching poor children were to stay with him throughout his political career. As he told Congress in 1965 during the debates on the Voting Rights Bill: 'Somehow you never forget what poverty and hatred can do when you see its scars on the hopeful face of a young child.'

Together with his sincere empathy, Johnson had a formidable array of political skills on which he could draw in his dealings with Congress. He was initially a member of the House of Representatives before running for the Senate in 1948. He was shrewd in choosing his friends and in taking up positions on legislation and soon became the Chief Democrat, or Minority Leader in the Senate. As Majority Leader from 1955, he honed his skills, cajoling and flattering, prodding and bullying in an effort to build support. Although no great speaker, he was the master of back-room politics, where difficult customers were given 'the treatment' and would often come away feeling as though they had been mugged. As President, Johnson drew on all his experiences, skills and knowledge of legislators to win over Congress.

He was aided in his task of building a reforming consensus by the shock and sympathy that stemmed from John F. Kennedy's death. He wisely chose to portray himself as the person to execute the late President's programme, thus harnessing the nation's grief in order to unite the country behind the quest to alleviate poverty. Kennedy had been a late convert to civil rights and Johnson himself had had reservations about the wisdom of sending the Civil Rights Bill to Congress due to the fear that it would wreck the rest of his programme. But once in the White House he successfully urged Congress to enact the legislation in Kennedy's memory. His predecessor's tax cut proposals were also realised in 1964, as was the long-standing Kennedy goal of giving federal aid to schools, in 1965.

Two of the greatest weapons a President can hold are a compliant Congress and a clear mandate from the people. The elections of 1964 delivered both to President Johnson. When faced with the competent inheritor of Kennedy's 'Camelot', Republican candidate Barry Goldwater's move to the extreme right, saw 61 per cent of voters opt for Johnson, the largest share of the popular vote a President had received. Now in power by his own right and with the mass of public opinion behind him, Johnson's confidence knew no bounds. The Democrats also consolidated their hold on both Houses of Congress (68 to 32 in the Senate and 295 to 140 in the House of Representatives). Johnson knew many members personally or had helped them to office as they were swept in on his coat-tails. This massive following in Congress made Johnson virtually unstoppable in the mid-1960s.

If Johnson was the right man to push through a programme such as the Great Society, it should also be said that it was the right time. Pressure had been growing since the turn of the twentieth century, when progressives had urged America to take collective action to provide a way out for the unfortunate. Franklin Roosevelt had made modest advances, but even though the New Deal of the 1930s had broken new ground it had fallen short on issues such as health care. Johnson, however, was not prepared to squander his glorious opportunity and, following his election, he oversaw the extension of medical cover to the elderly and low-waged, among many other reforms that had long been sought by liberals. It is somewhat ironic and fortuitous that it was a son of the South, a fiercely conservative region, who held office when the timing was right to pursue this type of agenda.

Finally, the nature of the legislation itself holds clues to its safe passage through Congress. With regard to health care, Franklin Roosevelt had been unwilling to take on the might of the medical community but Johnson ensured their consent by allowing doctors to charge the same rates for all patients irrespective of the basis of their cover. Furthermore, he sidestepped any charges of merely providing welfare when he insisted that Medicare would be made available to all elderly people, their financial status notwithstanding. Similarly on education, the issues that had dogged Kennedy's attempts at reform were avoided by providing help based on pupils' needs rather than the status of the schools themselves.

The safe passage of the Great Society legislation stands as a testament to Lyndon Johnson's will-power, political skill and the times themselves. Arguably it had to be a Southerner who managed to neutralise the entrenched power of the Democratic South in Washington and fashion a liberal agenda that would have surprised his 'political father', F.D. Roosevelt. A Washington insider from the age of 24 when he became assistant to a congressman, Johnson had a wealth of experience on which to draw. He never took Congress for granted and carefully cultivated the unity that he craved for his legislation. He once declared: 'Without constant attention from the administration, most legislation moves through the congressional process at the speed of a glacier.' He knew this better than anyone and would often instruct his staff to give a high priority to maintaining good relations with the legislature (Davidson and Oleszek). Throughout his Presidency, Johnson showed himself to be the most effective post-war President in winning support for issues on which he took a clear stance. Kennedy had performed admirably with Congress but Johnson, with his potentially more polarising Great Society agenda, gave a masterclass to all who would follow on how to manipulate the cumbersome American legislative process.

3   Was President Johnson's war on poverty a success? (20)

(AQA)

Essay plan

Introduction: Comment on the scale of the problem and LBJ's opportunity and willingness to tackle it.

Para 1:   The broad approach taken to reduce poverty. Tax Revenue Act (the bottom rate of tax was cut from 20 per cent to 16 per cent), Medicare Act (20 million elderly people eligible for federal health cover), Medicaid Act (cover for the low-waged), education measures, e.g. Head Start programme (helped young disadvantaged children with nutrition among other things).

Para 2:   Consider the position of African Americans and assess the Civil Rights Act (discrimination in employment illegal) and Voting Rights Act.

Para 3:   Assess self-help measures such as Economic Opportunity Act (loans for the development of rural and small businesses), Jobs Corps (work training programme for drop-outs), Vista (a domestic Peace Corps) and Community Action Programs.

Para 4:   Conservative historians, e.g. Charles Murray, have downplayed the advances made claiming that deficit spending slowed down the rate of growth, and giving federal tax dollars in aid amounted to nothing more than handouts encouraging dependency and anti-social behaviour.

Para 5:   Present the liberal historians' counterargument: low-waged not deterred from working by modest welfare payments, cost of Great Society was dwarfed by military spending, and the actual amounts spent were lower than those claimed by some conservative historians.

Conclusion: Use official poverty statistics to illustrate degree of success: 1959 – 21 per cent in poverty, 1969 – 12 per cent. Economic growth as well as LBJ's programmes contributed to this. The war on poverty had promised more than it ever delivered and had raised false hopes but the very real increase in living standards that millions of families experienced represents a significant amount of success.

The causes and consequences of Watergate

4 Assess the causes and consequences of Watergate. (20)

(AQA)

The political scandal that became known as Watergate was much more than a botched break-in at Democratic headquarters by people acting on behalf of President Nixon. In many ways it represents the zenith of an increase in executive power that had been under way for decades as the White House assumed more power over the governance of the United States. However, under Nixon the power of the Presidency went beyond accepted norms and took on an imperial feel as he sought to undermine challenges to his administration. The reasons for these transgressions can be partly explained by the social unrest at the time, which led Nixon to believe that America was under attack from within. But, arguably, they are more firmly rooted in the psyche of Nixon himself and his immediate advisers. In seeing opposition to his policies as a threat to national security, Nixon demonstrated his over-inflated opinions of self-worth and his resorting to underhand dealings illustrated a suspicious state of mind.

Nixon can aptly be described as an imperial President. He was not reserved in using the full powers of his office in pursuit of his goals. He had a strained relationship with Congress and is remembered as one of the most uncooperative Presidents for his blocking of Congressional hearings by refusing access to records or personnel. He also used the power of impounding funds from programmes more frequently than any of his forebears. This is exemplified best by his impounding half the funding in the Clean Water Act of 1972 after Congress had overturned his veto on the legislation.

Nixon was clearly willing to take strong action with Congress but it was his use of dirty tricks against his perceived enemies that led to his fall. The leaking of information on Vietnam to the *New York Times* in 1971 by an administration official had led to the formation of a team of 'plumbers' to fix such leaks. The use of surveillance and an illegal break-in to seize medical records with which to discredit the official duly followed. Nixon's reaction to the leaking of the 'Pentagon Papers' set a precedent that was to culminate in Watergate.

For the 1972 elections Nixon created a separate campaign group entitled the Committee to Re-elect the President (CREEP). Given the absence of an effective opposition this appears to have been a move based on fear rather than reality. With a fund of millions, much of which allegedly came from illegal contributions, they worked to secure Nixon's re-election in November. The break-in at the Watergate building occurred on 17 June 1972. Five men were apprehended while adjusting eavesdropping equipment in the Democratic Party headquarters. It was not headline news as a White House connection was not apparent and no one outside of Nixon's circle could have guessed what the story would become.

Over the coming months investigations by Congress, the federal judiciary and the *Washington Post* found evidence and testimony that linked the burglars to CREEP. It transpired that Nixon had not known of the break-in but had authorised a cover-up, which involved the manipulation and obstruction of the CIA and FBI. By July 1974 time was running out for Nixon. Tape-recordings existed of every conversation held within the Oval Office but Nixon had resisted their release by claiming executive privilege. In a unanimous decision, the Supreme Court demanded that they be handed over. The House voted three formal articles of impeachment against Nixon for the cover-up and abuse of office.

The most obvious consequence of the Watergate scandal was the resignation of President Nixon. It transpired that the Nixon administration had repeatedly resorted to dirty tricks and what can be deemed abuses of office, of which the break-in and the cover-up represented the final acts. Nixon did everything in his power and more besides to save his Presidency but the weight of evidence was far too great. He vowed to fight before the Senate, who, according to the Constitution, were to deliver the verdict on impeachment. But his closest aides knew the game was up and abandoned him. The Secretary of Defense went so far as to order military commanders to ignore Nixon's orders. The President realised that the Senate would vote a verdict of guilty and so on 8 August 1974 he announced to America and the world that he would resign. In his remaining twenty years, Nixon managed to regain a degree of respectability but failed to offer the nation an apology for his wrongdoings.

However, the most significant impact of Watergate was the damage that it did to the office of the Presidency itself rather than just the incumbent who had created the scandal. Congress had already acknowledged its intent to rein in the imperial Presidency in diplomatic and military affairs, largely due to Nixon's behaviour in Southeast Asia. In the aftermath of Nixon's resignation and with the White House's standing at an all time low, it was to be expected that the legislature would seek to enhance its position. It approached its role of overseer of the executive branch with renewed zeal. For example, the Senate launched a thorough investigation into the activities of the CIA both at home and abroad.

Bob Woodward, the journalist and writer whose name is the one most closely associated with Watergate after Nixon's, devoted a whole book to the impact of Watergate in 1999. In *Shadow*, Woodward examined how Presidents and executive agencies since 1974 have faced closer scrutiny from both Congress and the media. The Iran-Contra scandal during Reagan's second term and the never-ending investigations into Bill Clinton's financial and personal relationships that led to his impeachment, are the most notable episodes, but they can be viewed as part of a growing trend of increased Congressional scrutiny in the aftermath of Watergate. Although it should be borne in mind that Woodward had a vested interest in emphasising the importance of Watergate he nevertheless presents a thorough and compelling case for this increase in scrutiny and its source. The confirmation that even a President could be a crook forced Congress to increase its own surveillance of the executive. Woodward's analysis is certainly closer to the mark than the view expressed in Richard Nixon's autobiography that Watergate would prove to be only a footnote in history.

The fallout from Watergate was not confined within Washington DC's Beltway. It spread out across the nation invoking even greater levels of cynicism and mistrust of politicians within the American people. The November 1974 mid-term elections illustrated the public's estrangement from politics, with voter turnout falling to only 38 per cent. This should, however, be balanced against the fact that Americans have always held a certain amount of contempt for politics and Washington DC; it could be said that their existing views were simply confirmed by Watergate. The Nixon White House years did more than just amplify disillusionment with politicians; the nation's view of itself was affected as well. The bicentennial celebrations of the United States in 1976 were, untypically for the Americans, a somewhat muted affair, which represented the self-doubt that had entered the nation's psyche, as it could see itself falling short of the noble values from which it was born. But above all else, it was the devaluing of America's most prized institution, the Presidency, in the eyes of the people as well as the other branches of government that was the real legacy of Watergate.

It is clear that Watergate had a huge impact upon the United States in various ways and that its consequences in the short term, Nixon's resignation and the elevation of Gerald Ford to the White House, are equalled by the longer-term damage that it did to the Presidency. Can it be said that anything positive arose from Watergate? The suffix 'gate' subsequently entered the English language for scandals involving politicians (Irangate, Monicagate) thus ensuring the episode will remain in public consciousness. And at least America could console itself that the Constitution's checks and balances were demonstrated to be working well in the end. After all an incumbent President, the most powerful man in the world, had been brought down by a system designed nearly 200 years previously. James Madison would have approved.

PRACTICE QUESTION

5   **To what extent may factors other than Watergate be blamed for the loss of people's faith in the Presidency?** (20)

(AQA)

The problems that beset Gerald Ford

6   Why was Gerald Ford unable to make the Presidency his? (20)

(AQA)

The former House Minority Leader, Gerald Ford of Michigan, took over the Presidency when Richard Nixon left Washington on 9 August 1974. In a sense he was an illegitimate President given that he had not even been elected to the Vice-Presidency in the first place. Ford had replaced Spiro Agnew in October 1973 following the exposure of wrongdoings by the long-time Nixon cohort during his earlier governorship of Maryland. Ford had an impressive Congressional record and a reputation of being an honest and straightforward character. Throughout America there was a sense of relief that the crises of the last few years were drawing to a close and initially considerable goodwill was shown towards the likeable mid-westerner.

But the ghost of Nixon was to haunt the Ford White House and seriously undermine the new President's credibility. Ford's first month in office was dominated by the issuing of a Presidential pardon to Nixon. The latter's acceptance of such a pardon could be viewed as an admission of guilt and would, Ford hoped, draw a line under the affair. However, many suspected that the two had struck a deal during Nixon's final days, namely that Nixon would step down and hand the Presidency to his deputy in return for a full pardon. There had been a meeting that had hinted at this but afterwards, following advice from those around him, Ford had clearly outlined his position: that he was not amenable to such a proposal.

In retrospect it might have been wiser for Nixon to stand trial. It would have allowed a full and public closure to Watergate. The pardon spared the nation a traumatic trial and the indignity of jailing the former President but arguably blood letting of this nature was exactly what was required. Ford's view was that Watergate had done enough damage already and it was time for the nation to move on. Richard Nixon had paid for his misdemeanours with his job, reputation and health. But rumours of a deal between Nixon and Ford would not subside. On 17 October 1974 President Ford had to appear before a Congressional sub-committee to deny these suspicions. Congress wound down their investigation into Ford's accession to power, but the allegations tainted his Presidency from beginning to end.

The American people registered their displeasure in the mid-term elections of November 1974. As expected the Republicans fared badly, with their share of the House of Representatives falling to just 139. With opposing parties holding the White House and Congress the only foreseeable outcome was gridlock on the legislative front. But the 38 per cent turnout indicated that it was not just the Republicans whose standing had fallen. It was amply clear that the people were more disenchanted than ever with their politicians and federal institutions. These feelings were still evident nearly two years later as the nation approached its bicentennial. Under more favourable conditions, the 200th 'birthday party' of the United States would have been an epiphany of life, liberty and the pursuit of happiness. But the muted celebrations of 4 July 1976 illustrated the continuing self-doubt of the nation and did nothing to aid the standing of President Ford.

The last Vice-President to be promoted to the White House unexpectedly had been Lyndon Johnson, following the assassination of John F. Kennedy in 1963. Johnson had had little difficulty in making the Presidency his. He was the consummate back-room politician and had the advantage of having the consent of the nation and the cooperation of Congress. Furthermore he had a legislative programme, partly inherited and partly his own, to enact. Gerald Ford held none of these cards. Unlike Johnson, he had no burning desire to introduce legislation. He was essentially a reactive President, responding to events and the initiatives of Congress.

Domestically Ford the President was the same as Ford the House Minority Leader. He wished to see the degree of federal government intervention in people's lives decrease. He also sought to bring the economy under control by balancing the federal budget. But increases in unemployment in early 1975 prompted him to reduce taxation, which obviously represented a backwards step from this goal. He made great use of the power the President holds to check Congress with his liberal use of the veto on Congressional legislation. His opposition to Democratic spending programmes continued throughout his Presidency and did little to create jobs and endear him to the electorate. In fairness it should be borne in mind that Ford had inherited a grave economic situation with inflation and unemployment both rising to worrying levels. But his backtracking created a sense of confusion and his attempts to control inflation made him appear weak.

With only two years in the White House and lacking any sort of mandate, it was predictable that the Ford administration would be little more than a caretaker administration. But his brief tenure had the potential to be cathartic for the nation as it oversaw the end of the imperial Presidency, Watergate and Vietnam. Consequently the deep wounds that had opened up in America could start to heal, although Ford was too closely associated with the past to be able to prosper from this process. He attempted to draw a line under Vietnam by implementing a scheme whereby draft dodgers would be granted amnesty in return for undertaking a period of public service. The scheme came to a premature end due to its lack of appeal but not before it had aroused the anger of a proportion of veterans and the families of the 58,000 American casualties. And in April 1975, as the last American personnel were evacuated from Saigon, it was made evident to all that the war had been for nothing. At home and abroad the United States had been seen to fail in a manner that was both highly visible and humiliating.

Overall the Ford Presidency fell short of what America needed from its chief executive at the time. His low-key, humbler approach provided a timely departure from the imperialism of Nixon and helped arrest the degradation of the office in the eyes of the public. Real though this achievement was, more fundamental redemption was needed. It was vital that respectability be restored to the position that above everything else symbolises the United States and binds it together as a nation. Along with his pardoning of Nixon and constant vetoing, Ford is, rather unfairly, remembered best for his gaffes. He lived up to Lyndon Johnson's jibe 'That Gerald Ford. He can't fart and chew gum at the same time', when he fell down the steps of Air Force One. A rather cruel *Saturday Night Live* sketch showed the President stumbling around the Oval Office, his foot in the waste-paper basket and his head caught in the curtains. In keeping with the best comedy, it was just an exaggeration of the truth for millions of Americans. The media seemed to delight in making fun of the Yale Law School graduate whose eschewing of sound bites and glib remarks made him stand out from the typical type of politician.

The weak position of President Ford was reflected within the Republican Party itself. His Vice-President, Nelson Rockefeller, publicly announced that he would not stand alongside Ford if he chose to run for the Presidency in 1976 following an altercation with the President. Rockefeller had disagreed with Ford's decision to make personnel changes within the foreign and military departments. And when Ford finally made his decision to run for office, he faced a protracted battle from his party's right wing. When he eventually prevailed against challenger Ronald Reagan, the party still managed to get Ford to adopt policies with which he felt ill at ease. He nearly overcame a huge gap in the opinion polls to beat his Democrat challenger, Jimmy Carter, but it was not to be. In sum, Ford was a well-meaning stopgap President. The truth was that he had never really wanted the job and, by the time he had grown into the office, he had lost the position to Jimmy Carter in the elections of 1976.

 ## Was Jimmy Carter a Presidential failure?

7 How much truth is there in the commonly held assertion that Jimmy Carter represents another Presidential failure for the United States? (20)

(AQA)

Carter is usually portrayed as a President who presided over a period of ongoing transition, from the imperialism of Johnson and Nixon to the era of limited government in the 1980s. He suffered the indignity of being a one-term President, his tenure being brought to an end by Ronald Reagan's landslide victory in 1980. It is tempting to castigate Carter as another Gerald Ford, a caretaker President with few ideas of his own, whose main offering was his integrity. It is argued that after his four years in office America's self-image and economy had not improved, and the country delivered its opinion on his performance in no uncertain terms at the ballot box. But in recent times Jimmy Carter's Presidency and the legacy he left have received a less harsh hearing and some would claim that he has become 'America's best ex-President' – such is the gap between the usual contemporary verdict and more modern reappraisals of his impact.

Carter's background explains much of his appeal to the American people in the mid-1970s. The antithesis of a slick politician he was no Washington insider and was therefore able to present himself as exactly the kind of pure, honest candidate that was needed after Nixon and his pardoner, Ford. After a distinguished career in the navy, he had moved into the family business of peanut farming in his native Georgia. Following in the footsteps of his father, a local politician, he entered the Georgia Senate in 1962 before becoming governor in 1970. His first gubernatorial race in 1966 had failed, following which he had gone through a period of introspection and emerged a born-again Christian. His undoubted faith and the honesty he exuded, coupled with his reputation as an efficient manager, saw him win the Democratic nomination for the 1976 Presidential elections. In an age where a candidate's personality was coming to matter as much as their programme, Carter overcame his low national profile to defeat Ford, though the election was much closer than it should have been. Carter had seen his initial healthy lead in the opinion polls wither away which illustrates that he was not a gifted campaigner and communicator. These were indications of the weaknesses that would handicap his administration, but for now America wanted a chief executive in whom they could believe. After his inauguration, President Jimmy Carter walked down Pennsylvania Avenue to the White House.

In evaluating a President's performance the stewardship of the economy is high among the defining criteria. President Carter's unimpressive record on the economy seems beyond doubt to many commentators, though it can be said that the main problem, that of continuing energy shortages, was largely outside his control. Following the Yom Kippur War in 1973 oil prices had increased fourfold. A gas shortage during the severe winter of 1976/7 and a coal miners' strike worsened the situation under Carter. The energy crisis was a contributory cause of increases in inflation and interest rates. Inflation reached 13 per cent in 1979 and Carter's response of introducing credit controls resulted in a short recession. His economic record is remembered for headline-making inflation and 21 per cent interest rates but other economic indicators illustrate that things were not all bad. Underlying economic growth was strong, unemployment was relatively low and the budget deficit was reduced.

However, reducing spending in order to cut the deficit was not what everyone in Washington wanted to see. Relations between the administration and the Democrat-controlled Congress were characterised by Carter's gut feeling, according to Vice-President Walter Mondale, that politics was a sinful business and consequently politicians were best held at arms length. Accordingly, relations were not as warm as they could have been. After only a week, senior Democrats in both Houses were complaining to the press about a lack of consultation from the White House. The new President was not an outgoing character. Carter himself admits that he is a loner and his White House was certainly a contrast to the glitz of Kennedy's 'Camelot'. Building alliances between the executive and legislature and maintaining them is crucial to the success of domestic legislation. But Carter relied upon trusted Georgians rather than seasoned professionals who knew how to work Washington and were accustomed to its give-and-take nature. The administration's ineptitude in Washington is illustrated by their dealings with House Speaker Tip O'Neill. He was annoyed at not being allocated extra tickets for the inauguration and amazed that it took Carter's official in charge of Congressional liaison several months to drop by and introduce himself.

The administration's apparent ineptitude in dealing with Congress certainly had a detrimental effect on Carter's legislative agenda. In his memoirs *Keeping Faith*, Carter tells of the steep learning curve his team faced, and he attempts to redeem his reputation by relating at length how he sought the friendship and cooperation of key members of Congress from both parties. However, the wider context perhaps exonerates Carter to a greater degree. Power within Congress was becoming more dispersed as the number of committees and sub-committees multiplied. Concurrently the parties' strengths and abilities were declining and a new breed of 'Watergate Babies' in Congress were finding no shame in showing themselves to be independent-minded (King). So it comes as a surprise to find that Carter had a 77 per cent success rate with Congress on issues where he took a clear stance. Furthermore, this success rate was constant (Presidents usually suffer a drop during the latter half of their administrations).

Carter's domestic programme was characterised by attempts to promote efficiency and increase opportunity. He was not afraid to tackle a number of contentious issues head-on at the same time, even though contemporary wisdom was to deal with just one or two significant issues simultaneously. Presidential-inspired legislation under Carter made moves to overcome racial discrimination, protect the environment, create jobs, increase aid to students and reduce the federal budget deficit. The administration and Congress had serious disagreements over water projects such as the building of unnecessary dams in congressmen's districts. Carter did not approve of this blatant 'pork barrel legislation' and eventually won a hard-earned partial victory on the matter. Notable defeats for the President included welfare and tax reform and ambitious plans for a national health care programme.

Carter's policies often took on established interests and were introduced in a rush to a Congress that all too often had not been consulted to the degree to which it was accustomed. But he deserves credit for doing what he deemed to be right and history has shown that the many of the decisions he made were correct in the long term irrespective of the immediate consequences. A case in point is defence policy. Carter found himself under considerable pressure to authorise the construction of the B-1 bomber but he resisted because of the expense when compared to the number of jobs it would create and its limited future tactical use. He took on the powerful weapons manufacturers and their lobbyists in Washington and won the argument. His administration opted for the development and construction of cruise missiles and stealth jets, which proved their worth in the Gulf War of 1990–1.

Another example of Carter taking on the lobbies and congressmen was his drive to introduce his national energy policy. With the costs of energy rocketing and the level of consumption and oil imports increasing the President was determined to tackle an issue that made the US so vulnerable. He devoted his first 'fireside chat' to energy in an effort to win over the American people. But Congress was not involved in drawing up the resulting legislation and was presented with a complex bill on which they chose to dig in their heels. Carter was also disgruntled by the influence that the oil companies exerted through their lobbyists in the capital. Carter's poor tactical sense and the nature of the issue ensured that he would face an uphill struggle. It lasted for three years and the resulting total energy programme was, in true Washington style, a compromise that pleased no one completely. But, as a result, US consumption declined and oil imports fell. In fact by the mid-1980s the US had an oil surplus but it was too late for Carter to accept the political credit. Walter Mondale highlighted the dilemma succinctly: 'Under Carter we always front-loaded the pain and back-loaded the pleasure. We did what we had to do. We paid a heavy price for it and the country benefited, and so did Ronald Reagan' (Doyle).

If Carter is found wanting economically and politically, a strong case can be made for him restoring a good measure of the faith in America's leaders and institutions that had been lost through Vietnam and Watergate. In retrospect Carter was exactly what America needed at that moment in time. He had campaigned on the promise that he would 'never tell a lie to the American people', and the people had responded positively to the somewhat dour but genuine Georgian. His televised fireside chats from the White House library delivered in a cardigan, his lack of pomp and ceremony, and his frugal administration (for example, he charged officials $1.75 for breakfast during meetings) all helped restore America's faith in the office of the Presidency. By 1980 the people were ready to revert to type and elected a more traditional type of President.

Events abroad contributed a great deal to Carter's election defeat by Reagan in 1980. He had had some great successes in foreign policy, such as the Panama Canal treaties, the SALT II agreement with the Soviets, and the Camp David Accords, where he brokered a lasting peace between Israel and Egypt. But his response to the Soviet invasion of Afghanistan was to introduce export bans, which hit farmers and businesses, and a boycott of the 1980 Moscow Olympics, which hurt American athletes and national pride more than it did the Soviets, who simply won more medals. Carter was to suffer an agonising end to his term following a failed attempt to rescue hostages from the American embassy in Tehran, taken following the overthrow of the Shah in November 1979. Eight soldiers had died and the Secretary of State had resigned over the failed rescue. America appeared impotent and Carter was running out of credibility. Americans no longer wished to see their most potent national symbol appearing weak and discredited. They removed Jimmy Carter and replaced him with a chief executive who was able to make them feel good about themselves. Carter's last two days in office were spent trying to secure the release of the hostages but the Iranians cruelly waited until Reagan was sworn in before allowing them to leave their soil. Carter had had to be physically helped from the Oval Office that day to witness the swearing in of his successor.

8 **'The Reagan Presidency represents the triumph of style over substance.' Discuss.** (20)
(AQA)

From the outset it can be said that the quotation contains a large degree of truth. The Reagan years were characterised by the President's personal charm and attributes, namely his consummate ability to connect with the people via a medium with which he felt at obvious ease. And with regard to the substance of his two terms, Reagan's economic, social and defence policies represented a significant break with the past and it seems no exaggeration to talk in terms of a 'Reagan revolution'. But the success of these policies is open to question. Many claim that his early economic policies were instrumental in bringing prosperity in the mid-1980s and there can be no doubting the strong performance of the economy in these years. But this fact must be set against the social cost of his initiatives and the staggering increase in the national debt that would be bequeathed to future generations.

In terms of style, Ronald Reagan appeared to be almost everything America wanted from its leader. Very importantly, he was strong. He showed his willingness to stand tall against the 'evil empire' of the Soviet Union and to defend the United States with his Strategic Defense Initiative ('Star Wars'). Reagan's bold stance provided a contrast to the perceived impotence of American might under Carter and Ford, and from his strength the nation could repair its damaged self-esteem. He was even able to demonstrate his vigour and bravery in his personal life following an assassination attempt in 1981. Although he was the oldest man to be inaugurated as President he made a swift and thorough recovery from the shooting and charmed the nation with self-depreciating quips about the incident.

One of Reagan's appellations was 'the Great Communicator'. With over 50 minor films to his credit, numerous commercials and years on the corporate- and political-speaking circuit, he knew how to reach out to people with an ease and flair that no previous occupant of the White House ever had. He was a straight talker who instinctively put across his messages as simple, black-and-white issues: for example, the Cold War was a battle between good and evil – cowboys and Indians on the international stage. He avoided detail, opting instead to present generic visions to his audience. His folksy simplicity reassured people in good times and bad and suggested that the nation had a leader who was in control of the big picture and had a vision of where it was heading.

Reagan's communication skills were invaluable to achieving his vision. He would appeal directly to the people over the heads of Congress to win their backing for his proposals and thus reduce the ability of the legislature to stand in his way. But Reagan was only as good as the lines he was given to say and his success was not simply about presentation. He surrounded himself with an able team to whom he freely delegated. Unlike the Carter administration, Congressional liaison was placed in expert hands and his loyal cabinet and the Office of Management and Budget saw their status and role increase. Even the First Lady, Nancy Reagan, played an active role giving advice and looking for potential pitfalls for her husband's personal prestige. The administration was politically adroit and showed themselves to be experts at maximising their success during Reagan's first year in office. A key factor was speed. They acted quickly, emulating Roosevelt's 'Hundred Days' and capitalising on Reagan's personal popularity and his presumed mandate, although it was quite clear that a good proportion of his vote had been anti-Carter rather than pro-Reagan. To cap it all, the President himself hobbled into Congress on crutches following his shooting, and it appeared that Capitol Hill had little choice but to accept his unambiguous flagship policies that had been outlined during the election campaign to cut tax and reduce spending.

Reagan's economic policies were arguably his most significant achievement. Like his British contemporary Margaret Thatcher, Reagan sought a different approach to running the economy after the inflation and unemployment of the 1970s. Keynesian interventionist ideas were jettisoned in favour of the monetarist principles of Milton Friedman and the Chicago School of Economics. The idea was to set the economy free from government interference and reduce considerably the higher levels of taxation. Faced with fewer constraints and higher rewards, private enterprises would become more productive and the positive effects of this would trickle down for the benefit of all. During the primary season George Bush (who was to become his running mate) had labelled this theory 'voodoo economics'. Today it is recalled as 'Reaganomics', such is its identification with the Republican who instigated it.

The first of Reagan's two major economic policies was the Omnibus Budget Reconstruction Act of July 1981. It reduced government spending on social security, pensions and Medicare. The Economic Recovery Tax Act passed in August reduced the highest rate of income tax from 70 per cent to 50 per cent, cut capital gains tax from 28 per cent to 20 per cent as well as significantly reducing business taxes. They represented bold victories for the administration, but unlike the heady days of the New Deal the momentum could not be sustained and the White House found it much harder to get its own way. In 1982 House Democrats resisted social security cuts and in 1984 they rejected Reagan's call to support rebels in Nicaragua.

The immediate effect of Reagan's policies was to bring a deep recession in 1982 and taxes had to be raised. But by the following year, the economy recovered strongly and life was good for the rich until the stock market crash of 1987. Meanwhile for the less fortunate the welfare state had been scaled back, and in the cities homelessness and drug use were on the increase. But despite the social repercussions, Reagan's political achievement has to be acknowledged. He had come to Washington with a set of unambiguous policies and had overseen their swift enactment. For the first time since Nixon, he had shown that the Presidency was once more an effective institution for putting forward policies.

Although federal programmes were downsized, spending on defence rocketed. Echoing Kennedy's inaugural line, 'Let us never negotiate out of fear, but let us never fear to negotiate', Reagan initiated an escalation of the Cold War thus ending the détente of the 1970s. The Soviet Union simply could not match American spending and their spectacular economic and political collapse in the latter half of the decade duly followed. This was due in part to Gorbachev's reforms, but Reagan too must be given credit for, on the one hand, forcing their economic collapse and, on the other, for his willingness to find common ground with Gorbachev. It may have been inadvertent, but Reagan's military build-up paradoxically helped bring freedom and peace.

Reagan's political skills should, however, be called into question. He may have projected the image of an in-control visionary but behind the doors of the White House the reality was often quite different. Jimmy Carter had devoured paperwork and would immerse himself in every last detail of his administration's business, but Ronald Reagan was cut from different cloth. The President was lightweight in certain respects and those around him could always be counted on to move in to fill the void. Most notable of these was Donald Regan, the Chief of Staff from 1985 to 1987. According to insiders he cut off access to the President and called the shots himself (Doyle). Regan, the de facto 'president', was finally removed on the advice of Nancy Reagan. Ultimately Ronald Reagan's hands-off style and policy of delegation failed him in the end. The Iran-Contra scandal brought Reagan's White House into sharp focus and his Presidency to a sombre end.

Memories of Watergate were reawakened with the revelation that agencies of the federal government had acted illegally in pursuing what they considered to be the best interests of the United States. Weapons had been sold to Iran who in return would put pressure on hostage-takers in the Middle East. This flew in the face of the policy of refusing to deal with terrorists. The money from the arms deals was diverted to fund rebels in Nicaragua who were fighting their country's communist government. Giving aid to the Nicaraguan Contras broke laws that had been passed during Reagan's first term. Once more, an administration had demonstrated its disregard for Congress and the law, and in 1987 the Senate and House launched an investigation that would undermine Reagan's credibility.

The Iran-Contra hearings showed Reagan to be an ageing and forgetful President who was not in control of his administration. If it is to be believed that he genuinely could not recall anything about the secret deals that had been going on, then it showed his gross negligence in allowing a military officer to steer part of American foreign policy. With a haughty Congress intent on enhancing its own ability to check the Presidency and with the economy in trouble following a major fall in share prices in October 1987 (that became known as 'Black Monday'), Reagan withdrew from his job. He spent his days in the residency of the White House watching old films, depressed and seemingly disinterested in the affairs of state. There was serious talk of replacing him with Vice-President Bush, but Reagan managed to gather himself to see through his duties for the final year of his incumbency.

The flaws in Reagan's style became all too evident but when taken en masse his approach to politics must be considered a success. He oversaw the passing of his most important legislation and at the same time managed to restore some of the glamour and prestige to the White House. But Iran-Contra brought the administration back down to earth and Reagan's powers faded fast. He had a torrid time getting his nominations for the Supreme Court accepted by the Senate for example, but such was his popularity and the faith he inspired that his personal reputation was not damaged to the degree it might have been. Reagan led a charmed life as President; the mud refused to stick and it was not for nothing that he became known as the 'Teflon President'. Domestically he will be best remembered for his economic policies, which brought growth at a social cost. And in the last instance, the massive federal debt incurred by cutting taxes and increasing military spending must be questioned. Accordingly the most accurate sobriquet for Ronald Reagan is not the 'Great Communicator' but rather the 'Credit Card President'.

9   To what extent can 'Reaganomics' be described as a successful economic programme? (20)

(AQA)

Essay plan

Introduction: Outline the economic situation that Reagan inherited and state what he had pledged to do to improve the performance of the economy.

Para 1: Explain the theory behind supply-side economics and the personnel whom Reagan charged with enacting his vision of a smaller government drawing attention to the President's hands-off style.

Para 2: Assess Reagan's tax-cutting measures: 25 per cent over next three years alone with the hope that these cuts would pay for themselves as private investment grew. The relaxation of laws regulating industry and protecting the environment was also intended to stimulate growth.

Para 3: Outline the reductions in federal government spending ($35 billion in 1982) and their social impact.

Para 4: Describe the mid-1980s Reagan boom and his easy re-election in 1984. Can these be taken as signs of success?

Para 5: Explain the staggering increase in the federal budget deficit and the impact of higher interest rates and the increase in the value of the dollar.

Conclusion: A legislative triumph but an economic and social failure.

The domestic failure of George Bush

10 Assess the problems that beset the Presidency of George Bush. (20)

(AQA)

With the retirement of Ronald Reagan, his deputy, George Herbert Walker Bush, was finally able to step out of the shadows and become President in 1989. Bush was a former Director of the CIA and a noted party loyalist since the days of Nixon. He was not the automatic choice of many on the right of the Republican Party as he was viewed as something of a moderate, but he managed to win the important Primaries and the Republican nomination. Immediately Bush made a mistake that was to cause him embarrassment, and no doubt votes in 1992, by selecting a young senator from Indiana, Dan Quayle, to be his running mate. Quayle made numerous gaffes, misspelling potato in front of television cameras and a class of ten-year-olds, for example, and proved easy prey for the late night talk show hosts for the next four years. Although Americans could jokingly dismiss him as Bush's insurance policy against assassination, the Quayle factor did have a marginal political impact in 1992 when the incumbent Vice-President was pitted against the dour but infinitely more competent Al Gore.

In the largely negative Presidential campaign of 1988, Bush defeated the governor of Massachusetts, Michael Dukakis. The governor had squandered a healthy lead over Bush, as a result of Republican attacks as well as his own lacklustre campaign. The results of the elections demonstrated that Bush could hardly claim a convincing mandate from the people, a state of affairs compounded by the Congressional elections, where the Democrats won healthy majorities. The style Bush adopted, once in the White House, was reactive rather than proactive. He preferred to wait for Congress to act first and then use his power of veto where he felt necessary.

The Presidency of George Bush will be remembered on balance as a failure, such is the stigma of being a one-term President. This verdict is primarily due to domestic issues rather than foreign policy where he oversaw two important successes. Accompanying the collapse of communism in the Soviet Union and the territories it had occupied for decades, the Cold War came to a sudden end. The Berlin Wall was literally torn down overnight and central Europe was finally set free from Soviet subjugation. However, the dramatic decline of a once formidable enemy did little for the man in the White House at the time. In an uncharacteristically humorous moment in 1992, Al Gore summed up the situation thus: 'George Bush taking credit for the end of the Cold War is like the cockerel taking credit for the sunrise.'

With one long-term enemy defeated, another duly arrived in August 1990 when Iraq invaded its oil-rich neighbour Kuwait. Bush saw no other way out than to destroy Iraq's military capabilities. A five-week air campaign followed by a four-day ground war achieved this end. The conditional ceasefire that Bush announced in February 1991 saw the President act in accordance with prevailing international opinion by not interfering in internal Iraqi politics. Consequently Saddam Hussein remained both as Iraqi dictator and a thorn in America's side throughout the rest of the decade and beyond. Victory parades, the like of had not been seen since the Second World War, were held in the United States that summer – but in reality there was little to celebrate and Bush's post-war popularity soon plummeted. With continuing problems in the Middle East and the former Yugoslavia the world now appeared a more uncertain place to its only remaining superpower. At least with the Soviets things had been predictable.

But foreign policy was not where the 1992 elections would be fought. The economic boom of the 1980s had, unfortunately for Bush, come to an abrupt end. Unemployment rose and property values fell. The recession that blighted the Bush Presidency hit the middle classes in particular and seriously undermined his chances of re-election. In 1992 Bill Clinton would go out of his way to court this sector of the electorate. One of the more memorable events in the 1988 elections had been Bush's 'Read my lips, no new taxes' promise to the American people. But within two years he had reneged on it, owing to the size of the federal budget deficit and the downturn in the economy. In October 1990 he signed a bill that raised sales taxes on certain non-essential items and increased the highest level of income tax by 4 per cent. This volte-face had the dual effect of offending a good proportion of the electorate as well as his own party and can be considered a significant factor in his electoral defeat in 1992.

An indication of the domestic power of President Bush can be gained from controversies surrounding certain appointments to federal positions. Difficulties with Presidential nominations were evident from the start and were to dog him throughout his term. Bush nominated an old friend from Texas, former senator John Tower, for the prominent cabinet position of Secretary of Defense. Unverifiable allegations of drinking and womanising surfaced and, after a lengthy investigation, the Senate narrowly rejected the President's choice in March 1989. Bush believed that battering federal nominees had become a new sport in Washington and sure enough worse was to come from Congress and the media.

In 1990 Bush nominated a quiet, pro-choice New Hampshire judge, David Souter, for a vacant seat on the Supreme Court. As a 50-year-old bachelor the media considered him fair game and published allegations concerning his sexuality. Souter found the pressure and scrutiny unbearable and very nearly withdrew before the Senate finally and unequivocally confirmed him. The following year Bush nominated a black conservative judge, Clarence Thomas, when another vacancy arose. Thomas narrowly survived the spectacle of televised hearings over allegations of sexual harassment by a former colleague. Throughout Bush acted commendably, sticking by his nominees but still these problems had the effect of diverting attention and energy away from the real issues.

Outside Washington, President Bush's most pressing problem was the economy. But more vivid and divisive trouble was just around the corner. Racial tensions were brought into the spotlight in the worst possible way in the spring of 1992 when an all-white jury acquitted four Los Angeles police officers who had savagely beaten a black man, Rodney King. The unusual thing about the 'King Trial' was not the beating but the existence of videotape of the incident. It had been played time and again on television and with the evidence there for all to see it seemed incredible that the officers could escape unpunished. When the verdict came, South Central Los Angeles erupted in violence and looting that continued for three days. There were milder outpourings of indignation in several other cities across the US as well. Riots had not occurred on American streets since the 1960s and they came as a real shock to the American people.

The year 1992 was election year, and the timely reminder of social problems that had long existed in America could only harm the incumbent President. The campaign was going to be a hard battle for Bush and it did not start well when he lost his Chief of Staff, John Sununu, in December 1991, following media questioning about Sununu's travel expenses. With his re-election campaign about to begin, Bush felt that he could not afford to let one of his staff become an issue and so lost a trusted aide. The election was fought on domestic issues – and Bush had excelled in foreign affairs while appearing to neglect the problems facing millions of ordinary Americans. Faced with a charismatic Southern governor with an appealing programme, Bush fought in vain for a second term, losing by a landslide in November 1992 to Bill Clinton.

George Bush was, above everything else, a party loyalist who had been rescued from obscurity by Nixon, given his post at the CIA by Ford, before being selected by Reagan as deputy material after the Great Communicator had defeated him in the Republican Primaries of 1980. Bob Woodward, for one, has argued that Bush got where he was by playing by party rules and had not developed the necessary political skills to handle the obligatory scandals and conflicts of the office he eventually held. These weaknesses played a walk-on role in his election defeat but it was primarily his lack of a domestic agenda that cost him dear. And one thing mattered above all others, as the Clinton/Gore campaign repeatedly reminded themselves: 'It's the economy, stupid.'

PRACTICE QUESTION

11 To what extent were Reagan and Bush's domestic agendas different? (20)

(AQA)

Trends in the balance of power, 1960–1992

12 Outline and explain the shifts in the balance of power within the federal government and between the state and the people in America between the years 1960 to 1992. (20)

(AQA)

Relations between the executive and legislative branches of government in the US are quite different from the British example. In America the President is in a weaker position than the typical British Prime Minister, especially on the delivery of his domestic programme. The roots of this situation lie in the system of checks and balances that were integral to the Constitution of 1787. Essentially the Constitution holds a pessimistic view of human nature and the nature of power and therefore it set out to limit the ability to exercise power. The Founding Fathers devised two separations of powers in the United States that safeguard the nation and its people from possible tyranny from the apparatus of state. First, power is divided horizontally between the Presidency, the bicameral Congress and a Supreme Court, which swiftly assumed the power of judicial review. Second, power is split in a more vertical fashion between the federal government and the governments of the 50 states.

Throughout the nineteenth century, Congress was firmly in the ascendancy over the Presidency. It is interesting to note how people are frequently unable to recall the names of many Presidents of this era, other than that of Abraham Lincoln, who was President at a time when strong leadership was essential to the future of the nation. Furthermore, the scope of the federal government itself and its ability to affect the lives of the citizenry was quite limited. This can be seen as a contributing factor to the failure of Reconstruction following the Civil War, for example. The Presidency finally became the chief source of policy out of simple necessity during the Great Depression of the 1930s, and since this time Americans have come to expect that the President will take the lead role in proposing legislation for the common good. The scope of the government increased enormously under Franklin Roosevelt, as did the power of the Presidency over Congress. Over the intervening decades the United States has witnessed a constant shifting both in the powers of the Presidency and of Congress, and also in the degree of intervention in their lives that the people expect from their national government.

The 1960s began with the promise of more government intervention. John F. Kennedy had pledged that the federal government would tackle issues such as education and minority rights, although he made only modest progress towards these goals. Following Kennedy's assassination, Lyndon Johnson extended the scope of Kennedy's ideas in his Great Society programme that launched a war on poverty and saw the federal government take responsibility in areas it had hitherto ignored. The Civil Rights Act and the extension of medical cover to the elderly and low-waged represent a level of intrusiveness from the state that may be commonplace in Europe but has always lacked the same degree of consensus in the US.

The Presidency became imperial in manner under President Johnson with his Great Society and the escalation of the conflict in Vietnam and in 1968 Americans opted for what they expected to be a more restrained Presidency under Richard Nixon. However, his continued use of the military in Southeast Asia and the subversion of state agencies for his own ends led to bitter disappointment. It seemed as if the Presidency had become imperial in intent under President Nixon and following his downfall the balance needed to be redressed. The people and Congress demanded a humbler executive and that is what they received under Ford and Carter.

The 1970s saw Congress reassert its authority within the American political system to the detriment of the powers of the Presidency. The passage of legislation such as the War Powers Act, which bordered on unconstitutionality, enabled the legislature to check the President over diplomatic, military and budgetary matters in a more comprehensive manner than before. Johnson's Great Society had been on the wane since the early 1970s, which perhaps reflected the will for a less interventionist state. But it was also hampered by a faltering economy because of the cost of Vietnam and the increase in oil prices. Ford and

Carter stopped the rot as far as the public's perception of the Presidency, but it seemed that the balancing act had worked too well and that the Presidency was now impotent. This was especially apparent in their faltering attempts to steer the economy back on course.

By the late 1970s, fears concerning the 'imperial Presidency' were being replaced with worries about the 'post-imperial Presidency'. It appeared that the increasingly unhappy occupants of the White House had too little power and could only look forward to being frustrated in their efforts by Congress, the Supreme Court and the people. Anthony King has commented that during this period the public felt increasingly let down by their political system and were concerned that the institution of the Presidency appeared ineffectual and discredited.

There was a yearning for a successful Presidency after the years of turmoil and apparent failure. But Ronald Reagan's two terms in office cannot be considered especially successful, given his failed foreign policies in Lebanon and Nicaragua, the enormous public debt he left behind and the Iran-Contra scandal. In reality the Reagan years were not so far away from the perceived failures of the 1960s and 1970s. However, Reagan provided the people with what they needed: he was able to make Americans feel good about themselves and their nation. It was his manner that made him extremely popular rather than his policies and it was unsurprising that he easily won re-election in 1984.

Reagan's success was perceived rather than real. He oversaw a radical reduction in the scope of the federal government as social policies were neglected in favour of tax cuts. Together with these reductions, an enormous increase in defence expenditure saddled the nation with a horrific national debt. The introduction of so-called 'Reaganomics' firmly reversed the trend of the recent past when Presidents had sought to reduce the budget deficit. His successor, George Bush, promised a 'kinder, gentler America' but he too was inactive on social issues, and furthermore the economy was in recession. By the early 1990s America was ready to elect a candidate who promised to tackle issues at home, such as health care and the inner cities that had been sidelined for the previous two decades.

It appeared as if the United States had come full circle, from the promises of the Great Society, through the reduction of state intervention during the 1970s and 1980s, to a situation where the people were once again looking for the government to intervene on their behalf in the 1990s. Is there any way of explaining this cycle that America has been through? The work of Samuel Huntington can arguably shed light on the uneasy relationship Americans have with their state. In *The Promise of Disharmony*, Huntington argues that American politics is driven by a gap that exists between what is promised and what is actually delivered by its institutions. He states that being American is not an ethnic or cultural matter, rather it is ideological. The 'American creed' is captured in three pivotal documents: the Declaration of Independence, the Constitution and the Bill of Rights. The ideas contained herein, such as freedom, individualism and equality, form the basis of American nationality. These beliefs are united by the notion that limits should be imposed on power and the institutions of government. In other words, Americans are inherently suspicious of 'big' government.

Needless to say, the country does not manage to live up to these lofty ideals and its institutions are seen to fail in delivering what was promised. This 'ideals versus institutions' gap always exists but, from time to time, when the gulf becomes too wide, it is no longer tolerated. Huntington claims that the United States goes through a 'credal cycle'. Put simply this means that, when the people see the gap between promise and reality widening, they become more passionate about their system and demand that action be taken. This could explain why every generation or so the American people are willing to accept a more interventionist state. The New Deal of the 1930s, the Great Society of the 1960s and the election of Bill Clinton in the 1990s, despite his personal weaknesses, provide persuasive evidence for this theory about the workings of the governance of the United States.

Part 3: Historical skills

 1 Extracts from Ronald Reagan's speeches

Domestic policy from 1960 to 1992 is not currently examined using Sources. However, candidates should find the following extracts and accompanying questions a worthwhile exercise.

■ **Source A: Extract from Reagan's first inaugural address, January 1981**

For decades, we have piled deficit upon deficit, mortgaging our future and our children's future for the temporary convenience of the present. To continue this long trend is to guarantee tremendous social, cultural, political, and economic upheavals. You and I, as individuals, can, by borrowing, live beyond our means, but for only a limited period of time. Why, then, should we think that collectively, as a nation, we are not bound by that same limitation?

■ **Source B: Extract from Reagan's first inaugural address, January 1981**

It is my intention to curb the size and influence of the federal establishment and to demand recognition of the distinction between the powers granted to the federal government and those reserved to the states or to the people. All of us need to be reminded that the federal government did not create the states; the states created the federal government.

■ **Source C: Reagan's second inaugural address, January 1985**

Tax rates have been reduced, inflation cut dramatically, and more people are employed than ever before in our history.

■ **Source D: President Reagan's speech on the Challenger disaster, Oval Office of the White House, 28 January 1986**

The future doesn't belong to the fainthearted; it belongs to the brave . . . The crew of the space shuttle Challenger honored us by the manner in which they lived their lives. We will never forget them, nor the last time we saw them, this morning, as they prepared for the journey and waved goodbye and 'slipped the surly bonds of earth' to 'touch the face of God'.

1 **Examine Sources A and B. What do they show about President Reagan's intentions for his first term in office?**

Advice: *To reduce the federal budget deficit and the degree of intrusion from the federal government.*

2 **Using Sources A, B and C and your own knowledge assess the success of Reagan's economic policies.**

Advice: *There was a long period of economic growth from 1983 onwards. As promised Reagan cut taxes and government spending. However defence spending multiplied, which meant that his goal of reducing borrowing failed. Furthermore during the economic boom the poorest people were hit by the reductions in spending.*

3 **Using all the Sources and your own knowledge assess why Reagan remained so popular for so long.**

Advice: *Reagan owed much of his success to the presentation of his Presidency. He owes a debt to speech-writer Peggy Noonan as well as to the numerous films and other sources (e.g. the poem 'High Flight' by John Magee was used in his Challenger address) from which they took lines and anecdotes, often without crediting them or making clear that they were fictional.*

2 Research questions on domestic issues, 1960–1992

The Internet has become a useful research tool for History students but it should be realised that simply downloading relevant pages is of little benefit. It is necessary to actually do something with the vast amount of information available to you in order to facilitate your understanding. This exercise is intended to develop your ability to collate and condense information from a number of sources as well as extend your understanding of US domestic policy from 1960 to 1992.

Using search engines visit relevant sites to find out what you can about the following issues or events and produce a ten-line summary of each unless otherwise stated:

1   The 1960 Presidential elections including the Kennedy–Nixon debates and the role of JFK's father.
2   The 1964 tax cut.
3   Bobby Kennedy's final speech (Los Angeles 1968). Why did he criticise LBJ?
4   The various groups that demonstrated or rioted in the Johnson and Nixon years. Is Nixon's opinion that the nation was under threat from within understandable or a sign of paranoia?
5   The role of the media in taming the imperial Presidency.
6   The presentation of President Carter to the public and Congress. Under what name was he inaugurated?
7   The Iran-Contra scandal.
8   The messages of the 1992 Clinton–Gore campaign.
9   Produce a table to illustrate control of the House of Representatives, the Senate and the White House from 1960. Shade the Democrats and the Republicans in different colours. How often has one party been in control of all three institutions?
10 Produce graphs to illustrate trends in the following:
    (a) unemployment;
    (b) inflation;
    (c) the federal budget deficit.

Sources and references

G.H. Bennett, *The American Presidency, 1945–2000*, Sutton Publishing (2000).

Irving Bernstein, *Guns or Butter: The Presidency of Lyndon Johnson*, Oxford University Press (1996).

Hugh Brogan, *Kennedy*, Longman (1996).

Jimmy Carter, *Keeping Faith: Memoirs of a President*, Collins (1982).

Roger Davidson and Walter Oleszek, *Congress and its Members*, 8th edition, Congressional Quarterly (2002).

William Doyle, *Inside the Oval Office*, London House (1999).

Jim Heath, *John F. Kennedy and the Business Community*, University of Chicago Press (1969).

Samuel Huntington, *American Politics: The Promise of Disharmony*, Harvard University Press (1981).

Edmund Ions, *The Politics of John F. Kennedy*, Routledge and Kegan Paul (1967).

Doris Kearns, *Lyndon Johnson and the American Dream*, Andre Deutsch (1976).

Anthony King (ed.), *The New American Political System*, 2nd edition, AEI (1990).

Jane Mayer and Doyle McManus, *Landslide: The Unmaking of the President, 1984–1988*, Collins (1988).

Anthony Summers, *The Arrogance of Power: The Secret World of Richard Nixon*, Victor Gollancz (2000).

Mark White (ed.), *Kennedy: The New Frontier Revisited*, Macmillan (1998).

Bob Woodward, *Shadow: Five Presidents and the Legacy of Watergate*, Simon & Schuster (1999).

Chapter 12

General Conclusion: From AS to A2

The purpose of this book has been to prepare for essays and examinations at AS and A-level. Some of the topics studied and all of the historical skills acquired at AS lead naturally and logically to the next conceptual stage represented by A2. This includes two approaches which are rooted in AS but grow beyond it. One is *Historical Interpretation*, with an emphasis on historiography or the study of different historical viewpoints. The other is a *Synoptic Study* of a period of about 100 years. These are common to all the Examination Boards.

AS to A2: Historical Interpretation

An example of the approach to Historical Interpretation at A2 can be seen in the OCR Specifications for the paper entitled *Historical Investigations*.

> Investigations are built around topics of current interests to historians and the specific aim is to develop an understanding of how the past has been interpreted and represented, and how historical research generates controversies over interpretation. Candidates are expected to understand the principal arguments surrounding their chosen topic and to be able to offer their own explanations and interpretations.
>
> Extract from OCR Specifications for A2 History: Historical Investigations

One dimension of this has already been extensively covered. All AS students are familiar with at least one historical issue which is inherently controversial. They know how to interpret this issue in response to a specific question about it, making selective and creative use of the factual material relating to the topic.

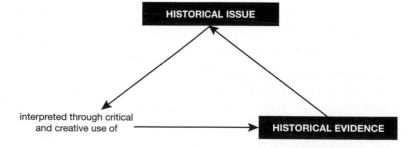

The AS approach to Historical Interpretation

HISTORICAL ISSUE

interpreted through critical and creative use of

HISTORICAL EVIDENCE

This has been the whole point of answering questions which begin with '*Why . . . ?*', '*How far . . . ?*', '*To what extent . . . ?*', '*Assess the reasons for . . .*' and many others. Use has been made of evidence from the period (factual knowledge) to consider possible reasons, to explain how these fit together and to weigh up which are the most valid.

This is the starting point for the A2 approach, which adds the extra dimension of assessing other *views* which have been put forward by different historians and groups of historians (who are part of 'schools of thought'). At A2 students have to be aware of the *real* controversy behind the issue as well as the *possible* interpretations which will have occurred to them at AS. Historiography is therefore added to History. But the whole process still has to take account of the historical evidence. Historiography does not replace History – it provides additional perspectives and further opportunities for creative and original thought.

The A2 approach to Historical Interpretation

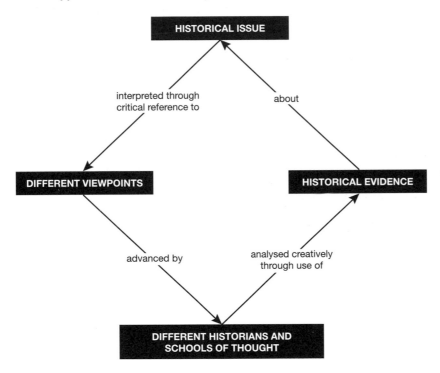

To give a practical example, an AS task might involve assessing how successful Roosevelt's 'New Deal' was. At A2 the emphasis would be more on explaining why there are major differences between historians over whether the New Deal was a success or not.

AS to A2: Synoptic Study

'Synoptic' in the context of A2 History has two possible meanings. The first is the connection *between* some of the different topics covered at AS and A2 to create a broader perspective on another paper; this is required by some specifications but not by others. The second is an approach *within* an A2 paper (whether or not it involves areas previously studied) which requires an analysis of the broad sweep of change over a period of approximately 100 years. The OCR Specifications, for example, refer to the Synoptic Study as *Themes in History*, which:

develop understanding of connections between different elements of the subject. They draw together knowledge, understanding and the values of diverse issues centred on Key Themes. The topics are based on Key Themes covering an extended period of approximately a hundred years with an emphasis on continuity and change within the topic. The emphasis is on developing a broad overview of the period studied. They are historical perspectives modules, so concern is centred on links and comparison between different aspects of the topics studied.

Extract from OCR Specifications for A2 History: Themes in History

As with the Historical Interpretation, the skills developed at AS lead to those needed at AS. This time, the change concerns the way in which perspectives are viewed. At AS the approach was to analyse a specific topic in a broad sweep (for example, the motives for writing the Constitution). At A2 the perspective is considerably extended, but the topic becomes much more selective (for example, assess the long-term impact of the Constitution on the outbreak of the American Civil War). The contrasting approaches can be seen as an open pair of scissors.

The A2 Synoptic approach and how it compares to AS

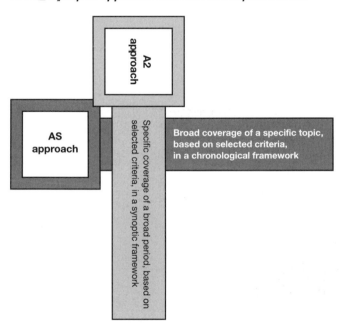

Coverage at A2 is based on 'themes', some of which cover the whole period; an example of a 'theme' might be 'The struggle for the Constitution, 1763–1877'. It also takes in comparisons – possibly between individuals and certainly between periods, for example between the leaders of African American civil rights movements. A2 coverage of this subject matter is less likely to be chronological than at AS: different periods are considered quickly and without necessarily looking at the connecting phases. Even this, however, will not be completely unexpected, since any AS essay depending strictly on chronology always runs the risk of narrative.

The Synoptic Study is so complex that it really needs a specific example of how it works and how it builds on the AS approach. Here are the stages by which an answer to a typical A2 question might be built up.

The first preparatory stage is to identify the significance of the parameters set by the question and to subdivide the two time periods into more manageable chunks which will allow more analysis.

Stage 1: A2 essay identifying the periods for coverage

To what extent did African Americans make more progress between 1877 and 1919 than between 1919 and 1980?

Stage 2: A2 essay identifying the periods for coverage

How far did African Americans make more progress between 1877 and 1919 than between 1919 and 1980?

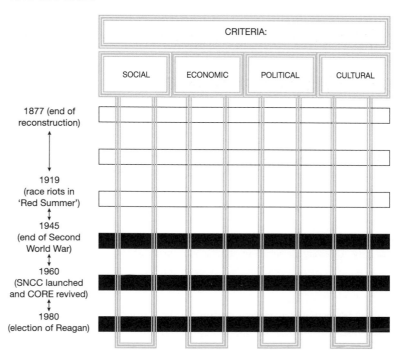

The second stage (see Stage 2, p. 306) is to select three or four key criteria for assessing the progress of African Americans between 1877 and 1980. These should be distinctive and examples should be drawn – overall – from the full time span 1877–1980. The themes selected should be fairly clear from the subject specification.

In terms of technique – if not of content – this could still be an AS essay. Many students would tend to use the criteria by working *chronologically* through the leaders. What would convert this into a full A2 approach is a direct comparison between them acting as the basic structure of the essay (see Stage 3). Although this may sound complex, it is actually using a skill already acquired at AS – but notching it up to a more demanding A2 approach.

Stage 3: A2 essay making comparisons through the whole period, using the criteria

The transition from AS to A2 is therefore entirely logical. In a sense, it represents the two main dimensions of History – the study of the past and an enquiry into methods used for that study.

Biographies of Important Personalities

Dean Acheson (1893–1971)
Dean Acheson was a Law graduate who worked his way up to the position of Secretary of State, and took a hard line on foreign policy, advocating intervention in Korea in 1950.

John Adams (1735–1826)
John Adams was born in Massachusetts, the son of a farmer. Having studied at Harvard, he became a lawyer and went on to lead the opposition to the Stamp Act in 1765. In 1774 he was a delegate to the First Continental Congress, and played a major role in the debates leading up to the signing of the Declaration of Independence. Having served the new Republic in France, Holland and England, in 1789 he became Vice-President of the United States to George Washington. In 1796 he was chosen as President, but following dissensions within the Federalist Party he was not re-elected in 1800.

John Quincy Adams (1767–1848)
John Quincy Adams, the 6th President of the US, was the son of the second President. He was groomed for high office at an early age, becoming Private Secretary to the American Envoy in St Petersburg at the age of 14. He went on to serve in a number of government posts, such as Secretary of State during which time he negotiated the treaty with Spain by which Florida was acquired. Some have suggested he was the real writer of the 'Monroe Doctrine'. In 1825 he was elected President by the House of Representatives, but failed to be elected on his second attempt. He continued to serve as a congressman until his death and became a notable opponent of slavery.

Louis Armstrong (1900–1971)
Louis Armstrong was a jazz trumpeter and singer who is regarded as one of the greatest jazz artists of all time.

John Brown (1800–1859)
John Brown married twice and had 20 children, most of whom he used as a private army in his crusade against slavery. He became involved in 'Bleeding Kansas' and was responsible for the murder of five pro-slavers in the 'Pottawatomie Massacre'. He gained greater notoriety with his 1859 raid on the Harper's Ferry armoury in Virginia from where he hoped to seize weapons with which he would spark a slave rebellion. Marines under Robert E. Lee captured Brown who then stood trial and defended himself eloquently and courageously before being sentenced to death and hanged.

William Jennings Bryan (1860–1925)
William Jennings Bryan went into politics after practising law, and was elected to Congress in 1890. He stood unsuccessfully as Democrat Presidential candidate in 1896 and 1900, and 1908. He was made Secretary of State by Woodrow Wilson but resigned during the First World War. He is perhaps best remembered for his 'Cross of Gold' speech and his prosecution of John Scopes in the Tennessee 'Monkey Trial' of 1925.

James Buchanan (1791–1868)

James Buchanan, the fifteenth and possibly worst President of the United States, was the son of an immigrant Irish farmer. Prior to his election as President in 1856 he had been out of the country for some time, and seemed ill-equipped to deal with the rising tensions over the slavery question, particularly regarding 'Bleeding Kansas'. His pro-Southern sympathies exacerbated the situation and he remained strangely inactive as Southern states seceded and war became increasingly likely.

George Bush (1924–)

George Bush was the 41st President of the US between 1989 and 1993. He enjoyed more success abroad than at home, with the expulsion of the Iraqi forces from Kuwait, and the formal ending of the Cold War. Domestically he had promised a 'kinder, gentler America' but the combination of rising unemployment, a tax rise and rioting in Los Angeles put paid to his chances of re-election in 1992.

James Byrnes (1879–1972)

James Byrnes was a former South Carolina senator and Supreme Court justice. As Secretary of State he had a conciliatory reputation and sought friendship with the USSR in 1945.

John C. Calhoun (1782–1850)

John Calhoun was born in South Carolina. He became Vice-President under John Quincy Adams and served in the same position under Jackson until he decided that he should resign in 1832 so that he could champion states' rights in the Senate with his great oratory. In 1829 he stated anonymously that a state had the right to nullify a federal law it regarded as unconstitutional. Despite annexing Texas as Secretary of State in 1844 and supporting the interests of the slave states, he opposed the war with Mexico in 1846.

Al Capone (1899–1947)

Alphonse Capone achieved notoriety as a gangster during the 1920s in Chicago. He based his empire on supplying alcohol during Prohibition, but was finally sent to prison in 1931 for tax evasion.

Andrew Carnegie (1835–1919)

Andrew Carnegie emigrated to America in 1848 with his family from Scotland. He personified the 'rags to riches' dream starting as a factory worker before the Civil War and then investing his savings eventually in iron and steel. Having made a fortune, Carnegie then began to give much of it away. It is estimated that he donated about $70 million mainly to educational projects.

Jimmy Carter (1924–)

Jimmy Carter was the 39th President of the US between 1977 and 1981. In the aftermath of Watergate and Vietnam, Carter represented a more low-key and humble Presidency and managed to restore the faith of the nation in the executive office. He achieved a moderate amount of success in foreign affairs before being voted out of office after one term following a rise in oil prices and an ongoing hostage situation in Iran involving US diplomats.

Henry Clay (1777–1852)

Henry Clay was a statesman of great stature, entering the House of Representatives in 1811, and serving as its speaker for many years. He played a significant role in bringing about the war of 1812 with Britain and also in ending it. Following his involvement in the Missouri Compromise of 1820, he won the title of 'the great pacificator'. He unsuccessfully contested the Presidency in 1824, 1831 and 1844, and was largely behind the Compromise of 1850.

Grover Cleveland (1837–1908)

Stephen Grover Cleveland served as the 22nd and 24th President of the United States. In 1895 he applied the 'Monroe Doctrine' to the area that is present-day Guyana.

Calvin Coolidge (1872–1933)

John Calvin Coolidge became the 30th President of the US in 1923 on Harding's death and served until 1929. His policies contributed to the Wall Street crash of 1929.

George Armstrong Custer (1839–1876)

General George Armstrong Custer, having graduated bottom in his class from West Point, went on to serve with distinction for the North in the Civil War, but has gone down in history as the headstrong, glory-seeking leader of the Seventh Cavalry whose command was wiped out in 1876 at the Battle of the Little Big Horn by a Sioux-Cheyenne force under Sitting Bull and Crazy Horse.

Clarence Darrow (1857–1938)

Clarence Darrow was a lawyer who defended socialist leader Eugene Debs following a strike by the American Railway Union, and was perhaps best known for his defence of John Scopes in the Tennessee 'Monkey Trial' of 1925.

Jefferson Davis (1808–1889)

Jefferson Davis became the only President of the Confederate States of America in 1861. Having served in the Mexican War, as a senator and as Secretary of War he appeared to be the best choice to lead the South, although he accepted the position of President reluctantly. He was put in prison for two years after the war but was never tried for treason.

Eugene Debs (1855–1926)

Eugene Debs, having been President of the American Railroad Union stood as a socialist candidate for the Presidency in 1904, 1908, 1912 and 1920, and was imprisoned between 1918 and 1921 for his outspoken pacifism.

Stephen Douglas (1813–1861)

Stephen Douglas, having been a Supreme Court judge, congressman and senator at various times, played as great a part as any individual in heightening sectional animosities in the 1850s, largely because of his failure to appreciate the extent of Northern anti-slavery feeling. Ironically he was not a sectional politician himself, but believed that the issue of slavery could be resolved by the settlers of a territory voting on whether slavery should exist or not. This alienated the North and also split his own Democrat Party making his chances of being elected President in 1860 very slim.

Frederick Douglass (1817–1895)

Frederick Douglass, having escaped from slavery and bought his freedom using money collected for him in Britain, became a leading figure in the abolitionist movement before the Civil War. His autobiography, first published in 1845 was an eloquent and influential book, and as well as becoming the first great leader of African Americans, he went on to be US Minister to Haiti in 1889.

W.E.B. Du Bois (1868–1963)

William Du Bois was a civil rights activist who was a founder member of the National Association for the Advancement of Colored People. He also wrote several books on the subject of civil rights.

John Foster Dulles (1888–1959)

John Foster Dulles as Secretary of State became notorious for using such phrases as 'massive retaliation', and felt that 'containment' was not an adequate policy, promoting 'brinkmanship' and liberation instead.

'Duke' Ellington (1899–1974)

'Duke' Ellington was a composer, conductor and pianist who is one of the most highly regarded jazz musicians of the twentieth century.

Gerald Ford (1913–)

Gerald Ford was the 38th President of the US. He was the Republican leader in the House of Representatives chosen to replace the disgraced Vice-President Spiro Agnew. Less than a year later he became President following Nixon's resignation. Ford is commonly considered to have been a caretaker President whose period in the Oval Office was undermined both by his pardoning of Nixon and also the fact that he was not elected to national office.

Henry Ford (1863–1947)

In 1899 Henry Ford founded his first motor car company in Detroit, and in 1903 set up the Ford Motor Company. He pioneered mass production and the 'assembly line' approach to manufacturing and by 1928 had turned out 15 million of his model T cars, helping to transform the habits of a nation by bringing cars within the price range of many ordinary workers. As a lifelong pacifist, he later clashed with F.D. Roosevelt over the use of the company for war production.

William Lloyd Garrison (1805–1879)

William Lloyd Garrison became one of the most famous opponents of slavery in the build-up to the Civil War. In 1831 he started production of an abolitionist newspaper *The Liberator*, and also set up the American Anti-Slavery Society.

Geronimo (1829–1909)

Geronimo, whose Indian name was Goyathlay, was an Apache leader who led resistance against the US government's policy of putting his people on reservations, until he surrendered in 1886 with the promise that he would be allowed to go back to Arizona.

Samuel Gompers (1850–1924)

Samuel Gompers was one of the most important labour leaders to emerge in the late nineteenth century, and set up the American Federation of Labor of which he was President.

Ulysses S. Grant (1822–1885)

Ulysses Grant was given overall command of Union forces in March 1864 and used it to good effect. His popularity after the war allowed him to become President of the US after the elections of 1868 and again in 1872, overseeing the period of Reconstruction, but making some bad appointments, which led to his administrations being tainted by scandal and corruption.

Alexander Hamilton (1757–1804)

Alexander Hamilton having fought with distinction during the War of Independence was returned to Congress, and then played a leading role in the Annapolis Convention, which led to the Philadelphia Convention the following year. He was behind the Federalist Papers which argued the case for the ratification of the Constitution. He became Secretary of the Treasury in 1789 but died following a duel with his rival Aaron Burr.

Warren Harding (1865–1923)

Warren Harding was the 29th President of the US. His death was possibly hastened by the scandals linked to the so-called 'Ohio Gang' of cronies he had appointed to various offices.

Benjamin Harrison (1833–1901)

Benjamin Harrison was active and ambitious in foreign policy, pursuing expansion in the Pacific, developing the US navy and improving trade links with Central and South America.

Rutherford Hayes (1822–1893)

Rutherford Hayes was the 19th President of the US. Having reached the rank of Major General during the Civil War, he was returned to Congress by Ohio, and, following the disputed election of 1876, a Congressional commission awarded him the Presidency. He effectively ended Reconstruction by withdrawing troops from the South in 1877.

Joseph Hooker (1814–1879)

'Fighting Joe' Hooker served in the Mexican War and became commander of the army of the Potomac in 1863. He was defeated by Lee at Chancellorsville and although replaced by Meade, he went on to march with Sherman through Georgia, and served until Atlanta fell.

Herbert Hoover (1874–1964)

Herbert Hoover was the 31st President of the US and one of the least popular by the end of his term in office. He had the misfortune to be in charge during the Wall Street crash and beginnings of the Great Depression. Despite being the most able of the Republican Presidents of the 1920s he remained unconvinced that the answer to economic problems lay in massive government intervention, so people never felt he had done enough.

Langston Hughes (1902–1967)

Langston Hughes was a writer who highlighted social injustice and the frustrations of African Americans through his articles, short stories and poems.

Andrew Jackson (1767–1845)

Andrew 'Old Hickory' Jackson was the 7th President of the US. Having served as a congressman and senator for Tennessee he became a Major General in the army before returning to politics and eventually being elected President in 1828. He has become associated with the concept of rewarding his supporters with the spoils of office and ushering in the era of the common man, but in reality Presidents before Jackson had also rewarded their supporters and 'Jacksonian Democracy' was an extremely limited type, which in the main extended only to white males. He opposed the US Bank and also stood up to South Carolina when the state threatened to secede.

Jesse Jackson (1941–)

Jesse Jackson is a civil rights activist who campaigned for the nomination to become the Democratic candidate for the Presidency in 1983/4.

'Stonewall' Jackson (1824–1863)

Thomas Jackson's stand at the First Battle of Bull Run in 1861 earned him the nickname 'Stonewall'. His Shenandoah valley campaign of 1862 against superior Union forces earned him great admiration, but he died after sustaining wounds inflicted by his own side at Chancellorsville in May 1863. Lee remained convinced that had Jackson been at Gettysburg he would have beaten Northern forces, and turned the tide of war.

Thomas Jefferson (1743–1826)

Thomas Jefferson became the third President of the US in 1801 having already had an illustrious career in many respects. He was a delegate to the First Continental Congress in 1774, and went on to draft the Declaration of Independence. He served in Washington's cabinet as Secretary of State despite effectively being head of the emerging Republican Party, which opposed the Federalists who dominated cabinet.

Andrew Johnson (1808–1875)

Andrew Johnson was the 17th President of the US and, according to a recent poll of American History professors, the second worst. Despite coming from Tennessee he regarded secession as treason and remained loyal to the Union. Following Lincoln's assassination in 1865 he took over as President and soon found himself at loggerheads with Congress over the course Reconstruction should take. His reluctance to see the point of view of Congress resulted in his impeachment, although he narrowly avoided a guilty verdict.

Lyndon Baines Johnson (1908–1973)

Lyndon Johnson was the 36th President of the US. Taking over after Kennedy's assassination in November 1963, he aimed to build a Great Society, which would see basic health care cover and an end to discrimination. The financial and human cost of American involvement in Vietnam on both Johnson and his reforms took their toll and he chose not to run again for the Presidency in 1968.

Joseph Johnston (1807–1891)

Joseph Johnston has been called the finest general the Confederacy had by some, but his talents were not appreciated by Jefferson Davis who blamed him for the fall of Vicksburg in 1863, and relieved him of his command in 1864. Having been recalled, he surrendered to Sherman in 1865.

John Fitzgerald Kennedy (1917–1963)

JFK was the 35th President of the US and the first one to be born in the twentieth century. He was arguably the first 'modern' President in terms of the glamour he brought to the post. An ill-advised decision to back the overthrow of Castro in Cuba in 1961 ended in embarrassment and made him seem naive in the eyes of the Soviet Union, an event which helped propel the superpowers towards stand-offs over Berlin and Cuba. Kennedy found it difficult to make headway on his domestic agenda due in part to the entrenched power of Southern conservative Democrats in Congress.

Martin Luther King (1929–1968)

Martin Luther King was a pastor and civil rights leader. He was a powerful orator who urged reform through non-violent protest.

Robert M. La Follette (1855–1925)

Under the leadership of Robert La Follette the state of Wisconsin became known as the 'laboratory of democracy' because of the experiments carried out in government. La Follette was a Progressive politician who stood unsuccessfully for the Presidency in 1924, but won nearly five million votes.

Robert E. Lee (1807–1870)

Robert E. Lee is generally regarded as the finest military leader of the Civil War. Despite beginning his military career as an engineer, having been appointed commander of Confederate forces in Virginia he gradually made a name for himself in a series of successful battles against superior Northern forces.

Abraham Lincoln (1809–1865)

Abraham Lincoln became the 16th President of the US in 1861 having come to national prominence in 1858 during a series of debates with Stephen Douglas in the Senate election campaign. His electoral victory for the Republican Party triggered the secession of the Southern states, and his determination to preserve the Union ensured that a Civil War would be fought. He eventually found the right combination of military leaders to win the war, but the chance of winning the peace was to be denied him by the bullet of assassin John Wilkes Booth, only days after Lee's surrender.

John Locke (1632–1704)

English philosopher John Locke's 'Treatises on Government' of 1689 argued that a government could be deposed if it offended against natural law, and talked of fundamental rights being 'life, liberty and estate' (i.e. property).

Douglas MacArthur (1880–1964)

Douglas MacArthur served in both world wars and commanded the campaign to defeat Japan during the period 1941–5. He went on to enjoy further success in South Korea in 1950.

James Madison (1751–1836)

James Madison became the 4th President of the US, having served in the Philadelphia Convention and become known as 'the father of the Constitution'. He co-wrote with Jay and Hamilton 'the Federalist Papers', but went on to support Jefferson's Republican Party when he became concerned about the power of central government.

George Marshall (1880–1959)

George Marshall was a US General and former army chief of staff who was seen as a more hardline Secretary of State than Byrnes. He is most famous for his Marshall Plan of 1947 that gave shape to US containment policy in Europe, and his role in the formation of NATO.

John Marshall (1755–1835)

John Marshall became Chief Justice of the US in 1801 following spells in the army and Congress and as Secretary of State. He played a seminal role in determining the position of the Supreme Court in the constitutional system.

Joseph McCarthy (1909–1957)

Joseph McCarthy served as a Republican senator for Wisconsin between 1947 and 1957, during which time he picked up on the issue of communist infiltration and subversion of US government. He intensified his accusations of US leaders including Marshall and Acheson and helped to generate hysterical 'witch-hunts' across the US. He was eventually censured by the Senate in 1954.

George McClellan (1826–1885)

In November 1861 George McClellan was made commander-in-chief of Northern forces, but was quickly replaced by Lincoln who believed that he showed far too much caution in prosecuting the war during his Peninsula campaign in Virginia, and in following up Confederate forces after Antietam. McClellan went on to run against Lincoln for the Presidency in the 1864 elections.

William McKinley (1843–1901)

William McKinley continued the more aggressive foreign policy of his two predecessors and led the US into its first war with a European power (the Spanish-American War of 1898) since 1812. He was re-elected but then assassinated.

George Meade (1815–1872)

George Meade served in the army against the Seminoles and the Mexicans before distinguishing himself in the Civil War by defeating Lee at Gettysburg.

Andrew Mellon (1855–1937)
Andrew Mellon used a huge fortune from his father to become a banker and businessman before going into politics and serving as Secretary of The Treasury from 1921.

John Mitchell (1870–1919)
John Mitchell was a self-educated miner who became President of the United Mine Workers Union in 1898. In 1902 he was particularly successful in uniting diverse immigrant workers to strike.

James Monroe (1758–1831)
James Monroe was the 5th President of the US. He opposed the Federalist interpretation of the Constitution, and was elected President in 1816, going on to serve a second term. He is perhaps best known for his 'Monroe Doctrine'.

J.P. Morgan (1837–1913)
J.P. Morgan turned his father's company into the most powerful private banking house in the US and set up the US Steel Corporation in 1901. He controlled the railways and many other business interests.

Richard Nixon (1913–1994)
Richard Nixon was the 37th President of the US, and one of the most controversial figures to occupy the White House. He presided over the American withdrawal from Vietnam and a thawing in the Cold War. However these achievements were overshadowed by rising domestic discontent and his eventual resignation in 1974 after the revelation of wrongdoings by his administration.

Thomas Paine (1737–1809)
Thomas Paine was an English radical who helped to inspire American independence with his pamphlet 'Common Sense' published in 1776. He went on to serve with the American army as well as becoming a deputy in the French National Convention following the revolution before returning to America.

Mitchell Palmer (1872–1936)
Alexander Mitchell Palmer, having been something of a Democrat Progressive who supported trade union and women's rights, changed his tune once appointed as Attorney-General. Convinced that communists were plotting to overthrow the government he embarked on a campaign against left-wing groups. Some have argued that he devised 'the Red Scare' to help his campaign to become President in 1920.

Rosa Parks (1914–)
Rosa Parks' refusal to give up her seat for a white man on a bus in Alabama sparked off the Montgomery Bus Boycott.

Terence Powderly (1849–1924)
Terence Powderly became the leader of the trade union the Knights of Labor in 1879, and pursued a policy of trying to work constructively with employers.

A. Philip Randolph (1889–1979)
A. Philip Randolph was founder of the Brotherhood of Sleeping Car Porters, an all-black union, who later became President of the National Negro Congress. His idea for a march on Washington was taken up by Martin Luther King and others in 1963.

Ronald Reagan (1911–2004)
Ronald Reagan was the 40th President of the US. The former actor became governor of California in 1967 before unseating Jimmy Carter in 1980. He is best remembered as the 'Great Communicator' due to his

ease and charm with the people and the media. Declaring government the problem rather than the solution to the nation's economic woes, he pushed through significant cuts in taxation and welfare spending. His foreign policy included a highly questionable invasion of Grenada and the illegal arming of Nicaraguan rebels as well as a renewal of the arms race with the Soviet Union.

Jacob Riis (1849–1914)

Jacob Riis became a police reporter for the *New York Tribune* and went on to publish his book *How the Other Half Lives* in 1890. The photographic images in the book, which portrayed the living conditions of the poor, prompted Theodore Roosevelt, then New York Police Commissioner, to close down police lodging houses in the city.

J.D. Rockefeller (1839–1937)

John D. Rockefeller established Standard Oil with his brother and ended up giving away over $500 million to various 'good causes'.

Franklin D. Roosevelt (1882–1945)

Franklin D. Roosevelt was elected 32nd President of the US in 1932, defeating Herbert Hoover by promising a New Deal to solve the Depression and also to repeal Prohibition. He won four elections and became America's longest-serving President. During the New Deal the scope and power of the state was extended and moderate success was achieved but it took the war to finally bring the US out of the Depression.

Theodore Roosevelt (1858–1919)

Theodore Roosevelt was the 26th President of the US. Having commanded his 'Rough Riders' during the Spanish-American War, he held the office of governor of New York state, before taking over as President when McKinley was assassinated. He was elected in his own right in 1904, regretted his decision to stand down in 1908, and fought the 1912 election unsuccessfully as a Progressive candidate.

Bayard Rustin (1910–1987)

Bayard Rustin was adviser to Martin Luther King. His homosexuality, links with communism and conscientious objection during the Second World War ensured that he always remained a background figure.

Nicola Sacco (1891–1927)

In 1920 Nicola Sacco and Bartolomeo Vanzetti were accused of robbery and murder. They were found guilty and executed seven years later. The judge in the case showed clear bias against the men throughout on account of their left-wing affiliations and the case became notorious worldwide.

Dred Scott (1795?–1858)

Dred Scott was the black slave who sued for his freedom on the grounds that he had lived in a free territory. The Supreme Court in 1857 ruled that Scott, as a slave, had no right to bring a case to court in the first place, and in any case was the property of his owner – in other words a slave could be taken anywhere and would remain a slave. The implications of this were that no state had the right to ban slavery.

William Seward (1801–1872)

William Seward started his political career as a Whig but became one of the leading figures in the Republican movement in the 1850s, and, having failed to gain his party's nomination for the Presidency in 1860, he became Lincoln's Secretary of State, and went on to purchase Alaska from Russia in 1867.

Daniel Shays (1747–1825)

Daniel Shays a veteran of the War of Independence led a rebellion of debtors in Massachusetts in 1786–7 in an attempt to get debts cancelled. His actions and the level of support he achieved led to great alarm among men of property and created much greater support for the Philadelphia Convention which met in 1787 to write a new constitution.

William Sherman (1820–1891)
William Sherman made his reputation in the Civil War, and gained notoriety for his destructive march from Atlanta to Savannah. He was made head of the army after the war.

George Shulz (1920–)
George Shulz was Secretary of State in the Nixon and Reagan administrations. He was dubious about SDI and developed a good working relationship with Gorbachev and his aides, facilitating the successful summit meetings of the late 1980s and the end of the Cold War.

Sitting Bull (1834–1890)
Sitting Bull (or Tatanka Iyotake in Indian) was a Native American chief of the Dakota Sioux who led his people in the Sioux War of 1876–7 that saw the defeat of Custer at the Battle of the Little Big Horn. He escaped to Canada but gave up in 1881 and went on to tour with Buffalo Bill's Wild West Show. He was killed by police during the 'Ghost Dance' uprising of 1890.

Alexander Stephens (1812–1883)
Alexander Stephens, having initially opposed secession, became Confederate Vice-President in 1861. He returned to the US Congress between 1874 and 1883, and in 1882 was elected governor of Georgia.

Thaddeus Stevens (1792–1868)
Thaddeus Stevens was a leading Radical Republican during Reconstruction and chaired the impeachment trial of Andrew Johnson.

Harriet Beecher Stowe (1811–1896)
Harriet Beecher Stowe gained fame through her novel *Uncle Tom's Cabin* which apparently had a major influence on Northern attitudes towards slavery.

William Taft (1857–1930)
William Taft became 27th President of the US in 1909 with the blessing of his predecessor Theodore Roosevelt, who then ran against him in the election of 1912. During his term in office a number of trusts were prosecuted.

Roger B. Taney (1777–1864)
Roger B. Taney was made Chief Justice of the Supreme Court in 1836. Taney's most famous judgement was in the case of Dred Scott where he ruled the Missouri Compromise of 1820 to be unconstitutional.

Frederick Jackson Turner (1861–1932)
Frederick Jackson Turner was a historian best known for his paper on 'The Significance of the Frontier in American History' in 1893.

'Boss' William Tweed (1823–1878)
William Tweed was the most notorious 'boss' of New York's Democrat machine, Tammany Hall, who lined his pockets at the expense of taxpayers. He was exposed by the *New York Times* in 1871 and sent to jail.

John Tyler (1790–1862)
John Tyler became the 10th President of the US following the death of William Harrison in 1841 only a month after his inauguration. He presided over the annexation of Texas in 1845 and became a member of the Confederate Congress when Civil War broke out.

Cyrus Vance (1917–)
Cyrus Vance was Secretary of State under Jimmy Carter and his rivalry with hardline security adviser Zbigniew Brzezinski led to contradictions in foreign policy. He resigned over the Iranian hostage affair in 1980.

William Vanderbilt (1821–1885)
William Vanderbilt was the eldest son of railroad financier Cornelius Vanderbilt, and extended his father's controlling interest in American railroads.

Bartolomeo Vanzetti (1888–1927)
Bartolomeo Vanzetti was accused with Nicola Sacco of a payroll robbery and murder in 1920, and was executed seven years later, with very little evidence having been produced to suggest he was guilty. It is generally felt that Sacco and Vanzetti were victims of the 'anti-red hysteria' of the time.

Benjamin Wade (1800–1878)
Benjamin Wade, having become a lawyer, joined the Whig Party and later the Republicans, and was elected to the Senate in 1851. He went on to champion votes for women and trade union rights, and was fervently anti-slavery. During the Civil War he became one of the Radical Republicans who criticised Lincoln. Wade was the presiding officer of the 40th Congress which meant that he would have become President had Johnson been successfully impeached. Some have suggested that this may have tipped the balance in Johnson's favour.

Booker T. Washington (1856–1915)
Booker T. Washington was a teacher and founder of the Tuskegee Negro National Institute. He wanted to provide essentially vocational education for African Americans and became a Presidential adviser on African American affairs.

George Washington (1732–1799)
George Washington was commander of American forces against the British during the War of Independence, President of the Philadelphia Convention in 1787, which wrote the Constitution, and subsequently became the first President of the United States in 1789.

Woodrow Wilson (1856–1924)
Thomas Woodrow Wilson became the 28th President of the US in the election of 1912. He served two terms in office and presided over a number of progressive reforms including women being granted the vote, and the amendment to the Constitution which introduced Prohibition, but tends to be remembered more for his role in the negotiations following the First World War and his part in creating the League of Nations.

Malcolm X (1925–1965)
Malcom X was an African American leader who initially rejected cooperation with white liberals. He became a leading spokesman for the Nation of Islam but was suspended from the movement after his conversion to orthodox Islam. Before his assassination he preached brotherhood between black and white people.

Glossary of Key Terms

African Americans Americans of African origin.

Anti-Federalist Term broadly used to define anyone who opposed the adoption of the Constitution in the late 1780s.

Appeasement The attempt by Britain and France in the 1930s to compromise with or meet the demands of the dictators of Germany and Italy.

Bicameral Literally means 'two chambers' – in the case of the US used to refer to the legislative two-house Congress established by the Constitution.

'Big stick' The nickname for Theodore Roosevelt's foreign policy, as in 'speak softly and carry a big stick'. It represented a build-up of military strength and a more assertive foreign policy in the early 1900s.

Black cabinet A group of highly educated and highly trained African Americans who advised Franklin Delano Roosevelt in the 1930s.

Black Codes Attempts made by Southern state legislatures to limit or avoid the extension of voting rights to freed slaves immediately after the Civil War.

Brinkmanship A term sometimes used to describe US foreign policy in the Eisenhower and Kennedy era. The US would take a tough approach towards the USSR and China, to the extent that it took relations to the 'brink' of open war. This proved successful in facing down the US's enemies but was a dangerous approach to Cold War diplomacy, e.g. the Cuban missile crisis of 1962.

Carpet-baggers A term of abuse adopted by Southerners for Northerners who moved into the South in the years following the Civil War, who in their eyes had come to exploit the South's position for personal gain.

Central Intelligence Agency (CIA) Created in 1947 as one of several US intelligence agencies, the CIA took responsibility for overseas espionage (spying) and was also used by the government to coordinate military intervention in Third World countries, thus allowing the President to conduct foreign intervention without involving Congress.

Civil rights The right of citizens to social and political equality.

Cold War The popular term to describe the state of mutual hostility and suspicion between the US and USSR (also China after 1949) during the 1940s and 1950s. While both sides fought wars during this period, outright superpower conflict never took place, hence a 'cold' rather than 'hot war'. 'Cold' also describes the chilly relations between the superpowers.

Communism The ideological belief in sharing all wealth, ownership and management of a state's resources among the working classes. Where practised (most notably in the USSR and China) it tended to lead to repressive, authoritarian governments acting 'on behalf' of the workers. Communist states regarded the West as corrupt, expansionist capitalists, whereas the West saw itself as the defender of human freedom against a dangerous, expansionist and repressive ideology.

Confederacy The name adopted by the Southern states which seceded from the Union in 1860 and 1861.

Confederation A union of states which created a loose system of alliance between them and did not involve the states giving up as much power to a central authority as the Constitution adopted in 1789 required.

Congress The bicameral legislature created by the Constitution in 1787, and consisting of the House of Representatives and the Senate. Prior to 1787 Congress was a unicameral body which had both legislative and executive functions.

Congressional Reconstruction The period roughly between 1867 and 1877 when Congress took the initiative in restoring the Union.

Constitution A set of rules to establish a framework for how a country or organisation might be run, which may prescribe the powers of government and freedoms for the individual.

Containment An approach to US foreign policy developed under Truman in the late 1940s. The US was not strong enough to risk attacking the USSR head-on but believed it should prevent the USSR from spreading communism to states which were not communist. This approach set the tone of US foreign policy through the 1950s and 1960s leading to costly interventions in Korea and Vietnam.

Dawes Plan Named after the US financier Charles G. Dawes, one of a team sent to Germany in 1924 to investigate German problems with repaying the cost of the First World War. The result was a plan to reschedule repayments over a longer period and grant Germany a large loan to aid economic recovery.

Détente A more conciliatory approach to US/USSR relations adopted for much of the 1960s and 1970s. The US sought summit meetings, arms limitations agreements and diplomatic solutions in an attempt to 'thaw' the Cold War. This policy was criticised as a failure by Reagan in the early 1980s, who argued it had left the US dangerously weak. He continued negotiations, but from a position of greater strength.

'Domino theory' The belief that if one Third World country were to turn communist, other neighbouring countries would be more likely to turn communist as a result. If you make an upright line of dominoes and push one over, the rest will be knocked over in turn. This belief supported the view that a policy of containment was necessary.

'Doves' US political jargon referring to politicians who seek peaceful solutions to foreign conflict, as opposed to 'hawks'.

Economic colonialism US policy in the late nineteenth century was to avoid the acquisition of colonial possessions, and instead to seek economic influence in independent states such as Hawaii (until 1898). A state would, in theory, govern its own affairs but much of its economic production would fall under the control of US business interests.

Enlightenment The movement beginning in seventeenth-century England inspired by such people as Isaac Newton and John Locke, and spreading to France in the eighteenth century, which stressed the importance of science and reason and argued that individuals could improve their lot rather than simply accepting it. The movement undermined much traditional authority and religious practice.

EXCOM Special committee set up by Kennedy in 1962 to provide advice during the Cuban missile crisis.

Federalists Initially used as a term for those who supported the adoption of the Constitution, and later used as a term for the political party which championed strong central government.

Fourteen Points President Woodrow Wilson announced a peace plan in January 1918 on which to base negotiations for an end to the First World War. The plan consisted of 14 separate points, including national self-determination and a League of Nations. Most of the plan did not survive the Paris Peace Conference in 1919, where a more vindictive mood predominated.

Free territories Land owned by the US which had not become organised into states, and in which slavery was barred.

'Great silent majority' A phrase used by Nixon in 1969 to undermine the credibility of anti-Vietnam War protesters. He claimed that most Americans supported his policy towards Vietnam and it was only a minority that was vocally protesting. The phrase has become a cliché in US politics and was even used more recently in response to protests against the 2003 invasion of Iraq.

'Green Berets' The nickname given to special US troops sent to South Vietnam by Kennedy to coordinate resistance against communist insurgency, prior to the start of the Vietnam War proper.

Harlem Renaissance The term given to the emergence of African American writers and musicians in Harlem during the 1920s.

'Hawks' US political jargon referring to politicians who readily seek military solutions to foreign conflict, as opposed to the 'doves'.

Hispanic Americans Americans of Spanish origin, including people from Mexico, Puerto Rico and Cuba.

Imperial Presidency Derogatory term used to describe the ability of Presidents to conduct foreign policy without proper restraint from Congress for much of the Cold War period. One of the key aims of the US Constitution is to impose checks upon Presidential power, so US Presidents should not be able to act like old-style emperors.

Inaugural speech The first speech given by a new President at his inauguration ceremony.

'Iron Curtain' Phrase first used by Winston Churchill in 1946. The USSR, having secured control of many central and eastern European states, had begun to deprive the people living in those states of the freedom to travel and communicate with the West, hence 'an iron curtain has descended across Europe'. Churchill's speech, delivered to a US audience, was controversial at the time but achieved its aim of warning the US not to withdraw its presence from Western Europe. Throughout the Cold War the West referred to countries such as East Germany, Poland, Hungary, etc. as being 'behind the Iron Curtain'.

Irreconcilables The name given to senators who absolutely rejected any involvement in a League of Nations after the First World War. They only numbered a minority in the Senate but when their votes were combined with those of more moderate 'Reservationists', this was enough to block the US from joining the League. This was an early sign of the US moving towards isolationism after the war.

Isolationism An approach to foreign policy that would reject binding commitments towards other states and international institutions, in effect 'isolating' the US from world affairs and thus avoiding costly foreign interventions such as the First World War. In practice, the US was never truly isolationist although there was public pressure to increase isolationism, especially in the early 1930s.

'Jim Crow' laws Laws passed in the Southern states in the 1870s and 1880s to limit the rights of African Americans and to segregate them from white Americans.

Ku Klux Klan Terrorist society that was formed in 1866 by a group of former Confederate soldiers. It was outlawed in 1871 but had re-emerged by the 1920s.

Lame duck The name given to the remaining time in office for an outgoing President or House of Representatives following a national election, before the incoming President or House actually take their seats. It implies that the remaining time in office is a period of weakness in which not much can be achieved.

Lend-lease In 1941 the US began to offer Britain a supply of arms on credit. This became known as 'lend-lease' and is an example of the US stepping away from isolation and towards involvement in the Second World War, some months before Pearl Harbor.

Linkage A term used by Kissinger to describe diplomatic initiatives that might solve more than one problem, e.g. a beneficial economic deal with the USSR might also encourage the USSR to reduce intervention in Third World countries and thus reduce the need for US 'containment'. Linkage took place in the context of 'détente' between the superpowers.

'Long telegram' An 8,000 word telegram sent to Truman's government in 1946 by Kennan, a US government agent based in the USSR. It warned of innate Soviet hostility towards the US and encouraged Truman to introduce his policy of 'containment' the following year.

Marshall Plan A plan to provide US economic aid to war-damaged European countries, put forward by Secretary of State George Marshall in 1947. The plan was rejected by the USSR but was applied with some success in Western Europe and helped to pave the way for the formation of NATO in 1949.

McCarthyism Named after senator Joseph McCarthy, this term describes the wave of anti-communist hysteria that led to reckless and often unsubstantiated accusations across US politics and society, an infamous example being the 'blacklists' circulating in the Hollywood film industry, between 1950 and 1954. McCarthy was by no means the sole cause of this persecution but he was the most prominent figure involved in making accusations.

'Merchants of death' One theory regarding the reasons the US went to war in 1917 was that arms manufacturers had stood to make a great profit. Such manufacturers were nicknamed 'merchants of death'.

Monroe Doctrine Formulated by President Monroe in 1823, a claim that all of the Americas lay within the US's sphere of interest. This attitude was evident in the US's intervention in several Caribbean, Pacific and Central and South American states during the nineteenth and twentieth centuries, including the Spanish-American War of 1898.

Muckraking Term given to a style of journalism which sought to expose a range of social problems and various other scandals and corruption, often in a sensationalist way, towards the end of the nineteenth century and early twentieth century.

Mutually Assured Destruction (MAD) The rationale that if both the US and USSR had sufficient nuclear weaponry to destroy each other, then this would act as a deterrent to both sides. If the USSR launched a nuclear attack on the US, or vice versa, then both sides would be utterly destroyed.

National Security Council (NSC) The NSC was a government department set up in 1947 in response to the onset of the Cold War. It studied national security issues closely and advised the President on foreign policy. In 1950 it advised huge increases in defence spending on conventional weapons in order to match and contain the USSR.

Native Americans A more politically correct term used in recent times to denote the inhabitants of America who were once referred to as Indians or Red Indians, descendants of the peoples who inhabited the Americas before white Europeans settled the continent.

New Look A proposal to shift the emphasis on US defence spending away from conventional weapons to nuclear weapons. The phrase was used by Eisenhower in the run-up to his election as President in 1952 and was promised to provide effective defence at less cost, 'more bang for the buck'. This escalated the superpowers' nuclear arms race.

North Atlantic Treaty Organisation (NATO) A military alliance, based on mutual assistance in case of attack, established in 1949 and comprising the US, Canada and most Western European states. The US responded with its own military alliance network of 'Iron Curtain' states ('The Warsaw Pact'), and the result was a divided, but also stabilised, Europe until the 1990s.

'Open Door' Proposal made in the 1890s that there should be no international restrictions of trade with China. China was a huge potential source of raw materials and market for US goods, but was too politically weak to prevent foreign powers from grabbing control over its foreign trade. Unrestricted trade was in the interests of the US but was increasingly threatened by Japanese expansion in the 1930s.

President The holder of this office created by the Constitution would be both the head of state and the head of the executive branch of government.

Presidential Reconstruction The period between 1863 and 1867 when Presidents Lincoln and then Johnson took the initiative in trying to restore the unity of the US.

Rebel states Term used to denote the Southern states that seceded from the Union prior to the Civil War.

Reparations Literally payment of damages. After the First World War, the Paris Peace Conference resolved that Germany would pay reparations but the figure was set very high and was hard to extract from a resentful and economically weak Germany. The US came up with financial plans to help German recovery in the 1920s but these were wrecked by the Great Depression of the early 1930s.

Reservationists The name given to senators who did not absolutely reject any involvement in a League of Nations after the First World War, but did wish to see amendments to the League so that the US's membership would not be too binding. This made agreement in the Senate difficult and when their votes were combined with those of the more hardline 'Irreconcilables' this was enough to block the US from joining the League.

Reservations Land allocated to Native Americans by the federal government in order to remove them from lands that white settlers wished to occupy.

Roll-back A more ambitious version of 'containment' whereby the US would work to remove communist or pro-communist governments in the Third World. Apart from an initial success in the Korean War in 1950, roll-back was not successful until the 1990s, and then generated by the internal collapse of the USSR rather than US foreign intervention.

'Roosevelt Corollary' A more assertive version of the Monroe Doctrine, introduced by President Theodore Roosevelt. The US would oppose any European imperialism in the Americas and would take pre-emptive action if necessary. This reflected US concern at the rapid expansion of European empires in the late nineteenth and early twentieth centuries, and was supported by continued development of the US navy.

'Rough Riders' The nickname for a volunteer cavalry unit that fought in the 1898 Spanish-American War. The unit was led by Theodore Roosevelt and made him a popular hero, helping him to rise rapidly to the US Presidency. The Rough Riders seem closer to the nineteenth-century 'Wild West' than to modern US warfare. Roosevelt was one of a number of US Presidents who have been elected following a successful military career.

Scalawags Term of abuse for Southern whites who collaborated with Northerners in the South during Reconstruction.

Secession The breaking away of Southern states from the Union to form the Confederacy.

Senate The 'upper house' of the US Congress in which every state is represented equally, by two senators.

'Separate but equal' The principle that established separate services and facilities, such as schools, seats on buses and park benches for African Americans. These segregated services and facilities were meant to be of an equal quality and standard to those enjoyed by white people but they rarely were.

South East Asia Treaty Organization (SEATO) A military alliance between the US, Australia, New Zealand and several Asian states (e.g. Thailand and Pakistan), established in 1954 and designed to contain the spread of communism.

Strategic Arms Limitation Talks (SALT) A series of summit meetings between the US and USSR between 1967 and 1979, which led to a major treaty known as SALT I in 1972. This treaty set a precedent for arms limitation. A further treaty, SALT II, was signed in 1979 but never ratified. SALT was the centrepiece of the 'détente' period of superpower relations.

Strategic Defense Initiative (SDI) A 1980s plan for a new defence system, to be based in space, that would in theory destroy enemy nuclear missiles before they could reach the US. It was championed by Reagan and often nicknamed 'Star Wars' after the film.

Supreme Court The highest court of the US judicial system, which, through the establishment of precedent, came to have the power to interpret the Constitution and on occasion to declare laws passed by Congress illegal.

Totalitarianism A system of government where the state has 'total' control over its people through a combination of indoctrination and repression. The term was used by the West to criticise communist government.

Truman Doctrine Another name for the policy of 'containment' introduced by Truman in 1947. It pledged the US to 'support free peoples who are resisting attempted aggression by armed minorities or outside pressure'. The doctrine was initially applied to US aid to the governments of Greece and Turkey.

'Uncle Tom' A term taken from Harriet Beecher Stowe's novel 'Uncle Tom's Cabin' to describe an African American who is considered to be excessively obedient or servile.

Unicameral Literally means 'one chamber' and in the case of the US it usually is used to refer to the idea of a legislative body with only one house, such as Congress prior to 1789.

Viet Cong A communist guerrilla force supported by North Vietnam, operating in South Vietnam. The central aim of the US's military intervention in South Vietnam in the 1960s was to drive out the Viet Cong. It failed.

'Vietnamization' The policy towards Vietnam introduced by Nixon. The US would reduce its forces in South Vietnam and instead train and encourage South Vietnamese troops to fight the Viet Cong.

Warsaw Pact More correctly named the Warsaw Treaty Organisation, this was a military alliance of the USSR and the communist 'satellite' states of central and eastern Europe, established in 1955. It was designed to counter the threat of NATO in Europe.

Select Bibliography

Stephen E. Ambrose and Douglas G. Brinkley, *Rise to Globalism*, 8th edition, Penguin (1997).

Colin Bonwick, *The American Revolution*, Palgrave (1991).

Peter Brett, *The USA and the World, 1917–45*, Hodder & Stoughton (1997).

Alan Brinkley, *The Unfinished Nation*, McGraw-Hill (2000).

Hugh Brogan, *The Penguin History of the USA*, Penguin (1985/1999).

Mark S. Byrnes, *The Truman Years 1945–1953*, Pearson (2000).

Henry Steele Commager, *The Blue and the Gray*, The Fairfax Press (1982).

Alan Farmer, *The American Civil War 1861–1865*, Hodder & Stoughton (1996).

Alan Farmer, *The Origins of the American Civil War 1846–1861*, Hodder & Stoughton (1996).

Eric Foner, *Reconstruction, America's Unfinished Revolution 1863–1877*, Harper & Row (1984).

J.K. Galbraith, *The Great Crash 1929*, Penguin (1975).

M.J. Heale, *The American Revolution*, Methuen (1986).

Michael Holt, *The Political Crisis of the 1850s*, Norton (1978).

Akira Iriye, *The Globalising of America 1913–1945*, Cambridge University Press (1993).

Maldwyn Jones, *The Limits of Liberty*, Oxford University Press (1994).

Walter LaFeber, *The American Search for Opportunity*, Cambridge University Press (1993).

Martin McCauley, *Russia, America and the Cold War 1949–1991*, Pearson (1998).

James McPherson, *Battle Cry of Freedom*, Penguin (1990).

John W. Mason, *The Cold War 1945–1991*, Routledge (1996).

John M. Murrin, Paul E. Johnson, James M. McPherson *et al.*, *Liberty Equality Power*, Harcourt (2001).

David Paterson, Doug Willoughby and Susan Willoughby, *Civil Rights in the USA 1863–1980*, Heinemann (2001).

Brian Holden Reid, *The Origins of the American Civil War*, Longman (1996).

Patrick Renshaw, *America in the Era of the Two World Wars 1910–1945*, Longman (1996).

Clinton Rossiter, *1787: The Grand Convention*, Norton (1987).

Robert D. Schulzinger, *US Diplomacy since 1900*, 5th edition, Oxford University Press (2002).

Richard Sobel, *The Impact of Public Opinion on US Foreign Policy Since Vietnam*, Oxford University Press (2001).

Kenneth Stampp, *The Causes of the Civil War*, Touchstone, Simon & Schuster (1991).

John Traynor, *Mastering Modern United States History*, Palgrave (2001).

Hugh Tulloch, *The Debate on the American Civil War Era*, Manchester University Press (1999).

Howard Zinn, *A People's History of the United States*, Longman (1996).

Index